SCC
$83.75

Developing
and Administering
a
Child Care
and **Education**
Program

SIXTH EDITION

Join us on the web at
EarlyChildEd.delmar.com

Chapter 8

Developing a Center Facility 179

Chapter 9

Equipping the Center 207

Chapter 10

Staffing the Center 249

Chapter 11

Marketing the Program and Selecting the Children 325

Chapter 12

Grouping and Enrolling the Children

339

Chapter 13

Managing the Food and the Health and Safety Programs

367

Chapter 14

Evaluating Center Components

405

Chapter 15

Providing for Personal and Professional Staff Development

441

C h a p t e r   1 6

Working with Families, Volunteers, and the Community   **471**

PREFACE

When we were first invited to write a text for early childhood administration courses, we were, of course, delighted. We had had experience in teaching and administering programs and eagerly began. Since that time, much has happened in early childhood education. The director's role has become even more complex, while many of the challenges have not changed.

With each edition, we have talked with directors, read relevant materials on early childhood and business, and submitted our work to anonymous readers from a wide range of programs across the country. Since leaving directorships and college teaching, we have kept current through our work on center boards, through training centers and conferences, through active participation in local and national professional organizations, and through working in classrooms with young children.

STATE OF THE DIRECTORSHIP

National recognition for the importance of the early childhood years continues to grow as educators, politicians, and community members express concern about the quality of our country's educational system. The realization that the quality of programs for the youngest children is often poor has led to demands for change. These factors have drawn increasing attention to the role of the director of programs for young children because directors set the standards for quality in the centers they lead.

No longer can a very good teacher be promoted to director with the expectation that assuming this leadership role will be simple. No longer can a person with business experience assume that it will be easy to step into the early childhood director's role. Specific preparation for the directorship is essential. Much more attention is now placed on acquisition of credentials, particularly the relatively new and still developing director's credential.

In keeping with the current movement to standards-based programs, directors must understand their role in curriculum selection and development and the related issue of assessment of young children. We continue to expect that the director who has not had sufficient preparation in child development and early childhood education will be responsible for obtaining that knowledge and understanding. Those components are too extensive and significant to be adequately included in a text on administration, yet they are essential if the director is to guide staff members to go beyond addressing academic standards or having no standards or inappropriate standards.

Similarly, the director who is well versed in early childhood education but has limited business knowledge and experience would do well to find opportunities for developing that knowledge and those skills.

OUR AUDIENCE

Developing and Administering a Child Care and Education Program, Sixth Edition was written to support students who are developing an understanding of the early childhood education field beyond the children's classroom. The book is geared to readers in associate and baccalaureate programs as well as master's degree students. Students in on-line programs are also using this text, and at least one program is being developed in Spanish. Readers who have come to the directorship with a business background will benefit from learning about the culture of early childhood education and be introduced to the priorities, practices, organizations, and resources that will guide them in their work.

Several states and institutions have developed director credentials. Our text provides the breadth of content that directors or prospective directors need to reach that goal. Our text is also being used by current directors who feel the need to upgrade their knowledge and by new directors, particularly those who have been promoted to administration because they were good teachers.

CONCEPTUAL APPROACH

The basic premise of this text is that the director must be both a manager and a leader. We see the managerial role as the business work to be done to support a high-quality program. Such work includes providing equipment and supplies, keeping financial records, and meeting licensing requirements. In large companies, separate managers may handle each of these components, but many programs for young children require directors who can handle all aspects of center administration. Recognizing that the program will not continue to exist if it is not well managed, we nonetheless emphasize equally the director's role as a leader of people. Staff must be supported and nourished rather than directed. Families, too, need a welcoming director who respects and values them. In the local community and beyond, the director advocates for children and for high-quality programs. Therefore, the second and equally important component of our approach is development of leaders who exhibit strong interpersonal skills.

Above all, we see the director as a well-prepared, ethical person who is authoritative and dedicated to meeting the needs of young children. We emphasize adopting and using the National Association for the Education of Young Children's Statement of Commitment and Code of Ethical Conduct whenever puzzling situations arise that may be of an ethical nature. We see the director's responsibility as educating the staff and families about the Code and how it can be used appropriately.

ORGANIZATION OF THE TEXT

The text includes 16 chapters, readily addressed in a semester course or modified for shorter courses. Each chapter contains practical information about the business aspect of the director's role while complementing that with attention to the interpersonal component. Throughout the chapters, information is provided about how the topics apply to both new and existing centers.

Chapter Contents

Chapter 1 provides a broad overview. The goal is to encourage the student to begin to think about the wide variety of tasks directors must be prepared to undertake. The chapter presents a range of roles the director plays at one time or another and demonstrates how complex the job can become. Here, and throughout the text, the reader is helped to understand the first of two equal themes, the need for strong management skills.

Chapter 2 depicts the second and equally important theme of the text. The director must have and use strong, effective interpersonal skills. These skills are based on the belief in the importance of each person, staff member, child, and family member. They play a major role in establishing the culture of the center, and they continue to be important as the director reaches out to the community.

Chapter 3 demonstrates to the reader that meeting community needs is essential if a program is to succeed. How a program is established is discussed. The authors discuss various types of programs, including those based on sponsorship, on the variety of purposes for which centers are created, and on those related to ages of children served. Whether an individual is beginning a new program or taking on work that has previously been established, principles of management and leadership apply.

Chapter 4 turns to components that may seem dry at first glance. Licensing, accreditation, and certification all play roles in establishing a program's credibility. Here, students consider ways of working with groups and individuals responsible for administering legislated regulation of all child care and education. They are also introduced to the idea of going beyond the basics, whether for center accreditation, teacher National Board certification, or director credentialing.

Chapter 5 again draws heavily on the combined themes of program management and leadership of people. Students consider how directors, even those who are young and inexperienced, must learn to work with and for a board of directors, while helping board members develop in their roles. Consideration of the business organization of the center is presented as a topic to be considered, whether the center is being created or is ongoing.

Chapters 6 and 7 examine handling financial matters and funding the program. Students who believe that they will always be unsuccessful in math often need extra time with these chapters. The authors have presented examples, rather than merely explaining the principles. When students actually do the math for each example, preferably using calculators, they begin to understand how challenging it is to balance reasonable tuition and reasonable teacher salaries. Both chapters make it clear that the director must be able to understand the financial management of a center.

Chapter 8 encompasses both starting anew and remaining in an existing facility. Practical information includes the kinds of planning that must be done as part of a director's role. In addition, the text describes what happens when a center opts to move or is forced to do so. Students are also encouraged to think about ways to enhance an existing facility.

Chapter 9 presents a topic, equipping the center, that on the surface seems simple and fun. When students realize they have to think about every single item that must be purchased, from waste cans and clocks to climbers and puzzles, it becomes more complex. Estimating need and managing supplies are additional important topics.

Chapter 10 demonstrates that staffing the center goes beyond finding and keeping a few good teachers. This topic also encompasses designing personnel policies, while considering legal and ethical issues, and orienting the employee. The authors stress the importance of extensive orientation for each new employee and continued support for each continuing employee.

Chapter 11 explains how and why centers are marketed so that families and community members understand the mission of the center. The relationship of marketing to funding is addressed, as is the connection between marketing and enrollment. The challenges involved in managing the many aspects of enrollment are included in terms of practicality, legality, and, above all, appropriate service to children and families.

Chapter 12 continues to address enrollment. This chapter describes the challenges the director faces in making decisions about grouping children. The authors explain approaches to bringing each child into the center, using a child- and family-focused approach that emphasizes both procedures and personal attention to each child's needs.

Chapter 13, the reader learns about creating and managing a food service program for young children. Topics include appropriate nutrition, meeting USDA standards, and encouraging children to develop healthful eating habits. A related topic, health and safety, explores the many possible risks in these areas and ways to prevent problems. Material about agencies that regulate child care and education programs is included.

Chapter 14 considers the terms *assessment* and *evaluation*. Students are introduced to expectations of the director as leader of both assessment and evaluation. This discussion includes assessment and evaluation related to children, staff, the director, and the program. A focus is the relationship between curriculum and assessment.

Chapter 15 demonstrates the importance of the director's relationship with staff in several significant areas. These include staff meetings and the roles that director and staff members play in those meetings, and staff training and professional development. Readers are encouraged to recognize that even when they are well prepared for a staff or director role, continuing learning is essential. In light of the challenges directors face as they deal with staff turnover, the authors emphasize the director's role as supervisor and coach of each staff member. In that work, the director is expected to be able to assess staff problems and to develop a plan to help bring about change.

Chapter 16 emphasizes the fact that the center's clients include family members. The chapter addresses creating and implementing a parent program, as well as providing a handbook for each family. The director also learns to work with volunteers, organizations and other agencies, and members of the community. Developing these relationships is explained in terms of benefits to both the children and the program.

Supportive Materials for Instructors and Students

After each chapter, Class Assignments and Class Exercises are provided. These are followed by Working Papers on which students can submit the work they complete relative to the assignments.

Each chapter is also followed by Director's Resources, documents that provide additional details on the chapter topic or samples of documents that directors have created. These give novice directors ideas about what is to be included and provide starting points as they create their own documents.

To maintain high readability, we have referred readers to an extensive list of books, Web sites, and resources. In the appendices, readers can find the specific information that meets their particular needs and interests.

NEW TO THIS EDITION

This updated edition covers a number of timely issues and includes the following:

- Working Papers now appear in the Online Companion™ so that students can submit assignments electronically.

- new and revised Director's Resources
- additional information on assessment and evaluation
- increased emphasis on diversity in all aspects of the program
- greater use of color and updated photographs throughout
- updated material on the new accreditation system
- additional material on technology
- new listings in the Director's Library, found in Appendix D
- updated sources of equipment and materials, found in Appendix A

USING THE TEXT

Developing and Administering a Child Care and Education Program, Sixth Edition can be taught using the existing order of chapters. Our reviewers and colleagues who regularly use the book have told us about a variety of ways in which they order the chapters for their students. Because each chapter is self-contained, a variety of usage orders works well.

Some instructors use the content as the basis of lectures, adding examples from their own experiences or inviting local directors to meet with the class to discuss a particular topic. Others assign students to interview directors on topics addressed in the text.

Many students who are enrolled in an administration class are involved in or will have completed an early childhood field experience. Many may be working in early childhood programs. Because (college level students) focus may be primarily on the classroom, instructors may use those experiences to help them consider how the director influences the program relative to the topic of the chapter being discussed. For example, in your center, how does the director's work affect the health, safety, and nutrition of the children?

Some instructors use the Reflections feature found throughout the text as a starting point for class discussions or as a topic for writing assignments. The Director's Corner feature, which presents quotes on the chapter topic, can also be used this way. Other instructors also use the Class Exercises to stimulate discussion. These exercises may take the form of role-playing or debates. One creative student group turned an exercise into a Jeopardy® game, divided the rest of the class into teams, and played their way through the content.

Most students are comfortable with the reading level. Terms that may be new to some students are explained in context.

Instructors whose students find text reading difficult may support them by encouraging them to

- read the objectives.
- read and study the chapter.
- summarize the chapter.
- return to the objectives to determine whether they can meet them.
- write down questions and list areas that they find difficult to understand.
- meet with the instructor or a study buddy or bring their questions to class.

The text lends itself well to related field experiences. Advanced students may be assigned as interns to work with directors, much as student teachers work with mentor teachers. Other instructors may assign students to form teams to create their own center on paper. This assignment may include creating an imaginary site, a mission statement, a funding plan, a tuition schedule, a budget, a marketing plan, a staffing plan, a policy and procedures manual, and a salary schedule. The assignment may be limited to one or more of these components.

Instructors may assign students to write a paper or prepare a class presentation on one of the topics discussed in the text, using related resources listed in the appendices or at the end of chapters.

ANCILLARY MATERIAL

Instructors Manual

An instructor's manual includes questions for each chapter that can be used for tests and exams. The essay questions may also be used for class discussions, presentations, or paper assignments.

Computerized Test Bank

The computerized test bank is composed of true-false, multiple-choice, short-answer, and completion questions for each chapter. Instructors can use the computerized test bank (CTB) software to create sample quizzes for their students. The CTB User's Guide provides more information on how to create and post quizzes on your institution's Internet or intranet server. Students may also access sample quizzes from the Online Companion™ to accompany *Developing and Administering a Child Care and Education Program, Sixth Edition*.

Online Companion™

The Online Companion™ to accompany *Developing and Administering a Child Care and Education*

Program, Sixth Edition provides a link to early childhood education on the Internet. The Online Companion™ contains many features to help students focus their understanding of child care administration.

 The Online Companion™ icon appears at the end of each chapter to prompt you to go on-line and take advantage of the many supplemental materials provided.

You can find the Online Companion™ at http://www.earlychilded.delmar.com.

Professional Enhancement Booklet

A new supplement to accompany this text is the Administration and Supervision booklet for students. This booklet, which is part of Thomson Delmar Learning's Early Childhood Education Professional Enhancement series, focuses on key topics of interest to future early childhood directors, teachers, and caregivers. Students will keep this informational supplement and use it for years to come in their early childhood practices.

WebTutor™

The WebTutor™ to accompany *Developing and Administering a Child Care and Education Program, Sixth Edition* allows you to take learning beyond the classroom. This Online Courseware is designed to complement the text and benefits students by enabling them to better manage their time, prepare for exams, organize their notes, and more. Special features include

- Chapter Learning Objectives: Correlated with textbook chapter objectives.
- Online Course Preparation: A listing of what students should have read or done prior to using on-line content.
- Study Sheets: Outline the content of each chapter and contain notes. Study Sheets can be printed to help students learn and remember important points.
- Glossary: Provides definitions for terms in each chapter or in the course as a whole.
- Flashcards: Allow students to test themselves on word definitions.
- Discussion Topics: Posted to encourage use as a threaded bulletin board and as assignments to develop critical thinking skills.
- FAQs: Provide questions and answers that students may have about specific content.
- Online Class Notes: Provide additional information about the chapter content.

- Online Chapter Quizzes: Given in various formats, including matching exercises, true-false quizzes, short-answer questions, and multiple-choice questions with immediate feedback for correct and incorrect answers. Multiple-choice questions also include rationales for right and wrong choices.
- Web Links: Provide students with practice searching the Web for information. Learners choose from a variety of Web links and report findings to their instructor through e-mail.

A benefit for instructors as well as students, the WebTutor™ allows for on-line discussion with the instructor and other class members; real-time chat to enable virtual office hours and encourage collaborative learning environments; a calendar of syllabus information for easy reference; e-mail connections to facilitate communication among classmates and between students and instructors; and customization tools that help instructors tailor their course to fit their needs by adding or changing content.

WebTutor™ allows you to extend your reach beyond the classroom and is available on either WebCT or Blackboard platforms.

ABOUT THE AUTHORS

Dorothy June Sciarra continues to be an active early childhood educator in a diverse variety of situations. She has served as director of the child development laboratory center at the University of Cincinnati, serving children and families from a wide range of backgrounds. Her work as director set the standard throughout the area for taking a stand for appropriate practice whether or not it was popular. Teachers who work with her understand their responsibility to the children and families and develop a clear understanding of early childhood education under her guidance. Dr. Sciarra's work as professor of child development/early childhood education has been highly prized. Former students still talk about her child development courses and her deep understanding of childhood. Dr. Sciarra served as department head with responsibility for early childhood associate, bachelor's, and master's degree programs and pioneered a system for career development as capable students were enabled to move seamlessly from the CDA to the associate and then on to the baccalaureate degree level. Currently she is involved in several community early childhood efforts, including board membership on the University of Cincinnati Child Care Center. She is active in 4C, a National Association of Child Care Resource and Referral Agency, and has participated tirelessly on many of its training committees. As an adviser at Children's for Children (Child Development Center at Children's Hospital Medical Center), her support was so highly valued that when a second center was built, the teachers' resource room was named in her honor. At the Cincinnati Early Learning Center, a large core of Sciarra's former students direct five programs. They look to her as their mentor and friend and call on her to guide them as they develop policy manuals, coach new teachers, and make decisions about environments at the centers. Dr. Sciarra is a recipient of the 4C early childhood award and was the first recipient of the Ohio Association for the Education of Young Children Early Childhood Teacher Educator Award. She has mentored many early childhood educators, including co-author, Anne Dorsey. Together they also wrote *Leaders and Supervisors in Child Care Programs,* published by Thomson Delmar Learning.

Anne Dorsey has also been a child development center director and followed in Dr. Sciarra's footsteps as professor and coordinator of early childhood programs at the University of Cincinnati. Dorsey has been active in local programs and served as chairman of the YMCA Child Development Services Committee of Management. On the national level, she has served on the NAEYC Ethics commission and panel and on the NAEYC Professional Practice Panel, and she has been a Board of Examiners member for the National Council for the Assessment of Teacher Education (NCATE). As a strong supporter of the National Association of Early Childhood Teacher Educators (NAECTE), she has served as president and was recipient of the NAECTE Early Childhood Teacher Educator award. Her publications include co-authorship of *Early Childhood Education: A Constructivist Approach* and *Early Childhood Curriculum: A Constructivist Approach.*

ACKNOWLEDGMENTS

Our book is the result of continuous support from friends and colleagues who have helped us immeasurably, even when they didn't realize the contributions they were making. We particularly want to thank the directors, many of whom are former students, who helped us understand their day-to-day work from a wide variety of situations and perspectives. Special thanks go to Chris Burroughs, Gretchen Estreicher, Patti Gleason, Jeanette Goertemoeller, Julie Hermes, Mary Marx, Louise Phillips, Cindy Sherding, and Sally Wehby. We appreciate the detailed work prepared by Chris Radel, who searched for and updated all the Web sites found in the book. We appreciate the guidance and encouragement given to us by our Delmar editors, Erin O'Connor, Stephanie Kelly, and Alexis Ferraro.

We hope our readers will find here the technical information they need to direct a viable program. Our greater desire is that they will recognize the significance of the leadership role of the director and the challenge and personal satisfaction derived from creating and implementing an excellent early care and education program for young children and their families.

Dorothy June Sciarra and Anne G. Dorsey

REVIEWERS

The authors and Thomson Delmar Learning would like to express their gratitude to the following professionals, who offered numerous, valuable suggestions:

Linda Aiken, MA
Southwestern Community College
Sylva, North Carolina

Jeanne W. Barker, MS
Tallahassee Community College
Tallahassee, Florida

Pam Boulton, EdD
University of Wisconsin-Milwaukee
    Children's Center
Milwaukee, Wisconsin

Toni Campbell, MEd
San Jose State University
San Jose, California

Irene Cook, MA
California State University at Bakersfield
Bakersfield, California

Jill E. Gelormino, PhD
St. Joseph's College
Patchogue, New York

Sylvia Hobbs, MS
Bellevue Community College
Bellevue, Washington

Leanna Manna, MA
Villa Maria College
Buffalo, New York

Elaine Boski-Wilkinson, MEd
Collin County Community College
Plano, Texas

Wayne Wolf, EdD
South Suburban College
South Holland, Illinois

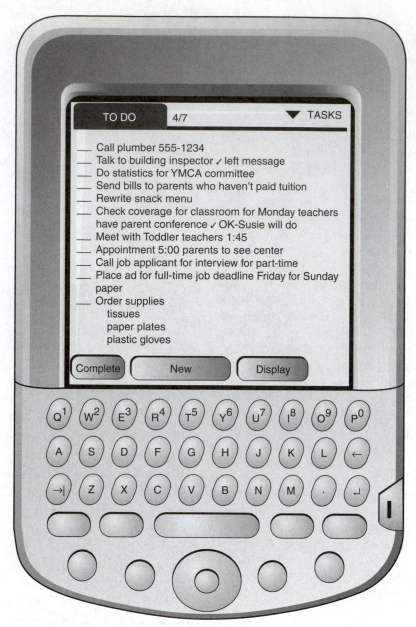

"Making a 'To Do List' is the only way I can come close to keeping track of the many things I must do each day. I recommend it to your readers who hope to become directors. By the way, I also recommend they learn something about plumbing!"
–Director, community agency center

C H A P T E R 1

The Working Director

Every director has a limited amount of time in which to do numerous tasks and develop many relationships. This work can be accomplished most effectively if the director is well organized.

OBJECTIVES

After reading this chapter, you should be able to:
- Identify administrative styles and roles.
- Describe the personal qualities needed to be an administrator.
- Describe two tools that enable the director to blend program management and people leadership.

Learning about the management and leadership of early childhood programs is important for staff and for current and prospective directors. The role of administrator requires knowledge and skills both in early childhood education and development and in business practices. With expertise in both of these areas, whether demonstrated by an individual or by a team, the program is likely to be successful for children, families, staff, and investors.

Any person who is doing an effective job as the director of an early childhood education center is involved in all the jobs that will be described in this text from enrolling children to evaluating staff, from budgeting to taking inventory, and from maintaining a physical plant to bandaging a child's scraped knee. The director's job includes all aspects of program and people management and leadership.

To do any one of these tasks, a director must have skills and knowledge; to do all of them requires stamina, understanding, and organization; and to do all of them effectively demands exceptional interpersonal skills as will be emphasized throughout this text. These skills enable the director to bring the best to parents, children, staff members, board members, and the community. In turn, serving as a model of these skills encourages those same people to give their best to the center. The effective director realizes that an early childhood education center can never be a one-person operation. There is a network of caring that transcends the day-to-day chores and makes being a part of a center worthwhile.

ADMINISTRATIVE STYLES AND ROLES

Although all directors are responsible for administering a program, their administrative styles are unique and, therefore, the outcomes of their programs differ. Some of the differences are based on the roles that are assigned to the directors, while others are based on the personalities, knowledge, skills, and attitudes of the directors.

Styles

Individuals who head an organization often begin the role using a managerial approach. They determine what has to be done, how it is to be done, and who should do whatever the task requires. The assigned staff member is expected to report back to the manager when the task is completed or at intervals along the way. If that does not happen, the manager takes responsibility for checking up on the staff member and commenting on the staff member's work or lack of success. This style may be appropriate in situations in which many staff members are relatively new in the field and have little background to draw upon. Even in that situation, however, when given opportunities, staff members may exceed expectations. Other managers use a more laissez-faire approach, leaving much of the decision making to the staff. Although they usually attend to essential paperwork, their interest may be directed more to building relations beyond the center for the benefit of the center. There is such a variety of managerial styles that it is impossible to categorize each one.

Some directors are natural leaders rather than managers. Others, over time and with mentoring, reading, and studying, become leaders. The director, who is a leader, looks to the staff for ideas, initiative, and implementation. Certainly, the leader does not turn over the running of the center to any staff member who steps forward. Rather, the leader supports and encourages staff to become part of the team that will help the center and its programs thrive. Directors realize that they must balance day-to-day reality with the vision that the center's stakeholders have prepared. (To read more about becoming a leader, see Covey, 2004; Lambert, 1998; McCrea, 2002; Sciarra & Dorsey, 2002).

Roles

If all the directors of centers in one state or county were to gather and discuss their roles, the job descriptions would undoubtedly cover a very wide range of categories. Some directors teach, perhaps spending half of every day in their own classrooms. Others never teach but are responsible for several centers; they travel between the centers, keeping abreast of two or more sets of circumstances, staff members, children, equipment lists, and so forth. Some may be responsible to an industry, to a corporate system, to a public school principal, or to a parent co-operative association, while others are proprietors and owners.

Some directors make all the policy and procedure decisions; others are in settings where some policy is set by a school system or corporate managing team. In other situations, every procedural detail is administered by a board. A director in a large center may have an assistant director, secretary, receptionist, and a cook; however, a director of a small center often does all the record keeping, supervising, answering of telephones, and meal preparation. Directors work with half-day programs, full-day programs, or perhaps even 24-hour care programs. The programs may offer care for infants and toddlers, or for older children, both before and after school. Sick child care or care of children with special needs also may be provided.

The financial plan may involve proprietary or agency operation and may or may not be organized to make a profit. Program goals range from providing a safe place where children are cared for to furnishing total developmental services for children, including medical and dental care; social services;

screening and therapy; and activities that promote intellectual, motor, emotional, social, and moral development.

Both the expectations of the clients served by the program and the expectations of the community will affect the center director's role. Some communities appreciate a director who is active in participating in the affairs of their community council, in lobbying for legislative reform, and in seeing that the cultural backgrounds of the children are preserved. Others prefer a director who focuses strictly on center business or on preparing children to deal with the demands of the elementary school. Directors must blend their personal philosophies with those of the community to achieve a balance. This blending can occur only if a potential director and a board explore each other's philosophies before agreeing on the responsibility for administering a particular program. If the philosophies of the director and those of the center truly are incompatible, one or the other must be changed.

DIRECTOR'S CORNER

"I had no idea how complex my role as director would be. Such a wide variety of people seem to need me immediately for such a wide variety of reasons. Meeting them all would probably be impossible (and maybe not even wise), but at the end of the day—most days—I know the challenges have been worthwhile. All it takes is one little pair of arms hugging me or one teacher smiling on her way out. 'See you tomorrow, Chris!'"

–Director, large suburban preschool

Sometimes, the director is confronted with a conflict between the two roles. The job description and the expectations of the people connected with the center may dictate that the director be present to greet teachers, parents, and children each day and to bid them good-bye each evening. In between, the director may be expected to be present in case an emergency arises. Simultaneously, however, there are obligations to the profession and to the community that must be met. The director may be asked to speak to a luncheon meeting of a community group that is ready to make a contribution to the center, to attend a board meeting of a local professional association, or to provide information at a session called by the diagnostic clinic to plan for one of the children with special needs who attends the early childhood education center.

Directors, especially those with experience, also have a responsibility to serve as child advocates. Although the National Association for the Education of Young Children (NAEYC) Code of Ethical Conduct calls on all who work with young children to "acknowledge an obligation to serve as a voice for children everywhere" (NAEYC, 2005), directors are more likely to have opportunities to see the broader picture of events in the community and beyond. They can keep informed about important legislative issues and about conditions affecting children and families by reading professional journals and newsletters and by being knowledgeable about local and national news. For example, NAEYC has an e-mail action alert system. Go to the NAEYC web site (NAEYC.org), visit the Public Policy section, and sign up for free regular updates. While at the site, explore the many other types and sources of information NAEYC provides. You can also subscribe to Educators Online Exchange as well as Exchange Everyday sponsored by the Child Care Exchange (www.childcareexchange.com). Children's Defense Fund (www.childrensdefense.org) will add you to its e-mail list if you request legislative updates.

Because directors are leaders and models, not only in their own centers but also throughout the community, staff, parents, and others often look to them for information about advocacy issues. Some directors may post information for staff and parents; others may make a concerted effort to involve people in an action plan. Some may write letters to the editors or to legislators, while others may testify before various governmental groups. In determining participation in advocacy efforts, each director must weigh responsibility to be an advocate against responsibility to the center, as well as consider personal time.

Although most directors work more than a 40-hour week, it is unreasonable and unwise to expect them to devote evening and weekend hours to their jobs on a regular basis. Directors who spend too much time on the job may become physically and emotionally exhausted, leading to ineffectiveness. As models for staff members, directors must demonstrate that they balance meeting personal and center needs. As you study this text, you may wonder how directors do it all. Knowledge, disposition, organization, and support all contribute to directors' success.

Personal Qualities

Directors may become enmeshed in unreasonable workloads because they have become personally involved in the center's work. An effective director should be involved closely with the activities of the center while maintaining distance, a difficult combination to attain. The primary reason for the difficulty in achieving this balance is that good directors assume their roles largely because they care about people. Yet at times, they find that there are overwhelming numbers of people who require care. This caring is exemplified in their willingness to do the mundane such as changing a diaper when a teacher is dealing with a crisis, or mopping up the kitchen when the dishwasher overflows just before lunch. Caring is apparent when the director assumes the role of learner as well as teacher and keeps abreast of current research while providing this information to staff when it is relevant. Caring is demonstrated by paying attention to detail, such as spelling an unusual name correctly, ordering the special food a teacher would like for a project, and seeing that each board and staff member is notified of an early childhood lecture that is being held in the community. Caring is regarding the operation of the center in a serious manner, yet maintaining a sense of humor.

For some people, caring is shown in an exuberant manner with lots of enthusiastic conversation, hugging, and facial animation. Others who are just as caring are quiet, seem somewhat reserved, and perhaps move into relationships more slowly. Directors may have other combinations of personal qualities, but the genuine and essential ability to care is the one that makes the difference.

An interesting aspect of caring is that it may be misunderstood. Because they are concerned for others, directors sometimes may have to adjust the style in which they relate to people. For example, some individuals may be uncomfortable about being touched; if the director unknowingly puts an arm around people who feel this way, they may be annoyed or insulted and be unable to accept the care and concern that is intended.

Being a caring person in the face of all the responsibilities of directing a center can be difficult. The caring director is constantly helping others by listening and providing emotional support for both children and adults and may well need people to respond in kind. Those individuals who become effective directors usually enjoy giving to others; they seem to thrive on it. However, because they are seen at the center as the source of so much giving, they must seek sustenance from either the caring network at the center, or a relative or friend outside the center. Even those people who freely and happily give of themselves need, at times, to receive support and encouragement through recognition and understanding.

Directing can be stressful because the director, although surrounded by people, is in a very real sense an isolate. She has no peers in the center and, no matter how loved and respected, is "the boss." It would be inappropriate for the director to confide in one particular staff member because some of the information with which she works cannot be shared with anyone at the center. Some directors have established a network of directors. They meet, perhaps monthly, for a relaxing lunch and conversation. There is reassurance in knowing that other directors have to report child abuse, experience staff turnover, have too many forms to fill out, and have considered quitting. As a group, directors can create ways to solve problems, to support one another, and to heighten community awareness regarding the needs of young children and their caregivers while maintaining confidentiality.

Directors realize they have the power to create healthy, supportive communities for children, families, and staff but also recognize that their early childhood training and classroom experiences have not prepared them to carry the vast array of responsibilities of running a center (Emmanuel & Elliott, 1997). Depending on the size, scope, and type of program, directors find they have duties that are as varied and complex as those of major corporate leaders. Yet they have had little or no preparation and often have no opportunity to prepare for the job. Limited mentoring is available.

To be effective leaders, directors must ensure that their own needs are met. Being a martyr, even a cheerful martyr, who never takes vacation or sick days may, in fact, lead staff to feel somewhat guilty when they recognize and meet their own needs. Competent directors serve as models of balance.

MANAGING THE PROGRAM

Although a broad range of roles may be assigned to directors, and although they may bring a variety of personal qualities to these roles, every director is responsible for program maintenance. This task, whatever its parameters, is possible only when the director is skilled and knowledgeable. Throughout this text, the information essential to doing the work of a center director is discussed. This information, when combined with some teaching and administrative experience, should help you meet the responsibilities that are required for appropriate program maintenance and enhancement. As with every other professional role, directors need to continue learning and developing. A list of typical responsibilities is included here.

1. Develop goals and objectives in relation to the center's philosophy, placing emphasis on the needs of clients.

CONTENTS

In memory of the love of my life, my husband, for his love, support, and encouragement in my personal and professional life throughout the 61 years of our marriage. His accomplishments and heroic spirit continue to inspire and sustain me, our children, and grandchildren, who loved him dearly and bless him for his gifts to all of us.   D.J.S.

To Robert Frost, without whom I may never have met Robert W. Dorsey.   A.G.D.

THOMSON

DELMAR LEARNING

Developing and Administering a Child Care and Education Program, Sixth Edition

Dorothy June Sciarra and Anne G. Dorsey

Vice President, Career Education SBU:
Dawn Gerrain

Director of Learning Solutions:
Sherry Dickinson

Managing Editor:
Robert L. Serenka, Jr.

Acquisitions Editor:
Erin O'Connor

Editorial Assistant:
Stephanie Kelly

Director of Production:
Wendy A. Troeger

Production Manager:
J.P. Henkel

Production Editor:
Rebecca Goldthwaite

Technology Project Manager:
Sandy Charette

Director of Marketing:
Wendy E. Mapstone

Channel Manager:
Kristin McNary

Cover Design:
Suzanne Nelson

Composition:
International Typesetting and Composition

Library of Congress Cataloging-in-Publication Data

Sciarra, Dorothy June.
    Developing and administering a child care and education program / Dorothy June Sciarra, Anne G. Dorsey.—6th ed.
        p. cm.
    Rev. ed. of: Developing and administering a child care center. 5th ed.
        c2003
    Includes bibliographical references and index.
    ISBN-13: 978-1-4180-0168-1
    ISBN-10: 1-4180-0168-6
        1. Day care centers—United States—Administration. I. Dorsey, Anne G. II. Sciarra, Dorothy June. Developing and administering a child care center. III. Title.

HQ778.63.S34 2007
362.71'2068—dc22
                                    2006001542

NOTICE TO THE READER

Developing and Administering a Child Care and Education Program

SIXTH EDITION

Dorothy June Sciarra

Professor Emerita, University of Cincinnati

Anne G. Dorsey

Professor Emerita, University of Cincinnati

THOMSON

DELMAR LEARNING ── Australia Canada Mexico Singapore Spain United Kingdom United States

2. Develop and maintain knowledge of standards created by professional and regulatory groups. Ensure that standards are being addressed appropriately throughout the center.

3. Work with staff to plan a curriculum to meet the objectives of the center.

4. Visit each classroom frequently.

5. Develop a positive working relationship with the board of directors and its committees, placing emphasis on communicating the center's accomplishments and needs to the board.

6. Establish policies for center operation, or become familiar with policies established by the center board, parent corporation, board of education, or other sponsor.

7. Draw up procedures for implementation of policies.

8. Prepare and maintain a manual for board and staff members.

9. Work with licensing agents to meet applicable licensing regulations.

10. Provide adequate insurance coverage.

11. Comply with all local, state, and federal laws relating to the center's operation.

12. Establish and operate within a workable budget.

13. Keep accurate financial records.

14. Pay bills and prepare payroll.

15. Collect tuition.

16. Write proposals and seek other funds for operation of the center.

17. Locate and maintain suitable physical facilities for the center's program.

18. Order and maintain equipment.

19. Develop and maintain a marketing plan.

20. Enroll and group the children.

21. Employ appropriate staff.

22. Orient staff.

23. Coach staff.

24. Develop knowledge levels and skills of staff so that upward mobility within your organization is feasible.

25. Evaluate the program, the staff members, and the children's progress.

26. Develop an effective communication system among staff members through regular staff meetings, conferences, and informal conversations.

27. Provide in-service training for staff and volunteers.

28. Fill roles of other staff members in emergency situations.

29. Plan and implement a family program that is responsive to needs and interests.

30. Explain the center's program to the community.

31. Participate in professional organizations; become an advocate for children.

32. Continue professional development through reading and attending pertinent courses such as workshops, conferences, and lectures.

Program maintenance requires that the director be organized. Just as the director expects teachers to have a plan for the year, month, week, and day, so too must the director have plans on a similar basis. Whether the plans are on a handheld device or on paper, they must be followed to a reasonable degree. Organization of documents is also essential. Although some paper forms are necessary, computerized systems often simplify documentation. If backed up and stored appropriately, they can be easy to locate, use, and modify. At the same time, discarding items that are no longer needed will make it easier to find working documents.

As you read other chapters of this text, you will notice the many types of files directors are expected to keep. These include policy manuals, staff records, child records, financial data, as well as numerous others. Most, if not all of these, can be available online. As with all important documents, it is essential to have a backup copy in a safe place.

Many of these program management jobs will be discussed in subsequent chapters. However, a key aspect of the center director's role to which this text gives very limited attention is that of developing curriculum. The director is the curriculum leader, but early childhood teacher preparation programs have at least one course devoted to curriculum. Directors who do not have an adequate early childhood background should expect to complete at least one course in early childhood curriculum. A section in an administration textbook and course could leave the false impression that that would suffice.

To aid in updating curriculum information, a wealth of books is available. Directors must assume responsibility for becoming familiar with curriculum for the young child, its sources, goals, and implementation approaches (see the Director's Library in Appendix D for suggested reading). Directors must be able to relate the curriculum principles in which they believe to the standards set forth by their state's education department and by early childhood professional organizations.

In addition, become familiar with the joint position statement from the NAEYC and National Association of Early Childhood Specialists in State Departments of Education (NAECS/SDE) titled *Early Childhood Curriculum, Assessment, and Program Evaluation: Building an Effective, Accountable System in Programs for Children Birth through Age 8* (2003). A related document issued by the same organizations, *Early Learning Standards: Creating Conditions for Success* (2002), also contains important professional information. Both documents have been posted on the NAEYC Web site in the position papers section. These documents appear to have been driven in part by public policy decisions, which have had major effects on early childhood programs, and in part by the realization that the quality of many programs is poor. One cause of low-quality programs is the lack of appropriately qualified teachers. The teacher market is tight and turnover is high, perhaps driven by the lack of realistic salaries. Rather than bemoan the situation, directors can get involved in the legislative process. But the decision to create a good-quality program is not really one a director is permitted to choose or reject. It is the heart of administration, hence of the director's role.

The director is responsible for instituting and maintaining a good-quality curriculum. Consulting with the teachers is expected, but the director must ensure that the goals and philosophy of the program are reflected in the curriculum. Directors who employ new teachers or teachers who have little or no background in child development and early childhood education will need to provide detailed coaching (Sciarra & Dorsey, 2002).

When choosing a curriculum, the director must recognize that it is highly unlikely that a curriculum that purports to have already done all the planning and provided all the necessary materials will be effective. Such programs are usually costly. They may also be unaesthetic, with "art" that should not appear in classrooms. Most important, it is impossible for the best teacher to plan every day's curriculum a year in advance. Such a plan cannot take into account the changing needs of the children. Nor can such a plan address the children's specific cultures, individual backgrounds, or current interests. In short, a pre-planned commercial curriculum should be examined carefully to determine whether it addresses the outcomes and uses the theoretical base that fits your organization's mission and goals and that will be significant for children's learning. Recall that when

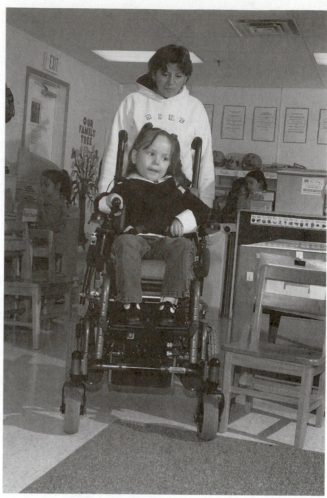

The director helps staff understand that all children can learn and that teachers must find ways to support each child's development.

developmentally appropriate practice was first being discussed, hundreds of manufacturers labeled their products, books, and curriculum kits "developmentally appropriate." Today, with the emphasis on research or evidence-based curricula, curricula are being labeled "research based." Before adopting a curriculum on the strength of that claim, make sure you see the research. Find out who the subjects were, what was done, and what the results were. Determine whether the results relate to your center's mission and goals.

The NAEYC and NAECS/SDE key curriculum recommendation suggests that early childhood professionals should "implement curriculum that is thoughtfully planned, challenging, engaging, developmentally appropriate, culturally and linguistically responsive, comprehensive, and likely to promote positive outcomes for all young children" (NAEYC & NAECS/SDE, 2003). The position statement defines curriculum as "a complex idea containing multiple components, such as goals, content, pedagogy, or instructional practices." When an appropriate curriculum is in place, children are actively involved, not just "on task." Children explore, create, plan, and implement. The curriculum the center has chosen helps the children reach comprehensive goals (cognitive, emotional, social, physical) and addresses academic standards in a planned way based on evidence that the child himself presents. For example, a child may be able to count to 10. After counting his 10 toy cars, he may respond by re-counting them when asked how many he has. This occurs not because he forgets how many he just counted, but because he has not yet created for himself the understanding that the last number stated in a counting sequence (in this case, 10) refers both to the tenth car and to the whole set. Teachers who understand this developmental sequence will plan classroom opportunities for him to encounter similar situations as he constructs this information for himself. These teachers demonstrate that they know the mathematics standards their children are expected to meet, that they understand mathematical development, and that they are helping children learn.

The NAEYC and NAECS/SDE position statement on standards cautions that "the development of high-quality curriculum and teaching practices—essential tools in achieving desired results—can be forgotten in a rush from developing standards to assessing whether children meet the standards" (2002). To address the challenge of meeting the needs of a diverse group of three- to six-year-olds, one idea is to provide broadly written content standards related to developmental continua but not to specific annual age-related goals (NAEYC & NAECS/SDE, 2002).

As directors address curriculum development and its relation to standards and to assessment, they must create a plan, perhaps even a curriculum, for ensuring that their staff are properly prepared to develop plans for their own classrooms and specific children. They must make certain that teachers are implementing the curriculum to the children's benefit and that the pedagogical approaches being used are developmentally appropriate. Teachers will need guidance and support to balance the children's developmental and individual needs with the expectations set by standards. In some centers, the director will assume most of the responsibility for working with families to ensure they have opportunities for input and for getting information about the center's curriculum. Families should be provided with information about standards set by the state or other organizations and how their children are being helped to move toward meeting standards. These topics are challenging for directors and teachers, but families are also interested and questioning what changes are being proposed and how they can be involved. (The Director's Library in Appendix D contains important curriculum references.)

LEADING PEOPLE

Directors sometimes acquire program management skills and stop there, failing to realize the importance of the skills of leading people. Centers can and do run, at least for a while, without people leadership; however, centers that lack program management quickly close their doors. People leadership and enrichment are at the very heart of a worthwhile early childhood education program.

Directors can enhance their effectiveness at leading people by developing an understanding of their own interpersonal styles. They also will benefit from studying various approaches to management, analyzing their own managerial styles, and determining their strengths and weaknesses in these areas. Most directors have had limited opportunities to acquire this information since they often move into administrative roles because they have been effective as teachers.

Fortunately, many seminars, books, and video and audio cassettes are available to enable directors to learn about interpersonal styles and management approaches.

The professional director understands that the role involves leadership as well as management. Beginning directors usually have to grow into the leadership role, but with motivation and support, they can attain the characteristics that will help them develop the entire center organization. Their major contribution will be creating and supporting a team that works effectively, efficiently, and positively with one another and with clients. For more information on this topic, see the companion volume, *Leaders and Supervisors in Child Care Programs* (Sciarra & Dorsey, 2002).

The center's board of directors may be willing to fund some training opportunities for the director, particularly if board members themselves understand and use this type of information. Possibly, a board member could furnish training or related materials.

Another option is to provide total staff or joint board-staff training in an approach such as conflict resolution. This training, if well done, should lead to confirming the director's role as leader, while establishing the responsibility of each staff member for the success of the center's program and the responsibility of the director to see that staff are involved in decision making and that their ideas are valued and accepted.

However, satisfaction obviously does not mean that everyone's demands will be met. For example, a teacher may be unhappy about working with a particular assistant whom she regards as lazy. When the teacher approaches the assistant with directions about what is to be done, the assistant does not complete the assigned tasks. In such a case, the director can facilitate a discussion between the teacher and assistant. However, had both of them been trained in conflict resolution, it is quite possible that they could solve the problem themselves. This situation certainly does not preclude the director from making a decision about retaining the assistant. However, helping a teaching team learn to work together is often more productive than terminating one and bringing in a new person. Only when the director is convinced that termination is in the best interest of the children and staff should that decision be made.

Because conflict in any organization is inevitable, preparing people to address it in a straightforward, rational manner can lead to satisfaction. Such an approach also goes a long way to eliminating gossip, dissension, and rumors. Everyone connected with the center—directors, board, staff, families, and children—realizes that their ideas will be respected. They begin to recognize that when disagreements occur, a people-centered approach to a solution is possible. The director does not have to be the judge in most situations. Individuals are empowered to work together to solve problems.

The basic ideas include bringing together the people who are experiencing conflict. This may be two individuals, the staff and director, or any other combination.

Once the people who are concerned are together, have them each state what the problem is. Depending on the situation, it may be helpful to write the results of each step for everyone involved to see. If two teachers want to use the playground at 10 a.m. and there is room for only one group of children at a time, the problem is "How can playground time be scheduled to everyone's satisfaction?" (Notice how similar this is to the problem of two children wanting the same toy at the same time.)

Next, brainstorm solutions. All solutions are presented for consideration. No comments about a potential solution are allowed at this point.

Examine the suggestions one at a time, eliminating any with which either party disagrees. Continue until a solution that is agreeable to each is reached.

Agree to try the solution for a set period of time and to renegotiate at the end of that time if necessary.

In summary, the process is as follows:

1. State the problem.
2. Generate solutions.
3. Select a solution agreeable to all.
4. Implement the planned solution.
5. Check after an agreed-upon time to determine whether the solution is working.
6. If it is not working, return to step 1 and continue the process.

The staff and board members who agree to commit to a conflict resolution type of philosophy use the concept that their customers (children and families) are their first priority as a starting point. By extension, a priority of directors must be staff satisfaction, and a priority of the board must be director and staff satisfaction. This approach works well when everyone understands it and accepts this basic principle.

Directors who are quite comfortable with an authoritarian role may find it difficult or impossible to relinquish that role, just as teachers who are convinced that a teacher-directed approach is the only appropriate way to work with children may be unable to provide choices for children. Directors who are willing to invest time and effort in learning about management usually will find that they are far more able to lead the staff and clients in ways that are more satisfying to everyone, and that the responsibility for the smooth running of the center will no longer rest primarily with one person.

The staff-oriented director plans time each day to visit each classroom, greet each staff member, and acknowledge their efforts and successes. She coaches and supports them as they develop new understandings and skills and provides honest, sensitive feedback. The staff-oriented director remembers and relates to events and incidents that are significant to staff, children, and families. It may be as simple as commenting to a teacher about how well she managed a frightened child during a thunderstorm by describing specifically the effective approach the teacher used. Perhaps the director stops to greet a child who is proudly bringing his rabbit to school for a visit. Maybe the director telephones a father to thank him for organizing a book fair to benefit the center.

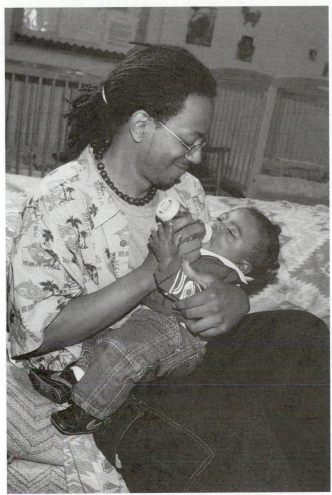 

In visiting an infant classroom, the director may comment to a staff member about the caring support provided for infants during feeding time and afterward.

Tending to the personal and professional development of the people associated with a center's program is seminal to the success of the program. The manner in which the director carries out people support tasks is a major contributing factor in program maintenance and vice versa. There is a delicate balance between successfully dealing with the mechanics of efficient program operation and simultaneously creating a caring environment for adults and children.

A director can have the human relations skills, care for others, ask for their ideas and opinions, encourage them to try new methods, and provide them with positive feedback. But if that same director does not have the skills and knowledge to accomplish the huge amount of work required of an administrator, the program cannot succeed. Similarly, the director who is task oriented, skilled, and knowledgeable may conduct a center that provides services but never really addresses or satisfies peoples' needs. Obviously, the director must combine work orientation skills with communication skills. If skills in either area are lacking, precious time will be wasted doing jobs or rebuilding relationships. Meanwhile, the children will not receive the excellent care they deserve.

Throughout this text you will read many more details about both program management and leadership that is required of all directors. You will begin by learning to manage a range of circumstances and tasks. Gradually, as you work at being a manager, if you are committed to developing your abilities and those of the staff, you will find yourself analyzing situations that occur in a child development program. As you reflect on what you do, why you do it, and the outcomes of your decisions, you will be creating new knowledge and understanding for yourself—something that no text or instructor can give you. You will be well on your way to moving from the role of manager to the role of leader.

Realizing that you may be feeling overwhelmed at the thought of the magnitude of the director's job, we turn now to a discussion of management tools that you can use to help you manage a challenging role.

MANAGEMENT TOOLS

Every director has a limited amount of time in which to do numerous tasks and develop many relationships. This work can be accomplished most effectively if the director is well organized. Then, when the inevitable unexpected event occurs, the director will be in a position that is stable enough to withstand the demands of the crisis. For example, the director whose financial records are in order may not have extra cash available to replace a broken water heater but at least is better prepared to adjust other budget categories to provide the funds. The disorganized director may not even know what funds and expenses will occur within the next few months in order to adjust the budget to meet the financial crisis. An efficient director can comfortably take time to listen to a group of excited children who burst into the office describing all the worms they found on the sidewalk. But a disorganized administrator may be too busy planning menus that are already overdue. It is obvious that administration will not always run smoothly for any director; however, the director who knows about appropriate techniques and uses them is certainly better prepared to cope effectively with the hubbub that often is evident in a child care center.

The use of several management tools can enable directors to administer programs effectively. These tools include policies and procedures manuals and time-use skills.

Policies and Procedures Manual

A manual containing all the center's policies and procedures facilitates the administrator's job. Generally, when there is a board, the board members make policies and the director develops procedures for implementation. For example, the board may establish a policy to admit any child between the age of three and five who can profit from the center's program. The director then establishes the procedures that are necessary to accomplish the child's enrollment such as plans for informing the community, distributing and receiving enrollment forms, and notifying parents that their child has been accepted or that the

center is full. The director also designs the necessary forms and includes copies in the manual.

When procedures are overly detailed or cover self-explanatory material, they become burdensome, and even may be neglected or circumvented by staff members. For example, teachers may be required to fill out a lengthy form to request permission to purchase something for which they will be reimbursed from petty cash; they also might be required to fill out another form after having purchased the item. At this point, some teachers may decide not to bother with purchasing needed items for their classrooms. They can carry their reaction one step further by disregarding the otherwise accepted procedures for using materials from the central storeroom. It is natural to anticipate that some established procedures will be unpopular with the staff, but if directors are open about why the procedures are important, and if they are careful about limiting the number of procedures to be followed, they will find that staff members are willing to comply.

Staff input prior to the establishment of procedures is usual, although the director still may need to make some independent decisions. When directors focus on their own need for power instead of on the establishment of procedures that will ensure the smooth running of an operation, it becomes impossible for the staff to feel respected. Staff members for whom every procedure is spelled out have no freedom. How, then, can they be expected to offer freedom to the children with whom they work?

Other Contents

In addition to policies and procedures, the manual contains the center's bylaws, job descriptions, salary schedules, and information about the center such as philosophy, goals, sponsorship, funding, and perhaps a brief history. If the manual is large, a table of contents and an index are helpful. Placing all materials in a loose-leaf binder enables staff members to add and delete pages as necessary. Each staff and board member receives a manual on initial affiliation with the center. It is the holder's responsibility to keep the manual up to date and to return it to the center when vacating the board or staff position.

Using Technology

Taking advantage of current technology can be a major time saver and organizer. Directors who are not already comfortable using computers will find that the initial learning period may be time consuming. Once users are confident, however, the benefits will begin.

One question often encountered when applying for financial assistance is "How will your company's financial records be maintained?" Financial record keeping and report generation are essential and time-consuming components of the director's role. Completing these tasks using software saves time and promotes accuracy once data is properly entered. Available software can provide computations for payroll deductions, billing, attendance, inventory, and a range of additional tasks. Nonetheless, many of the 364 directors responding to a survey conducted by the Center for Early Childhood Leadership (2004) were not taking advantage of this technology. Most of the directors had access to a computer and did use it for word processing tasks, but many did not use other components. More than half expressed interest in training in database management and spreadsheets. (Although the respondents came from 18 states and the District of Columbia, the survey was not designed as a random sample of all U.S. directors.)

In a similar study of readers of ChildCareExchange.com, 1341 responses to a Web site survey were received. Respondents, who found the survey because they were on line, reported greater use of technology for database management and accounting than that reported by the Center for Early Childhood Leadership study. In the ChildCareExhange survey, multicenter for-profit chains appear to be the most frequent users (Donohue, 2003).

Data for a more representative sample are more likely to show lower percentages of technology use. Kalinowki (2002) speculates that "about 15% of state licensed centers utilize a specialized child care management software package, meaning there is still a great untapped market" (p. 79). Purveyors of software have appeared at early childhood conferences for many years. Offering workshops, demos, free support, and a variety of other benefits, they have been unable to reach most of this large market.

As a director, you may be able to create your own system using software included in packages such as WindowsXP. You may choose to contract with a specialty business for payroll, fiscal reporting, and other functions, and you may find it reasonable to manage child information on paper. Nonetheless, analyzing staff time in terms of cost plus cost of contracted services compared with software cost and reduced staff time to generate comparable information may be surprising. Admittedly, initial learning time will increase costs. Another consideration is the professional appearance of computer-generated reports.

To find a software company that fits your center's needs, go to the Internet and do a search for "child care software." Read information provided by various purveyors, contact them, and ask for a demonstration. You can also check professional journals for reviews of child care software. *Child Care Information Exchange* and *Young Children* are potential sources, as are other directors who are experienced users of business software. At regional and national conferences, ask for demonstrations of software packages. Take a list of questions with you and jot down the answers and your impressions.

Consider which features you would like and which are essential. Ask whether you can buy components if you do not want or need a comprehensive package. For example, SofterWare's EZ-CARE2 has pages referred to as "drawers" for each family and each staff member. Data from the pages appear to be readily importable to other documents and easily modified as needed. Family drawer data flow to electronic fees collection and to receipts. Another example, ProCare Software has available a pocket attendance tracker, allowing teachers to have readily available emergency information for each child while on field trips. The data is imported from the children's files on the base computer. Another feature is a compact time clock that acts as a security device, requiring codes to enter the building and to clock in. For the food program, there is a menu planner, shopping lists, production sheets, and child food program eligibility and reimbursement amounts.

The director can set up a calendar of tasks to be completed, appointments, and so forth. Your staff may also benefit when you add computer technology to your center. Aside from paperwork that they may be able to complete more easily and professionally on a computer, they may also use the computer for continuing education courses. Explore these and other uses and packages thoroughly before buying. You may want to ask for a trial period.

Time-Use Skills

Some directors study time management as a tool to use in allocating available time wisely. The board may provide tuition or released time for a director to attend a time-management course or seminar. Several time-management techniques can be acquired easily and put to immediate use.

Analyzing Use of Time

As a beginning, directors can analyze how they spend their time by writing down in detail everything they do for several days. The next step is to make a judgment about which of the activities have not been enjoyed, have not been done well, or have not been related either to the personal goals of the director or the goals of the center. When time is frittered away on such activities, less time is available to invest in other, more productive activities. The individual alone can decide which activity should take priority. In some businesses, listening to a client discuss an emotional problem would be considered a waste of the administrator's time. In early childhood education, with its focus on children and families, time that the director spends listening may be the most effective use of the available administrative time.

Voice mail, e-mail, and other computer communication approaches help the director keep in touch while controlling the use of time. However, directors must be careful to avoid communicating with families and staff solely through technology. The sensitive director is alert to the need for a live, human contact and a handwritten note in some situations.

Although some of the director's tasks may not be appealing, they may need to be done. A director can, at least, recognize how much time must be devoted to undesirable tasks; then this amount of time can be put into perspective. The director also may decide to devise ways to make tasks more manageable. Of course, if the majority of tasks seem undesirable, the director may choose to change jobs.

Grouping and Assigning Tasks

The director who needs to economize on time also may decide to make an effort to read and answer all mail, place outgoing telephone calls, and record financial transactions at a specified time each day. Directors who allocate time for these types of chores and establish the policy that they are not to be disturbed during that time will probably have more time for meeting people's needs during the rest of the day.

Directors also should consider which jobs they must do and which jobs they can delegate to someone else. For example, could the janitor inform the director of supplies that are needed on a regularly scheduled basis instead of having the director do this checking? Perhaps the receptionist can be trained to respond to the general calls for information about the center instead of involving the director in a routine conversation about when the center is open and providing the ages of children who are served.

Once the center's operation is reasonably under control, additional staff people can be trained to fill the director's role in her absence, thereby allowing the director to move out into the wider community on occasion. It is not appropriate to insist that other staff people do the director's work, but it is appropriate to begin to train them to assume the role of director temporarily. In this way, both parties can benefit professionally.

Planning a Time Line

One of the ways a director develops efficiency is through the development of a time line. Jobs that must be done on a regular basis are scheduled, then the director does them according to the schedule. This simple concept curtails procrastination by helping the director recognize that when a job that is scheduled this week is postponed because it is distasteful, time and energy are going to be spent thinking about it anyway. Since the job must be completed eventually, no time is saved by waiting until next week; nor does the job become easier. In fact, the director then may be in the uncomfortable position of having to apologize.

REFLECTION

Imagine that you have planned to spend the evening writing a term paper that is due the following day. A friend telephones. He is terribly upset about his wife's serious illness. Think about what you might do.

Now imagine that at 3:00 P.M. you, as an early childhood center director, are greeted by a teacher who is leaving for the day and who wants to talk about her husband who has just lost his job. You had planned to spend the rest of the afternoon working on the major equipment order that is needed for a board committee report the following morning. You may choose

- to listen to the teacher.
- to tell the teacher that you do not have time to listen because of the report you must prepare.
- to schedule time the following afternoon to listen to the teacher.
- some other plan.

Any of these choices could be appropriate; the director must make the best choice. But the directors who always find themselves too busy to listen and those who always find themselves spending so much time listening that they must work all evening must analyze why their scheduling problems recur. Think about your own reaction to this situation.

A suggested time line for a working director appears in Working Paper 1–5. Each director must develop a time line based on the personal responsibilities that are unique to the type of program and the client's needs. No matter which jobs and time frames are included, writing a time line gives the director and others a clear picture of the work to be done. The time line can be flexible when circumstances warrant, but basically, the goal is to adhere to the plan so that regularly scheduled tasks will be completed and time for working with people will be made available.

In Chapter 2, you will learn about the importance of the director's interpersonal relationships and that they set the tone for the center. Now, as you prepare to learn more about the director's role, you will see this theme reemphasized. It may seem impossible that a director really could focus on establishing a "we" feeling when Chapters 3 through 16 will present an almost overwhelming set of director responsibilities.

Nonetheless, directors who know what is involved in the job, who work to acquire the necessary knowledge and skills, and who use a managerial approach that reflects an understanding of the needs of staff and clients are found in nearly every community.

These competent and successful directors know that being a director is exhausting,
and frequently challenging,
sometimes frightening,
never boring,
sometimes lonely,
many times hectic,
and, yes, even fun.

They also know that being a director—*a really good director*—
a leader,
a manager,
a model,

(A) Handling calls from prospective parents.

(B) Checking in with teachers and children.

(C) Maintaining the physical plant.

(D) Keeping up-to-date records.

The director's job includes all aspects of program and people support.

a coach,
and a supporter
is hard work and time consuming.
And being a director just often enough is
deeply satisfying,
even exhilarating,
and richly rewarding!

SUMMARY

An effective director is a person who combines skills, knowledge, and caring. Although directors fill a variety of roles in countless styles, no effective director can let either the management and operation of the center or the care of and communication with people occupy an inappropriate proportion of time. For each director in each situation, personal decisions must be made about the style of directing.

Two tools that enable the director to blend program management and leading people are the policies and procedures manual and time-use skills. Each director must develop an appropriate balance so that the program management—which must be done—does not override the importance of leading people. Because leadership can readily be overlooked by directors who find themselves in the throes of program management, directors must develop skills that enable them to excel at program management. Only then will they have the time and energy to devote to leading people that is the very essence of a quality child care program.

CLASS ASSIGNMENTS

1. Keep a log of how you spend your time for two days. Be sure to write down everything you do and the amount of time each activity takes. Look at your list. Did you do all the things you wanted to do during those two days? If not, which activities could you have omitted or shortened to provide time for other interests? Directors use this same technique in evaluating their use of time on the job. You can use it periodically to check on how much time you actually spend doing what you want and need to do, and how much time you devote to other activities.

2. Visit the director of an early childhood education center. Discuss approximately how much time is spent on various aspects of the job such as keeping financial records; communicating with parents, staff members, children, and board members; and handling emergencies. Write your findings on Working Paper 1–1.

3. Read the policy statement on celebration of holidays (Working Paper 1–2) and the outdoor play policy and procedures (Working Paper 1–3). Using Working Paper 1–4, write a policy statement for an early childhood education center on any topic of your choice. Then write procedures for implementation of that policy. Before doing this assignment, you may want to practice by writing some procedures for the above policy.

CLASS EXERCISES

1. Discuss with a classmate the activities on which each of you would like to spend more time. Were there any similarities between the activities you each mentioned? To what did each of you attribute your lack of time for your favorite activities?

2. Compare your findings from Class Assignment 1 with those of your classmates.

3. Discuss with three members of your class the kind of director you would like to be. Read the sample Director's Time Line (Working Paper 1–5). On which of the director's roles would you like to spend the most time? Put a check mark next to those tasks that you would enjoy doing. Put an X next to those you would not like to do. Compare your ideas with those of your classmates.

4. If you were the director, which of the tasks in the Director's Time Line could you assign to someone else? Why?

WORKING PAPER 1-1

(for use with Class Assignment 2)

DIRECTOR'S TIME FORM

Name of center _____

Name of person interviewed _____

Title of person interviewed _____

How much time is spent on keeping financial records? _____

How much time is spent communicating with parents, staff, board members, or children? _____

_____

How much time is spent handling emergencies? _____

Other information: _____

_____

Make a computer graph or diagram to depict these relationships.

WORKING PAPER 1-2

(for use with Class Assignment 3)

POLICY ON HOLIDAY CELEBRATIONS

The staff of the Children's Center met to discuss developmentally appropriate ways to celebrate holidays with three-year-old classes. We agreed that our policies are as follows:

1. Meeting the child's needs appropriately will be our first priority.

2. We will be sensitive to the interests and wishes of other school staff, parents, and the community.

3. We will inform parents, principals, and staff of our plans and of our rationale and welcome dialogue on these issues.

WORKING PAPER 1-3

(for use with Class Assignment 3)

POLICY STATEMENT FOR OUTDOOR PLAY

At Children's Learning Center, we believe that outdoor experiences should be provided for all young children through age eight on a daily basis. Because their physical development is occurring so rapidly, young children should go outside daily to practice large muscle skills, learn about outdoor environments, and experience freedom not always possible indoors. Outdoor time is an integral part of the curriculum and should be planned.

PROCEDURES FOR IMPLEMENTATION OF OUTDOOR POLICY

1. All children will go outdoors daily for at least 20 minutes. This time may be spent on the playground and/or going for a walk. The outside time is to be viewed as an integral part of the curriculum. Therefore, planning for and discussing that experience will be included in the Friday processing and lesson planning.

2. Parents will be informed that all children will be going out each day. Children not well enough to go outdoors are probably not well enough to be in school.

3. Plans will be made to provide caps, mittens, sweaters, and whatever other outdoor clothing is needed.

4. Circumstances that might preclude daily outdoor play are

   ■ a chill factor below freezing (32°F) at the time the children go outdoors.

   ■ a steady rain or downpour. Length of stay outdoors will be adjusted on drizzly or snowy days.

   ■ a tornado watch or tornado warning periods.

5. On days when circumstances preclude going outdoors, opportunity for large motor activity and/or walks within the building will be provided. Therefore, alternative plans will be discussed during the Friday processing and lesson planning.

WORKING PAPER 1-4

(for use with Class Assignment 3)

POLICY STATEMENT FORM

Policy on

_____

(Write the policy or policies on the topic you have chosen.)

Procedures: (Write the procedures for implementation of the above policy.)

WORKING PAPER 1-5

(for use with Class Exercise 3)

DIRECTOR'S TIME LINE

Directors complete a wide variety of tasks each year. The schedule depends on the center. In year-round centers, the budget/program year may begin in January. However, for many centers, the year begins in autumn when some children leave for kindergarten or first grade. Some directors find that enrollment is reduced in summer when older siblings may be available to care for young children.

Annual Tasks

Prior to Beginning of New Program Year
Prepare budget and get board approval (if needed).
Determine salaries for coming year.
Prepare staff contracts for coming year.
Assign teachers and children to groups and classrooms.
Interview substitutes and prepare sub list.
Recruit and orient volunteers.
Update policies and procedures.
Update marketing plan.
Confirm that all child and staff records are complete and up to date.
Order equipment and supplies.
Set up reminders on computer for renewal of the following:
  Individual medical forms (child and staff)
  Licenses (child care license, NAEYC accreditation renewal, food service, fire department license, first aid, communicable diseases, CPR, child abuse training, staff teaching licenses/certificates, bus driver's chauffeur's license, bus license)
  Insurance coverage
Check supply of forms needed throughout year.
Arrange for extra services such as medical, dental, social services if these are to be provided.
Set up calendar for coming program year, including items such as:
  Staff meetings and appreciation events
  Staff supervision and conferences
  Parent conferences
  Parent meetings
  Meetings with assistant director, educational coordinator, accountant, bookkeeper, other staff who assist with administration of center
  Meetings with board of directors and with chairman
  Periodic maintenance (heating/air conditioning, appliances, computers, bus, security system)
  Preparation of proposals for ongoing funding, such as Head Start, and United Way, and for special funding
  In-service training for self and staff

(continues)

WORKING PAPER 1-5
(continued)

(for use with Class Exercise 3)

Confer with student teachers and college supervisors.
Attend courses, professional conferences, and workshops.
Participate in professional organizations.
Make arrangements for special activities for children and families.
Conduct open house for potential clients.

Beginning of Program Year
Place new equipment and supplies.
Arrange with colleges for student teachers.
Conduct opening parent meeting.

End of Program Year
Clean, repair, and inventory equipment and supplies.
Conduct staff evaluations.
Prepare self-evaluation.
Arrange for program evaluation (may be done biannually).
Assist teachers in evaluating children's progress and in holding parent conferences.
Recognize volunteers.
Prepare annual report.
Thoroughly check building and grounds for needed maintenance and arrange to have work done.

Monthly Tasks
Review budget.
Prepare financial reports.
Report to board of directors (if applicable).
Plan menus.
Order nonperishable food.
Order supplies.
Read professional journals.
Check building, grounds, and equipment and schedule required maintenance.
Review teachers' classroom plans (may be done weekly).
Review attendance records.
Prepare billing.
Make payments.
Complete forms required by funders.
Prepare family newsletter.
Conduct fire drill.

Weekly Tasks
Prepare payroll.
Supervise staff (observe and confer).

(continues)

WORKING PAPER 1-5
(continued)

(for use with Class Exercise 3)

Order fresh food.
Conduct staff meetings (may be biweekly).
Maintain family and staff bulletin boards.

Daily Tasks

Greet each staff member at least briefly.
Talk with children and families.
Visit classrooms.
Record financial transactions.
Make and answer phone calls and e-mails.
Teach, including planning, implementing, and cleaning up (if included in job description).

As Needed

Advertise for, interview, and hire replacement or additional staff.
Orient new staff.
Enroll children.
Orient new children and parents.
Fill roles of absent staff.
Participate in fund-raising.
Conduct visitors' tours.
Conduct meetings to discuss individual children.
Contact other agencies to develop rapport.
Participate in community activities such as the opening of a neighborhood recreation center.
Obtain and disseminate information on legislation.
Inform legislators of issues related to early childhood education. Request support.
Recommend termination of employment of staff members, as necessary.
Deal with crises.
Deal with the mundane.
Take a break!

DIRECTOR'S RESOURCE 1-1

ESSENTIAL DOCUMENT CATEGORIES

–Building–

- Mortgage or lease or rental arrangements and contact person/s
- Insurance for building/contents (theft, fire, storm) and personal injury—agent's name and contact information
- Certificate of Occupancy (CO) from the municipality and related permits
- Fire extinguishers and smoke alarms—record of purchase and schedule for servicing
- Contact information and schedule for carpenter, cleaning contract, garbage collection, glazer, heat/air conditioning, locksmith, playground maintenance, plumber, snow removal (if needed)
- Paint, tile, carpet, fabric swatches with contact information

–Equipment–

- Keep a full inventory list of equipment by site location, classroom, office, kitchen, playground—includes dates of purchase, cost, depreciation of applicable, source of item and funding
- Prepare a file folder for the equipment in each location: kitchen, office, classroom A, B, C, etc., playground. Keep in each folder the information for each piece of equipment: purchase order or donation source, receipt, warranty, maintenance agreement, and operating instructions

–Program Operations–

- Incorporation papers
- Tax-related papers (tax-exempt letter from IRS, state-exempt certificate, corporate filing papers)
- Charitable organization records (if applicable)
- State and local licenses and accreditations (copies posted in visible location)
- Employment-related payments, tax records, payroll information
- Bank statements and account records—bank branch and contact information
- Investment accounts
- Bylaws, including original and each revision
- Attorney contract or agreement
- Accountant contract or agreement
- Medical personnel contract or agreement
- Insurance policies (copies of relevant policies should be in building and vehicle folders)
- Food documents and permits
- Fire drill procedures and records
- Corporate credit card records
- Funding sources, contracts, reports, etc.
- Journal and periodical subscriptions—payment and renewal schedules

–Vehicles–

- Title or proof of ownership (original in safe deposit box, copy in files) for each vehicle
- Registration documentation and renewal schedule for each vehicle
- Insurance policies (originals in safe deposit box, copies in files) for each vehicle
- Automobile club membership
- Authorized drivers, proof of age, copy of license with photo, etc.
- Service and repair arrangements and maintenance schedule for each vehicle
- Gas/oil credit cards (if applicable)
- Parking arrangements in garage or on parking lot

Republished with permission of CCIE (Neugebauer) from Exchange, permission emerged through Copyright Clearance Center, Inc.

DIRECTOR'S RESOURCE 1-2

THINGS TO DO TO REORGANIZE THE FILING SYSTEM FOR A CHILD CARE PROGRAM

Things to Do	Person Responsible
Conduct inventory of all files and place in a central location.	Director, Head Teacher, Secretary
Conduct inventory of office supplies.	Secretary
Order additional supplies.	Director and Secretary
Determine need for bank safety deposit box and make arrangements with a bank, preferably a complimentary box with the bank in which the program accounts are located.	Director and Finance Officer or Board Treasurer
Brainstorm essential document file categories and make a 5" x 8" sign for each one.	Director, Head Teacher, Secretary
Identify file cabinet drawer(s) or strong file boxes for storing only essential documents. Install a hanging file frame in each drawer and use hanging files. These may be color coded for each category if desired. In black ink, print each file category in BLOCK LETTERS on hanging file label (for example, **BUILDING**).	Director and Secretary
Review each file folder to discard duplicates and obsolete documents, and to archive necessary items. Allow enough time for this lengthy task; new directors should get advice from long-time staff before discarding documents.	Director and Head Teacher
Assign each file folder to one of the file categories.	Director and Secretary
In black ink, print each file folder label title in upper and lower case letters (for example, **Insurance**).	Secretary
Create an *Essential Document Directory* on a hard drive, and in a three-ring binder or a special color folder. Place hard copies in the front of the first EDD file drawer.	Secretary
Distribute copies of the Directory to the head teacher and board president	Director
Maintain the files by making changes as they occur and recording them in the Directory.	Director and Secretary

Reprinted with permission of CCIE (Neugebauer) from Exchange, permission emerged through Copyright Clearance Center, Inc.

DIRECTOR'S RESOURCE 1-3

PROGRAM ADMINISTRATOR DEFINITION AND COMPETENCIES

I. Program Administrator Definition

The program administrator is the individual responsible for planning, implementing, and evaluating an early care and education program. The role of the administrator covers both leadership and management functions. Leadership functions relate to the broad view of helping an organization clarify and affirm values, set goals, articulate a vision, and chart a course of action to achieve that vision. Managerial functions relate to the actual orchestration of tasks and setting up systems to carry out the organization's mission.

Functions of the program administrator include:

- *Pedagogical.* Creating a learning community of children and adults that promotes optimal child development and healthy families.

- *Organizational and Systems.* Establishing systems for smooth program functioning and managing staff to carry out the mission of the program. Planning and budgeting the program's fiscal resources. Managing organizational change and establishing systems to monitor and evaluate organizational performance.

- *Human Resources.* Recruiting, selecting, and orienting personnel. Overseeing systems for the supervision, retention, and professional development of staff that affirm program values and promote a shared vision.

- *Collaborative.* Establishing partnerships with program staff, family members, board members, community representatives, civic leaders, and other stakeholders to design and improve services for children and their families.

- *Political.* Advocating on behalf of high-quality services to meet the needs of children and their families.

The administrator may have different role titles depending on the program type or sponsorship of the program. Common titles include: director, site manager, administrator, program manager, early childhood coordinator, and principal.

II. Core Competencies

An Informant to Selection of Annual Professional Development Options Adapted from Illinois Director Credential

The core competencies needed for effective early childhood program administration fall into two broad categories: management knowledge and skills and early childhood knowledge and skills. These are not discrete categories; there is conceptual as well as practical overlap between and within each category.

Management Knowledge and Skills

Administrators need a solid foundation in the principles of organizational management including how to establish systems for smooth program functioning and managing staff to carry out the mission of the program.

(continues)

DIRECTOR'S RESOURCE 1-3
(continued)

1. Personal and Professional Self-Awareness

Knowledge and application of adult and career development, personality typologies, dispositions, and learning styles. Knowledge of one's own beliefs, values, and philosophical stance. The ability to evaluate ethical and moral dilemmas based on a professional code of ethics. The ability to be a reflective practitioner and apply a repertoire of techniques to improve the level of personal fulfillment and professional job satisfaction.

2. Legal and Fiscal Management

Knowledge and application of the advantages and disadvantages of different legal structures. Knowledge of different codes and regulations as they relate to the delivery of early childhood program services. Knowledge of child custody, child abuse, special education, confidentiality, anti-discrimination, insurance liability, contract, and labor laws pertaining to program management. Knowledge of various federal, state, and local revenue sources. Knowledge of bookkeeping methods and accounting terminology. Skill in budgeting, cash flow management, grant writing, and fund-raising.

3. Staff Management and Human Relations

Knowledge and application of group dynamics, communication styles, and techniques for conflict resolution. Knowledge of different supervisory and group facilitation styles. The ability to relate to staff and board members of diverse racial, cultural, and ethnic backgrounds. The ability to hire, supervise, and motivate staff to high levels of performance. Skill in consensus building, team development, and staff performance appraisal.

4. Educational Programming

Knowledge and application of different curriculum models, standards for high-quality programming, and child assessment practices. The ability to develop and implement a program to meet the needs of young children at different ages and developmental levels (infant/toddler, preschool, kindergarten). Knowledge of administrative practices that promote the inclusion of children with special needs.

5. Program Operations and Facilities Management

Knowledge and application of policies and procedures that meet state/local regulations and professional standards pertaining to the health and safety of young children. Knowledge of nutritional and health requirements for food service. The ability to design and plan the effective use of space based on principles of environmental psychology and child development. Knowledge of playground safety design and practice.

6. Family Support

Knowledge and application of family systems and different parenting styles. Knowledge of community resources to support family wellness. The ability to implement program practices that support families of diverse cultural, ethnic, linguistic, and socioeconomic backgrounds. The ability to support families as valued partners in the educational process.

(continues)

7. Marketing and Public Relations

Knowledge of the fundamentals of effective marketing, public relations, and community outreach. The ability to evaluate the cost-benefit of different marketing and promotional strategies. The ability to communicate the program's philosophy and promote a positive public image to families, business leaders, public officials, and prospective funders. The ability to promote linkages with local schools. Skill in developing a business plan and effective promotional literature, handbooks, newsletters, and press releases.

8. Leadership and Advocacy

Knowledge of organizational theory and leadership styles as they relate to early childhood work environments. Knowledge of the legislative process, social issues, and public policy affecting young children and their families. The ability to articulate a vision, clarify and affirm values, and create a culture built on norms of continuous improvement and ethical conduct. The ability to evaluate program effectiveness. The ability to define organizational problems, gather data to generate alternative solutions, and effectively apply analytical skills in its solution. The ability to advocate on behalf of young children, their families and the profession.

9. Oral and Written Communication

Knowledge of the mechanics of writing including organizing ideas, grammar, punctuation, and spelling. The ability to use written communication to effectively express one's thoughts. Knowledge of oral communication techniques including establishing rapport, preparing the environment, active listening, and voice control. The ability to communicate ideas effectively in a formal presentation.

10. Technology

Knowledge of basic computer hardware and software applications. The ability to use the computer for program administrative functions.

Early Childhood Knowledge and Skills

Administrators need a strong foundation in the fundamentals of child development and early childhood education in order to guide the instructional practices of teachers and support staff.

1. Historical and Philosophical Foundations

Knowledge of the historical roots and philosophical foundations of early childhood care and education. Knowledge of different types of early childhood programs, roles, funding, and regulatory structures. Knowledge of current trends and important influences impacting program quality. Knowledge of research methodologies.

2. Child Growth and Development

Knowledge of different theoretical positions in child development. Knowledge of the biological, environmental, cultural, and social influences impacting children's growth and development from prenatal through early adolescence. Knowledge of developmental milestones in children's physical, cognitive, language, aesthetic, social, and emotional development. Knowledge of current research in neuroscience and its application to the field of early childhood.

(continues)

DIRECTOR'S RESOURCE 1-3
(continued)

3. Child Observation and Assessment

Knowledge and application of developmentally appropriate child observation and assessment methods. Knowledge of the purposes, characteristics, and limitations of different assessment tools and techniques. Ability to use different observation techniques including formal and informal observation, behavior sampling, and developmental checklists. Knowledge of ethical practice as it relates to the use of assessment information. The ability to apply child observation and assessment data to planning and structuring developmentally appropriate instructional strategies.

4. Curriculum and Instructional Methods

Knowledge of different curriculum models, appropriate curriculum goals, and different instructional strategies for infants, toddlers, preschoolers, and kindergarten children. Ability to plan and implement a curriculum based on knowledge of individual children's developmental patterns, family and community goals, institutional and cultural context, and state standards. Ability to design integrated and meaningful curricular experiences in the content areas of language and literacy, mathematics, science, social studies, art, music, drama, movement, and technology. Ability to implement anti-bias instructional strategies that take into account culturally valued content and children's home experiences. Ability to evaluate outcomes of different curricular approaches.

5. Children with Special Needs

Knowledge of atypical development including mild and severe disabilities in physical, health, cognitive, social/emotional, communication, and sensory functioning. Knowledge of licensing standards, state and federal laws (e.g., ADA, IDEA) as they relate to services and accommodations for children with special needs. Knowledge of the characteristics of giftedness and how educational environments can support children with exceptional capabilities. The ability to work collaboratively as part of a family-professional team in planning and implementing appropriate services for children with special needs. Knowledge of special education resources and services.

6. Family and Community Relationships

Knowledge of the diversity of family systems, traditional, non-traditional and alternative family structures, family life styles, and the dynamics of family life on the development of young children. Knowledge of sociocultural factors influencing contemporary families including the impact of language, religion, poverty, race, technology, and the media. Knowledge of different community resources, assistance, and support available to children and families. Knowledge of different strategies to promote reciprocal partnerships between home and center. Ability to communicate effectively with parents through written and oral communication. Ability to demonstrate awareness and appreciation of different cultural and familial practices and customs. Knowledge of child rearing patterns in other countries.

7. Health, Safety, and Nutrition

Knowledge and application of practices that promote good nutrition, dental health, physical health, mental health, and safety of infants/toddlers, preschool, and kindergarten children. Ability to implement practices indoors and outdoors that help prevent, prepare for, and respond to emergencies. Ability to model healthful lifestyle choices.

(continues)

DIRECTOR'S RESOURCE 1-3
(continued)

8. Individual and Group Guidance

Knowledge of the rationale for and research supporting different models of child guidance and classroom management. Ability to apply different techniques that promote positive and supportive relationships with children and among children. Ability to reflect on teaching behavior and modify guidance techniques based on the developmental and special needs of children.

9. Learning Environments

Knowledge of the impact of the physical environment on children's learning and development. The ability to use space, color, sound, texture, light, and other design elements to create indoor and outdoor learning environments that are aesthetically pleasing, intellectually stimulating, psychologically safe, and nurturing. The ability to select age-appropriate equipment and materials that achieve curricular goals and encourage positive social interaction.

10. Professionalism

Knowledge of laws, regulations, and policies that impact professional conduct with children and families. Knowledge of different professional organizations, resources, and issues impacting the welfare of early childhood practitioners. Knowledge of center accreditation criteria. Ability to make professional judgments based on the NAEYC "Code of Ethical Conduct and Statement of Commitment." Ability to reflect on one's professional growth and development and make goals for personal improvement. Ability to work as part of a professional team and supervise support staff or volunteers.

Reprinted with permission of the National Association for the Education of Young Children.

REFERENCES

Center for Early Childhood Leadership. (2004, Spring). *Research notes.* Chicago: Center for Early Childhood Leadership, National-Louis University.

Covey, S. (2004). *The 8th habit: From effectiveness to greatness.* Rochester, NY: Free Press.

Donohue, C. (2003, November). Technology in early childhood education: An exchange trend report. *Child Care Information Exchange, 154,* 17–22.

Emmanuel, E., & Elliott, K. (1997, Summer). Director credentialling: An investment in quality care and education. *Leadership Quest: The journal for professionals in early childhood education, 1*(1), 18.

Kalinowski, M. (2002, July). The special nature of management software. *Child Care Information Exchange, 146,* 79–81.

Lambert, L. (1998). *Building leadership capacity in schools.* Alexandria, VA: Association for Supervision and Curriculum Development.

McCrea, N. (2002). Learning leading for authenticity. *Child Care Information Exchange, 147,* 10–14.

National Association for the Education of Young Children and National Association of Early Childhood Specialists in State Departments of Education. (2003). *Early childhood curriculum assessment, and program evaluation: Building an effective, accountable system in programs for children birth through age 8.* Retrieved from http://www.NAEYC.org.

National Association for the Education of Young Children and National Association of Early Childhood Specialists in State Departments of Education. (2002). *Early learning standards: Creating conditions for success.* Retrieved from http://www.NAEYC.org.

National Association for the Education of Young Children. (2005). *Code of ethical conduct and statement of commitment: Guidelines for responsible behavior in early childhood education.* Washington, DC: Author.

Sciarra, D. J., & Dorsey, A. G. (2002). *Leaders and supervisors in child care programs.* Clifton Park, NY: Thomson Delmar Learning.

Additional resources for this chapter can be found on the Online Companion™ at http://www.earlychilded.delmar.com. This supplemental material includes relevant Web links, Web activities, and case studies that apply the concepts presented in this chapter. In addition, the Working Papers and Director's Resources are available for download, allowing you to complete Class Exercises and Class Assignments electronically.

CHAPTER 2

Developing Interpersonal Relationships

The emotional tone at the center is set by the way the director feels about others and by the success with which those feelings are communicated to others in the setting.

OBJECTIVES

After reading this chapter, you should be able to:

■ Discuss ways to create a positive climate through:
    modeling
    community building
    communicating

■ List ways to motivate staff through:
    encouragement
    job enrichment

The following quotation is from the director of a community nonprofit child care center: "In order to be successful as a director of a child care center, I think, above all else, you have to be a *people person*. You have to realize that this job goes far beyond administrative policy and doing paperwork, that being *the boss* here is not really being a *boss* in the traditional sense. Being the boss here has to do with forming trusting relationships with your staff, respecting their individuality, being firm when you need to be firm and being gentle when they need a gentle hand. It's important to remember that you won't get respect if you don't show respect. Also, remember that others can do the paperwork, but you are the one who must build the relationships with your staff. Of course, you are also responsible for building relationships with parents and the community."

Clearly, the interpersonal issues and the time it takes to work them out are at the very core of every management position. Much of what follows in this text deals with budgets, boards, licensing, and record keeping, but the *real* task of the director as a manager is to work effectively with, and provide support to, those who will implement the program. The terms manager, director, administrator, and leader used throughout this book all refer to the person in charge of, and responsible for, the total program. The manager must relate to the staff and motivate them to do the tasks delegated to them. Members of the staff implement the total program, but the director, acting in the capacity of leader and motivator, orchestrates.

The student then legitimately may ask, "Why learn about boards and budgets? Why not focus on interpersonal skills?" These questions are, indeed, legitimate, but books about interpersonal skills and management strategies have been written by others with particular expertise in both management and communication. The Director's Library in Appendix D includes helpful suggested readings in the section titled "Leadership." Familiarize yourself with some of those books so that as you learn about budgeting and buying equipment, developing personnel policies, or planning a facility, you will be able to use that information in concert with effective interpersonal strategies.

The discussion in this chapter focuses on the importance of developing good management skills, then using these skills—coupled with good communication skills—as the basis for functioning as an administrator of a child care center or any other type of child care program. Obviously, the person in charge must have knowledge of how to draw up a budget, write policy and job descriptions, decide about equipment, and so forth. However, writing policy, hiring staff, making budgets, and ordering equipment all will be wasted efforts unless the manager has those special interpersonal and communication skills necessary to select, motivate, and relate to the people who are to carry out the program within the framework set by the program philosophy, the budget, and the personnel policies.

Once the policies are established, the staff are hired, and the children are enrolled, the function of the administrator parallels that of a classroom teacher. The administrator or director makes the total center program "go" much as the teacher makes the classroom "go" after the learning environment has been set up. E. Belle Evans suggests, "It is like leaping from one to another of a dozen different merry-go-rounds, each traveling at a different speed, each playing a different tune, and each blaring a separate cadence. Yet the administrator (*teacher*) must land gracefully, never missing a beat, always in perfect time with the music" (italics added) (Evans, n.d., p. 2). Once the program is operational, the function of the director becomes catalytic or facilitative. The total task of the director then is accomplished by creating an environment in which others may grow. Through the growth and development of staff members, the program is implemented and its goals are reached; the process unfolds in much the same way as in the classroom where the teacher attains the program goals through the growth and development of the children and their families.

CREATING A POSITIVE CLIMATE

As a leader, the director has the major responsibility for creating a climate of care, trust, and respect. This climate can be achieved best by demonstrating caring behavior, by taking steps to build a feeling of community or partnership, and by creating a climate for good communication among and between all members of the center community. The goal is to optimize the developmental potential of children, families, and staff in an environment that exemplifies respect for diversity.

Modeling

The emotional tone at the center is set by the way the director feels about others and by the success with which those feelings are communicated to others in the setting. The director creates a climate of warmth, caring, and acceptance by relating to staff members, parents, and children with honesty and openness. Mutual trust and respect will grow in an environment in which respect is earned, and the best way to earn respect is to show respect for others. When respect for diversity is modeled, the tone is set for the entire center.

Emotional stability, maturity, and a positive sense of self are the basic characteristics of a leader who has the potential for assuming responsibility and leading people in a caring manner. This leadership style creates a climate that, in turn, motivates others to imitate the pattern of acceptance and warmth in their interactions. The caring behaviors become contagious. Most of you have read about and observed "modeling" in young children. One child who is perceived as the leader displays a pattern of behavior, and others imitate it. Marcus says, "Yuck! Spinach!" and soon everyone at the table is saying such things as "Yuck, spinach!" "Slimy spinach!" "Yucky B. M. spinach!" However, if Marcus says, "Yummm, spinach!" other children are more likely to respond positively to the vegetable being served. Although this example is clearly an oversimplification of what typically happens in a group, behavior *is* contagious, and there is evidence that a leader who serves as the model does, indeed, control the behavioral climate of the setting.

Modeling begins with the very first encounter the director has with the new staff members as they come into the center for interviews, or when a newly hired director is introduced to the staff for the first time. The basic trust and mutual respect that are communicated and felt during this initial meeting are the building blocks for the relationships that will develop among the people in the center. The pattern established during these first meetings will set the stage for future meetings and will influence the ways in which staff members will interact with one another and with the families and children who come to the center.

Although warmth, acceptance, and mutual respect are clearly fundamental to creating a favorable environment for the growth and development of the people involved in the center program, other behaviors demonstrated by successful directors also facilitate personal and professional growth and lead to more favorable environments for children. The director who shows intellectual curiosity and is always seeking more information to do a better job can inspire others to do the same. A leader who does not serve as a model of professional commitment and enthusiasm for learning more about children, families, human relationships, and trends and issues in early childhood cannot expect staff members to invest energy in these areas. The leader's responsibility is to show interest and enthusiasm for what is going on in the program and in the profession and to serve as a resource for staff members and parents. They, in turn, will be stimulated to improve themselves as people and as caregivers of children. (A caregiver is "one who is responsive to the needs of children.")

Community Building

The director is responsible for developing and maintaining a sense of community among staff, parents, and children. Morale will be higher and the environment more conducive to growth for all involved if there is a "we" feeling, a feeling of belonging. As the feeling of belonging increases, anxiety, self-doubt, hostility, and feelings of rejection decrease.

Staff members who feel that it is *their* center and *their* program and who feel a sense of ownership about the program will be more self-assured and more enthusiastic about assuming responsibility. They not only will perform the tasks they are competent to perform but also will be willing to invest energy into learning more so they can extend their area of responsibility. The total task of serving children and families becomes *our* task, and *we* provide the richest and best service we can, given our human and material resources.

DIRECTOR'S CORNER

"I often think back on my own experiences in the classroom when I was there eight hours a day. I remember that I was expected to be nurturing and giving of myself *all* day long—it helps me remember how much I, in turn, needed to be nurtured. That's why I have an 'open door' policy for my staff—I take time to actively listen, to problem-solve with them, to encourage them. I often have to put my paperwork aside because I know that a staff person sometimes needs to talk *right now!* This job goes beyond, `I'm the boss and you're the staff person' relationship. The other side of this is knowing when and where to set the boundaries. When and how do I set limits on my availability to staff members or family members so that I can focus on what will be best for others and for me, as well as what is best for the company?"

—*Director, for-profit corporate center*

The "we" feeling radiates beyond staff to families and children. It becomes *our* center or *our* program, and children begin to talk about "my" school. The feeling of community permeates the entire environment; all who participate in the many aspects of the center program feel they play an important part in the total program. All participants feel that they *own* a piece of the program and contribute to its success or failure. Parents and children alike recognize that they, and their cultures and languages, are valued, that diversity is at the very core of the program, and that their contribution to the program is important. They come to understand that they are the very reason for the center's existence. There would be no reason for the center to continue if there were no families and children to serve.

All the discussion about a feeling of community or partnership in a child care environment surely produces questions about what a director can do to create and maintain that atmosphere. Some of it will grow out of the trust and mutual respect that result from the modeling behavior described previously. Community feeling also stems from good interpersonal communication.

REFLECTION

Take a moment to reflect on your own practicum experiences. Think about whether there was a sense of community in the center in which you gained experience. Consider whether you were made to feel that you were an important member of the community. If you recall feeling positive about the experience, who was most instrumental in creating that accepting environment for you? Did you sense the children also felt this was *their* place? Who was responsible for creating the "we" feeling in the classroom?

Communicating

Every director will engage in a certain amount of written communication. When there is a need to communicate in writing, the first question to ask is, "Who needs to know?" Interpersonal relationships often are damaged inadvertently because some members of the group do not receive information that they feel should be relayed to them. For example, although a change in next week's menu may, on the surface, affect only the cook in a child care center, a teacher who has planned a special science experiment around one of the foods to be served on a given day may be very annoyed to learn about the change in menu *after* implementing the special lesson. The message itself, including the exact wording, can be more easily drafted once the audience for the message has been determined. Therefore, the audience receiving the message will determine both the content and the wording.

Although some communication will be in writing, much of it will be face-to-face communication, verbal or nonverbal. To be an effective leader, the director must be a competent communicator and must take responsibility for helping the entire staff develop communication skills.

Verbal communication skills can be learned. The director can learn to send effective messages, to become a good listener, and to engage in effective problem solving. It is possible to define specific behaviors, both verbal and nonverbal, that block communication. It is possible to improve communication skills and, as a result, enhance interpersonal relationships. Note that we have said this is *possible,* but it is not easy. Unless directors believe wholeheartedly in the importance of open communication for good interpersonal relationships, they are unlikely to invest the energy necessary to develop the skills and to practice them until they become totally integrated into a personal communication style. However, once this integration has come about, the director's communication style inevitably will serve as a model for others. The model will set the pattern for all the other people in the center and will create an atmosphere more conducive to open communication.

It is important that verbal and nonverbal messages be congruent. Sensitive leaders will take care to convey the *real* message with both their words and their body postures. "Some communications researchers believe that fully 60 percent of all communication between people is based on body language" (*Child Care Information Exchange,* 1993, p. 5). Words that convey approval or acceptance but are accompanied by a frown and a closed body posture conveying rejection and hostility send a mixed message that is confusing to the receiver. Supportive, positive words and actions will help build trusting relationships among the people in the center. In a trusting relationship, criticism or negative reactions can be handled without destroying the relationship, provided they are given discreetly and are carefully timed. For the director to criticize a teacher in front of the receptionist when the teacher is on the way to the classroom to help a crying child is the epitome of poor communication skills and will have a negative impact on future attempts at open communication. Other, more subtle blocks to communication that will set the stage for a defensive response, hostility, or feelings of inadequacy include:

- demanding and controlling messages.
- put-downs.
- use of sarcasm or threats.
- flip humorous responses to serious concerns.

It is important to consider what needs to be said, how to say it, and when to say it, always being aware of the cultural nuances of language.

A sensitive leader is well advised to consider carefully whether a situation calls for *telling* or *listening*. Telling often comes more easily than listening but must always be done with full awareness of the cultural nuance of language. However, in many situations, listening is a better vehicle for maintaining open communication and strengthening a relationship. Dealing with the personal problems of families or professional issues of staff members often requires listening instead of telling. Such communication is energy draining and time consuming but when done well has a powerful and positive influence on the entire network of interpersonal relationships. It is time and energy well spent.

In spite of all the caring and planning that go into creating a supportive atmosphere, conflict will arise. This is human and does not necessarily mean poor management, nor does it imply weakness in the network. It does, however, require attention. There are communication skills that can be learned by the director and the staff to facilitate conflict resolution. It is beyond the scope of this book to train students in basic communication and problem-solving skills, but there are a number of excellent resources that provide basic information about effective communication and training exercises for practice purposes. Several suggested readings are included in the Director's Library (Appendix D) in the "Leadership" section.

MOTIVATING THE STAFF

The director does the orchestrating, but programs are effected through the efforts of other people. The staff of a center must be motivated to plan and implement the total program. Just as communication skills can be learned, so the skills for guiding mental and physical energies toward defined goals can be learned. Without training in how to guide and to motivate human energy toward shared goals, the director will follow some rules of thumb that may leave the role of director-as-motivator to chance. This practice may be compared to designing a program for young children based on knowledge gained from having been a child, having parented a child, or having been through a public school system. Although these experiences may be useful, they cannot substitute for theoretical knowledge and a sound educational background in the field.

As directors begin to think about ways to motivate employees, they usually think about salary increases, a better building, new equipment, more help in the center, and a number of other items that are related to money and budget. Certainly, low salaries and poor working conditions can lead to dissatisfaction, but the promise of more money—or the threat of less—probably will not have far-reaching or long-lasting effects on individual or group performance levels. However, if a leader is using dollars to control and motivate performance, it becomes increasingly more difficult to find the necessary supply to meet the demand. In addition, extrinsic incentives motivate employees to get the rewards but rarely alter the emotional or intellectual commitments that underlie behaviors.

What, then, is a director to do? There are a number of useful strategies for motivating people to commit themselves to a task and to actualize their potential. Two of the strategies that seem particularly applicable to the child care setting are use of encouragement and provision of job enrichment.

Use of Encouragement

Encouragement is a positive acknowledgment focused on a specific attribute of some action or piece of work completed (Hitz & Driscoll, 1988). Rewards or reinforcements may motivate the staff, but as with teaching, they tend to increase dependency on the one who controls the source of the rewards. They also heighten competition, thereby defeating the overarching goal of developing a sense of a cooperative community. Encouragement, on the other hand, tends to build self-confidence and a sense of intrinsic job satisfaction.

Just as the classroom teacher makes sure that encouragement is specific, focused on process, usually given in private, and neither judgmental nor evaluative, so the director keeps these same principles in mind when working with staff. To encourage a teacher who has just helped a screaming toddler, you might say, "I noticed how calm you managed to be with Tommy while he was having such a hard time in the bathroom. It worked out well." These words of encouragement are more specific and process oriented than, "I like the way you work with toddlers." Telling the teacher of four-year-olds, "You must have done some detailed planning for the graphing activity you did today to make it go so smoothly. It's surely fun for you to watch their progress" is more specific and less evaluative than, "That was a nice graphing activity."

Job Enrichment

Job enrichment is a management strategy that enhances job satisfaction by presenting more challenges and increasing responsibility, which, in turn, produce a sense of personal achievement and on-the-job satisfaction.

It is possible to design a job enrichment program for a child care center so that staff members are motivated to higher levels of commitment. As a result, they will experience greater intrinsic rewards. The job enrichment principles particularly applicable to child care centers are listed below:

1. Give new and added responsibilities to staff members so they are constantly challenged and empowered to control aspects of their work setting.

2. Provide opportunities for ongoing training and college-based education that will contribute to quality of performance and to personal and professional growth.

3. Give staff members special assignments such as occasional delegation of coworkers' or supervisor's jobs to broaden each person's understanding of the total operation of the organization. This is recognition but has no monetary reward. This procedure can bring more recognition from other staff members and open up greater opportunities for advancement.

Obviously, there is some overlap among the three stated principles, both in terms of the method used and the outcome expected. There also are other ways to enrich staff members' jobs that will broaden their experience and bring them both intrinsic and extrinsic rewards. The many possibilities are limited solely by the creativity and imagination of the person in charge.

At first glance, it may seem that added responsibility will lead to dissatisfaction and demands for more money or other material rewards. However, there is evidence to suggest that, more often than not, the person who is challenged and who "stretches" to assume more responsibility will feel a sense of pride and achievement. For example, the classroom aide who, at midyear, is given the added responsibility of meeting and greeting parents and children at arrival time, probably will find that job intrinsically satisfying. The aide will develop better skills for helping children make that first daily break from a trusted caregiver and acquire new skills for accomplishing the added responsibility. Assigning added duties can be accomplished best in an atmosphere of mutual trust, and it must be done through the use of positive communication skills.

The training needed to develop the skills necessary for managing a new task effectively often can be offered informally by other members of the staff, and by exposure to resources such as books, pamphlets, videos, PowerPoint presentations, or opportunities to observe. Ongoing training can be expanded to include more formalized in-service sessions on curriculum, child abuse, communication skills, working with children with special needs and their families, or other topics selected to serve a specific need within the center program. Release time or financial support for workshops and seminars, using on-line resources, and additional course work are still other ways to provide job enrichment opportunities for the personal and professional growth of staff members.

Delegating special assignments to staff members usually evokes a sense of achievement and recognition, even though it means extra work. A cook who is consulted about menu planning and buying, and who is later asked to help evaluate the total food service program when the center is undergoing a self-study for accreditation, not only gains an understanding of what is involved in the total food planning and preparation program but also is developing a greater potential for advancement, whether in the present job or in another work setting.

SUMMARY

The intent of this chapter is to point out the importance of good interpersonal relationships and trust within a center. Only through a feeling of community and a spirit of cooperation can a director create a supportive environment where both adults and children can grow to their fullest potential. There must be a strong element of acceptance and positive regard in the surrounding climate to establish a mutually helping relationship for staff, families, and children. It is the responsibility of the director as a leader to serve as a model of caring and respect for others in order to build a strong sense of community among all the diverse people involved in the center program. Effective interpersonal communication among the staff members, children, and families also is an important basic element in creating a supportive, comfortable environment at a center, and it is up to the director to be the model of good communication in order to create an atmosphere of openness, warmth, and acceptance.

The director uses encouragement and job enrichment to motivate staff members. Neither of these motivational means requires money; however, both require special interpersonal skills a director can acquire. Effective use of these support tools will not only facilitate personal growth and a feeling of positive self-worth but also will help move the center program forward.

CLASS ASSIGNMENTS

1. Read one of the books from the Director's Library, "Leadership" section in Appendix D. Write a short paper on the book including an analysis of how the material covered would be useful to you as a director of a child care center.

2. Write a brief essay on the "we" feeling or sense of community that prevailed (or was absent) in a center where you worked with children. Consider the following before you begin:
   - Who set the prevailing emotional tone of the setting?
   - What elements or daily happenings contributed to your feeling of belonging to the center staff?
   - How did the emotional tone affect your feelings about yourself, your peers, the children, and so forth?

CLASS EXERCISES

1. Think of yourself as a center director. In small groups with other class members, discuss the motivating factors that you as a director can control or change.
   a. List five effective, motivating factors directors can control.
   b. Compare the lists produced by the small groups, and develop a final list of strategies to encourage staff and enrich jobs that do not cost money.

2. Think about yourself as the director of a center where you have observed or taught. Using Working Paper 2–1, write appropriately phrased acknowledgments and create the job enrichment strategies requested.

WORKING PAPER 2-1

(for use with Class Exercise 2)

JOB ENRICHMENT STRATEGIES

1. Based on your understanding of the use of encouragement as a motivator, write an appropriately phrased positive acknowledgment for:

   the secretary

   the cook

   the custodian

   a volunteer

2. Describe a way you could use the job enrichment strategy with:

   the assistant infant teacher

   the van driver

   a student teacher

   a lead teacher

REFERENCES

Child Care Information Exchange: The Director's Magazine. (1993, January). *1,* 5.

Evans, E. B. (n.d.). *Day care administration.* Cambridge, MA: Educational Day Care Services Association.

Hitz, R., & Driscoll, A. (1988). Praise or encouragement? New insights into praise: Implication for early childhood teachers. *Young Children, 43*(5).

Additional resources for this chapter can be found on the Online Companion™ at http://www.earlychilded.delmar.com. This supplemental material includes relevant Web links, Web activities, and case studies that apply the concepts presented in this chapter. In addition, the Working Papers and Director's Resources are available for download, allowing you to complete Class Exercises and Class Assignments electronically.

CHAPTER 3

Assessing Community Need and Establishing a Program

Holding small group discussions with parents who express interest in having their children participate is a good way to obtain information about need.

OBJECTIVES

After reading this chapter, you should be able to:

- List the factors that influence the need for child care.
- Name the various types of child care used by families.
- Identify information that will help you determine the types of child services needed now and in the future.
- Use your knowledge of data collection methods and resources for assessing the need for child care in your area.
- Choose and explain your philosophy of early childhood education.
- Describe characteristics of different types of centers.

Creating a new institution is an exciting challenge that requires abundant creativity and energy and is overwhelmingly complex. The amount of activity inevitably taking place simultaneously during the early thinking and planning stages for establishing a center makes it impossible to outline a set pattern of sequential steps to be followed in these stages. Clearly, there must be a need for the program.

And there must be some driving force in the community, whether an individual or a group, that will generate the creative energy to

1. examine the need.
2. develop the program philosophy.
3. decide about the type of program that will fit the need and the resources.

These three major activities will be taking place simultaneously, and each will influence the type of program as well as the program philosophy. On the other hand, the type of program that is realistic to offer will influence the question of the ability to respond to the need.

The driving force might be an early childhood educator with a desire to open a center, or a group of parents who have an interest in providing child care services for their children. Sometimes community agencies choose to expand their services to include child care, and there also is an expansion of both employer- and public school–sponsored child care programs.

The nucleus of the driving force, whether it be an individual, an agency, or a corporation, must be prepared to carry out all preliminary tasks until a director is hired. They may have to deal with funding issues, undertake public relations campaigns, and carry out the needs assessment.

Program sponsors examine what services can be delivered realistically without diluting the quality of the program. Usually, it is unrealistic to try to set up a program that will be responsive to every demand and meet all needs. It is also unrealistic to expect to start a new program and have it fully enrolled immediately. It can take several years to bring a new program up to full enrollment. It is better to begin on a small scale, carefully weighing the assured need against the services that can be delivered under the existing financial and resource constraints. It is dangerous to overextend by trying to meet everyone's need or by providing a large-scale operation that overtaxes the resources. Problems also arise when the need is overestimated and a program is set up that is underenrolled. In either case, program quality diminishes and children become the victims of impoverished environments. Then families do not trust the program to deliver the promised services, and it is doomed to failure.

DIRECTOR'S CORNER

"I projected it would take us three years to reach capacity in this new center, which is licensed for 115 children. We are now at the beginning of the third year of operation and we are about two-thirds full—so my prediction was on target."

—Director/owner, franchised center

ASSESSING THE NEED

To ensure that the planned program is properly scaled to meet both the size and the nature of the community need, it is important to do a needs assessment during the preliminary planning period. The needs assessment can begin before or after a director is designated or hired, but it must be completed before any financial or program planning begins. The purpose of the needs assessment is to determine the number of families and children that will use a child care service and the type of service desired by those who will use it.

What Must You Know about Need?

The first step in the needs assessment process is to determine what you need to know. Once that has been decided, procedures for collecting the data can be worked out.

Number of Families and Children

First, you must find out how many families are interested in having their children participate in an early childhood education program and the number of eligible children in each family. It is useless to go beyond the earliest thinking or planning stage unless there are families available who will use the service. Simply assessing the *number* of children is not sufficient because number alone does not determine interest or need. If you currently are running a program for preschool children but get many calls for infant/toddler or school-aged child care, you are alerted to a need to expand your program offerings. However, between the time you assemble your waiting lists and accomplish the program expansion, many of those families on your list will have made other child care arrangements. One quick and informal way to decide whether to proceed with a needs assessment is to find out if other centers in the vicinity have waiting lists.

Some planners overestimate the number of families who need child care and fail to consider how many of those families will use or pay for center-based care if it is provided. Although the numbers of preschoolers in child care whose mothers work outside the home has increased sharply over the past four decades, it is difficult to determine who cares for the children of these working families. As of 2002, 64 percent of persons with children under six were in the workforce, and 61 percent of those children were cared for by someone other than the parents (Children's Defense Fund, 2004, p. 66). However, many of these children are with friends or family members, thus making it difficult to determine how many of these working parents would choose center-based care or family child care homes for their children if it became available to them.

Socioeconomic Level of Families

Many families may be interested in child care services but are unable to pay enough to cover the cost of the services they choose or need. When families are unable to pay the high cost of quality child care outside the home, operators cannot depend on tuition but must seek outside sources of funding if planned programs are to succeed. It is important to know how many families that express need for assistance actually qualify for state or federal subsidy. When families are able to pay, it is important to determine what they are willing to pay for center-based or home-based care. It is reasonable to expect that many families can afford to pay up to 10 percent of their total income for child care. However, low-income families could be forced to pay as much as 25 percent of their income for child care.

Ages of Children to Be Served

The ages of participating children affect all the program planning considerations and can make a considerable difference in the cost of delivering the service.

Determine the number of families who expect to have infants or toddlers participate in the group care program outside the home. Although early childhood education programs traditionally served three- and four-year-old children, the increase in the number of one-parent families and the number of working mothers has increased the demand for infant/toddler care for before and after school as well as for year-round programs for school-aged children. Therefore, when doing the needs assessment, inquire not only about three- and four-year-olds who may need care but also about older children and those under age three.

Type of Service the Families Prefer

In assessing the need for a program, one of the first things you must find out is whether families prefer full-day child care or a half-day program. Working families must have full-day care, and they often will need it for children ranging in age from birth through school age.

Families that choose half-day programs may use a program for toddlers and three- and four-year-olds (sometimes called preschoolers) but may prefer to keep infants at home. These families might select a five-day program for preschoolers but often prefer a two- or three-day program for toddlers. Parents who wish to become involved in the program may choose to place their children in a cooperative child care program. Other parents may not have the time or the interest in becoming directly involved in the school program.

In some situations, family child care homes may be more suitable than a center-based program because they can serve a broad range of needs, can be available for emergency care, and can provide evening and weekend care. The family child care home involves parents taking their children to someone else's home and paying for child care on an hourly, daily, or weekly basis. These arrangements usually are made individually, although there is often some regulation of the number of children for whom care can be provided in a given home. In a few cases, satellite programs are set up involving the coordination of family child care homes by a child care center staff member or an employer. Parents make arrangements through the child care center or the employer referral service for placement of their children in an affiliated family child care home. They make payments to the center or make use of this employer benefit. The center or employer, in turn, pays the caregiver and provides the parents with some assurance that the home and the caregiver have been evaluated and that placement for the child will be found if the caregiver becomes unable to provide the service due to illness or for other reasons. When the need for care is immediate and critical, it may be useful to locate and organize a few child care homes while the planning and financing of a center-based program is under way.

How Do You Find Out about Need?

Once you have determined the kind of data necessary to substantiate the need for a program, you are ready to decide how to collect the data. Some information for long-range planning can be obtained from census figures, Chambers of Commerce, or data on births from the Health Department. However, detailed information needed for decision making is best obtained through other means. The data must be collected, recorded, compiled, and analyzed so that the need for the program can be explained to anyone who is involved in initial planning, including members of a sponsoring group or funding agency. The data collection process might be formal and wide in scope to cover a broad potential population, or it can be informal and confined to a very small group of parents and community representatives. Mailed questionnaires, telephone surveys, or informal small-group meetings are possible methods of collecting needs assessment data.

Use of Questionnaires

When a large group of potential clients must be sampled, it is wise to develop a questionnaire that can be returned in an enclosed, addressed, and stamped envelope. Returned questionnaires provide specific data that can be recorded, compiled, and analyzed. These data are usually quite accurate; however, it is possible that some families will indicate interest in child care and then no longer need it or decide not to use it when it becomes available.

The major problems encountered with questionnaires used for data collection are the cost, the low percentage of returns, and the task of developing a good questionnaire. Enclosing an addressed, stamped envelope increases the number of returns, but it does not eliminate the problem of lack of response. Unreturned questionnaires create more questions because it isn't clear whether those families are not interested in the service, or whether they are interested but have neglected to return the questionnaire.

Good questionnaires are very difficult to develop. The questionnaire must be brief and understandable by the recipient, and the items included also must be carefully selected to provide precisely the data that are important to the needs assessment for any given program. Therefore, if you are involved in drafting a

questionnaire, it is imperative to analyze the potential audience first so that items are covered in terms that the audience understands and that it is family friendly; then you must be sure to include inquiries about *all* the information you need while keeping the form brief.

Review the sample needs assessment questionnaire in Director's Resource 3–1 to see what types of questions are asked for assessing need. Before planning location, type and size of program, and ages of children to be served, it is helpful to ask for the following information:

1. number of adults in the household
2. number of those adults employed
3. number and ages of all children in the household
4. number of children cared for outside the home
5. number and ages of children with special needs
6. estimate of family income
7. estimate of how much is or could be spent on child care
8. days and hours child care is needed
9. preferred location of child care
10. whether the family will use the proposed child care center when it becomes available

Use of Telephone Surveys

Since the percentage of returns on mailed questionnaires is costly and unpredictable, a telephone survey of potential users of a program may be a more accurate procedure for collecting needs assessment data. Telephone surveys are time consuming and costly if you expect to survey a large number of families. However, you can sample a large potential population and obtain fairly accurate information about the total group without calling each family. If you are involved in an extensive needs assessment program, you should consult a marketing specialist about appropriate sampling techniques. On the other hand, if you have access to a group of volunteers who can do some telephoning and if the population to be contacted is small, calling prospective families may yield accurate data, provided that the questioning is conducted uniformly and that the data collected are what you need to know.

To ensure uniformity, telephone surveys also must utilize a questionnaire. The survey caller verbally asks the questions and fills in the questionnaire. The same considerations that apply to mailed questionnaires apply to those used in telephone surveys: understandable wording, complete coverage of data, and brevity.

Small-Group Meetings

Holding informal group discussions with families who express interest in having their children participate in a program is a good way to obtain information about need. It is practical where the potential client population is defined (for example, church members, apartment complex dwellers, employees of a particular company), or where the size of the community or neighborhood limits the number of families who might use the center. Informal meetings have the advantage of establishing a basis of trust and open communication between the providers of the service and the families who will use it. Without the constraints of a specific questionnaire, parents are free to discuss their values and goals for their children, their unique needs and desires in terms of their family situation, and their feelings about different types of programs that might become available. However, this informal data collection process yields information that is often less valid and reliable as well as more difficult to tabulate and analyze than questionnaire data. You may find that it is beneficial to work out a combination of the informal discussion and formal questionnaire procedures by holding a series of small-group meetings in which parents fill out a brief questionnaire at the close of the meeting. Needs assessment data that are collected through both formal and informal channels can provide the basis for the decision about whether or not to have a program, and to furnish information about family values and goals that will enter into formulating the program philosophy. Of course, the values and the educational interests of the program planners and the director also will have a significant impact on the philosophy.

REFLECTION

Think for a moment about being called by someone doing a telephone survey. What was your reaction to the call? Was the call at a convenient time, or did it interrupt your study time or dinner? Did the caller get to the point quickly or waste your time, inquiring about your health or if you were having a good day? What led you to agree to participate in the survey, or decline and hang up? Recalling your reaction to a telephone survey can help you gain insights into how parents might respond to a needs assessment telephone survey.

PROGRAM PHILOSOPHY

The characteristics of an early childhood education program are based on the philosophy of the program. Program philosophy guides directors' decisions about hiring new staff and about selecting appropriate staff training because they want to ensure that all staff are prepared to implement a program that is consistent with the adopted philosophy. The program goals that determine what the curriculum and teaching strategies will be also are based on the program philosophy. If, for example, the program philosophy is based on the theoretical assumption that it is through the process of inventing ideas and developing hypotheses that children come to understand about things and people in their world, then the overarching program goal would be to have children become autonomous problem solvers. Therefore, in the classroom, in place of planned activities set up to teach letters or numbers, the adult would provide a print-rich environment that would include many books, charts, and a writing center, and children would enjoy the use of math games, measuring tools, and simple machines such as pulleys and pendulums. The two major questions to be answered in connection with the program philosophy are "Who decides about the philosophy?" and "What is the basis for deciding what the philosophy should be?"

Who Decides about Philosophy?

During the early planning stages, the individuals who make up the nucleus of the driving force must discuss and finally formulate a program philosophy. Occasionally, this discussion is delayed until a director is hired because it is important that the director feel comfortable with the adopted philosophy. However, when the planners have very specific ideas about program philosophy or a new director is hired for an ongoing program, the philosophy is written and a director is hired who can operate within the adopted philosophical framework. Frustrations over incompatible philosophies can create unworkable teaching situations for dedicated staff who need the support of the new director (Kuykendall, 1990, p. 49). If the adopted position is based on the assumption that the child is born a *tabula rasa* (meaning the mind at birth is a blank tablet to be written on by experience and the stated goal of education is to fill that tablet with experiences), it is helpful if the program director be committed to that same philosophy. A director with a cognitive-developmental or constructivist point of view who does not accept the a *tabula rasa* premise will find it difficult to develop or direct an educational program that would reflect the stated program philosophy. For a discussion of constructivism and a comparison of programs sharing the cognitive-developmental orientation, see DeVries and Kohlberg (1988).

The need for a philosophical position as a base for program design seems clear (Decker & Decker, 2005). Whether it is based on developmental theory, social learning theory, or the notion of multiple intelligences or behaviorism, it gives substance and validity to the program. The program philosophy underlies most programmatic decisions. It should reflect the values, beliefs, and training of the director, as well as the wishes and interests of the program planners and families who will participate in the program. When administrators carry out programs for which they are unable to state a philosophy, and substantiate that the curriculum and accompanying pedagogical strategies can be explained in terms of that philosophy, they risk internal confusion, lack of unity, loss of teamwork, and an inability to help parents understand their true purpose.

What Is the Basis for Choosing a Philosophy?

When programs are planned and implemented, the curriculum content and teaching strategies either consciously or unconsciously reflect a philosophy that is based on

1. assumptions about how children learn.
2. values of the program planners and the families involved.
3. views of the planners regarding basic issues in education.

Although the three areas that influence the philosophy of the program can be discussed separately, they interact with one another and, in reality, are almost impossible to identify and delineate.

Assumptions about How Children Learn

In the very broadest sense and in the most simplistic terms, assumptions about how children learn fall into three major categories: environmental, maturational, and interactional. The environmental position assumes that the child's learning is dependent on extrinsic motivators in the form of tokens, compliments, smiles, gold stars, and so forth. What the child is to learn is decided by the adult who then plans lessons designed to teach content and skills. One of the basic assumptions of this position is that anything worth teaching is also observable and measurable. Attempts to relate this particular assumption about learning to some theoretical base usually lead to the

mention of people such as Thorndike, Watson, and Skinner.

Goals based on the environmental assumptions about how young children learn might be that in preschool classrooms

- children learn to recite the alphabet through alphabet songs and stories.
- children practice rote counting during group time and while at play.
- staff help children with letter recognition by using flash cards and word games.
- group-time activities include color recognition and color naming exercises.
- children practice table manners at snack time and at lunch.

The maturational position assumes that there is an internal driving force that leads to the emergence of cognitive and affective systems, which, in turn, determine the child's readiness for mastery of developmental tasks. Mastery of the task is itself rewarding, so the reinforcement is based on intrinsic satisfactions derived from accomplishment and task mastery. Learning is controlled by an internal growth force and the child selects from various offerings, thereby learning what she is ready to learn. The theorists who are associated with the extreme maturational position are Freud and Gesell.

Goals based on maturational assumptions about how young children learn might be that children in the program

- show interest and select to work in various interest areas in the classroom.
- choose activities based on their interests and their rhythms.
- show evidence of satisfaction after having mastered a task (verbally, with actions or with body language that communicates pleasure in the accomplishment).

The interactional position assumes that learning results from the dynamic interaction between the emerging cognitive and affective systems, and the environment. The interaction with both the material and the human environment is not driven solely by an internal force but also is nurtured, facilitated, and intensified by the timely intervention of significant adults in the environment. The child is intrinsically motivated to select appropriately from the environment, but the adult is responsible for preparing the environment and for timely and appropriate questions and ideas to alert the child to the learning opportunities in each situation. The adult facilitates the development of intellectual competence. The impetus for the interactional approach came from Piaget's work. Rheta DeVries says, " . . . (the) theory of Piaget is . . . the most advanced theory we have of mental development" (DeVries & Kohlberg, 1988, p. ix). Additional insights into the interactive theoretical perspective come from Vygotsky's work. He emphasized the important connection between a child's social and psychological worlds for cognitive development (Berk & Winsler, 1995, p. viii).

Goals based on interactional assumptions about how young children learn might be that in all classrooms:

- play is cherished and play spaces are rich with learning opportunities.
- each child's rhythm is caught and given a warm response.
- children are encouraged to explore and create.
- children enjoy successes that lead to greater self-confidence and independence.
- staff members value and are responsive to each child's special abilities, learning style, and developmental pace.

REFLECTION

Think about a program you have taught or in which you have observed. Identify the assumptions about how children learn in this program. Try to formulate an example from that classroom experience that supports the assumption about how children learn. Think about activities you may have planned or behaviors you encourage, and try to determine the area of development you most value. What are your assumptions about how children learn?

Values of the Program Planners and the Families

The program philosophy is influenced by the priorities parents and planners set for the children. When questioned, most administrators would state that they value the optimum development of the whole child: the social, emotional, physical, and cognitive development of the child. However, when the philosophy or the ongoing program is analyzed, it may become clear that priorities do, indeed, exist. Concern for the development of the whole child is the stated position, but careful analysis reveals that cognitive outcomes are given priority over social/emotional goals or vice versa.

Views on Basic Issues in Education

A number of basic issues in education are implied, if not directly addressed, in the philosophy. One of these issues is the content versus process issue, sometimes interpreted as school orientation versus human orientation. Those who subscribe to the content orientation support the notion that the goal of education is to provide children with content that enables them to succeed in school as it exists. Their focus is on preparation for the next step in schooling, and achievement is evaluated by relating each child's progress to norms or to grade level. The goal of education for those who support human orientation is the upward movement of the child as an independent learner to higher levels of intellectual competence. The process of learning and the development of problem-solving skills are more important than content mastery. Autonomy, collaboration, and cooperation are valued, and the years in school are considered an integral part of life itself. The major goal is for children to become autonomous problem solvers (Kamii, 1982). Schooling is not viewed as either preparation for later school or preparation for life. Achievement is not dependent on reaching a norm or the next grade level but on the ability to cope with the here and now.

The philosophy dictates what the role of the teacher will be. If the focus is on content, the adult is expected to "teach" the children letters, numbers, shoe tying, manners, and the like. On the other hand, in a process-oriented environment, the adult as interactor is a questioner, role model, reflector, observer, and evaluator.

At first glance, this discussion about program philosophy may seem unrelated to the problems of starting a center or to taking over as director of an ongoing program. However, it is impossible to make program decisions without a commitment to an agreed-upon philosophy. Once that is in place, subsequent program decisions can be checked against the philosophy to ensure consistency with the stated position. After a program has been established, subsequent documents such as a mission statement and program goals are written, and these are based on the philosophy. The sample philosophies in Figure 3–1 will serve as a guide for writing a program philosophy.

The third major item to be determined, after the need has been assessed and the program philosophy written, is the type of program to be offered. After deciding on the type of program in terms of sponsoring agency and funding, the decision about ages of children to be served must be made before making arrangements for site selection, licensing, budgeting, staffing and equipping the center, and enrolling the children.

Program Philosophy #1

The program is based on the philosophy that most children can learn the skills necessary to succeed in school, that each child learns at her own rate, and that success in learning will develop the child's self-image.

Program Philosophy #2

The educational philosophy of the Child Development Center is based on meeting the developmental needs of children. The work of Erikson and Piaget provides the theoretical framework around which programs are planned to meet each child's emotional, social, cognitive, and physical needs.

This developmental program is based on the assumption that growth is a sequential and orderly process and that children do indeed pass through stages of development that occur in a predictable sequence in their physical, emotional, social, and cognitive growth. The adult's responsibility in a developmental program is to assist the child in growing to her fullest potential by recognizing each stage of development and fashioning a curriculum that will nurture and facilitate growth during that stage.

Program Philosophy #3

Our program is designed to meet the developmental needs of young children (three to five years). It provides experiences that enrich and enhance each child's cognitive, language, social, emotional, physical, and creative development. Within the center's daily schedule, each child has opportunities to create, explore the environment, learn problem-solving and personal interaction skills, and learn concepts through firsthand experiences. Children develop a positive self-concept through a balance of self- and teacher-directed activities. Opportunities for solitary play as well as group activities are provided. Staff serve as positive role models and provide care that is supportive, nurturing, warm, and responsive to each child's individual needs. We respect families as the primary and most important providers of care and nurturing, and we believe parents and teachers are partners in children's care and education.

Figure 3–1

Program philosophies.

TYPES OF PROGRAMS

The type of program that will be set up is certainly related to the assessed need and to the stated philosophy, but it also depends on the sources of available funds and the origin of the impetus for the program. Not-for-profit programs receive financial support through government funding or subsidies from sponsoring agencies, whereas proprietary programs are supported by capital investments of individuals or corporations. A wide range of program philosophies, including Waldorf, Reggio Emilia, and those based on Montessori's teachings, can operate under any of the program types discussed in the following section.

Not-for-Profit Programs

There are public and private not-for-profit programs (sometimes called nonprofit) that range in size and scope from the small cooperative preschool to the large, complex, agency-sponsored child care center. Although not-for-profit and nonprofit may be differentiated for legal reasons in some states, in most places the terms are used interchangeably.

Individual Cooperative Programs

Cooperative programs, often called parent co-ops, are owned and operated by a group. Since parents are expected to help in the classroom, the small co-op usually functions with one or two paid staff members, one of whom is usually a teacher/director. Costs are kept at a minimum and tuition is lower than in other centers. Most co-ops are half-day programs because they require parent participation; however, there are co-ops organized as child care centers.

Agency-Sponsored Programs

Many not-for-profit early childhood education programs are sponsored by community agencies such as church groups, labor unions, service agencies, neighborhood houses, and United Way organizations. These programs may be set up as full-day care centers for working families or as half-day enrichment programs. Such programs are found in both rural and urban areas and can serve both low-income and middle-income families depending on how much support is provided by the sponsoring agency. Agency-sponsored programs sometimes receive partial support from a sponsor such as United Way and obtain the remaining support from tuition, government funds, and/or grants.

Government-Sponsored Programs

Head Start is perhaps the best known of the federal government-sponsored, early childhood education programs. Head Start is a comprehensive *compensatory* program that serves children of low-income families. That is, it is a program intended to compensate for experiences the children from impoverished families may have missed. In addition to educational services, Head Start also provides comprehensive health and social services to children and families (Children's Defense Fund, 2004, p. 69). The funding for Head Start programs is allocated by the federal government from the U.S. Department of Health and Human Services, Administration for Children, Youth and Families (ACYF), Head Start Bureau (HSB). These funds are often distributed through and monitored by the local Community Action Agency. Funding for Head Start programs may go to public school systems, universities, and public or private not-for-profit agencies. Larger grantees such as public schools or universities often find creative ways to partner with other agencies to provide opportunities for more families to receive the benefits of this comprehensive government-sponsored child care program. For example, a public school may set up a partnership with a church child care program that serves a number of low-income families. The church, in collaboration with the public school, can offer Head Start income eligible families various health and social service benefits with the help of a Head Start family advocate. The Head State funding also helps the church cover program expenses for these families. Many unique collaborative arrangements are being worked out between and among various types of child care agencies across the country, all in an effort to better serve children and families.

Head Start programs may be center based or home based, may provide child care on a full-time or half-time basis, and usually serve four-year-olds. Those who receive funds from Head Start (grantees) are mandated to serve children with disabilities (10 percent of enrollment opportunities) who must be mainstreamed, and receive a total care package through direct services from the grantee or from other resources in the community. Innovative programs for younger children (Early Head Start) are funded through special Head Start grants. The Department of Defense and the Veteran's Administration also sponsor child care programs in some regions of the country, as do some state governments. Of course, there are many military programs (see section on military programs).

Public School-Sponsored Programs

Most states are funding some prekindergarten programs, and many of these are in public schools (Neugebauer, 2003). These programs are usually funded through local or state tax monies or other public funds. Full-day or half-day public school programs are staffed by people hired through public school personnel offices, and the programs are housed in public school buildings. Local school boards, public school administrators, and teacher unions typically have a voice in making policy as well as in teacher and program evaluation. The building principal is the appointed instructional leader, and at the state level, these programs fall under the jurisdiction of the superintendent of public instruction or the commissioner of education.

Practices in public preschools still tend to focus on academic success, school readiness, and standardized testing, but advocates for developmentally appropriate practice in preschools are challenging this academic readiness position of some public school instructional leaders. These philosophical differences are at the forefront of educational reform (Stegelin, 1992). The 1988 report of a task force of the National Association of State Boards of Education (NASBE) (NASBE Report, 1988), which advocates early childhood units in public schools, and *Eager to Learn: Educating Our Preschoolers* (National Research Council, 2000) will affect how young children are served in public schools in the next decades.

Before- and after-school programs for school-aged children often are housed in public schools. Some are also public school-sponsored, while others are run by community agencies or service groups such as the Salvation Army and YMCA. The public school-sponsored programs may be staffed by teachers in the building or by high school or college students who are free during early morning and late afternoon hours. Often, the person in the school

Many state funded preschool programs are housed in public schools

system responsible for the preschool programs also oversees these before- and after-school programs and other wraparound programs, and the building principal is the on-site administrator-in-charge.

Campus Child Care Programs

Laboratory schools and child care programs for children of students, faculty, and staff are two types of programs that can be found on college campuses. The programs may be sponsored and subsidized by the college or university, or by government funds. These programs often provide facilities for research, observation, and teacher training. They may be full day or half day and may charge full, or in some cases, partial, tuition for those affiliated with the university. In some places where student groups as well as the university itself offer support for the care of students' children, the students pay minimum tuition for their children and the program hours are flexible to accommodate the students' course schedules.

Privately Sponsored Not-for-Profit Programs

Many large industries, hospitals, and apartment complexes are including child care centers in their facilities and are offering services for the children of their employees and residents. These not-for-profit centers are set up for the comfort and convenience of the employees and residents. The hours are often flexible,

and in some cases, fees are on a sliding scale to encourage full use of the available facilities. In the case of hospital- and industry-operated programs, fees may be part of an employee benefit package implemented through the use of vouchers, direct payment to the caregivers, or a child care allowance to the employee.

Some employers offer a Dependent Care Assistance Program (DCAP) or Dependent Care Reimbursement Program (DCRP) that allows employees to set aside a certain amount of their yearly pretax salary for child care expenses, thereby providing a substantial tax savings to the employee.

Employers are realizing they cannot meet the challenge of fulfilling employees' child care needs on their own and are reaching out to the child care community for help in managing on-site centers. Some contract with centers for a reduced fee or funded slots for employees, whereas others prefer to contract for information and referral services in the area but are not involved in service delivery.

Profit-Making Programs (Proprietary)

Although much is written about not-for-profit programs such as Head Start, United Way centers, and public school programs, a large majority of the early childhood education programs in the United States are proprietary. These programs are set up to provide a service that will make a profit.

Independent Owner

Many full- and half-day child care programs are owned and operated by an individual or a small group (partnerships or small corporations). In the case of the proprietary center, tuition is usually the only source of income, and the operators frequently have budgeting and financial problems, although some proprietary and nonprofits can obtain supplementary funding from other sources including state funds. The proprietary operators may be able to draw a salary from the tuition that is paid by families using the service, but the operators rarely make a profit over and above that because of the high cost of operating a quality program. Sometimes, proprietors open more than one center in a community or region and begin a small chain operation. Although it is difficult to make a profit from the small chain, quantity buying and shared service costs sometimes can reduce the cost per child and increase the possibility of making a profit over and above operating expenses.

Corporate Systems

Large child care chains are operated by a parent company that develops a prototype and sets up a number of centers throughout a state or region, or across the nation and into Canada. Some of these corporations have gone public and their stock is traded on the New York Stock Exchange. These national child care chains operate under a central administration that furnishes the financial backing and is usually very powerful in setting the policy and controlling the program. There often is a prototype building and program that are publicized by identifiable slogans, logos, brochures, and advertisements. Some corporate systems operate all centers carrying the chain name, while others work on a franchised basis. In the latter case, an individual purchases a franchise from the parent company for a basic purchase price, then pays the company a percentage of gross intake for the ongoing use of the name and the program. In addition, the parent company supplies guidelines for fees, sample documents, brochures, advertising materials, and the like. Some of these sample documents must be changed by center operators in order to meet local regulations and/or be in line with local practice. The parent corporation often monitors the franchised centers to maintain the company standard of quality control. Since company policy often controls the program, directors are usually expected to adopt the program as outlined by the corporate body but also can adjust some practices based on their own philosophy. A list of "The Exchange Top 40" of America's largest for-profit centers is in Director's Resource 3–2.

Employer-Sponsored Programs

There is an increasing demand for employer-sponsored child care. Employers are analyzing the benefits of child care services and seeking creative ways to meet their employees' identified needs. During the 1990s, the top players among the child care management organizations involved in employer-sponsored care were Bright Horizons Family Solutions and Children's Discovery Centers/Knowledge Beginnings, now Knowledge Learning Corporation (Director's Resource 3–3). They accounted for the lion's share of the phenomenal growth in the employer-sponsored care in that decade. Much of their growth resulted from contracts to take over centers that employers were previously managing on their own in addition to some acquisitions of other independent child care providers. The employer-sponsored segment of the market had grown two or three times faster than the overall child care supply (Child Care Information Exchange/National Association of Child Care Resource and Referral Agencies, 1998). However, that growth rate has sharply declined since 2000 (Director's Resource 3–3). The concept of employer-sponsored care is not new. In the 1940s during WWII, the Kaiser shipbuilder corporation on the West Coast provided care for the children of women who were called into the workforce to support U.S. troops in the war effort. Stride Rite and Levi Strauss also were pioneers in the on-site employer-sponsored child care business. The availability of child care management corporations is relatively recent.

According to a Bright Horizons spokesperson, "Historically, the pharmaceutical, finance, insurance, and health industries dominated the landscape of clients. Now a number of new industries are involved, including retail, restaurants, and manufacturing. Also, there is an increasing demand for more customized services for clients, such as backup care and other creative services" (Neugebauer, 1999, p. 26). Some of these additional services include backup and sick child care, therapy services for children with special needs, crisis intervention, and a number of extracurricular programs including karate, gymnastics, music, and dance. Other creative ways to serve families is to offer dry cleaning pickup, UPS pickup, gourmet meal pickup, and even haircuts for children. In most cases, parents contract with these special service providers and the center is the appointed location for deliveries and pickups.

Centers are not involved in billing or receiving payments.

When unemployment is down, growing numbers of employers begin to view child care as a recruitment and retention tool. For example, hospitals sponsor on-site centers to help with recruitment and retention of nurses and other technical personnel. Although many employer-sponsored centers are run by the large management organizations, there are employers who seek out public or private groups such as universities or the YMCA to run centers for them. In some cases, the employers provide generous subsidies by building new facilities that are rent-free or offering low-cost leases for ground on which to build. Employers who strive to keep fees down for their employees, but value quality care and want fully qualified staff as well as low teacher-to-child ratios, subsidize their centers to make up the deficits.

When universities or other nonprofits such as hospitals or YMCAs are called on to manage centers for large for-profit corporations, it is important for the center director to be prepared for many discussions with the corporate partners about clarification of the mission and goals of the new program. Of course, families and children always will be the focus of those who manage and staff the center. However, it is important to keep in mind that recruitment, retention, employee productivity, and morale are major goals of the corporation that subsidizes and sponsors the center. Directors realize they have many customers, including families, children, and staff, but now directors must realize that one of the important customers is the sponsoring corporation. When issues and questions arise, the position of the corporate customer must be taken into consideration. They may have questions about curriculum or hiring practices, but they are likely to accept the decisions of the early childhood professionals whom they hired to deal with those aspects of the program. For the director, this is no different from handling the usual inquiries and concerns from parents in any type of center. But decisions about hours of operation, changing schedules for children by the week (or even the day), backup care, sick child care, late day or night care, and weekend care are the things a business sponsor may need to keep employees who work different schedules. They respect the early childhood professional and value the beautiful classrooms and rich programming offered the children. However, to meet the expectations the corporation has for its employees, the center staff may have to reconsider what they view as best for the children and adjust to the interests and schedules of their sponsor without compromising the integrity of their own ethical and professional values.

DIRECTOR'S CORNER

"I have been the director of an on-site center sponsored by a not-for-profit organization for almost 20 years. When that organization contracted with a large for-profit corporation to manage a new center they were ready to build, I was made the director of both centers. The corporation selected us because we had been the recipient of a national award and were well known for the quality program we offered in the on-site center. One of my greatest challenges when I began to work with the point people from the large corporate sponsor was to realize that they were now a customer of my not-for-profit employer. It really forced me to stretch my thinking and rethink what I valued and where I would draw the line on issues and not compromise."

—Director of two large employer-sponsored programs

Military Programs

The Department of Defense (DOD) operates child care programs at military installations across the country. Financed by a combination of government appropriations and sliding scale parent tuition fees, the programs may be full-day center-based care, part-day preschools, drop-in care, and, in some places, evening and weekend care.

Each of the military services (Air Force, Army, Marines, and Navy) operates its own child care service, but all must follow the mandates in the Military Child Care Act of 1989. The act addresses program funding, required training for staff, competitive pay rates for staff, and an internal inspection system. To meet the demand for child care services, the DOD has expanded preschool and school-aged child care options by increasing the number of programs on military installations. It accomplished this by using existing Resource and Referral Programs to help families locate available child care and by contracting with off-installation centers to guarantee spaces for DOD children.

Family Child Care Homes

Family child care is reminiscent of an extended family where a small group of children is cared for in the home of a child care provider (Gordon & Williams Browne, 2004). Although this type of child care service

Family child care homes offer care for a small group of children in the home of a child care provider.

is most popular for infants and toddlers, these home providers also care for preschool children and offer before- and after-school care. The provider may be an employee of a system but most often operates independently, contracting directly with families who choose home care over center-based care. In some states, family child care homes must be licensed, whereas in other places, they are certified or registered by a community agency authorized to pay for children of low-income families who are in the home. Many providers join employer or community agency Information and Referral Registries that take calls from parents seeking child care. Registered family child care homes may or may not be subject to inspection by a responsible community agency. In some places, inspections are made only after a complaint has been filed.

Standards of Practice for All Types of Programs

All types of programs listed in the previous section, whether for-profit or not, whether corporate or privately owned and operated, whether center based, school based or in-home care, are expected to provide high-quality programs for young children. It is assumed that all of these programs meet local licensing requirements because without a proper license, programs are not permitted to remain open for business. However, to provide the very best for children and to meet the accepted standards of quality based on expectations of fellow professionals, directors are expected to go beyond meeting minimum standards of excellence.

The best-known and most widely accepted standards for quality practice for any and all programs for children birth through kindergarten are those developed by the National Association for the Education of Young Children (NAEYC). School-age programs are accredited by the National After-School Association (NAA), while family child care programs are accredited by the National Association For Family Child Care (NAFCC), and in some places centers can receive accreditation from the National Association of Child Care Professionals (NACCP). (For additional information on accreditation, see Chapter 4).

SUMMARY

Starting a center is a challenging and exhausting undertaking. During the early planning stages, a number of concurrent activities interact with one another. The individual or group forming the nucleus of the driving force that gets a center started must assess the need for a program while developing a program philosophy and determining the type of program that will meet the expressed need. Many decisions must be made concerning how needs should be assessed, what philosophy will be most representative of the thinking of the planners and the prospective director, what type of program is feasible in terms of financing, and so forth. The people who are interested in starting a center must recognize that a great deal of time and energy must be invested before financial support is available and before a program can begin to deliver service to children and families.

CLASS ASSIGNMENTS

1. Review the sample needs assessment questionnaire in Director's Resource 3–1 and adjust it so you could use it for a telephone survey. Think about
   a. exactly what you would say to open the conversation.
   b. what incentive you would offer to encourage participation in the survey.
   c. what questions you would ask (or not ask) on the basis of answers you receive.
   d. how you would close the conversation.

CLASS EXERCISES

1. Using Working Paper 3–1, discuss and record the thinking of the group about the items listed.
2. Using Working Paper 3–2, write your own program philosophy based on your thinking about the items listed in Class Exercise 1 on Working Paper 3–1.
3. Reread Program Philosophy #1 (p. 48), and using Working Paper 3–3, rewrite it to make it more comprehensive and congruent with your own thinking.

WORKING PAPER 3-1

(for use with Class Exercise 1)

DISCUSSION FORM

In groups of four, discuss and record the thinking of the group about the items listed below:

1. What are your assumptions about growth and development?

2. How does learning or the development of knowledge come about?

3. During the early years of a child's life, what is the adult's role relative to:

   physical development?

   social development?

   emotional development?

   cognitive development?

   language development?

   moral development?

4. What goals do you have for the children in your care?

WORKING PAPER 3-2

(for use with Class Exercise 2)

Assume you have been hired as a director of a new center. Based on your own thinking about the items listed on Working Paper 3–1, write a program philosophy for your new center.

WORKING PAPER 3-3

(for use with Class Assignment 3)

Assume you have been hired as the director of a center that has been in operation for a number of years. The Program Philosophy they pass along to you to rewrite is presented below:

> The program is based on the philosophy that most children can learn the skills necessary to succeed in school, that each child learns at his own rate, and the success in learning will develop the child's self-image (Program Philosophy #1, p. 48).

Expand this stated philosophy and include your own ideas based on your training and the theoretical base on which you make program decisions.

DIRECTOR'S RESOURCE 3-1

SAMPLE NEEDS ASSESSMENT

1. How many adults are there in this household? _____

2. Do all adults in the household work?   ❑ Yes   ❑ No

   If yes,   ❑ part time   How many? _____   ❑ full time   How many? _____

3. What is the total number of children under the age of sixteen? _____

4. What is the number of children under age six? _____

   Check ages of children under six:

      ❑ Under one   How many? _____

      ❑ Between 1 and 2   How many? _____

      ❑ Between 2 and 3   How many? _____

      ❑ Between 3 and 4   How many? _____

      ❑ Between 4 and 5   How many? _____

      ❑ Between 5 and 6   How many? _____

5. Does any child in this family, younger than school age, regularly spend time away from home?   ❑ Yes   ❑ No

   If yes, how many? _____

6. Do any children in the family have special needs?   ❑ Yes   ❑ No

   If yes, how many? _____

   If yes, does the condition require attendance at a special school or program?   ❑ Yes   ❑ No
   If yes, describe program(s) needed:

   _____

   _____

7. Is/are your child(ren) regularly cared for every day in your home by someone who does not live with you?   ❑ Yes   ❑ No

   If yes, is the caregiver a relative?   ❑ Yes   ❑ No

8. How many children over five regularly spend time away from home before or after school?
   _____ What are their ages? _____

   Describe type of program:

   _____

   _____

(continues)

DIRECTOR'S RESOURCE 3-1
(continued)

SAMPLE NEEDS ASSESSMENT

9. For statistical purposes only, please give the total family income in this household:

   $0–$10,000 ❑

   $10,001–$18,000 ❑

   $18,001–$36,000 ❑

   $36,001–$50,000 ❑

   $50,001–$75,000 ❑

   $75,001–$90,000 ❑

   over $90,000 ❑

10. Approximately how much do you pay every week for the care of all your children? Give that figure in column A. In column B, mark how much you would be willing to pay for quality care for all of your children. Mark with X.

A	B	
_____	$0–50	❑
_____	$51–75	❑
_____	$76–100	❑
_____	$101–125	❑
_____	$126–150	❑
_____	$151–175	❑
_____	Over $175	❑

11. Many parents have a difficult time arranging for the care of their children. Indicate what has been your experience.

    ❑ Easy time

    ❑ Not very difficult

    ❑ Difficult time

    ❑ Extremely difficult

    ❑ No opinion

(continues)

DIRECTOR'S RESOURCE 3-1
(continued)

SAMPLE NEEDS ASSESSMENT

12. If you had a choice of arrangements for the care of your child, what would be your first choice?

    ❏ Care in child care center for four hours or less

    ❏ Care in child care center for more than four hours

    ❏ Care by another mother or someone in her own home

    ❏ Care by a sitter in your own home

    ❏ Care in a center before and after school

13. If you could have the type of arrangement you prefer, how many days per week would you want your child(ren) to spend there (insert number of days)? _____ Infant _____ Toddler _____ Preschooler _____ After school (Age_____)

14. Where would you prefer to have your child(ren) cared for?

    ❏ Near where you work

    ❏ Near where you live

    ❏ Other location: _____

15. Generally speaking, in selecting an ideal child care arrangement, which is more important to you? (Assume that quality is equal.)

    ❏ Cost more important

    ❏ Closeness to home more important

    ❏ Closeness to work more important

    ❏ No opinion

16. If a child care center opens across the street from your office (insert home, church, factory, as appropriate), for which age child would you be likely to use it?

    ❏ Your infant

    ❏ Your toddler

    ❏ Your preschooler

    ❏ Your school-aged child(ren)

DIRECTOR'S RESOURCE 3-2

THE EXCHANGE TOP 40
North America's Largest For-Profit Child Care Organizations

Organization	Headquarters	CEO	Centers*	Capacity*
Knowledge Learning Corporation	Santa Monica, CA	Tom Heymann	2,027	267,000
La Petite Academy	Chicago, IL	Gary Graves	643	89,000
Learning Care Group, Inc.	Novi, MI	Bill Davis	466	72,000
Bright Horizons Family Solutions	Watertown, MA	David H. Lissy	560	62,000
Nobel Learning Communities	West Chester, PA	George Bernstein	168	28,100
Child Care Network	Columbus, GA	James F. Loudermilk	130	17,618
The Sunshine House	Greenwood, SC	Dennis Drew	121	15,779
Children's Courtyard	Arlington, TX	Edward Follen	76	13,255
New Horizon Child Care	Plymouth, MN	Susan Dunkley	89	12,381
Minnieland Private Day School	Woodbridge, VA	Jackie M. Leopold	89	10,134
Mini-Skool	Scottsdale, AZ	Douglas MacKay	65	10,000
Allegheny Child Care Academy	Pittsburgh, PA	Harold Lewis	38	7,036
Children's Friend	Warner Robins, GA	F. Dewayne Foskey	40	5,824
Pinecrest Schools	Sherman Oaks, CA	Don L. Dye	14	4,332
Rainbow Child Development Centers	Lathrup Village, MI	Patrick G. Fenton	40	4,322
Action Day Nurseries/Primary Plus	San Jose, CA	Carole Freitas	15	3,450
Sunrise Preschools	Tempe, AZ	Robert Orsi	17	3,376
Hildebrandt Learning Centers	Wilkes-Barre, PA	William J. Grant	32	3,148
Children's Choice Learning Centers	Plano, TX	Nate McClintock	10	2,634
Crème de la Crème	Greenwood Village, CO	Bruce T. Karpas	8	2,512
Country Home Learning Center	San Antonio, TX	Sharon K. Ford	8	2,504
Stepping Stone School	Austin, TX	Rhonda Paver	14	2,389
Children's Lighthouse Management	Fort Worth, TX	George Michael Brown	10	2,050
Children's Creative Learning Centers	Sunnyvale, CA	Ty Durekas	17	2,041
Tot-Time Child Development Centers	Plymouth Meeting, PA	Donna M. Bongarzone-Fluehr	19	2,035
Creative World School	Tampa, FL	Billie McCabe	17	2,012
Creative Playrooms	Solon, OH	Joan P. Wenk	7	1,900
Kid's Country	Snohomish, WA	Lynnda Langston	11	1,778
Child Care Connection	Lincoln, RI	Kevin Fusco	17	1,746
Bobbie Noonan's Child Care	Frankfort, IL	Judith Nevell	13	1,663
Celebre Learning Centers	Bel Air, MD	Richard Huffman	12	1,548
Rogy's Learning Place	East Peoria, IL	Don Meyer and Rick Rogy	13	1,526
Seven Oaks Academy	Westminster, CO	Ronald S. Faillaci	11	1,497

(continues)

DIRECTOR'S RESOURCE 3-2
(continued)

THE EXCHANGE TOP 40
North America's Largest For-Profit Child Care Organizations

Organization	*Headquarters*	*CEO*	*Centers**	*Capacity**
Kiddie Kare Schools	Fresno, CA	James Fisher, Jr.	10	1,492
ChildrenFirst	Waltham, MA	John Marvin	32	1,354
Sunny Daze	Edmond, OK	Mike North	7	1,304

National Child Care Franchising Organizations

Organization	*Headquarters*	*CEO*	*Centers**	*Capacity**
Kids R Kids International	Duluth, GA	Pat Vinson	111	27,750
Goddard Systems, Inc.	King of Prussia, PA	Philip A. Schumacher	185	24,000
Tutor Time Franchise, LLC	Novi, MI	Bill Davis	130	24,000
Primrose School Franchising Company	Acworth, GA	Jo Kirchner	125	20,000
Kiddie Academy	Bel Air, MD	Michael J. Miller	75	10,172

*Data on capacity in above chart is the total licensed capacity for all centers as of January 1, 2005. Data for "Franchising Organizations" include both franchised and company-owned centers. Based solely on information supplied by organizations listed.

Reprinted with permission from Child Care Information Exchange, P.O. Box 3249, Redmond, WA 98073, (800) 221-2864, http://www.ChildCareExchange.com. Permission conveyed through Copyright Clearance Center, Inc.

DIRECTOR'S RESOURCE 3-3

THE EXCHANGE TOP 14
Largest Employer Child Care Management Organizations in 2003

Organization	CEO	Contracted Centers	Office Park Centers	Licensed Capacity
Bright Horizons Family Solutions	David H. Lissy	380	110	57,000
Knowledge Learning Corporation	Tom Heymann	98	82	20,176
La Petite Academy	Gary Graves	29	73	13,318
KinderCare Learning Centers	David J. Johnson	44	22	9,948
Hildebrandt Learning Centers	William J. Grant	28	0	3,049
New Horizon Child Care	Susan Dunkley	5	14	2,829
Children's Choice Learning Centers	Nate McClintock	4	4	2,325
The Children's Courtyard	Ed Follen	0	13	2,220
Easter Seals Child Development Center Network	Bob Siegel	22	0	2,011
Children's Creative Learning Centers	Ty Durekas	5	10	1,650
ChildrenFirst	Rosemary Jordano	8	23	1,345
Primrose Schools	Jo Kirchner	0	4	750
Imagine Early Learning Centers	Holly Saltzman	9	0	590
National Pediatric Support Services	Sheri Senter	5	0	290

NOTE: *Organizations listed by total licensed capacity of all contracted and office park centers as of September 1, 2003. The "Contracted Centers" column displays centers operated under contract to a single employer. The "Office Park Centers" column displays centers operated in office parks or other commercial settings serving more than one employer. Based solely on information provided by the organizations.*

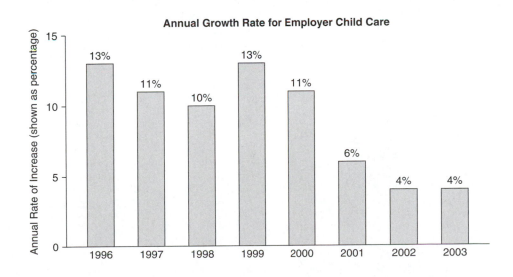

Annual Growth Rate for Employer Child Care

Reprinted with permission from Child Care Information Exchange, P.O. Box 3249, Redmond, WA 98073, (800) 221-2864, http://www.ChildCareExchange.com. Permission conveyed through Copyright Clearance Center, Inc.

REFERENCES

Berk, L. E., & Winsler, A. (1995). *Scaffolding children's learning: Vygotsky and early childhood education.* Washington, DC: NAEYC.

Child Care Information Exchange/National Association of Child Care Resource and Referral Agencies. (1998). *Inside child care.* Trend Report #4.

Children's Defense Fund. (2004). *The state of America's children.* Washington, DC.

Decker, C., & Decker, J. R. (2005). *Planning and administering early childhood programs* (8th ed.). Upper Saddle River, NJ: Prentice-Hall.

DeVries, R., & Kohlberg, L. (1988). *Programs of early education: The constructivist view.* Longman.

Gordon, A. M., & Williams Browne, K. (2004). *Beginnings and beyond* (6th ed.). Clifton Park, NY: Thomson Delmar Learning.

Kamii, C. (1982). *Number in preschool and kindergarten: Educational implications for Piaget's theory.* Washington, DC: NAEYC.

Kuykendall, J. (1990, July). Child development directors shouldn't leave home without it. *Young Children,* 49–51.

National Research Council—Executive Summary. (2000). *Eager to learn: Educating our preschoolers.* Washington, DC: National Academy Press.

NAEYC. (1998). *Accreditation criteria and procedures of the National Association for the Education of Young Children.* Washington, DC: Author.

NASBE Report. (1988). *Right from the start.* Alexandria, VA: NASBE.

Neugebauer, R. (1999). Competition shifting in expanding employer arena. *Child Care Information Exchange: The Director's Magazine, 127,* 26–28.

Neugebauer, R. (2003). Update on child care in public schools. *Child Care Information Exchange: The Director's Magazine,* 150, 66–71.

Stegelin, D. A. (1992). Kindergarten education: Current policy and practice. In D. Stegelin & T. G. Goffin (Eds.), *Changing kindergartens.* Washington, DC: NAEYC.

Additional resources for this chapter can be found on the Online Companion™ at http://www.earlychilded.delmar.com. This supplemental material includes relevant Web links, Web activities, and case studies that apply the concepts presented in this chapter. In addition, the Working Papers and Director's Resources are available for download, allowing you to complete Class Exercises and Class Assignments electronically.

CHAPTER 4

Licensing and Certification

The primary function of the licensing agent is to ascertain whether a program is in compliance with minimum requirements.

OBJECTIVES

After reading this chapter, you should be able to:

- Understand the purpose of licensing.
- Identify the steps in the licensing process.
- Understand various types of regulations and their specific purposes.
- Understand the difference between licensing and accreditation.
- Recognize the various levels of individual credentials available for staff in a child care and education center.

Child care center directors are responsible for understanding licensing, certification, and other regulations pertaining to provision of services for young children. Each type of regulation is developed by a governmental body and each has specific purposes. Directors must understand which regulations apply to their programs and ensure that all requirements are fulfilled in a timely manner. They also must be prepared to pay the requisite fees. In the future, people who assume responsible roles in children's programs probably will have to deal with more and more regulatory functions. This increase in regulation is related to the expanded use of public funds and the broader acceptance of the fact that programs for young children must provide care and protection for children and be educationally sound. Educational accountability points to greater focus on the need for also certifying or licensing the people responsible for children's programs, while protection of children's health and safety requires licensing of centers. The term "licensing" may cause confusion since it is used to signify that a governing body is giving permission to do something. In this case, what is being permitted is operating a child care program. Later in the chapter when we discuss licensing (or certifying) teachers, what is being permitted is the opportunity to obtain a teaching position.

After programs are in compliance with the minimum standards required for local or state licensing, they can move toward higher standards and gain some form of professional recognition. The National Association for the Education of Young Children (NAEYC) works with child care centers through its National Academy for Early Childhood Program Accreditation to administer "a national, voluntary accreditation system to help raise the quality of all types of preschools, kindergartens, and child care centers" which is how NAEYC describes its mission on its Web site (http://www.NAEYC.org). The National Association of Child Care Professionals (NACCP), the National Child Care Association (NCCA), the National After School Association, and the American Montessori Association also provide opportunities for accreditation.

On-site directors and boards are responsible for providing the necessary inspiration and leadership to improve the center. They work to move a program from compliance with minimum licensing requirements to meeting quality performance standards. Even beyond these standards lies the goal of dynamic development that continues to produce a quality educational program. Model program directors always are working to refine their programs as they move toward the goal of excellence. Since the knowledge base in child development and early childhood education is constantly growing, no program can afford to rest on its laurels.

LICENSING

Licensing of centers is required, but coverage varies from state to state. For example, in some states, only full-day child care programs are required to obtain a license, while in other states, all full-day care, half-day, and home-based programs must be licensed. Depending on the type of program being planned and the geographical location of the center, it is possible that both local and state requirements will need to be met. And where federal funding is involved, there will be additional requirements. In some states, program sponsorship determines program licensing. For example, programs affiliated with public schools may be licensed by the state department of education. Your licensing agent can provide updated licensing information. A directory of state child care regulatory offices is available from the National Child Care Information Center on-line at http://nccic.org. To obtain a copy of an individual state's child care licensure regulations, go to the National Resource Center for Health and Safety in Child Care at http://nrc.uchsc.edu. Both of these organizations provide numerous on-line documents and research results. In addition, the Children's Foundation

conducted a 2002 Child Care Licensing Study that is available at http://www.childrensfoundation.net. Other resources are listed at the end of this chapter.

The licensing function is a result of legislation, and its thrust is accountability for the health and safety of children. Licensing requirements are usually minimal and measurable, but they do not guarantee quality of care or protection for the children.

LeMoine, Morgan, and Azer (2003) describe three structural aspects of child care that are regulated by state licensing, all of which have been shown to relate to positive outcomes for children in child centers:

1. child-to-staff ratios
2. maximum group size
3. staff qualifications and ongoing training

However, licensing rarely addresses the educational quality of the program. The licensing function is essential and valuable, but often it is misunderstood. A license gives permission to operate rather than indicating quality.

The 2002 Child Care Center Licensing Study showed a 26 percent increase from 1991 in the number of registered centers nationwide, for a total of 117,284 regulated centers, while more than twice

After programs are in compliance with minimum standards required for local or state licensing, they can move toward higher standards that may lead to accreditation.

as many regulated child care homes were located in the 50 states, the District of Columbia, Puerto Rico, and the Virgin Islands (http://www.childrensfoundation.net). Family child care homes refer to places in which people care for one or more children in their homes instead of in a center or the child's own home. Some states divide these into categories based on the number of children permitted. In larger child care homes, perhaps 12 children may be cared for. At least two adults are needed and building regulations should be required. Many families prefer this type of care, particularly for infants and toddlers, because of the smaller setting. Although family child care (or family day care as it is sometimes called) has always been a frequently used source of child care, its regulation has been relatively recent.

A recent major increase in the number of states requiring preservice qualifications for family home child care providers was reported by LeMoine, Morgan, and Azer (2002). However, the mandated qualifications related to early childhood training are limited. For example, much of the training may be in first aid, collecting fees, or completing forms for Child Care Food Program reimbursement. Because of the limited hours available for training, information about young children's development and learning is minimal.

Child care center staff preservice training shows a trend toward emphasis on early childhood education.

Although not part of the regulatory system for child care centers, the American Association of Colleges of Teacher Education has called for all preschool teachers to have bachelor's degrees. This proposal far exceeds licensing requirements but is consistent with requirements for kindergarten teachers. As a future early childhood teacher or director, you may want to discuss this proposal with your peers or instructors.

In addition to the licensing department, in most localities the building department will review the plans, and the fire, building, and health or sanitation departments will send individual representatives to inspect the proposed space where the services for children will be offered. No matter what system is used in a particular state, an initial inspection and approval is required before the center can begin to operate. Even when the center is moving from one location to another, the inspection and approval must still be done. The regulating departments may be willing to send individual representatives to inspect the proposed space where the services for children will be offered. These inspections can alert the director to major and minor changes that would need to be made. The decision about moving to a particular facility may hinge on the cost and time line for making these changes, as well as on the deadline for exiting the current premises.

After initial inspection and approval, inspections and license renewals will be required on a regular basis. Directors are responsible for making certain that their programs are in compliance with regulations and for being familiar with appeal and grievance procedures if conflicts regarding compliance with the regulations arise.

The Children's Defense Fund (CDF) reports that several states made progress in enhancing programs for children during 2000. Among the CDF's examples are the Tennessee requirements increasing the number of unannounced visits to child care centers annually from one to six visits. North Carolina has provided 60 additional licensing staff and is beginning a system of rated licensing using a two- to five-star system (Children's Defense Fund, 2001). Many states also are adopting a tiered system of licensing with higher-rated centers eligible to receive higher subsidy rates.

Licensing Regulations

Local and state licensing regulations typically cover building safety and requirements for physical space and establish base teacher-to-child ratios. Although licensing regulations vary greatly from state to state, most licensing regulations include the following points:

1. *Building safety.* Licensing regulations always include at least the minimum fire, sanitation, and building safety standards that apply to all private and public services. Fire regulations usually cover the type of building construction, ease of evacuation from the building in the event of fire, alarm systems, smoke detectors, sprinkler systems, availability of fire extinguishers, and methods of storing combustible materials. Building codes usually cover wiring, plumbing, and building construction, including building materials. Health department regulations cover conditions in all areas of the building, with particular attention to the bathrooms and food service operations.

   When infants and/or children who are nonambulatory are enrolled in the program, the director must be sure to meet licensing requirements for those groups. Typically, these requirements focus on egress in case of emergency. Usually housing these programs on the first (ground) floor is required.

2. *Physical space.* Licensing regulations usually specify the amount of space necessary for programs for infants, toddlers, and preschool children. The requirement for three- to five-year-old children is typically a minimum of 35 square feet per child of indoor space and 60 to 75 square feet of space per child outdoors. Since programs for infants and toddlers require cribs, feeding tables, and diaper changing areas, such programs require more space per child than do programs for three- to five-year-olds. Levels and sources of light, levels of heat, sources of fresh air, fencing of outdoor areas, protection of radiators and low windows, and numbers of toilets also are included in regulations covering physical space. These standards are minimal, and good programs usually exceed them. Providing more than minimal space, particularly for children who will be at the center all day, is likely to make both children and staff more comfortable.

3. *Teacher-to-child ratios.* Some licensing regulations include minimum teacher-to-child ratios. These state or local ratios vary, but they are in the range of three to eight infants to one adult, 4 to 12 toddlers to one adult, and 6 to 20 preschoolers to one adult. The baseline licensing standards for child-to-staff ratios in child care centers in some states already meet the standards used by NAEYC, but most states are still below these significant ratios. Most regulations require that two responsible adults be on the premises at all times. The ratios are established to furnish a baseline standard for protecting the safety of children; however, group size is even more important and also is regulated by some states.

   A collaborative report from the American Public Health Association, the American Academy of Pediatrics, and the Maternal and Child Health Bureau (2002) recommends the group size and child-to-staff ratios shown in Figure 4–1.

   Licensing standards seem to be coming closer to these guidelines. Following are the most common child-to-staff ratios required by licensing in 2002 (LeMoine, Morgan, & Azer, 2002):

   - for infants, 4:1 in 33 states
   - for toddlers, 6:1 and 8:1 in 9 states each
   - for four-year-olds, 10:1 in 17 states
   - for five-year-olds is 15:1 in 15 states

   Accreditation Criteria, NAEYC provided the rationale for this staffing goal. "An important determinant of the quality of a program is the way in which it is staffed. Well-organized staffing patterns facilitate individualized care and support learning. Research strongly suggests

Child Age	Maximum Group Size	Ratio of Children to Teacher
Infant	6	3:1
Toddler	8	4:1
Three-year-olds	14	7:1
Five-year-olds	16	8:1

Figure 4–1

Recommended group size and ratio of children to staff.

(adapted from Caring for Our Children: National Health and Safety Performance Standards: Guidelines for Out-of-Home Child Care Programs, second edition, as reported by LeMoine, Morgan, & Azer (2003)).

that smaller group sizes and larger numbers of staff to children are related to positive outcomes for children such as increased interaction among adults and children, and less aggression, more cooperation among children" (NAEYC, 1998, p. 45).

4. *Staff qualifications.* Teachers' training in child development and their interactions with the children are key factors in creating a quality program. NAEYC's draft standards, scheduled to be approved and in effect by 2006, continue to uphold the importance of well-prepared staff and appropriate group sizes. These standards also call for teachers who "have high levels of formal education and specialized early childhood professional preparation." Check the NAEYC Web site for current information.

Although licensing regulations sometimes address staff qualifications, requirements are often minimal. Some states require that caregivers be able to read and write, while others require at least a high school diploma for anyone who is hired as a teacher, teacher assistant, and/or aide. Most states require a director to have at least a high school diploma, while a few states require some college training, which may or may not be in child development or early childhood education. Others, however, require specific training in early childhood education or attainment of the Child Development Associate credential. Professional organizations are working to upgrade the criteria for early childhood staff as one component of the effort to improve staff salaries. As this process evolves, we can expect licensing standards to continue to improve. Psychologists, nurses,

doctors on call, and other professionals must meet the appropriate credential requirements of their respective professions. Early childhood professionals also should be expected to meet standards.

5. *Transportation.* In centers where transportation service is provided, the service usually must meet the state motor vehicle department standards for school bus service. These standards regulate numbers of children, type of vehicle, types of lights on vehicles, proper identification on the vehicle, use of car seats and seat belts, and appropriate licensing and insurance coverage for the vehicle and the driver. Even when it is not required, it is wise to provide drivers with training in child development and management so that time spent on the bus will be positive as well as safe for both children and drivers.

It also is advisable to have a second adult on the bus to assist in an emergency. The driver, of course, should not leave even one child on the bus while seeking help or when walking a child to the door when that child's parent does not come out to meet the bus. Furthermore, some children have a difficult time leaving seat belts on. The driver, who must give full attention to the road, should not have to check constantly to ensure that all children are safely seated. The center also should establish a policy requiring the driver to check the interior of the vehicle thoroughly to be sure no child remains on board. This procedure should be in effect every time the driver leaves the vehicle. This procedure is required by law in some states.

6. *Other standards.* In centers serving infants, licensing usually requires detailed plans for diapering, including the surface on which the baby is placed, a plan for disposing of soiled and wet diapers, and hand washing by staff after each diaper change. Additional requirements for storing food, feeding babies, and washing toys also are included.

As you review this section on licensing regulations, it should become clear that depending on the size, location, and scope of the program for which you are responsible, you could find yourself working with local, state, and federal regulatory agencies. At times, the regulations from the various bodies are not totally compatible, and they even may be contradictory in some cases. It is your task to deal with all these regulatory agents so that your program is in compliance. If your program is not in compliance, you run the risk of having a fine imposed or of being unable to take full advantage of available funds and community resources. There also is the risk of having to delay the opening of a new program or having to close down an ongoing program because of failure to meet minimum licensing requirements. In some cases, noncompliance may jeopardize the well-being of children and staff.

The Licensing Process

Directors who are seeking initial licensing should allow plenty of time for the on-site visits and for conferences with inspectors from all the departments involved because the process is lengthy. It is wise to allow *at least* 90 days to complete the initial licensing process. All departments must provide clearance before the license is issued. On rare occasions, programs are permitted to continue operation when they are out of compliance because licensing specialists are trying to help provide sufficient child care in the community; but the regulatory agencies constantly monitor the work being done to bring the program into compliance with the minimum requirements. The burden is on the operator, who must present data to show that the program qualifies for a license or is working toward that goal within a well-defined, limited time line.

Since total compliance with all regulations may be very expensive, it is important to have a clear understanding about the changes that are essential before a program can operate and those that can be made as money becomes available. For example, the fire inspector may not allow children in the building until all required fire extinguishers are purchased, mounted appropriately, and made accessible. The health department might allow a child care program to begin before a separate sink for hand washing is available in the food preparation area, provided that adequate hand washing facilities are available elsewhere in the building and that there is a double sink in the kitchen. Monies must be budgeted to move toward compliance in areas that require further work. Therefore, the director and any board members who are involved in budget preparation should be well informed about any aspects of the program and the physical environment that might need modification to be in compliance with licensing standards. The time allowed for total compliance with all the licensing regulations will vary greatly and may be negotiable.

The steps involved in the licensing process are as follows:

1. Request a copy of licensing requirements from the appropriate regulatory agency.

2. Ensure that the zoning authorities in the area have approved the land use; that is, does zoning allow child care at the site you have chosen? Because child care may be considered a business instead of an educational program or school, neighbors may be reluctant to allow a zone change. Some may be concerned about setting a precedent that would allow additional businesses to locate in that immediate area. Others may be unhappy about increased traffic and noise, as well as about the compatibility of the building with others in the area. Whether or not a zone change is needed, one of the first jobs of the director is to reach out to neighbors and establish the center as a cooperative part of the neighborhood.

3. Obtain information from the licensing agent about contacting the sanitation inspector, the fire inspector, the building inspector, and the public health office.

4. Arrange for conferences with, and on-site visits from, representatives of all necessary departments.

5. When all inspections have been completed and the inspectors have provided evidence of approval, complete the application for the license and send it, with the required fee, to the appropriate licensing agent. You may be required to submit a detailed plan for operating the center, including number of staff, daily schedule, equipment list, and center policies and procedures. You also may have to show copies of forms you will use for gathering required information such as health and emergency data.

6. On receipt of the license, post it in a conspicuous place in the child care center so that it is visible to families and visitors.

7. Check the expiration date and establish a procedure to ensure that the renewal process will be set in motion in time to eliminate the possibility of having to interrupt the provision of services to the children or having to pay a fine.

A relatively new concept in child care licensing is one-stop licensing. The idea is that a director can contact one person to set the licensing process in motion. Such a plan eliminates most if not all of the frustration directors may feel they have experienced in the past as they tried to coordinate various departments and agencies. The goal of the various inspectors, as well as of the director, is to ensure that the standards are met.

The director, or in special cases a designated member of the board, is responsible for obtaining a license for the child care center. Renewals, although less time consuming for both the director and the licensing agents, must be taken care of on a regular basis. The cost of a state or local license itself is minimal when considered in light of a total budget, but it is an item that must be included in the budget. Although some states do not charge a fee, others charge varying amounts based on the number of children served. Some states have additional fees for special services such as review of a particular building prior to a decision to obtain that building.

The Licensing Specialist

The primary function of the licensing specialist is to ascertain whether a program is in compliance with the licensing regulation and to issue, or recommend issuing, a license to those programs that meet the minimum requirements. When programs do not meet minimum requirements, the function of the licensing specialist is to provide support and suggest resources that will help bring the programs into compliance rather than to close them. The specialist's goal is to improve services for children and families. Licensing specialists are being viewed more and more as people who provide services instead of as people who simply issue licenses or close centers. In one Midwestern community, a licensing specialist noted that she actually issues licenses for the equivalent of only two months of the year, but that she is available to directors to provide resource information and support throughout the year.

Knowledge of the community combined with a thorough knowledge of the licensing regulations makes the licensing specialist a valuable resource for directors who are seeking training for staff; looking for educational program consultants; and exploring the best and least expensive ways to meet the fire, health, or building regulations. The licensing specialist also may be available as a consultant when a director is petitioning to have an unusual or unrealistic restriction varied or adjusted. In situations where licensing regulations are inappropriate for children's programs, licensing specialists are available to support community efforts to have the regulations changed. Often, specialists are not in a position to initiate an action to change a very restrictive regulation. However, they may provide support and information to a group of lay or professional people who organize to bring about changes that will allow quality service to children, and at the same time, free the programs from unrealistic restrictions. If you find yourself confronted with a local or state regulation that seems impractical or unworkable, enlist your licensing specialist's help in making contact with other directors who feel as you do about the regulation, and form a task force to investigate the process necessary to have the regulation changed.

In one locality where all staff people were required to hold first aid certificates, center operators and licensing specialists worked together to adjust the requirement and make it more realistic without jeopardizing the health or safety of the children. Having a first aid license is valuable for everyone, whether at the center or elsewhere. However, when a center experiences high rates of staff turnover, paying for training and providing paid time to complete the training can be a major burden. In some cases, centers require staff to meet this requirement during their own time and at their own expense. The key is ensuring that appropriate numbers of staff are prepared and properly certified to administer first aid at the center, while children are being transported, and on field trips.

An unreasonable or outdated requirement may be included in licensing and may need to be changed, but the regulation may remain until some very pragmatic, energetic director comes along who is willing to organize the forces necessary to create change. You may find yourself interested in doing just that with the help of other directors, related agencies, and your licensing specialist.

CORNER

DIRECTOR'S

"I spend a lot of time keeping track of paperwork. I know that I have to have all the staff and child medical records as soon as a new child or staff member comes to the center. That's one of the first things I do. I also make a calendar each year that reminds me when to apply to renew our license, to get our fire inspection, and our kitchen inspection."

—Director, private not-for-profit center

You also may find yourself in a situation in which the licensing requirements have little effective protection of children. In this case, even though your center exceeds minimum standards, it is your responsibility to advocate for appropriate standards. The NAEYC Code of Ethical Conduct (1998) states in Section IV our, Ethical responsibilities to community and society and points out our obligation "to support policies and laws that promote the well-being of children and families." Often, licensing specialists support the need for more appropriate requirements, yet their authority allows them to enforce only the written rules.

The licensing specialist also can help you work through a grievance process if you encounter a unique problem with licensing. For example, one specialist explained a situation in which the fire inspector was holding to the letter of the law by requiring that an expensive, special type of glass be installed in the windows of a center building that was not the required 30 feet from an adjacent building. The regulation requiring 30 feet is appropriate and necessary for adequate fire protection, but in this case, the center windows were 28 feet away from an all-brick, fire-resistant building separated from the center by a grassy area. There was no real hazard to the children in this particular center. The licensing specialist provided special help to the director to expedite the grievance process, and the requirement was waived for the center.

In another situation, a new, all-day program was to begin for a one-year period on an experimental basis. The kitchen facility was totally inappropriate for cooking lunches for children who were to stay all day. The director, with the help of the licensing specialist, was able to obtain a temporary permit to operate the experimental program for one year by having the children bring brown-bag lunches. Bag lunches are strictly forbidden in this particular locality under the center licensing regulations, so this particular experimental program could not have been implemented without the understanding support of the licensing specialists. It was agreed that the conditions in the center's food service area would have to meet minimum standards if the program were to be extended beyond the first experimental year and that the bag lunches would have to be appropriately stored each day during that period. The center provided information to parents about appropriate nutritional content of sack lunches.

Licensing specialists are well acquainted with many directors and teachers in the community, so they can serve as a communication bridge between centers by taking ideas and news from one center to another. For example, sharing the news about how a director in a neighboring community solved a budget or staffing problem (without breaking confidentiality) can be very helpful to the director who is dealing with what seems like unsolvable problems and who is isolated from contact with colleagues facing similar problems. The specialist can assist directors who are trying to effect budget adjustments or staffing changes but who are meeting resistance from board members or influential community groups. Occasionally, for economic reasons, some board members will pressure the director to overenroll a group to increase revenue. Overenrolling is a risk because there are days when all the enrollees appear and the classroom becomes overcrowded and understaffed on those days. It may be difficult to convince some board members that overcrowding or understaffing for a few days a month can be demoralizing for staff members and disruptive for children. In some states, overenrolling is illegal.

Although some prefer fewer government regulations, keep in mind that the quality of child care would almost certainly diminish rapidly if state regulations were reduced or eliminated. If child care center licensing were not in place, an individual could assume responsibility for large numbers of children. This is an unsafe condition and one that would jeopardize children's health, safety, and development.

ACCREDITATION

While licensing implies meeting minimum standards, accreditation implies performing at a higher level and meeting additional standards. Directors volunteer to have their center reviewed by an accrediting agency, and those programs that are accredited are deemed worthy of the trust and confidence of both the private and professional community.

Groups such as the American Montessori Society, the Association Montessori Internationale, the Child Welfare League of America, the National Association of Child Care Professionals (NACCP), and the YMCA have various programs to ensure that their centers provide good-quality child care. The NACCP also accredits centers. However, the most far-reaching effort is that of the National Academy, a division of NAEYC. One facet of this professional organization's attempt to improve the quality of life for young children and their families is the accreditation system, based on criteria developed over several years with input from a wide range of early childhood educators. Further information about this process appears in Chapter 14. Accreditation materials may be obtained by sending an e-mail or writing to NAEYC (see Appendix B for address).

DIRECTOR'S CORNER

"We were a little bit leery of going for NAEYC accreditation. It was a lot of work, but the staff and parents really got interested. And when we got the letter saying we were accredited, I felt like we'd accomplished something as a team."

—Director, agency center

Since licensing is intended to ensure that a center meets minimum standards, engaging in the accreditation process is productive for the director, staff, parents, and ultimately for the children. The self-study process may be revealing to the director since it requires reviewing all facets of the center's operation. The process also can provide opportunities for the director and staff to work together in achieving the quality they desire.

A number of states are encouraging early childhood programs to seek accreditation by

- providing differential pay rates for child care subsidies.
- providing funding, training, and technical assistance for centers undergoing accreditation.
- setting expectations that funded programs will be accredited (Warman, 1998).

CREDENTIALING

Individuals who work in a profession may be awarded a credential indicating they have demonstrated the capabilities necessary for successful participation in that profession. While licensing is required for an agency to operate a program, credentials are related to the educational preparation of individual staff members. Credentials may or may not be required by licensing, but they are an indication that the individual has had appropriate preparation for the early childhood profession. There are several types of credentials in the field of early childhood education.

State Teacher's Licensure

Licensing or certification of early childhood personnel has been under discussion in many states for a number of years, and more and more states are creating pre-kindergarten or early childhood teaching licenses. Some people refer to the credential as a certificate, meaning a license to practice the profession of teaching, just as doctors, lawyers, real estate agents, or beauticians may obtain a state license to practice their professions. Although the term certificate was more widely used earlier, licensing now is considered to be the base. A certificate may be earned from the National Board for Professional Teaching Standards, which indicates that the individual exceeds minimal requirements for teaching. This system is parallel to center licensing and center accreditation. The license usually is issued by the state department of education. In some cases, the state provides enabling legislation; that is, the license is available, but the state does not require that everyone who teaches preschool children be licensed. Although more than half the states offer early childhood licenses, there are many different configurations that include birth to five years, birth to eight years, three to five years, and so forth. Individual center policies may require that teachers be licensed, but often directors find that they are unable to find licensed teachers willing to work in child care centers at the salaries offered. Directors who require licensure as a qualification for their teachers must be aware that there are many kinds of teaching certificates. Preparation for elementary or secondary teaching licenses, for example, does not include attention to most of the knowledge, skills, and attitudes necessary for those working with younger children. Therefore, these licenses usually are not good criteria for early childhood teachers.

National Board Certification

Teachers who desire to demonstrate that they are accomplished in their field may apply to become National Board Certified Teachers through a voluntary program organized by the National Board for Professional Teaching Standards. This nonprofit organization is governed by a board primarily composed of classroom teachers.

Eligibility for the certificate requires the applicant to have

- at least three years' experience working with children ages three through eight.
- a baccalaureate degree.
- a valid teacher license or certificate in the applicant's state.

Applicants prepare a portfolio and a videotape and go to one of the many assessment centers around the country. There they respond in writing to prompts about their specialization, early childhood. Like any worthwhile effort, the process is time consuming and is, itself, a valuable learning experience for teachers. About 4,000 early childhood educators have obtained this credential. In addition to the recognition the certification carries, a number of states have begun programs to provide compensation to board-certified teachers. For more information, check http://www.nbpts.org, the Web site for the National Board for Professional Teaching Standards.

Director Credentialing

During the early 1990s, a movement toward director credentialing began. The credential evolved through the work of advocates in the profession who recognized the importance of specific training, education,

Directors who are working toward a credential may review their understanding of child development by observing in the classroom.

and recognition of center leaders. Work/Family Directions, with funding from the American Business Collaborative, was one of the initiators. Roger Neugebauer of *Child Care Information Exchange* took a leadership role in a Director Credential Caucus by scheduling meetings at various conferences. And the Center for Career Development at Wheelock College created the Taking the Lead Project and set up pilot projects in four states (Status Report on Director Credential Movement, 1998).

Director credentialing "certifies that an individual has mastered a specific set of defined skills and knowledge, and has demonstrated competencies to perform as a director in any early care and education or school-age setting" (Morgan, 2000). The body that awards the credential may or may not be the same organization that delivers the training. A credential may be awarded by a professional association, a state agency, a higher education consortium, or other organization and signifies a consensus by those groups of the validity of the standards set forth (Morgan, personal communication, November 18, 2004). Thanks in large measure to the support of 17 foundations, including $1.5 million from the American Business Collaborative, a number of states established director credentials or are in the planning stage. Since this movement is evolving quickly, check with your licensing specialist or other leaders in your state to determine the status of your state's progress toward the credential. Illinois in particular, under the leadership of Paula

Jorde Bloom at National Louis University, continues to provide specific director training programs accompanied by mentoring. The National Black Child Development Institute has created an African American Early Childhood Resource Center. A major goal is the development and mentoring of leaders (Neugebauer, 1999a).

Neugebauer (1999b) also reports that the Mississippi Forum on Children and Families has developed a director credentialing program that trains 250 directors a year. Directors complete 135 hours of class work after which their centers are eligible for a 10 percent increase in reimbursement rates.

State legislation in Florida and North Carolina requires that the director or person responsible for day-to-day operations of a center have a director credential. Optional credentials are available or are in the process of being developed in many other states by governmental bodies and professional or educational organizations.

This credential is important because it increases the knowledge and skill level of administrators, particularly in the business and management roles they must assume. As a result, the quality of centers is likely to improve and staff turnover under the leadership of a knowledgeable administrator may be reduced. The director makes the decisions that influence child outcomes while helping to create the culture of the center. Components such as staff-to-child ratios, provision of appropriate resources, and selection of well-qualified teachers lead to high quality. Being credentialed creates value for the role of director and encourages individuals to consider this position as a career. The credential can also promote public and private support as the directorship becomes recognized as a valid professional role (Rinker, 2001). Because much early childhood education being offered today is of poor quality, the need for well-prepared directors is being given more attention.

Child Development Associate Credential

Another type of credential is the Child Development Associate (CDA) credential offered by the Council for Early Childhood Professional Recognition. Established in 1985, the Council has awarded more than 100,000 credentials to caregivers in three categories.

1. center-based infant/toddler or preschool
2. home visitor
3. family child care

A bilingual credential is also available. This national credential is included as one of the possible qualifications for directors and/or teachers throughout the United States. Candidates for the credential demonstrate their skill in six competency areas, including 13 functional areas such as advancing physical and intellectual competence (physical, cognitive, communication, creative). A combination of experience and training prepares candidates for assessment based on procedures established by the Council. Now, more than 25 years since its inception, the credential is still tied closely to Head Start, the program that led to its creation. The CDA is widely recognized by the entire early childhood community as a valuable addition to professional development. In fact, Bredekamp (2000) relates the CDA to "an entry-level qualification that is equivalent to 9–12 credits of professional education." She reports on a survey of CDA recipients over the last 10 years. Of the 1,000 respondents, 877 are still in the field up to 10 years after having received the credential. This positive report has encouraged large numbers of teachers to enter the CDA program at a wide variety of sites. In some cases where college credit has been granted for CDA courses, students have gone on to associate and higher degrees using the CDA credits as a starting point (Lynch & Shupe, 2000).

To be eligible for assessment, candidates must

- be 18 years of age or older.
- hold a high school diploma or GED.
- have 480 hours of experience working with children.
- have 120 clock hours of formal education.

Candidates must be prepared to demonstrate their understanding of the following areas:

- safety
- health
- learning environment
- physical
- cognitive
- communication
- creative
- self
- social
- guidance
- families
- program management
- professionalism

Although there are fees associated with participating in this credentialing process, scholarships are available, and some agencies pay all or part of the fees. Contact the Council for application materials and a list of fees (see Appendix B).

SUMMARY

The director of a child care program is responsible for initiating licensing procedures and carrying through with on-site visits from building, fire, and health inspectors. If program adjustments or building changes are necessary to bring a center into compliance with local, state, or federal regulations, the director must take steps to bring about the changes or risk a delayed opening date or denial of a license renewal. The licensing specialist is a good source of information and advice through the initial licensing process, as well as the renewal process.

Accreditation through a reputable organization is an important approach for improving quality in child care centers and for involving staff in the process. Since licensing is designed to ensure that minimal standards are met, centers that have participated in the accreditation process demonstrate to families that they are interested in exceeding minimum requirements and that they are attempting to provide high-quality care for their children.

Although licensing of child care programs is mandated in most localities, few states require licensure of prekindergarten teachers, a college degree-based credential. Through special training programs and after specific assessment procedures, some caregivers are qualified to receive the Child Development Associate credential. Directors' credentials also are becoming more prevalent, an added indication of professionalism in the early childhood field.

CLASS ASSIGNMENTS

1. Use the Internet to locate the contact information for state child care licensing agencies and write for a copy of state licensing regulations (your professor may assign you a specific state). Request a copy of the state licensing requirements and ask for copies of the forms needed to apply for a license to operate a program for young children in the state. You also may obtain this information from your state's Web site. After you receive this information, answer the following questions:

   a. What is the allowable adult-to-child ratio in the state?

   b. What qualifications are staff required to meet?

   c. Were the materials you received understandable and easy to read? Was it easy to find the information you needed?

   Write your answers on Working Paper 4–1.

2. Write to the appropriate state department or check your state's Web site to establish the status of early childhood licensure in that state (your professor may assign you a specific state). Ask for the following information and record it on Working Paper 4–2:

   a. Does the state provide licensure for prekindergarten teachers?

   b. What are the requirements for obtaining this license?

   c. Does the state require that prekindergarten teachers have this license?

3. Interview a child care center operator and write his responses to the following questions on Working Paper 4–3:

   a. Have you asked your licensing specialist for help?

   b. Has the licensing specialist been helpful? In what ways?

   c. What kinds of experiences have you had with the fire inspectors? Health and/or sanitation inspectors? Building inspectors?

Note: Your instructor may have you present the name of the director you plan to interview in order to ensure that no director is interviewed multiple times. It is also important that you prepare for the interview in advance and that you thank the director.

CLASS EXERCISES

1. Invite the licensing specialist from the community to come to a class session to discuss all the services provided by the licensing agency. Request copies of the local licensing regulation for class members. Then complete the following activities:

   a. As a group, review the licensing regulations and determine which sections of the code would help you do a more effective job as a center director.

   b. Evaluate the regulations and determine which sections (if any) should be revised so that more effective service could be delivered to children.

2. Divide the class into small groups to consider the pros and cons of licensure for prekindergarten teachers.

   a. Can you think of any individuals or groups that provide services for young children who would be opposed to licensure? Discuss why.

   b. Does licensure guarantee quality service to young children? Discuss the reasons for your conclusion.

   c. What are the best ways to guarantee quality service to children? Report your conclusions to the class.

3. Use the data class members obtained in Class Assignment 1. Create a table showing similarities and differences. Analyze the data.

4. Using Director's Resource 4–1, read the "Background" and the section on "The Importance of an Effective System of Public Regulation."

   a. Read and discuss the fire work an "Effective Licensing System Falls Short." Consider how your state rates in these fire areas.

   b. Read and discuss "NAEYC's Position" and "NAEYC's Principles for Effective Regulation." Write a short paper supporting or disputing one of the 10 principles.

WORKING PAPER 4-1

(for use with Class Assignment 1)

STATE CHILD CARE CENTER LICENSING REQUIREMENT FORM

Name of state _____

1. Staff-to-child ratios:

    a. The staff-to-child ratio for infants is _____ .

    b. The staff-to-child ratio for toddlers is _____ .

    c. The staff-to-child ratio for three-year-olds is _____ .

    d. The staff-to-child ratio for four-year-olds is _____ .

    e. The staff-to-child ratio for five-year-olds is _____ .

    f. The staff-to-child ratio for school-age children is _____ .

2. Staff qualifications are:

3. Were materials understandable and easy to read, and was it easy to obtain the information? If not, give an example.

WORKING PAPER 4-2

(for use with Class Assignment 2)

EARLY CHILDHOOD LICENSURE

To whom did you write regarding state early childhood teacher licensure or which Web site did you use?

Name _____

Address _____

    a. Does the state provide licensure for prekindergarten teachers?

    b. What are the requirements for obtaining this license?

    c. Does the state require that prekindergarten teachers have this license?

WORKING PAPER 4-3

(for use with Class Assignment 3)

DIRECTOR INTERVIEW FORM

Name of director whom you interviewed: _____

    a. **Has the director asked the licensing agent for help?**

    b. **Has the licensing agent been helpful? In what ways?**

    c. **What kinds of experiences has the director had with:**

       ■ **fire inspectors?**

       ■ **health and/or sanitation inspectors?**

       ■ **building inspectors?**

DIRECTOR'S RESOURCE 4-1

(for use with Class Exercise 4)

LICENSING AND PUBLIC REGULATION OF EARLY CHILDHOOD PROGRAMS

A position statement of the *National Association for the Education of Young Children*
Adopted 1983; revised 1992 and 1997.

One of the most dramatic changes in American family life in recent years has been the increased partici-pation of young children in nonparental child care and early education settings. Between 1970 and 1993 the percentage of children regularly attending these types of arrangements soared from 30 to 70% (Department of Health and Human Services, n.d.). Much of the demand comes from the need for child care that has accompanied the rapid rise in maternal labor force participation. Increased demand for early childhood care and education services also comes from families who—regardless of parents' employment status—want their children to experience the social and educational enrichment provided by good early childhood programs.

Background

Families seeking nonparental arrangements choose among a variety of options: *centers* (for groups of children in a nonresidential setting*), small family child care homes* (for 6 or fewer children in the home of the care provider), *large family or group child care homes* (typically for 7 to 12 children in the home of a care provider who employs a full-time assistant), *in-home* care (by a nonrelative in the family home), and *kith and kin* care (provided by a relative, neighbor, or friend to children of one family only).

The responsibility to ensure that any and all of these settings protect and nurture the children in their care is shared among many groups. Families are ultimately responsible for making informed choices about the specific programs that are most appropriate for their own children. Early childhood profession-als and others engaged in providing or supporting early childhood services have an ethical obligation to uphold high standards of practice. Others within the community, including employers and community organizations, who benefit when children and families have access to high-quality early childhood pro-grams also share in the responsibility to improve the quality and availability of early childhood services. Government serves a number of important roles, including:

- ■ **licensing** and otherwise regulating so as to define and enforce minimum requirements for the legal operation of programs available to the public
- ■ **funding programs and supporting infrastructure,** including professional development and supply-building activities
- ■ **providing financial assistance** to help families with program costs
- ■ **supporting research and development** related to child development and learn-ing and early childhood programs, as well as data gathering for community planning
- ■ **disseminating information** to inform consumers, service providers, and the public about ways to promote children's healthy development and learning, both at home and in out-of-family settings

While many of these functions can and should occur at multiple levels of government, the licensing func-tion is established by laws passed by state legislatures, creating offices that traditionally play the primary

(continues)

DIRECTOR'S RESOURCE 4-1
(continued)

(for use with Class Exercise 4)

role in regulating the child care market by defining requirements for legal operation. States vary considerably in the methods and scope of regulation, using processes that may be called licensing, registration, or certification. These terms can have different meanings from state to state.

The importance of an effective system of public regulation

The primary benefit from public regulation of the child care and early education market is its help in ensuring children's rights to care settings that protect them from harm and promote their healthy development. The importance of these rights is underscored by a growing body of research evidence that emphasizes the importance of children's earliest experiences to their development and later learning (Center for the Future of Children 1995; Hart & Risley 1995; Bredekamp & Copple 1997; Kagan & Cohen 1997). Emerging research on brain development indicates that the degree of responsive caregiving that children receive as infants and toddlers positively affects the connections between neurons in the brain, the architecture of the brain itself (Newberger 1997; Shore 1997). Given the proportion of children who spend significant portions of their day in settings outside their family, ensuring that these environments promote healthy development becomes increasingly important.

Research documents that those states with more effective regulatory structures have a greater supply of higher quality programs (Phillips, Howes, & Whitebook 1992; Helburn 1995). Additionally, in such states, differences in quality are minimized between service sectors (e.g., nonprofit and proprietary programs) (Kagan & Newton 1989).

Children who attend higher quality programs consistently demonstrate better outcomes. These differences are apparent in many areas: *cognitive functioning and intellectual development* (Lazar et al. 1982; Clarke-Stewart & Gruber 1984; Goelman & Pence 1987; Burchinal, Lee, & Ramey 1989; Epstein 1993; Helburn 1995; Peisner-Feinberg & Burchinal 1997); *language development* (McCartney 1984; Whitebook, Howes, & Phillips 1989; Peisner-Feinberg & Burchinal 1997); and *social development* (McCartney et al. 1982; Clarke-Stewart 1987; Howes 1988; Whitebook, Howes, & Phillips 1989; Peisner-Feinberg & Burchinal 1997). The demonstrated outcomes appear in cross-sectional studies conducted at a specific point in time as well as in longitudinal studies over time (Carew 1980; Howes 1988; Vandell, Henderson, & Wilson 1988; Howes 1990; Schweinhart et al. 1993; Barnett 1995). The differences in outcomes occur even when other family variables are controlled for, including maternal education and family income level (Helburn 1995; NICHD 1997).

Research is also consistent in identifying the structural factors most related to high quality in early childhood programs:

- small groups of children with a sufficient number of adults to provide sensitive, responsive caregiving
- higher levels of general education and specialized preparation for caregivers or teachers as well as program administrators
- higher rates of compensation and lower rates of turnover for program personnel (Whitebook, Howes, & Phillips 1989; Hayes, Palmer, & Zaslow 1990; Galinsky et al. 1994; Helburn 1995; Kagan & Cohen 1997; Whitebook, Sakai, & Howes 1997). Many of these factors can be regulated directly or influenced by regulatory policy.

Despite widespread knowledge of what is needed to provide good quality in early childhood programs, many programs fail to do so. Two large-scale studies of licensed centers and family child care

(continues)

DIRECTOR'S RESOURCE 4-1
(continued)

(for use with Class Exercise 4)

homes found that only about 10 to 15% of the settings offered care that promoted children's healthy development and learning. For infants and toddlers, the situation is grave: As many as 35 to 40% of the settings were found to be inadequate and potentially harmful to children's healthy development (Galinsky et al. 1994; Helburn 1995).

Support for an effective licensing system falls short

An effective licensing system minimizes the potential for harmful care, but regulatory systems in many states receive inadequate support to fully protect children's healthy development and learning. The lack of support can be seen in five broad areas: (1) some states set their basic floor for protection too low, failing to reflect research findings about the factors that create risk of harm; (2) a large number of settings in some states are exempt from regulation; (3) the licensing office in some states is not empowered to adequately enforce the rules; (4) multiple regulatory systems may apply to individual programs, resulting sometimes in overlapping or even contradictory requirements; and (5) policymakers may view licensing as unnecessary because they believe it seeks the ideal or imposes an elitist definition of quality rather than establishing a baseline of protection. Each of these issues is discussed briefly below.

1. *Some states set their basic floor for protection too low, with licensing rules that fail to reflect research findings about the factors that promote or hinder children's healthy development.* Clear links exist between the quality of early childhood programs in child care centers and homes and the quality of the public regulatory systems governing these services. Not only is the overall quality level of services provided to children higher in states with more stringent licensing systems (Phillips, Howes, & Whitebook 1992; Helburn 1995), but also demonstrable improvements can be seen in program quality in states that have worked to improve aspects of their licensing processes (Howes, Smith, & Galinsky 1995). Despite such compelling evidence as to the importance of strong licensing systems, a 1997 study looking at grouping, staff qualifications, and program requirements found that "the majority of states' child care regulations do not meet basic standards of acceptable/appropriate practice that assure the safe and healthy development of very young children" (Young, Marsland, & Zigler, in press). Similar findings also have been reported on licensing standards for the care of four-year-olds (Snow, Teleki, & Reguero-de-Atiles 1996).

2. *A large number of settings in some states are exempt from regulation.* Many children are unprotected because they receive care outside their families in programs that are legally exempt from regulation. Exemptions affect both centers and family child care homes. Among centers the most common licensing exemptions are for part-day programs (roughly half of the states) and programs operated by religious institutions (nine states) (Children's Foundation 1997). Programs operated by or in public schools are sometimes exempt from licensing, although in some cases public school programs must meet comparable regulatory standards. Many states exempt family child care providers from regulation if they care for fewer children than stipulated as the threshold for regulation. About half of the states set such a threshold, ranging from 4 to 13 children (Child Care Law Center 1996).

(continues)

DIRECTOR'S RESOURCE 4-1
(continued)

(for use with Class Exercise 4)

3. *States do not always provide the licensing office with sufficient funding and power to effectively enforce licensing rules.* A 1992 report found that "many states face difficulties protecting children from care that does not meet minimum safety and health standards" (General Accounting Office 1992, 3). According to the report, staffing and budget cuts forced many states to reduce on-site monitoring, a key oversight activity for effective enforcement. These cutbacks occurred during a time of tremendous growth in the number of centers and family child care homes. The number of centers is estimated to have tripled between the mid 1970s and early 1990s, while the number of children enrolled quadrupled (Willer et al. 1991). An indicator of the growth in the number of regulated family child care providers is found in the recorded increase in the number of home-based participants in the USDA Child and Adult Care Food Program (regulation being a requirement of participation) from 82,000 in 1986 to nearly 200,000 in 1996 (Morawetz 1997).

   Lack of meaningful sanctions makes enforcement of existing regulations difficult (Gormley 1997). Licensing offices in all states have the power to revoke licenses, but some states have a much broader range of enforcement tools. Others lack funding to adequately train licensing personnel and fail to receive appropriate legal backup for effective enforcement.

   Although most states require that a facility license be prominently posted, many states do not require prominent posting or public printing of violation notices when facilities fail inspections. Information about licensing violations is only available in some states by checking the files in the state licensing office (Scurria 1994). The high demand for child care and early education services can exert pressures to keep even inadequate facilities open (Gormley 1995).

4. *Multiple regulatory layers exist, sometimes with overlapping or even contradictory requirements.* Different laws have created different inspection systems for different reasons, all affecting child care programs. Programs typically must comply with local zoning, building and fire safety, and health and sanitation codes in addition to licensing. A lack of coordination of requirements can frustrate new and existing providers and undermine the overall effectiveness of the regulatory system. For example, state and local regulatory structures sometimes impose contradictory requirements on family child care providers (Gormley 1995). If providers react by "going underground," children suffer.

5. *Policymakers may view licensing as unnecessary because they believe it seeks the ideal or imposes an elitist definition of quality rather than establishing a baseline of protection.* By definition, licensing rules represent the most basic level of protection for children. Licensing constitutes official permission to operate a center or family child care home; without this permission, the facility is operating illegally. Licensing rules combined with other regulatory requirements, such as environmental health codes, zoning provisions, and building and fire safety codes, define the *floor* for acceptable care that all child care programs must meet. In the current deregulatory climate, efforts to improve licensing rules and provide better basic protections for children's healthy development have sometimes been misrepresented as attempts to impose a "Cadillac" or ideal of quality child care that is too costly and unrealistic for all programs to achieve. When such misrepresentations

(continues)

DIRECTOR'S RESOURCE 4-1
(continued)

(for use with Class Exercise 4)

succeed, the floor or safety net that licensing provides to protect children in out-of-family care is weakened.

Drawing upon a conceptual framework first espoused by Norris Class (1969), Morgan (1996) distinguishes multiple levels of standards needed to achieve quality in early childhood programs. As the strongest of governmental interventions, licensing must rest on a basis of the prevention of harm. Other regulatory methods, including approval of publicly operated programs, fiscal control and rate setting, and credentialing and accreditation, provide additional mechanisms that, building upon the basic floor of licensing, can encourage programs to achieve higher standards.

Nonregulatory methods can also promote higher quality services: for example, public and consumer awareness and engagement, professional development of teachers/caregivers and administrators, networking and information sharing among professionals, and dissemination of information regarding best practices. These standards can interact and be dynamic. For example, licensing rules can reference credentialing standards, or fiscal regulation can reflect higher rates for accredited programs. Also, greater knowledge of the importance of various factors in preventing harm to children's healthy development and learning can result in changes in licensing rules so as to raise the level of basic protection over time.

NAEYC's position

The National Association for the Education of Young Children (NAEYC) affirms the responsibility of states to license and regulate the early care and education market by regulating centers, schools, and family and group child care homes. The fundamental purpose of public regulation is to protect children from harm, not only threats to their immediate physical health and safety but also threats of long-term developmental impairment.

NAEYC recommends that states continue to adopt and improve requirements that establish a basic floor of protection below which no center, school, or family child care or group home may legally operate. Basic protections should, at a minimum, protect children by striving to prevent the risk of the spread of disease, fire in buildings as well as other structural safety hazards, personal injury, child abuse or neglect, and developmental impairment.

Licensing rules should be coordinated statewide and streamlined to focus on those aspects that research and practice most clearly demonstrate as reducing these types of harm. Licensing rules and procedures should be developed in a context that recognizes other strategies and policies that encourage all programs to strive continuously for higher standards of quality. Such strategies and policies include application of levels of funding standards and rates for the public purchase or operation of services; maintenance of broadly accessible registries of programs or providers who meet nationally recognized standards of quality (such as NAEYC accreditation); provision of a broad array of training and technical assistance programs to meet the varied needs of different types of providers; and development and dissemination of model standards or best practices.

Public regulation of early childhood program facilities, including licensing, represents a basic level of protection afforded to all children in settings outside their family. Additional strategies and policies along with licensing are needed to support the provision of high-quality services for all families who want or need them. These strategies and policies, however, cannot substitute for licensing in providing basic protection.

(continues)

DIRECTOR'S RESOURCE 4-1
(continued)

(for use with Class Exercise 4)

NAEYC's principles for effective regulation

NAEYC offers the following 10 principles for implementing an effective regulatory system.

1. **Any program providing care and education to children from two or more unrelated families should be regulated; there should be no exemptions from this principle.**

   NAEYC believes that all types of care and education programs within the child care market should be regulated to provide basic protections to children. These protections must apply to all programs, without limiting definitions, exemptions, or exceptions. Whenever programs are exempted, not covered, or given special treatment, children are vulnerable and the entire regulatory system is weakened. NAEYC believes that programs should be regulated regardless of sponsorship, regardless of the length of program day, and regardless of the age of children served. NAEYC explicitly opposes exemption of part-day programs or programs sponsored by religious organizations because such exemption does not provide an equal level of health and safety protection for all children.

   NAEYC's definition of licensed care specifically excludes care by kith and kin when a family engages an individual to care solely for their children. A family support/education model that provides helpful information and support to individuals caring for children is likely to be more effective and meaningful in reaching kith-and-kin providers than a formal licensing model. Programs targeted to parents of young children to help them in their role as their child's first teacher should also be accessible to kith-and-kin caregivers. If kith-and-kin providers are paid with public funds, NAEYC supports the application of funding standards to these arrangements.

2. **States should license all facilities that provide services to the public, including all centers, large family or group child care homes, and small family child care homes (i.e., grant permission to operate).**

   NAEYC recommends that all centers or schools (serving 10 or more children in a non-residential setting) be licensed facilities. Facility licensure should include an on-site visit prior to licensure and periodic inspections to monitor continued compliance. Licensing rules should focus on the aspects deemed most critical to maintaining children's safety and their healthy development, both in terms of their immediate physical health and well-being and their long-term well-being in all areas of development. NAEYC supports the use of *Stepping Stones to Using "Caring for Our Children"* (National Resource Center for Health and Safety in Child Care 1997) to identify those requirements in the National Health and Safety Performance Standards (APHA & AAP 1992) most needed for prevention of injury, morbidity, and mortality in child care settings.

   Licenses are typically granted to privately administered programs rather than publicly operated programs, although some states do require publicly operated programs (such as those administered by the state department of education) to be licensed. If licensure is not required of publicly operated programs, the administering agency should ensure that the program's regulatory standards and enforcement procedures are at least equivalent to those applied to licensed facilities. Such language should be written into law to empower the administering agency to develop statewide policies for implementation.

(continues)

DIRECTOR'S RESOURCE 4-1
(continued)

(for use with Class Exercise 4)

States currently vary widely in their definitions and procedures for regulating family child care homes. NAEYC recommends the adoption of consistent definitions of *small family child care homes* as care of no more than 6 children by a single caregiver in her home, including the caregiver's children age 12 or younger; and of *large family child care homes* as care in the caregiver's residence employing a full-time assistant and serving 7 to 12 children, including the caregiver's children age 12 or younger. When infants and toddlers are present in a small family child care home, no more than three children should be younger than age three, unless only infants and toddlers are in the group and the total group size does not exceed four. Large family child care homes should meet the same ratios and group sizes recommended for use in centers.

For small family child care homes, NAEYC supports licensing methods that are designed to achieve full regulatory coverage of all home-based care providers in a state. These methods sometimes do not require an on-site inspection prior to operation. NAEYC believes that such methods—whether called registration, certification, or another form of licensing—are viable ways to license small family child care homes provided that (1) standards are developed and applied; (2) permission to operate may be removed from homes that refuse to comply with the rules; (3) parents are well informed about the standards and the process; and (4) an effective monitoring process, including on-site inspections, is in place. NAEYC believes that large family child care homes should be licensed in the same way as centers, with an inspection prior to licensure.

3. **In addition to licensing facilities, states should establish complementary processes for professional licensing of individuals as teachers, caregivers, or program administrators (i.e., grant permission to practice).**

The skills and qualifications of the individuals working in an early childhood program are critically essential to creating environments that promote children's healthy development and learning. Establishing licenses for the various roles included in early childhood centers and family child care homes not only protects children's healthy development by requiring the demonstration of key competencies but also enhances early childhood professionalism and career development. In addition, individual licensure holds promise for increasing the compensation of staff (Kagan & Cohen 1997). Licensing of individuals is also a more cost-effective way of regulating qualifications centrally rather than through a licensing visit.

A number of states are implementing career or personnel registries (Azer, Capraro, & Elliott 1997); individual licensure can build upon and complement these efforts. Personnel licensure should provide for multiple levels and roles, such as teacher/caregiver, master or lead teacher/caregiver, family child care provider, master family child care provider, and early childhood administrator. Attaining a license should require demonstration of the skills, knowledge, and competencies needed for the specific role. (For further information, see NAEYC's *Guidelines for Preparation of Early Childhood Professionals* [NAEYC 1996] and "A Conceptual Framework for Early Childhood Professional Development" [Willer 1994]).

Multiple licenses are needed because of the diversity of roles and functions fulfilled by program personnel; multiple levels help to establish a career ladder with meaningful

(continues)

DIRECTOR'S RESOURCE 4-1
(continued)

(for use with Class Exercise 4)

opportunities for career advancement, with higher levels of compensation linked to higher levels of qualification and demonstrated competence. In states in which early childhood teacher licensure or certification already exists for public school personnel, early childhood personnel licensing should be coordinated with these efforts. Individual licensure efforts may also be used to provide a form of consumer protection for families using in home care by enabling them to check the credentials of a potential employee.

4. **Licensing standards should be clear and reasonable and reflect current research findings related to regulative aspects that reduce the risk of harm.**

Licensing rules reflect public policy, not program specifications. Highly detailed descriptions of program implementation are inappropriate for inclusion in licensing rules. Such areas are better addressed through consumer education and professional development. For example, requiring programs to establish a planned program of activities to enhance children's development and learning would be an appropriate licensing rule; specifying the number of blocks to be available in a classroom would not.

NAEYC recommends that the licensing standards address health and safety aspects, group size, adult-child ratios, and preservice qualifications and inservice requirements for staff (referencing individual licensing standards). Periodic review and revision (every five years) are needed to ensure that rules reflect current issues as well as the latest knowledge and practice. Licensing rules should be widely publicized to parents and the public; these groups, along with service providers, should also participate in the review and revision of the rules.

5. **Regulations should be vigorously and equitably enforced.**

Enforcement is critical to effective regulation. Effective enforcement requires periodic on-site inspections on both an announced and unannounced basis, with meaningful sanctions for noncompliance. NAEYC recommends that all centers and large and small family child care homes receive at least one site visit per year. Additional inspections should be completed if there are reasons (such as newness of the facility, sanction history, recent staff turnover, history of violations, complaint history) to suspect regulatory violations. Unannounced visits have been shown to be especially effective when targeted to providers with a history of low compliance (Fiene 1996).

Clear, well-publicized processes should be established for reporting, investigating, and appealing complaints against programs. Parents and consumers especially should be informed of these processes. Staff should be encouraged to report program violations of licensing rules. If whistle blowing laws do not exist or do not cover early care and education workers, such legislation should be enacted. Substantiated violations should be well publicized at the program site as well as in other venues (such as resource and-referral agencies, newspapers, public libraries, online, etc.) easily accessible to parents and consumers. Lists of programs with exemplary compliance records also should be widely publicized along with lists of programs that meet the requirements of recognized systems of quality approval, such as NAEYC accreditation.

Sanctions should be included in the regulatory system to give binding force to its requirements. Enforcement provisions should provide an array of enforcement options

(continues)

DIRECTOR'S RESOURCE 4-1

(continued)

(for use with Class Exercise 4)

such as the ability to impose fines; to revoke, suspend, or limit licenses; to restrict enrollment or admissions; and to take emergency action to close programs in circumstances that are dangerous to children. When threats to children's health and safety are discovered, sanctions should be promptly imposed without a delayed administrative hearing process. The vulnerability of children mandates the highest level of official scrutiny of out-of-family care and education environments.

6. **Licensing agencies should have sufficient staff and resources to effectively implement the regulatory process.**

    Staffing to handle licensing must be adequate not only to provide for timely processing of applications but also to implement periodic monitoring inspections and to follow up complaints against programs. Licensing agencies must consider a number of factors in determining reasonable caseloads, for example, program size and travel time between programs. NAEYC believes that, on the average, regulators' caseloads should be no more than 75 centers and large family child care homes or the equivalent; NAEYC recommends 50 as a more desirable number. States that do not make on-site inspections prior to licensing small family child care homes may assume larger caseloads, but allow for timely processing of licenses, periodic on-site inspections, and prompt follow-ups to complaints.

    Regulatory personnel responsible for inspecting and monitoring programs should have preparation and demonstrated competence in early childhood education and child development, program administration, and regulatory enforcement, including the use of sanctions. These criteria should be included in civil service requirements for licensing staff.

7. **Regulatory processes should be coordinated and streamlined to promote greater effectiveness and efficiency.**

    Rules and inspections should be coordinated between the licensing agency and those agencies responsible for building and fire safety and health and sanitation codes so that any overlap is reduced to a minimum and contradictions resolved. In many cases, coordination will require reform at a statewide level, as different requirements derived from different laws are implemented by different agencies and respond to different constituencies (Center for Career Development 1995). Coordination with funding agencies is also crucial. Licensing personnel can provide program monitoring for the funding agency, thus eliminating duplicate visits; funding possibly can be withheld in cases of substantiated violations.

    Other methods for consideration in streamlining the regulatory process include (1) establishing permanent rather than annual licenses for centers, allowing for the revocation of the license for cause at any time and conducting inspection visits at least annually to determine continued compliance; (2) coordinating local teams that monitor and inspect for licensing and regulation of health, fire, and building safety codes; and (3) removing zoning barriers. NAEYC believes that centers and family child care homes should be regarded as a needed community service rather than as commercial development and should be permitted in any residential zone. Planning officials should take into account the need for these services as communities develop new housing and commercial uses.

(continues)

DIRECTOR'S RESOURCE 4-1
(continued)

(for use with Class Exercise 4)

8. **Incentive mechanisms should encourage the achievement of a higher quality of service beyond the basic floor.**

    In addition to mandated licensing rules that establish a floor for quality below which no program is allowed to operate, governments can use incentive mechanisms to encourage programs to achieve higher levels of quality. Examples of incentive mechanisms include funding standards, higher payment rates tied to demonstrated compliance with higher levels of quality, and active publicity on programs achieving higher quality. Given the nature of the early childhood field as severely underfunded, these mechanisms should be implemented in conjunction with funding targeted to help programs achieve and maintain higher levels of quality, or else the strategy simply enlarges the gulf between the *haves* and *have-nots*. Differential monitoring strategies, whereby programs maintaining strong track records and experiencing low turnover in personnel receive shortened inspections or are eligible for longer-term licenses, also may serve as incentives to programs for providing higher quality care.

9. **Consumer and public education should inform families, providers, and the public of the importance of the early years and of ways to create environments that promote children's learning and development.**

    Actively promoting messages about what constitutes good settings for young children not only encourages parents to be better consumers of services in the marketplace but also, because these messages will reach providers outside the scope of regulation (family members and in-home providers), may help improve the quality of other settings. Public service announcements, the development and dissemination of brochures and flyers that describe state/local standards, open workshops, and ongoing communication with organized parent groups and well-care programs are all excellent ways for the regulatory agency to raise the child-caring consciousness of a community. A highly visible regulatory system also helps to inform potential and existing providers of the existence of standards and the need to comply with the law.

10. **States should invest sufficient levels of resources to ensure that children's healthy development and learning are not harmed in early care and education settings.**

    NAEYC believes that public regulation is a basic and necessary component of government's responsibility for protecting all children in all programs from the risk of harm and for promoting the conditions that are essential for children's healthy development and learning and must be adequately funded. Additionally, government at every level can and should support early childhood programs by ensuring sufficient funding for high-quality services, opportunities for professional development and technical assistance to service providers, consumer education to families and the general public, and child care resource-and-referral services to families.

Early childhood regulation in context

An effective system of public regulation is the cornerstone of an effective system of early childhood care and education services because it alone reaches all programs in the market. But for the regulatory system to be most effective, other pieces of the early childhood care and education services system

(continues)

DIRECTOR'S RESOURCE 4-1
(continued)

(for use with Class Exercise 4)

also must be in place, including (1) a holistic approach to addressing the needs of children and families that stresses collaborative planning and service integration across traditional boundaries of child care, education, health, employment, and social services; (2) systems that recognize and promote quality; (3) an effective system of professional development that provides meaningful opportunities for career advancement to ensure a stable, well-qualified workforce; (4) equitable financing that ensures access for all children and families to high-quality services; and (5) active involvement of all stakeholders—providers, practitioners, parents, and community leaders from both public and private sectors—in all aspects of program planning and delivery. NAEYC is committed to ensuring that each of these elements is in place. As early childhood educators, we believe that nothing less than the future of our nation—the well-being of its children—is at stake.

References

APHA & AAP (American Public Health Association & American Academy of Pediatrics). 1992. *Caring for our children—National health and safety performance: Guidelines for out-of-home child care programs.* Washington, DC: APHA.

Azer, S.L., L. Capraro, & K. Elliott. 1997. *Working toward making a career of it: A profile of career development initiatives in 1996.* Boston: Center for Career Development in Early Care and Education, Wheelock College.

Barnett, W.S. 1995. Long-term effects of early childhood programs on cognitive and social outcomes. *Center for the Future of Children* 5 (3): 25–50.

Bredekamp, S., & C. Copple, eds. 1997. *Developmentally appropriate practice in early childhood programs.* Rev. ed. Washington, DC: NAEYC.

Burchinal, M., M.W. Lee, & C.T. Ramey. 1989. Type of day care and preschool intellectual development in disadvantaged children. *Child Development* 60: 128–37.

Carew, J. 1980. *Experience and development of intelligence in young children at home and in day care.* Monographs of the Society for Research in Child Development, vol. 45, nos. 6–7, ser. no. 187.

Center for Career Development in Early Care and Education at Wheelock College. 1995. *Regulation and the prevention of harm.* Boston: Author.

Center for the Future of Children. 1995. Long-term outcomes of early childhood programs. *The Future of Children* 5 (3).

Child Care Law Center. 1996. *Regulation-exempt family child care in the context of publicly subsidized child care: An exploratory study.* San Francisco: Author.

Children's Foundation. 1997. *1997 Child care licensing study.* Washington, DC: Author.

Clarke-Stewart, K.A. 1987. Predicting child development from child care forms and features: The Chicago Study. In *Quality in child care: What does research tell us?* ed. D.A. Phillips. Washington, DC: NAEYC.

Clarke-Stewart, K.A., & C. Gruber. 1984. Daycare forms and features. In *Quality variations in daycare,* ed. R.C. Ainslie, 35–62. New York: Praeger.

Class, N.E. 1969. Safeguarding day care through regulatory programs: The need for a multiple approach. Paper presented at the NAEYC Annual Conference, Seattle, Washington.

Epstein, A. 1993. *Training for quality: Improving early childhood programs through systematic inservice training.* Ypsilanti, MI: High/Scope Press.

Fiene, R. 1996. Unannounced versus announced licensing inspections in monitoring child care programs. Paper developed for the Cross-systems licensing project, Pennsylvania State University at Harrisburg and Pennsylvania Department of Public Welfare.

(continues)

DIRECTOR'S RESOURCE 4-1
(continued)

(for use with Class Exercise 4)

Galinsky, E., C. Howes, S. Kontos, & M. Shinn. 1994. *The study of children in family child care and relative care. Highlights and findings.* New York: Families and Work Institute.

Goelman, H., & A. Pence. 1987. Effects of child care, family and individual characteristics on children's language development: The Victoria day care research project. In *Quality in child care: What does research tell us?* ed. D.A. Phillips, 89–104. Washington, DC: NAEYC.

Gormley, W.T., Jr. 1995. *Everybody's children: Child care as a public problem.* Washington, DC: Brookings Institution.

Gormley, W.T., Jr. 1997. Regulatory enforcement: Accommodation and conflict in four states. *Public Administration Review* 57 (4): 285–93.

Hart, B., & T. Risley. 1995. *Meaningful differences in the everyday experiences of young American children.* Baltimore: Paul H. Brookes.

Hayes, C.D., J.L. Palmer, & M.J. Zaslow, eds. 1990. *Who cares for America's children? Child care policy in the 1990s.* Washington, DC: National Academy Press.

Helburn, S., ed. 1995. *Cost, quality, and child outcomes in child care centers.* Technical report. Denver: University of Colorado at Denver.

Howes, C. 1988. Relations between early child care and schooling. *Developmental Psychology* 24: 53–57.

Howes, C. 1990. Can the age of entry into child care and the quality of child care predict adjustment in kindergarten? *Developmental Psychology* 26 (2): 292–303.

Howes, C., E. Smith, & E. Galinsky. 1995. *The Florida child care quality improvement study. Interim report.* New York: Families and Work Institute.

Kagan, S.L., & N. Cohen. 1997. *Not by chance: Creating an early care and education system.* New Haven, CT: Bush Center for Child Development and Social Policy, Yale University.

Kagan, S.L., & J.W. Newton. 1989. Public policy report. For-profit and nonprofit child care: Similarities and differences. *Young Children* 45 (1): 4–10.

Lazar, I., R. Darlington, H. Murray, J. Royce, & A. Snipper. 1982. *Lasting effects of early education: A report from the Consortium for Longitudinal Studies.* Monographs of the Society for Research in Child Development, vol. 47, ser. no. 201.

McCartney, K. 1984. The effect of quality of day care environment upon children's language development. *Developmental Psychology* 20: 224–60.

McCartney, K., S. Scarr, D. Phillips, S. Grajek, & C. Schwarz. 1982. Environmental differences among day care centers and their effects on children's development. In *Day care: Scientific and social policy issues,* eds. E.G. Zigler & E.W. Gordon. Boston: Auburn House.

Morawetz, E. 1997. Personal communication in July. Unpublished data, Child and Adult Care Food Program, U.S. Department of Agriculture, Food and Consumer Service, Child Nutrition Division, Alexandria, VA.

Morgan, G. 1996. Licensing and accreditation: How much quality is *quality?* In *NAEYC accreditation: A decade of learning and the years ahead,* eds. S. Bredekamp & B.A. Willer, 129–38. Washington, DC: NAEYC.

NAEYC. 1996. *Guidelines for preparation of early childhood professionals.* Washington, DC: Author.

National Resource Center for Health and Safety in Child Care. 1997. *Stepping stones to using "Caring for our children: National health and safety performance standards guidelines for out-of-home child care programs."* Denver: Author.

Newberger, J.J. 1997. New brain development research—A wonderful window of opportunity to build public support for early childhood education. *Young Children* 52 (4): 4–9.

(continues)

DIRECTOR'S RESOURCE 4-1
(continued)

(for use with Class Exercise 4)

NICHD Early Child Care Research Network. 1997. Mother-child interaction and cognitive outcomes associated with early child care: Results of the NICHD study. Paper presented at the 1997 Biennial Conference of the Society for Research in Child Development, Washington, DC.

Peisner-Feinberg, E.S., & M.R. Burchinal. 1997. Relations between preschool children's child-care experiences and concurrent development: The Cost, Quality, and Outcomes Study. *Merrill-Palmer Quarterly* 43 (3): 451–77.

Phillips, D., C. Howes, & M. Whitebook. 1992. The social policy context of child care: Effects on quality. *American Journal of Community Psychology* 20 (1): 25–51.

Schweinhart, L.J., H.V. Barnes, & D.P. Weikart with W.S. Barnett & A.S. Epstein. 1993. *Significant benefits: The High/Scope Perry Preschool Study through age 27.* High/Scope Educational Research Foundation Monograph, no. 10. Ypsilanti, MI: High/Scope Press.

Scurria, K.L. 1994. Alternative approaches to regulation of child care: Lessons from other fields. Working paper prepared for the Quality 2000: Advancing Early Care and Education Initiative.

Shore, R. 1997. *Rethinking the brain: New insights into early development.* New York: Families and Work Institute.

Snow, C.W., J.K. Teleki, & J.T. Reguero-de-Atiles. 1996. Child care center licensing standards in the United States: 1981 to 1995. *Young Children* 51 (6): 36–41.

U.S. Department of Health and Human Services. n.d. *Blueprint for action. Healthy Child Care America campaign.* Washington, DC: Author.

U.S. General Accounting Office. 1992. *Child care: States face difficulties enforcing standards and promoting quality.* GAO/HRD-93-13. Washington, DC: GPO.

Vandell, D.L., V.K. Henderson, & K.S. Wilson. 1988. A longitudinal study of children with day-care experiences of varying quality. *Child Development* 59: 1286–92.

Whitebook, M., C. Howes, & D.A. Phillips. 1989. *Who cares? Child care teachers and the quality of care in America. The National Child Care Staffing Study.* Oakland, CA: Child Care Employee Project.

Whitebook, M., L. Sakai, & C. Howes. 1997. *NAEYC accreditation as a strategy for improving child care quality, executive summary.* Washington, DC: National Center for the Early Childhood Work Force.

Willer, B. ed. 1994. A conceptual framework for early childhood professional development: NAEYC position statement. In *The early childhood career lattice: Perspectives on professional development,* eds. J. Johnson & J.B. McCracken, 4–23. Washington, DC: NAEYC.

Willer, B., S.L. Hofferth, E.E. Kisker, P. Divine-Hawkins, E. Farquhar, & F.B. Glantz. 1991. *The demand and supply of child care in 1990.* Washington, DC: NAEYC.

Young, K., K.W. Marsland, & E.G. Zigler. In press. *American Journal of Orthopsychiatry.*

Reprinted with permission from the National Association for the Education of Young Children.

REFERENCES

American Academy of Pediatrics, American Public Health Association, & Maternal and Child Health Bureau. (2002). *Caring for our children: National health and safety performance standards: Guidelines for out-of-home child care programs, second edition.* Denver, CO: National Resource Center for Health and Safety in Child Care.

Bredekamp, S. (2000). CDA at 25: Reflections on the past and projections for the future. *Young Children, 55*(5), 15–19.

Children's Defense Fund. (2001, April). New CDF report highlights state developments in 2000. *Child Advocacy Newsletter,* http://cdfchildcare@childrensdefense.org

The Children's Foundation. (2002). *The 2002 Family Child Care Licensing Study.* Washington, DC: Author.

LeMoine, S., Morgan, G., & Azer, S. (2003, Winter). A snapshot of trends in child care licensing regulations. *Child Care Bulletin, 28.* Retrieved September 28, 2004, from http://nccic.org.

LeMoine, S., Morgan, G., & Azer, S. (2002). *Child care licensing and regulation trends.* Vienna, VA: National Child Care Information Exchange. (Retrieved from http://nccic.org/April, 2004).

Lynch, E., & Shupe, M. (2000). Building bridges and tearing down walls: Constructing an early childhood career ladder through university-Head Start collaboration. *Journal of Early Childhood Teacher Education, 21*(1), 5–11.

Morgan, G. (2000). The director as key to quality. In M. Culkin (Ed.), *Managing quality in young children's programs: The leader's role* (pp.40–58). New York: Teachers College Press.

National Association for the Education of Young Children. (1998). *Accreditation Criteria and Procedures of the National Association for the Education of Young Children.* Washington, D.C.: Author.

National Association for the Education of Young Children. (1998). *Code of ethical conduct and statement of commitment: Guidelines for responsible behavior in early childhood education.* Washington, DC: Author.

Neugebauer, R. (1999a, January). Update of director development initiative. *Child Care Information Exchange, 125,* 81–85.

Neugebauer, R. (1999b, July). No poverty of ideas in Mississippi. *Child Care Information Exchange, 128,* 68–71.

Rinker, L. (2001, November). Raising the bar: Director credentialing initiatives flourish across the nation. *Child Care Information Exchange, 142,* 14–18.

Status report on director credential movement. (1998, May/June). *Child Care Information Exchange 121,* 93.

Warman, B. (1998). Trends in state accreditation policies. *Young Children,* 53(5), 52–55.

WEB SOURCES CITED

http://www.childrensfoundation.net
http://www.naeyc.org
http://nccic.org
http://nrc.uchsc.edu

Additional resources for this chapter can be found on the Online Companion™ at http://www.earlychilded.delmar.com. This supplemental material includes relevant Web links, Web activities, and case studies that apply the concepts presented in this chapter. In addition, the Working Papers and Director's Resources are available for download, allowing you to complete Class Exercises and Class Assignments electronically.

CHAPTER 5

Organizing Center Structure and Working with a Board

The board carries out some functions related to personnel, finance, facilities, and program and keeps in touch with the director who is also working on fiscal and program matters.

OBJECTIVES

After reading this chapter, you should be able to:

- Describe ways in which centers can be organized.
- Explain the function and purpose of boards.
- Identify roles of committee members of a governing board.
- Describe articles of incorporation.
- List the components of bylaws.

Many child care centers have a governing body that is ultimately responsible for the total program. This group is usually constituted as a policy-making body called a board of directors or a board of trustees. The center director, who is responsible to this policy-making body, implements the center program as mandated by the board. In practice, board involvement runs the gamut from heavy involvement with the center to leaving all the work to the director. In the former situation, the board carries out all the functions described in this chapter and then charges the director with full responsibility to act on decisions that the board has reached. In the latter case, the board does not question the rationale or philosophical basis for the recommendations presented by the director for board review and gives carte blanche approval. Ideally, a board should function somewhere between these two extremes by carrying out some functions related to personnel, finance, facility, and program and by keeping in close contact with the director who also is working on fiscal and program matters. Although some proprietary centers operate without the guidance of a governing group, the organizational structure of most agency-sponsored and public-funded programs includes a board of directors.

When the center is an arm of another agency such as a church-sponsored child care program, the agency board may serve as the governing board, sometimes with representation from the center. In other cases, an advisory committee for the center is formed. As the name implies, the role of the advisory committee is much less structured and the committee has less authority than a board. When child care is part of a public school system, the principal often assumes many of the director's responsibilities and a lead teacher assumes others. The actual board then would be the elected board of education.

ORGANIZATION OF THE CENTER

When a new center is being created, the driving force behind the idea, whether one person or a group, must make some key decisions. First, will the center be created as a sole proprietorship, partnership, or corporation? Second, will the center be operated for profit or not for profit? These decisions will affect whether or not there is to be a board and the roles that board will take.

Sole Proprietorship

Individuals who create centers and maintain ownership are sole proprietors. They can make all the decisions and they bear all the responsibility. They provide the financing, often through bank loans using their own property as collateral. Some individuals may obtain loans from friends or relatives. This type of operation usually is rather small but may later grow, perhaps then becoming a partnership or a corporation.

Being the decision maker has benefits but also can be lonely, particularly when a crisis hits. When the center's furnace must be replaced on the coldest day of the year, or the lead teacher leaves and a replacement can't be found, the proprietor may second-guess the organizational decision. When the waiting list is long and a child gives the owner a hug, the decision seems just right. The owner is at risk, however, in the case of a lawsuit, for example, when a child is injured on the playground. All the owner's assets are in jeopardy. Carrying liability insurance is essential, even for small proprietary programs.

Creating a sole proprietorship is relatively easy once the financial hurdles have been resolved. Papers must be filed with federal, state, and local governments. Usually a form indicating the name of the business is required. Even if Mary Smith decides to open Smith's Child Care Center, she must file the paperwork stating that she is doing business as Smith's Child Care Center.

Partnerships

Sharing responsibility and finances is another possibility. Two or more individuals can enter into a partnership and typically determine the percentage of involvement of each. Two people might be equal partners, 60–40, or any other combination. This decision usually impacts the amount of decision making and responsibility each assumes and the amount of financial involvement of each. Being a silent partner also is a possibility. That occurs when one contributes financially but is not involved in decision making. When profits are available, they usually are allocated according to the percentage of investment. In case of a lawsuit, each partner is liable on a percentage basis, although personal assets are at risk. The liability issue is based on the way in which the partnership is legally constituted.

Because setting up a partnership is somewhat more complicated than setting up a sole proprietorship, employing a lawyer is essential. The paperwork must be prepared with care. Furthermore, even the best of friends or relatives may disagree and decide to end the partnership. Or one or more of the partners may decide that this is no longer the business investment desired. In addition, it must be made clear, in writing, what happens to the partnership in the event of the death of a partner.

Franchise

A model may be developed by a person or a group who then decides to sell the right to use that model, its name, logos, and so forth to others. The franchisees then must continue to pay a percentage of their gross income from the centers to the franchisor. Parents can expect that each franchise will be the same as others of the same name with which they may be familiar. The franchisor ensures that the franchisee follows company policies and standards. You may be familiar with this model based on some of the fast-food restaurants that you patronize. If you like certain foods prepared a certain way, you expect to find the same product at other franchises of that restaurant.

Corporation

To form a corporation, articles of incorporation must be filed with the state (usually with the secretary of state); bylaws, also referred to as regulations or a constitution, must be adopted; and a governing body, usually called a board of trustees, must be formed to set policy and assume overall responsibility for the operation of the corporation.

A corporation is owned by one or more shareholders. The shareholders elect directors to manage the affairs of the corporation, and the directors, in turn, elect officers to handle the day-to-day business of the corporation. Both federal and state laws regulate registration of stock issued to shareholders. Stock refers to shares or parts of ownership of a corporation. A stockholder provides an amount of money to a company through a broker, thereby becoming part owner of the company. Large companies have thousands of shareholders whereas a corporate child care center's stock may be held by a very small number of friends of the center. Some child care centers, however, become major corporations by creating or acquiring a large number of centers under one corporate name. Examples of large corporate child care programs are Knowledge Learning Corporation and Bright Horizons. Knowledge Learning provides a good example of acquisition of existing corporations. In 2003, Knowledge Learning Corporation acquired Children's World Learning Centers, which had been the third-largest chain. About one year later, Knowledge Learning, a privately held company, paid approximately $550.3 million for Kindercare Learning Centers, Inc. and took on Kindercare's $490 million debt. Kindercare operated more than 1,200 early childhood and care centers, serving about 118,000 children in nearly 40 states (retrieved from http://kkr.com).

Furthermore, federal, state, and local branches of government are taking on a larger share of the child care role. In some cases, a governmental body will provide funding for child care and education programs. In other cases, a business will be chosen or created to run a government early childhood program. For example,

a school board might hire a corporation that manages a number of children's programs. That corporation would provide staff and equipment, usually at the school, and be paid to run child care for preschoolers and for older children before and after school. Increasingly, public schools are offering their own preschool programs, staffing them, and creating the curriculum. Many parents appreciate this, believing that it is easier to have preschoolers in the same building as older siblings and feeling that the young child will not have to transition to a new place for kindergarten. The program may be partially or totally funded by tax dollars. One drawback may be that some programs may operate on the typical school schedule, with no provisions for before- and after-school care, nor for holidays and vacations. In some cases, the program for young children and for after-school care may be primarily academic rather than focusing on the whole child. Infants and toddlers are rarely included in public school programs. An exception occurs when a school creates a program for the very young children of high school students.

One aspect of the increased direct involvement in preschool education by public schools is the effect on child care businesses. Because the need for infant and toddler care will still be strong, centers may find that the high cost of care for the youngest children may no longer be balanced by the lower cost of care for three- to five-year olds. As you read more about financing programs for young children in a later chapter, this idea will become more clear.

When a center is to be operated as a corporation, it is a board responsibility to initiate the incorporation process. Because laws vary from state to state, an attorney should be consulted. The law does not require that child care centers incorporate, but it is desirable.

Although initially setting up a corporation is more complex and more costly than setting up a sole proprietorship or partnership, there are advantages. Corporations may attract funding more easily and may be more stable because they may be less dependent on the involvement of one or a few individuals. However, a corporation can be very small and consist of only a few family members.

One advantage that accrues to corporations is the limitation on financial responsibility. The liability of the corporation is limited to the assets of the corporation; therefore, individuals holding positions in the corporation are generally protected from personal liability for acts or debts of the corporation. A corporation can be sued and lose all of its assets, in effect, putting it out of business. However, the personal assets of the director or owners are not included.

No matter how the center is organized, individual attention to each child is essential.

On the other hand, corporate assets of small child care centers often are obtained by using personal assets as collateral. In that case, individuals' assets are jeopardized.

Profit or Not-for-Profit Corporations

When a center management plan is to incorporate, the decision to be for profit or not for profit must be made. In the case of a not-for-profit corporation, the corporate structure is different. For example, there are no shareholders in a nonprofit corporation. Instead, there are members who elect trustees to manage the affairs of the corporation. The required number of trustees and officers varies from state to state. Once incorporated, the corporation must function in accordance with the state laws, the articles of incorporation, and the bylaws.

Not-for-profit corporation status does not automatically result in tax-exempt status. Based on Internal Revenue Code 501, it is necessary for the corporation to apply to the Internal Revenue Service (IRS) for tax-exempt status and to demonstrate that the organization's purpose is educational or falls under one of the other IRS exempt categories. A specified Department of the Treasury form must be completed accurately. This form requires a statement of the organization's sources of financial support, fund-raising program, purpose, activities (past, present, and future), relationship to other organizations, and policies (for example, nondiscrimination). This lengthy form also requires a statement of revenue and expenses and a list of governing board members. The process is time consuming and expensive, taking up to six months and costing $2,500 or more in legal fees (Neugebauer, 1999). However, centers that operate on a not-for-profit basis are subject to fewer taxes. For example, with the proper documentation, they usually are exempt from sales tax as well as some federal taxes. Exemption from state and local taxes, including sales tax, is often tied to exemption from federal income tax, but application for exemption must be made to each taxing body.

Because tax law is subject to change, the director and board must keep abreast of new requirements. New directors moving in to existing centers must check to see that the documents are in order and that proper procedures are being followed.

When donors make contributions to a not-for-profit center, they may deduct the amount on their federal income tax subject to applicable tax laws. In the event that a not-for-profit program ceases operation, its assets must be donated to another not-for-profit organization. Although nonprofits can obtain grants, writing these takes time, effort, and skill. Typically, grants do not cover the capital needed to start a program or cover operating costs.

Both for profit and not-for-profit centers benefit to an extent from the child and dependent care tax credit, which allows parents a credit for part of their child care expenses. In some cases, parents then are more able to afford child care tuition. Although nonprofits can receive funds from donors and foundations, less than 1 percent of all child care funding today comes from philanthropic sources (Behrman, quoted in Neugebauer, 1999). Although government funding often goes to not-for-profit programs, funding that follows the child can be provided to for-profit centers.

The profit versus not-for-profit issue is complex. Organizations are advised to consult with attorneys and tax advisers before making this type of decision.

The corporate center board will have an important role to play in the decision making.

THE CHILD CARE CENTER BOARD

Board membership, board duties, committee structure, and board operations vary, depending on the size and type of center and on the relationship of the center to a sponsoring or funding agency. In spite of the inevitable variation in the structure and function of center boards, you will be better equipped to assist in establishing a board or to work with an existing board if you have some basic information about governing boards and how they operate.

Board Membership

Most well-planned boards consist of from 10 to 20 members who are either elected or appointed to board positions. A board operates most efficiently when its size is small enough for members to know each other and feel comfortable about speaking out when issues are being discussed, yet large enough for members to cover all the committee assignments that are required to conduct business without overworking any board members. Tenure for board members is specified in the bylaws. Requirements for board membership are based on program philosophy and needs, state laws, and sponsoring agency mandate.

When for-profit corporations involve very large organizations, usually the parent organization manages all the centers by providing regional supervisors (a variety of titles may be used). In this case, since the corporation operates on a major business model and may be traded on a stock exchange, the board also operates commensurate with the rest of the organization. Board members are chosen from a national perspective and usually are paid. Shareholders vote for the board members. Their vote is weighted, based on the number of shares they own. Shareholders are invited to the company's annual meeting, although rarely do small shareholders attend due to lack of knowledge, lack of influence, and inconvenience of travel distance. The boards described in the next sections refer to boards affiliated with individual centers or small groups of centers.

Selection of Board Members

At the outset, boards may be made up entirely of appointed members, but after the bylaws are developed and incorporation is accomplished, ensuing boards usually are elected by a regulated process required by law and stated in the bylaws. When a director, a board, or a nominating committee chooses persons to be appointed or elected to a child care center board, the background and personality of the candidates and the current board composition must be considered.

The nominating committee may create a process that will allow them to fill board positions effectively and efficiently. They may begin by deciding the types of people who are needed on the board. Although it may be advisable to have a physician on the board, that person's role should be one of commitment to the whole program rather than to the health needs only (Bess & Ratekin, 1999). As the organization's circumstances change, the kinds of board members needed also may change. Although a variety of professionals can be valuable board assets, their expertise should not be exploited. Their perspectives will help guide the board, but when particular professional advice is needed, the board should allocate funds and employ a nonboard member. When an organization and a board are small and in a start-up phase, some professionals may be willing to join the board and provide guidance that would not be needed for an established program. They may be serving out of friendship for the director.

Professionals from the fields of health, education, finance, and law often are asked to serve on child care center boards. These professionals can provide support in decision making in their areas and often volunteer time and expertise to help solve problems. For example, the physician who is a board member may direct the board to accurate information about health practices in the center, or the accountant may help draw up the budget and prepare for an audit. A media specialist or a board member who can write effective proposals and who has contacts with various funding sources can be a real asset. A person with knowledge of special education may support the board in its efforts to meet requirements of the Americans with Disabilities Act and may help the center staff address issues related to inclusion of children with special needs. A computer specialist also may be a valuable asset as a director ponders what types of hardware or software would be best for the center. Some boards reserve a percentage of slots for parents, and a teacher also may be a member although usually a nonvoting one.

Once the nominating committee has decided on the types of members needed, it may solicit suggestions from existing board members. After creating a master list, the committee begins contacting potential candidates, explaining that it is considering board and committee nominees to determine interest. The committee may send interested persons an information sheet about the organization, including the purpose and philosophy, as well as job descriptions of board and committee members. Then, it may interview several potential candidates and recommend putting them on the board slate or on a committee until a board opening occurs. No new board member should be surprised when asked to serve on a committee or when asked to contribute and solicit funds for the organization. Board members should be prepared to be active and committed to the organization.

Large agencies usually provide liability coverage for board members, but smaller organizations may be unable to afford this coverage. Nonetheless, board members usually are legally liable for center operation. Prospective board members should be informed that they will need to provide their own liability coverage if that is the case. Director liability is controlled by state law. Additional information on this important topic can be obtained from your insurance agent or attorney.

Orienting Board Members

New board members should be expected to participate in an orientation program led by the chair of the nominating committee. Board officers may be asked to participate, both to welcome the new members and to explain their components of the organization. Before this session, each should receive a board book, preferably a loose-leaf binder, containing the following:

- welcome
- board members' names and addresses
- mission statement
- bylaws
- strategic plan
- board committees
- minutes from the past year
- fiscal statements from past year

- current year budget
- center information, including philosophy, number of children and ages served, and calendar

At the orientation, new members should learn about the role of the nonprofit agency board and should be alerted to the differences between the roles of board and staff. As a result, new members should be ready for their first meeting with a basic understanding of current and recent issues and decisions. They should enter the meeting knowing a few of the members and should be greeted individually by others. This approach helps new members recognize that they are valued and that the board functions in a businesslike manner with positive interpersonal interactions (Bess & Ratekin, 2000).

Terms for Board Membership

Continuity in board membership is important. Therefore, many boards elect members for a three-year term, allowing for one-third of the members to be new each year. To achieve this ratio, the initial board members draw lots to determine who will hold three-, two-, and one-year terms. This time frame may not be workable for parent members who may not feel comfortable about joining the board until their child has been at the center for a while or who may no longer be interested once their child has left the center.

Although continuity is valuable, stagnation may occur when board members serve for too long. Consequently, bylaws should contain a provision for a limited number of terms of board service. Provision also should be made for replacing members whose attendance is poor. When a board member resigns, an exit interview may provide insight regarding possible changes in board operation. Members who feel overworked or undervalued may choose not to complete a full term.

Board Duties

Initially, the board is responsible for drawing up the bylaws for the center's operation. Subsequently, the board makes policy decisions and provisions for the operation of the center.

Drawing Up Bylaws

Bylaws for operation of the center are written by the board and should contain the following points:

1. name and purpose of the organization
2. composition of the board of directors, including information about when and by whom its members are elected or appointed

3. officers to be elected, their duties and terms of office, and description of the procedure for elections

4. method of replacing a board member or officer when necessary

5. frequency of meetings or minimum number of meetings to be held annually

6. standing committees and their composition and duties

7. relationship of staff to board

8. rules governing the conduct of meetings

9. provisions for an annual meeting

10. procedures for amending the bylaws

11. procedures for dissolution of the corporation

Other items may be added to meet the needs of a particular board.

Bylaws should be extensive enough to meet legal requirements and to guide the board. However, when bylaws are too detailed, the board's operation is hampered. Furthermore, changes to bylaws appropriately involve rather detailed procedures that become burdensome if changes must be made frequently. Therefore, bylaws may not list the specific month of the annual meeting or the exact number of board members.

Along with the establishment of bylaws, the board works on developing or revising (if needed) the organization's mission statement. The board may also create a vision statement, describing the future to be expected if the mission is carried out according to strategic planning.

Making Policy

After the mission and philosophy (see Chapter 2) have has been established, the board sets goals for the program based on the philosophy and purpose. If goals have already been established prior to the formation of the board, the board formally adopts them. The board then informs the director and staff about the philosophy and goals that form the basis for establishing the objectives for the daily program. In some cases, a knowledgeable director can take a leadership role in guiding the board's decision making about philosophy and goals that reflect sound theories. In any case, the board establishes policies and the director uses these policies as the basis for formulation of procedures. A *policy* is a course of action that guides future decisions. A *procedure* is a series of steps to be followed, usually in a specific order, to implement policies.

Written policies for the center's major components such as personnel policies, policies relating to the children's program, and policies about parent involvement are essential. Ensuing decisions then will be consistent because they will be based on established policy.

Important policy decisions include who will be authorized to write checks, receive funds, and make deposits. Will these persons be bonded? Will regular audits be required? Who will oversee audits? Policies regarding board membership and responsibilities should be in place in addition to the statements included in the bylaws. And a policy regarding when the bylaws will be reviewed for possible revision should be included. Since the policies should not be changed without serious consideration, the board should make them general and flexible enough so that the director is able to implement them without disregarding the goals of the center and without being required to request policy changes every time a new circumstance arises. Procedures are more detailed than the policies. Their purpose is to provide an implementation plan that is clear and uniform. Fire drill procedures or procedures for checking out material from the storeroom are good examples. Procedures also may be written for using the building after the children leave, for using equipment in the multipurpose room, or for filling a staff vacancy.

Policy decisions regarding personnel and program are ultimately subject to board approval; but in practice, they are often made by the director with official board approval becoming a mere formality. Occasionally, an involved, knowledgeable board will scrutinize carefully policies presented by a director, often asking for the rationale to support each policy. In some instances, staff and program policies are actually written by board members.

The type of program offered and the population served are both program policies subject to board approval. Decisions about the number and age span of children, the method of selection, and the population served are all board decisions. Examples include decisions about setting up the program schedule to include after-school care or care for children on a part-time basis. Although these policy decisions are usually based on the director's recommendations, the board makes the final determination.

Operating the Center

The board is responsible for making provisions for the operation of the center. The major decisions in this category are as follows:

1. selecting a director

2. providing for appropriate staff members and for their suitable, in-service training opportunities

3. providing facilities and equipment

4. preparing or approving the budget and overseeing the finances of the center

5. writing proposals and obtaining funding, including setting rates of tuition

6. complying with local, state, and federal laws

7. evaluating the operation of the program and the work of the director and assisting the director in the evaluation of other staff

8. arranging for an annual audit of financial records

9. arbitrating problems between the staff and the director that cannot be resolved by the director

10. replacing the director, as needed, and dismissing the director as the situation warrants

After provisions are made for operating the program, it becomes the director's responsibility to implement the program. At this point, the director becomes accountable to the board for the total program operation.

Board Committees

Board work is usually done by committees. Each standing committee has a charge that is spelled out in the bylaws. When all the standing committees are in place and working, the basic board functions are carried out. As special needs arise, ad hoc board committees are appointed by the board chairperson to perform specific, short-term tasks and report to the board. When the task has been completed, the committee is dissolved.

The board chairperson appoints members to each standing committee based on their interest and expertise and makes an attempt to balance the membership on committees by gender, race, age, point of view, and type of skill. Some boards have special requirements for committee membership. For example, the bylaws may state that each committee must have a parent member or a community representative.

Board committees convene at intervals that correspond to meeting the demands of their workload. When a center is being formed, most committees are extremely active; however, in an ongoing program, some committees have activity peaks. For example, the building committee deals with building maintenance, which is fairly routine. But if a decision is made to remodel, relocate, or build a new facility, the building committee would become very active.

Decisions about the number and types of standing committees needed to carry out the board functions are made when the bylaws are written. Some of the typical standing committees are executive, personnel, finance, building, program, and nominating.

DIRECTOR'S CORNER

"My business partner and I decided to add a second site and to incorporate since our business was growing. At first, the board was just a few relatives. But gradually we realized that we needed people who could really help with the management and oversight of the corporation, particularly when we needed additional investors. Now we have a working board that helps keep us focused on the fact that an early childhood program that is good for children and families must be run as a business."

−Director and president, incorporated for-profit center

Executive Committee

The executive committee is composed of the board's officers with the center director often serving as an ex-officio member. The executive committee advises the chairperson on actions to be taken, on changes to be made, and on committee assignments. This committee conducts board business between meetings and acts in place of the total board in emergency situations. However, it is critical that the executive committee plan far enough in advance to avoid as many "emergency" situations as possible, lest the way be opened for making important decisions without total board participation. Board members will become disgruntled and fail to contribute time or energy to board business if they find that crucial decisions are being made outside official board meetings. Whenever possible, board decisions should be made by the total board. In some situations it may be illegal for the executive committee to make decisions.

Personnel Committee

The personnel committee is responsible for hiring a director who will adhere to the philosophy of the center and implement the policies established by the board. To accomplish this task, the committee advertises the position, conducts the interviews, and prepares the director's contract. The personnel committee also is responsible for firing the director if that becomes necessary.

Personnel committee members usually assist the director in writing job descriptions, interviewing job candidates, and discussing the merits of each applicant. After these steps are completed, the hiring recommendations are made to the total board for final approval. Other boards set the basic criteria for staff members and set hiring and terminating employees as the director's responsibility.

In small centers where there is no evaluation committee, personnel committee members may be asked to conduct the evaluation process. In this capacity, the committee determines the method of evaluation, carries out the evaluation of the director, and monitors the director's evaluation of the center staff and program.

Finance Committee

Because they prepare the budget and appropriate the funds, finance committee members must have an understanding of the program's overall operation and of the way in which the operation relates to the program philosophy. In situations where the director prepares the budget and secures the funds, the finance committee approves the budget, monitors the record keeping, and arranges for the annual audit. In some centers, the finance committee sets salary schedules and reviews bids for major purchases. This committee also should teach board members how to read financial statements and what they mean.

Building Committee

The responsibility for finding and maintaining a facility suitable for the type of program being offered rests with the building (or facility) committee. Prior to starting a center or establishing a new facility, the committee spends an extraordinary amount of time making decisions about purchasing, constructing, or leasing a building. The committee is responsible for locating the new facility or the construction site. Building committee members work closely with the architect when the construction or remodeling is in progress and must remember to involve the director who presumably has the most knowledge of what the center needs.

It is the building committee's responsibility to see that the building and grounds are clean, safe, and attractive. Preventive maintenance and emergency repairs also are authorized by this committee. Although directors usually manage the details of applying for a license and arranging for necessary changes at the center to keep the program and facility in compliance with licensing standards, the building committee may be the one designated by the board to monitor licensing.

Many boards also assign the building committee responsibility for the center's equipment. The director must obtain the approval of the committee on major equipment orders, and the committee sanctions orders after considering whether the suggested purchases are suitable, in both type and quantity, and are within the budget. The committee members also ascertain whether the equipment is properly stored, maintained, and inventoried.

The building committee makes long-range plans by considering questions such as the center's future building needs. It projects the type and amount of space that will be needed and plans for ways to meet those needs. Equipment needs are considered in a similar way. Long-range planning prevents the board from suddenly finding that a major addition or repair is needed when no funds are available. Long-range planning also enables the center to stagger the purchase of equipment so that the quality and quantity are constantly maintained at a high level and so that the budget is not suddenly unbalanced by the need to replace large quantities of worn-out equipment.

Program Committee

The responsibility for all center programs ultimately rests with the program committee; however, in practice, any work on the program is handled completely by the director and the staff. The children's program, the parent program, and the in-service program for staff all may be under the auspices of the program committee. The committee recommends policies to the board focusing on the enrollment and grouping of children; the hours and days of operation; and the offering of ancillary services such as health, nutrition, and social services. Some boards set up separate committees for medical services and social services if these are major components of the center's program. These separate committees are responsible for working with the director to determine what services are needed, where, and at what cost they can be obtained. The committees also may help with transportation arrangements to the medical center if required, and with recruitment of volunteers to assist children and families needing special social or educational services.

Nominating Committee

The nominating committee's function is twofold. Potential members of the board are screened by the committee, which also prepares the slate of board officers for election by the board. The process should be open, and the committee should check with prospective members for permission to nominate them.

A separate committee may be set up for the orientation of new board members, or the nominating committee may serve in this capacity. Continuing the process begun at nomination, the committee ensures that new board members understand their duties and the operating procedures of the board.

Board Communication

From the committee descriptions, it should be obvious that the functions of the committees are interrelated and that communication among committees is essential. For example, the building committee must know what kind of plans the program committee is making in order to provide an appropriate facility. However, the building committee cannot choose a facility without an understanding of how much the finance committee plans to allocate for physical space. To avoid duplication of efforts, each committee's task must be delineated clearly. Sometimes, a board member may be assigned to two closely related committees to facilitate communication between them. Care must be taken to divide the work of the board equitably among its members and to see that every board member is involved in and aware of the operations of the board and of the center.

DIRECTOR'S CORNER

"Our staff seemed rather mystified about the board—who they were and what they did. Many board members needed to know more about the center. One of our teachers volunteered to take pictures of the staff and board members and to make a montage of the photos. Afterward, we had an old-fashioned ice cream social, with board members serving the ice cream."

–Director, child care center

The board shares responsibility with the director for maintaining open communication within the board itself and maintaining open communication among the board, the sponsoring agency, the staff, and the families who use the center's services. The most successful boards are those whose members communicate effectively with the center's director and with each other. Both the board and the director have responsibilities here, and it may be worthwhile to provide training in interpersonal communication for all concerned. If staff and board members both attend the training sessions, communication skills

are improved, staff and board members become better acquainted with each other's values, and the outcome is a greater sense of community among those people who are responsible for the center's operation. An obvious place to start is to make sure that new board members are introduced and that continuing board members also introduce themselves. Perhaps taking new board members on a tour of the facility and introducing them to the staff also could be planned. When board members and staff members have developed effective communication skills, all will be expected to use the skills. Ideas will be expressed and considered openly; likewise, disagreements will be stated specifically and objectively. Board and staff members lacking these skills may be less willing to address problems directly, with the result that disagreements may not be resolved and factions may develop within the organization.

As with all good communication, that between the board and the staff is two-way. The board informs the director of policies that have been formulated because the director is responsible for seeing that the policies are executed. The board also explains the reasons for its decisions and approaches any necessary changes in a positive way instead of in a dictatorial manner. The director, in turn, communicates to the board any difficulties the staff is having with the existing policies or suggests policy changes, providing reasons for these changes. For example, if the director finds that there are a number of parents asking for a program for their two-year-olds, the suggestion is presented to the board and is supported with arguments for or against the admission of two-year-olds. Facts concerning the type of services that could be provided, the facilities available, the cost of such a program, and the advisability from an educational standpoint also should be presented to the board. Considering the data and the recommendation of the director, the board makes the final decision about the admission of two-year-olds.

It is the responsibility of the board to use the director's recommendations and all other pertinent data in formulating policy. Policy decisions must be based on sound data so that they are fiscally responsible, educationally sound, and legal. They must also be realistic. For example, a policy requiring the director to be on duty whenever the center is open may be educationally sound but will be unrealistic in practice in a child care center that operates for 10 hours a day. Similarly, a board policy requiring the director to hire only well-qualified, trained teachers would make the hiring task nearly impossible if available salaries are held at or near the minimum wage level. Since the director is mandated to carry

Board members may be invited when a special activity is planned at the center, and they are always welcome to visit.

out board policy, the board ideally gives careful consideration to her recommendations to ensure that final policy is mutually agreeable and feasible.

DIRECTOR'S CORNER

"I know that our board members are really interested in our program, but they aren't early childhood educators. So I have to make sure they understand the needs of the center and of our staff. I put a lot of effort into making sure key persons are well informed. Maybe I'll have lunch with the board chairperson or talk about an idea I have over coffee. You definitely don't want to surprise your chairperson with a new idea during a meeting."

—Director, agency-sponsored child care center

The board serves as the communications liaison between the center program and the sponsoring agency. The director keeps the board informed about the center's functioning by sending the board members copies of newsletters, special bulletins, and meeting notices; by reporting at board meetings; and by presenting a written report to the board at least annually. Board members may be invited when a special activity is planned at the center, and they are always welcome to visit. The board, in turn, communicates to the sponsoring agency by reporting regularly to the agency board. This type of communication is two-way in that the board also receives information from the sponsoring agency concerning the expectations of the sponsoring group. For example, a community group may provide partial funding for the center with the stipulation that it be used to provide training for a staff member or parent program, or a church sponsor may expect preferential admissions for members' families. As long as these stipulations and expectations are compatible with the center's philosophy and are legal, they should be fulfilled.

Board Operation

When a new center is starting up, the board must meet frequently—even daily—during very busy planning periods. However, in ensuing years, boards may meet monthly, quarterly, or in some cases annually. When the board is working closely with the director and is intimately involved in policy making, monthly meetings are essential. On the other hand, the board that assigns most of the decision making to the director may meet only annually to receive the director's report; approve the budget for the ensuing year; and make any adjustments in goals, policies, or procedures that seem necessary. Notice how unrewarding service on such a board might be.

The board that meets frequently contributes to the operation of the center by working closely with the director and by utilizing fully the skills of all board members. The board that meets less frequently provides the director with maximum freedom to operate on day-to-day matters, although within definite guidelines. Each board must decide which alternative seems to be more appropriate for the type of center being planned, and the director is chosen to fit into the selected method of operation.

Although each board has its own style, board meetings must be conducted according to recognized parliamentary procedures that may be covered in the bylaws. In large, formal organizations, a parliamentarian who is appointed or elected ensures that business meetings are conducted according to the procedures adopted. Although too much formality may be uncomfortable for some board members, total informality leads to loose practices, with disputes arising over decisions that are based on improper voting procedures or other points of order.

REFLECTION

Consider how you might work most effectively as a director. Would you prefer a board that left the decision making to you and expected an annual report about what you had done? Or would you prefer to be in a situation where you had to check back with people in authority on a regular basis to get the benefit of their thinking, after which you would follow their lead as you continued your work? You may be able to relate this idea to college classes in which you operated independently and received feedback from your instructor only on the final exam, compared to classes in which you regularly submitted written work throughout the course and regularly received information from your instructor about your work. It would be wise to give careful consideration to your own needs and administrative style before accepting a directorship.

The board of an incorporated center is obligated by law to conduct its business in an organized manner and to keep accurate records of all transactions. In situations where record keeping is not required by law, it is just sensible business practice to operate an agency in an orderly manner. Therefore,

minutes of all board meetings, committee reports, and financial records should be kept. Copies of contracts and agreements, job descriptions, and correspondence also should be in the files.

SUMMARY

Key decisions to be made when new centers are planned include structure (sole proprietorship, partnership, or corporation) and the profit or not-for-profit consideration. A board of directors must be formed as the governing body of an early childhood education center that is incorporated. When members are chosen carefully in terms of the contribution they are capable of and willing to make, the director can receive excellent guidance from them. A well-organized board operates with a group of committees whose functions relate to the major components of the center's operation. Records of ongoing operations keep information about the functioning of the board open to everyone involved, and good communication between the board and the director produces a well-run organization. The board creates policies and the director implements those policies, but it is the ultimate responsibility of the board to see that its plans are brought to fruition.

CLASS ASSIGNMENTS

1. Find out how many people are on the board of directors of your college or local public school district.

    a. How did they become board members?

    b. What are their duties?

    c. How often do they meet?

    If possible, talk with a board member or attend a board meeting. Write your findings on Working Paper 5–1.

2. Arrange to talk to the director of an early childhood education center and ask whether there is a board of trustees.

    a. How are members chosen?

    b. How long is a member's term?

    c. What are the duties of board members?

    d. How often does the board meet?

    e. Are minutes of each meeting kept?

    f. What is the relationship of the director and the board?

    g. Is the director a voting member of the board?

    Report your findings on Working Paper 5–2.

3. Obtain a copy of the bylaws of an organization with which you are associated or of any type of community agency. (Consider your sorority or fraternity, your church group, PTA, and so forth.) Compare the bylaws of the group you select with the bylaws provided by another student.

   a. How are they similar in structure?

   b. What are the substantive differences?

   c. How do the differences in the documents reflect the differences in the purposes of the organizations?

   Write your answers on Working Paper 5–3.

4. Locate the forms you would need to incorporate a center. You may choose to write to the secretary of state in your state, check the Internet, or use library resources. Your instructor may assign each class member a different state. You may create your own information as you complete the forms, or you may base your responses on a center with which you are familiar.

CLASS EXERCISES

1. Involve the whole class in role-playing a meeting of the board of directors of a center that provides full-day child care for three- to five-year-olds. If your class is large, two simultaneous meetings may be held. Appoint a president, a secretary, a treasurer, and a director of the early childhood education center. Assign other class members to be early childhood education specialists, doctors, lawyers, accountants, parents, and community members at large. Include members of any other group that you feel should be represented.

   The agenda for the meeting is to consider whether to apply for funding to renovate and equip the outdoor area that is blacktopped and surrounded by a rusty fence. There is no permanent equipment. Think about what board members would need to know in order to make an informed decision and from where that information should come.

WORKING PAPER 5-1

(for use with Class Assignment 1)

BOARD MEMBERS FORM

How many people are on the board of directors of your college or local public school district?

How did they become board members?

What are their duties?

How often do they meet?

WORKING PAPER 5-2

(for use with Class Assignment 2)

BOARD OF TRUSTEES FORM

Is there a board of trustees for this center?

How are members chosen?

How long is a member's term?

What are the duties of board members?

How often does the board meet?

Are minutes of each meeting kept?

What is the relationship of the director and the board?

Is the director a voting member of the board?

WORKING PAPER 5-3

(for use with Class Assignment 3)

BYLAWS FORM

1. For which organization did you obtain bylaws?

2. Compared with the bylaws provided by another student:

    How are they similar in structure?

    What are the substantive differences?

    How do the differences in the documents reflect the differences in the purposes of the organizations?

DIRECTOR'S RESOURCE 5-1

CHARITABLE LAW SECTION

GUIDE FOR BOARD MEMBERS

FIDUCIARY DUTIES OF TRUSTEES AND DIRECTORS OF CHARITABLE ORGANIZATIONS

JIM PETRO

ATTORNEY GENERAL

STATE OF OHIO

A publication of the state of Ohio

(continues)

DIRECTOR'S RESOURCE 5-1
(continued)

TRUSTEE/DIRECTOR:
THEY ARE NOT HONORARY TITLES

Charities depend greatly on volunteers for their governance. Volunteers donate their time for a variety of reasons: Some are interested in the charity's programs, while others may feel that the position brings them some level of prestige. Most often, the motivation is a sense of civic duty and the satisfaction that comes from making a contribution to the community.

Charities often seek prominent members of the community to serve on their boards, perhaps because of that individual's business and management reputation. This could also be a means of honoring that individual and boosting the image and credibility of the charity by having well-known names listed among its trustees. Whatever the motivation of the individual or the charity, joining a board of trustees is a decision not to be taken lightly.

Prospective board members should investigate what such a commitment will entail, and understand the role, function, and responsibilities of a charity's governing body. This guide is intended to assist in that endeavor.

THE LEGAL DUTIES

Trustees and directors of a charitable organization, whether or not the organization is formally incorporated as a nonprofit corporation, have specific legal duties owed to the organization. The primary duties are:

The duty of care.

The duty of loyalty.

The duty to maintain accounts.

The duty of compliance.

THE DUTY OF CARE

The duty of care requires that a trustee be active in the charity's affairs by attending board meetings and meetings of committees on which the trustee serves. A board member must keep himself or herself informed to determine if the policies established by the board are being followed and should understand how the charity is functioning.

This duty must be discharged diligently and in good faith. Board members must act with knowledge and after adequate deliberation. They should carefully establish organizational policy and regularly oversee its administration by a competent staff.

Board members who are regularly absent from meetings, are inactive, or who fail to conduct adequate research prior to making decisions are not fulfilling their duties of care. Board members should conduct themselves with the level of care, skill, and diligence exercised by prudent persons in the handling of their own affairs. Generally, a board member who knows the facts, analyzes the probable result

(continues)

DIRECTOR'S RESOURCE 5-1
(continued)

of an action, exercises sound judgment, and keeps reasonable records acts prudently and fulfills his or her duty of care. Some ways you can meet your duty of care include:

- Understand the charity's mission by familiarizing yourself with the charity's articles of incorporation, constitution, by-laws, or other governing documents.
- Attend board and committee meetings and be prepared for those meetings by reading and reviewing reports, minutes, and other materials distributed for the meeting.
- Be prepared to ask questions and obtain the information needed for you to make informed decisions in approving and disapproving proposals. Included in your responsibilities is the oversight and review of the performance of the charity's executive director or chief executive officer. You should exercise your independent judgment and not merely acquiesce to the staff's requests.

THE DUTY OF LOYALTY

Many problems can be avoided if board members keep the duty of loyalty foremost in their thoughts. The duty of loyalty requires that the interest of the charity, and, as a consequence, the interest of the public, take precedence over the board member's personal interests. A trustee must, loyally and **without self-interest,** further the charitable objectives of the organization by acting fairly and in the best interest of the charity.

Trustees may breach the duty of loyalty when they engage, directly or indirectly, in transactions between themselves as trustees and themselves as individuals. They may also violate this duty by being involved in transactions with family members or businesses in which they hold an interest. Board members should not engage in any transaction that is adverse to the charity, engage in any competing enterprise to the detriment of the charity, divert an organizational opportunity for personal gain, or derive any kind of secret profit or other advantage in dealing with or on behalf of the charity. **Caution should be exercised in entering into any business relationship between the organization and a board member.** This should be avoided entirely unless the board determines that the transaction is clearly in the charity's best interest. Ways to avoid trouble:

- Ensure that the interest of the charity is always first.
- Establish a written policy for dealing with conflict of interest situations, which should include procedures for written disclosures from board members concerning business dealings with the charity or those seeking to do business with the charity.
- Disclose your financial interest whenever the charity proposes to enter into a business relationship with you, a member of your family, or a business in which you hold an interest. Don't vote on the transaction or participate in any debate or decision on the merits of the transaction.
- Don't divert an opportunity available to the charity for your own gain.
- Avoid transactions involving potential conflicts of interest, appearance of impropriety, and self-dealing situations.

(continues)

DIRECTOR'S RESOURCE 5-1

(continued)

THE DUTY TO MANAGE ACCOUNTS

Board members are responsible for assuring the financial accountability of the charity. Procedures should be established to keep the organization fiscally sound and ensure that it operates in a fiscally responsible manner. Care must be taken for the proper use of any restricted funds. Trustees should oversee the executive director and determine that the charity's purposes are fulfilled without waste. Preparation of a budget is important for providing clear directions for spending and translating program and management goals of the board into financial projections.

The organization should be able to demonstrate the wise use of its funds. Accurate records of all income, expenditures, transactions, and activities must be maintained. Accurate minutes of board meetings should be taken in order to demonstrate board approval of certain expenditures and investments and to show that informed decisions were made with regard to these transactions.

- Keep accurate records of income, investments, expenditures, and transactions, and accurate minutes of board meetings.
- Develop annual budgets that provide clear direction for spending at all levels of activities. The budget should be a blueprint of the board's program plans.
- Establish appropriate internal accounting systems, including a system of checks and balances. No one person should retain total control over finances.
- Prudently invest and reinvest assets.
- Assist the organization in acquiring resources for its programs. Develop fund-raising goals and policies. Make certain that fundraising appeals are presented honestly and fairly, and monitor the performance of fund-raising professionals.
- Shop around for the best values in goods and services through comparisons and informed bidding processes. This process should also be applied to contracts entered into with fund-raising professionals.

THE DUTY OF COMPLIANCE

Board members have a duty to be faithful to the organization's purposes and comply with the charity's governing documents. They are also under a duty to be familiar with the laws that apply to the charity and to comply with those state and federal laws that relate to the charity and its business operations.

- Be familiar with and follow the provisions of the charity's articles of incorporation, constitution, by-laws, or other governing documents.
- Familiarize yourself with state and federal laws relating to nonprofit entities, fund-raising, and tax-related issues.
- Comply with state and federal registration and reporting requirements, which may include filings with the Ohio Attorney General, the Ohio Secretary of State, and the Internal Revenue Service.

(continues)

DIRECTOR'S RESOURCE 5-1
(continued)

KEEPING THE BOARD VIGOROUS

To ensure the continuing vitality of the charity and its awareness and responsiveness to community needs, board members should look for ways to continue to breathe new life into the board. Choose board members who have an interest in the charity's mission and represent diverse viewpoints. Actively recruit individuals whose skills and commitment will enhance the charity. Consider term limits and rotation off the board to other assignments as a means of avoiding stagnation, tunnel vision, and the perception that the board is merely an insider's club.

CONSEQUENCES

There can be severe consequences to trustees for breaches of fiduciary duty. Trustees can be held individually responsible to charities for breaches of fiduciary standards. For example, if charitable assets are sold at less than their fair market value, trustees may be held accountable for any shortfalls.

IS IT WORTH IT?

Serving the community and its needs is a worthy act of stewardship. However, a board member who feels that his or her position as trustee is merely honorary is in for a shock. Service on a charity's board requires your acceptance of responsibility for the funds donors have contributed. Donors are placing their trust in you; the public that benefits from the charity's services is depending on you; and regulators are watching you.

These responsibilities need not deter any prospective board member. You need only to be active and involved, use sound judgment, act responsibly and in fairness to the charity, and always have the charity's best interests foremost in all actions. For board members who take their responsibilities seriously, the rewards of voluntary service are immeasurable.

REFERENCES

Behrman, R. (Ed.). (1996). Financing child care. *The future of child care.* Los Altos, CA: The David and Lucille Packard Foundation.

Bess, G., & Ratekin, C. (1999, May). Recruiting effective board members. *Child Care Information Exchange, 127,* 14–20.

Bess, G., & Ratekin, C. (2000, November). Orienting and evaluating your board of directors. *Child Care Information Exchange, 136,* 82–87.

Kindercare Learning Centers and Knowledge Learning Corporation Announce Merger Agreement. Portland, OR: November 05, 2004. (retrieved from http://www.kkr.com.)

Neugebauer, R. (1999, July). To profit or not to profit: That is the tough question. *Child Care Information Exchange, 128,* 76–81.

Additional resources for this chapter can be found on the Online Companion™ at http://www.earlychilded.delmar.com. This supplemental material includes relevant Web links, Web activities, and case studies that apply the concepts presented in this chapter. In addition, the Working Papers and Director's Resources are available for download, allowing you to complete Class Exercises and Class Assignments electronically.

CHAPTER 6

Handling Financial Matters

Often, the director is responsible for the center's financial management, but when an additional staff member assumes this role, the director must still be involved in decision making.

OBJECTIVES

After reading this chapter, you should be able to:

■ Describe the budget process.
■ List items to be included in a budget.
■ Analyze and prioritize the budget categories.

The director's role as one who sets the tone for the center has already been established, but he also must be a pragmatist capable of dealing with all the financial obligations of running a center. The financial operation of a center should be as smooth as possible to ensure that the director can maintain control of the finances. Poor financial management leads to constant lack of funds and continuously hinders personnel as they work to achieve program goals.

The two major components of the financial plan are developing a system for managing financial resources and obtaining adequate funding. The latter will be discussed in Chapter 7.

Every center needs a long-range financial plan and a plan for the upcoming year. A money management system including both policies and procedures is essential. Although many aspects of a good early childhood education program cannot be purchased at any price, high-quality care for young children is expensive, and funds must be allocated properly to provide a developmentally sound program on which children and parents can depend. No matter how good the intentions of the staff, a program cannot continue to operate for long without a balanced budget.

In a new center or one that is reorganizing, a decision must be made regarding who will be responsible for the center's financial management. Usually, the director is selected for this job, although sometimes a board member, parent (particularly in a parent co-op), or an assistant director carries all or part of the load. If there is a board with a finance committee, the staff member responsible for financial management works closely with this committee. A corporate system may have a regional or national operation of all the system's centers, and in a public school system the finances usually are handled through the central office.

BALANCING INCOME AND EXPENSES

A major task of the director or finance committee is the preparation of a budget. A budget is a plan or financial forecast usually set up for a period of one year. One section of the budget contains a list of income categories and dollar amounts; the other section shows a list of categories and dollar amounts for expenditures. The director's goal is to balance income and expenses, and in some cases, to show a profit. However, the cost of the desired early childhood education program is often higher than the total income available. The director prepares a budget by

- estimating how much the program will cost (based in part on the center's goals).
- determining how much income will be available (Chapter 7).
- seeking more income to equal expenditures, adjusting expenditures to equal income, or doing both.

Estimating Costs

The financial director's first task is to figure program cost. The task requires an overall understanding of the early childhood education program and its goals and objectives. It also requires reviews of the child care industry spending patterns nationally and locally. At the macro level, the Washington Quality Child Care Think Tank, which began its work in 1996, estimates that quality child care costs $8,300 per child per year (Center for the Future of Children, 1996). However, costs vary widely, in part, based on the area of the country. For example, in 2000, the average annual cost of child care for a 12-month-old in Conway/Springdale, Arkansas, was $3,900. At the same time, parents of a 12-month-old in Boston encountered an average cost or $12,978 per year for the child's

center-based care (Shulman, 2000). At the local level, the director determines what is needed for children in the particular community and program, then analyzes the cost of meeting these needs. These data will be needed in order to prepare a realistic budget. If other people are preparing the budget, the director works with them in interpreting program needs. In this planning model, some objectives may have to be postponed or omitted because of a lack of funds. Priorities should be established on the basis of the program goals, while the cost and the availability of funds determine the scope of the program. For example, a center may select improving salaries as a primary goal. If new playground equipment is also desirable, the decision about providing equipment in addition to improving salaries will be made based on the availability of funds, as well as on which is the greater need.

Another question that has an impact on both program and finances is: What is the population to be served? For example, does the program serve children from infancy through preschool age? If so, the director will have to recognize that costs for infant programs are considerably higher than costs for preschoolers, based largely on the staff-to-child ratio infants need. Decisions will have to be made about holding places for children as they are ready to move up to the next age group. How long can the center leave a toddler slot vacant when the toddler leaves the center or moves to a preschool classroom? The center director may realize that Baby Jones will be ready to move from the infant group to the toddler group in six weeks. Can he afford to tell a waiting list toddler parent that there is no room, thereby forgoing six weeks of toddler income? Should the slot be filled right away, if possible? And then in six weeks, when Baby Jones is ready to move, should that baby be kept in the infant room even though he is old and mature enough to move to the toddler area? And if that happens, should the Jones family pay infant tuition or the less expensive toddler tuition?

Should three- and four-year-olds be in the same classroom? Aside from the educational issues and the pros and cons of multi-age classrooms, the director may recognize that many three-year-olds need more adult assistance than four-year-olds. Licensing may require that the ratio needed for the youngest children in the group be maintained. If so, the director would have to provide the three-year-old ratio even if the majority of children in the class were four-year-olds. Would it then be cost effective to maintain separate groups for three- and four-year-olds? Would the expected cost savings be worth sacrificing the presumed child benefits a mixed-age group would provide?

Other questions include: How many teachers will be needed and for what hours? Will it be necessary to have aides? A cook? A janitor? A secretary? A bus driver? Answers to these and dozens of additional questions should be available from the people who are responsible for designing the program. By using this method, the director keeps the goals and philosophy of the center paramount.

Some directors have difficulty with the initial phase of budgeting. Instead of starting with the goals and objectives, they start with the dollars available and attempt to determine what can be done with them. Such a center is truly ruled by the budget (or by the finance director), and maintaining an educationally and financially sound program under these conditions is extremely difficult.

Although program and financial decisions may be made at the national or regional level, in a corporate system, the director of each center is responsible for implementing these decisions. The national or regional financial officer provides information about how much money is budgeted for each category; each local director then orders equipment and supplies through the main or regional office and is responsible for generating the required tuition.

Determining the dollar amount of a budget is a major part of the overall financial plan. This figure is arrived at by listing the items needed to operate the program for a year in categories such as salaries, rent, and equipment. Next, the budget director determines how much each of these categories will cost with as much accuracy as possible. The sum of the costs for each category is the amount of income needed for a year. A sample budget in Director's Resource 6–1 provides an idea of the costs of each category and of the costs of the total program for a hypothetical center. This sample budget is not meant to be utilized in the form presented here but may be used as a guide to budget preparation. Center directors, and other professional groups and organizations in each community

such as gas and electric companies, kitchen equipment suppliers, toy suppliers, and business associations, can furnish more specific and relevant cost information for individual centers.

Factors that will influence the total amount spent by a center and the ways in which that amount is allocated are listed below:

1. number, ages, and special needs of children enrolled
2. teacher-to-child ratio
3. staff training
4. type and location of building
5. amount of equipment already owned or available
6. type of program and services provided
7. section of the country in which the center is located
8. general economic conditions
9. amount and type of in-kind contributions

REFLECTION

Think about the tuition that is paid by parents, particularly in regard to its relationship to the salaries that are paid by a center. Consider a situation in which a teacher's annual salary is $27,000 and the assistant teacher's annual salary is $18,000. With a total of $45,000 a year for salaries, 15 families would each pay $3,000 a year to cover these salaries alone. Unless the center has other sources of income, tuition costs also must cover costs of equipment, supplies, food, facilities, utilities, benefits, administration, and so forth. Since the last child will leave the center from 10 to 12 hours after the first child has arrived, staff members will have to be present on a staggered schedule and additional help will be needed, all of which will increase salary costs. What would tuition have to be to produce a profit for the program sponsors?

Think about how much you will probably earn as a teacher in a child care center. If you were to earn minimum wage as a child care center teacher, working eight hours a day, five days a week for 52 weeks, what would your total salary be? If you were a parent earning minimum wage, how much could you afford to pay for child care?

The sum of the costs for each category is the cost of running the center for one year. Dividing this figure by the number of children to be served establishes the cost per child, a figure that can be further examined on a monthly, weekly, daily, or hourly basis. The cost of various program components, such as infant or school-age programs, can be figured this way also.

It is important to consider whether the center is a nonprofit organization or whether one of the goals is to make a profit. This question is sometimes a hotly debated issue among early childhood educators, many of whom feel that early childhood education centers should not be operated for profit because someone then makes money at the expense of the children. Admittedly, early childhood education costs are high and it is difficult to make a profit. Nonetheless, if a person or group can provide a good program, meeting the needs of both children and staff while showing a profit, there is no reason to discourage such a financial plan. It is the director's responsibility to ensure that children are not shortchanged in the interest of making a profit. This ethical issue may become even more challenging if the director's salary is tied to the amount of profit.

Adjusting Budget Figures

While it is relatively easy to change the budget figures on paper, chronic budgetary problems will drain staff energy from the daily operation and will remain unless the center can actually pare costs to the level of income earned.

REFLECTION

It may be easier to think about the financial aspects of an educational program by looking at your own educational finances. Think about the following questions: How is your college course work being financed? If you are paying tuition, what percentage of the actual cost of your education do you pay? Who finances the balance? Taxpayers? Endowments? How are other school expenses (high school and elementary school) financed?

Each expense must be analyzed with an eye toward its relative importance to the overall program. Can the equipment budget be lowered by substituting some free or inexpensive materials? Can food costs be lowered by cooperative buying? Can the consumable supply budget be reduced without a major effect on program quality? What effect will a particular cut have on the quality of the children's program? How will the cut affect the staff? Keep in mind that reductions that work on paper may be unfair to children and staff. The point at which budget cutting becomes an ethical issue has to be considered.

When no cost reductions are feasible, both new and current funding sources can be approached with clear documentation of the need in relation to goals because expenses must not exceed income. If professional early childhood educators take the approach that it is better to have a poor program than none at all, the problem of adequately funding child care never will be solved. When a center's financial management is poor, the director may continue operating past this point without becoming aware that the inevitable outcome will be a poor-quality program or bankruptcy.

PREPARING THE BUDGET

Well before the end of each fiscal year, the director or finance manager begins preparing the budget for the coming year. In the case of a new center, a realistic budget will determine whether or not opening the center is feasible.

Types of Budgets

Budgets are classified in several ways. They may be based on the stage of development of the center or they may be categorized according to the stage to which the budget itself has been carried. The creation of a new center demands one kind of budget while the ongoing operation of a center requires a budget of a different type. Budgets also may reflect the center's accountability mechanism.

Start-up Budgets

When a center is being created, the director prepares two budgets: the start-up budget and the operating budget. The *start-up budget* consists of all the expenses incurred in starting the center. These expenses include initial building expenses (down payment on the purchase of the building, the cost of building renovation, or rent deposit), the purchase of major equipment, the cost of publicizing the center, the director's salary for several months prior to the children's attendance, the deposit on telephone service, and the utility charges during the start-up period. Salaries for any additional personnel needed to assist the director of a large center also must be provided. Total start-up costs vary widely. When these costs are incurred, the usual sources of revenue ordinarily have not become available. In these cases, a special grant may be needed or the organizers of the center may arrange for a loan or invest their own funds. When a loan is obtained, the cost of the interest must be recognized as constituting a very real budgetary item.

Occasionally, suppliers will permit purchasers to defer payment for 90 days and the center can schedule purchases so that the first tuition is received before the 90-day period ends. However, the first receipts certainly will not cover all the expenses. If receipts are due from agency or government funds, those first payments usually are made after the services have been provided. In the meantime, suppliers may charge interest on unpaid bills. Therefore, it is important to obtain as much assurance as possible that funds for start-up will be available when needed.

The United States General Accounting Office (GAO) report on child care costs found start-up costs of $8,000 to $90,000, with a median of $48,500. These costs included, in descending order of amount spent, costs for space, supplies and equipment, planning and administration, and teacher training (United States General Accounting Office, 1990). Today's figures obviously would be higher.

Area of the country, projected size of the center, ages of children to be served, in-kind support (such as free or reduced-price space offered by a church), and amount of money to be borrowed all contribute to start-up costs for new centers. Therefore, it is difficult to project the cost of a specific center. The Small Business Administration (SBA) recommends that persons interested in starting a center create a business plan. Using this approach, the prospective owner can determine whether his plan is realistic in terms of potential resources (loans, etc.) and potential success of his plan. More information about the SBA is available in Chapter 7 and on-line at http://www.SBA.gov.

Operating Budget

The *operating budget* consists of an income and expense plan for one year, and is used when centers enroll children and begin the program, and annually thereafter. The center may operate on a calendar year (from January 1 to December 31) or on a fiscal year, a 12-month period chosen for ease of relating financial matters to other operations of the center. Centers funded by agencies that operate on a fiscal year running from July 1 to June 30 find it easier to work on the same schedule as the funding agency, but many early childhood education centers choose September 1 to August 31 for their fiscal year because those dates

relate closely to the start of their school year. Once a center has selected its fiscal year, no change should be made without serious reason. Planning one year's budget from January 1 to December 31, then changing to a September to August fiscal year in the following year, causes confusion and may need to be justified for tax purposes.

Before spending can begin, the budget must be approved by the board and the funding sources. The budget must balance, that is, income and expenses must be equal. When there is a surplus in the income side of the budget, it is categorized as profit or may be put in a reserve fund for large expenses that may occur in a future year. Because not-for-profit businesses obviously do not show a profit, such funds would be added to appropriate budget categories or would be put in a reserve fund. However, if the budget projects a loss, serious attention must be paid to immediate financial trimming or funding. Believing that "something will turn up" is a poor way to conduct business and should not be accepted by a board or funders. At this point, conflict may arise among the board, the funding agency, and the director as each group may have varying interpretations of the center's goals and of the means for reaching these goals. Once a consensus has been reached and the budget has been approved, the budget becomes the working financial plan and the director must see that it is followed.

Analyzing Budget Categories

Most boards of directors have a finance committee that oversees the preparation and implementation of the budget. However, even when this committee assumes major responsibility, the director still is responsible for understanding and articulating what is needed to operate the program successfully. Many board members have limited knowledge of the actual cost of child care. The director must help them develop this understanding.

DIRECTOR'S CORNER

"Our needs assessment indicated that over 100 children would use our center. Two major corporations in the neighborhood worked with us and many of their employees expressed interest in enrolling their children. We were shocked when we spent the whole first year with only nine children enrolled. Luckily, we had strong financial backing, and we have now reached capacity enrollment."

–Director, private not-for-profit center

Some centers budget by function rather than simply by category; that is, administrative costs and the costs of each aspect of the program are budgeted separately. For example, if 20 percent of the director's time is spent working directly with the children and 80 percent is spent on administration, then 20 percent of the director's salary would be allocated to the children's program salaries category and 80 percent would fall under administration. A complex center may provide and budget several separate functions such as infant program, preschool program, and after-school program. This budgeting method clearly delineates the actual cost of the children's program. And when coupled with a description of the services offered, it provides a mechanism for comparing costs with other programs and for including the value of the services provided in relation to the costs incurred. This method also provides information used in determining tuition. However, ever-changing tax laws make it essential for even small centers to have the services of an accountant to guide the director in setting up fiscal systems and to provide information about new governmental requirements. An attorney also may be needed to help ensure that the center is operating within legal limits. The cost of these services must be included in the budget.

Although requirements at each center are different, new directors may be given a general idea of costs if they consider the following rough estimates:

- 70 percent personnel
- 10 percent facility, utilities
- 5 percent equipment
- 3 percent supplies
- 3 percent food
- 9 percent other categories

Attempting to design a budget to fit these percentages would be inappropriate since these figures are provided as general guides.

The following budget categories will provide a rough idea of the costs of early childhood education and the formats used for presenting a budget.

Salaries

In any early childhood education budget, the major component is salaries (www.ccw.org). A center can expect to spend up to 80 percent of its operating costs for personnel. This figure includes salaries and wages for full- and part-time staff members (such as director, teachers, cooks, janitor) and for substitutes. It also includes fringe benefits for the full-time staff. In determining the budget for salaries, the personnel policies should be consulted in regard to pay rates and fringe benefits. The salary policies may address issues such as staff members' education level, previous experience, or meritorious service. The director also must comply with the minimum wage laws, tax laws, and laws regarding employer responsibility. Other factors that may influence salaries are public school affiliation, union membership, and salary standards of the sponsoring agency. Center directors must ensure that they meet the Fair Labor Standards Act (FLSA). A number of complex issues and conflicting results of court cases make it difficult to determine who is considered a teacher for the purposes of FLSA. This determination can make a difference in whether or not an employer is required to provide overtime pay and pay for hours spent in in-service training and parent meetings "after hours" (The Child Care Law Center, 1996).

U.S. Department of Labor regulations that went into effect in 2004 consider exempt (from FLSA) those staff members who are paid a regular salary of at least $23,660 annually, no matter how many hours they work. Their work must relate directly to the management or general business operations of the organization. For more details, go to http://www.dol.gov. Keep in mind that professional advice is still important, especially when addressing complex legal matters.

DIRECTOR'S CORNER

"Recently, a local employer built a brand new on-site center and employed a director. She is a company employee. Her salary and all building costs, including rent, maintenance, and utilities, are covered by the company. We had to increase our salaries because we were losing staff to the new center, which could, of course, pay higher salaries. But it meant we had to raise tuition, and we really didn't want to do that."

—*Director, full-day child care center*

Based on the National Child Care Staffing Study (Whitebook, Howes, & Phillips, 1998), NAEYC reported that the highest paid teachers averaged $10.85 an hour while the lowest averaged $7. Assistant teacher pay ranged from $6 to $7 per hour. An important additional consideration is benefits. Only 20 percent of centers offered fully paid health care to teachers, and fewer than 23 percent of these covered dependents. As expected, independent nonprofit centers had the lowest staff turnover rates (28 percent), which seems to be related to their highest salaries of $12.27 hourly (NAEYC, 1998).

By 2003, little progress had been made. The Bureau of Labor Statistics report separated salaries of preschool teachers and child care workers for analysis and reported salaries by mean (average) and median (the midpoint of all figures in the group.) Results were as follows:

- The mean hourly wage for preschool teachers was $10.67.
- The median hourly wage for preschool teachers was $9.53.
- The mean hourly wage for child care workers was $8.37.
- The median hourly wage for child care workers was $7.90 (Center for the Child Care Workforce, 2004).

Personnel costs to the center over and above the salaries and wages paid to employees consist of the percentages of these wages that are imposed as taxes by various governmental agencies and that the employer may be required to pay. For example, the employer pays percentages of the employee's salary for Social Security, workers' compensation, and unemployment compensation. The center also incurs the bookkeeping costs that are involved with maintaining accurate records for each employee and filing reports with a variety of government agencies. Benefits such as health insurance are included in personnel costs, and provision must be made for substitute staff who work during employees' sick and vacation leave. Although benefit costs may seem expendable, they often mean the difference between a stable and a transient staff. Keep in mind that high staff turnover means additional costs for advertising, additional training time, and perhaps loss of clients. More important high staff turnover has a negative effect on the quality of child care.

In addition to the benefits just described, the agency also is required to withhold certain taxes from each employee's paycheck, to accrue these funds, and to submit them to the appropriate governmental body in a timely manner with accurate records. Although these taxes are not paid by the employer, here again, the cost of record keeping does contribute to the overall cost of operating the center. Even though these funds may be available for several months before you must pay them out, it is not wise to spend them with the assumption that you will replace them. Employers are required to maintain sufficient funds to meet their government-imposed obligations.

Because payroll preparation has become so complex, some directors find that hiring a company to handle all payroll issues is cost effective. However, computer software packages are available for directors

Despite the need to attend to business matters, directors recognize that the center exists to support children's development.

who choose to handle this function. The staff member responsible for payroll types in the employees' information, pay rates, tax rates, other deductions, and anything else that impacts pay. The software handles the formulas created by the computer operator, and the checks are printed by the attached printer.

Consultants

A second component of a center budget that is closely related to salaries is contract services or consultant fees. This category covers payments to people who agree to perform specified services for the center or its clients such as accountants, lawyers, doctors, dentists, social workers, psychologists, nutritionists, and educational consultants. These types of professionals could be employees of a large center or system. However, they usually serve as consultants by agreeing, for example, to give dental examinations

In planning a budget, directors must be aware of the day-to-day needs of everyone in the center.

to all children enrolled in the center or to provide workshops for teachers one day a month. When the center's staff is not well trained, or when a broad range of services is provided for children, many consultants are needed. Although some centers do not hire consultants and most will hire only a limited number, the overall quality of the program may be increased by the services they provide.

When consultants come from out of town, their transportation, meals, and lodging may be additional costs. Sometimes, consultants are paid a per diem rate to cover meals and lodging. The current per diem rate of the federal government might be used in budgeting. Both the center and the consultant should agree in writing on all financial arrangements and performance expectations in advance of any services rendered. Under no circumstances should the director attempt to classify a staff position as a consultancy to avoid paying taxes and benefits. Serious legal ramifications may be the result.

Plant and Equipment

The largest cost in the physical plant category is rental, lease, or mortgage payments on the facility. The costs for the maintenance of, and the repairs to, the building and grounds also are part of this budget item. When maintenance work is done on a regular basis, the costs usually will be lower in the long run. However, since it is impossible to predict all maintenance and repair needs in advance, a lump sum for this purpose should be allocated each year. A preliminary assessment of the main components of a building

foundation (roof, plumbing, wiring, heating and cooling system, termite damage, and so forth) will provide a rough idea of when major repairs may be expected.

Also included in physical plant in the operating budget are utilities (heat, electricity, and water). In some cases, one or more of the utility charges may be covered in the lease, a point that should be fully understood and in writing before an agreement to lease is made. Some centers also may have to pay for garbage removal. When utilities are not included in the lease, an approximate budget figure can be obtained by checking with previous tenants or with the utility companies.

In budgeting for a new center, equipment for the office, the kitchen, and the children is a major part of the start-up budget. For a continuing center, the operating budget includes supplementary pieces, as well as repair and replacement where needed. Leasing and rental charges for equipment are included here. For example, a center may rent a carpet cleaner for a day or two, or lease a copy machine for a year. The continuing equipment budget will be about 10 percent of the start-up equipment budget, so if the start-up equipment budget is $1,000 per child, the continuing equipment budget would be $100 per child per year.

Depreciation

One of the costs of doing business that may be overlooked is depreciation of major equipment. When a center purchases major playground equipment or furniture such as tables, chairs, and shelves, it would appear that the center had added that amount of

Year	Worth =	New Value
1	$2,000–$400*	$1,600
2	$1,600–$400*	$1,200
3	$1,200–$400*	$800
4	$800–$400*	$400
5	$400–$400*	$0

*$2,000 ÷ 5 years = $400 depreciation per year.

Figure 6–1

Depreciation chart showing five-year depreciation of a $2,000 computer

dollar value to its assets. However, once an item is purchased and put into use, its value begins to drop or depreciate. Let us assume that the children's furniture will last 15 years, whereas the computer and copy machine will have to be replaced in 5 years. Dividing the initial cost of the item by the anticipated length of its useful life yields the annual depreciation amount. A $2,000 computer divided by 5 years results in depreciation of $400 a year. That is, the computer is worth $400 less each year. Figure 6–1 depicts the annual value of the computer. Although the computer may still be functioning adequately, it now has little or no value. When you consider the assets of your child care business, this computer is no longer an asset even though you may continue to use it.

REFLECTION

Think about purchasing a new car. As soon as you drive it away from the dealer's showroom, it becomes a used car and is worth less than you are paying. Every year, therefore, it is worth less, partly because it is being used and gradually wearing out and partly because newer models with different features are being produced. At some point, it may be worth a lot more to you than to anyone else. You may continue to drive it. But if the cost of repairs becomes very high, you will probably decide that it would be more economical to get a different vehicle.

In listing assets, the annual amount of depreciation is deducted so that the value of the equipment is more realistic than if the full cost were listed. At the same

time, wise directors build an equipment replacement fund so that when eight infant cribs must be replaced, the center is somewhat prepared for that expense.

Supplies

Three types of supplies must be purchased: office and general supplies, classroom supplies, and food supplies. The first category—office and general supplies—includes items such as pencils, stationery, toilet paper, paper towels, cleansers, and brooms. Construction paper, paint, crayons, pet food, and doll clothes are included in classroom supplies. Food supplies encompass all items available for human consumption. Usually, two meals and two snacks per child per day are served in full-day centers, with one snack offered in a half-day program. In any case, sufficient food should be provided so that teachers can eat with the children. Food costs vary depending on the availability of federal food subsidies and on factors in the economy. A nutritionist engaged as a consultant can aid the director in setting up a nutritionally and financially sound food plan.

All consumable supplies should be ordered in large quantities when that is more economical, assuming that there is sufficient storage space and that the supplies will be used while they are still in top condition (for example, paint dries out when it is stored too long). The cost of providing storage space and the possibility that plentiful supplies will be used more freely by the staff must be weighed against the savings accrued from purchasing in quantity.

Transportation

This category may include the purchase or lease of several buses for transporting children to and from school and on field trips. In such cases, insurance, gas, maintenance, and license fees must be budgeted. Some centers contract with a company to provide transportation for children, and others may rent a bus for special occasions. Vehicles must be equipped with child safety seats or seat belts, depending on the size and age of the child, and other governmental regulations regarding vehicles must be followed. Centers may have to purchase or lease buses instead of vans based on a ruling by the National Highway Traffic Safety Administration. They must follow both federal and state laws. Your state may require that you transport children in vehicles meeting special school bus regulations and that drivers have special licenses. The many financial, safety, and liability issues involved frequently lead centers to require parents to provide the child's transportation to and from school.

Costs for staff members to travel to professional meetings, other centers for observation, and homes for home visits are included in the transportation category. The mileage rate for automobile travel reimbursement is usually based on the current federal government mileage rate.

Communication

Telephone costs can be determined by checking with the telephone company. In deciding on the number of telephones to order, consider the center's staffing pattern. For example, if a classroom staffed by one adult is located on another floor away from other classrooms, an extension or cell phone is needed to allow that teacher to get help when necessary. When a teacher is outside or on a field trip, even though at least one other adult is present, it is a good idea to provide a cell phone. In an emergency, the teacher can get help. Licensing requirements in some states specify where a telephone is required. In any case, enough lines should be provided to enable parents and other callers to reach the center without undue delays. Call waiting, often less costly than a second line, improves accessibility for outside callers but can be annoying to some.

Getting emergency messages through immediately is a priority item, and providing staffers with access to a telephone for personal calls during breaks is a benefit that recognizes their needs and helps them feel that they are respected members of the organization.

Many centers rely on e-mail for much of their in-house communication, as well as contact with families, colleagues, vendors, home offices, and others. The director and other staff also will use various Web sites for gathering information, contacting legislators in their roles as advocates, and marketing the center. The monthly charge for this access is included under communication. In arranging for Internet connection, make sure that you will have access to phone service and the Internet simultaneously.

DIRECTOR'S CORNER

"One of our teachers and her assistant took their class on a field trip about 10 miles from the center. As lunch time approached, I began to worry. I had been assured they would return for lunch. Just then a telephone call came in. There was a huge wreck on the expressway and traffic wasn't moving. A driver in a car in the next lane lent the teacher his cell phone to call me. As soon as I realized that all the children were safe, I made a note to order cell phones to be used on field trips."

—Director, church-based preschool

Staff Training

Even when a center is fortunate enough to have a staff of well-prepared teachers and assistants whose education was in the early childhood field, continuous in-service training still will be needed. Recognizing that learning is lifelong and that research continues to provide new information about children's development, both directors and staff members need opportunities to participate in conferences, classes, and visits to other programs. When the staff is underprepared, the director must begin their in-service program immediately. State licensing regulations may require a particular number of hours of training annually, usually a minimal level. It is the director's responsibility to determine what is needed and to facilitate the acquisition of that training or education. Some centers provide partial scholarships for classes and may reimburse the staff member on successful completion of a course.

Insurance

Insurance agents can quote rates and provide information about appropriate kinds of insurance. A center usually needs at least fire, theft, and liability insurance. If the center provides transportation or owns vehicles, various types of insurance are required. A child accident policy is valuable and inexpensive. If the center has a board of directors, directors and officers insurance is important. Be sure to read each policy carefully and ask questions about any items you do not understand. Find out whether your legal expenses would be covered if, for example, you were sued by a family who claimed that you were negligent. What are realistic deductibles for your situation? What exclusions, if any, are written in your policy ("Does Your Insurance," 2002)?

Postage

Postage covers the cost of mailings to parents and prospective client families. The cost of shipping and other business mailing is included. In some cases, fax or e-mail may be appropriate and less costly, but in all cases, a record of important communication should be maintained.

Billing, especially notices of overdue accounts, usually are mailed. Some centers establish the policy that payment is due on a particular date each month and no bills are sent. Postage costs can be held down to some extent if information is distributed by sending notes home with the children, but keep in mind that these items may not always reach the parent.

Marketing

Marketing includes newspaper and telephone book advertisements, brochures and fliers, and radio or television announcements. Some agencies design a logo and use it on various products such as T-shirts, stationery, business cards, and beverage mugs. Once a center is well established, the marketing budget may be minimal, but in the initial stages and in highly transient neighborhoods, it is an income-producing expense. All centers are wise to maintain a good public relations plan so that the community knows about and supports their work. But perhaps the best marketing tool is a satisfied customer.

Licensing

Information about licensing costs can be obtained from the licensing agent; these costs will vary according to the center's location. Other professional fees, such as those for NAEYC accreditation, also belong in this category.

Audit

Yearly audits are essential. They assure the board and funders that the center's financial matters are being handled properly. You should ask your accountant for a cost estimate and build that into the budget.

Miscellaneous

This category includes funds for small items that do not fall under any of those previously mentioned. However, attributing expenditures to a particular category provides a more accurate picture of the center's financial status and eliminates slippage in expenditures. For example, if postage and advertising were both included under miscellaneous, postage expenditures could skyrocket and not be recognized as a budgetary problem.

In-Kind Contributions

Some budget items are not received in cash and are not paid for in cash. These are called *in-kind contributions* and should be shown in the budget so that the true cost of operating the center is known. For example, a center may rent two 600-square-foot-rooms in a church building for $200 per month per room. This would cost the center $4,000 for a 10-month program. If the fair rental cost is at the rate of $10 per square foot (a total of $12,000), then the church is, in effect, contributing $8,000 to the center program.

Consultants may volunteer their services, and such services also should be shown as in-kind contributions. For example, assume that a child development specialist conducts one half-day workshop without charging the center. The specialist's contribution is valued at $300, which is the hypothetical per diem rate for professional services.

Sometimes, directors expect staff to volunteer to work additional hours without pay. This practice is usually inappropriate. Many teachers already spend time at home planning and preparing materials. Furthermore, staff salaries usually are alarmingly low. If staff members are expected to attend meetings and programs outside regular work hours, these conditions should be spelled out in the job descriptions. Some centers include policies relating to staff caring for children who are center clients outside of work hours. At the very least, staff members who are required to work more than 40 hours in a week must be paid overtime rates for the additional hours, unless they are exempt under U.S. Department of Labor regulations.

Budgeting for Second and Subsequent Years

Several months prior to the end of the year, the director and members of the finance committee meet to review the budget the director has prepared for the ensuing year. For the second and subsequent budgets, the previous year's figures can serve as a guide, but the new budget figures, based on experience and on program changes, will differ from those of the previous year. Still, the income and expenses must balance.

OTHER FINANCIAL RESPONSIBILITIES

The budget is the major tool used by the financial director for management of center finances, but balancing income and expenses is only one aspect of an overall, ongoing financial system. The director has a number of continuing financial responsibilities, all of which relate ultimately to the budget.

Designing Budget Systems

Once the sources and amounts of income have been determined, these facts must be written down along with the plan for spending discussed earlier in this chapter. This written plan must be prepared in such a way that the people who need to read it will be able to understand it.

Small centers can use a very simple format. Centers that are publicly funded may be required to use whatever system is designated by the funding agency. Many centers use budget codes or account numbers, assigning a code number to each budget category and using separate numbers for each item within that category. For example, if the budget item equipment is coded as 110, then the subcategories might be:

111 office equipment
112 classroom equipment
113 kitchen equipment

Similarly, personnel might be coded as 510, with:

511 salaries
512 social security
513 worker's compensation

Such a system enables the financial director to record transactions according to appropriate budget categories and to ascertain quickly how much has been spent and how much remains in a given category.

An additional consideration in keeping accurate records is the responsibility to maintain ethical and legal practices. Having access to large sums of money is tempting to some people. If safeguards are not in place, the director or an employee who has access to financial records may manipulate them in unethical and illegal ways. A system of checks and balances can deter this behavior. For this reason, board members should be tenacious in insisting on current and thorough financial reports and should not hesitate to question any items they do not understand.

To have an accurate picture of the center's current financial position, accrual rather than cash accounting is essential. This means that revenues and expenses are recorded as they are incurred. By using this system, the director avoids the inaccurate picture presented when expenses are recorded only when they are paid instead of when the money is encumbered. This information is reported on a monthly cash flow report, an estimate of how much you expect to receive and spend each month. The director estimates receipts and disbursements for the year, month by month. The amount of cash expected to be on hand at the end of one month becomes the amount of cash expected to be on hand at the beginning of the following month. As actual figures become available, these are entered in the "actual" column so that monthly comparisons can be made between anticipated and actual expenses for the month and year to date (Stephens, 1991). A sample cash flow report appears in Director's Resource 6–2.

DIRECTOR'S CORNER

"I thought we were in good financial shape. We were showing a solid bank balance and we had full enrollment. What our cash accounting system didn't show was that we had several thousand dollars in bills that the bookkeeper hadn't paid yet. I learned that checking the cash on hand and even looking at how much we had budgeted for a category weren't necessarily appropriate ways to make decisions about what I could spend."

—*Director, for-profit proprietary center*

Whenever a financial transaction occurs, it should be recorded promptly in a specific form. Access to a personal computer and appropriate software makes this task relatively easy and provides clear, readily available reports that show the financial position of the center on a monthly, weekly, and even daily basis.

Managing Cash Flow

To be sure that you will have enough cash on hand to pay staff and order the equipment for which you budgeted, you will need to keep track of cash flow. Often, budgets are divided into monthly components with the assumption that each month you will spend approximately one-twelfth of the annual amount. Income may be assumed to be received in a similar pattern: one-twelfth of the annual income is expected each month. But suppose your budget includes $1,200 for classroom supplies. Does that mean you can spend $100 a month or can you place a $500 order in March? You need to know whether the cash will be available.

To accomplish this, you make a cash flow chart, showing each income and each expense item on a monthly basis. Often, these amounts are shown on a one-twelfth per month basis. At the end of January, you record the amount actually received and disbursed in each category. In another column, you show the difference between what you expected to receive or spend in that category, and what actually happened.

REFLECTION

You have $120 in your checking account. An item of clothing that you have desired for a month has just gone on sale for $100. What factors will you take into account in determining whether to buy it?

Now assume that you direct a center. In examining your records for this month, you note that

- income for March 2006 = $20,359.
- expenses for March 2006 = $15,250.

Can you, as the director, therefore, purchase $5,000 of needed equipment for the center? Why or why not? If you were using the accrual method, you would know that you had already encumbered $5,000 for equipment that hadn't arrived yet.

You also may record year-to-date expenses and receipts, as well as year-to-date expectations. Let us assume that you listed $100 each month for classroom supplies for an annual total of $1,200. If you spent $0 in January, $50 in February, and $0 in March, you would have a $250 favorable balance in the supplies line. Unless your funder requires it, it is not necessary to spend money only as it is available in that line. However, you must be sure you can meet all expenses and not exceed the annual amount allocated without either receiving unexpected, unbudgeted income or decreasing the amount to be spent for the year on another item. Using a good software package to help you keep these records will simplify your task.

Ordering Goods and Services

With an approved budget in hand, the director or purchasing agent (or someone else assigned to this role) can begin to order supplies, equipment, and services. The first step is to consult the person or people who will use the item or services. The janitor may be consulted about a waxing machine, while the teachers should be involved in decisions about tables and chairs for the children. Both janitor and teachers could participate in selecting carpeting for the classrooms. However, when it comes to the actual ordering of the goods and services, as few people as possible—one is preferable—should be involved.

Several methods of ordering goods and services are utilized, depending on the nature of the purchase. Major purchases usually are approved by the director, the board, or a committee. If outside funding has been received, the center's contract may require that bids be submitted for large items or for large quantities of items such as food or paper goods. The purchaser writes out required specifications to suppliers or advertises for bids in the case of a large order. Then, the purchaser examines the bids and contracts that each supplier offers. The lowest bid must be accepted unless the bidder does not meet the specifications. Specifications can refer to a description of the item in question (for example, a commercial dishwasher) to the performance of the item (with water temperature of 180 degrees), or to its delivery date (to be delivered by September 1, 20xx).

Smaller purchases or those that are routine such as art supplies may be ordered from a wholesaler. However, some centers require that price information on such items be obtained and that the item of appropriate quality having the lowest price be purchased. Sometimes, purchases are made with particular outlets because they allow credit, but this choice will be false economy if the quality is not satisfactory.

In some large cities, several centers may band together to purchase large quantities of items at reduced prices in a plan called *cooperative buying*. Each center may contribute to the salary of the person who manages the co-op and must transport items from a central location to its own center.

Making Payments

The director (or someone so designated) is responsible for making all payments. When shipments arrive, they are checked then paid for as soon as possible within the terms of agreement. For example, if the vendor gives 30 days to pay, the center should use the money until the payment is due but should monitor bill payment carefully so that unnecessary interest is not incurred. In cases where a discount is offered for prompt payment, that may be a wise course to follow. Before paying for any item, it is important to verify that the items received are proper in quantity and quality and that the price on the invoice is correct.

A center should establish a checking account immediately so that payment for goods and services can be made promptly and safely. If the center is small, there may be the temptation to pay expenses directly from cash income. This practice is a major mistake because under such a plan, money can easily be lost or stolen, and errors or misunderstandings are more likely to occur. Furthermore, no audit trail of these items is available. Most centers use checking accounts and some centers require two signatures on each check, perhaps the signatures of the board treasurer and the director. In small centers or in proprietary centers, the director signs all checks. Even more important is to appoint a person other than the bookkeeper to reconcile the bank balance.

When specific procedures for money management are in place, fewer errors are likely to occur. There must be a specific place to store bills and a specific time set aside to pay them. In small co-ops, a parent may work at home recording transactions. In large, complex organizations, all finances may be handled through a central administrative office that may be in another city or state.

Recording Transactions

Whenever a financial transaction occurs, it should be recorded promptly in a specific form. Access to a personal computer and appropriate software makes this task relatively easy and provides clear, readily available reports that show the financial position of the center on a monthly, weekly, or even daily basis.

In fact, many directors who now use computers for record keeping wonder how they managed without these tools. At first, using this technology can be time consuming, particularly if you are completely unfamiliar with the way these machines can work for you. However, once the system is set up, it takes no more time (and probably less time) to enter figures by means of the keyboard as opposed to pencil and paper. The result usually is easier to read, may be

converted readily to chart form on the computer, and can be cross-referenced. For example, you can enter in each child's record the tuition received that month from that family, and without rewriting all the amounts, query the computer for the total amount of tuition received that month.

Billing is easy. Once you have enrolled a child, and entered the parent(s) names and addresses, you can direct your computer to print bills to each family customized with the specific amount owed. You also may want to add a message to each bill such as a reminder about registration for the following autumn or an advance notice of the date of the school picnic.

Although not directly related to the center's fiscal operation, you may want lists of center children or families by child's birth date, health checkup due date, zip code, or by class at the center. You can print out attendance (often required by funders), a task that is made even easier if the parent signs the child in and out using a computer. Clip art or your own creative graphics add zest to notices. Just remember that you are directing a professional program and not a "Kutesy Korner."

Getting your payroll out on time can be much simpler with a computer. Once programmed with the hourly or monthly rates, the percentages to be withheld or deducted for various purposes, and other data to be recorded such as sick days used and available, your computer will do the calculations and print the checks. You'll have a record of the transactions, but, as with any other document, you'll make a backup disk and keep it in a secure place.

As you work on budgets, reports to funders, cash flow statements, and any other data, you can use a password that will prevent those who do not need access to the data from viewing or modifying it. For example, a parent may not want the child's address published on the class list, or you may not want the staff to see the proposals for salary increases until the board of directors has approved them.

Every year, hardware and software manufacturers develop new capabilities for this technology. If you are relatively new to computer usage, finding a knowledgeable board member, volunteer, or consultant to assist you is essential. Choosing computer components requires understanding how you will use your computer. Most centers can't afford to buy a more powerful computer than they will need in the next few years, yet buying strictly on price will probably prove to be false economy. If your computer cannot run the software you need, you may wind up with not much more than an expensive typewriter.

If you are going to use a computer for communicating by e-mail, using the Internet to gather information, or faxing documents, you'll need a telephone line. It should be a separate line so that parents can have telephone access to the center while you are using the computer. Don't forget to budget charges for Internet access.

Purchasing software also can be challenging, though not as costly as the hardware. Just as you can add hardware components as you acquire the need and the funds, so too can you add software packages. For example, you may add an accounts receivable package. You may also modify or customize existing programs, or you might purchase a basic program and create your own system.

When purchasing software, some of the items you'll want to consider include the following:

1. What kind of hardware is needed to run this software?
2. Can you try out the software?
3. Does it do what you need?
4. What kind of support is available and at what cost?
5. Are seminars available? Where and when are they held?
6. Is there a telephone help line? What are the hours in your time zone?
7. Are upgrades provided?
8. How long has the company been in business?

Since both computer hardware and software are changing so rapidly, it's a good idea to check with colleagues about what has worked effectively and what they would like to add. Professional journals such as *Child Care Information Exchange* provide regular reviews. Most reputable software companies will permit you to try out the software instead of watching someone else work with it and telling you about it as they go. ProCare from Professional Solutions and Kids Care from Softerware are two of the most active players in this market. However, you also may find an excellent package developed by individuals who have been or are directors and have worked with computer programmers to design software that meets specific needs. Of course, whether a center uses computerized records or handwritten reports, these will be timely and accurate only when timely, accurate information is recorded.

Shortly after a fiscal year ends, the financial director should prepare an income statement for that year. This statement shows all revenue and expenses for the past year and points out the net income or loss. Director's Resource 6–3 provides an example of an income statement.

To monitor the center's financial position, the financial director lists all assets and all liabilities as well as the equity the owner or owners have in the center. Directors need this total picture to enable them to understand their total financial position. For example, if the assets are much less than the liabilities, the center is obviously in financial trouble. Notice how important accrued accounting is in creating the statement of financial position. Director's Resource 6–4 provides a sample statement of financial position.

Auditing

In most businesses, including early childhood education centers, an auditor reviews the books annually. The director makes the financial records available to the auditor, whether on computer or in a ledger. Also included are the checkbook, canceled checks, receipts, and invoices. The director or bookkeeper must keep these documents in an organized manner, and they must be regularly updated. Shoe boxes or laundry baskets full of invoices are totally unacceptable and certainly are unprofessional. At the very least, such lack of organization leaves the impression that the financial transactions of the center are not accurately maintained.

Auditors can perform several levels of audit or verification that the financial operation of the center is based on generally accepted procedures. The board will determine which level is needed, but in any event, the auditor will not verify each individual transaction. An annual audit protects the financial personnel of the center by making sure their job is being done according to procedures and protects the entire operation by ensuring that the use of funds is being recorded as planned.

Handling Petty Cash

The director also regulates the petty cash fund, setting the procedures for its use and maintaining sufficient cash to keep the system working effectively. This fund is usually small because serious losses by theft or carelessness may occur when large amounts are kept on hand.

There are several ways to operate the petty cash fund. Each teacher may receive a specified sum of money to spend for the classroom, or the director may allocate a certain sum per staff member, paying cash when the staff member presents an appropriate receipt. Some centers use petty cash for all unexpected small needs. The director keeps a sum of cash on hand and gives it to staff members who present legitimate requests. For example, if the cook has run out of bread, petty cash may be used to purchase a loaf or two. Petty cash should be used as little as possible to avoid obscuring substantial program expenditures under its heading. If $20 worth of food is purchased weekly with petty cash, then the item *food* in the budget is underrepresented. All expenditures should be recorded (or allocated) to the correct account. This can be accomplished by the bookkeeper when the user presents receipt documentation.

Handling Salaries

Once the budget is approved, the financial director informs the personnel committee of the allocation for salaries. In a new center, the committee then may begin the employment process in accordance with the personnel policies. In continuing centers, raises should be considered.

The director keeps additional records relating to the budget category *salaries*. Professional staff may be paid monthly, biweekly, or weekly, but their salaries are a fixed expense regardless of the number of hours worked as long as that individual remains on the payroll. Other staff receive wages based on number of hours worked during the pay period. Employees who are paid hourly must have some way to record the amount of time spent on the job if that is the basis on which they are paid. Some centers have employees record their working time on weekly time cards or by signing in and out on the computer. These records are referred to when paychecks are prepared. The director keeps a record of the sick days and the professional days used for all employees, including those who are salaried. Payments are made to each individual employee on the basis agreed on in the employment contract. In small centers where staff have the same schedule daily, time sheets may not be kept. In any event, the director is responsible for keeping track of hours worked, sick leave, and vacation time. Here again, entering this information into a computer database enables the fiscal officer to prepare up-to-date reports and facilitates preparation of the payroll.

The employer must obtain a federal taxpayer identification number from the IRS because before the employee is paid, the employer must make the appropriate deductions from the amount earned. These deductions may include federal, state, and local income taxes; Social Security tax; retirement; and medical insurance. Some centers, at the employee's request, deduct union dues, parking fees, or contributions to the United Way and other fund-raising groups. When these categories are part of a computer program, changes in percentages or dollar amounts can be made simply and accurately. An explanation of each deduction must be provided to each employee with each paycheck.

Information is available from the Internal Revenue Service regarding federal income tax. Each employee is required to file a W-4 form with the center upon employment and to update it as needed. These forms, available from the IRS, enable the employer to determine how much tax must be withheld from each paycheck, based on that employee's income and exemptions. The employer also must check with state and local governments about income taxes that may have to be withheld. The person in charge of preparing the payroll is responsible for learning what the deductions are and for seeing that they are made correctly. Your accountant can list the taxes for which your business is liable.

The director must give each employee a W-2 form by January 31 of each year, showing how much the employee earned during the previous year and how much was paid in taxes. The form may also include information about how much the center provided for health insurance, retirement, or any other monetary benefits. Many employers also provide an annual summary of benefits, including in-kind benefits such as meals provided by the center.

The employer serves as a collection agent, turning over the deducted money to the appropriate agency. Tax dollars are sent to the nearest IRS center, the state treasury, and the local government treasury. For Social Security, the employer contributes an amount equal to the amount deducted from the employee's pay; this amount is based on a rate determined by the federal government, and both the employer's and the employee's portions are sent by the employer to the IRS. Workers' compensation is paid entirely by the employer. This program covers payments to the employee for job-related injuries, diseases, and disabilities that occur as a result of working conditions.

The director must check with each taxing body to determine the amount of taxes to be withheld and the time at which they must be reported and paid. Penalties and interest are charged if payments are late or inadequate, and these costs are paid by the center, not the employee. If the center provides benefits such as medical insurance or collects fees for these benefits from employees' pay, the director is responsible for making the payments at the appropriate time.

Staff members also may be on unpaid leave. Current laws require that certain leaves be available to staff for circumstances such as child rearing. The returning staff member is not guaranteed the exact job but is guaranteed employment when the legal leave concludes. Centers also may create additional opportunities for leave. In any case, accurate records must be kept of leaves requested, granted, and used, and the director or designee is responsible for knowing and following related laws.

Payroll checks must be delivered to the employees at the agreed-upon time. Staff morale is lowered considerably when paychecks are not ready on the appointed day. Accuracy is essential.

Even in a small center, the magnitude of fiscal record keeping may seem overwhelming to many directors. Conceivably, the director could keep up with the day-to-day records, but even a part-time assistant would be a wise investment in terms of accuracy and currency.

If you are not already knowledgeable about financial planning and record keeping, gaining this knowledge is essential, at least at a basic level. Even when a director has no direct responsibility for financial records, being unable to understand them is unacceptable. Many books and articles are available to guide you. If you are a real financial beginner, Gail Jack's book *The Business of Child Care: Management and Financial Strategies* will start you off with the basics (Jack, 2005). It contains several sample forms to give you an idea of how they look and what they include. The numbers included are not meant to be used by a center. Rather, you will need to create your own budget and, therefore, your own financial reports.

SUMMARY

To provide a good program for young children, a center must delegate the responsibility for developing and carrying out a financial plan to a competent financial director or committee. The overall plan must be carried out by a person who has knowledge of basic accounting and budgeting procedures and an understanding of the requirements of a good program for young children.

The plan must be based on the priorities for meeting children's needs and on the available funds. The major tool used by the financial director is the budget, a plan for balancing income and expenses. The director is responsible for all other financial matters, including designing budget systems, ordering goods and services, making payments, recording transactions, and preparing the new budget. An appropriate computer program can save time and money and, if used correctly, can provide timely, accurate data in a readily accessible format.

Perhaps your personal checkbook is seldom balanced. However, a center director must record all transactions immediately or see that the person responsible is doing so. Even when another staff member is in charge of financial record keeping, it is the director's responsibility to keep apprised fully of the center's finances on a frequent and regular basis.

CLASS ASSIGNMENTS

1. Prepare a start-up budget for a center designed to serve 40 preschoolers. Decide where your center will be housed, whether it will be for-profit or not-for-profit, and who will be implementing the start-up plan. Record your answers on Working Paper 6–1.

2. Using Working Paper 6–2, list the facilities, goods, and services you will need to purchase for a year of operating a child care program for 60 children and provide the cost of each category. Assume that the start-up equipment is already in place, and include in your plan only replacement and supplementary equipment. Provide for classroom, general, and office supplies and for food for one year. Also list the number and type of personnel needed for one year and include benefits and other items that will cost money. If you feel that some items could be donated, list those as in-kind contributions. Then total all the costs. How much will your year's budget cost per child?

3. Ask an insurance agent about the types and the cost of insurance recommended for an early childhood education center in your area. Report your findings on Working Paper 6–3.

4. Check with several early childhood education directors in your community about the cost per child per week for their centers. Find out what services are provided for this amount of money. Record your findings on Working Paper 6–4.

5. Survey four centers to determine the salary ranges for various positions such as teacher, assistant teacher, and director. Is there much difference among these salary ranges? To what do you attribute the differences or similarities? Report your findings on Working Paper 6–5.

Note: To avoid overburdening individuals in your community, your instructor may assign you names of people to contract.

CLASS EXERCISES

1. Using the budget provided in Working Paper 6–6, answer the following questions.

   a. What is the overhead cost per child per week?

   b. What are the weekly expenses for the infant program on a per-child basis?

   c. What are the weekly expenses for the toddler program on a per-child basis?

   d. What are the weekly expenses for the pre-school program on a per-child basis?

   e. Consider the overhead cost per child plus the infant expenses per child. What is the total cost to provide care for an infant? What is the difference between that cost and the amount received in tuition for one infant for a year?

   f. Consider the overhead cost per child plus the toddler expenses per child. What is the total cost to provide care for a toddler? What is the difference between that cost and the amount received in tuition for one toddler for a year?

   g. Consider the overhead cost per child plus the preschool expenses per child. What is the total cost to provide care for a pre-schooler? What is the difference between that cost and the amount received in tuition for one preschooler for a year?

   h. How do you think the difference is accounted for? How does this director balance the budget?

2. Using the Sample Cash Flow Statement (Director's Resource 6–2) as a guide, complete Working Paper 6–7. Assume these January estimates: cash at beginning of period is $1,600, total cash available is $30,000, and total cash paid out is $29,000. Fill in the rest of the chart with hypothetical figures to show cash at the end of March. Explain what the figures mean.

WORKING PAPER 6-1

(for use with Class Assignment 1)

List the items you will include in a start-up budget for a center preparing to serve 40 preschoolers. Indicate whether your center will be for-profit or not-for-profit, where it will be housed, and who will be responsible for implementing the start-up plan.

WORKING PAPER 6-2

(for use with Class Assignment 2)

FACILITIES, GOODS, AND SERVICES FORM

List the facilities, goods, and services you will need for one year of full-day child care for 60 children. Assume that start-up equipment is already in place. List the cost of each category. You may refer to online or print services.

Total: Cost per child for one year. $ _____

WORKING PAPER 6-3

(for use with Class Assignment 3)

INSURANCE COSTS FORM

1. What types of insurance are recommended for an early childhood center in your area?

2. What is the approximate cost of this coverage?

WORKING PAPER 6-4

(for use with Class Assignment 4)

COST VERSUS SERVICE

1. Center A:

   Cost per child per week is $ _____

   Services provided:

2. Center B:

   Cost per child per week is $ _____

   Services provided:

3. Center C:

   Cost per child per week is $ _____

   Services provided:

WORKING PAPER 6-5

(for use with Class Assignment 5)

SALARY RANGE FORM

Salary	*Center A*	*Center B*	*Center C*	*Center D*
Director:				
Teacher:				
Assistant teacher:				

Similarities or differences may be attributed to:

WORKING PAPER 6-6

(for use with Class Exercise 1)

SAMPLE BUDGET BY PROGRAM

Director	$31,000	
FICA, FUTA, WC	3,100	
Health Insurance	2,000	
Cook	10,000	
FICA, FUTA, WC	1,000	
Maintenance and Repair	4,000	
Cleaning Service	10,000	
Custodial Supplies	500	
Insurance (Liability and Building)	4,000	
Bookkeeping/Audit	12,000	
Rent	20,000	
Food	30,000	
Education Supplies	5,000	
Utilities/Telephone	15,000	
Office and Paper Supplies	2,000	
Training/Consultants	2,000	
Licenses	700	
Travel/Field Trips	1,500	
Advertising	500	
TOTAL		$154,300
Overhead Charge per Child ($154,300/73)		$2,114

INFANT EXPENSES (BASED ON A 3:1 RATIO):

Infant Primary Caregivers (3)	54,000	
Infant Aides (2)	14,000	
FICA, FUTA, WC	6,800	
Health Insurance	6,000	
Substitutes	4,000	
Vacancy (5%)	3,861	
TOTAL		$88,661
Overhead (9 × $2114)		19,026
TOTAL INFANT EXPENSES		$107,687
TOTAL INFANT INCOME (9 × $165 × 52)		77,220
TOTAL INFANT PROFIT/<LOSS>		($30,467)

(continues)

WORKING PAPER 6-6
(continued)

(for use with Class Exercise 1)

TODDLER EXPENSES (BASED ON A 5:1 RATIO):

Toddler Head Teacher	24,000		
Toddler Assistant Teacher	17,000		
Toddler Aide	7,000		
FICA, FUTA, WC	5,000		
Health Insurance	4,000		
Substitutes	3,000		
Vacancy (8%)	6,240		
TOTAL		$66,240	
Overhead (10 × $2114)		21,140	
TOTAL TODDLER EXPENSES			$87,380
TOTAL TODDLER INCOME (10 × $150 × 52)			78,000
TODDLER PROFIT/<LOSS>			($9,380)

PRESCHOOL EXPENSES (BASED ON A 9:1 RATIO):

Head Teachers (3)	78,000		
Assistant Teachers (3)	51,000		
Preschool Aides (3)	21,840		
FICA, FUTA, WU	15,000		
Health Insurance	12,000		
Substitutes	9,000		
Vacancy (8%)	29,661		
TOTAL		$216,501	
Overhead (54 × $2114)		114,156	
TOTAL PRESCHOOL EXPENSES			$330,657
PRESCHOOL INCOME (44 × $140 × 52)			320,320
PRESCHOOL INCOME (SUBSIDIZED) (10 × $97 × 52)			50,440
TOTAL PRESCHOOL INCOME			$370,760
PRESCHOOL PROFIT/<LOSS>			$40,103
TOTAL CENTER PROFIT/<LOSS>			$256

WORKING PAPER 6-7

(for use with Class Exercise 2)

CASH FLOW TRACKING

Period: Year ____

	January		February		March		Total	
	Estimate	Actual	Estimate	Actual	Estimate	Actual	Estimate	Actual
1. Cash at Beginning of Period								
2. Add: Cash Received from:								
Tuition-Parents								
Dept. Human Services								
USDA								
Donations								
Community Chest								
Other sources ____								
Total Cash Received								
Total Cash Available								
3. Subtract: Cash Paid out:								
Payroll								
Supplies								
food								
educational								
office								
miscellaneous								
Insurance								
Taxes								
Employee benefits								
Other expenses								
Equipment								
Total Cash paid out								
Cash at End of Period								

DIRECTOR'S RESOURCE 6-1

SAMPLE CHILD CARE CENTER BUDGET

INCOME

TUITION

Infants (8 × $160 × 51)	$65,280	
Toddlers (12 × $150 × 51)	91,800	
Preschooler's (51 × $135 × 51)	351,135	
Total Gross Tuition		508,215

DISCOUNTS
Vacancy (3%)

Total Discounts		<15,246>

OTHER INCOME

Application Fees (30 × $20)	600	
Interest on account	600	
Fund-raisers	1,000	
Grant award (literacy program)	2,500	
Total Other Income		4,700
TOTAL INCOME		**$497,669**

EXPENSES

PERSONNEL

Director	30,000	
Head Teachers (5)	135,000	
Teachers (5)	100,000	
Assistants (10 part time)	46,800	
Substitutes	2,000	
Secretary	8,000	
Custodian	7,000	
Cook	8,000	
FICA, Workers' Comp., Unemploy. and Insurance	62,500	
Total Personnel		$399,300

RENT	31,000	
UTILITIES AND TELEPHONE	17,465	
ADVERTISING	1,000	
FOOD	35,000	
OFFICE SUPPLIES	1,000	
CUSTODIAL SUPPLIES	700	
CLASSROOM EQUIPMENT & SUPPLIES	5,200	
C.P.A. FEES	1,000	
INSURANCE	3,500	
LICENSES	500	
STAFF DEVELOPMENT/TRAINING	1,500	
TEACHERS' PETTY CASH	504	
Total Non-personnel		98,369
TOTAL		**$497,669**

DIRECTOR'S RESOURCE 6-2

SAMPLE PROJECTED CASH FLOW STATEMENT

Period: Year 20xx

	January Estimated	January Actual	February Estimated	February Actual	March Estimated	March Actual	Total Estimated	Total Actual
1. Cash at Beginning of Period	$1,430	$1,500	$1,071	$1,074	–$983	–$730	$1,518	$1,844
2. Add: Cash received from:								
Tuition-Parents	28,595	28,395	26,600	26,800	30,590	30,400	85,785	85,595
Dept. Human Services	520	507	520	520	520	494	1,560	1,521
USDA								
Donations			100				100	
Community Chest								
Other Sources								
Total Cash Received	$29,115	$28,902	$27,220	$27,320	$31,110	$30,894	$87,445	$87,116
Total Cash Available	30,545	30,402	28,291	28,394	30,127	30,164	88,963	88,960
3. Subtract: Cash Paid out:								
Payroll	20,400	20,400	20,400	20,400	20,400	20,400	61,200	61,200
Supplies								
food	2,800	2,753	2,600	2,614	2,800	2,817	8,200	8,184
educational	100	102	100	79	100	94	300	275
office	50	–	50	84	50	27	150	111
miscellaneous	100	20	100	123	100	131	300	274
Insurance	500	500	500	500	500	500	1,500	1,500
Taxes	–	–	–	–	–	–	–	–
Employee benefits	3,060	3,060	3,060	3,060	3,060	3,060	9,180	9,180
Other expenses								
rent	1,000	1,000	1,000	1,000	1,000	1,000	3,000	3,000
utilities	1,264	1,264	1,264	1,264	1,264	1,264	3,792	3,792
Equipment	200	229	200	–	200	305	600	534
Total Cash paid out	$29,474	$29,328	$29,274	$29,124	$29,474	$29,598	$88,222	$88,050
Cash at End of Period	$1,071	$1,074	–$983	–$730	$653	$566	$741	$910

DIRECTOR'S RESOURCE 6-3

SAMPLE INCOME STATEMENT
FOR THE YEAR ENDED DECEMBER 31, 20XX

Income Statement
For the Year Ended December 31, 20xx

Revenues

Infant Program Income	$70,500	
Toddler Program Income	64,500	
Preschool Program Income	247,120	
Federal Child Care Food Program	41,500	
Donations/Contributions	500	
Parent Fund-raising	1,100	
Other Income	50	
Total Income		**$425,270**

Expenses

Salaries/Wages	267,100	
Health Benefits	19,650	
Employment Taxes and Insurance	21,840	
Management Services Fee	15,000	
Training/Consultant Fees	7,200	
Food/Beverage Supplies	21,300	
Educational Supplies	4,100	
Office & Paper Supplies	3,300	
Rent	16,000	
Payroll Service Fees	1,420	
Cleaning Service Fees	8,920	
Custodial Supplies	950	
Equipment Expense	2,800	
Utilities/Telephone Expense	11,300	
Garbage Removal	650	
Advertising	850	
Travel/Field Trips	1,600	
Bookkeeping/Audit Service Fees	11,500	
Licenses	625	
Maintenance & Repair Expense	5,920	
Insurance Expense	3,200	
Total Expense		425,225
Net Income (Net Loss)		**$45**

DIRECTOR'S RESOURCE 6-4

SAMPLE STATEMENT OF FINANCIAL POSITION
AS OF APRIL 30, 20XX

Assets

Cash–Operating	$7,000
Cash–Payroll	8,000
Accounts Receivable	11,200
Educational Supplies	900
Office Supplies	400
Property, Plant, and Equipment	42,000
Total Assets:	$69,500

Liabilities

Accounts Payable	$11,000	
Wages Payable	5,000	
Mortgage Payable	32,000	
Long-Term Liabilities	11,000	
Depreciation	4,000	
Total Liabilities:		63,000

Equity

Capital	6,500
Total Liabilities and Equity	$69,500

REFERENCES

Center for the Child Care Workforce. (2004). Retrieved November 2004, from http://www.ccw.org.

Center for the Future of Children. (1996, Fall). *Financing child care: The future of children.* The David and Lucile Packard Foundation. Los Altos, CA: Author.

The Child Care Law Center. (1996, September). The fair labor standards act and the child care industry. *Child Care Information Exchange, 82–86.*

Current data on the salaries and benefits of the U.S. early childhood education workforce, 2004 edition. Retrieved October 27, 2005, from http://www.ccw.org.

Does your insurance coverage fit your needs? (2002, November). *Child Care Information Exchange, 148,* 80–83.

Jack, G. (2005). *The business of child care: Management and financial strategies.* Clifton Park, NY: Thomson Delmar Learning.

National Association for the Education of Young Children. (1998). Quality, compensation and affordabiliy: The updated staffing study: A valuable resource for advocates. *Young Children, 53* (5), 42–43.

Shulman, K. (2000). The high cost of child care puts quality care out of reach for many families. Washington, DC: Children's Defense Fund. Retrieved April 11, 2005, from http://www.futureofchildren.org.

Stephens, K. (1991). *Confronting your bottom line: Financial guide for child care centers.* Redmond, WA: Exchange Press.

United States General Accounting Office. (1990, January). *Early childhood education: What are the costs of high quality programs?* Briefing report of the chairman, Committee on Labor and Human Resources, U.S. Senate.

Whitebook, M. C., Howes, C., & Phillips, D. (1998). *Worthy work, unlivable wages: The national child care staffing study,* 1988–1997. Washington, DC: Center for the Child Care Workforce.

Additional resources for this chapter can be found on the Online Companion™ at http://www.earlychilded.delmar.com. This supplemental material includes relevant Web links, Web activities, and case studies that apply the concepts presented in this chapter. In addition, the Working Papers and Director's Resources are available for download, allowing you to complete Class Exercises and Class Assignments electronically.

CHAPTER 7
Funding the Program

The director is responsible for ensuring that funds are available, but board members often assist in securing needed loans or grants.

OBJECTIVES

After reading this chapter, you should be able to:

- Describe the director's role in funding a center.
- Explain the difference between start-up funds and operational funds.
- List several resources available for child care financing.
- Describe several types of financial reports that must be prepared by the child care center director.

A major component of the director's responsibility is ensuring sufficient funds to establish and operate the program. Although this assignment is ongoing, peak times occur when a new program is created and when additional components are to be added to an existing program. Of course, every director annually addresses the upcoming year's funding, and experienced directors recognize the need for long-range fiscal planning. Certainly, seeking additional funding is important, but shepherding carefully the funds one has is essential. In child care, there are no dollars to waste or lose through carelessness.

Typically in child care centers, the director's role is demanding in terms of time, energy, and talent. Throughout this text, you have read about the wide range of expectations placed on the director. When it comes to funding, it often is wise to obtain needed assistance in one of several ways. First, the director may assign other staff to assume some additional responsibilities such as organizing equipment orders or conducting inventory. Second, the director may enlist the aid of one or more volunteers to take on some responsibilities, thereby providing time for the director to engage in fund-raising. For example, a volunteer may conduct center tours for prospective clients. An enthusiastic parent may do an excellent job of pointing out things parents are especially interested in knowing. Or a volunteer may answer the telephone one afternoon a week to provide the director with uninterrupted proposal writing time. Finally, volunteers may participate in the fund-raising process in myriad ways that will be discussed throughout the chapter.

Directors of several centers may support each other by creating a joint fund-raising plan. They even may be able to hire a fund-raising consultant to guide their efforts, particularly if they have limited knowledge of the process. In the long run, such an expense may be quite productive.

It is essential to recognize that the director alone cannot manage the entire fund-raising process. Were that the expectation, the probability of limited funds would be likely.

FUNDING A NEW CENTER

Obviously, starting a new center or expanding an existing center requires a significant amount of money. Before seeking a loan or investing personal assets, remember that you are starting a business. The U.S. Small Business Administration (SBA) and the Service Corps of Retired Executives (SCORE) are good resources (their Web sites are http://www.sba.gov and http://www.score.org, respectively).

A prospective center developer who does not have a strong business background should seek assistance. The SBA recommends that before starting a business you answer the following questions:

- What niche or void will my business fill?
- What services or products will I sell?
- Is my idea practical and will it fill a need?
- Who is my competition?
- What is my business's advantage over existing firms?
- Can I deliver a better-quality service?
- What skills and experience do I bring to the business?
- What will be my legal structure?
- How will my company's business records be maintained?
- What insurance coverage will I need?
- What equipment or supplies will I need?
- How will I compensate myself?
- What are my resources?
- What financing will I need?

- Where will my business be located?
- What will I name my business?

Another possibility is purchasing an existing business. Such a purchase involves real estate, possibly equipment, the name of the center, and the good will the center has established (if that is the case). Linsmeier (2003) explains how a child care business is valued. As a buyer, you will need to research the value that the seller uses and how that amount was calculated. At the same time, maintaining confidentiality is essential so that the current enrollment is not diminished based on parents' anxiety about changes in ownership. You would not want to buy a center whose status was being compromised by rumors.

In any case, check with your state department of labor about specific policies that will govern your business. For example, you may need to register your business name and get a business license and sales tax number, and you must definitely open a separate business bank account. You will need to know the federal and state laws governing employees and stay current with business publications in your area. Gather data on whether the market for child care is growing or declining in the area in which you are planning your business. Your local chamber of commerce may be able to help with information and may provide valuable contacts. Even when your business is going well, stay current with your community and its needs.

To obtain money, you must know exactly how much you need, why you need it, when you will need it, and how you will pay it back. You must also commit sufficient capital such as a second mortgage on your home. The lender will obtain your credit report; therefore, it is wise to check your own credit report before applying for a loan.

Start-Up Funding

Start-up capital is the money that must be available before the program begins and the money needed to support the initial program operation until the flow of tuition and other funds is sufficient to support the ongoing program. Once a director is hired, it takes a minimum of two to three months to complete the necessary preliminary planning before the program begins. Money for space, equipment, office supplies, and some staff salaries must be available during these early months before the center opens. Programs often are underenrolled during the first few months of operation. Checks from funding sources are sometimes delayed until the program operation is well under way. Therefore, it also is wise to have sufficient capital on hand at the outset to operate the program for at least six months. These operating monies to cover costs for three months of planning and six months of operation are in addition to the capital needed to finance the purchasing or remodeling of a site and to purchase equipment and supplies for the children's program. In other words, it takes a considerable amount of money to start a program, and it is important to make careful calculations to ensure that the start-up money is adequate to cover the costs until regular operating funds become available.

A director who has been a teacher and is now planning to open a center will notice that lenders, suppliers, inspectors, and insurers will not ask about what kind of relationships she plans to establish with children and families, what the curricular objectives are, or what kinds of special activities will be provided. They are interested in business. The teacher-turned-director will have to have or develop this new focus while continuing to focus on children and families and their needs and interests. Although the director may have a close relationship with families since she and they care about their children, she is still the administrator. She must be careful to avoid crossing an invisible line. At some point, the director may have to follow up on a slow tuition payment. A family may decide to dispute the way an injury was handled or to complain about the food being served.

Directors who have moved up from teaching must remember that as teachers they were authoritative. They knew what was appropriate for children and classrooms. Now they must also become authoritative about business. They must understand the finances of operating a center even if they don't have day-to-day responsibilities for that aspect of the work.

Most agency-sponsored centers are nonprofit, and many are eligible to receive funding from other community or governmental agencies once there is an established, ongoing program to fund. To get started, however, the agency may need to apply to foundations for funding. A sample grant application is shown in Director's Resource 7–1. Often agencies conduct campaigns, soliciting first from their own board members, who are expected to contribute. Next, businesses and others who have expressed interest in the work of the agency are approached. Some corporations that operate many centers, or very large centers, obtain funds from investors. Operators of small proprietary centers that are established for profit or that have no sponsoring agency must invest personal capital or arrange for a loan in order to get started. Foundation money is rarely offered to proprietary centers; instead, it is reserved for serving particular populations chosen by the foundation that meet specific foundation-determined goals.

DIRECTOR'S CORNER

"The bank wouldn't lend me the money to start a center. They said it would take too long to show a profit. Finally, we put our house up as collateral and we got the loan. But I didn't get any salary for three whole years. We're in good shape now after five years and we're expanding."

—Director, private for-profit center

Community Support

When the community expresses great interest in getting a program started, it may be possible to promote a successful fund-raising program. However, only relatively small amounts of money can be obtained through raffles, bake sales, or paper drives. Established philanthropic groups such as Kiwanis, Lions, various community groups, and fraternal organizations sometimes are willing to donate money to cover start-up costs such as equipment or to support a capital improvements fund-raising campaign. They may fund specific activities such as field trips. But like other funders, they seldom provide operating expenses.

A company may provide start-up funding for a center for its employees' children with the understanding that the director will need to secure adequate funding for operating costs from other sources, including tuition. If the company makes something the center could use, such as diapers or packaged food products, they may offer a continuing supply to the center. Other companies may offer a flex plan, a benefit that allows employees to set aside before-tax income to pay for child care. This benefit makes child care more affordable for families. In turn, it provides relatively reliable tuition payments for centers because an employee must show a paid receipt from the center or caregiver to collect his own before-tax dollars. If, by the end of the year, the employee has not used all of his child care benefit fund, the money reverts to the employer. Centers in public schools are usually funded through special government grants and the central administration may manage the budget. In the case of large chains of centers, the corporate office secures investors and funds the start-up of new centers based on its market research.

Programs that start without a sufficient funding base are in fiscal trouble from the outset. Since it is very difficult to maintain a balanced budget for an early childhood education program, it is paramount to keep a balanced budget at the outset by finding enough capital to cover start-up costs.

OPERATING FUNDS

Operating funds refers to the amount needed to run the center and must include all the regular budget items described in Chapter 6. Once the facility is established and the basic equipment has been purchased, income must be adequate to ensure daily program operation. Many centers have depended heavily on tuition, government funds, and United Way monies to provide most or all of their operating funds. An analysis of these sources for the 21st century indicates that in most cases, it is unlikely they will be sufficient to maintain the quality that centers must provide.

Fund-raising for operating costs must be planned carefully in terms of the benefit to be derived from the contributor's dollars. Imagine a contribution being used to pay for rather mundane, yet certainly essential, categories such as utilities and office supplies. Such usage may not encourage the giver. The creative fund-raiser frames requests in terms of projected program accomplishments. One director in an annual fund-raising letter labeled contributions as "your opportunity to nourish the minds and bodies of 62 of our youngest children." During the preceding weeks, she had sent the local newspapers (with parental permission) pictures of several children engaged in interesting projects such as writing invitations to their parents to visit their classroom, then walking to the post office to mail them and to meet the postmaster.

In determining the amount of funds needed, a breakeven chart is useful. You and your accountant can prepare such a chart by first determining the fixed costs of operating the center such as rent, utilities, and director's salary. These are costs that will remain at the same level, regardless of enrollment.

Next, variable costs are calculated. These are the costs for operating the program that change as children are added or subtracted. For example, when 4 or 5 children are added, the cook probably orders more food, more art materials are needed, and so forth.

Based on licensing requirements and center policies, when a certain enrollment is reached, an additional teacher must be employed. A simple example would be to think of a center with 30 children in which a 1:10 ratio is required. When the 31st child is added, the center must provide an additional teacher, even though the additional tuition generated by 1 child surely will not pay a teacher's salary. However, if 6 new children are added, it may be feasible financially to have four groups of 9 children. Of course, if tuition from 10 children is required to pay the expenses, then the director should not add children until she can ensure a class of 10 or realize that money will be lost on that class.

The director or accountant can figure a breakeven analysis, that is, how many children and at what tuition will be needed to offset costs. To get an idea of how this works, use the following steps:

1. First, calculate fixed costs. These must be paid no matter how many children are enrolled (rent, phone, utilities, insurance, equipment, salaries and benefits for director, cook, maintenance staff, and secretary and any other nonclassroom staff).

2. Determine the number of children you will serve.

3. Based on the number of children per teacher, calculate the number of teachers and the cost of teacher and assistant salaries and benefits.

4. Based on the number of children, estimate the cost of food and supplies.

5. Add the costs to be incurred (items 1, 3, and 4).

6. Divide the total (from line 5) by the number of children.

7. The dollar figure in line 6 represents the amount you will have to receive in tuition to break even.

8. If at any time you do not have full enrollment, you will lose money.

9. Therefore, you will want to build into your budget a cushion that will allow for underenrollment and overspending. One way to

accomplish this is to charge higher tuition than required to break even. However, if any of your tuition comes from government vouchers, you will be limited to the current voucher rate, which will almost certainly be below your tuition costs.

Costs for infants and toddlers are higher than for preschoolers while costs for school-age care are lower, based primarily on the teacher-to-child ratio. To determine breakeven costs when you serve a variety of age groups, do the following:

1. Divide fixed cost by the total number of children in all age groups (as described previously). The fixed cost for every child, regardless of age, is the same.

2. Calculate the variable cost for each age group separately (teaching staff, food, supplies).

3. Divide each age group's variable cost by the number of children in that age group to find the variable cost per child.

4. Add the variable cost per child and the fixed cost per child. This amount is the tuition that must be collected from that child to break even.

To carry this further, you may want to investigate how you would figure costs for a center serving eight infants and 36 preschoolers. Notice that although the variable costs for infants will be considerably higher than those for preschoolers, the fixed cost for each child remains the same. Therefore, preschool tuition, although spread over more children in this example, must, in effect, cover part of the cost of caring for infants. (The sample budget in Chapter 6, Working Paper 6–6, demonstrates that a center may lose money on infant care but cover that loss with tuition from preschoolers. Nonetheless, infant care is important for at least two reasons: (1) there is a major need for infant care in many communities, and (2) when children start in a center during infancy, the center hopes to retain them throughout their preschool years. If the number of preschool children in a center is decreased, the cost of infant care may have to increase.

By the same premise, school-age care can potentially balance the cost of care for younger children. Centers must carefully plan school-age tuition to be reasonable for families. However, because fewer staff are needed, before- and after-school care is less costly than preschool and may be financially helpful to centers serving preschoolers. The key factor remains retention of high quality care for all age groups.

Using a breakeven chart, the director projects the income based on the enrollment. She then looks for the points at which the total costs meet the income and checks to see at what enrollment levels that occurs (Stephens, 1991).

Despite the best effort of early childhood educators nationwide, the issue of funding child care centers presents several dilemmas. First, many parents simply cannot afford to pay the cost of care. Although government already provides large sums of tax revenues, that has never been enough to provide even basic quality for all the children who need care. At the same time, by far the largest part of the child care budget goes to staff salaries. Yet most staff salaries are deplorably low. "We know there is an overall quality problem. And the question is why. Why, when investments in early care and education are soaring, does quality remain low?" (Kagan, Brandon, Ripple, Maher, & Joesch, 2002.) Brandon, Kagan, and others are proposing a plan for financing universal early care and compensation. Major ideas include delineating a career lattice that would allow entry-level child care staff to begin work with limited previous training and then participate in professional development at no cost. Staff members with bachelor's degrees would be paid salaries in line with those of public school teachers. All staff would be expected to continue to participate in professional development activities. Directors need to be aware of such initiatives, to contribute ideas, and, above all, to work for improved quality in child care.

Tuition

When the center is largely dependent on tuition for operating funds, it will be necessary to balance the number of children to be enrolled, the amount of tuition their families can reasonably be expected to pay, and the amount of money needed to operate the program. The program will not always be fully enrolled; therefore, the budget should have at least a 3 percent to 8 percent vacancy rate built in. Programs just beginning may have only a few children enrolled for many months, necessitating close management of the initial budget and reduction of variable costs to the lowest possible level. Even some fixed costs can be reduced. For example, a director may employ one or two salaried teachers until the tuition receipts warrant the addition of more staff.

Since the salaries of most preschool teachers are unreasonably low, and since salaries comprise the biggest expenditure by far in an education budget, it is sensible to charge an amount that will provide the fairest possible salary to the staff. Therefore, the tuition rate should be based on a number of facts, including:

- the amount needed to meet professional commitments to staff.

- the amount that is reasonable in terms of the type of program offered to families.
- the amount charged by comparable centers in the area.

To assist parents or to attract clients, centers may decide to offer lower tuition when two children from the same family attend, or they may choose to offer one or more weeks' tuition free for vacation or illness. The director must balance this loss of income against the potential loss of two children or else must make the initial tuition rate high enough to cover such factors. However, since these costs are quite variable depending on how many two-child families are enrolled in the center at a given time, they may add to budget instability. Holding a space for an expected infant for partial tuition has a similar budgetary effect. Giving a free vacation week may negatively affect cash flow if most parents decide to take advantage of this plan during the same week, thereby severely curtailing income. This event would be particularly damaging in a center that used the cash, rather than accrual, method of accounting.

Some centers charge tuition on a sliding scale based on the parents' ability to pay. Often, these centers receive government or agency funds to supplement tuition income. A sliding fee scale formula is prepared that takes into account the amount of income, the number of dependents, and other circumstances such as extraordinary medical bills. However, whenever a family pays less than the actual cost of care, the difference must be covered by making the top of the scale higher than the cost so that some families pay more than the cost of care, or by securing outside funds. A sample sliding fee scale appears in Director's Resource 7–2.

Many center directors encounter situations in which parents would like to enroll their children but are unable to afford the tuition. You may want to plan for some sort of aid for either partial or full tuition. This can be accomplished by establishing a scholarship fund created by soliciting contributions, by charging more tuition than the cost per child and using the excess for scholarships, or by contacting agencies and foundations to ask them to support full or partial scholarships.

Think about the purpose of a scholarship. Do you want to assist families who are temporarily unable to afford tuition, families whose income falls between eligibility for government support and the ability to pay tuition, children from other cultures, or children with special needs? In any event, the purpose must be clear. To create a scholarship program, you will need an application process, a review process, and a system for record keeping of funds contributed and disbursed. If the tuition assistance program is large, particularly in a multiple-site organization, additional staff time may be needed (Vast, 2003).

Tuition charges are set by estimating what families are willing and able to pay for services and by considering what rates are charged by competing agencies in the community. Local professional organizations or the local or state universities may have information about the amount of tuition that reasonably can be charged in a particular community. Unless a program offers something very different from that offered by nearby centers (such as NAEYC accreditation), it may be difficult to convince parents to pay significantly higher tuition for one program over another; therefore, tuition rates must be reasonably competitive. On the other hand, if tuition is lowered to attract clients, it may be difficult to cover costs and compete with other centers in offering teachers appropriate salaries and in hiring competent staff. Directors of quality centers often have to educate members of the community about the differences in program quality and, in particular, about the value of well-prepared and more costly staff.

Although most programs charge tuition, sometimes that charge is even higher than tuition at a college. A typical range in a community might be $115 to $215 per child per week. Infant tuition is higher than tuition for preschoolers because of the higher teacher-to-child ratio in infant rooms. Usually parents of children needing child care have had limited opportunity to save for tuition because they are just beginning a career or because they are working in low-paying jobs. College tuition is often supplemented by governmental support, endowments, and grants. Completing college is important for many people, but more and more attention is now being given to the importance of the early childhood years as the foundation for future learning.

Community Resources

Many early childhood education programs are subsidized by local charities and church groups or by United Way funds. Church groups or other charitable sponsoring agencies typically do not provide cash to help meet the operating budget. Instead, they provide in-kind contributions such as free rent, janitorial service, coverage of utility bills, volunteer help, and so forth. If the director and the board find themselves with an unbalanced budget at the end of the year because of unforeseen problems with enrollments or unexpected expenditures, some sponsoring agencies will cover the losses. This practice is particularly prevalent in situations where one of the sponsoring agency's goals is to provide child care services to low-income members of the community. However, the director who is not managing her budget well is not likely to be bailed out more than once.

Boards and directors may want to respond to newly identified needs and to creative ideas. To meet these needs, seeking funding is almost inevitable. Occasionally, whoever funds operating costs also may fund special projects. More often, special funding must be sought. Consider the program that served several children—Mindy, Dashawn, and Ronnie—with developmental delays. The teacher observed that they seemed very interested in caring for classroom plants. She asked the director for gardening supplies and a section of playground so that her whole class could create a garden. Mindy, Dashawn, and Ronnie were to be assigned special responsibilities. Recognizing a creative idea, the director went to a local nursery for help. The owner not only contributed tools and seeds but also volunteered to help the class create the garden and joined them at circle time to discuss her job. Later, the class visited the nursery. Having been so delighted with the children's interest and the positive response from parents, several of whom later made purchases from her, the owner made a follow-up call to the director. She offered to provide a small greenhouse for the school so that the children could start plants earlier the following year. Imagine how much everyone benefited from one idea and one director's efforts to provide funding.

United Way funds, raised through a United Appeal campaign, are available for child care services in many communities. Eligibility for these community funds varies depending on the locale, the amount of money available, and the demands placed on that source of funding.

As a director of a program that may need community support money, you should familiarize yourself with eligibility requirements in your community so that you can plan accordingly. Often, a number of preliminary steps must be taken before a program can be presented for funding consideration. Also, some United Way agencies will not give start-up money or operating funds to new programs. Eligibility requirements for funds typically include the following points:

1. The agency must be an incorporated, voluntary, nonprofit, charitable organization possessing tax-exempt status under Section 501 (c)(3) from the Internal Revenue Service. The agency must be licensed by the appropriate authority; must carry on a needed health, welfare, or social service; and must have a qualified and representative governing body that serves without compensation.

2. The agency must have and must implement a written policy of nondiscrimination and non-segregation on the basis of race, ethnic origin, disabling condition, sex, or religion regarding its governing body, its employees, and the people it serves.

3. The agency must have been established and must have continued to function for a minimum of three years (number varies here) before applying for funds.

4. The agency must be willing to cooperate in the United Way fund-raising campaign and to abide by all the policies of the United Way agency.

Once the minimum eligibility requirements have been met, the necessary steps for funding consideration must be taken by the director of the center or by a designated board member. The director usually is the only person who has all the necessary information for completing application forms and, therefore, is the one ultimately responsible for filing the numerous ongoing attendance and financial records most United Way agencies require. If a board member assumes this responsibility, the director still must provide the necessary data. Therefore, it is important that the director be familiar with the application procedures and clearly understand the ongoing reporting requirements for funded programs *before* entering into any agreements with this or any other funding agency.

The application for funding may seem intimidating to some directors and hinder them from applying for available funds. The process does become easier as the director gains more experience in applying and finds that many applications require similar information. Once it has been gathered, some of the data can be reused in subsequent proposals. Nonetheless, directors must be prepared to spend a great deal of time and energy on routine reporting if they expect to use outside funds.

Foundations

A *foundation* is a fund administered by trustees and operated under state or federal charter. Foundation funds sometimes are made available to child care centers for major equipment purchases or for a special project. Occasionally, a foundation will provide funds for building or remodeling a facility or for training staff. Foundation support for a program depends on whether the trustees of the foundation have declared education, or more specifically, early childhood education, as an area of interest.

Large philanthropic foundations such as the Ford, Carnegie, and Rockefeller Foundations have broad-ranging programs with specific interest areas that change periodically. For example, there may be a general interest in funding innovative educational programs, but monies may be going into literacy or single-parent programs during one funding period, only to shift to programs for preschool children with developmental delays or to innovative child care models during the next funding period. Smaller foundations may limit support to programs in a certain geographic area or to a given problem area that may change every few years, while other special-interest foundations limit support efforts to very specific interest areas that do not change.

The Foundation Center is an organization with branches in several major cities. Free classes on various aspects of funding are frequently offered at its sites. In addition, individuals may register to receive regular e-mails from the center (http://www.fdncenter.org). The center has published three research reports, which you can view at its locations or purchase online. The reports include *Foundation Growth and Giving Estimates: 2004; Foundation Giving Trends: Update on Funding Priorities;* and *Foundation Yearbook: Facts and Figures on Private and Community Foundations.*

Money from corporate foundations is available in many communities. In smaller cities, it is wise to solicit funds from small, local corporations that often have some funds set aside for use by local agencies. Frequently, the small corporate funds are controlled by corporate managers who are very sensitive to the public relations value of making a gift to local agencies that in turn, will give due credit and recognition to the funder.

In an earlier example, a small-business owner recognized a creative and worthwhile idea. She was interested in helping children learn about plants and, therefore, responded to the center's request. Foundations, too, are looking for innovative ideas and approaches to solving problems. You can approach foundations with your opportunity for them to support a good cause (Mitchell, 1996). Your well-prepared and enthusiastic presentation, as well as your strong interpersonal and communication skills, will improve your chances of obtaining funding. Keep in mind, however, that foundations provide only a small portion of the large amounts of money required to provide good child care.

When directors plan to approach a foundation for money, they must know precisely what they expect to do with the money and how they expect to do it. Their appeal for money must be tailor-made to the foundation's interest areas, and all funding requests must move through the proper channels. However, personal contacts with foundation trustees or other people connected with the foundation are considered very helpful. Perhaps a member of the center's parent group or a board member has personal contacts with a foundation or can help find the best channels to use for personal contacts.

Funds tend to flow toward challenging and interesting programs in well-run organizations rather than to needy institutions that are faltering.

Government Funding

Federal, state, and local governments all have a commitment to the care of the children of working mothers, with the federal government being the forerunner of that movement as far back as the early 1940s. Although state and local government agencies have been involved in licensing and monitoring early childhood education programs for some time, the availability of state and local money for child care for working mothers is relatively recent when compared to federal monies available on a somewhat sporadic basis for about 50 years. Government monies typically are available for programs that serve low-income families or those that serve children with special needs. Currently, the Head Start program and the proliferation of programs for young children with special needs serve as evidence of the federal government's focus on these children's education. California was the first state to establish an extensive network of state-supported child care centers. However, New York, Ohio, and several other states are moving to expand their state-supported systems. Although some funds are available, many children, particularly in certain areas, are underserved or receive no services.

A number of major sources of federal funding were established during the 1960s and continue to provide some basic support for child care and for children with special needs. Early in 2001, Congress passed an appropriations bill. Ten million dollars was appropriated for training early childhood staff in high-poverty areas. A loan forgiveness program for higher education for child care workers received a $1 million appropriation, and the Child and Adult Care Food Program was extended to some for-profit centers (Children's Defense Fund, 2001).

The Child Care and Development Block Grant general funds provided $1.9 billion for after-school programs and included some set-asides (portions of funding that must be spent in specific ways). Head Start was funded at more than $6 billion. In 2004, more than $2 billion in tax dollars was allocated to the Child Care and Development Block Grant, while more than $7 billion went to Head Start. Approximately $7 million was allocated for training and technical assistance (retrieved from U.S. Government Web site, April, 2005).

Often, legislation involving child care is controversial. As more women work outside the home and more children grow up in single-parent families, child care has taken on new political importance.

Center directors need to keep informed of current and pending legislation, and make their views known to state and federal legislators who can provide up-to-date information. Local and national organizations such as NAEYC are good sources of information on legislation related to young children, and local libraries can help you find the names of your legislators. The Children's Defense Fund provides a newsletter available through e-mail. Regular updates and bulletins on pending legislation are provided. Governmental bodies, individual government officials, and a myriad of organizations related to funding, education, and similar issues are found on the Internet.

Center directors are responsible for maintaining current knowledge of how federal, state, and local dollars are being allocated. They should make their opinions known to their legislators and determine whether their programs or the children they serve might be eligible for various types of funding. If so, they certainly should give serious consideration to applying for those dollars.

Some programs are funded almost entirely by state or federal government tax dollars. Although one might argue that three-year-olds are just as entitled to government funds as are seven-year-olds who attend public schools, relying on tax monies to support a program totally is risky. Funding for some programs or individuals has been eliminated rather abruptly, and there is no guarantee that funds will continue from year to year. Many public elementary and secondary schools engage in additional fund-raising for aspects of the program that are usually considered integral parts of schooling such as music, athletics, field trips, and library books. Depending solely on government (taxpayer) dollars is unwise and unrealistic.

Loans

At some point, you may have to apply for a loan in order to make desired or essential improvements or to enable you to grow your center. Banks often are not interested in child care centers because the margin of profit is quite low, particularly in the case of small, new centers. Nonetheless, enterprising directors have obtained loans, in large measure because they were prepared to answer a range of financial questions. Obviously, you will need to be able to explain why you are asking for a loan. You may be asked to provide a business plan, a document that explains your company or agency to the funder. Such a plan includes an overview of the center, its purpose, and basic operation procedures. You may include a list of the staff, a description of insurance carried by the center, an inventory of major equipment, and fiscal records. The Small Business Administration can help you with this (see Director's Resource 7–3). Providing clear financial records and realistic projections is essential. If you do not have every record with you, demonstrate your organizational skills by following up quickly with the requested documentation. Keep in mind that you are arranging a business deal for which your agency will pay in interest. Even if you are applying for a grant from a foundation or governmental body, a good business plan will allow the funder to assess whether the funds granted will be used wisely.

Individuals who have visited the center can tell potential contributors about its strengths and needs.

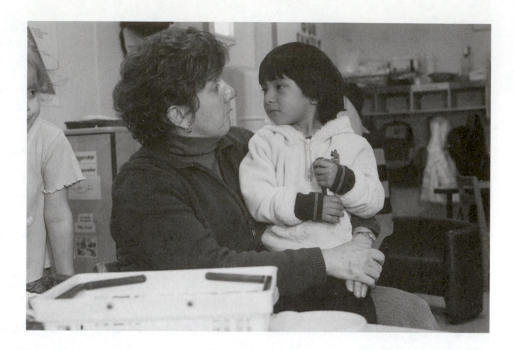

FUND-RAISING

Since most directors will need to be involved in annual and special fund-raising, they must establish policies and procedures regarding this responsibility. These policies and procedures then can be used to create individual funding campaigns. Step one is to find the people who will be the fund-raisers. If board members have been selected with this activity in mind, at least some of them will be able to contribute significantly, monetarily or in service, to the fund-raising program. All board members should understand their responsibility to make a contribution to the center, no matter how small. Some board members may have connections with community members or corporations who are prospects for center support. All should be willing to ask for contributions.

Preparing for Fund-raising

Before beginning any fund-raising program, the board and director must make sure that the center has been formally chartered by the state and has IRS exemption. Forms for the latter can be obtained from the IRS. This status permits individual donors to deduct the amount contributed to the center as a charitable contribution. Specific procedures must be followed depending on the size of the contribution and the value (if any) that the contributor receives in return such as a dinner, book, or ticket to an event. Written reports are required in these cases, and it is the director's responsibility to know and follow the law or to see that the person assigned to this task has complied. Many agencies disseminate this type of

information in a special brochure. When the contributor does not receive the proper documentation from the agency, future contributions may be jeopardized.

Whether the center retains an attorney, relies on the volunteer services of an attorney who also is a board member, or keeps abreast of legal requirements in some other manner, the board is responsible for knowing and following the law. Professional organizations and journals are helpful in alerting directors to potential changes and to those that have been adopted. But not knowing the law is not accepted as an excuse for not following it.

Once the agency is in a position to seek contributions, the board approves the plan to conduct a fund drive. Next, the director prepares attractive and informative materials that make the case for the program's current and future operation. The information must be free of jargon and accurate, not overblown or overly dramatic. Important points must stand out with clarity to aid the busy reader who initially may be totally unfamiliar with the center and its mission. Be sure to include the purpose of the request, the total amount being sought, and information on current funding. If the document is based on a request for proposals (RFP) created by a funder, the proposal must state clearly how the funds will be used and relate that information to the funder's goals. RFP guidelines must be followed closely, and meeting the funder's deadline is essential.

References

A number of reference sources are available to help you plan your fund-raising strategies and to help you target foundations, corporations, and government agencies that are likely contributors to your type of request. One of these groups is listed on the reference page at the end of this chapter.

Your local library will have other resources, and you will find it helpful to conduct a computer search for books, journal articles, and requests for proposals.

Requesting Contributions

The director is responsible for ensuring that board members are prepared to speak knowledgeably about the agency and the fund purpose and that they know how to ask comfortably and specifically for funds. Board members (or whoever will request contributions) should determine who will be approached, by whom, and in what time frame. Then the designated person either telephones or writes for an appointment. The latter is usually more successful and may be followed with a brief letter of confirmation. Targeting a specific amount or range for an individual or organization gift is necessary. You may receive a "no" followed by "but I can contribute a lower amount." A request for a vague amount or for a contribution may net you $100 when a specific request for $1,000 may have produced that amount. Many people are uncomfortable discussing money, and even more cringe at the thought of asking someone else for funds. Good fund-raisers focus on the value of the contribution to the agency's clients and on providing the prospective funder an opportunity to engage in important work. In most cases, the enthusiasm and sincere approach of the requesters go a long way toward eliciting a positive response.

Let us assume that you called on someone for funds. Whether or not the response was favorable, writing a brief thank-you letter will win friends for the agency and is common courtesy. If a contribution is made, your appreciation is certainly warranted, and if the prospective funder chose not to contribute, appreciation for the time spent with you is in order.

REFLECTION
REFLECTION

Think about a time when you needed a loan from a bank, your parents, or a friend. Did you plan ahead what you would say and how you would explain your need? Did you mention the amount you needed and the purpose of the loan? How did you decide who to approach for a loan? A director who writes a proposal must answer similar questions.

Reporting to Funders

Whether the funders are organizations providing support to assist needy families, stockholders investing for profit, members of a parent co-op, school board members, or individuals who own and direct the center, every funder needs to know how the business is doing. Accurate, timely, and understandable reports are essential. The director uses the daily transaction records to prepare monthly financial reports for the funders as well as for internal use in making budgetary decisions. (These reports also should be available to those staff members who choose to read them.) The director may present this information at a board meeting or may mail it to board members and other concerned persons. Either way, the information should be presented in clear, neat, and concise form. Computer-generated reports can be revised readily so that the most current information is available. The director must be prepared to answer questions regarding the month's operating budget and to justify the figures in the report.

Since the purpose of the report is to inform the reader, it is meaningless to present a highly technical report to a group with no background in reading such reports. On the other hand, large organizations may require that each center follow a particular reporting format. In any event, the income and expenses must be presented in such a way that the reader can grasp easily the financial situation of the center. If a report indicates the need for changes in the budget (for example, an unpredictable expense such as a furnace that must be replaced immediately), the person or the people who have to approve such changes can review the budget and make appropriate revisions.

The director prepares or oversees the preparation of several types of reports.

Center Enrollment Report

How many children are enrolled and how many are on the waiting list? If the center serves various age groups, the report should be subdivided into the various subgroups such as infants, toddlers, preschoolers, and after-school care. The director also may project the number of children expected to move up to the next age group on a month-by-month basis. For example, if six children will no longer be eligible for the toddler group in March, based on licensing rules will there be room for them in the preschool classrooms?

Accounts Receivable

The director should receive a report at least weekly of accounts receivable. In a child care center, this figure will consist primarily of tuition owed. Repeated

In funding the center, the director works to maintain full enrollment with an appropriate number of children.

billing on a specific schedule (usually weekly) is essential.

Budget Comparison Report

Each month, the director prepares or receives a report from the bookkeeper showing what was spent the preceding month in each category. The report also shows budgeted spending for that month, as well as actual and budgeted spending for the year to date. The director or board then can spot cash flow problems, analyze expenditures, project remaining expenses, and revise the budget if necessary.

Statement of Financial Position

On a monthly basis, a statement of financial position should be prepared, showing assets (what you own) and liabilities (what you owe).

Income Statement

The director or accountant must create an income statement at the end of each year. This statement reflects the total of all revenue earned and all expenses incurred during the fiscal year. The difference between revenue and expense is net income if revenues are greater than expenses, and net loss if expenses are greater than revenues. The income statement is widely considered the most important financial statement because it is a measure of how well a business is doing at the end of the year. The statement shows whether the company has generated a profit or is incurring losses. The income statement represents the actual figures for each of your previously budgeted categories. It can be used as a tool to evaluate monies allocated to specific categories on your budget. For example, if maintenance and repair expense was actually $7,000 for the year according to the income statement but was budgeted at $2,500 on your operating budget, you would want to reevaluate your budgeted figure, provided that the dollars spent for maintenance and repair were not one-time, unusual expenditures. In addition to this latter example, the income statement can be helpful for other kinds of statistical analysis.

Annual Report

At the end of the fiscal year, the director presents a final report showing the amount budgeted in each category and the amount actually spent. Up-to-date cash flow statements make it relatively easy to prepare the annual report.

A computer is an invaluable tool in preparing financial and other reports. A computer with basic word processing and spreadsheet software can be utilized for budgets, enrollment reports, budget comparison reports, cash flow statements, income statements, statements of financial position, annual reports, and virtually any other financial statement that a child care program would ever need. Examples of word processing software are Microsoft Word® and WordPerfect®. Examples of spreadsheet software are

Quicken® and Microsoft Excel®. Although all four of these are well known and widely used, there are many other brands of software available for word processing and spreadsheet applications. In addition to financial reporting, a computer also can be utilized for a multitude of other functions such as preparing the case for your request for funds, preparing professional correspondence with funders, and maintaining records of contacts made and responses received. When the director or a board member has the opportunity to do a presentation about the agency, software that supports this demonstration such as PowerPoint® can help make a good impression. Keep in mind, too, that you will save hours of proposal preparation as you prepare materials for fund-raising. You will be able to use modifications of your basic information to meet the objectives of different funders by highlighting various aspects of your program. Not having to type everything over will lead you to value technology highly on the day the proposal is due or when you are working hard to meet a deadline.

SHEPHERDING EXISTING FUNDS

Although obtaining additional funds often requires a significant portion of a director's time and effort, putting into place policies and procedures to manage available resources also is essential. Of course, the director must make it clear to staff and families that these policies and procedures will be followed. A knowledgeable, skilled director does this without rancor and without antagonizing anyone. The director helps all concerned recognize that lax procedures can lead to reduced resources. From the staff point of view, this can mean reduction in salary, staff, or supplies and equipment. For families, it can mean a lowering of program quality. And for everyone, it can mean eventual closure of the center.

Following are three areas that can lead to unexpected diminishing of funds:

1. collections
2. fraud
3. lawsuits against the center

Collections

It is not uncommon for a family to have difficulty paying bills. Recognizing this, center policies and procedures must be explained clearly and agreed to during the enrollment procedures. State verbally and in writing when payment is due and how it can be made (check, credit card, cash, voucher). Establish procedures regarding timing, method, and number of overdue reminders, and whether a penalty will be charged for late payment. Consider a plan for accepting partial payment when a family is hit with a crisis, but keep in mind that the money is needed to meet your budget and that some families will fail to pay when their children leave the center.

Your policy may be to inform the parents that the child may not attend the center program until all past due payments have been made and will be readmitted only if the space has not been filled. Because positive relationships have presumably been established with every child and family, this is one of the most difficult tasks a director faces. It should never be turned over to the classroom teacher. In fact, neither the teacher nor any of the other staff need to have this confidential information.

If your policy is to require a week or two of tuition in advance, when a problem occurs, you will have payment for that period of time while you try to replace the child who must leave. This policy also will help when a family decides to move out of the area or finds another child care arrangement.

Fraud

Clear policies and procedures must be in place to protect against fraud. Huge amounts of money are embezzled each year, and a large percentage of that occurs in small businesses. Fraud refers to legally wrong "misrepresentation of a material fact the perpetrator knew was false and made with the intention that the misrepresentation be relied on and the the victim did rely on and, as a result incurred a loss" (Lukaszewski, 1997). Some examples of fraud include theft of cash and charging for more hours than actually worked. An employee who has access to the financial records can commit fraud by keeping an employee on the payroll for a period after they leave, writing extra checks to themselves, or charging personal expenses to the business.

Fraud occurs when a person of low integrity is unwittingly given the opportunity to steal. For example, when one person is in charge of receiving, recording, and depositing funds, it may be easy to keep some of that money for personal use. Not accepting cash will limit this opportunity to an extent.

To prevent fraud, the director must be aware of what is happening with the financial records and periodically must cross-check records such as time cards and payroll. The board must review all financial statements carefully. Members must know how to read and understand their reports and must not be afraid to question items that seem out of line to them.

However, the most important deterrent is clear enforceable and enforced policies and procedures.

Lawsuits

Directors also should establish and enforce policies that will reduce the likelihood of being sued. For example, training staff and documenting that the training occurred, coupled with adequate ongoing staff supervision, will help prevent accidents. Regularly scheduled checking of equipment, buildings, and grounds, as well as maintenance, is another preventive component. Policies regarding who has access to the premises and who may take children from the center are essential and must be followed strictly. Hand washing, food storage, and serving procedures should be reviewed regularly, as should all other health and safety policies and procedures.

Maintaining positive relations with all families and keeping them informed on a regular basis and whenever anything out of the ordinary occurs also may lessen the probability of a suit. Certainly, centers should carry insurance that will cover families' expenses in the event of an accident at the center.

The well-prepared director takes a proactive stance in seeking funds for the center and using existing resources wisely. The director also assumes responsibility for coaching the staff to follow the policies and procedures that are essential to the maintenance of a financially stable organization.

SUMMARY

Operating a good quality center requires a significant amount of funding, and dependence on tuition and government support is unlikely to provide sufficient resources. Many programs in early childhood education depend on outside funding for partial or total support. Knowledge of the sources of funding and some skill in writing proposals are important for directors who may be forced to find funds to operate their programs when tuition is not sufficient to support a high-quality program. Some programs receive funds from their sponsoring agencies, while others depend on United Way funds, grants from foundations, or government grants.

When a center operates with a board, the board makes policies about tuition, usually to balance the need to retain enrollment and meet budgetary requirements. Tuition for child care programs is set based on cost of the program, parents' ability to pay, availability of other funds, and the marketplace. Board members also participate in securing funds and in creating the three- to five-year financial plan for the center.

The breakeven analysis, budget comparison report, statement of financial position, and income statement are important financial management tools for the director and provide a clear, accurate picture for funders.

CLASS ASSIGNMENTS

1. Find out who provides money for early childhood education in your community. Are any programs funded by the federal, state, or local governments, United Way, private individuals, chain or franchised centers, universities or colleges, businesses, or proprietors? Is anyone else funding early childhood education in your community? Write your findings on Working Paper 7–1.

2. Contact a rural or inner-city child care center director (not a Head Start center). Inquire about the funding base. Try to find answers to the following questions and write them on Working Paper 7–2.

   a. How much tuition do parents pay?

   b. How much of the total budget is covered by tuition?

   c. What outside funding sources are available to support the program, and how much money is available through those sources?

   d. How were outside funds obtained?

3. Use the figures in Working Paper 7–3 to determine how many children will be in each group for the next six months. If licensing requires one adult for each four infants, one for each eight toddlers, and one for each 12 preschoolers, what effect will the changing enrollment have on your budget?

4. Read the Business Plan Questionnaire in Working Paper 7–4. Fill out the form using a hypothetical situation.

   Write a paragraph about your reaction to these questions.

CLASS EXERCISES

1. Work with a group of your classmates to make the following decisions. Assume that your center serves 60 preschoolers in four classes of 15 children each. Your operating expenses are $360,000.

a. How much will the annual tuition be? How much will the weekly tuition be?

b. Will you take into account bad debts and a vacancy factor?

c. Assume that 10 families can pay only $1,000 a year ($20 a week) for their 10 children. How much tuition will every other family have to pay to make up the difference if you don't get scholarship funds from other sources?

2. Form a small group with several of your classmates to decide on a policy based on the following information. Four families at the center you direct announce they are expecting babies in about six months. They want you to hold places for them, and they want to keep the older siblings home for three months (without paying tuition) while the mother is on maternity leave. What will your policy be?

WORKING PAPER 7-1

(for use with Class Assignment 1)

FUNDING FORM

Who provides money for early childhood education in your community?

Federal government?

State government?

Local government?

United Way?

Private individuals?

Chains or franchised centers?

Universities or colleges?

Businesses?

Proprietors?

Other?

What sources of information did you use?

WORKING PAPER 7-2

(for use with Class Assignment 2)

FUNDING BASE FORM

1. Name of the center you contacted:

2. Funding base

   How much tuition do parents pay?

   How much of the total budget is covered by tuition?

   What outside funding sources are available to support the program, and how much money is available through those sources?

   How were outside funds obtained?

WORKING PAPER 7-3

(for use with Class Assignment 3)

ENROLLMENT FIGURES

February

Enrolled

Infants	10
Toddlers	16
Preschool	24

Waiting List

Infants	12
Toddlers	3
Preschool	0

Ready to Move Up

Infants to Toddlers

March	1
April	0
May	2
June	1
July	1
August	0

Toddlers to Preschool

March	0
April	1
May	0
June	2
July	0
August	0

Effect on Budget?

WORKING PAPER 7-4

(for use with Class Assignment 4)

BUSINESS PLAN QUESTIONNAIRE

Financial Analysis

1. Will you need a loan to start or expand the center? If so, approximately how much?

2. What will the loan be used for?

3. What sources will you use to obtain the loan? (bank, credit union, state, city, etc.)

4. What is (are) the item(s) to be purchased and at what cost(s)?

5. Who will be supplying these items?

6. Do you have a personal savings, checking, or business account with a local bank? If so, which one, and who is your banker?

7. Have you approached them about your loan request? What was their response?

8. Do you own any assets or items of value? If so, what?

9. Would you be willing to use your personal assets as collateral against a loan to provide your center with a stable equity base?

10. Have you prepared a projected profit and loss statement showing the potential revenues versus expenses of your center during your first three years of operation?

11. Will you need assistance in preparing such statements?

12. Can you provide personal tax returns for the past three years?

13. How will a loan make your business more profitable?

Adapted from "Business Plan Questionnaire," The Ohio Department of Development, Small and Developing Business Division, Office of Management and Technical Services, Columbus, OH 43216-0101.

DIRECTOR'S RESOURCE 7-1

SAMPLE GRANT APPLICATION*

Doe Learning Center Inc. is a nonprofit corporation that operates four child care centers in the greater metropolitan area. The centers provide quality child care for children ages three months through five years and also offer school-age care at two of the sites. As a United Way agency, the centers' common goal is to work toward alleviating the current crisis of child care, as outlined in the Long Range Plan for Child Care of the United Way in 2000. This study shows that there is an urgent need for quality programming for children identified as having special needs. Doe Learning Center Inc. has responded to this need by operating four centers whose common goal is the inclusion of all children.

Statement of Agency Commitment

Metropolitan Learning Center (MLC) is located in the central area of the city. The program serves 67 children ages three months through five years. In the summer we enroll an additional 20 children in our school-age program. Established in 1984, MCL was the first full-day program in this city to be accredited by the National Association for the Education of Young Children.

Largely based on the theories of Piaget and Erikson, the center's philosophy reflects a focus on the development of the whole child and the formation of strong, trusting relationships. The developmental constructivist approach holds the belief that children develop sequentially from one stage of development to another. Because of this we believe that children must be provided with opportunity that will challenge them and aid in their progression from one stage to the next. It is a necessity that learning be based on actual experience and participation. Talking without doing is largely meaningless to young children.

We believe that for children to grow, they must be placed in a setting that meets their basic needs. Therefore, it is our utmost concern that our program provide a nurturing, comfortable environment that is specifically structured to meet the physical, emotional, and cognitive needs of each individual child.

This philosophy was the foundation for the development of the agency. Due to this commitment, the question of inclusion was never discussed, only how to do it well.

In this time of severe staff shortages in the ECE field, MLC feels fortunate to have an outstanding quality of professionals.

- four preschool head teachers—M.Ed.
- one toddler head teacher—Associate in Early Education
- two infant teachers—Bachelor Education and two infant teachers—Associate Education
- Dr. John Jones, professor emeritus at the Metropolitan University, has been consulting with our agency for three years. This past year Dr. Jones is working strictly at MLC, coordinating our educational services.

MLC has worked extensively with the Early Childhood Education Department, Metropolitan University. The program has been a training site for the past five years and works with an average of three to four students per quarter.

According to Washington County Child Day Care: The State of Today and Plans for 2010, "Special needs children are still at a great disadvantage. Most child care providers feel ill-equipped to serve children with developmental problems and physical disabilities." MLC has successfully integrated approximately 25 children identified as having special needs. One family called more than 60 child care centers before finding a placement at MLC for their child with cerebral palsy. The center has served many children with a wide variety of special needs, including, but not limited to, pervasive development disorder, fragile X syndrome, autism, mild mental retardation, receptive language disorder, and visual impairments, to name a few.

*Names of people and places are fictitious.

(continues)

DIRECTOR'S RESOURCE 7-1
(continued)

One of the primary goals of the organization is to meet the needs of the family, parent, and child. MLC has identified its ability to meet these needs as follows:

Needs of the Child–

- placement in a program meeting the standards of developmentally appropriate practice
- master-level staff capable of identifying and working with high-risk children

Needs of the Family–

- providing high-quality care for their children
- providing quarterly parent education/training programs
- providing assistance in identifying (or working with existing) available services (i.e., early intervention) for their children

MLC has been identified in the community as a program that will not only serve children with special needs but also give them access to the services they need or support the work of other service providers as part of the daily program. Metropolitan University acknowledged the endeavors of the center by placing students from the Special Education department under the guidance of our experienced staff. We have worked with many agencies in order to provide more comprehensive services to these children. These agencies include the following:

- Washington County Department of Human Services
- Special Education Regional Resource Center (SERRC)
- Cerebral Palsy Services Center
- Center for Developmental Disorders
- Speech and Hearing
- Speech Pathology
- Child Advocacy Center
- Association for the Blind
- Metropolitan University–Early Childhood/Special Education Department
- Foster Grandparent Program
- The Council on Aging
- The Single Parent Center

Statement of Need

There are currently eight children enrolled in the program who have been identified as having special needs. There are several children that are integrated into the environment and are receiving services from support agencies. MLC feels confident that we can meet their needs without additional services. There are two children that pose challenges to our existing program. One child is currently enrolled in our infant program; he is 20 months old and has cerebral palsy. When we enrolled Ed, we assessed that we could meet his needs in the infant program. Though Ed is nonmobile and nonverbal, he uses smiles, cries, and coos to communicate with his caregiver.

(continues)

DIRECTOR'S RESOURCE 7-1
(continued)

To continue serving Ed,

■ we need to be able to meet the challenge of facilitating his growth through experiences with the toddlers.

■ we need to acquire the equipment to encourage his further development.

■ we need release time for his caregiver to meet with his therapist to learn how to use specialized equipment and participate in his IEP meeting.

Our second child has been identified with pervasive developmental disorder and mild characteristics of autism. Communication has been the primary barrier in the progression of Ryan's development. This aspect of his disorder carries over into other areas of his growth, including the development of self-control. Ryan has been enrolled in our program for one year and within that period has gone from single word utterances to communicating in four- to five-word sentences. Because of this increased ability to communicate, the agency believes that a transition to the oldest preschool classroom is the next step. The goal of this move is to place Ryan in an environment of his same-age peers where he might benefit from the modeling of age-appropriate behaviors and participation in activities. Any changes in daily schedule and transition times are extremely difficult for Ryan, and separation from his current classroom teacher will be a tremendous undertaking.

Our belief is that in order to best aid in this transition, MLC will need the assistance of an additional staff person for the following reasons:

■ to meet the needs of Ryan during the period of transition so that classroom staff may continue to meet the needs of his peers

■ to act as a facilitator, giving Ryan assistance with social interactions so that he might form relationships with his peers and staff

■ to give the classroom staff opportunity to focus on forming trusting relationships with Ryan, without concern that the experiences of his peers are being limited

Purpose of Funding/Budget

The purpose of our funding breaks into three categories: equipment, consulting/training, and additional staff to decrease ratios.

Equipment

Type	Purpose		Cost
Outdoor swing	seat for severely challenged student allows		$126.95
Floor sitter	a nonmobile child to interact with peers but have necessary support		$150.00
Button switch toy			$42.00
Jelly bean switch toy			$42.00
Circus truck			$27.00
Bumper car			$25.00
Brontosaurus			$29.50
Oversized ball	easier to manipulate than typical ball	18"	$24.35
		34"	$69.50

(continues)

DIRECTOR'S RESOURCE 7-1

(continued)

Consulting/Training

Topic (we would like to open these to public)

How to adapt "typical" equipment to meet the needs of physically challenged children	$100.00
How to use switch toys	$80.00
How to write an appropriate IEP and how to make the IEP meeting work for the child	$100.00

Consulting

How to arrange the toddler environment to meet the needs of a physically challenged child	$100.00
How to encourage positive peer relationships with typical and atypical children	$50.00

Support Staff

Enrolling a physically challenged child into the infant program was within the abilities of our staff. Allowing time for this child to interact with peers of his own age and slowly transitioning him into the toddler room will be a challenge for us. We need time for his caregiver to visit the toddler room with him, and then time for the toddler teacher to have one-on-one time for him. This cannot be done without additional staff. Any choice we make with the current staff situation will either shortchange Ed or the other children enrolled. We are requesting a part-time assistant for six months.

Cost $6,656

Having children that model age-appropriate behaviors has been the most vital ingredient to Ryan's development. To continue his progress, it is imperative that he be surrounded by children exhibiting the behaviors that Ryan is striving for. As mentioned earlier, any transition is very difficult for Ryan. To continue servicing Ryan and meet his needs by transitioning him to be with children of his own age, we will need additional staff.

We are requesting a part-time assistant for six months. Cost $6,656

TOTAL REQUESTED $14,278.30

Expected Outcome

This grant will enable us to purchase equipment that will

- allow physically challenged children to become more accessible to the other children by being positioned near them on the floor.
- provide stimulation and encourage peer interaction.
- lessen isolation so that relationship with peers will increase.

This grant will enable us to provide sufficient staff to

- allow challenged children to be surrounded with children of their own age providing appropriate models.
- allow staff to meet the needs of our children with special needs without denying other children the attention they need.
- facilitate smooth transitions that encourage success with meaningful relationships with other children.
- make inclusion a successful experience that will encourage staff to include additional children.

(continues)

DIRECTOR'S RESOURCE 7-1
(continued)

This grant will provide technical assistance that will

- give the staff and management the knowledge to include these children and additional children in the future.
- encourage other early childhood programs to attend these training sessions and build support through networking with other teachers participating in inclusion.

We will be asking staff who are working with Ed and Ryan to fill out a short questionnaire before we provide additional services, and again after. We would like to see if these support services change any possible insecurities or feelings of being overwhelmed that had previously occurred.

DIRECTOR'S RESOURCE 7-2

SAMPLE SLIDING FEE SCHEDULE

Parent pays:	20%	30%	40%	50%	60%	70%	80%	90%
Infant	$30/wk	$45	$60	$75	$90	$105	$120	$135
Toddler	$25	$37.50	$50	$62.50	$75	$87.50	$100	$112.50
Preschooler	$20	$30	$40	$50	$60	$70	$80	$90

DIRECTOR'S RESOURCE 7-3

UNITED STATES SBA BUSINESS PLAN

To obtain funds from any source, the (SBA) recommends creating a business plan. What goes in a business plan? The body can be divided into four distinct sections:

1. Description of the business
2. Marketing
3. Finances
4. Management

Addenda should include an executive summary, supporting documents, and financial projections. Although there is no single formula for developing a business plan, some elements are common to all business plans. They are summarized in the following outline:

Elements of a Business Plan

1. **Cover sheet**
2. **Statement of purpose**
3. **Table of contents**

    I. The Business
    A. Description of business
    B. Marketing
    C. Competition
    D. Operating procedures
    E. Personnel
    F. Business insurance

    II. Financial Data
    A. Loan applications
    B. Capital equipment and supply list
    C. Balance sheet
    D. Breakeven analysis
    E. Pro-forma income projections (profit & loss statements)
    Three-year summary
    Detail by month, first year
    Detail by quarters, second and third years
    Assumptions upon which projections were based
    F. Pro-forma cash flow

    III. Supporting Documents
    Tax returns of principals for last three years; personal financial statement (all banks have these forms)
    For franchised businesses, a copy of franchise contract and all supporting documents provided by the franchisor
    Copy of proposed lease or purchase agreement for building space
    Copy of licenses and other legal documents
    Copy of resumes of all principals
    Copies of letters of intent from suppliers, etc.

Sample Plans

One of the best ways to learn about writing a business plan is to study the plans of established businesses in your industry.

Retrieved from http://www.sba.gov

DIRECTOR'S RESOURCE 7-4

HYPOTHETICAL BUDGET BY MONTH CREATED ON SPREADSHEET

Felton Family Preschool
Monthly Budget

	"Reasonable" Budget A3	September	October	November	December	January	February	March	April	May	June	July	August
INCOME													
Tuition	344,235	25,000	28,000	30,000	30,000	30,000	30,000	30,000	30,000	30,000	27,078	27,078	27,078
Fund-raising	3,500	292	292	292	292	292	292	292	292	292	292	292	292
County Grant	27,000	2,250	2,250	2,250	2,250	2,250	2,250	2,250	2,250	2,250	2,250	2,250	2,250
Other	2,000	167	167	167	167	167	167	167	167	167	167	167	167
TOTAL INCOME	376,735	27,708	30,708	32,708	32,708	32,708	32,708	32,708	32,708	32,708	29,787	29,787	29,787
EXPENSE													
Payroll Expense													
Salaries-Staff	270,000	22,759	23,793	20,690	23,793	23,793	20,690	21,724	22,759	22,759	21,724	23,793	21,724
Payroll Taxes	24,300	2,048	2,141	1,862	2,141	2,141	1,862	1,955	2,048	2,048	1,955	2,141	1,955
Worker's Comp	13,500	1,138	1,190	1,034	1,190	1,190	1,034	1,086	1,138	1,138	1,086	1,190	1,086
Staff Benefits													
Health Ins.	27,250	2,271	2,271	2,271	2,271	2,271	2,271	2,271	2,271	2,271	2,271	2,271	2,271
Dental Ins.	4,000	333	333	333	333	333	333	333	333	333	333	333	333
Education Allow.	875	73	73	73	73	73	73	73	73	73	73	73	73
Rent	4,800	400	400	400	400	400	400	400	400	400	400	400	400
Janitor	6,000	500	500	500	500	500	500	500	500	500	500	500	500
Insurance													
Liability	2,914	243	243	243	243	243	243	243	243	243	243	243	243
Accident	1,575	131	131	131	131	131	131	131	131	131	131	131	131
Directors Ins.	944	79	79	79	79	79	79	79	79	79	79	79	79
Supplies	15,000	1,250	1,250	1,250	1,250	1,250	1,250	1,250	1,250	1,250	1,250	1,250	1,250
Utilities	2,835	236	236	236	236	236	236	236	236	236	236	236	236
Capital Improvement	2,000	0	0	1,000	0	0	0	1,000	0	0	0	0	0
TOTAL EXPENSES	375,993	31,461	32,640	30,102	32,640	32,640	29,102	31,282	31,461	31,461	30,282	32,640	30,282
SURPLUS (DEFICIT)	742	(3,753)	(1,932)	2,606	68	68	3,606	1,427	1,247	1,247	(495)	(2,854)	(495)

From "The Business of Child Care, Management and Financial Strategies," by Jack ©2005. Reprinted with permission of Delmar Learning, a division of Thomson Learning: http://www.thomsonrights.com.

DIRECTOR'S RESOURCE 7-5

HYPOTHETICAL BUDGET TRACKING CREATED ON SPREADSHEET

	A	B	C	D	E	F	G	H	I	J	K
1											
2				Felton Family Preschool							
3				Two Months Budget Vs. Actual							
4											
5				"Reasonable"	September	September	September	October	October	October	2 Mos.
6				Budget A3	Budget	Actual	Variance	Budget	Actual	Variance	Variance
7		**INCOME**									
8		Tuition		344,235	25,000	25,375	375	28,000	27,000	(1,000)	(625)
9		Fund-raising		3,500	292	50	(242)	292	0	(292)	(533)
10		County Grant		27,000	2,250	2,250	0	2,250	2,250	0	0
11		Other		2,000	167	200	33	167	100	(67)	(33)
12											
13		**TOTAL INCOME**		376,735	27,708	27,875	167	30,708	29,350	(1,358)	(1,191)
14											
15		**EXPENSE**									
16		Payroll Expense									
17		Salaries-Staff		270,000	22,759	24,410	(1,651)	23,793	25,130	(1,337)	(2,988)
18		Payroll Taxes		24,300	2,048	2,197	(149)	2,141	2,262	(120)	(269)
19		Worker's Comp		13,500	1,138	1,220	(83)	1,190	1,256	(67)	(149)
20		Staff Benefits									
21		Health Ins.		27,250	2,271	2,000	271	2,271	2,000	271	542
22		Dental Ins.		4,000	333	350	(17)	333	350	(17)	(33)
23		Education Allow.		875	73	0	73	73	100	(27)	46
24		Rent		4,800	400	400	0	400	400	0	0
25		Janitor		6,000	500	500	0	500	500	0	0
26		Insurance									
27		Liability		2,914	243	250	(7)	243	250	(7)	(14)
28		Accident		1,575	131	125	6	131	125	6	12
29		Directors Ins.		944	79	75	4	79	75	4	7
30		Supplies		15,000	1,250	640	610	1,250	2,000	(750)	(140)
31		Utilities		2,835	236	200	36	236	200	36	72
32											
33		Capital Improvement		2,000	0	0	0	0	0	0	0
34		**TOTAL EXPENSES**		375,993	31,461	32,367	(906)	32,640	34,648	(2,008)	(2,914)
35											
36		**SURPLUS (DEFICIT)**		742	(3,753)	(4,492)	(739)	(1,932)	(5,298)	(3,366)	(4,105)
37											

REFERENCES

Center for the Future of Children. (1996, Fall). *Financing child care: The future of children.* The David and Lucile Packard Foundation. Los Altos, CA: Author.

Children's Defense Fund. (2001, January 8). Addition to FY 2001 appropriations for children and families. *Child Care Advocacy Newsletter.* CDFCHILDCARE@childrensdefense.org

Kagan, S. L., Brandon, R. N., Ripple, C. H., Maher, E. J., & Joesch, J. M. (2002, May). Supporting quality early childhood care and education: Addressing compensation and infrastructure. *Young Children, 57*(3), 58–65.

Linsmeier, D. (2003, May). Valuing your child care business. *Child Care Information Exchange, 151,* 56–59.

Lukaszewski, T. (1997). Who can you trust? *Child Care Information Exchange, 116,* 20–24.

Mitchell, A. (1996). Fishing for dollars in philanthropic waters. *Child Care Information Exchange, 111,* 7–10.

Neugebauer, R. (2001, September). Employer child care growth and consolidation continues. *Child Care Information Exchange, 141,* 14–16.

Neugebauer, R. (2001, September). Keys to success in raising funds. *Child Care Information Exchange, 141,* 76–78.

Stephens, K. (1991). *Confronting your bottom line: Financial guide for child care centers.* Redmond, WA: Exchange Press.

Vast, T. (2003, July). Establishing and managing a tuition aid program: Guidelines for helping families with financial difficulties. *Child Care Information Exchange, 152,* 27–32.

 Additional resources for this chapter can be found on the Online Companion™ at http://www.earlychilded.delmar.com. This supplemental material includes relevant Web links, Web activities, and case studies that apply the concepts presented in this chapter. In addition, the Working Papers and Director's Resources are available for download, allowing you to complete Class Exercises and Class Assignments electronically.

CHAPTER 8

Developing a Center Facility

Directors work with architect and contractors before and during the building or renovation process.

OBJECTIVES

After reading this chapter, you should be able to:

- Describe an early childhood space that meets the needs of children, staff members, and parents.
- Incorporate licensing guidelines when designing a new space.
- Identify the individual consultants involved in planning an early childhood facility.

An early childhood education program should be housed in a spacious, attractive facility that has been created or redesigned for children and that also meets the needs of staff members and parents. The director is responsible for ensuring that appropriate space is available; therefore, space needs are analyzed carefully for both ongoing and new programs. This job may be done in cooperation with the board building committee, or the director may assume full responsibility for analysis of space needs. These needs then are submitted to the board for action. Corporate systems often have a prototypical design for all centers in the system, and they usually designate an employee to provide and manage the physical facilities for the system's centers. Similarly, preschool facilities in public schools usually are planned by central administration, although the principal may have a major decision-making role.

ANALYZING SPACE REQUIREMENTS

In providing a suitable facility, the first task is to analyze the space needs. When a program is already in operation, this analysis is made periodically to ensure the availability of proper facilities for both present and future needs. If the center program or enrollment change, it may be necessary to move to a different location or add or eliminate space in the existing center. When a new center is created or when a move is proposed, the director usually assumes major responsibility for locating appropriate facilities. All renovation, relocation, or initial facilities choices should be based on the space needs analysis.

Space needs are based on consideration for the users (children, staff, and parents), program requirements, and governmental regulations. Therefore, the director must have up-to-date information in all these areas.

Of course, the desired number of children to be enrolled will be of major importance. Very small centers may be more costly (per child) to operate while those that serve hundreds of children may overwhelm the child. Large centers must be especially and carefully designed so that children have private spaces. What the child encounters on a daily basis, in terms of both facilities and people, must be manageable for the child.

Moore (1996) recommends 42.5 square feet of usable activity space per child and 50 square feet for infants and toddlers because more adults are involved with the younger children. He also suggests two smaller motor activity spaces for use by different age groups in place of one larger room. Even when the space is not used at the same time by different groups, the equipment must be changed or its use curtailed when very young children enter.

Users' Needs

"One of the greatest challenges in designing institutions is to transform a physical plant into a human environment. One part of the transformation has to do with discovering ways to allow impersonal rooms and hallways reflect the lives of the children and adults who spend so many active hours in that space" (Gandini, 1994). Lella Gandini, official liaison in the United States for the Administration of Early Childhood Education of the Municipality of Reggio Emilia, Italy, also emphasizes the importance of recognizing the "special qualities of local life."

REFLECTION

When you visit a friend's home or apartment, how does the space reflect who they are? Does your home convey to others your own culture? What was the place in which you grew up like? Was there a community feeling? Think about schools you attended. Recall whether or not they were influenced by the surrounding community. Did you feel welcome there?

Both children and adults are bombarded with stimulation. Using decorations judiciously can minimize environmental "noise." For example, limit what is on walls and windows (Kielar, 1999). Children's art and photographs, documentation of projects, and information for parents are all legitimate items to be posted. When space surrounds each posting, it is more likely that someone will notice the item. When displays are changed frequently, the newness draws children and adults alike to inspect them.

Users of an early childhood education facility fall into three groups: children, staff, and families. An analysis of space requirements must be based on the needs of each of these users. Since a child care center is planned primarily to meet the needs of children, all child care facilities should be comfortable and convenient, both in terms of children's sizes and their developmental levels. School-aged programs require space for larger children and must take into account the need for active play as well as relaxation, studying, and preparing and eating snacks. Children who spend six or seven hours in a school classroom need a change of pace and should not feel they are in a school room before and after school.

Each child needs an individual space for outdoor clothing and for a change of clothes. Infants and toddlers need separate storage areas for diapers, which are provided by parents. Preschoolers need a place to store special items they bring to show others but not to share with them. And school-agers need a place for books, musical instruments, and sports equipment.

The building also must be comfortable and convenient for adult users, if they are to work effectively with the children.

The primary needs that planners must consider for each of these users are

- health and safety.
- accessibility of facilities.

■ controlled traffic flow.
■ personal space.
■ opportunities for independence and growth.
■ aesthetic character.

Meeting the needs of each group of users has a cumulative and reciprocal effect because when the needs of one group are met, a step is taken toward meeting the needs of the other two groups. The dynamics of a human environment involve the impacting of each group on the others. In a well-run center, the three groups interact effectively because each is involved in the joint, sensitive process of child development.

Health and Safety

Center planners must be aware of the safety aspects above and beyond those stipulated in licensing regulations. A hazard-free building meets the needs of staff and parents, as well as children. Directors must keep abreast of environmental issues. For example, asbestos and lead paint, once considered appropriate building materials, now are not used in child care centers. Some sealed buildings in which air is recirculated may be simply redistributing poor-quality air. Recently, several schools have extensively renovated sections of buildings in which mold had developed, usually from a leaking pipe. Although not ordinarily visible on the surface, mold may cause children and teachers to become ill. The solution is to close off the area while qualified personnel remove contamination.

Governmental regulations usually will determine the type of building and decorative materials (such as carpeting) to be used, the number and type of exits (including panic hardware and lighted exit signs), the number and location of fire extinguishers, smoke detectors and fire alarm systems, and location of furnace and water heaters relative to the children's play area. All these regulations protect children and staff from dangers associated with fire.

Children also must be protected from such hazards as tap water that is too hot, slippery floor surfaces, unsafe or unprotected electrical outlets and wiring, and poorly lighted spaces. Covered convenience outlets or specially designed safety outlets are needed throughout the classroom for audiovisual equipment, computers, aquaria, and so forth. The director must ensure that the flooring is even; that there are no protrusions to cause falls; that stairs are provided with sturdy, low rails; and that protective screening is installed on all windows. Although the director is primarily responsible for establishing and maintaining a basic safety plan for the center, every staff member must remain alert to potential hazards and must teach children simple safety procedures such as reshelving toys and mopping up spilled water.

In public schools where older children use the hallways, plans for entering and exiting the building and moving about must be made so that young children experience minimal encounters with large groups of grade schoolers. Although older children can move about the building independently, additional staff may be required so that small children will have escorts when they go to the library, the office, or the restroom. Ideally, each classroom for young children will have its own adjoining bathroom.

In any building, many safety practices revolve around the enforcement of center safety rules such as prohibiting children from climbing on window sills, but it is preferable to adapt the building itself so that it is a safe place for children. Placing locks on the furnace room door is less disturbing to everyone and far safer for children than telling them they must not enter the furnace area. Be sure, however, that security devices such as locks or gates do not block an emergency exit. Guidelines for fire safety can be obtained by consulting the fire inspector.

For safety reasons, programs for children usually are housed on the ground-floor level of the building, even where licensing regulations do not require this. In the event of a fire or other emergency that requires building evacuation, preschool children may become confused easily and may need individual guidance to

Staff work space includes space to prepare materials to use in the classroom.

reach safety. In such situations, staff members caring for infants, toddlers, and nonambulatory preschoolers will be able to remove only the one or two children they can carry. Some centers place several babies in a crib and roll the crib to safety. Therefore, stairways are dangerous obstacles to quick and safe building evacuation. Remember that it is usually unsafe to use elevators in an emergency.

Over and above promoting the ease of evacuation, other safety considerations make ground-level facilities immediately adjacent to fenced outdoor space very advantageous. When children can go directly from their classrooms to a fenced outdoor area, the teaching staff can supervise both those children who choose outdoor play and those who remain indoors. The outdoor space is viewed as an extension of the indoor. Fenced-in play areas prevent children from leaving the play space and prevent others from entering and damaging equipment, interfering with children's play, or leaving dangerous materials such as broken glass around the area. A covered outdoor space provides an additional advantage because it can be used on rainy days or on very hot, sunny days.

All exits from the building and the outdoor playground should be in locations where supervision of who comes and goes can be maintained readily. While the center may welcome community visitors, strangers should not be permitted to wander through the building. Similarly, children should not be able to leave unnoticed, either alone or accompanied by anyone other than authorized personnel. Panic hardware must be provided on all exit doors, but they should be locked so that visitors cannot enter without being admitted. Parents and staff probably will have to be reminded that holding the door open for an arriving visitor is unwise since that person's presence in the center may go unnoticed.

Accessibility of Facilities

All users must have access to the building, its program, and its materials. Many parents do not want to subject their children to long daily trips to and from the center, and they prefer a center close to home. Others will look for a center close to the workplace so that they can visit the child during the day. Location near public transportation also is desirable for staff and parents.

Access to the center is increased when people feel comfortable about entering the building; therefore, the scale of the building is another consideration. As children approach the center, they should feel that it fits them. Even a large building should have some features that indicate to the children that the building is theirs. Entranceways and the areas surrounding them can be scaled to the children's requirements so that the children are not overwhelmed by a huge, heavy door or a stairway wide enough for a regiment.

Because parents and visitors often form opinions about a program on the basis of external appearances, the grounds must be well maintained, and the building itself must be inviting. A building welcomes people through its scale, color, texture, and design. When the building is compatible with other buildings in the neighborhood, the center can begin to establish itself as a positive force in the community and be considered as an integral part of the total community. Understandably, an ultracontemporary building might not be welcome in a traditional residential neighborhood.

When a child care center is housed in a building shared by other users, the center should have a separate entrance that is clearly marked so that families and visitors can find it. Entrances used by older students, agency clients, or other tenants may mean heavy traffic that can intimidate children and may make supervision of their arrival and departure more difficult.

The parking area should be located near the center's entrance and should be large enough to accommodate the cars of staff, parents, and visitors. A safe walkway from parking to entry is essential because many parents will arrive with several children, diaper bags, and favorite toys.

Inside the building, there should be clear indications of where to proceed. Signs, supergraphics, or pathways incorporated in the flooring (such as tile arrows) can lead visitors to the proper place, even if no receptionist or secretary is available. A pleasant greeting from a receptionist is ideal, especially when the child and parent are called by name, but many centers are unable to afford a staff member to fill that role.

When the receptionist's or secretary's office has a large glass window overlooking the entry, visual contact can be made with people as they arrive, and parents or visitors will feel more comfortable about asking for assistance. In the office adjacent to the entry, the center staff can greet people and receive forms and payments from families. If parents or visitors find no one with whom to communicate when they enter the building, they may become disgruntled and leave, feeling that no one cares about their needs. Or a visitor may search out the classrooms and begin a conversation with a busy teacher, disturbing activities there and probably inviting a cursory response that is detrimental to good public relations. The entry also should be accessible to the director's office so that he is highly visible and readily available. Furthermore, it is imperative that all visitors be screened to ensure that everyone who enters has a legitimate purpose.

A pleasant greeting from a receptionist makes everyone feel welcome.

DIRECTOR'S CORNER

"This morning Mrs. Adams stopped in to see me. She just wanted to let me know how much she and Ralinda missed Marion, our receptionist, who has been home with the flu for a week. She said, 'Marion always calls everyone by name. She greets us with a smile and, especially on days when I'm rushing, I really enjoy the welcome.'"

—Director, urban center

In any case, the entry itself should say "welcome." The colors used in the entry should indicate that this is a place for growth and vitality; grayness and drabness do not belong here. Lighting is as important here as it is in the classrooms. The area should be bright but not harsh. Sunshine is ideal, but when that is not available, an artificially brightly illuminated area sets the tone for the real warmth that children and families can expect to experience throughout the center. Entry surfaces also are important and must be designed to withstand muddy shoes or boots and dripping umbrellas. Although the entry should be large enough to accommodate several people without being crowded, it should not be too large since such space has minimum use but still costs about as much per square foot as areas that are heavily used. Furthermore, large entranceways may overwhelm a child or intimidate an unsure parent. Some children will interpret large open spaces as an invitation to run.

The required minimum number of entrances and exits is determined by fire laws, but to determine the best locations for these doors, the planners should take into consideration the traffic patterns of people who come to the building. Teachers like to greet parents as they arrive with their children; therefore, locating the arrival point close to the classroom helps parents and children as well as teachers. Similarly, when the children leave, teachers can see the parents. Just as children should be able to reach their classrooms without walking through long, uninteresting, and perhaps frightening hallways, adults should be able to get to their areas conveniently and without disturbing children's play. For example, deliveries to the kitchen or other service areas should be easy to make without having to negotiate stairs and moving through the children's space.

Accessibility carries an additional importance for those who have special needs. The Americans with Disabilities Act (ADA) protects them by requiring that facilities be designed so that all services can be used by all clients and employees. Entrances and exits, traffic flow patterns, and facilities throughout the building and grounds should be designed for ease of use by people who have disabilities. People (children included) in wheelchairs or on crutches should be able to move about comfortably; to use bathrooms, drinking fountains, and telephones; and to participate in all aspects of the center's program. Seemingly small items such as the type of faucet on sinks or the handles on cabinets can be designed to facilitate use by persons who otherwise would have to ask for assistance. The ADA requires these accommodations for most centers that meet certain conditions, but even in situations where the accommodations are optional, concern for the comfort of all individuals necessitates that efforts be made to modify buildings. The Child Care Law Center in San Francisco also can help with information. Refer to Director's Resource 8–1 for additional ideas.

Control of Traffic Flow

Planners should consider the children's daily traffic patterns between indoor and outdoor spaces, as well as within those spaces. For example, children will move from classroom to multipurpose room and back, and from classroom to outdoor area and back. They may leave from the outdoor area if they are playing there when their parents arrive. A good floor plan takes into account the fact that young children should be able to go directly outdoors, preferably from their own classroom, or at least with minimal walking in hallways or in areas used for other purposes.

Coat storage should be near the door where the children enter. When coats are stored in the classroom, shelving may be used to create a coat area separate from the play space.

REFLECTION

Think about how the traffic pattern of a building you use frequently affects you. When you arrive at this building, which room do you go to first? Where is that room in relation to the door you use to enter the building? Think about the directions in which you move through the building during the day. Are there any places that could be rearranged to save you steps? Classrooms can be arranged for variety and ease of traffic flow if areas within the room are clearly demarcated and exits are located so that traffic does not cross through a number of areas. Shelves for blocks are excellent room dividers that can be used to separate the block area from the housekeeping area and from the heavy traffic area, thereby providing a special space for undisturbed block building. Reading and writing areas can be separated from noisy carpentry or music areas by shelves or dividers; then children can find quiet, secluded spaces for solitude and concentration. Children can work comfortably without being disturbed when traffic patterns in the classroom are taken into consideration in planning their space needs.

Well-planned children's areas are designed so that teachers can supervise all areas from almost any vantage point without excessive walking. A teacher supervising in a room with an alcove may have to walk over to that area repeatedly to know what is happening there. An L-shaped outside area may be spacious, but such an area becomes impossible to supervise because as soon as children turn the corner, they are out of sight and beyond the reach of supervising adults.

Serving meals to children further complicates the traffic flow in the center. Because preschool children usually eat in their classrooms, there is no need for a separate cafeteria. In fact, in a public school, the noise and confusion of a cafeteria is inappropriate for preschoolers and the furniture is too large to accommodate them comfortably. Preschool classrooms, therefore, must be large enough to contain tables and chairs for all the children and teachers without crowding the play space, and the kitchen should be nearby. Steps or doorways between the kitchen and the classrooms make moving food carts or carrying trays difficult, and long distances between kitchen and classrooms may mean long walks for teachers and long waits for children when something extra is needed during mealtime.

The kitchen must function primarily in relation to the classrooms and secondarily in relation to adult areas. The amount of kitchen space required varies according to the activities to be conducted. The center that uses a catering service for lunches may need very little space, while the center in which hot lunches are prepared will require additional equipment and space. In very large centers, a kitchenette may be provided for staff use, for preparation of refreshments for various meetings.

Licensing laws regulate the number of toilets and sinks required, but the location of the bathroom is equally important. Children need bathrooms immediately adjacent to their classrooms, multipurpose room, and outdoor play areas so that they can get to them quickly. Each of these areas may not need a separate bathroom, but planning can include location of one bathroom to serve two areas. Since prekindergarten boys and girls are comfortable sharing the same bathroom, doors in front of each toilet can be eliminated. However, the philosophy of some programs and the requirements of some governmental bodies now necessitate separate toilet facilities for boys and girls. Certainly these are needed for school-age children. As with all other areas, restrooms require adequate adult supervision.

Location of adult bathroom facilities is often determined by designing a plumbing core around which the

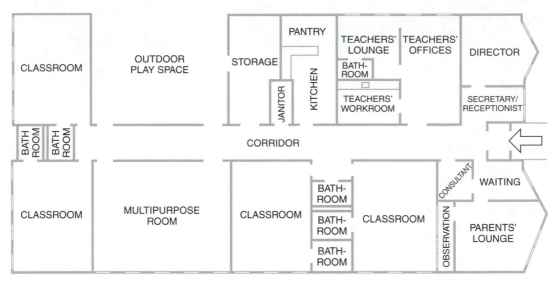

Figure 8–1

Hypothetical center floor plan showing relation of staff space to child space.

bathrooms and kitchen are built. Although a plumbing core design is economical, it may not be practical in terms of the traffic pattern and the program needs because adult bathrooms must be placed appropriately to serve the people in classrooms, offices, meeting rooms, and kitchen. It is particularly important that classroom teachers have easy access to adult bathrooms while children's programs are in session.

Figure 8–1 shows an example of a plan for a child care center, but because each center should be designed to meet the needs of its clients and staff, it is not meant as a model. Several of this plan's characteristics are worth imitating, however. Note that as families arrive, the receptionist (or director) can greet them and then they can go directly to the classrooms. An observation booth is shown overlooking one classroom. When space is available, this feature may be desired for all of the children's spaces. Note, too, that each classroom has an adjoining restroom and that a multipurpose room is available for large-muscle activities.

In planning for traffic flow, the staff's daily traffic patterns also must be considered with attention focused on which areas they use in what sequence on a typical day. Figure 8–1 shows the relationship of staff members' spaces to children's spaces in one center. Teachers need a conveniently located general storage room to enable them to set up the day's activities efficiently. They must be able to move comfortably and quickly from the storage areas to the classroom, the outdoor area, or the multipurpose room, depending on where the equipment or

the supplies are needed. Teachers also need a cabinet that they keep locked for storing the solutions used to sanitize the tables and for other cleaning supplies.

Sometimes, with proper written documentation from parents and the child's physician, a teacher will be asked to administer medication at school. Paying attention to licensing guidelines as well as center policies and procedures related to these issues is essential. And, of course, teachers need coat storage that is readily accessible when they go outdoors with children.

Office space sometimes is placed close to the classrooms so that immediate additional supervision can be provided in an emergency situation; but planners may decide to place the offices farther away from the classrooms to eliminate distractions for the director, off-duty teachers, or other staff members. An intercom system can be installed to facilitate communication in emergency situations and to eliminate disturbances. The intercom or a telephone may be a necessity if a classroom or any other area used by children is isolated from direct contact with the rest of the center. For example, all classrooms may be located on the ground floor while the multipurpose room is a level above them. A teacher using the multipurpose room needs a telephone to reach additional help if a crisis occurs.

Figures 8–2 and 8–3 show additional ideas for arranging center facilities. If you have ever browsed through magazines showing floor plans of various

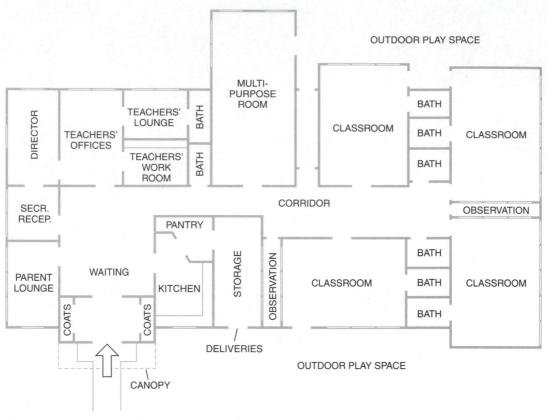

Figure 8–2

Hypothetical floor plan.

homes, you may have found yourself saying, "There's a feature I like" or "I'd never want to have a room like that." Consider these floor plans in the same way. Examine them to see what you would like and why. Keep in mind that the ages and numbers of children to be served will have a major effect on the plan for the building and grounds. Geography and topography also will play important roles. For example, on a sloping lot, both the front and the back of a building may be at least partially at ground level. This condition is an important planning issue.

Personal Space

A comfortable and convenient classroom for young children includes enough space for each child to work and play without being disturbed by other activities. Thirty-five square feet per child is considered minimum, so a classroom for 10 three-year-olds must have at least 350 square feet, measuring about 18 feet by 20 feet. Fifty square feet per child is more realistic, and more space should be provided whenever

possible. However, extremely large classrooms are difficult to supervise and may feel overwhelming to children.

Children need cozy places where they can relax while they look at books, examine interesting objects, or just daydream. These spaces should be small enough to promote a sense of privacy and intimacy, yet large enough to be shared with a friend or two. Sometimes, a loft can meet this need. It must be quite sturdy and have some kind of siding to prevent objects from falling to the floor and hitting anyone below. The space under the loft can be used for storage or small group activities. In any event, the teacher must be able to supervise the area. Furthermore, it would be wise to build a loft that is accessible to a child with special needs.

The classroom also must include a meeting area that is large enough for a number of children to gather for a story or special activity. Furniture can be moved for these occasions. Movable shelving and furniture facilitate such rearranging. These movable pieces also will be valued when teachers are placing

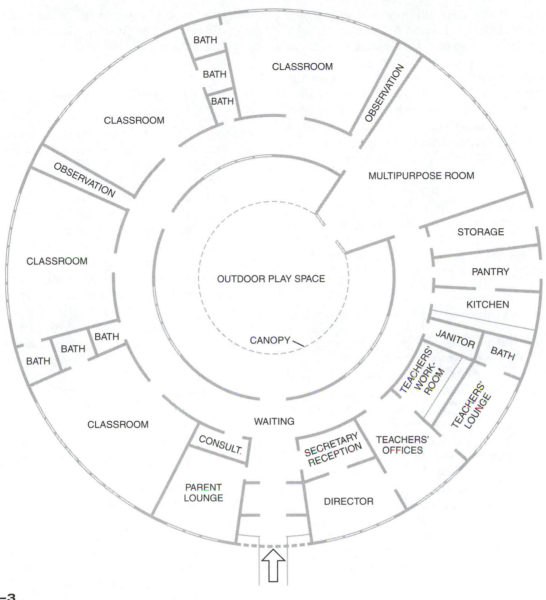

Figure 8–3

Alternate hypothetical floor plan.

cots for children's naps. Most centers do not have a separate nap room and must consider how to place cots so that children will not be too close to one another (a requirement of many licensing rules). When cots are too close together, children may find it difficult to rest. Space also must be available for cot storage.

Staff members have a variety of space needs. These include personal space for storing their belongings, bathroom facilities separate from those used by the children, and a lounge area in which to have refreshments during break times. Work space includes places

in which they work with children, places in which they prepare materials for classrooms, and places in which they do paperwork or hold conferences. Work space that meets the staff members' needs assists them in performing their duties well. Some personnel have specialized work spaces (maintenance staff, the cook, or the nurse). Each work place must be of a size suitable for the activity in question. For example, full-time office staff each need approximately 100 square feet of office space. This space should be arranged to provide for some privacy and sound control so that work can be accomplished with minimal interruption.

Parents and visitors need a comfortable lounge area in which to wait for their children or to talk with each other. Parents also need a space that is large enough for group meetings and space that is small enough for individual conferences with a teacher or the director. Even if a whole room is not available, centers at least can provide some seating in another area. Fire laws may preclude having furniture in hallways. Facilities for observing the classrooms, while going unnoticed by the children, represent both a convenience and a learning experience for parents and visitors.

Often, employer-sponsored child care is provided near the work site. Parents will appreciate an area in the classroom where they can spend quiet time with their own children, sharing a book or puzzle. In infant centers, a private space for nursing offers a relaxing time for mother and baby.

REFLECTION

Think about a place to which you often go. Maybe it's a library, a store, or a college building. What kind of experience do you have as you approach the building? Is it easy to find the entrance? Is it accessible? Do you feel comfortable entering, or are you a little bit intimidated? Once you enter, can you find the area you need? If not, is help available (a receptionist, signs, a computer information kiosk)? How do you feel when everything seems quite unfamiliar and no one seems to care that you have arrived?

Children who come to the center for before- and after-school care will treasure some personal space. Imagine spending 10 hours a day in a relatively small space with 30 people primarily following someone else's directions. Although many adults do spend 8 hours in a work environment crowded with equipment and people, they have the opportunity to go out for lunch or take a short break. Children in schools usually are required to stay with their class for the entire day. After school, having some private space provides a welcome respite. Before and after school, elementary grade children also need spaces for organizing clubs and playing games, for informal sports, and for creating and carrying out their own wonderful ideas. They need adult supervision, but at the same time, they need much more independence in organizing and reorganizing the space, perhaps

decorating it so it is theirs. Because these needs are quite different from those of younger children, it is clear that they need separate spaces.

Opportunities for Independence and Growth

The facility should be planned to promote the independence of both children and staff. An environment for children fosters independence and growth when it is arranged so they can make decisions and solve their own problems. Such a setting has child-size appointments, including sinks, toilets, drinking fountains, doorknobs that children can reach and operate (where that is desirable), and wall decorations that are placed at the children's eye level. Planners must keep in mind that independence is equally important for children with special needs.

A setting that encourages independence also has classroom storage that is directly accessible to children, enabling them to find and reach all the materials and equipment they use. When such storage is adequate, each piece of equipment is displayed so that the children can see it easily, remove it from the shelf without moving other items stacked on top of it, and return it to its proper place. Clearly marked storage space for children's personal belongings, located so that children can get to it, also will promote independence. In addition, however, storage space that is out of children's reach also is needed in each classroom so that teachers can store materials and supplies they do not want the children to obtain, such as gallon jugs of glue.

Single-purpose buildings allow programming to be based on users' needs (especially those of children) rather than requiring that the program be planned based on the needs of a range of occupants. A center allows teachers to feel independent when the design of the facility enables them to plan programs for their children without constantly checking with other teachers. For example, teacher independence is curtailed when a preschool class is housed in a public elementary school where the young children must use the bathroom, lunchroom, or outdoor play space for specific time blocks because older children use these facilities at other times. Even if the children's needs suggest a deviation from this schedule, the teacher may be required to follow it. Some teachers in centers that move children from room to room for various activities find that they are not able to plan as independently if they have to direct children from the art room to the music room and then to the playroom on a daily basis at a predetermined, scheduled time rather than having the children move at their own pace.

Trees and grassy areas enhance the children's playground.

The environment that fosters independence and growth is one in which variety is apparent, offering children an *appropriate* number of choices. They are not overwhelmed with choices or bored with repetitive sameness in design of space. Variety in color, texture, floor level, and building materials, if not overdone, can give children a sense of vitality that can be stimulating. Noise level is another area in which variety can be appropriate. Some spaces may be set aside for noisy play while others are retained for quieter activities. Although acoustical ceilings, carpeted floors, and curtains all absorb sound and contribute to the auditory comfort of everyone in the center, children still can learn to use appropriate sound levels in each space and to choose their activities accordingly. The environment leads to cooperation as well as to independence.

Aesthetic Character

An environment for children should be aesthetically pleasing to them. The factors relating to other users' needs and to program requirements can be designed so that they appeal to the children's sense of beauty. For example, it is just as easy to have an interesting painting in the classroom as it is to put up a fake window with curtains over the play sink. Both are intended to make the room more attractive. Children can enjoy a wide range of art, but the value of a fake window is limited, at best.

Provide as much natural light as possible while avoiding glare. Artificial lighting should be bright enough for children's activities but also adjustable. Lamps that cannot be tipped over, ceiling lighting that can be controlled with dimmer switches, and area lighting all contribute to a feeling of physical and emotional well-being and help foster productivity, relaxation, and comfort. Incandescent lighting and full-spectrum lighting seem more appropriate than fluorescent.

Wall surfaces can provide texture and color that contribute to the room's vitality. Garish decorations or "cute" wall coverings, emblems, or cutouts contribute little to children's appreciation of beauty. Carpets replete with numbers and letters add "busyness" to the environment and provide neither aesthetic nor intellectual stimulation. Children and staff probably will be more inclined to take care of an attractive environment. It is easy to develop messy habits when the surroundings are poorly designed with inadequate facilities and unappealing spaces. It is equally easy and more satisfying for everyone to develop good habits and an appreciation of beauty when the facilities are well designed. Note that the touches a teacher adds may be inexpensive or free: a single flower from her garden, attractively mounted pictures of the children at play, or a crystal hanging in the window to catch the light and project interesting colors and patterns throughout the room.

Having analyzed the facility requirements for a high-quality early childhood education program, and the information provided by a specific needs assessment, the director can determine the center's current facility needs and project the building and grounds needs of the center for several years. This long-range planning is useful in enabling a center to coordinate program, facility, and financial decision making. Whether the director is analyzing need in terms of possibly rearranging or remodeling the existing center's facilities, or of leasing or constructing a new center, the users' needs are kept in the forefront when working toward a decision about the facility.

DIRECTOR'S CORNER

"Our entire staff spent hours discussing what our ideal center would look like. We listed all the criteria for each space, including details such as height and depth of classroom sinks, number of feet of shelving in the toy storage room, and types of doorknobs. We couldn't have everything we wanted because of the cost, but we all felt like we had helped design our new center."

–Director, agency-sponsored center

Programmatic Requirements

The director and building committee members must be thoroughly familiar with the early childhood education program before they attempt to evaluate an existing or proposed facility. They must understand the types of activities planned, the program goals, and the enrollment projections. For example, in contrast to a half-day program, a full-day program must provide a place for resting and for eating meals. Many children who spend the entire day at a center also need room in which to seclude themselves from the group for short periods of time, a quiet place supervised by the teacher but free from the intrusion of other children.

The center's philosophy influences the type and arrangement of space. If the philosophy places heavy emphasis on parent involvement, space will be needed for meeting rooms and a lounge, and additional parking will have to be provided. The prevailing climate also affects the type of building. If children are able to be outdoors most days on a year-round basis, they will need more outdoor space and slightly less indoor space. On the other hand, a center located in a region with temperature extremes will put emphasis on indoor areas and will give major consideration to effective heating, ventilating, and air-conditioning systems. Floor-level temperature in the children's areas is critical since children frequently play on the floor.

Planning for carpeting and tiling sections of the classroom floor should be done with activities in mind. Cleaning is facilitated when art and food activities take place on hard surfaces, and teachers will be able to focus on the children's needs instead of protecting the carpeting. A sink in the classroom is a much-used and much-desired convenience and also should be on the tiled area.

Keep in mind the importance of the outdoor environment. Just as children need to test ideas in the classroom, so too do they need to test ideas outdoors. They also need opportunities to test what they can do physically as they explore an environment created to challenge and stimulate them. Similarly, children need time to try new ways of doing things, new ways of interacting with water, mud, plants, and people. As more and more information becomes available on the problems caused by childhood obesity, directors must plan for spaces and opportunities for children to engage in significant periods of large motor activity. When the outdoor environment is aesthetically pleasing for children and adults, well maintained, and designed with lots of movement in mind, it beckons them to come out and be involved.

Admission policies will have an impact on the facilities requirements. For example, centers that accept infants must provide space for infant cribs and a number of feeding tables, as well as safe places where infants can explore their environment freely. Spaces for infants and toddlers must be designed for them instead of being scaled-down versions of preschool classrooms. Ramps, wide doorways, and low light switches are necessities for children who have a disability. When planning a facility, it is mandatory to provide for children and adults with special needs so that they can be served effectively and so that the requirements of federal and state laws can be met.

Governmental Regulations

In communities that have zoning laws, an early childhood education center that is operated for profit may be limited to locating in a business or less restrictive zone, while a nonprofit educational facility generally may be located in any zone. Prior to signing a lease or contract to purchase property, the director must check with the local zoning board to see if usage of the particular piece of property is in compliance with the zoning code. In some cases, a zoning variance may be allowed; that is, the director may petition to use the location for a center if it can be shown that the presence of the center will not have a negative effect on neighboring sites. Zoning ordinances also may include parking requirements, and off-street parking provisions may have to be made for center staff and visitors, including those who have special needs.

When a new facility is built or an existing building renovated or put to a new use, current codes usually apply. For example, a building being used as a public school would be inspected based on the codes in existence when that building was put into use. However, if a child development center leases the space, the owner will be required to meet the *current* regulations. When a building is renovated or a new facility is constructed, the Americans with Disabilities Act (ADA) must be followed. Some requirements include access by means of ramps instead of stairs, accessible restroom facilities, doors that can be opened by a person in a wheelchair, and low drinking fountains.

Other governmental regulations pertain to licensing. These are discussed in Chapter 4 and include number of square feet of space for children's use both indoors and outdoors, fencing, exits, building materials, and toilet and hand-washing facilities. Before you purchase, lease, or renovate a building, ask your licensing agent to ensure that the facility is in compliance with governmental regulations or can be renovated appropriately and at an affordable price. There may be a charge for this consultation.

PLANNING A NEW CENTER

In planning for a new center, the director, who sometimes works along with a building committee of the board, must decide on a site early in the planning stage. The decision may be to construct a building; to buy, rent, or lease an existing building; or to locate space that would be donated by the owner on a temporary or permanent basis. Planning for a new center involves the same analysis of space requirements that is done when an ongoing program facility is assessed. The one item that stands out as being conspicuously important in decisions about planning a new center is cost. Although cost is a major factor, the key concept is the value of the setting to both children and staff. When staff find themselves working in a well-designed, appropriate space, they are happier, which leads to a better program for children (Sussman, 1998).

The director who has started facilities planning with a needs assessment has applicable information about zoning, licensing, program requirements, and clients. These data, combined with the availability of a particular amount of money, are applied as criteria in the search for appropriate facilities. Some centers

assess needs, locate facilities, and then mount a fund drive, anticipating that sufficient money will be obtained. The director or building committee must assess realistically the amount of money that will be *available* for establishing and maintaining the center facility and the amount of money that will be *required* to meet the assessed need.

The building committee works closely with the budget committee to determine the amount of money needed and available for constructing, purchasing, renovating, or leasing a building. Costs of real estate and construction vary widely depending on geographical location, and within a given city they vary from the inner city to the suburbs. Costs must be checked for each locale. Careful planning is essential because once construction starts, changes are costly.

Considering New Construction

Both land and building costs must be considered. The lot must be large enough for a building of the required size; for a playground of at least 75 square feet per child (groups of children may use this area at different times); and for parking for staff, parents, and visitors. The cost of the building will depend on the size of the building, on the quality and elaborateness of the materials used, and on the intricacy of the design. A major advantage of new construction is that the building can be made to look like a place for children. And if it is well designed, it will be a place in which the program can be delivered efficiently, effectively, and with a high level of comfort for all users.

Using Existing Buildings

Costs involved with the use of an existing building are purchase price, lease or rent, and renovation. A center may incur none, one, or two of these costs, depending on the owner and on the condition of the building.

Sometimes, a church or community service organization will permit an early childhood education center to use its facilities at little or no charge. Available rooms also may be found in school buildings. This contribution is a major cost benefit to the program. Before agreeing to this use of the building, however, both the contributor and the center board should have a clear written understanding of the rights and responsibilities of each party. For example, both will need to know how liability insurance will be handled.

If funds are available, a down payment on the purchase of a lot or a building, or plans for extensive remodeling, may be made. The board must be certain that funds for monthly payments, including interest as well as principal, will be available. A bank or savings and loan company can provide information on interest rates, length of mortgage, and payment procedures. It also can explain penalties, foreclosures, and insurance requirements.

Renting or Leasing

Because purchasing a building involves high initial costs, most centers rent or lease all or part of a building. Both renting and leasing involve periodic payments. Under a lease, the lessor and the lessee agree that the space will be available and paid for during a specified length of time, usually at least a year. A longer lease is preferable since moving can be expensive and clients may be lost if the center changes locations. Relocation costs include staff time spent in the following activities:

- Fund-raising
- Attending additional board committee meetings
- Locating a new site
- Negotiating the lease
- Arranging loan for additional costs
- Communicating with staff and families about the move
- Arranging for required and desired renovations
- Planning logistics of move
- Working with licensing specialist
- Arranging for reaccreditation as needed
- Managing the unexpected

Following are direct costs of relocation:

- Attorney fees
- Architect and contractor fees
- Materials needed for renovation
- Cleaning prior to move
- Movers
- Changing address or other information on stationery, brochures, Web site
- Reaccreditation fee
- Paying staff overtime to prepare new site just before center opens

One of the most challenging aspects of moving a center is making the move so that service to children and families will be interrupted as little as possible. Another challenge is the possible loss of families if the new location is not as convenient for them.

The director is then faced with recruiting new families quickly while managing the settling-in period in the new center. When a space is rented, the renter may have to pay only for the period during which the space is actually used. For a nine-month preschool program, this savings could be important and significant. Such a situation occurs primarily when renting from a church. The school's equipment may have to be moved out during the summer months or may be used by other groups as part of the rental agreement. If you are renting space, can you negotiate limitations on rent increases?

A lease should spell out these conditions and include items such as

- the beginning and ending dates of the lease.
- whether or not the lease is renewable.
- if renewable, what limits, if any, will be set on a fee increase: whether or not the lease can be terminated early; if terminated, what penalties apply; whether or not you can sublet.
- who is responsible for maintenance and repairs: what is included; who pays for it; who provides materials, supplies, and tools; when maintenance and repairs will be done; who is responsible for compliance with building code.
- who pays for utilities.

For example, if the board of health requires the addition of a hand-washing sink (a permanent fixture), will the center or the landlord pay for the sink and its installation? The center cannot operate a program without the sink because a license will not be granted; but if the center should move, the landlord will still have the sink.

If the landlord is responsible for maintenance, can an agreement be reached that the grass is not cut during children's regular playground hours? Think about securing a written agreement about spraying for insects. Will it be done when children are present, meaning you will have to move them to another area? Will all materials to be used be safe for areas used by children?

If the facility is shared because the landlord uses part of it or rents part of it to someone else or because the center owns a building and rents or leases part of it to someone else, all the preceding items must be considered. In addition, the building committee or director will settle the matter of who has access to the building and when they may have access. For example, if a teenage group uses the building in the evenings, will they be allowed to use the playground during the late afternoon before all the children have left? Other points to be considered include the following:

- Who may have master keys?
- Who may use what equipment and supplies?
- Who is responsible for ordering and paying for shared equipment and supplies?
- Who pays the telephone bill? Internet service?

Other questions involve use of the center's space by other organizations or individuals when the children are not present, such as during the evenings or on weekends. The use of the facilities (their own and that of others) by center staff members and the parent group during evening, weekend, and holiday hours also must be considered.

It is easier to reach agreement on these issues before the building committee signs a lease and takes occupancy. If a lease has been signed, the center usually cannot be moved without financial penalty, which could mean that an uncomfortable situation exists for a number of months. When the lease clearly details the rights and responsibilities of each party, most questions can be settled amicably.

Renovating

Renovation costs also vary widely depending on the location of the building and the type of work to be done. Complex changes such as relocating plumbing; rewiring electrical circuits; or installing exits, stairways, and fire-resistant surfaces are costly. The type and amount of renovation to be done will be based on the particular licensing requirements, including fire and building codes, and on the requirements of the planned program. If the center owns the building, renovation usually is a worthwhile investment.

DIRECTOR'S CORNER

"When the renovation was initially being planned and the architects were working up the drawings, the chairperson of the committee and I went in and talked about what we would like to see happen. It seemed to break down after the initial meetings, and there were some outcomes that we were not that pleased with. Everything was ordered and halfway done before I realized what was happening. There wasn't any way that we could go back and ask for changes."

—Director, preschool in a church facility

WORKING WITH OTHER PROFESSIONALS

A variety of professionals outside the field of early childhood education can be helpful in planning a space for young children. Usually, the cost of their services is relatively high on an hourly rate, but in the long run, the expertise they contribute to the center's development is worth far more than the actual expenditure. However, checking references and credentials before you sign an agreement with the individual or company is critical. Written agreements with each service provider also are essential.

Licensing Agent

Because most programs must be licensed, the first professional that the building committee contacts is the licensing agent. This specialist often provides free services and is funded through state or local taxes. Through this agent, the committee works with other professionals in the building, sanitation, and fire departments. Community planners also may be involved, either at the governmental level or through community councils. Even though these professionals are not paid by the center, the licensing and inspection fees must be paid as required.

Architect

During the very early planning stage, retaining an architect can produce positive results. An architect can evaluate a site in terms of a center's needs or can examine an existing building and make recommendations about the renovations that are necessary for safety, efficiency, and aesthetics.

Ongoing architectural services can be contracted at an hourly rate, flat fee, or on a percentage basis. The architect should spell out clearly in a contract the services that are to be provided—such as survey, site selection, design, working drawings from which a building can be built or remodeled, contractor selection, construction supervision, and/or final inspection.

Your architect also will assist you in selecting materials if that is part of your contract. For instance, gypsum wallboard (which is inexpensive) is readily dented, gouged, and subject to corner damage. An architect whose firm specializes in school facilities recommends applying "a skim coat of 'diamond hard' plaster" to a height of four feet to increase durability" (Caples, 1996). If you are not familiar with building materials, this addition to your contract could save you much more than the added fee. The architect also should include in the contract the fee for services rendered and the dates that payments are due.

When selecting an architect, choose someone with whom you feel comfortable. Many architects are unfamiliar with child care center needs, and you will want to choose one who is willing to listen to your concept and incorporate your ideas. Keep in mind, however, that architects have knowledge about design and construction that can help you attain a more attractive, more functional building within your budget. A few architects will want to put a great deal of emphasis on the exterior of the building, using such a large portion of the budget there that little money remains for finishing and furnishing. Listen to your architect with an open mind, but be willing to insist on components essential to your program.

Also be sure to let your architect know what kind of budget you are working with. You may have dreams of an elaborate center with all kinds of wonderful enhancements, but your budget may dictate that you have a much more straightforward approach. A good architect can help you get the most for your money. Figure 8–1 shows a very simple, relatively inexpensive design. Only the essential spaces are included for this hypothetical half-day program. A rectangular building is often the least expensive to build.

When the plans are complete, asking a colleague to review them with you may help uncover details you hadn't considered. Changes made at this stage are relatively easy; changes made once construction begins may be impossible. At the very least, they usually are quite expensive.

Generally, the architect will oversee the job, but the general contractor is responsible for scheduling subcontractors, ordering materials, and so forth. Some architects also serve as construction managers, and some contractors offer building design services.

Contractor

A contractor may plan the construction or remodeling of the center's building and carry the work through to completion. Parts of the job may be subcontracted such as the electrical or plumbing work, but the contractor retains responsibility for the satisfactory and timely completion of that work. Nonetheless, the director must pay attention to the job as it moves along. Balancing frequent site visits with allowing the contractors to do their work is necessary, but asking questions is essential when you aren't sure about an aspect of the construction or when the work is not as promised. Sometimes, directors feel intimidated because they don't understand the drawings and specifications for the work. Part of the contractor's job is making sure that the work is done to the client's specifications as determined by the written contract.

Accountant

The building committee works with an accountant to determine the amount of money that can be invested responsibly in construction, purchase, or rental. The accountant also may help locate a lending agent and may help the building committee find the best interest rate. Information about depreciation and taxes also may be provided. An accountant may charge an hourly rate or a flat fee for a particular piece of work. Some centers pay an accountant a monthly retainer in exchange for whatever services are needed, including preparation for the annual audit.

Attorney

When the building committee decides to enter into a contract or sign a lease, its attorney reviews the document to ensure that the center's needs are being met and that all legal aspects have been covered. The attorney also participates in settling disputes in relation to payment, failure to perform work satisfactorily, and so forth. In a few cases, these disputes may be taken to court. In those special situations, the attorney would represent the center in court. The attorney may be on retainer or paid an hourly fee.

SUMMARY

Whether it is a brand-new building or one that was constructed years ago for another purpose, the ideal early childhood education center environment is created to meet the needs of the children, the staff members, the parents, and the visitors while satisfying all licensing requirements. Health and safety, accessibility of facilities, traffic patterns, personal space, opportunities for independence, and aesthetic character are the guidelines for determining the design. Professional services from the architects and contractors who work with building committee members, staff members, parents, children, and other professionals provide these aspects within the framework of the budget to create a center that is best suited for carrying out the program for which it has been designed.

CLASS ASSIGNMENTS

1. If you do not know how to compute the number of square feet in an area, find out how to do it. When you determine the square footage of a room for a center, include all of the area except those spaces that are used for permanent fixtures. For example, if a playroom has a sink that is 2 feet by 3 feet, you would have to deduct

6 square feet from the size of the room. However, it is not customary to deduct square footage for movable pieces such as tables or shelves. Record your answers to the following scenarios on Working Paper 8–1:

1. **a.** Assume that your center has a room 20 feet by 30 feet with a sink that is 2 feet by 3 feet. How many children could use the room? Consider first the minimum requirements in terms of square feet.

   b. Refigure the number of children that could be accommodated in terms of 50 square feet per child.

2. You want to have 20 children in a group at your center. What might the dimensions of the room be if you were to provide the minimum amount of space required?

3. What dimensions might the room have if you wanted to allow 50 square feet per child? (Assume you want to have 20 children in the group.)

2. With the director's permission, visit an early childhood education center (or use your student-teaching or work site). Use the information in Director's Resource 8–2 to guide you. Record information on Working Paper 8–2 about the following areas:

   ■ parking
   ■ exterior appearance of building and grounds
   ■ identifying sign
   ■ identifiable entrance
   ■ entry area
   ■ location of offices (director, teachers, secretary)
   ■ waiting room or lounge
   ■ adult bathrooms

   ■ classrooms (number, size, ease of supervision, arrangement of areas, attractiveness, neatness, noise level, temperature, relation to other areas used by children)
   ■ multipurpose room (size, arrangement of equipment, ease of supervision, attractiveness, temperature, noise level)
   ■ outdoor play area (size, fencing, arrangement of equipment, attractiveness, ease of supervision, variety of surfaces, shelter)
   ■ children's bathrooms in relation to classrooms, multipurpose room, and outdoor area

3. Draw a floor plan of the center where you student-teach or work. Include all indoor and outdoor spaces that are used in any way by children, staff, and parents. Make your drawing approximately to scale. Now draw the traffic patterns. Use red to show the children's pattern, blue for teachers, and green for parents. Complete your floor plan on Working Paper 8–3.

CLASS EXERCISES

1. Work with a classmate to design a floor plan for a child care center for 44 children (6 infants, 8 toddlers, 14 three-year-olds, and 16 four-year-olds). Also show the spaces that are used by adults. Be prepared to explain your design to the class.

2. Work with a classmate to design a building plan for a half-day preschool for 14 three-year-olds and 16 four-year-olds. Make your drawing approximately to scale.

3. Compare the drawings in Exercise 1 and Exercise 2. Are any of the differences attributable to full-day versus half-day child care?

WORKING PAPER 8-1

(for use with Class Assignment 1)

AREA FORM

1. Your center has a room 20 feet by 30 feet with a sink that is 2 feet by 3 feet.

    a. How many preschool children can use the room?

    b. How many children can the room accommodate if you decide to allot 50 square feet per child?

2. What might the dimensions of the room be if you were to provide the minimum square footage required for 20 children?

3. What might the dimensions of the room be if you were to provide 50 square feet per child for 20 children?

WORKING PAPER 8-2

(for use with Class Assignment 2)

FACILITIES VISITATION FORM

Name of center:

Record information about the following:

- parking

- exterior appearance of building and grounds

- identifying sign

- identifiable entrance

- entry area

- location of offices (director, teachers, secretary)

- waiting room or lounge

- adult bathrooms

- classrooms (number, size, ease of supervision, arrangement of areas, attractiveness, neatness, noise level, temperature, relation to other areas used by children)

- multipurpose room (size, arrangement of equipment, ease of supervision, attractiveness, temperature, noise level)

- outdoor play area (size, fencing, arrangement of equipment, attractiveness, ease of supervision, variety of surfaces, shelter)

- children's bathrooms in relation to classrooms, multipurpose room, and outdoor area

WORKING PAPER 8-3

(for use with Class Assignment 3)

CENTER FLOOR PLAN

Draw a floor plan of the center where you student-teach or work.

DIRECTOR'S RESOURCE 8-1

EVALUATING AND ADAPTING THE ENVIRONMENT

When we design an appropriate environment for children with diverse abilities and needs, two ground rules should apply:

- ■ The environment needs to be safe for all children. Special accommodations will be needed to make it accessible and safe for some children.
- ■ The environment impacts all children's abilities to participate, learn, and communicate. Special adaptations may be needed to help some children participate, learn, and communicate.

Since children use their bodies and their senses to explore, learn, and play, and since special needs often relate to differences in how children use their bodies or their senses, using our senses to evaluate the environment can help us organize, capitalize on, and adapt for diverse abilities and needs.

Physical Environment

Questions to think about:

- ■ How do different children use their bodies or the space around them for learning?
- ■ How can we enhance or adapt the physical environment for children who have difficulty moving (or who move too much)?
- ■ How can we capitalize on the physical environment for children who learn by moving?

Accessing the environment safely:

- ❏ Are doorway widths in compliance with local building codes?
- ❏ Ramps in addition to or instead of stairs?
- ❏ Low, wide stairs where possible (including playground equipment)?
- ❏ Hand rails on both sides of stairs?
- ❏ Easy handles on doors, drawers, etc.?
- ❏ At least some kids' chairs with armrests?
  - ■ "Cube" chairs are great!
  - ■ Often a footrest and/or seat strap will provide enough stability for a child to do fine motor activities.
- ❏ When adapting seating, mobility, and/or gross motor activities for a specific child with physical disabilities, consult a physical therapist.

(continues)

DIRECTOR'S RESOURCE 8-1
(continued)

Learning through the environment:

❑ Do the environment and equipment reflect variety?

- Surfaces, heights (textured, smooth, low, high, etc.)
- Space for gross motor activity (open spaces, climbing structures, floor mats)
- Quiet/comfort spaces (small spaces, carpet, pillows)
- Social spaces (dramatic play area, groups of chairs or pillows, etc.)

❑ Are toys and equipment physically accessible?

- Glue magnets to backs of puzzle pieces and attribute blocks and use on a steel cookie tray.
- Attach large knobs or levers to toys with lids, movable parts.
- Attach tabs to book pages for easier turning.

❑ An occupational therapist can provide specific suggestions for adapting materials and activities so a child with physical disabilities can participate.

Visual Environment

Questions to think about:

- How do different children use their vision for learning?
- How can we enhance the visual environment for a child with low or no vision?
- How can we capitalize on the visual environment for children who learn by seeing?

Accessing the environment safely:

❑ Are contrasting colors used on edges and when surfaces change (e.g., tile to carpet, beginning of stairs, . . .)?

❑ Can windows be shaded to avoid high glare?

- Also consider darker non-glossy floors and table tops.
- Some children's behavior and learning may improve dramatically once a strong glare is eliminated.

❑ Is visual clutter avoided on walls, shelves, etc?

- Visual clutter can interfere with learning, predictability, and safety.

❑ Is "spot lighting" (e.g., swing arm lamp) in a dimmer room available?

- Spot lamps help some children pay attention and work better on table tasks.

❑ Orientation and mobility specialists help children with visual impairments learn to navigate the environment.

(continues)

DIRECTOR'S RESOURCE 8-1
(continued)

Learning through the environment:

❏ Are objects and places in the environment labeled?

❏ Are the size and contrast of pictures and letters adequate for the children with visual impairments in your program?

❏ Are visual displays at the children's eye level?

❏ Are large print materials, textured materials, and auditory materials available (e.g., big books, sandpaper letters, books on tape)?

❏ Is the daily schedule represented in words and pictures?

  ■ A velcro schedule which allows children to post the schedule and then remove items as activities are complete can help children to stay focused and transition more easily from one activity to the next.

❏ Are children with low vision seated close to the center of activity and away from high glare?

❏ Teachers for the visually impaired assist in selecting and adapting materials for children with low vision.

❏ Children who are blind may need a "running commentary" of events, places, etc. Pictures in books and food on plates, for example, should be described.

Auditory Environment

Questions to think about:

  ■ How do different children use their hearing for learning?

  ■ How can we enhance the auditory environment for a child who is deaf, hearing impaired, or has poor auditory discrimination skills?

  ■ How can we capitalize on the auditory environment for auditory learners?

Assessing the environment safely:

❏ Does background noise (from indoor or outdoor sources) filter into the area?

❏ Is there a way to eliminate or dampen background noise (using carpeting, closing windows and doors . . .)?

  ■ Some kids are unable to do the automatic filtering out of background noises that we do so unconsciously.

❏ Is "auditory competition" avoided?

  ■ Raising one's voice to compete with a roomful of noisy children is rarely as effective as "silent signals" such as holding up a peace sign and encouraging children who notice to do the same until the room is full of quiet children holding up peace signs!

(continues)

DIRECTOR'S RESOURCE 8-1
(continued)

❑ Are non-auditory signals needed to alert a child with a hearing impairment?
   ■ Turning the lights on and off is a common strategy.
   ■ Ask the child's parents what strategies are used at home.

Learning through the environment:

❑ Are auditory messages paired with visual ones (e.g., simple sign language, flannel boards, picture schedules)?

❑ Are children with hearing impairments seated so they can see others' faces and actions?

❑ Teachers for the hearing impaired can provide strategies for modifying activities for children with hearing impairments.

❑ A child who is deaf will need a teacher or aide who uses sign language.

Social Environment

Questions to think about:

■ How do different children use social cues for learning?

■ How can we adapt the social environment for children with impulsive behavior, attention deficits, or behavior problems?

■ How can we capitalize on the social environment for children who learn by relating to others?

Accessing the environment safely:

❑ Is the schedule predictable? Are children informed of schedule changes?

❑ Does the schedule provide a range of activity level (e.g., adequate opportunities for physical activity)?

❑ School psychologists and behavior specialists can help analyze misbehavior and modify the environment or schedule to minimize problems for children with attention deficits or behavior problems.

Learning through the environment:

❑ Does the environment have a positive impact on self-esteem?
   ■ Allows all children to feel safe?
   ■ Invites all children to participate?
   ■ Maximizes all children's opportunities for independence?

(continues)

DIRECTOR'S RESOURCE 8-1
(continued)

❑ Do learning materials and toys include representation of all kinds of people, including children and adults with disabilities?

    ■ People with disabilities should be represented in active and leadership roles, not just as passive observers.

❑ Does the schedule include opportunities for a variety of groupings (pairs, small groups, whole class) as well as quiet time or time alone?

    ■ Pairing or grouping children with complementary abilities eases the demands on the teacher and enables children to help one another.

    ■ When given a chance, peers often come up with the most creative ways for children with disabilities to participate.

    ■ Creative use of staffing may be needed to provide additional support for some children during some activities.

❑ Does the schedule provide both structured and open activity times?

    ■ Children who have difficulty with a particular type of activity may need extra support at those times.

Additional Strategies When Adapting the Environment for Individual Children:

❑ Make use of the diverse strengths of the various people on the child's team.

    ■ Early childhood educators are among the most sensitive and creative when it comes to developing multisensory, inclusive activities that take individual children's skills and needs into account!

    ■ Be on the lookout for how kids modify environments and activities for themselves and their peers. They often come up with the most creative solutions!

    ■ Include parents when making accommodations for children with special needs. Parents know their own children better than anyone else.

    ■ Some children qualify for special education services through state-wide infant or preschool intervention services. The specialists in these programs can assist in assessing a child's needs and providing suggestions and/or parameters for modifying the environment (and instructional strategies).

❑ Respect for each child's strengths and needs is the most important ingredient in creating appropriate environments for all children.

Clearly, there are many ways to break down how we view the environment in order to adapt and/or capitalize on the qualities of an early childhood environment. Different people will find different views more or less helpful, and often particular children will inspire us to see the world in new ways. The key is to open our eyes—and ears, hands, and feet—to new possibilities for participation and learning.

Reprinted with permission from Child Care Information Exchange, P.O. Box 3249, Redmond, WA 98073, (800) 221-2864, http://www.ChildCareExchange.com. Permission conveyed through Copyright Clearance Center, Inc.

DIRECTOR'S RESOURCE 8-2

FACILITY CHECKLIST

What do you see?...

Yes	No	**Building and Landscape**
❑	❑	Building is without peeling paint, loose shingles, or graffiti
❑	❑	Shutters or other building adornments are in place
❑	❑	Window panes are without cracks or holes
❑	❑	Blinds and other window treatments are even, and show no tears or slats missing
❑	❑	Landscape is attractive and well kept
❑	❑	Gates are operable, easily opened by adults, but prevent children from leaving
❑	❑	The area for drop-off and pick-up of children is safe

Entrance

❑	❑	Entrance door is attractive and without dirt and fingerprints
❑	❑	Doors or alarm prevent children from wandering out of the center unnoticed
❑	❑	Intercom or other security system allows visitors to be screened before entering
❑	❑	Lobby is clean, attractively decorated, and welcoming for adults and children
❑	❑	Lobby furniture is in good shape, unstained, and attractive

Hallways and Common Space

❑	❑	Carpet is clean, secured to floor, and without buckling or tears
❑	❑	Tiles are clean, secured to floor, and without chips or missing pieces
❑	❑	Waxed floors are clean and show no buildup in corners or around molding
❑	❑	Items on bulletin boards are current and placed so as to be easily read
❑	❑	Names and/or information about classroom staff are posted outside of room
❑	❑	Walls are clean and without lots of tack holes or tape residue
❑	❑	There is no evidence of vermin

Classrooms

❑	❑	Furniture is clean, in good shape, stable, and child-sized
❑	❑	Classes are attractively arranged and inviting to children
❑	❑	Toys and materials are in good shape and have all parts and pieces
❑	❑	There is labeled space for children's belongings
❑	❑	Teacher supplies not in use are out of sight or neatly stored
❑	❑	Children's work is displayed and looks original
❑	❑	Pet cages are clean and do not smell
❑	❑	Dangerous substances are out of reach
❑	❑	There is minimal clutter

(continues)

DIRECTOR'S RESOURCE 8-2
(continued)

Yes	No	Playground
❏	❏	A variety of equipment and/or activities are available for all ages of children
❏	❏	Equipment is age-appropriate and in good condition
❏	❏	Areas beneath equipment provide cushioning for falls
❏	❏	Separate play areas are designated for toddlers and older children
❏	❏	The playground enclosure has an exit of egress
❏	❏	The area is free of debris, animal waste, thorny plants, or trees with fruit to ingest

What do you hear? . . .

Yes	No	From Children
❏	❏	Children laugh and appear to be relaxed and happy
❏	❏	Children ask adults for help without fear
❏	❏	Children are not afraid to approach staff

Yes	No	From Staff
❏	❏	Voices are pleasant and in moderate tones
❏	❏	Language is correct and spoken clearly
❏	❏	Staff encourage children to express themselves
❏	❏	Children are called by name
❏	❏	There are no adult conversations held in front of the children
❏	❏	Children's accomplishments and efforts are acknowledged with words of
❏	❏	encouragement
❏	❏	Laughter and "happy" talk are spontaneous

Reprinted with permission from *Child Care Information Exchange, P.O. Box 3249, Redmond, WA 98073, (800) 221-2864, http://www.ChildCareExchange.com. Permission conveyed through Copyright Clearance Center, Inc.*

REFERENCES

Caples, S. E. (1996). Some guidelines for preschool design. *Young Children 51*(4), 18–19.

Gandini, L. (1994, March). Not just anywhere: Making child care centers into particular places. *Child Care Information Exchange*, 48–50.

Kielar, J. (1999). An antidote to the noisy nineties. *Young Children, 54*(5), 28–29.

Moore, G. T. (1996). How big is too big? How small is too small? *Child Care Information Exchange, 110*, 21–23.

Sussman, C. (1998). Out of the basement: Discovering the value of child care facilities. *Young Children, 53*(1), 10–15.

Additional resources for this chapter can be found on the Online Companion™ at http://www.earlychilded.delmar.com. This supplemental material includes relevant Web links, Web activities, and case studies that apply the concepts presented in this chapter. In addition, the Working Papers and Director's Resources are available for download, allowing you to complete Class Exercises and Class Assignments electronically.

CHAPTER 9

Equipping the Center

Supplying appropriate equipment contributes significantly to the success of early childhood education programs.

OBJECTIVES

After reading this chapter, you should be able to:

- Identify the necessary equipment that will meet children, adult, and service area needs.
- Identify criteria for choosing vendors and equipment.
- Compile a list for maintaining and storing equipment.
- Provide justification of needs when preparing an order requisition.

It is both challenging and rewarding to equip a child development center. Your personality will be reflected in the physical environment you create as you strive to meet the needs of the children and as you select things that enable you to set up a program congruent with your program philosophy. Although many programs are being implemented with inadequate, unsuitable materials, supplying equipment that is appropriate contributes significantly to the success of early childhood education programs and is necessary for successful program implementation. Creating rich learning environments that are replete with abundant opportunities for children to be actively involved with age-appropriate and individually appropriate materials requires thoughtful, careful selection of classroom equipment and supplies. Also, staff members are able to do their assigned jobs more efficiently and comfortably when they work in adequately equipped environments.

Equipping a center is costly, and when mistakes are made, replacements are doubly costly. Many companies charge about 30 percent of the cost of items that have been returned unless, of course, they arrived damaged. In addition, the center pays the return shipping. Impulse buying is irresponsible when you are in charge of purchasing equipment. Therefore, plan your purchases carefully by first assessing your needs, next developing criteria for equipment selection, and finally relating needed and desired items to your budget. After selections are made, decide on ordering procedures, and develop a maintenance and storage system to reduce unnecessary repairs and losses.

ESTABLISHING NEEDS

There are three major areas to equip in a child care center, and a director must determine the type and amount of equipment needed for each one.

1. children's spaces, both indoors and outdoors

2. adult spaces, including offices, waiting rooms, conference rooms, and lounge areas

3. service areas

Equipment includes not only furniture but also appliances, computers, and other durable goods. Also included in the budget are supplies consisting of items that have a relatively short useful life or that are disposable. Examples are computer disks, finger paint, food, and paper towels. The equipment and supplies budgets should provide for initial purchases, as well as for long- and short-term replacement of both basic furnishings and consumable supplies.

Directors entering an ongoing program begin by taking inventory of what is on hand, setting up a priority system for securing new equipment, replacing worn-out items, and replenishing supplies of consumable materials. Directors of new centers are confronted with the somewhat overwhelming task of equipping an entire center.

Many equipment suppliers will be happy to provide sample equipment and supplies lists. Even more valuable is the Association for Childhood Education International (ACEI) publication listing suggested purchases for various age groups from infants through school age (Moyer, 1995). (See Director's Resource 9–1) These comprehensive lists are not intended as mandatory purchases but as guides to be adjusted and supplemented, based on the needs of particular children, staff, and families. As new materials become available, they can be considered, based on their appropriateness for the children who will use them. For example, although vinyl records were widely available in preschools some years ago, today centers are more likely to purchase CDs or DVDs.

Children's Spaces

Program philosophy and the needs of children dictate what will be ordered for the children's spaces in the center. Most programs are set up in basic curricular areas such as art, music, blocks, books, science, manipulative, and pretend play and spaces for math games and writing materials. All of these curricular areas require special furnishings and materials. Provisions also must be made for water and sand play, carpentry, cooking, building, and large-muscle activities. Furniture for working, resting, and eating is needed, including such accessories as clocks, plants, wastebaskets, and curtains. If the director is not familiar with early childhood curriculum and the associated equipment, room arrangement, and scheduling, the center definitely will need an education coordinator who has this knowledge and who is an experienced early childhood teacher. She must also be familiar with programs for infants, toddlers, and school-age children if those groups are to be served. Taking courses in early childhood education curriculum and child development will also enable the director to develop a better understanding of why some materials are important and why others are not supportive of program goals and children's needs. Curriculum courses also provide information on how and why to integrate curriculum. Suggested books on curriculum and child development are included in the Director's Library in Appendix D.

Adult Spaces

Even a very small center requires some office space with a locked file cabinet for records at the very minimum. Since adult desks are not used in classrooms for young children, some space for teachers to use as they plan their curriculum and prepare reports is essential. Furnishings that facilitate curriculum development include shelving for a teacher resource library and a work table with paper cutter, laminator, and storage for supplies such as poster board, scissors, and markers.

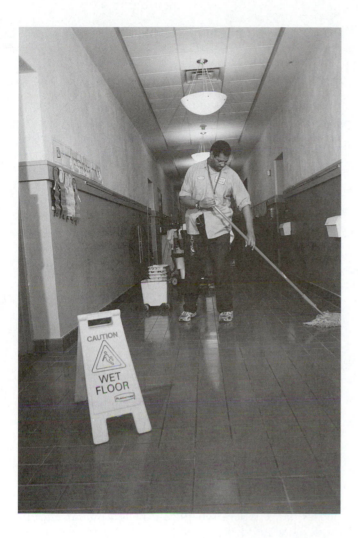

Almost every professional child care center director now relies on a computer for record keeping, billing, correspondence, writing reports, information gathering, and e-mail. Some teachers also use computers to maintain professional currency through the use of the Internet. Therefore, purchasing appropriate software becomes a significant contribution to the smooth running of a center. A survey of the CCIE panel of directors by editor Roger Neugebauer led to a list of questions directors should ask before purchasing software.

1. Does it meet my needs?
2. Is it easy to use?
3. Is it flexible?
4. Is help available?
5. Is the software guaranteed in writing?
6. Can you provide references whom I can contact? (Neugebauer, 1997).

You should also find out whether updates are provided and at what cost. Directors should be assertive about getting answers to these questions before purchasing software. In some cases, the vendor will allow you to try out the program before purchasing it. If your knowledge of computer use is limited, recognize that everyone has experienced this beginning stage and avoid saying you understand if that is not the case. Although it is not uncommon to find glitches in computer software, you still should expect the vendor to provide needed support in rectifying the problem.

The director is responsible for equipment for adult, child, and service areas.

When office space is provided, the basic furnishings for each occupant include two chairs, a desk, a file cabinet, and a bookshelf. A desk and cabinet can be shared by two teachers who spend most of their time in the classroom. Teachers need access to a telephone for parent contacts and for limited personal calls when they are on break. The location of the telephone should allow for quiet talks and for privacy. Staff also need a few comfortable chairs for lounging during breaks, a refrigerator for storing snacks, and any other amenities that the center can provide.

Directors of larger centers find that a copy machine is a worthwhile investment in terms of the time and money saved in duplicating such items as newsletters, menus, and forms. Although these machines are initially expensive, they pay for themselves over time by saving staff time and enable the center to produce materials of professional quality.

When the families who are affiliated with your center have access to the Internet, you may want to send information via e-mail. This process may be used for communicating with the entire center's population, with families from a particular classroom, or with an individual parent. Setting up a listserv with the e-mail addresses of those families who choose to be included makes communication easy and quick. However, other ways of reaching those who are not using this technology must be provided. Remember, too, that personal face-to-face communication is still highly desirable whenever possible. You may also want to communicate with members of the broader community by creating and maintaining a Web site. In some areas, this approach can be developed into a successful marketing tool.

The staff needs a place for meetings. When staff meetings are held after children leave, the classrooms can be used. However, it certainly is more comfortable for the adults attending meetings to have a space furnished with adult-size chairs and tables. Comfortable furniture should be provided for use by parents who come to the center for conferences and by consultants who come to meet with staff members. Bulletin boards and coat racks are convenient accessories for adult spaces. Since some adults who come to the center have disabilities, consider the seating and other furnishings and equipment in terms of their needs.

Some centers provide a separate lounge for parents and visitors. This area should have comfortable seating, lamps, tables, a bookshelf for pertinent reading materials, and perhaps facilities for coffee or other refreshments. Wall hangings or pictures, plants, a rug or carpet, and curtains all enhance the appearance of the space. A shelf of toys and books for visiting children indicates that the center is sensitive to children's needs.

Service Areas

Basic equipment in the bathrooms, kitchen, laundry, and janitor's closet is usually built in and, therefore, is not purchased from the equipment and supplies budget. In a new facility, some appliances may be included in the equipment line. Consumables for service areas must be furnished, and, of course, appliances must be replaced over time. Dishes, cutlery, cooking utensils, and serving carts must be provided in centers where lunch is served. In large centers, special appliances such as commercial dishwashers, rug shampooers, heavy-duty automatic washers and dryers, and large refrigerators and freezers are needed. The local board of health may have very specific requirements about the type of kitchen equipment that must be provided.

USING SELECTION CRITERIA

Selection of all equipment should be based on a set of preestablished criteria. The primary consideration is usefulness; that is, will a specific piece of equipment meet the needs of this center? Other criteria are versatility, safety, suitability, durability, ease of maintenance, attractiveness, and user preference. Some equipment for children should encourage and even necessitate cooperative play. All equipment should work the way it is supposed to and should be durable and economical. Although these criteria apply to all equipment purchases, this chapter primarily covers information about equipment that children will use. Refer to Director's Resources 9–2 and 9–3 for further information.

The goals and objectives of a particular center will dictate some purchases. A center that emphasizes academic development with a special focus on mathematics and problem solving will purchase a wide variety of materials suitable for helping children attain knowledge about math. In this case, some advanced math games will be included with the expectation that the comprehensive program in math will enable the children to enjoy these more complex materials. On the other hand, a center that emphasizes social development may concentrate more heavily on materials for pretend play and on equipment that can be used simultaneously by a number of children. Most early childhood programs will focus on these two areas equally, and only a few, if any, will exclude either area. The focal points of a program will be based on its philosophy, which will determine, in part, the types of equipment and the quantity of equipment of various types to be purchased.

Today's standards-driven educational approaches require that administrators and staff become familiar with standards set forth by state departments of education and national professional organizations. In some cases, working to ensure that all children meet these standards will be mandated. For example, in some states, even preschool centers that receive state funds will be expected to be guided by the standards. More and more, children entering kindergarten are being tested to determine what they have learned. Directors who have a good grasp of developmentally appropriate curriculum will be able to help teachers work toward the standards within the context of routines, schedules, and plans that meet each child's needs while supporting children's acquisition of the content standards. Eliminating play and the related materials and equipment is not an option.

Suitability of specific curricular materials will not be discussed here since a number of texts include this information in the context of program development.

REFLECTION
REFLECTION

Think of yourself as a director who is responsible for equipment purchases. Did you realize that you would pore over classroom equipment and materials, Web sites, and catalogs and would find yourself searching through office equipment and restaurant supply catalogs, Web sites, and ads? Your duties now have expanded from educator and administrator to purchasing agent. This responsibility probably seems like an overwhelming undertaking at the moment because many of you have been responsible for purchasing only personal items and, in some cases, basic household equipment. You are, no doubt, beginning to realize that the role of the director has many facets and requires a wide variety of special skills.

Usefulness

The usefulness of a piece of children's equipment is measured first by how well it meets the developmental needs of the children in the program and second by whether the equipment can be put to multiple uses by those children.

Developmental Needs

The developmental levels, capabilities, and the age range of the children enrolled influence what will be purchased. A center serving two-year-olds will need some pull toys and small climbers that would not be needed if the youngest child were three. Infants require special furnishings such as cribs and changing tables. Although younger infants are always held during feeding, infants who are able to sit independently are also ready to help feed themselves and should be encouraged to do that. High chairs had been standard equipment for this purpose, but because of the danger of the child's falling from the chair, they are usually replaced by low feeding tables, similar to high chairs but with shorter legs. Infants also require washable and chewable toys, bibs, sheets, blankets, and disposable diapers. Parents may be asked to furnish some of those necessary items and to take responsibility for their infant's laundry.

When center bathrooms have adult-size toilets and sinks, children will need step stools to be able to use the equipment independently. Preferably, the center will have installed child-size, toddler-height toilets and sinks. Toddlers also need toys that provide opportunities for filling and dumping, big toys that can be carried during early walking stages, and lots of duplicates so that sharing will not be necessary.

School-aged children in after-school care programs need games and crafts that are far too complex and frustrating for younger children. They also may need well-lighted working areas for homework, larger furniture in which they can sit and work comfortably, and equipment for active, semiorganized sports and games. They also need a place to store and eat snacks and an area where they can be away from the group for a while when they need time to relax alone.

Programs for school-age children should enable them to participate as fully as possible in activities that other children their age enjoy. When the center is well equipped to meet these needs, it will provide not only what the children could have been doing at home after school but also enriching group activities that encourage children to develop new interests and hobbies.

Children with special needs may require modified equipment or equipment that has been specifically designed to meet a particular need. A director who has established contact with agencies serving people with disabilities can seek their assistance in providing modifications or special equipment. The equipment should enable the child to do as much as possible independently.

Versatility

A piece of equipment that can be used in several ways is a bonus, both financially and in terms of enriching the learning environment for children. Such a piece saves space and money and gives children the opportunity to use their imaginations in creating different functions for one object. An example would be the large hollow blocks that can be used to make a puppet stage or a grocery store or can serve as individual work spaces for children's small projects. A bookshelf can be a room divider and a storage facility. Two-year-olds may find the water table to be a relaxing place for splashing while four-year-olds may be more interested in using this equipment for constructing a water maze. Many pieces of equipment may be shared by two or more classes for the same or different purposes, eliminating the purchase of duplicate materials and freeing up money for other purchases.

Some equipment can be used both indoors and outdoors, a practice that is economical and provides a wider variety of learning experiences for children. Easels, water tables, and movable climbing equipment are a few items that may be moved outside if the building and play area have been planned to facilitate such indoor-outdoor movement. When that planning has not occurred, teachers will not be able to leave the children in order to make several trips to carry equipment, and the children will not have access to those items. Perhaps a janitor, or in elementary settings older children, may be able to help set up outdoor equipment. In communities where theft is a problem, equipment must be locked away when children are not in the outdoor area.

Despite the challenges and expense of equipping an outdoor play area, doing so is essential. Our recognition that many young children are already obese demands that we provide many opportunities for movement, particularly involving sustained large-muscle activity. When weather does not permit outdoor play, space and equipment indoors for similar activities must be available.

Safety

No matter how versatile, attractive, durable, economical, and suitable a piece of equipment may be, it must be rejected if it is not safe. A climber with protruding bolts, blocks of soft wood that splinter, and tricycles that tip over easily should not be used in the center. A kitchen appliance that requires a long extension cord is a hazard to the cook and to the children and should be avoided. All equipment used by the children must be of nontoxic material and must not have sharp or pointed edges. Safety is maintained by staff members who make a point of being constantly alert to the condition and the arrangement of the equipment that is placed in the learning environment (Wortham & Frost, 1997).

However, a safety issue may be inadvertently overlooked. Three areas to which staff must give special attention are fall zones, entrapment, and protrusions (Wardle, 1999). Fall areas occur under climbers and swings. Entrapment refers to the possibility of a child getting a body part trapped in a piece of equipment (for example, when fence slats are close together but not close enough a child may get an arm or a leg caught). Look carefully at elaborate climbing towers with tunnels. It is possible for a child to become frightened while in the tunnel, yet the tunnel may be too long for the adult to reach the child. Protrusions also may lead to safety issues. Sharp corners on furniture or screw heads extended from a flat surface may injure a child. Some furniture may tip over and is particularly dangerous if a heavy object such as a television or CD player has been placed on top. A child may try to climb on the furniture, causing it to tip over.

A U.S. Consumer Product Safety Commission study (1999) found that two-thirds of the child care centers participating had at least one potential safety hazard. These included the use of clothing with drawstrings at the neck (38 percent of settings), lack of safe playground surfacing (24 percent), and cribs with soft bedding (19 percent).

Realizing that lead paint has been banned for consumer use for many years, directors may not realize the lead hazard lurking in playground equipment. Commercial users still coat products with paint containing lead, and children need consume only small quantities on a regular basis to create a harmful lead level. Even the surface under the equipment may contain lead. Having a trained inspector check a playground periodically for lead and other hazards is a wise investment (Aronson, 1997).

Suitability

Some equipment must be provided in several sizes to meet the needs of each user. For example, the secretary must have a standard adult-size chair, but chairs for children are usually 10, 12, and 14 inches high, depending on the child's age and height. Children's chairs that are so large that seated children cannot put their feet on the floor are not suitable for them. Children's chairs also should have a wide base so they will not tip.

For meals, school cafeteria tables and chairs are not at all suitable for toddlers and preschoolers. If these children are to use a school cafeteria, they must have low tables and chairs. Eating in their own classroom is often a better option. When older children are also present, the noise and activity level may be distracting for preschoolers and toddlers. Children in before- and after-school programs should never be expected to use preschool-size chairs and tables. They need their own furniture, space, and equipment designed to fit their needs.

Stereotypes

Equipment must be chosen with the understanding that it may be used equally by all children. Staff members who plan curricula in a stereotyped way will need special guidance on this point so that boys are not relegated to playing with blocks and trucks and girls are not always expected to dress dolls and play quiet table games. People with special needs should be depicted in books, puzzles, and classroom displays, and they should be shown participating in a variety of activities. Classroom materials should reflect many cultures and depict a variety of roles being chosen by members of various cultures and of both genders. For example, dolls of many races should be available. The play figures that are used as block accessories should include female postal workers and black doctors. Books, music, foods, and posters should be carefully selected to avoid any stereotyping and to depict the culturally pluralistic society in which the children live. This principle applies even when the center serves only one race, a situation that may occur when students all come from a segregated neighborhood.

Special Needs

In determining the suitability of equipment, you must consider children with disabilities. Children who cannot walk, for example, may need easels and water tables that can be used while the children sit in a chair or a wheelchair. Sometimes, such equipment is very low to enable children who are sitting on the floor to use it. In selecting the equipment, you should consider the height of the chair or wheelchair that is used and the length of the children's arms. In this way, you can determine the optimum height of the working space for a particular child.

If children are crawling in body casts or leg braces, they need comfortable floor surfaces. Wheeled equipment such as a sturdy wagon or a special buggy with seat belts will make it possible for children with physical disabilities to enjoy tours around the center neighborhood with the rest of the class. Other children may need an augmentative communication system so they can interact with staff and children.

Children with hearing loss need ample visual cues such as pictures attached to storage areas so that they can tell where equipment belongs, even though they cannot hear the teacher's directions. Children with visual impairments need some toys that vary in terms of weight, texture, and sound. Balls with a bell inside and storage containers covered with different materials (for example, velvet on a container of beads or corduroy on a box holding small blocks) are especially appropriate for these children. When children who do not have disabilities use these same materials, they may develop greater insights into the experience of children with disabilities.

In purchasing equipment for a center, the director will need to know, in general, what the lifestyles of the families are and what the learning styles and interests of individual children are. Children must be provided with enough ordinary, simple equipment so that they need not be bombarded nine hours a day with novelty. A balance of the familiar with the novel creates a learning environment that is neither overstimulating nor boring; the proper balance may be different in full-day child care centers than it is in half-day programs.

Some directors purchase packaged kits or curricula for their centers, particularly when the staff members have had little early childhood educational background. In such cases, it is essential that the materials be appropriate since they may be used with the belief that because they were included in a curriculum package, they must be good. The director has a major responsibility for ensuring that the components meet the needs of children and teachers. Often, materials can be purchased separately at lower cost.

It is the director's responsibility to determine who prepared the curriculum and what premises about teaching and learning are supported through its use. Keep in mind that it is unlikely that someone who does not know the children in your center could develop a day-to-day curriculum or set of materials with a plan for when and how to use them that would meet the needs and interests of your children.

Ease of Maintenance

Ease of maintenance also should be a consideration in choosing equipment. Sinks, toilets, and drinking fountains that must be cleaned daily and table tops that must be washed several times each day should be extremely simple to clean. The surfaces should be smooth and all areas easy to reach. Small pieces that are hard to clean around may cause problems and harbor dirt and germs. Equipment parts that are cleaned separately, such as feeding table trays, should be easy to remove and replace. Some plastic chairs have surfaces that are slightly roughened or ridged. And although the surface feels relatively smooth to the hand, there are actually shallow indentations that attract and hold dirt. It is almost impossible to wipe or even scrub these chairs so that they look clean. This type of furniture may be slightly less expensive than other furniture, but maintenance problems outweigh the possible savings. A clean, well-maintained environment is important for all children and staff, but it may be critical for children and staff who have allergies or asthma. In those cases, it may be helpful to have curtains, drapes, and carpeting cleaned frequently.

Outdoor equipment that must be repainted frequently should be designed so that it can be sanded and painted easily. Places that are difficult to reach are a nuisance, and surfaces that catch and hold rain increase the need for maintenance. Equipment that will rust or rot easily should not be purchased for outdoor use.

Attractiveness

Child care center equipment should be well designed and aesthetically attractive. Most parents and teachers would like their children to appreciate beauty, and one of the best ways to help children acquire this appreciation is to surround them with beauty. An attractive environment also carries the subtle message that children, families, and staff who enter the setting are much appreciated and that great care is taken to make their environment beautiful. A material that is aesthetically appealing need not be expensive. In fact, it often is the ability of the director or teacher to find beauty in nature that provides the most attractive places for children. A colorful tablecloth on the housekeeping area table with a small vase of wildflowers in the center makes that classroom area attractive and inviting. A large square of interesting gift-wrapping paper or a square yard of fabric serves as an attractive and inexpensive wall hanging and can be changed or cleaned often.

Be aware of the wide variety of art forms and styles developed by each culture. Displaying these introduces children and families to beauty that they may not have had the opportunity to experience and provides an interesting and appropriate way to begin discussions and explorations of other cultures.

> **REFLECTION**
>
> Think about the art that appeals to you. Where did you find it? Do you know who created it? Is there a story behind it? What does beauty mean to you? Can you remember how you developed your ideas about art and its value? What ideas do you have for bringing art to young children?

When equipment is made for the classroom, it should be prepared with special attention to its visual appeal. A math game, for example, can be made using well-designed stickers or beautiful pictures cut from duplicate copies of magazines instead of cartoonlike gimmicky stickers or drawings. The cardboard should be cut evenly and laminated or covered with a plastic coating instead of being presented to children with rough, crooked edges. Preparing beautiful materials takes a little longer and may require initial costs that are somewhat higher, but the product is worth the investment. It is the director's job to help staff and children value quality rather than quantity and appreciate and care for the beauty in the objects around them.

User Preference

Sometimes, teacher preference determines the type of equipment ordered. One teacher may choose to buy many books while another depends heavily on the library; or one sees an autoharp as a necessity while another finds this instrument encumbering. One teacher may choose a guinea pig as the ideal classroom pet, another prefers fish, and still another considers all pets to require an inordinate amount of the teacher's time. As long as these teacher preferences do not mitigate against appropriate classroom practice, they are legitimate and should be honored if at all possible. When budgeting constraints or other equipment needs make it impossible to fill all teachers' requests, the director must notify teachers that their preferences are under consideration and that plans are being made to fill all requests as soon as possible. The teacher who wants an autoharp may have to wait until next year's budget provides it, but meanwhile, the director can support that teacher by informing the staff of planned equipment purchases. Each teacher's preference deserves careful consideration because each teacher will ultimately set the stage for learning through the use of the center's equipment. Of course, the director will have to intervene if a teacher chooses to order inappropriate items such as toys and games with very small pieces for toddlers or workbooks for preschoolers.

DIRECTOR'S CORNER

"Our board is meeting today to discuss how to spend the $600 they earned by selling coupon books. They asked each teacher to keep a wish list on hand. When the order comes in, we have a celebration, with the board and staff gathering to open the cartons."

—Director, agency-sponsored child care center

Children enjoy working with some found materials such as leaves found on the playground.

WORKING WITHIN A BUDGET

Major considerations when working with an equipment budget are durability and economy. Often, they go hand in hand. The climbing apparatus that costs three times as much as a competitor's product is worth the original investment if it lasts three times as long or is safer and sturdier. When more durable items are purchased, the center is not faced with the problem of replacement so often, and considerable shipping costs are saved, particularly with large pieces of equipment. Price and durability are not always perfectly correlated, but it is safe to say that inexpensive tricycles, which may be appropriate for home use, are inappropriate for group use. When used at a center, the standard equipment that is used at home will be in the repair shop far sooner and more frequently than will the sturdier, more expensive equipment that is designed for school use. Keep this fact in mind when well-meaning board members want to donate items

their children have outgrown instead of including sufficient dollars in the equipment budget.

In child care center kitchens, many adults (and occasionally children) use the equipment. This heavy usage (and perhaps misuse), coupled with lack of care, may lead to the need for earlier replacement. Refrigerator and freezer doors are opened frequently and often are left standing open while children take out ice cubes or put in trays of sloshing Jell-O™. Dishwashers may be improperly loaded or overloaded, and sinks are sometimes scoured with rough scouring pads or abrasive powders. It is important to provide heavy-duty kitchen equipment because equipment made for home use will require costly service calls when it is subjected to the hard use it inevitably will get in a center. A prepaid maintenance agreement may be a cost-effective way to manage equipment repairs. Checking the total cost of the maintenance agreement against the record of repairs typically needed over time for a particular type of equipment is a smart practice. Two possible sources of such information are consumer guides, usually available at libraries, and discussion with other directors. Furthermore, instructions on how to use equipment may be posted on each item, and a short in-service session may be helpful.

In setting up a new center, the director can expect to spend $10,000 to $30,000 per classroom on equipment. The variance is due to the number of children in each classroom and the quality of the items purchased. A typical budget for manipulatives (puzzles, table toys, and small blocks) for a center of about 75 children is about $4,000, assuming that the items are centrally stored so that teachers can share them. To reduce this cost, directors often search for free materials and supplies. However, the director then may have to pick up the items or enlist a volunteer for this service.

ORDERING EQUIPMENT

Decisions about what, when, and where to buy equipment are usually left to the director. In any case, directors are consulted and they have considerable control over what is bought with the money that is budgeted for equipment and supplies.

Equipment Requisition

Directors usually develop an equipment request procedure. Staff members notify the director, in writing, of the type of equipment that is needed or desired, providing additional information such as the rationale to support the need, a possible vendor, and an estimated purchase price. All of these data are helpful when final purchase decisions are made. Some centers use purchase order or requisition forms, which are nothing more than request forms that can be sent to vendors with a duplicate retained for center records (see Working Paper 9–1). Even though this request procedure is formal and perhaps cumbersome, it puts the purchase of equipment on a businesslike basis and gives each staff member an equal opportunity to bid for the equipment dollars in the budget.

In corporate systems, requisitions are processed through a central purchasing agent and shipments are made directly to the center from the manufacturer. The central office handles all the orders and saves money through collective, quantity buying and careful selection of suppliers. This approach cuts costs but limits the options for those staff members selecting equipment. Public school programs usually have specific purchasing procedures to follow, requisitioning their supplies through the principal or through a supervisor responsible for the preschool or after-school programs.

In centers where directors are fully responsible for receiving staff requests and placing orders, they check requests against the established selection criteria and the budget allowance before completing order forms. All order forms should include quantity, price, catalog order number (if available), and name or description of each item. When making final decisions on purchases, make certain that careful consideration is given to possible savings through bulk buying. For example, newsprint for painting can be bought from some vendors for much less per ream when bought in 48-ream packages. Economies realized through bulk buying are practical only if adequate storage space is available for the unused materials.

Equipment costs also can be reduced in nonprofit centers by applying for tax-exempt status. When orders are sent to suppliers, the center will not be charged sales tax if the order includes the center's tax-exempt number.

Some centers have provisions for teachers to purchase specified dollar amounts without permission and within a given time period. For example, a teacher may receive $100 to spend for the classroom each year (in addition to the centerwide purchases that the director makes). In some cases, the purchase is made, and the teacher is reimbursed on presentation of the receipts to the board treasurer or the director. The practice of giving teachers some petty cash to spend for classroom materials gives them some freedom to provide for special program needs and, more important, communicates trust in their ability to make appropriate choices for their children.

REFLECTION

Assume that your classroom is stocked with basic equipment for your 15 four-year-old children. You have received $200 from petty cash. Think about how you might spend the petty cash allocated for your classroom.

Purchase Time Line

Equipment purchasing occurs in three different time frames:

1. start-up
2. supplementary
3. replacement

First, there must be a major start-up equipment purchase when a center is opened so that all the basic aspects of the program can function with appropriate equipment. This phase obviously is the most expensive of the three, but extensive purchases at this point are absolutely essential because it is unfair to children and staff to operate a program without basic equipment. To save money, some secondhand, borrowed, or homemade equipment can be used, keeping in mind the criteria described earlier. There is no formula that can tell a director exactly what must be provided, but the staff will need equipment of the type, quantity, and quality that will allow them to focus on the children and their needs instead of on the equipment or the lack thereof. Children in a classroom with inappropriate or inadequate equipment will be quite likely to engage in inappropriate behavior as they seek to create something interesting to do.

Providing enough appropriate storage is also essential. In the classroom, teachers need storage for supplies that they will use later in the day or week. Major classroom storage space should be available to the children so that they can independently choose and put away materials. Crowded shelves and cluttered spaces make it difficult for children to find the materials they are interested in using. Children are also more likely to leave materials strewn about the classroom when it is not clear where they belong.

The second phase of equipment purchasing is the supplementary phase that provides for additional equipment purchases throughout each year. When supplementary equipment purchases are spaced throughout a program year, both children and staff members enjoy greater variety and a change of pace. Furthermore, teachers can adjust equipment requests to meet the needs of particular children such as a child with special needs who enrolls midyear and requires a chair with particular supports, a prone board, or a walker. Although outside funding may be available for some of these larger items for an individual child's use, teachers still need to consider books with large print, puzzles with large knobs, or writing tools that have been adapted for easier handling.

Last, the replacement phase helps maintain a constant supply of equipment that is in good repair and allows for adjustments in available equipment and materials as program needs change or as new items come on the market. For example, a few years ago, all African-American dolls had Caucasian hairstyles and facial features, but newer dolls have features that match the ethnic group being represented. Vinyl records were the major source of recorded music for children, followed by audio tapes and now compact discs. Similarly, filmstrips have been replaced by videos and DVDs. At the same time, the 50th anniversary edition of the much-loved children's book, *Goodnight Moon* (Brown, 1947), reminds us that new isn't always better.

The budget also should include enough money for emergency replacements. Although careful usage, combined with a maintenance plan, minimizes the need for emergency replacements, unexpected breakage or loss is sure to occur. When a copier repair is too costly, it is sometimes more economical to buy or lease a new model than to repair the old one.

Sources of Equipment

Much of the equipment for early childhood education centers is purchased from catalogs. If the dealers are reliable, this arrangement is satisfactory. It is wise to check with other directors, professional organizations, or the Better Business Bureau to determine the suitability of making purchases from a particular company. Among the advantages of purchasing by catalog are the wide variety of merchandise that is available and lowering of costs with bypassing the retailer. On the other hand, shipping costs may be charged and return of unsatisfactory merchandise may be cumbersome. It is helpful to have a supply of catalogs available to the staff. Most companies will be pleased to put your center on their mailing list, and most major suppliers now have Web sites. Refer to the list on Appendix A.

When you are placing a large order, request a discount. Another opportunity for price reduction is prompt payment. Vendors who establish a relationship with your center are more likely to inform you of upcoming special prices. Then it is up to you to purchase items because the center needs them instead of because they are on sale.

Equipment purchased from local retail outlets can be seen and tried out, which has obvious advantages. But most retail outlets cater to home users and carry a limited stock of classroom equipment. If a local outlet has access to a manufacturer of school equipment, it may be possible to order from a catalog through a local retailer. A buying co-op is another equipment source that is worth investigating because group buying can be very economical. In this system, the co-op group buys in quantity at a wholesale price and sells items to co-op members at just enough above cost to pay the co-op operating expenses.

Exhibit areas at state or national early childhood conferences provide great opportunities to view a huge range of products for early childhood classrooms and to talk with the vendors. Keep in mind that their goal is to sell their products, but a careful

All children need ready access to a wide range of books, some of which may be obtained from the local library.

shopper can garner a wealth of information and sometimes a special price. Particularly at the end of the exhibit hours, vendors would just as soon give you a discount as ship materials back to their home base. Remember also that conference sponsors rarely endorse products being displayed. Conferees are responsible for using their own good judgment since what is available is not always appropriate for early childhood education.

Toy libraries are popular equipment sources in some areas. A center director or teacher may borrow anything from a puzzle to a complete set of housekeeping equipment, just as one borrows library books. Sometimes, a group of center directors finds it worthwhile to help establish a toy library for their mutual benefit, and it is especially helpful to have toy-lending programs that furnish materials for special-needs children. Occasionally, toy-lending or toy-sharing systems are set up by community organizations to make equipment available to centers and parents.

Secondhand shops, discount stores, antique shops, and garage or yard sales frequently are excellent sources of equipment or raw materials for pieces needed by the center. The buyer may discover a garlic press that can provide an interesting physical knowledge experience for children. With imagination and effort, large ice cream cans can become storage places for musical instruments or some other equipment that demands a number of relatively small, easily accessible spaces. Perhaps a used desk or file cabinet for the center office can be located. When such discoveries need to be put into finished, usable, and attractive

form, it sometimes is possible to enlist the help of the parent group, a high-school vocational class, or a senior citizens' organization whose members enjoy repairing and painting. In some regions, high-school woodworking, metal working classes, or Junior Achievement groups make new equipment and sell it to centers at reasonable prices.

Another way to obtain equipment is to solicit the help of parents, teachers, board members, or residents of the community in equipment-making parties. This activity enhances the feeling of community in the center's program. Child care center staff members often take advantage of the children's nap time to make classroom materials. Encouraging staff members to make some materials is important because few centers have unlimited resources, and commercial equipment cannot always be suitably adapted to meet individual children's needs.

Gifts of equipment are usually welcome but their suitability must be measured against the same criteria employed for equipment purchases. A gift such as a toy gun in a center where pretend gun play is discouraged or the gift of an animal that induces allergic reactions in some children must be refused graciously.

MANAGING EQUIPMENT

Even before equipment is delivered to the center, the director must consider how it will be managed. All equipment must be checked and inventoried on delivery, and before it is stored or put into use, a maintenance plan should be set up to minimize repair and replacement needs.

Checking and Inventorying Equipment

When equipment is received, it must be checked against the order to ascertain whether or not it corresponds with the order in terms of quantity, size, color, and so forth. It also is important to make certain that only the items actually received are listed on both the order and the packing slip and that prices are correct. If discrepancies are found, the vendor must be notified immediately. It is wise to keep original packing materials in case any equipment needs to be returned.

Most center directors keep a record of at least the major items purchased, and some directors keep a running account of all small items and consumables as well. An inventory of purchases can be recorded as items are unpacked by listing each item on the computer or a file card, noting the description, supplier, price, date of purchase, and location in which the item is to be used. Some directors mark equipment with the name of the center, with an inventory number, or with an identifying number so that if a center owns five identical tape players, each is individually identifiable. In public schools, the usual practice is to put the room number on each piece of equipment. The labeling practice is helpful when pieces are sent out for repair, when school buildings are cleaned during vacation periods, or when items are stolen. Of course, valuable equipment should be insured. When equipment is added or removed from the center, the inventory should be updated.

An accurate record of equipment will always be available when the inventory is updated regularly. Working Paper 9–2 shows a suggested inventory form. A backup disk of the inventory should be kept in a safe place—a fire-resistant file cabinet or other storage unit if possible—so that losses can be reported accurately in the event of fire or theft. Furthermore, an ongoing, updated inventory minimizes the work of taking an annual inventory (usually necessary for insurance purposes) for annual reporting to the board or the sponsoring or funding agency or for reporting to a corporate central office that must have an accurate annual inventory to determine the assets of the corporation. Updated inventories also give directors a clear picture of what is available in the center and help pinpoint center areas or types of equipment that are incurring heavy damage. This information is useful in determining how much and when to reorder and in making decisions about changing vendors or brands of equipment ordered. Information about persistent damage in certain areas should lead to a careful examination of the storage and maintenance system.

After the equipment is checked in and inventoried, the director must notify the staff that the new equipment is available for use. No doubt everyone will know when a new climbing tower arrives or when a new microwave oven is available, but if 12 new puzzles are placed on the shelves or a fresh supply of felt markers is stored, it could be weeks before all teachers in a large center discover the new materials.

Maintaining and Storing Equipment

As soon as equipment is placed in the center, the job of maintenance begins. In the very act of placing equipment, maintenance decisions are made. For example, an untreated wooden climber that is placed outdoors in a rainy area is doomed to rot. It will need immediate treatment, followed by periodic coatings of a penetrating, nontoxic stain if it is to withstand weathering. Carpeting under an easel will become stained with paint unless additional floor covering such as a rubber or plastic mat is placed on top of the carpet under the easel.

Equipment used by the children must be checked daily and removed if it is in need of repair, even if immediate replacement is impossible. Children need attractive, usable equipment and should not be subjected to the frustration of trying to make sense out of broken or incomplete classroom materials. Puzzles with missing pieces, tricycles with broken pedals, or books with torn or defaced pages should not be left in the classroom.

Storage of equipment also is directly related to its maintenance. It is easy to return equipment after it has been used when each piece has a specific, clearly delineated storage space. The space, whether in a storage room or on a classroom shelf, must be large enough so that the object does not have to be jammed into place and perhaps damaged. The space must be accessible to staff members (and in many cases, to children) to ensure that it will be used for storage purposes. When storage is far from a classroom or the teachers have to go through another area such as the director's office to get to the storage room, it is more likely that the equipment and materials will be shoved out of the way in the classroom rather than returned to the storage room. Each center must work out a method for storing certain equipment and supplies that are used daily and must remain in the classroom. Other supplies should be designated for return to a central area. Storage also must be provided for

Date	Item	Teacher	Date Returned
10/7/06	Large Legos	Denice	10/29/06
10/7/06	Magnetic letters	Sam	
10/10/06	CD: Ella Jenkins	Maria	10/30/06
	CD: Elgar violin		

Figure 9–1

Sample checkout sheet for equipment and materials.

items such as tricycles that are used daily but must be protected from weather and theft. Additional storage is needed for items that are purchased in quantity for long-range use such as paper towels and paint.

When a large number of people have access to the central supply storage areas, there is some tendency for each person to assume that someone else will maintain order and cleanliness in the area. Therefore, many of the users feel little or no responsibility for maintaining the area. When this happens, some users return materials in a haphazard way, fail to place them on the correct shelves, or return them in poor condition. Other staff members become irritated when they try to find what they need and have to cope with a messy storage area. These frustrations lead to conflict and a breakdown in positive staff relationships. Sometimes, this problem can be avoided by assigning each teacher the responsibility for maintaining a specific storage area such as for art materials, outdoor equipment, or books and records for a given length of time. In other centers, periodic work sessions are scheduled to involve the entire staff in cleaning and straightening central storage areas. Some centers institute a system for checking equipment in and out of the storage room that is similar to the practice conducted in a library an example is shown in Figure 9–1. In a large center, putting the checkout list on a computer may be helpful, but in most centers, posting a clipboard with a checkout sheet is more likely to be convenient for teachers. A few centers keep all the equipment in classrooms on shelves available to the children or in closed cabinets available to the teacher, but this practice is expensive because it requires so much duplication.

In whatever way equipment is stored, its placement should be neat and easy to find so that children and teachers alike will be encouraged to maintain some degree of order in their attractive environment. The director's job is to establish and follow routines that lead to the easy accessibility of all equipment to everyone. These routines make putting things away

far less burdensome for both teachers and children. Orderliness does not have to be an obsession; rather, it is an appropriate way to manage a large variety of equipment that is used in a number of ways by a wide range of people.

SUMMARY

Appropriate equipment allows the staff to focus on the essentials of their work as they provide an excellent early childhood program. Initial purchases are made when a center opens, and additional items for children's and adults' spaces and for service areas are purchased to supplement and replace this equipment. Most centers acquire equipment from a variety of sources, but all equipment should be considered in terms of its usefulness, durability, economy, ease of maintenance, attractiveness, teacher preference, and safety. Once equipment is made available, it must be properly maintained and stored. A plan for use and care of equipment must be developed for both children and staff as a component of the center's program.

CLASS ASSIGNMENTS

1. Visit a local toy store. Select two dolls for possible use in a class of four-year-old children. Compare the two dolls using the following criteria:
   - suitability
   - durability
   - economy
   - ease of maintenance
   - attractiveness
   - safety
   - your preference as a teacher

   Repeat this assignment using two tricycles for child care center use. Make a third set of comparisons using infant rattles. Using Working Paper 9–1, prepare a purchase order for the doll or the tricycle.

2. Visit local stores or check equipment catalogs and Web sites to find the current prices for enough equipment to supply one classroom serving 15 children. List the sources. Compute the total cost. What is the cost per child? Enter five of the major items on your list on the sample inventory form found in Working Paper 9–2, or create an inventory form using a software package.

3. Visit two centers (or draw on your previous or current experiences in two centers). Write a comparison of the equipment in general, using the information provided in this chapter. Use a separate sheet of paper for this assignment.

CLASS EXERCISES

1. Work with fellow students on the following role-playing situations. Have several students role-play, using different approaches to each problem. Discuss the strengths and weaknesses of each group's approach.

   a. You are a preschool director. Mrs. Jane Jones has just given you 24 coloring books with an advertising message for her husband's business on the cover. You never use coloring books at the center because you believe that they are not developmentally appropriate and would not meet NAEYC guidelines. How might you handle this?

   b. Suppose that the same situation in problem (a) occurred but that the donor is Mrs. Thomas Vanderbilt. Last year, she gave your center $5,000 for equipment. What might you say to Mrs. Vanderbilt?

2. Your preschool class is in the planning stage and will be held in a public school building. Discuss with your principal your four-year-olds' needs and ways in which their equipment will be different from that of older children.

WORKING PAPER 9-1

(for use with Class Assignment 1)

PURCHASE ORDER FORM

REQUISITION/PURCHASE ORDER
THE CHILDREN'S CENTER

To: _____

_____

_____

Catalog No.	Description	Quantity	Price	Total

Ship to:
The Children's Center
1099 Main Street
Centerville, CA 00000–0000

Account charged: _____

Approved by: _____

Date ordered: _____

Date received: _____

WORKING PAPER 9-2

(for use with Class Assignment 2)

SAMPLE INVENTORY FORM

INVENTORY FORM					
Date Purchased	Description	Identifying Number	Source	Price	Location in Center

DIRECTOR'S RESOURCE 9-1

SUGGESTED EQUIPMENT AND MATERIALS

Suggested Order of Acquisition

Essential Items—A	Extensions—B

Note: Items, quantities, and priorities suggested on the following pages of this section are to be thought of as guides rather than inventories.

SUGGESTED ITEMS	A	B	SUGGESTED ITEMS	A	B
PRESCHOOL, AGES 3–5			Peg board with pegs for storage/display	1	
			Pillows	4	
I. BASIC ENVIRONMENTAL			Plants	X	X
EQUIPMENT			Refrigerator	1	
Bookcase for children's books, on casters, 1 or 2 slanted shelves on top	1		Rugs, if room not carpeted, indoor/ outdoor, approx. 9' x 12'	1	1
Bookshelf, for adult books, up high	1		Sand table (see Psycho-Motor Development)		
Bulletin boards, portable	2		Shed, outdoor, with cupboards, for storage of maintenance supplies and items such as hollow blocks, vehicles, sand-box toys, art materials, etc., rain and vandal-proof	1	
Cabinets:					
Movable, sturdy, with adjustable shelves for storage of curriculum, materials, cleaning supplies, foods, etc.	4				
Movable, sturdy, with rigid shelves, child height for self-help equipment and displays	2		Shelf unit, for blocks, so individual sizes and shapes can be easily seen, chosen and put back by children and adults	1	
Chairs:			Sinks:		
Adult size:			Indoor, with counter space	1	
Desk	1		Outdoor, with counter space		1
Folding, for meetings	10	20	Smoke alarms	X	
Rocking	1		Step-stool	1	
Child size, stackable, lightweight but sturdy, 1 per child, several for staff and visitors	30		Stove	1	
			Tables:		
Chalkboard, portable, with chalk and erasers	1		Adult size, seating 4, folding	1	
			Child size:		
Clock, wall	1		Seating, 4–8, same height, so can be combined, 18" to 20" high	4	
Counter or shelf for preparation of craft materials and food	2		Seating 8–10 children and adults, for outdoor use	1–2	
Cubbies, indoor, wood, with bottom shelf, hooks above and 1 or 2 shelves at the top, 1 per child	20		Serving cart	1	
Drinking fountain, child height	1		Trash cans, with lids, large	2	
Filing cabinet, 2–4 drawers	1		Trays, storage, non-toxic, impact resistant/lids	X	
Fire extinguishers	X		Wastebasket, large with lid	1	
Laundromat (See Housekeeping Supplies—Cleaning)			Wastebaskets for recyclable items	X	

(continues)

DIRECTOR'S RESOURCE 9-1
(continued)

SUGGESTED ITEMS	QUANTITIES A	B
II. GENERAL MAINTENANCE, INDOOR/OUTDOOR		
Broom, push, heavy duty for outside	1	
Buckets, 1 metal, 1 plastic, flat bottom, large	2	
Electrical extension cord and plug, heavy duty	1	
Hardware kit: nails, nuts, bolts, sandpaper, screws, staples, washers, etc.	1	
Iron, electric	1	
Ironing board	1	
Plunger	1	
Rakes:		
Garden	1	
Leaf	1	
Rope, 4' to 8'	1	
Shovel or spade	1	
Tool box	X	
Trash bins	1	
Twine, cone	1	
III. HOUSEKEEPING SUPPLIES		
Brooms:		
Push	1	
Regular	1	
Cleansers:		
Disinfectants	X	
Glass cleaner, can	1	
Scouring powder, cans	12	
Cloths, cleaning	6	
Dishpan	2	
Drying rack, folding	1	
Dust pan with brush	X	
Garbage bags/ties	X	
Garbage can with lid	1	
Mops:		
Dust	1	
Wet	1	
Soap:		
Bar, doz.	3	
Liquid, qt.	3	
Powder, box	3	

SUGGESTED ITEMS	QUANTITIES A	B
Sponges, several sizes	6	
Strainer, sink	1	
Toilet paper, carton of 3000 sheets	5	
Towels:		
Bath, each child brings own	X	X
Dish	12	
Hand	12	
Paper, case of 3000	6	
Vacuum cleaner, if floor is carpeted		1
Vacuum cleaner bags, as needed		X
IV. HEALTH AND SAFETY		
First aid supplies:		
Cotton blankets, one per child	24	
First aid cabinet stocked in accordance with individual school regulations or with the following items:		
Antiseptic soap (Phisoderm™)	2	
Bandages, plastic strips, boxes	6	
Eye bath	1	
Gauze, sterile, boxes	4	
Gauze pads, sterile, boxes	4	
Gloves, latex, for use when in contact with all body fluids	X	
Hypoallergenic adhesive tape	2	
Ice pack	1	
Medicine glass	1	
Red Cross first aid manual	1	
Rubbing alcohol, bottle	1	
Safety pins, pkg.	1	
Thermometer strips	3	
Tweezers	1	
Flashlight	1	
Handkerchiefs, paper, small hospital size, boxes	18	
Rugs, plastic covered foam mats or cots for resting, 27" x 48", or towels from home	24	
Towels, paper, junior size, pkg. of 150	10	

(continues)

DIRECTOR'S RESOURCE 9-1

(continued)

SUGGESTED ITEMS	QUANTITIES A	B
Food preparation and service:		
Food and cooking are considered part of the education program for children and adults, as well as serving nutritional needs. Health standards and regulations must be observed. Items are suggested only for schools that serve hot meals daily.		
Blender	1	
Bottle opener	2	
Bowls:		
Serving, unbreakable, assorted sizes	3	
Soup/cereal, plastic	30	
Sugar	2	
Bowl scrapers, various sizes	2	
Cake pans, unbreakable	4	
Canisters, or other food containers, with lids	6	
Can openers:		
Electric	1	
Hand	1	
Colander	1	
Cookie:		
Cutter, assorted sizes, special shapes for holidays	12	
Decorator	1	
Sheets	4	
Corn popper, hand or electric	1	
Cups, paper, flat bottom, box of 100, 5 oz.	6	
Cutlery:		
Forks:		
Heavy plastic, reusable, for special events	60	
Long handled	2	
Salad, stainless steel, for children and adults	36	
Serving	3	
Knives:		
Bread	1	
Butcher	1	

SUGGESTED ITEMS	QUANTITIES A	B
Dinner, heavy plastic, reusable, for special events	60	
Paring	2	
Stainless steel, for children and adults	12–20	
Spoons:		
Cooking, with long handles, unbreakable	3	
Serving:	6	
Soup, stainless steel	6	
Teaspoons, stainless steel	36	
Double boiler	2	
Egg beater, hand	1	
Electric mixer	1	
Flour sifter	1	
Fry pans:		
Electric	1	
Regular, 6", 8", 10", 12"	1	
Funnels:		
Large	1	
Small	1	
Glasses, unbreakable:		
Large, 10 oz.	6	
Small, 6 oz.	24–36	
Hot pads	4	
Hot plate, electric stove, if full day	1	
Ladles	2	
Measures:		
Bowls, nesting set, unbreakable	3	
Cups, unbreakable, sets	2	
Spoons, sets	2	
Napkins, paper, buy in quantity	X	
Oven, portable, if no stove available	1	
Pie pans, unbreakable	6	
Pitchers, unbreakable:		
Cream	1	
Pt. size	4	
1–2 qt. size	4	
Plates:		
Dessert, paper	48	
Dinner, heavy plastic	36	

(continues)

DIRECTOR'S RESOURCE 9-1
(continued)

SUGGESTED ITEMS	QUANTITIES A	B	SUGGESTED ITEMS	QUANTITIES A	B
Dinner, paper	36		Bars for hanging	2	
Serving, assorted sizes	4		Bean bags	20	
Pot holders	4		Boards:		
Rolling pins, additional ones for children's use	2		Cleated, 1'–6'	1	
Salad bowl and servers	1		Plain, 6'–8'	3	
Salt shakers, incl. one for stove	4		Resilient, for jumping	2	
Sauce pans, 1 qt., 4 qt., 6 qt., with lids	4		Bowling pins set	X	
Sieves:			Boxes, large, wooden	2	
Large	1		Climbing structures: old tires, empty electrical reels, concrete culvert units	2	
Small	1		Crates, packing boxes	1	
Spatulas, assorted sizes	3		Crawl-through tunnel or cubes, large	1	1
Storage containers:			Dollies, hand	1	
Freezer	2		Folding mats, anti-bacterial, anti-fungal, reinforced seams to place at the end of the indoor slide, etc.	5	
Refrigerator	4		Hoops, 18" to 24" in diameter	20	
Tablecloths, plastic, to be used for meals or cooking activities, one for each table	X		Hose, length as needed	1	
Table mats, plastic, if desired	24		Ladder, lightweight, sturdy for children, 4' to 6'	1	
Teakettle	1		Net, cargo, for climbing		1
Tongs	1		Pails, assorted sizes, for outdoor play	3	
Trays, assorted sizes	6		Parachute, sturdy, 6' diameter, hand-held strap	X	
Vegetable peeler	1		Pulleys	1	

V. AUDIOVISUAL EQUIPMENT

SUGGESTED ITEMS	QUANTITIES A	B	SUGGESTED ITEMS	QUANTITIES A	B
CD and cassette recorder/player, dual cassette decks, separate speaker with 3' extension cord, auto-reset tape counter	X		Rakes	2	
CDs		X	Recordings, suggesting gross and fine muscle activities	4	
Filmstrip projector	1		Ribbon sticks for ribbon dance	20	
Filmstrips (access to)	X		Rocking boat	1	
Movie and sound projector (access to)	X		Rope, 6' to 8' length	1	
Projection screen	X		Sandbox frame with sand (water faucet and hose nearby)	1	
Record player	X		Sand toys, variety	X	
Records	X		Shovels, small but sturdy	4	
Tape recorder	1		Spades	2	
Tapes or cassettes for listening and recording	4		Swing set, double with canvas or rubber seats	1	

VI. PSYCHO-MOTOR DEVELOPMENT

SUGGESTED ITEMS	QUANTITIES A	B
Balls, rubber, assorted sizes (10)	X	
Barrels	1	
Trampoline, rubber, attached to climbing structure, low enough for children's safety	1	

(continues)

DIRECTOR'S RESOURCE 9-1

(continued)

SUGGESTED ITEMS	QUANTITIES		SUGGESTED ITEMS	QUANTITIES	
	A	B		A	B
Wheel toys:			VIII. BUILDING AND		
Tricycles	2		CONSTRUCTION		
Tricycle trailers	1		Blocks:		
Wagons	2		Hollow	30	
Wheelbarrow	1		Parquetry, set	2	
			Table, choose from cube,		
VII. PERCEPTUAL DEVELOPMENT			interlocking, nesting, regular		
Bead laces	12		small sets in variety of		
Beads, wooden, $\frac{1}{2}$" cubes and			materials: wood, plastic, rubber	3	
assorted shapes, box of 1,000	1		Unit, full school set (protected		
Counting rods, sets	2		floor space and appropriate		
Dressing frames	4		shelving important)	150	
Games, matching:			Boards, small, flat 24"–36" long, to		
Block: attribute, design, domino,			use with blocks	4	
number, property, etc.	4		Building sets: (choose from such as		
Card: animals, geometric shapes,			the following in school size sets of		
flowers, vehicles, etc.	4		sufficient quantities to satisfy needs)		
Frame: bingo and lotto type with			Crystal Climber	1	
birds, flowers, food, clothing,			Giant tinker toys	2	
zoo animals, etc.	4		Lego	2	
Lacing toys	X		Lincoln Logs	1	
Linking toys	X		Rig-a-jig	1	
Magnetic board, 18" x 36"	1		Rising Towers	1	
Magnetized figures, 50 items, set	1		Tinker toys	1	
Mechanical board: bolts, nuts,			Carpentry: (all tools real, not toy)		
locks, etc.	1		Bench	1	
Nest of rings or boxes, 6 to 8 items	1		Bits, $\frac{1}{4}$", $\frac{1}{2}$" and $\frac{3}{4}$"	1	
Olfactory materials: spices, foods,			Block plane	2	
greenery, etc. in plastic bottles with			Boiled linseed oil	2	
perforated, tightly sealed lids	X		Brace, adult size, $1\frac{1}{2}$ lbs.	1	
Shape or sorting box with			Brushes	5	
interchangeable panels	1		Clamps, vise or c-clamps	6	
Sound cylinders, approx. 3" high,			Coping saw, wooden handle	1	
2" diameter, set of 5	2		Coping saw blades	1	
Tactile materials: sandpaper, cloth,			Crowbars	3	
wood, metal, sponge, rocks, etc.,			Goggles (eye protection), adult		
in container	X		and child-sized	X	
Taste materials: sugar, flour, salt,			Hammers, 7–13 oz., flat head with		
fruit juices, etc., in plastic			claws	2	
containers with removable lids	X		Hand drill and drill sets	1	
Water table with water toys	X		Hinges, 1" and 2" with screws	X	

(continues)

DIRECTOR'S RESOURCE 9-1
(continued)

SUGGESTED ITEMS	QUANTITIES A	B
Measuring rod, tape, ruler, one of each	3	
Nails, assorted sizes, $1/2$" to 2", some very long, lbs.	5	
Nuts and bolts, assorted, box	1	
Pliers	1	
Sandpaper, medium grit, pkg.	1	
Saws, crosscut, 14" blade, 18" blade, 8 teeth per inch	2	
Screwdrivers, 8", 12", regular and Phillips	2	
Screws, steel, flat head, assorted sizes, box of 50	2	
Washers, assorted sizes, box	1	
Cloth, yds.	2	
Corks, supply accumulated	X	
Foam rubber pieces, supply accumulated	X	
Glue, tubes	1	
Lumber:		
Assorted shapes and sizes, soft, scrounged (often available from lumber yard disposal bins and carpentry shops) 50–75 pieces	X	
Assorted sizes, rough measure footage, 30'–60', purchased	1	1
Sand/water play materials, all unbreakable:		
Brushes, large	3	
Containers, wide variety	6	
Dishes, variety	4	
Dishpans	1	
Floating toys and objects	4	
Funnels, assorted sizes	2	
Hose, small pieces, can be scrounged	2	
Measuring sets:		
Cups	2	
Spoons	2	
Molds, assorted	3	
Pitchers	1	

SUGGESTED ITEMS	QUANTITIES A	B
Scoops	4	
Sieves	2	
Sand/water table or tray	1	
Straws, plastic, pkg.	1	
Tongue depressors or craft sticks, pkg. of 1,000	1	
Toothpicks, colored box	1	
Vehicles:		
Construction, large, sturdy, variety	3	
Transportation, unbreakable, in various sizes	6	
Wheels, wooden disks	6	

IX. CREATIVE ARTS

SUGGESTED ITEMS	QUANTITIES A	B
Aprons, plastic or cloth, homemade	10	
Beads, and other objects for stringing	500	
Brushes, glue, $1/2$–1" thickness handle length, 6"–9"	2	
Brushes, paint $1/2$–1" thickness handle length, 6"–9"	12	
Brush holders	2	
Cans, cookie cutters, for cutting dough, assorted sizes	4	
Chalk:		
Assorted colors, large box	2	
White, box	1	
Clay, gray and red, lbs. each	25	
Cloth:		
Burlap and/or heavy weight mesh for stitchery, yds.	2	
Old sheeting to paint/draw on, supply accumulated	X	
Plastic drape, one for each table	X	
Clothespins, for hanging art work	48	
Coffee filters, box of 100	1	
Collage materials, scrounged, such as pieces of cloth, paper, leather, plastic, old greeting cards, buttons, Styrofoam, yarn, ribbon, sequins,		

(continues)

DIRECTOR'S RESOURCE 9-1

(continued)

SUGGESTED ITEMS	QUANTITIES A	B	SUGGESTED ITEMS	QUANTITIES A	B
glitter, beads, etc., supply accumulated	X		Powdered tempera, assorted colors, boxes	6	
Containers:			Watercolors, boxes with brush	2	
For clay, plastic with lid	2		Paint jars, plastic with lids	16	
For collage materials: old boxes, baskets, jars, etc., supply accumulated	X		Paper:		
			Brown, wrapping, 15 lb. roll with dispenser	1	
For paint: small cans, cut down cartons, plastic, with lids	10		Construction, colored, 9" x 12", pkg. of 50 sheets	20	
Cookie cutter, for use with play dough	12		Construction, colored, 12" x 18", pkg. of 50 sheets	8	
Corks for painting	6		Manila for drawing, 12" x 18", reams	8	
Cotton balls, bags	4		Mural paper, white, roll	1	
Crayon holders	2		News, unprinted, 18" x 24", pkg.	15	
Crayons, jumbo, assorted colors, boxes	10		Poster, colored, 9" x 12", pkg. of 100 sheets	20	
Drying rack for art materials, if needed	1		Poster, colored, 12" x 18", pkg. of 100 sheets	4	
Easels, double adjustable	2		Tagboard, medium weight, 24" x 36", sheets	10	
Fabric scraps (assorted box)	1		Tissue, 20" x 30", pkg. of 24 sheets	4	
Garlic presses for use with clay	2				
Hole puncher	1		Paper bags, approx. 8" x 14"	20	
Kiln (access to)	X		Paper brads or fasteners, boxes	2	
Knives, plastic (box of 25)	1		Paper clips, box of 100	4	
Knives, table, for use with clay and dough (can be old)	6		Paper cutter, 12" blade	1	
			Paste, semi-liquid, gal.	2	
Looms, handmade out of cardboard, paper plates, wood and nails, for simple weaving	2		Paste jars, 2" diameter, 1½" deep, with covers	10	
Marking pens, non-toxic	6		Pastesticks, hardwood, pkg. of 500	1	
Masking tape, roll	4		Pencils, soft, thick lead, without erasers	12	
Natural items for collage and painting (e.g., acorns, corks, dried flowers, herbs, leaves, feathers, seeds, etc.)	X		Pencil sharpener	1	
Newspapers	X		Pie tins or other containers, for children to use in mixing paint	6	
Paint:			Pins, safety, medium size, box of 100	1	
Finger, commercial, pts.	6		Pipe cleaners, assorted colors, pkgs.	2	
Finger (make as needed out of starch, water, tempera and soap flakes)	X		Plasticine, single color, lbs.	5	
Liquid tempera, assorted colors, qts.	10		Play dough, can be made or purchased, as needed	X	

(continues)

DIRECTOR'S RESOURCE 9-1
(continued)

SUGGESTED ITEMS	QUANTITIES	
	A	B
Printing materials for play dough, clay and paint, assorted kinds: cut vegetables, spools, blocks, etc., supply accumulated	X	
Rolling pins for play dough	4	
Salt, for cooking and making play dough, boxes	2	
Sand:		
Indoor sandbox, white, fine (lbs.) or cornmeal or sawdust in comparable amounts	200	
Outdoor sandbox, coarse, lbs.	800	
For painting, lbs.	2	
Scissors:		
Double-handled training, child-size	2	
Rounded, left-handed, child-size	8	
Semi-pointed, right-handed, child-size	8	
Shears, pair, adult-size	1	
Scotch tape, rolls	4	
Sponges, to be cut into pieces approx. 1" x 2" x 2" for painting	2	
Spray bottles	5	
Squeeze bottles, supply accumulated	X	
Staple remover	1	
Stapler, adult-size	2	
Stapler, child-size	4	
Staples, box	2	
Starch for mixing finger paint, boxes	2	
Straws for blow painting (box)	1	
Tape, Mystic, cloth with plastic finish, 3" wide x 108", roll	1	
Water color markers, non-toxic, water soluble, pkg.	3	
Wax	1	
Wheat paste, lbs.	1	
Wood pieces for collage and construction, scrounged, supply accumulated	X	
Yarn for collage, stitchery and weaving, scrounged balls	4	

SUGGESTED ITEMS	QUANTITIES	
	A	B
X. DRAMATIC PLAY		
Animal:		
Figures, small, plastic/rubber, a variety, in quantity for use with blocks and sand/water play	16	
Puppets, assorted	6	
Stuffed animals	4	
Camping:		
Backpack, from surplus store	1	
Lantern		1
Pup tent		1
Sleeping bag		1
Utensils	4	
Doctor/Nurse:		
Bandages, kit	1	
Clip board and pencils	2	
Cot		2
Instruments:		
Sphygmomanometer for blood pressure	1	
Stethoscope	1	
Mirrors	1	
Mask	1	
Grooming-toilet articles, male and female: comb, hair brush, hair rollers, hand mirror, nail brush, manual razor without blades and/or electric razor with plug off, shampoo bottles, hair spray bottles, shaving brush, soap	X	
Home management and family living:		
Bathing and cleaning:		
Broom, child size	1	
Dishcloth	2	
Dry mop	1	
Dustpan	1	
Iron, wood or plastic	1	
Ironing board	1	
Pail	1	
Soap flakes, sample boxes	1	
Towels:		
Bath	1	
Dish	2	

(continues)

DIRECTOR'S RESOURCE 9-1

(continued)

SUGGESTED ITEMS	QUANTITIES A	B	SUGGESTED ITEMS	QUANTITIES A	B
Hand	2		Furniture for playhouse area, sturdy,		
Washcloths	2		unbreakable:		
Wet mop, 30" handle	1		Bed and mattress, big enough		
Cooking and eating equipment, real,			for child to curl up on	1	
unbreakable:			Chairs:		
Baby bottle	2		High chair with tray	1	
Cutlery: forks, knives, spoons,			Rocking	1	
place settings	4		Straight	4	
Dishes: bowls, cups, saucers,			Curtains, as desired	X	
small glasses, plates, plate			Dresser or chest	1	
settings	4		Mirror, full-length, child height	1	
Food containers, empty	X		Refrigerator	1	
Food, pretend	X		Sink	1	
Utensils: cake pan, colander, frying			Sofa	1	
pan, kettle, ladle, large spoon,			Stove	1	
measuring cups and spoons,			Table, to seat four children	1	
mixing bowls, pie pan, sauce			Telephone	1	
pan, sieve, toaster (each)	2		T.V. frame, scrounged	1	
Doll equipment:			Office and school:		
Baby bottles	2		Attache case, scrounged	1	
Bed	1		Computer monitor/keyboard		
Buggy and stroller	1		(scrounged)	1	
Clothes, assorted, male, female,			Paper pads	2	
baby, older, various fastenings	12		Paper trays	2	
Dishes, place settings	2		Pencils and erasers	2	
Doll house, open on sides, top			Typewriter, scrounged	1	
removable	1		Waste baskets	2	
Doll house dolls: families, multiethnic,			Playhouse, outdoor	1	
multicultural, bendable preferred,			Puppets, family, hand or finger	4	
to use also with blocks, vehicles,			Repair and yard work:		
sand/water play	4		Carpentry apron	1	
Dolls, baby boy, girl, multiethnic,			Paintbrushes	X	
multicultural, unbreakable,			Paint cans containing colored		
washable	X		soapsuds	3	
Dress-up properties, male and			Sewing materials: buttons, cloth		
female: aprons, belts, billfolds,			pieces, decorations (pieces		
blouses, boots, uniforms, dresses,			of lace, ribbon, beads), large		
hats, hose, overalls, jackets, jewelry,			needles, rounded scissors,		
pants, purses, scarves, shawls,			thread, yarn, scrounged	X	
shoes, skirts, suitcase, ties, watches,			Transportation/Occupations: buy		
wigs, supply accumulated	X		and scrounge		

(continues)

DIRECTOR'S RESOURCE 9-1
(continued)

SUGGESTED ITEMS	QUANTITIES A B
Dress-up clothes: hats, uniforms, tools for a variety of occupations, such as bakers, bus drivers, carpenters, divers, engineers, fire fighters, air pilots, police officers, sailors, taxi drivers, train engineers, postal workers, construction workers	X
Model sets: airport, camper, fire station, garage, space center, etc., with proportioned buildings, figures, furnishings, tools, vehicles	4
People figures, proportioned, plastic, rubber, wood, representing a variety of workers	6
Puppets, representing different workers	4
Traffic signs for air terminals, highways, railroad crossings, waterways	5
Note: Additional dramatic play centers such as the following could also be provided based upon the children's needs and experiences: animal hospital, bakery, dentist office, farm, fire station, flower shop, gas station, grocery, hair salon, laundromat, pizza restaurant, police station, post office, repair shop, etc. Materials for the above can be easily scrounged by parents, teachers and community friends.	

XI. MUSIC

SUGGESTED ITEMS	QUANTITIES A B
Autoharp	1
Cassettes	X
CDs	X
Cassette player for children to handle	X
Claves	6
Dancing clothes: scarves, skirts, streamers, supply accumulated	X

SUGGESTED ITEMS	QUANTITIES A B
Guiro tone block	1
Guiro with scraper	1
Rhythm instruments:	
Bells, variety: ankle, cow, wrist, melody, set, supply accumulated	X
Castanets	2
Drums, variety: snare, tom-tom, etc.	2
Guitar	1
Kazoo	2
Keyboard, can be homemade	2
Maracas	4
Piano	1
Recorder, wind instrument	1
Sticks, rhythm, flat/fluted sets	12
Tambourines	2
Triangles	1
Ukulele	1
Wind chimes	1
Wood blocks	2
Xylophone	2

XII. LANGUAGE ARTS

SUGGESTED ITEMS	QUANTITIES A B
Alphabet letters, movable, sandpaper, tactile, in several sizes	300
Books:	
Permanent collection of 30 or more, and circulating collection borrowed from library. Choose high quality children's books, look for multicultural, multiethnic, non-sexist content.	X
Topics to include:	
Animals	
Child activities	
Community	
Fairy tales	
Fantasies	
Holidays	
Mother Goose	
Seasonal	
Sensitive topics—adoption, divorce, illness	

(continues)

DIRECTOR'S RESOURCE 9-1
(continued)

SUGGESTED ITEMS	QUANTITIES A	B
Easy to read books	X	
Picture books, including alphabet books and dictionaries	X	
Poetry to read aloud	X	
Resource books on such topics as biological science, community, crafts, cultures, family, geography, holidays, physical sciences, space science	X	
Camera for snapshots of children, etc.	1	
Chalkboards, portable, with chalk and erasers	1	
Chart paper, large, for experiences	2	
Computer (for exploration)	1	
Felt board	1	
Felt board pieces: alphabet, stories, animals, familiar objects, etc., pkg. of 50 items	1	
Games, simple, such as lotto and other picture games	4	
Notebooks for dictated stories	3	
Perception cards, set	1	
Puzzles, wooden, 9 to 16 pieces	8	
Typewriter, primary	1	

XIII. MATHEMATICS

Counters, unbreakable: animals, beads, blocks, buttons, cards, color chips, nails, napkins, marbles, sticks, etc.	X	
Food to cut and divide	X	
Geometric figures, wooden, 3" units, approx. 6 items, set	1	
Matching sets	X	
Measuring equipment, English and Metric:		
Dry units	4	
Liquid units	4	
Rulers	2	
Tape	1	
Thermometers:		
Hand manipulated model	1	
Indoor/Outdoor	1	
Money, play, homemade	X	

SUGGESTED ITEMS	QUANTITIES A	B
Number games	4	
Numerals, tactile in variety of sizes and materials	20	
Objects: any in environment to examine their properties, likenesses and differences	X	
Peg boards, 12" x 12"	4	
Pegs, hardwood, $\frac{1}{8}$" diameter, 2" long, box of 1,000	1	
Shapes, basic sets, tactile, unbreakable, variety of sizes and materials, supply accumulated	X	
Sorting containers, unbreakable: baskets, boxes, cans, glasses	3	
Timers, buy or scrounge, as needed for curriculum:		
Calendars	2	
Clocks:		
Alarm, hand-wound	1	
Electric, wall	1	
Watch	1	
Weights, English and Metric:		
Bathroom scale	1	
Kitchen scale	1	

XIV. SCIENCE

Air experiments: (obtain as needed each year)		
Balloons	6	
Bubble pipes	20	
Squeeze bottles, supply accumulated	X	
Straws	24	
Tubing, 3' length	1	
Windmills for water and sand	4	
Animal foods that are appropriate for below	X	
Animals: Follow all public health and safety laws and regulations, provide adequate food, medical care, shelter. Choose from:		
Baby chicks		

(continues)

DIRECTOR'S RESOURCE 9-1

(continued)

SUGGESTED ITEMS	QUANTITIES A B		SUGGESTED ITEMS	QUANTITIES A B	
Ducks			Grow chart, height, weight	1	
Fish			Light and heat:		
Gerbils (when permitted by law)			Electricity: batteries, bulbs, buzzers,		
Guinea pigs			simple circuits, supply		
Hamsters			accumulated	X	
Mice			Magnifying glasses, hand	2	
Parakeets			Magnifying glasses on stand	1	
Rabbits			Mirrors, unbreakable	2	
Snails			Prisms, assorted	2	
Snakes			Liquids and supplies:		
Sponges, living			Liquids:		
Aquarium	1		Ice	X	
Books dealing with science			Oil, $\frac{1}{2}$ pt. can	1	
concepts	X		Other liquids	X	
Eggs and incubator	4–6		Supplies:		
Food and gardening:			Containers, plastic, supply		
Use of food in science is essential			accumulated	X	
to a child's experiencing the			Kettle	1	
changes of state in matter.			Medicine dropper	2	
Children's cookbook	1		Paper:		
Containers: bottles, cartons, flower			Blotting, odds and ends	X	
boxes, flower pots, jars, etc.,			Filter, pkg.	1	
supply accumulated	X		Sponges	2	
Cotton, box	1		Sprayer	1	
Dirt box or dirt plot	1		Squeeze bottles, supply		
Fertilizer, lbs.	5		accumulated	X	
Food:			Squirt bottles, for spraying, supply		
Natural foods, fruits, nuts,			accumulated	X	
vegetables	X		Mechanics and physics:		
Packaged mixes and processed			Inclined planes	1	
foods, pkg.	4		Magnets, variety of shapes and		
Raw ingredients: flour, salt, soda,			sizes, and things to try to pick up	2	
spices, sugar, etc., in tightly			Picture collection: animals, plants,		
covered containers, one for			geography, astronomy,		
each item	X		machines, etc.	X	
Garden tools, child size: hoe, rake,			Siphon	1	
spade, set	1		Soda bottles for experiments	X	
Plants, cultivated and wild	X		Take-apart equipment (donated):		
Seeds, collected from nature and			old clocks, typewriters, vacuum		
purchased, supply accumulated	X		cleaners, etc., supply		
Stakes and string or wire fencing	X		accumulated	X	
Terrarium	1		Wheels	4	
Watering cans or hoses	2		Minerals: rocks, stones, etc.	X	

(continues)

DIRECTOR'S RESOURCE 9-1
(continued)

SUGGESTED ITEMS	A	B	SUGGESTED ITEMS	A	B
XV. OFFICE SUPPLIES AND RECORD KEEPING			Chairs:		
Bulletin board	1		Adult-sized:		
Calendar	1		Comfortable	1	
Correction fluid for typewriter (bottle)	1		Rocking	2	
Diskettes for computer	X		Child-sized:		
Diskette tray	1		High	3	
Fax machine (access to)	1		Rocking	1	
File cabinet	1		Stackable	6	
Index cards	X		Clock, wall hung	1	
Key organizer	1		Clothes rack for drying clothes		1
Manila envelopes, 2 sizes	36		Cots or mats for resting	4	
Manila folders	36		Cribs, one per infant	X	
Marking pens, several colors	4		Cubbies or tubs for personal belongings	8	
Message pads	10		Cushions, washable, plastic	4	1
Microcomputer	1		Dishwasher	1	
Paper clips, 2 sizes, boxes	2		Electrical outlet covers, as needed	X	
Paper hole puncher	1		Feeding and play table	1	
Pencils, boxes	6		File cabinet	1	
Pens (boxes)	5		Front pack, for carrying young infant	1	1
Photocopier (access to)	1		Hamper for soiled clothes (See Health Materials)		
Rubber bands, assorted sizes, boxes	4		Infant bounce seat (floor model, not mobile)	1	
Scissors	2		Infant stroller	1	1
Stationery, letterhead and plain, 2 sizes, quire of each	10		Infant swing	2	
Thumbtacks, boxes	8		Microwave oven		1
Writing paper tablets, ruled and unruled, in several sizes	8		Mirror, unbreakable:		
Yardstick	1		Horizontally mounted at floor level	1	
			Vertically mounted at child's eye level	1	
INFANT/TODDLER			Photocopier, access to	X	
I. BASIC ENVIRONMENTAL EQUIPMENT			Playpen or similar structure to allow young infants protection from and visual access to older infants and toddlers	1	
Box, wooden or plastic on rollers with handles		1	Portacrib	2	
Bulletin boards, staff and parent	2		Refrigerator	1	
Cabinet, closed and locking for storing adult supplies out of children's reach, such as first aid or cleaning supplies	1		Safety gate	1	
Carpet or other resilient floor covering	X		Screens, low sturdy folding panels for use as area dividers	2	
			Serving cart	1	

(continues)

DIRECTOR'S RESOURCE 9-1
(continued)

SUGGESTED ITEMS	A	B
Shelves:		
High, closed for toys and supplies not in use	1	
Low, open, for children's toys and supplies	2	
Storage bins on rollers for outdoor toys	1	
Tables:		
Changing table at adult height	1	
Adult height for food preparation	1	
Child height	2	
Toilet facilities:		
Dressing table	1	
Sink, tub, or plastic tub for bathing	2	
Lavatories	2	
Toilet seat	1	
Training chairs	3	
Tote tubs for play materials	6	4
Trash cans, covered	2	
Vacuum cleaner	1	
Washer and dryer	1	
Wastebaskets, covered	3	
Window coverings as needed	X	
Work station on wheels, for adults	1	

II. HOUSEKEEPING EQUIPMENT AND SUPPLIES

SUGGESTED ITEMS	A	B
Brooms:		
Adult size, straight & push, one each	2	
Child size, straight	2	
Brushes:		
Bottle	2	2
Counter	1	
Hand	2	
Cleaners, scouring powders, cans	3	
Dishpan	2	
Dishtowels	6	3
Dishwasher (See Basic Environmental Equipment)		
Disinfectants, bottles, replace as needed	X	X
Dustcloths, replace as needed	X	X

SUGGESTED ITEMS	A	B
Dust mop	2	
Hand held portable vacuum	1	
Heating and serving dishes	4	2
Soap, liquid hand and dishwasher, as needed	X	X
Sponges	3	
Towels, paper, case of 3000	2	
Trays		4
Vacuum cleaner (See Basic Environmental Equipment)		
Washer and dryer (See Basic Environmental Equipment)		
Wastebaskets (See Basic Environmental Equipment)		

III. HEALTH AND SAFETY MATERIALS

SUGGESTED ITEMS	A	B
Diapers, disposable and unscented (if not provided by parents or if diaper service is not used), pkg. of 1 doz.	400	
First aid and toilet supplies:		
Bandages, adhesive, boxes	2	
Butterfly bandages, boxes	1	
Calamine lotion	1	
Cotton, sterilized, boxes	2	
Cotton tip swabs, boxes	4	
Eye bath	1	
Gauze, sterilized, boxes	2	
Gauze, sterilized, pads	2	
Gloves, disposable	X	
Ice pack	2	
Lotion, nonallergenic	3	
Medicine dropper	1	
Nonallergenic adhesive tape, rolls	2	
Paper towels, package	25	
Petroleum jelly	3	
Powder, talcum, cans	8	
Ointment, antiseptic	1	
Red Cross first aid manual	1	
Rubbing alcohol	1	
Scissors	1	
Soap, antiseptic	3	

(continues)

DIRECTOR'S RESOURCE 9-1
(continued)

SUGGESTED ITEMS	QUANTITIES A	B
Temperature strips	X	
Tissue:		
Facial	18	
Toilet	25	
Tweezers	1	
Food service:		
Bibs, disposable dental, used with clips	300	
Bottles, spare:		
4 ounce	2	
8 ounce	2	
Bowls, plates, cups, glasses, unbreakable sets	12	
Flatware:		
Forks, juvenile	6	
Knives, juvenile	2	
Paper cups	200	
Paper napkins, packages of 100	5	
Place settings, adult	6	
Spoons, juvenile	12	
Spoons, serving	4	
Toddler trainer cup, two handled	4	
Hamper for soiled clothes	1	
Resting facilities:		
Blankets	12	
Cots (See Basic Environmental Equipment)		
Cribs (See Basic Environmental Equipment)		
Mattress pads, assorted sizes	18	
Sheets:		
Cotton, assorted sizes, patterns and colors	18	
Rubber, assorted sizes	12	
Sanitation:		
Diaper changing pads, vinyl	6	
Diaper changing paper rolls, hygienic	X	
Smocks, infant	4	
Sprays:		
Air freshener, cans	2	
Disinfectant, cans	4	

SUGGESTED ITEMS	QUANTITIES A	B
Towelettes, disposable, as needed	X	
Towels:		
Bath size	12	
Fingertip size	18	
Trash cans (See Basic Environmental Equipment)		
Washcloths	18	
Washer and dryer (See Basic Environmental Equipment)		
Wastebaskets (See Basic Environmental Equipment)		
IV. GROSS MOTOR EQUIPMENT (Indoor/Outdoor)		
Apparatus:		
Boxes of various sizes for climbing	5	
Crawl-throughs: oil drum, lined barrels, cardboard tubing, perception box	1	
Indoor stair and slide combination	1	
Pads to place under climbing and sliding apparatus	2	
Rocking boat	1	
Tumbling mat	1	
Wading pool		1
Walking boards—planks slightly raised at one or both ends	1	1
Dramatic play:		
Dishes, soft, unbreakable	12	
Dolls, soft, unbreakable, washable, multiethnic, with Velcro® clothes	4	
Foods, unbreakable plastic, multiethnic	2	
Furniture: stove, table, sink, cupboard, bed, baby carriage, high chair, shopping cart	4	
Housekeeping: (child-sized) broom, dustpan, one each		2
Housekeeping: pots, pans, spoons and other kitchen utensils, multiethnic	4	
Playhouse, child-sized, dividers or low screen		1

(continues)

DIRECTOR'S RESOURCE 9-1
(continued)

SUGGESTED ITEMS	QUANTITIES A	B
Large muscle activity toys:		
Balls, various sizes, 3", 6", 12", 20" diameter, rubber or plastic	4	
Blocks, large foam, plastic or cardboard	10	6
Pounding peg board and mallet	2	
Pull toys, commercial or teacher-made	4	
Push toys	4	
Riding toys, propelled by arms or feet		3
Rocking horse		1
Throw toys: Bean bags, textured foam balls, yarn balls	4	
Wagon, small	1	
Sand play: (can be used with materials)		
Cups, spoons, plastic bottles and other measuring devices	6	
Dump and fill containers: bowls, cans, pails, measuring cups and spoons, sieve, funnel, scoop, sand shovel	10	
Indoor sandbox or table approximately 24" x 24" x 5", filled with sand	1	
Outdoor sandbox with cover	1	
Umbrella or other shade	1	
Water play:		
Container: plastic bathtub, dishpan or water table	1	
Dump and fill containers: bowls, cans, bottles, pails, watering cans, pitchers	10	
Manipulative materials: corks, floating tub toys, soap, sponge, sprinkler bottle, lotion dispenser, bottle, funnels	X	X
Vinyl sheet to place under water container	1	
V. MANIPULATIVES		
Infant:		
Clutch balls, large with finger holds in soft materials	2	

SUGGESTED ITEMS	QUANTITIES A	B
Infant gyms, floor model	2	
Rattles, securely enclosed, pleasing to the ear, including measuring spoons on a ring, spools in a box, sound makers contrived from juice cans and large plastic beads	4	
Squeeze toys, soft washable	4	
Teething toys, durable	6	4
Toys to wear:		
Bell bracelets, securely made with a strip of elastic and a small bell	4	
Colorful wrist and ankle bands	4	
Foot sock with a smiling face	4	
Toddler:		
Beads, jumbo, plastic, set	1	
Duplos®, set	1	
Peg board, giant plastic, set	1	
Pop-up toys	2	
Mazes, commercial beads on wire tracks	1	1
Vehicles, plastic	2	2
VI. SENSORY PERCEPTION		
Listening materials:		
Bell blocks, wood, with bell inside each block, set of five	1	
Bell bracelets	6	
Chimes, wind		2
Mobiles, musical		2
Music boxes, pull-a-cord or wind-up	1	1
Paper to rattle and tear	X	X
Records and tapes, children's music, classical, multiethnic, bilingual	X	X
Smelling materials:		
Fresh flowers	X	X
Spices, sealed, in plastic bottles with perforated lids, set	1	
Tasting materials:		
Foods, new and familiar in identical containers, for identification games	X	X

(continues)

DIRECTOR'S RESOURCE 9-1
(continued)

SUGGESTED ITEMS	A	B
Foods for tasting: fruits, vegetables, breadstuffs, cereals	X	X
Touching and feeling materials:		
Cuddle toys, animals, dolls	5	2
Flannel covering for babies' bottles to encourage feeling while feeding		3
Poke boxes (shallow boxes with hand holes on lid through which infant can touch variety of textures)	1	1
Texture ball (cloth ball covered with textures such as velvet, fur, cotton, sandpaper, etc.)	1	1
Texture glove made from a variety of materials, to be worn by an adult		1
Wall hangings, textured and touchable	1	1
Warm and cold materials: hot cereal, ice cubes, etc.	X	X
Visual materials:		
Color paddles, set		1
Mirrors, unbreakable, hand held	2	
Mobiles, brightly colored	2	1
Pictures, laminated or covered with clear contact paper, multiethnic	X	X

VII. COGNITIVE

SUGGESTED ITEMS	A	B
Aquarium with fish		1
Bird feeding shelf		1
Blocks, unit set of foam or plastic	1	
Books on numbers		2
Coffee cans, empty, with clothes pins to be clipped on the rim	4	
Counting cubes and disks, large enough not to be swallowed	100	
Floating and sinking objects	6	
Form boards	2	1
Gear turning toys, wood or plastic	2	
Hardware fixture board with workable parts: hinges, door bolts, knockers, knobs, etc.	1	
Locks and attached keys, large	2	
Magnetic board and accessories	1	

SUGGESTED ITEMS	A	B
Magnifier on tripod		1
Nature objects: autumn leaves, snow, flowers, fruits, nuts	X	X
Nesting toys, commercial and teacher-made	4	2
Number puzzles	X	
Number sorters		2
Nuts and bolts, large, wood or plastic, set	1	
Plants, living, non-toxic	X	X
Puzzles, variety, some with handled pieces	6	6
Shells and rocks, wide assortment, set of 8–10	1	
Stacking toys, commercial and teacher-made	4	2
Sorting toys, commercial and teacher-made	4	2
Terrarium with plant and amphibian life		1

VIII. CREATIVE

Music

SUGGESTED ITEMS	A	B
Autoharp		1
Bells, melody, hand and wrist, set	1	
Chimes, set	1	
Instruments: multiethnic		
Drums		
Bongo	2	
Handcrafted drums, such as coffee can with plastic lid or innertube top, oatmeal box with lid glued on	4	
Maracas	2	
Rhythm sticks, pair	2	
Tambourines	2	
Xylophone	1	
Record player	1	
Songbooks:		
Nursery rhymes	1	
Traditional, multiethnic selections	2	1
Tape recorders, adult and child	2	

(continues)

DIRECTOR'S RESOURCE 9-1
(continued)

SUGGESTED ITEMS	A	B
Tapes and records: multiethnic		
Blank cassettes	2	2
Musical: listening, activity	4	2
Narrative: talking stories and poems	4	2
Sounds: animals, city noises, farm noises	1	
Art		
Accessories:		
Brushes, large for water painting and painting with color	5	
Crayon holders	2	
Easel	1	
Smocks (use old shirts worn backwards or aprons)	X	X
Tray, plastic for finger painting	2	
Illustrations of pleasing line, form, color, such as designs on wallpaper samples, gift wrap, wall decorations of mounted fabrics, calendar photographs and drawings	X	X
Media:		
Chalk, soft, white for chalkboard or paper, white, chubby sticks, box	1	
Crayons, large assorted colors, box	1	
Markers, washable, non-toxic, assorted colors including multiethnic skin tones, box	2	2
Play dough for modeling (cooked and uncooked recipes)	X	X
Poster paint: red, yellow, blue, white, black, brown, quart each	1	1
Soap suds, colored, made with vegetable coloring	X	X
Natural objects: flowers, plants, rocks, shells, wood	X	X
Paper:		
Assorted colors for mounting display materials, pkg.	4	4
Assorted sizes, shapes and colors	X	X
Computer print-out, recycled	X	X
Magazines, recycled	X	X

SUGGESTED ITEMS	A	B
Newsprint, pkg. of 100 sheets	3	3
Wallpaper, samples	X	X
Movement and pretend play		
Dramatic play props (See Gross Motor Equipment)		
Hats, washable	X	X
Scarves and ribbons, as movement props	X	X
Telephones	2	
IX. COMMUNICATION		
Books:		
Cloth and paper, with squeeze and feel pictures, various sizes and shapes	10	2
Nursery rhyme books	2	
Story, to read to children, plus access to library books, include multiethnic	10	10
Discussion pictures about foods, health, safety, science, social learning, everyday objects, some laminated	X	X
Feel box (use small box with child hand-size hole, fill with objects child can feel, take out, talk about and put back)	1	
Flannel board	1	
Flannel board accessories: animals, numerals, letters, geometric shapes, multiethnic people	18	6
Language games involving identifying, sorting, matching	4	
Puppetry, familiar figures:		
Hand puppets, multiethnic	4	
Homemade puppets, stick, sack, cloth	4	
Screen or stage behind which puppets can operate	1	1
X. RECORD KEEPING		
Attendance record sheets, weekly	52	
Booklets, to record children's verbalizations	8	

(continues)

DIRECTOR'S RESOURCE 9-1
(continued)

SUGGESTED ITEMS	QUANTITIES A	B	SUGGESTED ITEMS	QUANTITIES A	B
Budgeting record book	1		Health and general information reporting sheets	X	X
Card file for anecdotal records	1		Portfolios of children's work	12	
Daily "communication with parent" forms	250		Progress reporting sheets on specific behaviors	12	
File cards, 6" x 4" or to fit available file drawers, pkg. of 100	5		Teacher planning book	1	

Reprinted by permission of Joan Moyer, Editor, and the Association for Childhood Education International, 17904 Georgia Avenue, Suite 215, Olney, MD. Copyright ©1995 by the Association.

DIRECTOR'S RESOURCE 9-2

GUIDE TO PURCHASING CLASSROOM FURNITURE

Furniture purchases are important decisions for child care centers. Good choices will reward you, and mistakes may haunt you for years to come. To help improve your decision making, we have compiled the following checklist of questions to pursue in evaluating any furniture purchase. These questions were formulated based on the input of furniture manufacturers and dealers. In researching these questions, it may be helpful to secure the advice and support of parents or friends who are carpenters or engineers, as well as other center directors who can offer feedback on their experiences with various vendors and types of furniture.

Center Needs

- Do you have an overall plan for furnishing each classroom?
- Does the furniture you are now considering fit into this plan?
- What is your purchasing strategy? Do you purchase low cost items with short life expectancies, or do you invest more up front for quality items that last longer?
- Do you have an aesthetic concept? Do you want the furniture to foster a certain look or image? Do you have a color scheme for each classroom?
- What materials do you want your furniture constructed from? [Quality hard woods (birch, maple, oak) are durable, long lasting, and aesthetically pleasing. Softer woods (pine and low quality plywoods) are less expensive, but much less durable. Hardwoods with quality laminates are highly durable and easy to maintain. Metal is the sturdiest material, but needs suitable plating or painting to prevent rust. Hard plastic is colorful, lightweight, and, in some cases, easy to maintain.]

Health and Safety

- Does the furniture meet or exceed state licensing requirements?
- Does the product meet Consumer Product Safety Commission standards?
- Does it present any barriers for use by children with special needs?
- Can it tip over easily?
- Does it have sharp edges or rough surfaces?
- Are there nails, splinters, or staples in exposed areas?
- Are screws inset and out of harm's way?
- Will it splinter or crack?
- Were environment-friendly materials used in furniture manufacture?
- Can children find ways to use the furniture that may be perilous? [Toddlers, for example, will hang onto anything within reach while toddling about.]
- Does it have ornaments or knobs that are dangerous or flimsy?
- Are the doors and hinges safe for children's fingers?
- Can children's feet be caught underneath the furniture?
- How difficult will it be to keep sanitary?
- Can it be cleaned and sanitized easily?

(continues)

DIRECTOR'S RESOURCE 9-2
(continued)

Child Appropriateness

- Is the furniture appropriate for the age of children who will be using it?
- Is it the right size for children? [For example, when a child uses a chair, her feet should rest squarely on the floor, and the table should be waist high to a standing child.]
- Can it be used appropriately by children of different ages?
- Is it designed for children, or is it simply scaled down adult furniture?
- Do chairs promote good posture?
- Can children move it themselves easily?
- Is its intended use clear to children?
- Does it support child centered learning?
- Does it promote the discovery of independence and motor development?
- Will the children find it comfortable?
- Does it provide a variety of textures for children to experience?

Construction and Design

- How solidly is the furniture constructed?
- If assembly is required, are all the required tools and parts included?
- Are the joints well engineered and secure? [For wood furniture, the least stable joint construction is side-to-end construction, and the most preferred are: (1) peg, glue, and screw; (2) dado and screw; and (3) glue and screw.]
- Is the furniture flexible—can it perform more than one function?
- Can it be purchased in modular units that build on one another?
- Can it easily be moved for different room arrangements?
- Can it easily and compactly be stored?
- Will it attain its look and feel under frequent cleaning?
- How do the materials in the furniture contribute to the overall acoustical environment?

Vendor Reliability and Support

- Do the salespersons from the vendor really understand early childhood environments?
- Can they help evaluate your needs and explore alternatives?
- Do they understand furniture manufacture so they can answer questions about safety and durability?
- Can the vendor make modifications to the furniture to meet your needs?
- Is the furniture in stock—can the vendor guarantee delivery dates?
- Does the company have a reputation for timely deliveries and solid follow-up support?
- Who will the contact person be after the sale—a local representative or a toll free service?

(continues)

DIRECTOR'S RESOURCE 9-2
(continued)

- How long a warranty is available on the furniture? [Warranty periods vary widely—from one year to lifetime—with five years an average length. Higher quality materials and construction methods generally yield longer warranty periods.]
- Are there any exceptions or limitations on the warranty?
- When defective items or items damaged in shipping need to be returned, will the customer be responsible for shipping or restocking fees? [The answer should be "no."]
- Does the vendor have a reputation for standing behind its warranty? [The answer should be "yes."]

DIRECTOR'S RESOURCE 9-3

GUIDE TO EARLY CHILDHOOD CURRICULUM PRODUCTS

Today, in designing and refining the curriculum of your early childhood organization, you have a myriad of resources to support you. These range from packaged comprehensive curriculum kits that address all aspects of children's development to targeted curriculum packages that address specific curriculum areas such as self-esteem, multicultural programming, or health and safety.

Having such a rich base of support can be reassuring, but it can easily become overwhelming. In this guide, we are going to share with you questions to pose in evaluating curriculum products. These questions are based on the insights of curriculum product developers.

Underlying Assumptions

- Is the product founded on research-based principles of learning?
- Does it respect the social nature of learning?
- Are activities proposed appropriate for the age of children?
- Does it realistically take into account the limited amount of planning time available for teachers?
- Is it easy to use by teachers with diverse levels of training?
- Does it help teachers construct knowledge of effective practices without being overly prescriptive?
- Does it encourage teachers to utilize their own creativity?
- Does it provide guidance on organizing an effective learning environment?
- Does it maintain a consistent focus on a particular philosophy, goals and objectives?
- Does it value diversity in culture, linguistics, gender, and ability?
- Does it describe the teacher's role in observing children, planning experiences, and interacting in ways that promote social competence and learning?
- Is it well organized and easy to use?
- Does it involve families as partners in the learning process?
- Are materials aesthetically pleasing?
- Does the product include a user-friendly teacher's guide?

Approaches to Learning

- Are activities likely to engage the interests of the children?
- Does it place the child in the role of an active, independent learner?
- Does it offer support for children with all forms of learning disabilities?
- Does it provide opportunities for different learning styles?
- Is there a logical progression of learning experiences?
- Does it incorporate routine tasks, such as toilet training, eating, dressing and sleeping, to teach self-help and social skills?
- Does it promote success through cooperation and teamwork in an all-inclusive social and physical community?
- Does it encourage children to proceed at their own pace?

(continues)

DIRECTOR'S RESOURCE 9-3
(continued)

- Is it fun for the children and the staff?
- Are appropriate learning materials available to support the curriculum?
- Does it provide experiences for large groups, small groups, and individuals?
- Are the activities challenging and slightly beyond the children's skill levels?
- Does it provide measures for assessment?
- Does it allow for coincidental, spontaneous learning?

Content Areas

- Does it develop a child's imagination and sense of wonder?
- Does it develop a child's cognitive thinking skills?
- Does it develop a child's gross and fine motor skills?
- Does it develop a child's socialization ability?
- Does it develop a child's language skills?
- Does it foster a child's positive self-image?
- Does it encourage creative and artistic expression?
- Does it encourage good health, safety, and nutritional practices?
- Does it encourage the appreciation of music and the arts?
- Does it expose children to differences in people?
- Does it provide experiences to all five senses?
- Do activities give children a sense of accomplishment?
- Does it help the child learn to reason?

Vendor Capabilities and Support

- Do the products' developers have specific and extensive training in child development?
- Do they have extensive and current experience in working with children in a variety of real life settings?
- Do they keep informed on the latest research?
- Can the vendor supply you with names of current users for reference checks?
- Does a customer have an opportunity to try the product out before purchasing?
- Does the vendor listen to users and make changes where needed?
- Does the vendor offer initial hands-on training in the use of the product?
- Does the vendor provide ongoing, nearby in-service opportunities?
- Does the vendor provide support via a toll-free support line or Internet access?
- Does the vendor offer a money back guarantee if the customer is not satisfied?

Reprinted with permission from Child Care Information Exchange, P.O. Box 3249, Redmond, WA 98073, (800) 221-2864, http://www.ChildCareExchange.com. Permission conveyed through Copyright Clearance Center, Inc.

REFERENCES

Aronson, S. (1997, January). Lead paint poisoning from playground equipment. *Child Care Information Exchange*, 79–81.

Brown, M. W. (1947). *Goodnight moon.* New York: Harper.

Moyer, J. (Ed.). (1995). *Selecting educational equipment and materials for school and home.* Wheaton: Association for Childhood Education International.

Neugebauer, R. (1997). Child care center management software buying guide. *Child Care Information Exchange, 116*, 64–66.

U.S. Consumer Product Safety Commission. (1999). Washington, DC: U.S. Government Printing Office.

Wardle, F. (1999). The story of a playground. *Child Care Information Exchange, 128*, 28–30.

Wortham, S. C., & Frost, J. L. (Eds.). (1997). *Playgrounds for young children: American survey and perspectives.* Reston, VA: American Alliance for Health, Physical Education, Recreation and Dance.

Additional resources for this chapter can be found on the Online Companion™ at http://www.earlychilded.delmar.com. This supplemental material includes relevant Web links, Web activities, and case studies that apply the concepts presented in this chapter. In addition, the Working Papers and Director's Resources are available for download, allowing you to complete Class Exercises and Class Assignments electronically.

CHAPTER 10

Staffing the Center

The director may take full responsibility for interviewing all job candidates for available staff positions.

OBJECTIVES

After reading this chapter, you should be able to:

■ Describe the major sections of a personnel policy.
■ Write a job description for each position in a child care center.
■ Understand the interview process.
■ Develop an orientation process for new employees.

The basic tools used in developing plans and procedures for hiring the child care center staff are written personnel policies and job descriptions. On the surface, these documents and procedures appear to be easily drawn and delineated; at a more subtle level, they reflect the philosophy of the overall program as it focuses on individuals and their worth as human beings. As policies and procedures are adjusted and changed, they will reflect the ability of responsible administrators in the organization to make optimum use of available human resources.

An analysis of each center's purposes and manner of operating will determine the broad policy areas to be covered in the personnel policies. The center that employs large numbers of professional and ancillary staff may have policies with separate sections for each category of employee and other personnel, including substitutes, resource teachers, and other support staff. In all cases, every policy statement should contain an affirmative action section that verifies the center's intent to adhere strictly to acceptance of all personnel regardless of race, age, sex, creed, national origin, sexual preference, or disability. (For information regarding employment discrimination and affirmative action issues, contact the U.S. Equal Employment Opportunity Commission, 800-669-3362, http://www.eeoc.org, or call 800-669-4000 to be connected to your state EEOC office.)

DESIGNING PERSONNEL POLICIES

Directors of new centers are faced with the daunting task of developing new personnel policies while directors of existing centers must deal with the recurring task of reviewing and revising these policies. When writing or revising personnel policies, it is important to consider the purpose served by the policies, the best interests of all parties covered and affected by the policies, and what is to be included in the policies. Although each center's documents are individualized and program specific, personnel policies from other centers can serve as helpful guides while writing or revising these policies.

Purpose

The need of personnel for security and confidence in their daily job performance should be balanced with the center's need to function effectively in the establishment of carefully conceived personnel policies. When staff members are unsure of their rights and their responsibilities, some of them may tend to probe and test to determine where the limits lie. The dissension among staff members that ensues drains energy from child care. On the other hand, the staff members who know what is expected of them can recognize how their assigned roles fit into the overall organizational structure and can, therefore, function more comfortably in those roles. Administrators also can function more assuredly when there is little doubt about policies because questions can be handled by referring to policies instead of by involving individual personalities. When the rights and responsibilities of each staff member are understood by the entire staff, friction is eliminated and negotiations can be conducted between members.

Inclusive personnel policies tailored to a specific child care operation, whether staffed by a few or by many, serve two purposes.

1. They reduce procedural errors and free administrators from unnecessary involvement in resolution.

2. They reduce anxiety by helping each staff member to understand expectations and move, independently and as part of the team, toward efficient operation of the program.

A written statement of the personnel policies and procedures should be given to each employee at the beginning of the term of employment. These policies will set the parameters within which the total staff will function. Of course, there may be situations in which a new employee may require time on the job before fully understanding all that is written in the policy statement. Nonetheless, distribution of the written policy to everyone is a tacit statement on the part of administrators that communication is open and that there are no secret or hidden agreements or rules at any level in the staff hierarchy. The administrator should make a point of checking periodically with employees to ascertain whether the policies are understood. Although these policies must be tailored to the needs of each program, the samples in Director's Resource 10–1 can serve as a guideline for their preparation.

DIRECTOR'S CORNER

"During my new staff orientation program, I sit down with each new employee and read through the personnel policies, leaving time for questions and discussion. I give special attention to the section on holidays, sick days, personal days, and vacation time. It helps me feel comfortable that this new staff person has at least looked at the personnel policies once and not just put the document in a file or on her night table to read later when she has more time."

–Director, private not-for-profit center

Source

Since the task of writing personnel policies is complex and the sphere of their influence is extensive, the decision about who writes them requires careful consideration. They must not only be precise, well written, and inclusive but also take into consideration the best interests of staff, children, and families. The interest of the sponsoring group, whether it be to make a profit or not, deserves consideration as well. For example, a one-year probationary period for a new teacher may be agreeable to a sponsoring agency and provide good protection for a new staff member, but it could turn out to be devastating for the children if a newly hired individual clearly demonstrates a lack of skills in the classroom. In turn, the reputation and the income of the sponsoring group could suffer. Therefore, those who are responsible for writing the policies must have both an understanding of the scope of the program and insight into the vested interests of all involved.

Depending on the size and the organizational structure of a center, the personnel policies might be prepared by the hired director of a community-sponsored center, an owner of a proprietary center, a personnel director of a center sponsored by an industry, or the personnel director of a national child care chain. Existing public school personnel policies for teachers or, in some cases, for civil service employees often will be applicable in public-school-sponsored programs. When the center staff is part of a labor union, the union contract supersedes all policies and procedures for the bargaining staff, so policies and procedures are rewritten to reflect any changes in the contract after negotiations are completed. This will affect procedures such as reassignments and layoffs more than hiring policies or job descriptions.

The more usual practice in child care settings is to have policies drawn by a subcommittee or a standing personnel committee of the policy-making board. The bylaws, as drawn up by the policy board, should contain the mechanism for creating a personnel committee and should detail the manner in which the membership of that committee will be selected. The center director serves on the committee and represents the staff's interest. Other members of the committee might be parents, people from the community, and representatives of licensing and/or certifying groups who would, in each case, represent a special-interest group.

INCLUSIONS

In general, personnel policies cover all matters relating to employment and include job responsibilities, tables of organization, schedules of reimbursement for services, evaluation and grievance procedures, and description of the steps necessary to change the policies themselves. They must conform to union requirements, where applicable, and to all regulations that apply to employment practices. For example, as of July 1994, employers with 15 employees or more must comply with the Americans with Disabilities Act (ADA), which covers nondiscrimination practices related to recruitment, advertising, tenure, layoff, leave, fringe benefits, and all other employment-related activities (The Americans with Disabilities Act: Questions and Answers, 1991; see Director's Resource 10–2). Since many of these elements are included in the personnel policies, it is important to understand the implications of the ADA for you and your staff to ensure compliance with these regulations, as well as to protect your program. Personnel policies specifically spell out the rights of employees and what they may expect from the employer; therefore, they should include the following items:

Career Ladder

Developing the career ladder for a center is a challenge to the director and/or the board. Each center must develop its own version of a career ladder after reviewing the roles and responsibilities of each staff position, budget limitations, and the professional goals of the center. The career ladder clearly defines education and experience and corresponding salaries and benefits for every step in the hierarchy (see Bloom, Sheerer, & Britz, 2005 for a discussion of career ladders).

Contract

The contract usually is a bilateral agreement signed by both parties that mutually binds the employee and the employer to acquire certain rights from each other. In this case, the employee agrees to provide a service (as defined by the appropriate job description) and the employer agrees to reimburse the employee for the service at a given rate for a specific length of time. Of course, those employers who have an at-will policy do not use employment contracts.

Employment at Will

Employment at will is operative in most states unless you have contracted with an employee and your contract says something other than that the employee is an employee at will. When the personnel policies state that employees are employees at will, it means either the employer or the employee may terminate the employment relationship for any reason or without reason. "Even in states which allow for 'at will' employment (as opposed to states which require 'good cause'), an employer may still be found liable if the employer violates its own personnel policies" (Cohen, 1998, p. 86). The sample personnel policies in Director's Resource 10–1 provide exact wording for those who choose to use the employment at will provision. But that being the case, it is important to use caution in wording the staff handbook so nothing in that document can be viewed by the court as a contract. Since employment law is changing all over the country and regulations vary state by state, it is wise to consult an attorney on these employment-related questions and issues.

Job Description

The job description is a detailed outline of what is expected from the person who fills a specific job opening, including director, head teacher, teacher assistant, cook, custodian, and so on. Job descriptions are discussed in greater detail later in this chapter.

Salary Ranges

Salary range for each position on the career ladder should be indicated clearly. Salary then will be based on the training, experience, and years of service that the person brings to the particular position. Details about overtime pay, merit pay, raises, vacation pay, pay for holidays, sick leave, or professional days should be detailed under salary and salary range. The federal government has instituted new rules that clarify employee rights and employer obligations relative to overtime pay. The Child Care Law Center can furnish the latest information on these rules (see Appendix B). If salary increases are performance based, the plan for those increases is stated in the personnel policies.

Each state may have its own laws regulating minimum wage and overtime pay, but all state regulations must be compatible with the federal Fair Labor Standards Act (FLSA). In that act, employees classified as "exempt" from FLSA are professional, salaried staff while those who earn an hourly wage and are entitled to overtime pay are considered "nonexempt" and are covered by the FLSA. Because these definitions and rules are scrutinized and revised regularly, it is important to consult an attorney with expertise in labor law when making decisions concerning questions related to compliance with government regulations. The Child Care Law Center can provide information on the current status of the issues around how the FLSA affects child care employees in different states (see Appendix B).

Staff and Fringe Benefits

Staff and fringe benefits available to employees must be stated clearly in the personnel policies. Retirement plans, health insurance, educational opportunities for personal or professional staff development, reduced tuition for family members, Social Security, Workers' compensation, liability coverage while working in the center with children, family and medical leaves, and any other items that might be covered under staff and fringe benefits should be included.

Health and Safety Measures

A health examination for all staff members is required in most centers. In many localities, the law requires the health examination of center administrators who are viewed as being ultimately responsible for the health and safety of the children in the center. Those who work with children should be free of any infectious disease, whether or not there is a local certifying or licensing group responsible for monitoring health regulations. In addition, they all should have bloodborne pathogens and hazardous materials training. It also is recommended that child care staff be advised to update their immunizations because intimate contacts with children puts them at risk for contracting a variety of infectious diseases. Furthermore, since the work is often physically demanding, the examination protects members of the staff by exploring their health limitations and by reminding them to follow basic healthful practices such as getting adequate rest and proper food.

Child abuse and other child safety issues are a major concern among child care professionals. Therefore, there is an increasing trend to seek ways to certify that employees do not use drugs and have no criminal records. Some states and/or government-funded programs require that prospective staff be screened for one or more of these. Employers with more than 15 employees must comply with the ADA when dealing with employment issues. Employers must avoid job related discrimination based on an employees' disability, but ". . . may prohibit use, or working under the influence of, alcohol or illegal drugs as well as smoking in the workplace" (Surr, 1992). The problem of AIDS is one that is causing concern as well. Congress intended that the ADA protect persons infected with AIDS and HIV. Therefore, employers may not ask candidates about it on applications or during the prehiring process (Director's Resource 10–2). The sample form in Figure 10–1 that covers the criminal record issue will serve as a guide for a way of obtaining information from staff members as well as job candidates about some sensitive areas of inquiry. If there are questions about the legality of making inquiries of this nature, contact the EEOC or seek legal counsel.

Personnel policies should state clearly that professional staff must submit certified copies of credentials and that personal and professional references furnished by all new employees will be contacted before job offers are made.

For use by Head Start Agencies to comply with 45 CRF Part 1301, Subpart D, Head Start Grants Administration, Personnel Policies, Section 1301.31(c) and (d).

Name of Prospective Employee: _____

Federal policies now require that Head Start agencies require all prospective employees to sign a declaration prior to employment which lists:

1. All pending and prior criminal arrests and charges related to child sexual abuse and their disposition
2. Convictions related to other forms of child abuse and/or neglect
3. All convictions of violent felonies

The declarations may exclude:

- Any offense, other than any offense related to child abuse and/or child sexual abuse or violent felonies committed before the prospective employee's 18th birthday, which was finally adjudicated in a juvenile court or under a youth offender law
- Any conviction for which the record has been expunged under Federal or State law
- Any conviction set aside under the Federal Youth Corrections Act or similar state authority

Note that individuals who declare, through this form, that they have been arrested, charged with or convicted of any of the offenses listed above are not automatically disqualified from being hired. Head Start agencies must review each case to assess the relevance of an arrest, charge or conviction to a hiring decision.

Please provide your signature on the appropriate category below:

I *have not been* arrested, charged and/or convicted on one or more of the three types of offenses listed above.

_____   _____
Signature   Date

OR

I *have been* arrested, charged and/or convicted on one of more of the three types of offenses listed above.

If so, please attach information listing the offense(s), the date(s) of the arrest, charge and/or conviction, and other relevant information.

_____   _____
Signature   Date

IMPORTANT:
Each Head Start agency must take necessary steps to assure the confidentiality of this form.

Figure 10–1

Sample declaration form for prospective employees in Head Start programs.

Daily Hours and Employment Period

The daily schedule and the total employment period should be stated in the personnel policies. Careful scheduling of personnel is critical for effective and efficient operation of all centers. This schedule should be stated in the personnel policies and should be reiterated in each contract or letter of employment if these are used. Daily hours will not coincide exactly with the hours the children are present in the center and will not be the same for each staff member. Obviously, some staff members must arrive before children to prepare the learning environment. Furthermore, a large child care center will need extra staff to cover peak hours. For example, if school-aged children come to the center before and after school, or for lunch, the staffing needs will be increased during those hours. A key staff member must be present late in the day to chat with people who pick up the children near closing time. When all children have gone, the center must be in order for the early arrivals the following day; therefore, some of the staff must stay beyond the time that all children leave.

The complexity of the staffing plan and the format used to lay out the plan in an understandable way will vary. The major consideration is to set it up so it provides sufficient coverage to meet the licensing requirements, where applicable, and to guarantee safety of children and adequate staff to maintain high standards of quality throughout each day. In planning the staffing patterns, directors should keep in mind the concerns about child abuse in child care centers and take preventive measures. Schedule at least two caregivers to be present at all times, particularly early and late in the day and during nap and toileting routines. This will help protect children and staff should one be unjustly accused of abuse (Cohen, 1998). The sample staffing plans in Director's Resources 10–5 and 10–6 will serve as guidelines for setting up staffing patterns. Use of graphing, listing by staff member, listing by room, or listing by program are a few of the ways to record a staffing pattern so it is clear to those who are interested in it, including staff, board members, licensing agents, and especially parents.

In addition to information on staffing plans, the policy statement also indicates methods for obtaining tenure if that is a possibility within the system.

Relief Periods

A planned system of daily relief periods should be stated. The policy on rest periods may be very flexible or carefully scheduled; but in either case, the policy clearly states and includes the designated space where staff may take breaks. Staff will be more comfortable knowing that it is acceptable to need to be away from the children for a time each day and that it is acceptable to go to the bathroom now and then, although some administrators fail to provide that option. In half-day nursery schools, it is rare to find a set policy on rest periods due to the short time span of concentrated effort required by staff members. On the other hand, in child care programs in which a teacher may work an eight- or nine-hour day that includes having lunch with children, it is essential to provide time to rest and be away from the children. Some centers prefer to have some staff members work a split shift to provide time for rest, shopping, or study at midday. This serves to reduce costs at a time of low need.

Vacations, Holidays, and Sick Leave

A statement on vacations and holidays should appear in the personnel policies. Specific details about lead time for vacation applications and the length and timing of vacations is advisable for larger, year-round centers, but smaller centers in session only during the typical school year may not require the same specificity in their policy. However, both large and small centers observe certain holidays. These holidays will vary depending on the religious and ethnic orientation of the staff and/or the children served, the agency with which the school is affiliated (church, public school, and so on), and the community mores. All employees should know exactly which holidays will be observed by the center.

Sick days and personal days, maternity leave, child-rearing leave for either parent, and special leave days for jury duty or voting should be included in the personnel policies. Directors can check the Family and Medical Leave Act (FMLA) regulations when dealing with these requests. It also is wise to cover details like use of unused leave days, the necessity for documenting illness, and policies about closings due to bad weather. Some employers allow "earned time" over and above holidays, and each employee decides how and when to take that time. This flexible earned time plan may make it difficult for a director who must find substitutes, and it could be detrimental to the well-being of the children. A variation on this plan is to give one Friday or Monday off each month to each staff person, thereby guaranteeing one long weekend a month. Staff members decide when they want their long weekend; and in a large center, the director can hire a regular substitute to work every Monday and Friday, which gives greater continuity to the program for the children.

The center's plan for hiring substitutes for each staff position during vacation periods, for special holidays, and for sick days must be spelled out clearly. The policy should state that all health, safety, and training

Staff members are entitled to know evaluation procedures as well as evaluation criteria.

qualifications for staff also apply to substitutes. Maintaining a substitute file that includes the necessary personnel information and payroll paperwork on available persons will make it easier to find substitutes on short notice. A plan for hiring substitutes avoids confusion when emergencies occur and also facilitates budget planning for these special needs.

Meeting Schedules

Scheduled staff meetings, parent meetings, and board meetings should be listed in the personnel policies. Most programs, regardless of size, have a series of meetings at various levels to gather individuals together to discuss plans and mutual concerns. In some cases, only selected personnel are expected to attend meetings. The personnel policies state which meetings each employee is expected to attend and the frequency of such meetings, as well as those meetings that are open to any interested staff member. Whether there will be reimbursement or comp time for attending meetings outside the working day should be made clear.

Probationary Periods

Many programs include probationary periods after initial employment to allow an adjustment period for both adults and children in the program. A director may be appointed on an "acting" basis for as long as a year. The time period must be long enough for the new employee to demonstrate competency in a given position but not so long that valuable aspects of the program can be undermined by an incompetent individual.

Teacher competency can be validated in a three- to six-month probationary period by an experienced

director who operates under a clearly defined philosophy of education and evaluates with an experienced eye. Since the teacher works directly with the children and any incompetence could have direct detrimental effects on them, the probationary period for teachers should be delineated carefully and understood clearly at the time of employment. This practice not only protects the welfare of the children but also is more equitable for the teachers in the long run because they come into a new role with a clear understanding of the time allowed for initial review and evaluation.

Evaluation and Grievance Procedures

Evaluative review of personnel should be scheduled on a regular basis. Evaluation and grievance procedures are included in the personnel policies (Figure 10–2). These procedures should be made available to all center personnel. Ideally, they will include details about the following:

- who evaluates whom
- when the periodic evaluation will take place
- what techniques or instruments will be used in the evaluation
- who makes the decision on whether or not the criteria are met
- what the consequences are of not meeting the stated criteria

Not meeting stated criteria could mean no recommendation for a raise, no opportunity for advancing to a higher-level position, or termination. When there are other actions that could cause dismissal such as use of corporal punishment, these should be

Evaluation and Grievance Procedures

1. Frequency of Evaluation

Performance evaluations will be made twice during the probationary period for every new staff member—at the midpoint and the end of the probationary period—and annually thereafter. It is the responsibility of the Personnel Committee to evaluate the work of the Director and the responsibility of the Director to evaluate all members of the staff. All evaluations will be shared with the employee and then become part of the employee's file.

2. Purpose of Evaluation

The primary purpose of the annual evaluation is to create a mutual understanding between the Director and each member of the staff of what is expected and how they both view the best way to move toward fulfilling those expectations.

Annual evaluations will be used as a basis for continued employment, horizontal or vertical movement on the career ladder, salary increments in cases where the job descriptions allows for merit raises, and demotion or dismissal.

3. Basis for the Evaluation

Staff members will be evaluated on knowledge of the job as described in the job description, quality of skill demonstrated in fulfilling the job, interest and initiative, dependability, personal and professional growth, attendance and punctuality, and ability to work effectively in cooperation with other staff members.

Evaluation forms for each staff position in the center are included in these personnel policies.

4. Evaluation Procedure

Each staff member will be notified as to when his/her evaluation will take place. The evaluation will be discussed with the staff member, at which time the staff member will be given the opportunity to express his/her disagreement or agreement with the evaluation. The outcome of this discussion will become part of the staff member's record.

5. Review of Grievances

The staff member who wishes to present a grievance must present it first to the Director. Failing to reach settlement with the Director, the staff member may submit to the Chairperson of the Personnel Committee a written statement of the situation, requesting that the grievance be reviewed by the Personnel Committee. The Personnel Committee will review the grievance and report with recommendations to the Board of Directors for action.

Figure 10–2

Townville Child Development Center (a United Way Agency) evaluation and grievance procedures.

in writing. In some situations, there may be no recourse once a decision to deny a raise or to terminate an employee has been made. Although that may seem unfair, it is better to state it at the outset than to deal with all the negative feelings generated by the decision when an employee is unaware that there is no way to appeal it.

Performance Evaluations

Staff members are entitled to know evaluation procedures as well as evaluation criteria. Therefore, performance evaluations for all staff positions should be part of personnel policies and/or the orientation materials and discussed during staff orientation. Teaching staff is usually evaluated by the director who, in turn, may be evaluated by the personnel committee of the board or by the personnel director in cases where centers are part of a larger organization. Other support staff may be reviewed and evaluated by the director or by other designated staff. The sample Annual Performance Evaluation paired with a Lead Teacher Job Description (Director's Resource 10–8) might be used as a prototype for performance evaluation tools. Although there may be some overlap in areas covered by the evaluation forms such as physical and mental health, ability to work well with other adults, and personal attributes such as enthusiasm or sense of humor, some are unique to a given position. For example, the cook must be able to manage time well in order to have meals ready for serving at a given hour whereas a teacher must adjust the daily schedule based on changing needs of children. Performance evaluation forms usually are based on job descriptions. Knowledge of evaluation criteria helps build a sense of trust and partnership between staff to be evaluated and the evaluator, who is either the director or another staff member (see Chapter 14 for more information on evaluation).

Organizational Chart

An organizational chart that is sometimes part of the personnel policies and is made available to all members of the staff can clarify lines of communication and responsibility for everyone in the center. For a newcomer, even a very simple organizational pattern may be difficult to see unless it is presented in a diagram or flow chart (Figure 10–3). An organizational chart enables an employee to determine how each position meshes with other positions in the center. This information, coupled with complete job descriptions, performance evaluation procedures and forms, and open staff communication, leaves little doubt about expectations, areas of responsibility, and who will be the evaluator for each position.

Amending and Changing the Policies

The personnel policies should contain a section that details the procedure for amending the policies. The amending procedure presumably parallels the one that was used initially for developing the policies and that is stated in the bylaws, but the policy-making body now may be expanded to include staff members or parents who were not available during the initial stages of development. As the center undergoes its regular evaluation period, the personnel policies also should be checked to determine whether changes are needed. Then the board or the policy-making staff can follow the amendment procedures when it becomes necessary to make changes. Once a change has been adopted, it is important to inform all personnel of the changes, and the director is charged with implementing the new policy.

Clearly, small private centers will not use all the preceding items in their personnel policies. However, large, complex organizations undoubtedly will include all of these and more. Policies are drawn and shaped to the unique needs of each center and are constantly evaluated and changed to meet the ever-changing and growing needs of the program for which they are written.

DRAWING UP JOB DESCRIPTIONS

One mechanism for reducing conflict and uncertainty for staff members is to provide a clear definition of the role of each member on staff. Each role requires a thorough description so that no matter who fills the role, the same basic job will be done. The description can be written to clarify expectations yet retain the personal freedom of all staff members to follow through in the performance of their roles according to their own unique style. Well-written job descriptions provide a framework within which an individual can function creatively while performing the tasks required for the program. Detailed descriptions of required knowledge, skills, and physical abilities are important because subsequent performance evaluations are based on the job description. For teaching staff job descriptions, include the idea that staff will be able to supervise children within sight and sound and have the ability to physically attend to the children. For infant and toddler teachers, also add that the staff person will have the ability to lift at least 40 pounds regularly during an eight-hour period. The applicants then are asked if they can perform the duties as described in the job description.

A sample job description (Director's Resource 10–7), provides a prototype for writing descriptions

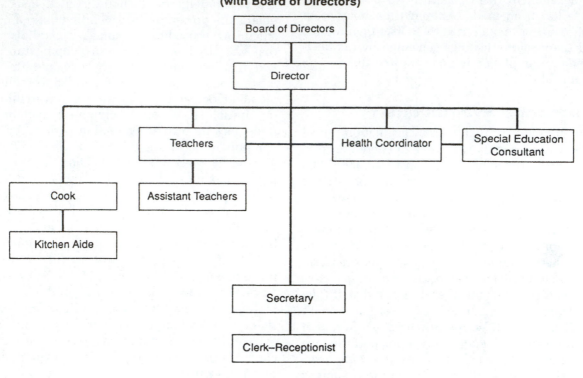

SAMPLE ORGANIZATIONAL CHART
(with Board of Directors)

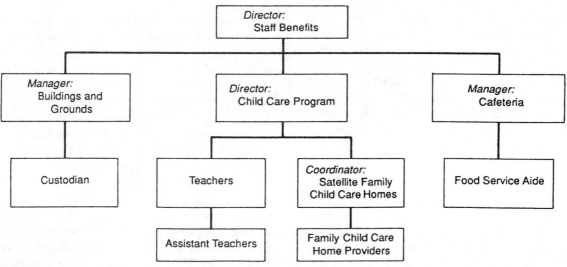

SAMPLE ORGANIZATIONAL CHART
(Employer-Sponsored Program)

Figure 10–3

Sample organizational charts.

for various staff positions, including full-time and part-time professional and support staff for both agency-sponsored and proprietary child care centers, as well as public school preschools. Job descriptions may cover some of the following or other items as needed:

- job title
- person to whom responsible
- people for whom responsible
- qualifications (education, experience, personal health, physical abilities, and so forth)
- duties and responsibilities
- salary schedule
- work schedule

Job descriptions should be reviewed on a regular basis to determine whether changes are necessary. Such periodic review is useful because the director or governing body can deal with changing rules or regulations governing practices, adjust the policies as role expectations at different levels shift, and change job descriptions when new personnel bring changing talents and skills to a staff. For example, menu planning and shopping may be part of a director's job description, but a new cook who has been trained to plan meals may take over that function. Job descriptions for both the director and the cook can be adjusted accordingly, allowing staff members to perform at their highest creative level.

REFLECTION

Think about yourself as a practicum student or a new teacher, and remember the uncertainty and accompanying anxiety you felt when you did not have a clear understanding of what was expected of you. How did you feel when you were unsure about who was to set up the snack or who was to straighten up the storage room? How did you manage when you were not sure about who to call when you knew you would be late because you had missed the bus? How did you react to criticism when you did not put all the blocks on the shelf while another adult had the children outside, and you had not been informed that you should do that? Can you remember how energy draining these experiences were and how they interfered with your creative work with children? A carefully written job description for your position might have helped you have a clearer understanding of your role.

Initial writing of job descriptions is only the first step in an ongoing process. This process requires expertise in using information from the program evaluation and an ability to adjust to changing and growing strengths of personnel in order to make efficient use of available talent for a more effective program.

Recruiting

Once the job descriptions have been written, the major hiring procedure begins. In fact, in many large centers or in programs with a board, the first task assigned to a new director is to initiate staff-recruitment procedures. Each center establishes and follows some general procedures regarding advertising, interviewing, and selecting employees to use during initial hiring in a new center and in filling vacant staff positions for an ongoing program.

Advertising for new staff is usually the director's responsibility. However, in some public schools and in corporate settings, the personnel office may set up school district or company advertisements that cover available positions throughout the organization. If the center program is ongoing, the director first should notify current staff members, board members, and parents about job openings as they become available. People in the organization may choose to apply for the new job, or they may know qualified individuals who would like to apply. For employees to learn of openings in their own center from an outside source is disconcerting, and it exemplifies poor communication within the center.

Affirmative action statements must be included when advertising for center personnel. It is helpful to have advertising appear in a range of publications to make the information available to diverse segments of the population. Figure 10–4 shows examples of some advertisements. Local professional organizations that publish classified ads in their newsletters are good places to advertise for classroom staff, as are high schools, colleges, or universities that have child care training programs. Ads also may be placed in national professional journals or put on their Web sites if there is sufficient time to meet publication deadlines. Some colleges and vocational high schools maintain placement services, and some hold placement conferences so that employers can interview applicants. Notices of job openings also can be posted on community bulletin boards and in community papers that reach special segments of the population such as the African-American or Native American community, non-English-speaking groups, and on various appropriate Web sites.

The classified section of newspapers is frequently used for advertising, but the result may be

Sample Classified Advertisement for the *Waynesburg Chronicle*
Teacher Assistant in a Child Care Center. Responsibilities include assisting the classroom teacher in the planning and implementation of the daily program for children, assisting in the family involvement aspect of the program, and taking responsibility for some designated record keeping. Must have an Associate Degree in Early Childhood Education or equivalent. Experience preferred. Job available immediately. Send written resume to P. O. Box 320, Waynesburg, Iowa 36103, or e-mail wayneecce@aol.com. Our employees know about this opening. We are an Equal Opportunity Employer.

Sample Classified Advertisement for the *Local Association for the Education of Young Children Newsletter*
Director wanted for the Community Head Start Center. Responsibilities include hiring and supervision of entire staff for a program serving 75 children, record keeping, proposal writing, working with Center staff, Community Action agency, parents, and other community agencies. Applicant must have a Master's Degree in Early Childhood Education with some training in at least one of the following: social work, special education, administration. Three years' administration experience required—Head Start teaching experience preferred. Send resume to Community Head Start Center, 352 Ninth St., Sioux City, Iowa. Deadline for applications, July 1. We are an Equal Opportunity Employer.

Sample Classified Advertisement for *The New York Times*
Preschool teacher wanted for suburban church-affiliated preschool. Responsibilities include planning and implementing an age-appropriate developmental type early education program for a group of 15 three- and four-year-old children. Bachelor's Degree required—early childhood education teacher experience preferred. Write for application to Ms. D. L. Jones, Director, Upper Plains Christian Church, 130 Meadows Place, Upper Plains, New York 11112, or call (713) 431-6037 Monday through Thursday from 1:00 to 3:00 P.M., or e-mail upperplains @hotmail.com. We are an Equal Opportunity Employer.

Sample Classified Advertisement for the *Parkville Times*
Cook wanted for child care center at outskirts of town. Responsibilities include preparing snacks and lunch for 65 preschool children, cleaning kitchen appliances and cupboards, and making weekly shopping list. Experience preferred. Please send resume to P. O. Box 932, Parkville, VA 23221. Equal Opportunity Employer.

Figure 10–4

Sample advertisements.

large numbers of unqualified applicants who then must be screened before interviewing can begin. Nonetheless, when a position must be filled quickly, advertising in both small community weekly newspapers and large city daily newspapers is helpful because information is quickly disseminated to large numbers of people.

Personnel ads should include enough information to minimize the number of applications from completely unqualified persons but should not be so narrowly written that qualified persons fail to apply. If you are expected to write the advertising copy, you must be completely familiar with all the qualifications that are essential for performance of the job. Careful review of the job description is a good way to become familiar with the desired qualifications for

potential candidates. Each advertisement should include the following:

- the job title
- a brief job description
- the essential qualifications
- the method of applying (telephone, letter, application blank)
- the name of the person to contact with a telephone number, street address or e-mail address

Starting date, working hours, starting pay, fringe benefits, and goals of the organization also may be included.

Advertisements that clearly state all nonnegotiable items will eliminate practically all unqualified applicants. On the other hand, negotiable items stated equivocally tend to attract a more diverse pool of candidates from which to choose. For example, "experience necessary" is much more restrictive than "experience preferred." If experience is a nonnegotiable qualification, then say, "experience necessary." However, if the position could be filled by a person with good training and a variety of life experiences that may or may not have been with children, then say "experience preferred." The latter phrase appeals to a broader population and will increase the number of applicants.

The director should be cautious about luring people into the field by presenting a glowing picture of life in a child care center. Hiring staff members under false pretenses can lead to job dissatisfaction quickly. Rapid staff turnover disrupts program continuity and is very hard on the families and children who must constantly establish new relationships. During the last decade, the staffing crisis in the early childhood field has increased the challenge for directors who prefer to wait until they find qualified candidates to fill vacancies but are unable to meet required teacher-to-child ratios because of staff shortages. Many well-qualified early childhood teachers are choosing to move into public school or Head Start programs where pay and benefits often are better than those in other child care settings. The availability of qualified staff is limited and the competition for their services is keen. But dealing with the consequences of hiring staff who are unable or unwilling to do a good job inevitably leads to more turnover that is hard on other staff, families, and children. Therefore, a job opening notice that lists the required job qualifications in specific and realistic terms and careful hiring increase the probability of getting the best match between applicants and available positions and reduces turnover.

Careful consideration must be given to the best method for receiving applications. If the need is urgent and immediate, it may be necessary to accept applications by telephone. This option means that a new employee can be found quickly because an interview can be scheduled moments after a notice is seen. But it also means that current staff members may have to spend hours on the telephone, which detracts from their work with the children and puts them in the position of answering questions from people who are not seriously interested in the job.

Listing a post office box number in an ad places fewer demands on the director and the staff because potential candidates do not know the identity of the center and are unable to call. On the other hand, qualified people may decide not to apply if they are unsure of the source of the ad. Others may feel that they could be applying to the center in which they work, another reason for notifying all employees of every opening. In fact, occasionally ads read, "Our employees know about this advertisement."

Allowing applicants to apply in person can be very inconvenient and is inappropriate for some positions. Unless the center has its own personnel director or is affiliated with a sponsoring agency such as a public school, having applicants appear at the door during the hours in which children are present is awkward. However, this problem can be handled by setting specific hours during which interviews may be scheduled. In neighborhoods where many people do not have telephones and where writing letters is difficult for some adults, it may be appropriate to have people apply in person. If the job does not entail making written reports such as in the case of a cook or a housekeeper, then the ability to communicate effectively in writing may not be a criterion for selection, and there is no need to see a resume or written application. On the other hand, in the case of a teacher, teacher assistant, or special education resource teacher, writing skills are important. For these positions, a written response offers helpful data for initial screening of applicants and should be made mandatory before an interview is scheduled.

The advertiser also will have to decide whether to have the candidates request an application form or send a resume. If a secretary is available to answer requests for application blanks, the process can be speeded up. If the director will be distracted from work by recording the name and address of applicants and mailing out applications, it is wiser to have candidates mail in resumes and fill in a formal application when they are interviewed. Sample application forms (Figures 10–5 and 10–6) show how applications are adjusted depending on availability of a resume from the applicant.

When all the applications have been collected, they must be screened to eliminate obviously unsuitable candidates. If no suitable candidates have applied and attempts to recruit staff from other centers has failed, the advertising and application process is reopened. The director or the chairperson of the personnel committee usually screens the applications for those that meet the job requirements, particularly in the areas of education, health, or experience. Then interviews can be arranged. Interviewers should not be burdened with candidates who have no qualifications for the job. Therefore, the careful writing of the job opening notices to interested qualified candidates and the initial screening process to eliminate totally unqualified candidates are both important steps in the recruiting process.

Sample Application Form
(Suggested for use when no resume is on file)

Application for Employment

Jewish Community Child Care Center—Fairmount, Pennsylvania

Name of Applicant _____
　　　　　　　　　　　Last　　　　　　First　　　　　　Middle or Maiden

Address _____

State _____ Zip _____

Telephone _____ Social Security No. _____

Citizenship:　USA _____ Other _____

Record of Education

School	Name and Address of School	Check Last Year Completed	List Diploma or Degree
High		1 2 3 4	
College		1 2 3 4	
Other (Specify)		1 2 3 4	

Figure 10–5

Sample application form (no resume).

List below all present and past employment, beginning with your most recent

Name and Address of Employer	From Mo./ Yr.	To Mo./ Yr.	Describe in detail the work you did	Weekly Starting Salary	Weekly Last Salary	Reason for Leaving	Name of Supervisor

List all professional and community organizations with which you are affiliated. *(Indicate if you hold office in the organization.)*

Write your educational philosophy.

What do you feel most qualifies you for this position?

What are your professional goals?

List names and addresses of three references.

_____

_____

_____

I give permission to contact references _____
                                                (signature)

Figure 10–5

(continued)

Sample Application Form
(Suggested for use when a resume is on file)

Application for Position

University Day Care Center—Ogden University, Ogden City, Michigan

Name of Applicant _____
　　　　　　　　　　　　Last　　　　　　First　　　　　　Middle or Maiden

Address _____

State _____ Zip _____

Telephone _____

Title of position for which you are applying. _____

What do you feel best qualifies you for this position? _____

_____

_____

Would you be willing to continue your education by taking college courses or in-service training if recommended to do that? _____

_____

_____

What satisfaction do you expect to receive from this position? _____

_____

_____

List three references (preferably one former employer, one former teacher, and one community person).

　　　　1. _____

　　　　2. _____

　　　　3. _____

I give permission to contact references _____
　　　　　　　　　　　　　　　　　　　　　　　　　　(signature)

Figure 10–6

Sample application form (resume on file).

Applications that are received from people who are not subsequently called for an interview should be retained so that affirmative action procedures can be completed where that is a requirement. A record must be kept listing the reasons why any applicant was not interviewed, and they should receive written notification that they will *not* be interviewed. Applicants who are called for an interview should be advised to bring identification to prove citizenship. A candidate who is not a U.S. citizen will be required to prove eligibility to work in this country. To be in compliance with the Immigration Reform and Control Act of 1986, every person hired must complete Form I–9, available from the Immigration and Naturalization Service (INS). A copy of Form I–9 can be found in Director's Resource 10–9.

Interviewing

Interviewing is essential and should not be eliminated no matter how urgent the need for obtaining a staff member may seem. Even though a candidate can make an excellent impression during an interview and then turn out to be an ineffective staff member, interviewing will provide insights that cannot be gleaned from written applications or resumes and will facilitate judicious hiring decisions in the majority of cases. The relative amount of time spent interviewing can be extremely profitable when compared to the amount of time that might otherwise be spent solving personnel problems and higher staff turnover because a poor candidate was hastily selected. "Although not a magic solution to cure all turnover woes, effective interviewing is a step in the right direction" (Hamrick, 2000). The person or group responsible for staffing the center must decide who will review applications and interview the candidates and must develop the plan for the interview.

Reviewing Applications

Reviewing applications is the first step in the total interviewing process. The director or group in charge of staffing the center first must make sure that the job description for the position being filled is up to date. It also is helpful to think about what type of person will best fit the position. Consider not only what the job description defines as required for the position but also the center culture, the match with other staff, and the comfort level for working with the center families. Using a systematic approach for application screening makes the job easier and will cover you later if anyone questions your hiring decision.

Begin the application review process by developing a form that covers the required qualifications for the job, including education, experience, and specialized training. Add qualifications that may not be required for the position but are preferred and could contribute to the candidate's ability to do the job. For example, experience at working with diverse populations may be a requirement, but special experience on a Native American reservation or student-teaching in Latin America could be a plus, depending on the location of your program and the population served. Include items on the form that would cover those special experiences by having a place to check whether or not the candidate has had experience with diverse groups and a place to note which ethnic, cultural, and socioeconomic groups were part of that experience. The screening form should include all the items that are on the application and also cover the job description.

Develop a rating scale for the items on the screening form so each reviewer can arrive at a total score for each applicant (Hamrick, 2000). A three-point scale can be used for this purpose. It is helpful to provide reviewers with some definitions for the three levels on the scale. If the candidate does not meet the requirement at all, the score on that item would be 0. Ratings might be defined as follows:

1 = barely meets requirement
2 = meets requirement
3 = exceeds requirement

Definitions of ratings will vary, depending on exactly how the requirements or criteria for the job are stated. In any case, it gives those who screen the applications a way to evaluate the qualifications of the candidates and provides a score for each one. There should be places on the screening form for comments and recommendations of reviewers and a place where they can note that the candidate does not have the qualifications to fill the position that is open. All applications are kept on file should there be any question about the hiring procedures.

When the reviewers meet to discuss the next step in this process, they can eliminate those candidates who do not have the qualifications for the job as described in the job description and use their scores on the screening forms to rank the remaining candidates. The next steps are to decide who will be interviewed and who will do the interviewing.

Interviewers

While applications are being collected and screened, decisions are made about who will interview the viable candidates. In a very small program, the director may take full responsibility for all interviewing or may do it with the help of one or more of the following:

- staff person
- member of the board
- community person
- other professional (social worker, special educator, physician, school principal)
- person responsible to the new employee
- parent representative

In some programs, the interviews are conducted by committees, often by the personnel committee.

The composition of the interview committee may be established by the board beforehand as in the case of the personnel committee; or the committee can be set up by the director to pertain specifically to the job being filled. For example, when there is an opening for a teacher, the committee might include the director, a teacher, and a parent. The expertise of a teacher on the interviewing team is very valuable. Including teachers also makes them feel valued and appreciated. Community people could be included as well as people from other professions, such as community health or special education. There might be more than one person from a given category, but if the committee is too large, its effectiveness will diminish. It can be difficult for large numbers of people to interview a given candidate at one time and the procedure can be very threatening for the candidate. Nonetheless, it is best if the committee is representative of the center staff with whom the person will work, of the families who use the center, and of the people who represent the sponsoring agency if all who have a vested interest in the position to be filled are to be represented.

Although the committee makeup may vary depending on the type of center and on the position to be filled, both the committee members and the candidates must be aware that the organizational structure of the center takes precedence in making hiring decisions. For example, if a janitor is being hired, it may be appropriate to have the teachers express a preference for the candidate who would be most able to meet their needs for classroom maintenance. However, if the person who becomes janitor is going to be responsible to the center director, then the director's opinion must weigh heavily in the final hiring decision.

A major exception to this hiring and interviewing procedure is in public-school-sponsored programs where hiring is based on established school district policies. Public school union contracts often dictate hiring policies and procedures. Sometimes, the personnel office will handle advertising, interviewing, and hiring. Involving teachers or parents in the process is unlikely. This could result in a team that will have to spend time building a workable partnership and work through possible philosophical differences.

Preparation for the Interview

Just as candidates should come to the interview prepared to express their strengths, weaknesses, goals, expectations, and past experiences, so the interviewers should be prepared for each interview. Their questions should reflect a thorough knowledge of the center, its program, its staff, and the clients served by the program. Interviewers should be familiar with the information in the candidate's resume, application form, and reference letters, and they should look for evidence of warmth, good-natured calmness, and ease of relating to others. As Greenberg notes, it is important to select caregivers who have "the right stuff" to start with because "you can teach people to conform to certain schedules, perform specific acts, use assorted tips and techniques—but you cannot develop an entirely different character, personality, and self-esteem in a staff person" (Greenberg, 1991). An interview is conducted most productively when all parties are well prepared and when the environment has been set up for a meaningful dialogue between interviewers and interviewee.

Interviewer Information

Each interviewer should be totally familiar with the job description for the vacant position and should have copies of the candidate's application and references. A letter or questionnaire that has been prepared in advance for submission to all listed references will provide comparable data for all candidates and make it easier for reference people to respond. If reference letters are not received promptly, the candidate may be asked to contact the reference person. Sometimes, it is necessary to proceed with interviewing before information has been received from all references. Although it is important to have written information from the candidate's references, a follow-up call to discuss the written responses can provide valuable information. A sample reference letter is shown in Figure 10–7.

Interview Plan

Interviewers plan the type of interview they will conduct. Sometimes, a predetermined list of questions is developed so that all candidates will respond to the same questions. This procedure provides uniform data

TO: Mr. L. N. Davidson
                      University Court - Rm. 416
                      Midtown University
                      Midtown, KY 35231

FROM: Mr. John Wilkins, Director
                      Midtown Child Development Center
                      414 Main Street
                      Midtown, KY 35231

_____ has given us your name as a reference. We are interested in having any information from you about this applicant that will help us in hiring the best person available for an assistant teacher position on our staff. Your cooperation is greatly appreciated.

In your opinion, what is this applicant's ability in each of the following areas?

Working with other staff members

Working with young children

Working with families from the inner city

Capacity for personal and professional growth

Ability to evaluate self

In what capacity did you know this applicant?

How long have you known this applicant?

Comments:

                      Signature: _____
                      Title: _____
                      Date: _____

Figure 10–7

Sample reference letter.

but is somewhat inflexible and may not elicit the most useful data from each candidate. Sometimes, questions are developed as the interview progresses. This spontaneous procedure is more likely to give rise to potentially constructive data but requires more skill on the part of the interviewers.

The person who develops the questions should keep in mind the parameters of the job description and should understand the requirements of Title VII of the 1964 Civil Rights Act, the EEOC, and the ADA. There must be a "business necessity" for all questions asked during the interview. Questions to avoid include the following:

- date of birth or age
- marital status
- spouse's occupation
- pregnancy issues and number of children
- child care arrangements
- religious affiliation
- membership in organizations (except pertaining to the position)
- union memberships
- disabilities

The first question should be open ended and require more than a simple yes or no answer. Furthermore, it should focus on previous jobs, education, hobbies, or any other subject matter with which the candidate is very familiar. This technique puts the candidate at ease and creates an environment for more focused probing later in the interview. For example, the interviewer might say, "I see in your resume that you have worked for Head Start in California and that committee was made up of Mexican and Asian parents. What were the aspects of that job that you liked best?" or "I see you studied at Wheelock in Boston. Tell us about that program." From these questions, it is possible to cull out material that can be examined at greater depth. "You said you enjoyed working with the Parent Policy Committee in California. What did you do with that group that you think is applicable to this job?"

Interviewers can learn a great deal about the ways in which a teacher candidate would fit into their center's program by posing hypothetical situations and asking questions such as, "What would you do if a child kicked you?" or "How would you work with a toddler who is not yet talking?" This type of question can produce ideas about curriculum, classroom management, parent involvement, staff relations, and understanding of the development of young children. Of course, the questions should relate to the job for which the person is applying. For example, a prospective cook might be asked, "What would you do if sandwiches were on today's menu and the bread

delivery had not been made by 10:00 A.M.?" A list of sample questions in Director's Resource 10–4 can give you some ideas for questioning both degreed and nondegreed job candidates.

Interview Setting

Before the interview, give careful thought to the setting:

- Will the candidate be as comfortable as possible?
- Will everyone be able to see and hear everyone else?
- Is the seating arrangement comfortable and planned so that desks or large tables do not separate the candidate from the interviewers?
- Is the interviewing room free from distractions?
- Has the time of the interview been chosen appropriately so that everyone can focus on the interview instead of on the next appointment and are all cell phones turned off?
- Is adequate time available for developing rapport and exploring details of the answers to the questions?
- Has provision been made to offer water or some refreshments to the candidate?

When the goal is to make applicants feel welcome and at ease, the interview setting becomes a matter of central concern. The interviewers are revealing to the candidate a major part of the center-culture and philosophy as they create an accepting environment for an interview and are more likely to obtain an accurate picture when the candidate is at ease.

REFLECTION

Can you recall your first job interview? If so, you may be able to remember some of your reactions during that interview. Were you put at ease when you entered the room? Were you introduced to everyone before the questioning began? Did you feel the interviewers had prepared for the session by reviewing your resume and credentials? Were you given time to ask questions? How did they close the interview? As you think about being interviewed and recall the stress you experienced, you will increase your sensitivity to an applicant's feelings.

The director sets the nonverbal tone for the interview by being relaxed and friendly. It is important to sit back, smile, and maintain an open posture with arms down in the lap and body facing the candidate.

The Interview

At the beginning, candidates should be given some idea about the length of the interview and informed that there will be a time at the end of the interview to ask questions. Interviewers should be prepared to present information about the program's philosophy, the job, and the center and should clearly and honestly answer the applicant's questions. The interviewers should maintain eye contact and let the applicant do most of the talking. They can refer to the personnel policies and clarify thoroughly the expectations that are held regarding performance standards for the position.

The interviewers will look for an applicant who plans to stay with the center for a number of years because staff stability provides continuity for children and nurtures a sense of community at the center. Nonetheless, caution should be used about requesting any information in sensitive areas mentioned earlier. It is recommended that employment records be limited to that information relevant to employment decisions and that disclosures of that information to third parties be strictly limited where not authorized by the candidate or employee. It is advisable that child care centers develop written policies and procedures concerning this issue. Also, since federal law provides only a portion of the employment discrimination picture and many states have their own discrimination laws, it is wise to consult an attorney regarding applicable state laws for your center and to clear up uncertainties about content of interview questions.

Interviewers should obtain as much information as possible during the interview, but note taking or discussing the candidate's qualifications should be done after the interview. Some discussion about the candidate is useful and reaching a group consensus serves a worthwhile purpose. Discussion provides the opportunity for interviewers to share their impression of the candidate as they draw on each other's perceptions. Confidentiality is a critical issue, and all committee members must understand that information on candidates and any committee discussion must be kept confidential.

Teaching Interview

Observing a teacher or assistant teacher candidate in a classroom setting provides the committee with additional data on classroom presence and skills with children. Some candidates are able to give interviewers all

Observing a candidate in a classroom setting provides the interview committee with data on classroom presence.

they want to hear in an interview, but when observed in a classroom, it becomes obvious they are not comfortable with children. It is unfair to have the regular classroom teacher leave a new person alone in the classroom because of the anxiety that would be produced in both the candidate and the children, but a great deal can be learned by observing a prospective teacher read a story to a few children or join a small group for snacks. Asking to see sample lesson plans, resource files, or picture files also provides useful information to the interview committee. Some centers select candidates from the substitute list or from among a pool of student teachers whom they know. In this case, the center staff will have worked with the candidate before the interview.

Second Interview

A second interview for prospective candidates after the teaching interview can be helpful when there are several candidates with comparable training and credentials or when more information is needed prior to making the final hiring decision. Having a second interview also offers opportunities to discuss the teaching interview and to answer questions the candidate may have at this point in the interview–hiring procedure. Additional questions that focus on the candidate's opinions and personal style also can be discussed at a second interview. Director's Resource 10–4 gives sample interview questions for first and second interviews.

SELECTING THE EMPLOYEE

When interviewing is completed, the person or committee responsible for selecting the employee uses material such as the personnel policies and the job description, combined with all the information from the interview and the observation, to reach a final decision. All data are weighed and balanced until the best match among job description, current staff composition, and candidate qualifications is obtained. It also is important to review the nondiscrimination prohibitions in this decision-making process, especially if you have an applicant who is disabled. An employer is not required to give preference to a qualified applicant with a disability over other applicants; however, the employer may not consider the candidate with disabilities unqualified if that person can perform the essential functions of the job. More information on this subject can be found in Director's Resources 10–2 and 10–3. It may be helpful to have a second interview with selected candidates from the pool who seem best qualified for the position in order to further narrow the choice. The procedure for making a decision should be clear to all interviewers. Will the director ultimately choose the employee? Will the director present two or three names to the board, and the board will make the decision? If there is a board, will that group make the decision, or will the committee rule by majority vote? Generally, the director will make the decision, taking into account the recommendations of the interviewing committee. Final approval from the board sometimes is part of the hiring policy.

The selected candidate should be notified of the job offer by the director or the chairperson of the committee. On acceptance, the new employee may be asked to sign a contract stating the salary and the length of time covered by the contract, provided the personnel policies do not state that all employees are employees at will. Immediately after the new employee has been informed of the job and has accepted it, all other interviewees are informed of the selection, thanked for their interest, and told that their resumes will be kept on file if another vacancy should occur.

ORIENTING THE EMPLOYEE

The director is responsible for introducing the new employee to the work environment. The new person will need to know where to find work space, what storage facilities and materials are available, and what schedule is to be followed. A tour of the building and introductions to all other staff members, either during the tour or at a staff meeting shortly thereafter, are essential to the orientation procedure. The person who conducts the tour and makes the introductions sets the tone for the employee's future interpersonal relationships with the other staff members. Each staff member has an obligation to become involved with making the new employee's transition to the staff position as smooth and satisfying as possible. For an in-depth discussion of staff orientation, see Sciarra and Dorsey (2002).

The new employee also should be introduced to parents at the earliest possible time. Some directors notify parents of staff additions or changes by mail; others use their bulletin boards, e-mail, Web Site, or newsletters; and still others introduce the new member informally as the occasion arises or at a regularly scheduled meeting.

During the initial weeks of employment, it is important for the director to check with the new staff member to answer any questions and make a conscious effort to build a positive relationship. At the same time, the director can continue to reiterate expectations and expand on ways to follow and implement the program philosophy. A carefully planned staff orientation program can promote better staff relationships and reduce staff turnover.

DIRECTOR'S CORNER

"We do a five-day orientation for each new staff person before we finalize the hiring process. The prospective employee is paid for those hours of classroom participation, meetings with me, joint reading of dos and don'ts in the classroom, etc. It's well worth the time and money and has helped us make good hiring decisions."

—Director, private not-for-profit center

Sometimes, it is difficult for the director to be available to the new teacher often enough. It can be helpful to establish a mentor program or assign a staff member to watch over the new staff person. Mentors can help new staff with basic orientation questions like where to find and file various forms, and introduce them to all staff and support persons such as the van driver and custodian. Mentors also can provide new staff with information about special talents of other teachers such as planning effective group times, planning, and carrying out smooth transitions, or making challenging math games. A mentoring system assists the director with orientation of new staff and enriches and enhances the self-esteem of the mentor (Carter, 1998).

A mentoring system assists the director with orientation of new staff.

It also helps for the director to leave a note in the teacher's box asking questions like, "What went well today?" or "What did I miss today in your room that you would like to share with me?" The director also might leave a message about being available the next day at nap time or a plan to stop in before lunch to see how things are going. These steps help make the new teacher feel that the director really is available to give support and help.

Some centers have handbooks for each employee. In corporate centers, the parent firm may prepare a handbook for use in all centers, whether franchised or run by the corporation. Guidelines in this handbook may detail how many children should be permitted in blocks or dramatic play at any given time, or exactly how the daily cleaning is to be done by the classroom teachers. However, handbooks are rarely that detailed and usually do not include expectations for teachers to clean the premises. More often, they include items such as the following:

- philosophy of the center
- bylaws of the board (if applicable)
- personnel policies
- policies and procedures for the children's program
- copies of forms used by the center
- information about the community the center serves
- information about the staff (job titles, home addresses, telephone numbers, and so forth)
- NAEYC Code of Ethical Conduct

A handbook is useful because it gives everyone a common reference point and provides new employees with materials that familiarize them with the center.

REFLECTION

Perhaps you can recall your first day as a new student or employee in a child care center. How did you feel on that first day? What else do you wish you had known about the center or the program? Do you recall what it was like not to know where the extra paper towels were kept or how awkward it was when you could not find the easel paper? As you recall those feelings, consider what you would tell a new teacher in your center if you were responsible for orienting the new employees.

HANDLING TURNOVER

"At least one-third of the child care workforce leaves the job each year, nearly double the U.S. job turnover rate" (Whitebrook & Bellm, 1999). It is estimated that staff turnover can cost, at a minimum, $3,000 for each lost employee. Centers cannot afford the high cost of staff turnover, especially when those are not only financial costs, but also damaging to employee morale, customer satisfaction, and center image (Hamrick, 2000). Although some would say low wages and poor benefits are the major causes of turnover, it is important to recognize that there are many different ways to think about turnover. As Hamrick (2000) points out, poor hiring decisions are a major factor along with compensation concerns.

In making hiring decisions, take time to reflect on what type of person would best fit the position. What are we looking for in this person in terms of the fit with

- the center culture?
- the parent group?
- the support staff?
- the teaching staff?
- the administrative staff?

The first step in reducing turnover is to hire the right people.

Although compensation and careful hiring have an impact on turnover, they are not the only factors affecting staff stability. There is evidence that highly trained teachers are more likely to remain at their jobs. It follows that these teachers are usually compensated at a higher level and work with other highly trained staff who are also inclined to stay with a job. These qualified staff persons are also more often in accredited centers, and there is also evidence that accredited centers have a more stable workforce and less turnover.

When unemployment is low, scarce resources make turnover seem an impossible problem to solve (Whitebrook & Bellm, 1999). Finding dollars to offer the kind of wages and benefits to keep qualified staff is difficult. Although some staff turnover is inevitable, and some may even allow for positive changes, clearly, much of the time, loss of a staff member is disappointing and traumatic for the families, children, and staff who remain.

The director's task is to try to reduce staff turnover by attending to variables that can be adjusted and changed. There are a few inexpensive perks that may compensate staff and help them feel good about their job. Consider the following:

- flex time
- treats in the staff lounge for break times
- occasional personal use of the office copier (limits are necessary here)
- token gifts for birthdays and other special days
- opportunities to attend conferences as well as take additional education courses

This last item does involve some cost to the center, but there may be tax breaks for this benefit (check with your tax adviser or attorney).

Striving to give staff higher wages and more benefits is worthy, but stabilizing the workforce by refining hiring practices, improving the work environment, and making sure there is a thorough orientation plan in place for all new hires can all be done without great cost. Because there are no magic solutions to solving the problem of staff retention, directors are almost always involved, at some level, in looking for and hiring new staff.

Work Environment

Work environment is an inclusive term covering the physical space, and more important, for our purposes, the interpersonal climate—that is, relationships with coworkers. An involved director constantly evaluates the quality of the work environment and makes adjustments where possible. (See Chapter 14 for more discussion on evaluating work environment.) Sometimes, alterations in the physical environment are costly and can happen only if the budget allows. However, adjustments can be made to alter other aspects of the work environment with little or no added expense. For example, it is very important for every staff member to feel respected and valued. Offering staff opportunities to write for the newsletter, help with the design and equipment choices for the new playground, join an advocacy group, or serve on the committee to plan the center's tenth anniversary celebration are but a few ways staff can feel a sense of ownership in the center's total program. There is pride, commitment, and collegiality among those who share ownership in a successful enterprise.

"In child care we tend to spend very little time on adult development. We are often more democratic and participatory in spirit with children than we are among ourselves" (Whitebrook & Bellm, 1999). Although classroom teachers are encouraged to help children problem-solve, resolve conflicts, and make decisions, in some programs, major decisions are made by administrators with minimal input from staff who are very much affected by those decisions. Adults may initially need a lot of support and encouragement from the director who really wants active participation in writing articles, planning center events, leading staff meetings, or joining focus groups because they are accustomed to top-down management. When staff are invited to help plan meeting agendas and submit their questions and concerns for group meetings, they feel they are valued and important to the organization. When directors seek staff participation in decision making and help teachers feel valued, they are nurturing loyalty and commitment in the work environment.

Issues of race, class, and culture also are aspects of the work environment that impact interpersonal relationships and can affect staff turnover. Directors like to describe their programs as color blind, but on careful analysis of the reasons for turnover, they may find that issues of class, color, or culture contributed to friction that led to resignations. Constant attention to open communication with a focus on understanding and acceptance of diversity is essential because diversity can never be taken for granted. Adults go through stages of unlearning bias and you, as the director, are obliged to shepherd that journey for your staff (Whitebrook & Bellm, 1999).

Adults often are unaware of their own biases and sometimes unintentionally perpetuate biases in the environments they create for families and children. When children make comments about others in the classroom with different skin color or difficulty speaking English, teachers may comment that the other child simply is different. These may be brief conversations about hurting the other child's feelings, but rarely is there a challenge like, "Why do you feel that way?" The problem is not so much the differences but the fact that the teacher is not comfortable discussing the differences.

REFLECTION

Think about the best and the worst job you ever had. What made you stay with the best one? What made it appealing? What was bad about the worst job? How much were your feelings about the best and worst jobs affected by the relationships you had with other adults in the setting?

SUMMARY

The staffing process in a child care center is based on the personnel policies and job descriptions that define the staffing requirement to operate the center's program. Decisions about the content of recruiting advertising, interview questions and procedures, and final hiring should be based on specific job requirements that are detailed in the job descriptions. Interviewing may be done individually or in a group and should be a time for two-way communication between the candidates and the representatives of all

aspects of the center's programs. Questioning should focus on the requirements of the position and the candidate's potential for fulfilling those requirements. The purpose of the entire process is to provide the employer with the information that is necessary for selecting the best available person for each staff position. Directors can minimize costly and disruptive staff turnover by improving the work environment.

CLASS ASSIGNMENTS

1. Write a resume of your training and experience up to this point in your education and professional career, and bring it to class. Use Working Paper 10–1 to complete this assignment.

2. A job description for a cook in a Head Start center can be found in Working Paper 10–2.

   a. Write the qualifications for that position based on the job description.

   b. Write an advertisement for the position of cook in the Head Start center based on the qualifications you have written for that position plus information in this chapter on content of advertisements.

3. Fill in the application form in Working Paper 10–3. Apply for the position of preschool teacher.

CLASS EXERCISES

1. Review the job description for the preschool teacher in Director's Resources 10–7 and develop a list of questions that would be appropriate to ask candidates applying for the job.

2. Select three class members to serve as interviewers of applicants for the preschool teacher's position. Select one class member as a candidate for the position.

3. After the three interviewers review the candidate's application for the position (Class Assignment 3), have them role-play an interview with the candidate using questions based on those developed in Exercise 1 in addition to information from the application.

4. After the interview, have all class members participate in summarizing, in writing, the candidate's qualifications for the job. Use Working Paper 10–4 to complete this exercise.

WORKING PAPER 10-1

(for use with Class Assignment 1)

RESUME FORMAT

Name: _____

Permanent Address   **Present Address**

_____   _____

_____   _____

_____   _____

Telephone: _____   Telephone: _____

Position objective:

Education:

Employment experience (in chronological order):

Honors and activities:

References (names, addresses, and telephone numbers of three):

1. _____

   _____

   _____

2. _____

   _____

   _____

3. _____

   _____

WORKING PAPER 10-2

(for use with Class Assignment 2)

JOB DESCRIPTION

Cook

Schedule: Monday through Friday—7:30 A.M. to 3:30 P.M.

Responsible to the Head Start director.

Responsible for the following:

1. safely preparing all food (breakfast, lunch, and snacks)

2. requisitioning appropriate amounts of foodstuffs based on designated menus

3. checking food deliveries against orders

4. storing foods appropriately, before preparation, in refrigerator, freezer, bins, cupboards, and the like

5. preparing all foods using methods that maintain food value and freshness

6. following menus, recipes, or other directives furnished by Head Start nutrition consultant

7. recording amounts of food used daily and maintaining an inventory of staples on hand

8. washing and sterilizing dishes and all utensils according to sanitarian's directions

9. cleaning appliances and storage areas according to a designated schedule

10. supervising assistant cook

Qualifications:

Advertisement for cook:

WORKING PAPER 10-3

(for use with Class Assignment 3)

SAMPLE APPLICATION FORM

Application for Employment

Jewish Community Preschool—Fairmount, Pennsylvania

Name of Applicant _____
                                      Last   First   Middle or Maiden

Address _____

State _____ Zip _____

Telephone _____

Citizenship: USA _____ Other _____

Record of Education

School	Name and Address of School	Check Last Year Completed	List Diploma or Degree
High		1 2 3 4	
College		1 2 3 4	
Other (Specify)		1 2 3 4	

(continues)

WORKING PAPER 10-3
(continued)

(for use with Class Assignment 3)

List below all present and past employment, beginning with your most recent

Name and Address of Employer	From Mo./ Yr.	To Mo./ Yr.	Describe in detail the work you did	Weekly Starting Salary	Weekly Last Salary	Reason for Leaving	Name of Supervisor

List all professional and community organizations with which you are affiliated. *(Indicate if you hold office in the organization.)*

_____

_____

Write your educational philosophy.

What do you feel most qualifies you for this position?

What are your professional goals?

List names and addresses of three references.

1. _____

2. _____

3. _____

I give permission to contact references _____
                                                        (Signature)

WORKING PAPER 10-4

(for use with Class Exercise 4)

INTERVIEW SUMMARY

Candidate Qualifications for Preschool Teacher

Education:

Experience with children:

Other relevant experience:

Ability to express ideas verbally:

Congruence of philosophy to that of the center:

General appearance:

Evidence of ability to work as part of the teaching team:

Other comments:

DIRECTOR'S RESOURCE 10-1

CINCINNATI EARLY LEARNING CENTERS INC.

Human Resource Policies And Practices

(continues)

DIRECTOR'S RESOURCE 10-1
(continued)

TABLE OF CONTENTS

(continues)

DIRECTOR'S RESOURCE 10-1
(continued)

(continues)

DIRECTOR'S RESOURCE 10-1
(continued)

INTRODUCTION AND PURPOSE

Responsibility

The Executive Director of Cincinnati Early Learning Centers Inc. (CELC) has responsibility for administering written personnel policies, which have been approved by the Board of Directors. To handle situations not covered by written policies, the Executive Director may take problem-solving action without Board approval, keeping the Board informed of any significant outcome which may indicate need for future development of formal policies.

Each employee with supervisory responsibility is expected to be familiar with these personnel policies and should consult with the Executive Director or Associate Executive Director on questions of interpretation before decisions are made or actions are taken. All employees will receive a copy of these personnel policies.

Notice of Employment

This Summary of Policies, including other matters addressed in it, is presented only as a matter of general information. This is not a contract of employment. Your employment with Cincinnati Early Learning Centers Inc. (CELC) is an employment-at-will relationship. Any individual may voluntarily leave employment or may be terminated by CELC at any time for any reason or without reason. Any oral or written statement or promises to the contrary are hereby expressly disavowed and should not be relied upon by any prospective or existing employee. Statements in this handbook, specifically including but not limited to those concerning discipline or reasons for discharge, are only general guidelines used by CELC. CELC may take disciplinary action other than that outlined in a particular case and may discipline or discharge an employee for reasons not listed in this handbook.

In addition, certain employee benefit plans are defined in legal documents such as insurance certificates or plan documents. Such legal documents are controlling. Should there be any conflict between this handbook and the certificate, plan, or other legal document, the legal document governs and not the descriptions contained in this handbook or in any other description or notice provided by CELC. This handbook and/or any policy or provision contained herein may be revised, modified, altered or revoked by CELC at any time with or without notice.

GENERAL RULES

Confidentiality

Records of all children are confidential and only staff and referral agencies may have access. A file may not leave the Directors office without approval. **An employee may be dismissed for discussing children outside of the school, staff, or referral agencies.**

Open Door Policy

An open door philosophy is an essential part of maintaining strong communication and a positive work environment. We are interested in knowing our employees' ideas, questions, suggestions, problems or concerns.

In most instances, your immediate supervisor is the person best qualified to solve a problem or answer a question. Therefore, we urge you to initially contact your supervisor and discuss anything that is on your mind. Give your supervisor the first opportunity to resolve any questions or conflicts you may have before taking it to the next level of supervision.

(continues)

DIRECTOR'S RESOURCE 10-1
(continued)

However, there may be times when you wish to discuss a concern or problem with someone other than your immediate supervisor. You are encouraged to bring these matters to another member of the management. *Where feasible, you should still advise your immediate supervisor that you wish to meet with another member of management.*

Reference Inquiries

All reference inquiries about current or past employees must be forwarded to the Executive Director. This is the only person authorized to share employee reference information with anyone outside the company. A current or ex-employee must provide a signed release for reference information to be shared with another party.

No Solicitation

In order to avoid interruption of your work and to protect you from unnecessary annoyance, solicitation and/or distribution of literature on CELC premises is limited to the following rules:

Non-employees of CELC have no right to distribute materials or solicit our associates on CELC property at any time.

Employee-to-employee solicitation, distribution or acceptance of literature by employees during work hours and in work areas is prohibited. Work time does not include time before or after employees scheduled work hours, meal periods, or paid break periods.

This policy includes solicitation and distribution of literature for all purposes, such as lotteries, raffles, charitable or political organizations and the like. The Executive Director of CELC must make any exceptions to this policy.

Resignation

If you choose to resign your employment, it is requested that you submit a written two-week notice.

EMPLOYMENT

Nondiscrimination

Cincinnati Early Learning Centers Inc. recognizes our employees as one of our greatest assets. We are committed to provide equal employment opportunity to all qualified persons, consistent with applicable federal, state and local equal employment opportunity laws prohibiting discrimination based on race, gender, age, handicap and/or disability, religion, ancestry, sexual orientation, marital status, color, or national origin.

These opportunities include, but are not limited to, recruitment, hiring, training, promotion, compensation, benefits and all other terms and conditions of employment.

Harassment

It is CELC's policy to maintain a working and learning environment free from all forms of harassment or intimidation including, but not limited to, race, gender or religion. This policy pertains to employees, supervisors, students, parents, suppliers and other non-employees. Unwelcome sexual advances, request for sexual favors and other verbal or physical conduct of a sexual nature are serious violations of our policy and will not be condoned or permitted. Not only is sexual harassment a violation of our policy, but it may violate Title VII of the Civil Rights Act and other federal and state laws.

(continues)

DIRECTOR'S RESOURCE 10-1
(continued)

If you are subjected to sexual harassment or intimidation, you should contact your supervisor, any other supervisor, or any member of management with whom you feel comfortable, for immediate help. All complaints of sexual harassment will be promptly and confidentially investigated and appropriate action will be taken against anyone found to have violated this policy. No employee who reports unlawful harassment or who assists in any investigation by CELC will be subjected to retaliation of any sort, and such retaliation will not be tolerated and is itself a violation of CELC policy. Submission to such unwanted conduct will never constitute a condition of employment. Any employee violating this policy will be subject to disciplinary action up to and including termination; sexual harassment of CELC employees by parents may result in the child being dismissed from the center; harassment by suppliers or other outside parties may result in termination of business relationships with CELC and will also be addressed in accordance with applicable state and federal laws.

Employee Classifications

Every employee is classified appropriately for the purpose of determining uniform standards for benefits, conditions of employment, and compliance with applicable wage and hour laws.

Non-exempt (hourly) positions are paid on the basis of "pay for work performed". Non-exempt employees are entitled to overtime pay under specific provisions of federal and state laws.

Exempt positions are paid on a salary basis due to the nature of their position. Such employees are excluded from specific provisions of federal and state wage and hour laws and are not eligible for overtime pay.

Full-time employees are those who are regularly scheduled to work 35 hours or more a week and are considered to be eligible for full employee benefits.

Part-time employees are those who are regularly scheduled to work between 10 and 34 hours per week on a regular basis and will be eligible only for reduced vacation benefits and holidays.

There may be times, or even periods of time when CELC permits a part-time employee to work more than part-time hours during a workweek. This does not change an employee's part-time status or their eligibility for certain benefits. An employee keeps their part-time status until CELC specifically notifies the employee in writing that it has changed.

Unclassified employees are those regularly scheduled to work less than 10 hours per week or workers hired as interim replacements to temporarily supplement the work force, to assist in the completion of a specific project, or in a seasonal position. Employment assignments in this category may be of a limited duration. Unclassified employees are paid under the company's normal payroll system and must adhere to the company rules and policies. Unclassified employees are not eligible for benefits.

Probationary Period

Your first ninety (90) days of employment is considered a probationary period. During your first ninety (90) days, your director/supervisor will provide information regarding your job duties and responsibilities. You will also receive feedback on your job performance throughout this period. If any performance problems develop during the probationary period, you may be counseled. If at any time during the probationary period it becomes obvious to either the employee or CELC that the employment relationship is unsatisfactory, separation from employment will occur, without regard to reason.

Licensing Requirements

All employees must meet current Ohio Department of Jobs & Family Services child care licensing requirements for their positions. For example: current medical exam every three years.

(continues)

DIRECTOR'S RESOURCE 10-1
(continued)

Personnel Records

Your personnel record contains information pertinent to your employment. Generally, your file contains such things as your application, resume, tax forms, and performance appraisals/development plans. The file is confidential and is the property of the organization. If you would like to see your file, contact center director/department head.

Termination of Employment

Certain circumstances, depending on the seriousness of the offense, may result in a final written warning, suspension or a termination without any prior notice or corrective counseling.

Certain types of conduct are offensive to our employees and children and cannot be permitted. The following examples illustrate some (but not all) types of conduct that may result in immediate dismissal without warning:

- Direct refusal to comply with legitimate request from a supervisor.
- Flagrant discourtesy to a child, parent, or employee. This includes, but is not limited to, fighting, or inciting a fight, using obscene or abusive language, or threatening an employee, parent, or child.
- Immoral, indecent or illegal conduct reflecting negatively on the company or violating the rights of the employees or children.
- Reckless conduct resulting in injury or harm.
- Falsification of any company records, such as employee records, timekeeping records, activity reports, etc.
- Misuse or unauthorized removal of company, employee, or children's records, or confidential information of any nature.
- Unauthorized use, blatant misuse, destruction, removal or embezzlement of property or money belonging to CELC, its employees or the children.
- Possession, sale, distribution or use of alcohol or illegal drugs while on work time or company property.
- Possession or storing of firearms, weapons, ammunition, or explosives on company property.
- Violation of the company harassment policy.

OPERATION OF OUR FACILITIES

Working Hours

Teaching Staff—Employee's hours will be set upon hiring. Schedules will change according to enrollment and all teachers are required to sign in and out each day. If an employee should be late for any reason, he/she must call the center to notify staff as early as possible. Employees are required to attend all staff meetings and are expected to attend parent meetings when scheduled, along with any activities to improve parent-teacher relationships. When staff meetings are scheduled after shift hours, non-exempt employees will be compensated for this time in accordance with applicable wage/hour laws. All employees are required to have time sheets signed and approved by their supervisor or Center Director.

(continues)

DIRECTOR'S RESOURCE 10-1
(continued)

Administrative/Management Staff–CELC currently maintains a regular scheduled workweek of 35 hours or more for full-time employees. Employee's hours will be set upon hiring. Individuals may adjust their scheduled daily hours only by prior agreement with their supervisor.

Meal and Rest Breaks

If you are a non-exempt employee and you work 4 hours but less than 7 hours, you are entitled to a paid 15 minute rest break. When you work at least 7 hours, you will receive a paid 30 minute break. Break time is to include meals and/or rest. Break time is calculated from the time you stop performing assigned tasks until the time you resume them.

Children and Closing

It is the closing employee's responsibility to confirm that all children have been picked up before leaving the building. Two employees must always be present when a child is in the center. In the event that a child is not picked up at the closing of the center, the remaining employees will follow these guidelines:

If attempts to reach parent at work and home are unsuccessful, call emergency contact number.

If attempts to contact emergency contacts are unsuccessful, contact the director immediately.

YOU ARE A PROFESSIONAL: AT NO TIME MAY YOU TRANSPORT A CHILD OR LEAVE A CHILD UNATTENDED.

Dress Code

All employees are encouraged to wear comfortable clothing. A professional appearance must be maintained at all times. An employee reporting to work in inappropriate clothing may be asked to go home and change before returning to work.

Attendance and Punctuality

CELC employees are expected to be on the job, on time, on a regular basis. Our work schedules are based upon the understanding that all employees will be at work and at their workstations on time. We recognize that on occasion, it may be necessary for an employee to be tardy or absent from work due to illness or personal problems; however, absence or tardiness can hamper or prevent others from performing their jobs properly. Repeated or chronic tardiness will subject an employee to discipline (up to and including discharge) at the discretion of CELC.

If you are unable to come to work on a scheduled or regular work day, you must give notice to your supervisor or director as soon as you are aware that you will be absent. If your absence is due to illness, injury, or other personal reasons, you must call in as soon as possible. If you know that you will be absent for more than one day, you must advise your supervisor or director of that fact and the expected duration of your absence. Otherwise, you must call each day of your absence.

Subject to the provisions of the Family/Medical Leave Act, the Americans with Disabilities Act, or other applicable laws, any employee who is absent more than 15 days in a calendar year, whether for reasons of illness, injury, personal reasons or otherwise, will be subject to discharge. In the case of serious illness or injury, unpaid leave may be granted at the discretion of the Director, however, no such leave will exceed 30 days and any employee who is absent for more than 30 days for any reason shall be subject to discharge.

(continues)

DIRECTOR'S RESOURCE 10-1
(continued)

Outside Employment

While employed at CELC you may decide to seek employment outside of your regular working hours at your center. CELC has no objections to this type of work, provided it does not interfere with your assignments and responsibilities at CELC. Furthermore, you cannot be employed by a competitor of CELC that would create a conflict of interest in your employment.

At times the families enrolled in the program request teachers to provide child care in their homes after program hours. This is not encouraged or endorsed by CELC. Each parent and teacher is asked to sign a disclaimer releasing CELC of any liability if they enter into an arrangement.

COMPENSATION

General Compensation Policy

Our goal is to attract, retain, and reward competent employees. To accomplish this we will provide you with a series of potential rewards, including competitive pay and competitive benefits. The CELC compensation program is competitive within the early childhood education profession and the local markets within which we conduct business. Increases to compensation will be based on the individual employee's performance and the overall performance of the company.

Overtime

Exempt Salaried Employees are paid the same pre-determined amount for each period that they perform any work. The salary is paid for the work done, not for the number of hours worked. Therefore, these employees are exempt for overtime pay.

Non-Exempt Hourly Employees who work in excess of the normal workweek, which has been previously assigned or approved by their supervisor, will be compensated accordingly. Any work in excess of 40 hours will be compensated at 1-1/2 times the hourly rate. Sick leave, personal days, vacation, or other non-worked time off are not to be used in calculating hours worked per week.

Compensatory time can be authorized under special circumstances for work which cannot be done within the usual working hours. Non-exempt hourly employees must first have approval by their supervisor. Final approval shall be with the Executive Director. Accrued compensatory time may not exceed 40 hours, unless approved by the Executive Director for extraordinary circumstances. At time of termination, there is no cash reimbursement for unused compensatory time.

Pay for overtime is included in the semi-monthly payroll. Overtime must be authorized in advance by the supervisor.

Split Shift

Split shift is a schedule where an employee agrees to work a minimum of eight (8) hours and where those hours are divided with at least a two (2) hour break. (Example: 7 a.m.–1 p.m. and 3 p.m.–5 p.m.) Employees will earn an extra two dollars ($2.00) per hour for working a split shift when it is not a standard or regular work schedule.

Wage Reviews

Wages are reviewed at least annually and will be based on individual and/or team performance and external market conditions. Your individual supervisor can provide more information on wage reviews.

(continues)

DIRECTOR'S RESOURCE 10-1
(continued)

Payday

Employees are paid on a semimonthly basis, on the 15th of the month and the last day of the month. Payment on the 15th of the month will cover the period from the 1st to the 15th of the month for salaried exempt employees and for the period from the 16th to the last day of the previous month for hourly employees. Payment on the last day of the month will cover the period from the 16th to the last day of the month for salaried exempt employees and for the period from the 1st to the 15th of the month for hourly employees. *If the 15th or last day of the month falls on a holiday or weekend day, pay will be issued on the last workday before the holiday or weekend.*

For your protection, your paycheck or direct deposit stub will be released only to you unless you provide advance written authorization. The person picking up your check will be required to present photo identification proving his/her identity.

Your paycheck is confidential; you should never show it to, or discuss it with, another employee. To do so will be considered a violation of confidentiality. Questions or concerns should be discussed with your supervisor. You should inform your supervisor of any possible errors in your paycheck. CELC reserves the right to adjust subsequent checks if an error is discovered.

Payroll Deductions

Federal and state laws require that certain deductions be withheld from the pay of all employees. Among these are Social Security and Medicare taxes, federal income tax, and state and local taxes, where applicable. Should your wages be legally garnished or other court ordered deductions be required, the payroll function will reduce your pay as required.

When eligible, you may authorize the following deductions:

- Benefits (i.e. medical, dental, life insurance, etc.)
- Charity (i.e. United Way, etc.)
- Savings (maximum $150 direct deposit)

EMPLOYEE BENEFITS

Protection For Your Future

At CELC, we strive to offer you a comprehensive and competitive benefits package. The company offers plans that are available to *assist you in preparing for your future.* You can join the plans after satisfying the eligibility requirements designated for each plan.

Section 125 Flexible Benefits Plan

CELC offers a Section 125 Flexible Benefits Plan. This plan allows employees to have payroll deducted health, dental and other insurance premiums deducted from their paychecks on a pre-tax basis. This allows employees to have their taxable income reduced by the amount of these deductions.

Health Insurance

Employees who regularly work 35 or more hours per week as a permanent schedule are eligible for paid health insurance. CELC offers quality health care plans to eligible employees to ease the burden of costs associated with illness. *New employees will become effective on the first billing*

(continues)

DIRECTOR'S RESOURCE 10-1
(continued)

date after becoming eligible with completion of 30 days of employment. Should an employee choose other than standard coverage or to include other family members, all costs above the employee's basic cost will be the obligation of the employee through payroll deduction. (Single standard plan costs are paid by CELC.)

The design of our health-care plans is guided by:

- A commitment to make cost-efficient health care possible
- An expectation that employees are responsible for personal health as a function of life style, prevention, dietary habits, and self-care, taking responsible precautions to ensure good health
- A cooperative effort to work toward influencing external factors to control health-care costs
- A review of health-care plans on a continual basis to satisfy the needs of CELC and its employees

Life Insurance

Employees who regularly work 35 or more hours per week as a permanent schedule are eligible for paid life insurance and accidental death & dismemberment benefit coverage. CELC provides eligible employees with financial protection through term life insurance for their families in case of the employee's death or amputation or loss of a body part (dismemberment).

New employees will become effective on the first billing date after becoming eligible with completion of 30 days of employment. The plan provides each employee with coverage of $50,000. Plan coverage is provided at no cost to the employee.

Retirement Savings Plan

The company participates in a 403(b) Retirement Savings Plan. All employees are immediately eligible to participate in the plan on a voluntary basis. You may contribute on a pre-tax basis between 1–20% of your gross salary each calendar year up to an annual maximum set by the federal government. Your taxable income is reduced by the amount you save through your pre-tax deferral.

Vacation/Sick Days

Each employee may take vacation/sick days with full salary at such time is mutually agreed upon by his or her supervisor. The eligibility for paid vacation/sick days is based on the status of employment and length of continuous service.

Full-time staff employees After thirty (30) days of employment they will receive three (3) vacation/sick days to be used in his/her first year of employment. After six (6) months of employment, they will receive four (4) additional vacation/sick days to be used in his/her first year of employment. After one year of employment, vacation/sick day entitlement is as follows:

Upon 1st year anniversary	10 days
Upon 2nd year anniversary & forward	12 days

(continues)

DIRECTOR'S RESOURCE 10-1
(continued)

Part-time staff employees After thirty (30) days of employment they will receive two (2) vacation/sick days to be used in his/her first year of employment. (*Part-time employees are to be paid only the number of hours they would regularly be scheduled to work. For example, a part-time employee regularly scheduled to work four (4) hours would be paid four (4) hours for the vacation/sick day.*)

Upon 1st year anniversary & forward   5 days

Full-time management employees After thirty (30) days of employment they will receive six (6) vacation/sick days to be used in his/her first year of employment. After three (3) months of employment, they will receive six (6) additional vacation/sick days to be used in his/her first year of employment. After six (6) months of employment, they will receive fifteen (15) additional vacation/sick days to be used in his/her first year of employment. After one year of employment, vacation/sick day entitlement is as follows:

Upon 1st year anniversary & forward   27 days

An employee may accumulate up to a maximum of ten (10) vacation/sick days that may be carried over into the next benefit year based on their service anniversary to be used to cover planned medical reasons. Proper physician authorization is required. Unused accumulated vacation/sick days will be paid out upon termination of employment.

Personal Days

After thirty (30) days of employment **each full-time staff employee (excluding full-time management employees)** will receive one personal day each month. The director or scheduler will schedule these days no more than three (3) months before, and no less than one (1) month before. The center reserves the right under special circumstances to reschedule personal days. An employee may save up to three (3) personal days per year to be used as paid time off. They must be used within the same year. *These days are not accrued vacation and no paid compensation will be due to staff that resign or are terminated.* If, due to a staffing shortage, an employee elects to forfeit a personal day within twenty-four (24) hours of their scheduled day off, and they come in to work, they will be paid time and a half for the hours worked.

Holidays

Eligible full-time and part-time employees are paid for the following recognized holidays where it is a regularly scheduled work day for them: New Years Day, Martin Luther King Day, Memorial Day, July 4th, Labor Day, Thanksgiving Day, and Christmas Day. Part-time employees are to be paid only the number of hours they would regularly be scheduled to work. For example, a part-time employee regularly scheduled to work four (4) hours would be paid four (4) hours for the eligible holiday.

Tuition Reduction

Center employees may be granted a reduced tuition rate as follows:

All full-time employees: 20% tuition reduction

Reduced tuition slots are limited based upon available accommodations and management's discretion. **Tuition under this policy must be paid with employee payroll withholding.**

(continues)

DIRECTOR'S RESOURCE 10-1
(continued)

Jury Duty

Jury duty is considered a civic duty; therefore, no deduction from salary will be made for time actually served, subject to the procedures as indicated following. As a full-time employee and once you have completed your 90-day introductory period, you will receive your regular pay for each regularly scheduled work day you are on jury duty. You must show the court summons to your supervisor before commencing jury duty leave. Any income received for jury duty will be returned to the agency. You will be required to furnish a court prepared work statement or similar documentation form the court to authorize your request to receive your regular pay. Upon completion of jury duty for the day or after being excused from any service for the day, the employee must call their supervisor to determine whether they must report for work for the remaining period of the day. Should an employee not call to allow their supervisor to make such determination and it is found that they did not complete a full day of jury duty, they will no longer be eligible to receive regular pay for each regularly scheduled work day they are on jury duty.

COBRA

CELC reserves the right to treat any leave as a triggering event as defined under the Comprehensive Omnibus Budget Reconciliation Act ("Cobra") and to notify the employee of his/her right to continue any group health insurance coverage at the employee's cost for the duration of such leave.

Subject to the provisions of the Americans With Disabilities Act, the Family and Medical Leave Act, or other applicable state or federal laws, time spent on leave of absence shall not be counted as actual service time for purposes of calculating such items as vacation or sick time accrual, or any other fringe benefits. Further, an employee on leave of absence may not engage in any form of gainful employment or occupation without prior written approval from the Director. Violation of this policy will result in cancellation of the leave and termination of employment.

LEAVES OF ABSENCE

Medical Leave

For absences due to serious personal illness or injury that exceed 5 days in length, an employee may be eligible for medical leave of absence. Any employee, full or part-time, who has completed 90 days of service, is eligible. To initiate a medical leave, the employee must submit a doctor's note that indicates the nature of the situation and the expected dates of leave to their supervisor. The supervisor will notify the Executive Director as soon as possible. The Executive Director is responsible for final approval of medical leave requests.

Generally, a medical leave may not exceed 13 weeks, including any portion that would be covered by vacation pay, sick pay, personal days, or unpaid leave. Should the employee reach an unpaid status during the leave, the employee must submit payments for insurance premiums that would normally be deducted from pay in order to keep the coverage intact.

Every effort will be made to hold the employee's position open during the leave. Should business conditions require that the position be filled, every effort will be made to restore the employee to a position of similar pay and status upon return to work. In no event shall the employee be replaced without first being notified. A doctor's note releasing the employee to return to work may be required for any illness of 5 days or more. Failure to return from scheduled leave will be considered a voluntary resignation.

(continues)

DIRECTOR'S RESOURCE 10-1
(continued)

Family & Medical Leave Act (FMLA)

Pursuant to the Family and Medical Leave Act of 1997, employees may be entitled to up to twelve (12) weeks of unpaid leave per year under certain circumstances as set forth in the Act. During leave taken under the terms of the Act, medical insurance and certain other benefits in which the affected employee is a participant will be maintained on the same basis as for active employees. While the employee does not continue in "active service" for purposes of accruing vacation, retirement or other benefits related to length of service, leave taken pursuant to the Family and Medical Leave Act does not constitute a "break in service" for such purposes. At the completion of leave taken pursuant to the Act, the employee will be restored to his or her former position or, if necessary and appropriate in light of the needs of CELC and at CELC's sole discretion, to a position substantially similar in terms of pay, benefits, and conditions of employment.

Under the Family and Medical Leave Act, employees who have been employed by CELC for at least twelve (12) months and who have been credited with 1250 hours of active service during the year immediately preceding the requested leave period are eligible for this leave.

The Act provides that eligible employees may take up to twelve (12) work weeks of leave during any twelve (12) month period for one or more of the following: (1) birth of a child of the employee, in order to care for such child; (2) placement of a child with the employee, either through adoption or foster care; (3) to care for the employee's spouse, child or parent with a serious health condition; (4) a serious health condition of the employee that makes it impossible for the employee to perform the functions of his or her employment.

Leave taken pursuant to the Act will be offset by paid or unpaid leave otherwise available to the employee, i.e., accrued vacation, personal, medical and/or sick leave must be used as the first part of the twelve (12) week maximum leave period.

In the event of the birth or placement of a child, the employee's entitlement to leave to care for such child expires twelve (12) months after such birth or placement. Further, if a husband and wife are both employed by CELC, the maximum leave for both spouses combined will be twelve (12) weeks in any given year for the birth or placement of a child or the care of a parent with a serious health condition. Under the Act, any employee requesting leave must give CELC thirty (30) days advance notice if the need for the leave is foreseeable. Otherwise, notice is required as soon as practicable. An expected date of return shall be determined prior to the commencement of any leave, and may be extended for good cause but in no event past the maximum leave period allowed by the Act. If the leave is requested because of serious health condition, certification signed by a bona fide health care provider shall be provided and a request for a second opinion may be required at CELC expense. CELC may also require re-certification on a reasonable periodic basis. During any such leave, the employee shall be required to check in with his or her supervisor on Monday of each week to determine the employee's status and to discuss possible changes in the employee's expected date of return.

While the employee is on leave under the Act, CELC will continue group health coverage on the same basis as though the employee continued to be in active service. If the employee fails to return to work after the leave period has expired for reason other than a continuing serious health condition or other circumstances beyond the employee's control, CELC will be entitled to recover from the employee the cost of any health coverage provided during the leave period. Employee co-payments or contribution for such coverage will be required to keep coverage in force during leave under the Act.

Consult with your supervisor or the Director for more details about the terms and procedures applicable to leaves under the Family and Medical Leave Act.

(continues)

DIRECTOR'S RESOURCE 10-1
(continued)

Personal Leave

An employee may be eligible to take a leave without pay for personal reasons, other than those covered by medical leave or the Family and Medical Leave Act. Any employee who has completed 90 days of service is eligible. The employee must submit a written request to the supervisor stating the reason for the request and the proposed dates of leave. The supervisor will notify the Executive Director as soon as possible. The Executive Director is responsible for final approval of personal leave requests. A personal leave may be approved for up to 13 weeks. Every effort will be made to hold the position open during the leave. In no event shall the employee be replaced without first being notified. Eligible accrued time off available to the employee, i.e., accrued vacation, personal, medical and/or sick leave must be used first as part of the requested leave period. When taken in conjunction with a medical leave, vacation, or other paid time off, the total time away from work may not exceed 13 weeks. When the employee is on unpaid status, he/she must submit payments for the employee's portion of insurance that would normally be deducted from pay in order to keep coverage intact.

EMPLOYEE DEVELOPMENT

Performance Development Requirements

Regardless of their previous education or experience, employees will be expected to continue studies of and training in early childhood education practices in order to keep abreast of new developments in the field. This continued study and training may take place on the employees own time outside of regular working hours, and as recommended by the director. Methods employed may include, but are not limited to, in-service training classes at the center, attendance at a recommended professional conference or meeting, membership in a professional organization and attendance at its monthly meetings, and/or enrollment in pertinent courses offered by local colleges and universities.

Child Development Training

Each non-degreed (ECE) employee must complete a minimum of fifteen (15) hours of child development training each year. Also, associate teachers must be enrolled in a Child Development Associate (CDA) credential program after one year of employment. Each degreed employee must complete a total of six (6) hours of annual training, four (4) of which will be child development topics. These requirements may be waived by the Director if the employee is taking a university credit course of one (1) to three (3) hours.

In certain circumstances, management may require employees to take other courses or training that broaden their knowledge and help them further contribute to the goals of the corporation.

In-Service Training

Two (2) days each year, typically on Good Friday and the Friday after Thanksgiving, the center will be closed for in-service training. The in-service days will consist of training and individual time for planning, goal setting, etc. Every employee must attend. If someone misses due to illness they must make this time up on a Saturday and replacement training will be at their own expense. This in-service must be made up within thirty (30) days of it being offered/scheduled.

(continues)

Corrective Counseling

CELC recognizes that on occasion it may be necessary to discuss specific areas of an employee's performance or conduct that are below the expected standards. These discussions are designed to help the employee correct whatever problem may exist. The corrective counseling may range from a verbal discussion to written warnings to termination.

Recruitment

Applications are always to be accepted and filed. The center works with local universities and vocational schools to provide placements for students in teacher training programs. When a position becomes available within the corporation, employees are notified and can be considered for the position if qualified.

Performance Appraisal

Employees are evaluated on an annual basis. Details regarding these procedures are included in the Orientation Manual.

Position Descriptions

Job descriptions are reviewed with the employee at the time of hire and a copy of their job description will be maintained in their personnel file. Job descriptions can be revised by the Director/Supervisor with the approval of the Executive Director.

Promotions and Transfers

Upon notification from an employee of his/her interest in another position or transfer to another location, the Director/Supervisor over the position or location will determine the eligibility for promotion and/or transfer. The employee must meet the following criteria to be eligible:

Minimum of six (6) months in current position.

Current job performance is satisfactory, meeting expectations or above.

No pending corrective counseling or disciplinary warnings in effect.

Recommended for the position by their current Director/Supervisor.

Once the above criteria are met, the employee can be interviewed for the open position or transfer opportunity. The receiving Director/Supervisor will make final determination on the promotion and/or transfer.

STANDARDS OF CONDUCT

Arrest, Indictment, or Conviction

If you are arrested, indicted or convicted, you must notify your supervisor as soon as possible and we will consider all available facts before taking action.

You may be:

A. Allowed to continue employment until conviction. If you are convicted, your employment status will be reviewed by management at that time.

B. Suspended because your presence at work could cause substantial disruption to the workplace.

C. Terminated from employment.

(continues)

DIRECTOR'S RESOURCE 10-1
(continued)

The termination decision will be made on an individual basis and may be based on the following:

A. You are unable to return to work due to incarceration.

B. Your presence at work could cause substantial disruption.

C. The crime for which you are accused is of such a grave nature that it adversely affects our legitimate business interests.

D. The nature of the crime is such that allowing you to continue to work results in a "good faith" probability of future harm to your co-workers, our customers, visitors, or business interests.

If you are exonerated, consideration may be given to reinstatement.

If you have information of a co-worker's arrest, indictment or conviction, you should immediately inform an appropriate supervisor.

It is CELC's policy that all employees obey local, state, and federal laws.

Confidentiality

All business information, practices and records, including any that pertain to customers and employees, are considered confidential. The release of confidential information to unauthorized persons could result in disciplinary action and possible termination from employment. If someone asks you for information and you are unsure whether to give it or not, ask your supervisor first.

Smoking

In keeping with our intent to provide you and our children with a safe and healthful work environment, smoking by employees, visitors, or any parties, is prohibited within our facilities.

Substance Abuse Control

We are committed to providing a healthful and safe workplace for everyone. Consistent with that commitment, we have established a policy which promotes a drug and alcohol-free work environment. We understand that some problems related to drugs and alcohol are more than one person can handle. Therefore, we encourage you to talk with your supervisor should you need help.

We expect you to report to work in the mental and physical condition necessary to perform your job in a satisfactory manner. The legal use of prescribed drugs is permitted on the job only if it does not impair your ability to perform the essential functions of the job effectively and safely.

The use, possession, sale, or transfer of illegal drugs or alcohol are prohibited on company premises, while using company vehicles, or while you are taking part in any company business.

Under the Drug-Fee Workplace Act, you must notify the company within five days of any criminal conviction for drug-related activity occurring in the workplace.

If any supervisor has reason to suspect that you may be:

1. under the influence of alcohol or drugs while at work or your job performance is being adversely affected by the possible abuse of drugs or alcohol, or

2. keeping drugs or alcohol on your person, in your desk, locker, or other personal belonging or company area

(continues)

DIRECTOR'S RESOURCE 10-1
(continued)

We may ask you to:

1. open the area for inspection
2. consent to be tested
3. leave the premises

If you are found to be in possession of illegal drugs or alcohol, refuse to consent to testing or leave the premises if requested, or test positive, you may be disciplined up to and including termination of employment. Pre-employment and post-employment drug testing may also be conducted.

Use of Company Property

Use company property for business only. Do not use company property for personal reasons. Also, office supplies and other company property must never be taken from the facility (unless authorized to do so). This shall include all business and computer related files and/or records.

CONFLICT RESOLUTION PROCEDURE

Employee Questions, Concerns or Complaints

CELC, Inc. acknowledges that circumstances may arise about which an employee may desire to seek formal assistance in resolving questions or concerns about employment. CELC wishes to provide all employees with considerate supervision and fair treatment. To that end, the following conflict resolution procedure has been adopted to resolve such questions or concerns.

1. Every employee question or complaint should first be discussed with the director within three (3) days of the occurrence of the cause of the complaint. (If the director is the cause of the complaint, the employee may begin at Step 2.) It is hoped that a satisfactory resolution of the complaint can promptly be reached between the employee and the director. In any event, what the director proposes shall be given in writing to the employee with a copy sent to the Executive Director and the Associate Executive Director.

2. If the employee is not satisfied with the resolution of the complaint proposed by the director, the employee may appeal his or her complaint in writing to the Executive Director and the Associate Executive Director. They will jointly render a written decision within ten (10) working days after the filing of the appeal.

3. The decision of the Executive Director and the Associate Executive Director shall be final and binding on all parties and not subject to any further appeal. They shall keep the President of the Board informed of personnel concerns involving such formal complaints.

4. In the case of a complaint either against or by a management employee, including the Associate Executive Director, the Executive Director shall hear and review evidence presented by the complaint. In the case of a complaint either against or by the Executive Director, the President of the Board shall hear and review evidence presented by the complaint; if deemed necessary by the President of the Board, he/she shall appoint a committee of the Board to hear the complaint. If this committee fails to satisfy the parties involved, an appeal may be made in writing to the President for a hearing before the entire Board. Decision by the Board will be final.

(continues)

DIRECTOR'S RESOURCE 10-1
(continued)

The Associate Executive Director and the Executive Director shall maintain an "open door policy," in which any employee may, in private, present a complaint or other agency concern.

EMPLOYEE'S ACKNOWLEDGMENT

I have received and read the *"Cincinnati Early Learning Centers Inc. Human Resources Policies and Practices."* I expected to be guided by the policies contained therein. I further understand and agree that my employment with Cincinnati Early Learning Centers Inc. (CELC) is at will and may be terminated by me or CELC at any time for any reason or without reason. I understand that nothing in the Human Resources Policies and Practices or in any oral statement or representation by any employee or representative of CELC shall be deemed to create a contract of employment or any other modification of the at-will employment relationship. I also understand that any or all of the provisions contained in the Human Resources Policies and Practices may be modified, amended, or eliminated by CELC at any time with or without notice.

_____

Print Name

_____   _____

Signature   Date

_____

Employee SSN

_____   _____

Director/Supervisor Signature   Date

_____

Employment Location

Reprinted with permission from Cincinnati Early Learning Centers, Inc., 1301 McMillan Avenue, Cincinnati, OH 45206.

DIRECTOR'S RESOURCE 10-2

ADDITIONAL QUESTIONS AND ANSWERS ON THE AMERICANS WITH DISABILITIES ACT

Q. What is the relationship between the ADA and the Rehabilitation Act of 1973?

A. The Rehabilitation Act of 1973 prohibits discrimination on the basis of handicap by the federal government, federal contractors and by recipients of federal financial assistance. If you were covered by the Rehabilitation Act prior to the passage of the ADA, the ADA will not affect that coverage. Many of the provisions contained in the ADA are based on Section 504 of the Rehabilitation Act and its implementing regulations. If you are receiving federal financial assistance and are in compliance with Section 504, you are probably in compliance with the ADA requirements affecting employment except in those areas where the ADA contains additional requirements. Your nondiscrimination requirements as a federal contractor under Section 503 of the Rehabilitation Act will be essentially the same as those under the ADA; however, you will continue to have additional affirmative action requirements under Section 503 that do not exist under the ADA.

Q. If I have several qualified applicants for a job, does the ADA require that I hire the applicant with a disability?

A. No. You may hire the most qualified applicant. The ADA only makes it unlawful for you to discriminate against a qualified individual with a disability on the basis of disability.

Q. One of my employees is a diabetic but takes insulin daily to control his diabetes. As a result, the diabetes has no significant impact on his employment. Is he protected by the ADA?

A. Yes. The determination as to whether a person has a disability under the ADA is made without regard to mitigating measures, such as medications, auxiliary aids and reasonable accommodations. If an individual has an impairment that substantially limits a major life activity, she is protected under the ADA, regardless of the fact that the disease or condition or its effects may be corrected or controlled.

Q. One of my employees has a broken arm that will heal but is temporarily unable to perform the essential functions of his job as a mechanic. Is this employee protected by the ADA?

A. No. Although this employee does have an impairment, it does not substantially limit a major life activity if it is of limited duration and will have no long-term effect.

Q. Am I obligated to provide a reasonable accommodation for an individual if I am unaware of her physical or mental impairment?

A. No. An employer's obligation to provide reasonable accommodation applies only to known physical or mental limitations. However, this does not mean that an applicant or employee must always inform you of a disability. If a disability is obvious, e.g., the applicant uses a wheelchair, the employer "knows" of the disability even if the applicant never mentions it.

(continues)

DIRECTOR'S RESOURCE 10-2

(continued)

Q. How do I determine whether a reasonable accommodation is appropriate and the type of accommodation that should be made available?

A. The requirement generally will be triggered by a request from an individual with a disability, who frequently can suggest an appropriate accommodation. Accommodations must be made on a case-by-case basis, because the nature and extent of a disabling condition and the requirements of the job will vary. The principal test in selecting a particular type of accommodation is that of effectiveness, i.e., whether the accommodation will enable the person with a disability to perform the essential functions of the job. It need not be the best accommodation or the accommodation the individual with a disability would prefer, although primary consideration should be given to the preference of the individual involved. However, as the employer, you have the final discretion to choose between effective accommodations, and you may select one that is least expensive or easier to provide.

Q. When must I consider reassigning an employee with a disability to another job as a reasonable accommodation?

A. When an employee with a disability is unable to perform her present job even with the provision of a reasonable accommodation, you must consider reassigning the employee to an existing position that she can perform with or without a reasonable accommodation. The requirement to consider reassignment applies only to employees and not to applicants. You are not required to create a position or to bump another employee in order to create a vacancy. Nor are you required to promote an employee with a disability to a higher level position.

Q. What if an applicant or employee refuses to accept an accommodation that I offer?

A. The ADA provides that an employer cannot require a qualified individual with a disability to accept an accommodation that is neither requested nor needed by the individual. However, if a necessary reasonable accommodation is refused, the individual may be considered not qualified.

Q. If our business has a health spa in the building, must it be accessible to employees with disabilities?

A. Yes. Under the ADA, workers with disabilities must have equal access to all benefits and privileges of employment that are available to similarly situated employees without disabilities. The duty to provide reasonable accommodation applies to all nonwork facilities provided or maintained by you for your employees. This includes cafeterias, lounges, auditoriums, company-provided transportation and counseling services. If making an existing facility accessible would be an undue hardship, you must provide a comparable facility that will enable a person with a disability to enjoy benefits and privileges of employment similar to those enjoyed by other employees, unless this would be an undue hardship.

Q. If I contract for a consulting firm to develop a training course for my employees, and the firm arranges for the course to be held at a hotel that is inaccessible to one of my employees, am I liable under the ADA?

A. Yes. An employer may not do through a contractual or other relationship what it is prohibited from doing directly. You would be required to provide a location that is readily accessible to, and usable by your employee with a disability unless to do so would create an undue hardship.

(continues)

DIRECTOR'S RESOURCE 10-2
(continued)

Q. What are my responsibilities as an employer for making my facilities accessible?

A. As an employer, you are responsible under Title I of the ADA for making facilities accessible to qualified applicants and employees with disabilities as a reasonable accommodation, unless this would cause undue hardship. Accessibility must be provided to enable a qualified applicant to participate in the application process, to enable a qualified individual to perform essential job functions and to enable an employee with a disability to enjoy benefits and privileges available to other employees. However, if your business is a place of public accommodation (such as a restaurant, retail store or bank) you have different obligations to provide accessibility to the general public, under Title III of the ADA. Title III also will require places of public accommodation and commercial facilities (such as office buildings, factories and warehouses) to provide accessibility in new construction or when making alterations to existing structures. Further information on these requirements may be obtained from the U.S. Department of Justice, which enforces Title III. (See page 22.)

Q. Under the ADA, can an employer refuse to hire an individual or fire a current employee who uses drugs illegally?

A. Yes. Individuals who currently use drugs illegally are specifically excluded from the ADA's protections. However, the ADA does not exclude:

- persons who have successfully completed or are currently in a rehabilitation program and are no longer illegally using drugs
- persons erroneously regarded as engaging in the illegal use of drugs

Q. Does the ADA cover people with AIDS?

A. Yes. The legislative history indicates that Congress intended the ADA to protect persons with AIDS and HIV disease from discrimination.

Q. Can I consider health and safety in deciding whether to hire an applicant or retain an employee with a disability?

A. The ADA permits an employer to require that an individual not pose a direct threat to the health and safety of the individual or others in the workplace. A direct threat means a significant risk of substantial harm. You cannot refuse to hire or fire an individual because of a slightly increased risk of harm to himself or others. Nor can you do so based on a speculative or remote risk. The determination that an individual poses a direct threat must be based on objective, factual evidence regarding the individual's present ability to perform essential job functions. If an applicant or employee with a disability poses a direct threat to the health or safety of himself or others, you must consider whether the risk can be eliminated or reduced to an acceptable level with a reasonable accommodation.

Q. Am I required to provide additional insurance for employees with disabilities?

A. No. The ADA only requires that you provide an employee with a disability equal access to whatever health insurance coverage you provide to other employees. For example, if your health insurance coverage for certain treatments is limited to a specified number per year, and an employee, because of a disability, needs more than the specified number, the ADA does not require that you provide additional coverage to meet that employee's health insurance needs. The ADA also does not require changes in insurance plans that exclude or limit coverage for pre-existing conditions.

(continues)

DIRECTOR'S RESOURCE 10-2
(continued)

Q. Does the ADA require that I post a notice explaining its requirements?

A. The ADA requires that you post a notice in an accessible format to applicants, employees and members of labor organizations, describing the provisions of the Act. EEOC will provide employers with a poster summarizing these and other federal legal requirements for nondiscrimination. EEOC will also provide guidance on making this information available in accessible formats for people with disabilities.

What Are My Obligations to Provide Reasonable Accommodations?

Reasonable accommodation is any change or adjustment to a job or work environment that permits a qualified applicant or employee with a disability to participate in the job application process, to perform the essential functions of a job, or to enjoy benefits and privileges of employment equal to those enjoyed by employees without disabilities. For example, reasonable accommodation may include:

- acquiring or modifying equipment or devices
- job restructuring
- part-time or modified work schedules
- reassignment to a vacant position
- adjusting or modifying examinations, training materials or policies
- providing readers and interpreters
- making the workplace readily accessible to and usable by people with disabilities

Reasonable accommodation also must be made to enable an individual with a disability to participate in the application process and to enjoy benefits and privileges of employment equal to those available to other employees.

It is a violation of the ADA to fail to provide reasonable accommodation to the known physical or mental limitations of a qualified individual with a disability, unless to do so would impose an undue hardship on the operation of your business. Undue hardship means that the accommodation would require significant difficulty or expense.

What is the Best Way to Identify a Reasonable Accommodation?

Frequently, when a qualified individual with a disability requests a reasonable accommodation, the appropriate accommodation is obvious. The individual may suggest a reasonable accommodation based upon her own life or work experience. However, when the appropriate accommodation is not readily apparent, you must make a reasonable effort to identify one. The best way to do this is to consult informally with the applicant or employee about potential accommodations that would enable the individual to participate in the application process or perform the essential functions of the job. If this consultation does not identify an appropriate accommodation, you may contact the EEOC, state or local vocational rehabilitation agencies, or state or local organizations representing or providing services to individuals with disabilities. Another resource is the Job Accommodation Network (JAN). JAN is a free consultant service that helps employers make individualized accommodations. **The telephone number is 1-800-526-7234.**

(continues)

DIRECTOR'S RESOURCE 10-2
(continued)

When Does a Reasonable Accommodation Become An Undue Hardship?

It is not necessary to provide a reasonable accommodation if doing so would cause an undue hardship. Undue hardship means that an accommodation would be unduly costly, extensive, substantial or disruptive, or would fundamentally alter the nature or operation of the business. Among the factors to be considered in determining whether an accommodation is an undue hardship are the cost of the accommodation, the employer's size, financial resources and the nature and structure of its operation.

If a particular accommodation would be an undue hardship, you must try to identify another accommodation that will not pose such a hardship. If cost causes the undue hardship, you must also consider whether funding for an accommodation is available from an outside source, such as a vocational rehabilitation agency, and if the cost of providing the accommodation can be offset by state or federal tax credits or deductions. You must also give the applicant or employee with a disability the opportunity to provide the accommodation or pay for the portion of the accommodation that constitutes an undue hardship.

Can I Require Medical Examinations or Ask Questions About an Individual's Disability?

It is unlawful to:

- ask an applicant whether she is disabled or about the nature or severity of a disability
- require the applicant to take a medical examination before making a job offer

You can ask an applicant questions about ability to perform job-related functions, as long as the questions are not phrased in terms of a disability. You can also ask an applicant to describe or to demonstrate how, with or without reasonable accommodation, the applicant will perform job-related functions.

After a job offer is made and prior to the commencement of employment duties, you may require that an applicant take a medical examination if everyone who will be working in the job category must also take the examination. You may condition the job offer on the results of the medical examination. However, if an individual is not hired because a medical examination reveals the existence of a disability, you must be able to show that the reasons for exclusion are job related and necessary for conduct of your business. You also must be able to show that there was no reasonable accommodation that would have made it possible for the individual to perform the essential job functions.

Once you have hired an applicant, you cannot require a medical examination or ask an employee questions about disability unless you can show that these requirements are job related and necessary for the conduct of your business. You may conduct voluntary medical examinations that are part of an employee health program.

The results of all medical examinations or information from inquiries about a disability must be kept confidential and maintained in separate medical files. You may provide medical information required by the state workers' compensation laws to the agencies that administer such laws.

Do Individuals Who Use Drugs Illegally Have Rights Under the ADA?

Anyone who is currently using drugs illegally is not protected by the ADA and may be denied employment or fired on the basis of such use. The ADA does not prevent employers from testing applicants or employees for current illegal drug use, or from making employment decisions based on verifiable results. A test for the illegal use of drugs is not considered a medical examination under the ADA; therefore, it is not a prohibited pre-employment medical examination and you will not have to show that the administration of the test is job related and consistent with business necessity. The ADA does not encourage, authorize or prohibit drug tests.

(continues)

DIRECTOR'S RESOURCE 10-2
(continued)

How will the ADA Be Enforced and What Are the Available Remedies?

The provisions of the ADA which prohibit job discrimination will be enforced by the U.S. Equal Employment Opportunity Commission. After July 26, 1992, individuals who believe they have been discriminated against on the basis of their disability can file a charge with the Commission at any of its offices located throughout the United States. A charge of discrimination must be filed within 180 days of the discrimination, unless there is a state or local law that also provides relief for discrimination on the basis of disability. In those cases, the complainant has 300 days to file a charge.

The Commission will investigate and initially attempt to resolve the charge through conciliation, following the same procedures used to handle charges of discrimination filed under Title VII of the Civil Rights Act of 1964. The ADA also incorporates the remedies contained in Title VII. These remedies include hiring, promotion, reinstatement, back pay, and attorneys fees. Reasonable accommodation is also available as a remedy under the ADA.

How Will EEOC Help Employers Who Want to Comply with the ADA?

The Commission believes that employers want to comply with the ADA, and that if they are given sufficient information on how to comply, they will do so voluntarily.

Accordingly, the Commission conducts an active technical assistance program to promote voluntary compliance with the ADA. This program is designed to help employers understand their responsibilities and assist people with disabilities to understand their rights and the law.

In January 1992, EEOC published a Technical Assistance Manual, providing practical application of legal requirements to specific employment activities, with a directory of resources to aid compliance. EEOC publishes other educational materials, provides training on the law for employers and for people with disabilities, and participates in meetings and training programs of other organizations. EEOC staff also will respond to individual requests for information and assistance. The Commission's technical assistance program is separate and distinct from its enforcement responsibilities. Employers who seek information or assistance from the Commission will not be subject to any enforcement action because of such inquiries.

The Commission also recognizes that differences and disputes about the ADA requirements may arise between employers and people with disabilities as a result of misunderstandings. Such disputes frequently can be resolved more effectively through informal negotiation or mediation procedures, rather than through the formal enforcement process of the ADA. Accordingly, EEOC will encourage efforts to settle such differences through alternative dispute resolution, providing that such efforts do not deprive any individual of legal rights provided by the statute.

(continues)

DIRECTOR'S RESOURCE 10-2
(continued)

The ADA: Questions and Answers

For More Information

For more specific information about ADA requirements affecting Public Services and Public Accommodations contact:

Office on the Americans with Disabilities Act
Civil Rights Division
U.S. Department of Justice
P.O. Box 66118
Washington, DC 20035-6118
(202) 514-0301 (Voice)
(202) 514-0383 (TDD)

For more specific information about ADA requirements affecting employment contact:

Equal Employment Opportunity Commission
1801 L Street NW
Washington, DC 20507
(800) 669-4000 (Voice), (800) 669-6820 (TDD)
(202) 663-4900 (Voice, for 202 Area Code)
(202) 663-4494 (TDD, for 202 Area Code)

For more specific information about ADA requirements affecting transportation contact:

Department of Transportation
400 Seventh Street SW
Washington, DC 20590
(202) 366-9305 (Voice)
(202) 755-7687 (TDD)

For more specific information about ADA requirements affecting public accommodations and state and local government services contact:

Department of Justice
Office on the Americans with Disabilities Act
Civil Rights Division
P.O. Box 66118
Washington, DC 20035-6118
(202) 514-0301 (Voice)
(202) 514-0381 (TDD)
(202) 514-0383 (TDD)

(continues)

DIRECTOR'S RESOURCE 10-2
(continued)

For more specific information about requirements for accessible design in new construction and alterations contact:

**Architectural and Transportation Barriers
Compliance Board**
1111 18th Street NW
Suite 501
Washington, DC 20036
800-USA-ABLE
800-USA-ABLE (TDD)

For more specific information about ADA requirements affecting transportation contact:

Department of Transportation
400 Seventh Street SW
Washington, DC 20590
(202) 366-9305
(202) 755-7687 (TDD)

For more specific information about ADA requirements for telecommunications contact:

Federal Communications Commission
1919 M Street NW
Washington, DC 20554
(202) 634-1837
(202) 632-1836 (TDD)

For more specific information about federal disability-related tax credits and deductions for business contact:

**Internal Revenue Service
Department of the Treasury**
1111 Constitution Avenue NW
Washington, DC 20044
(202) 566-2000

This booklet is available in Braille, large print, audiotape and electronic file on computer disk. To obtain accessible formats call the Office of Equal Employment Opportunity on (202) 663-4395 (voice) or (202) 663-4399 (TDD), or write to this office at 1801 L Street NW, Washington, DC 20507.

DIRECTOR'S RESOURCE 10-3

EQUAL EMPLOYMENT OPPORTUNITY COMMISSION (EEOC) QUESTIONS AND FACTS

The U.S. Equal Employment Opportunity Commission

Facts About Age Discrimination

The Age Discrimination in Employment Act of 1967 (ADEA) protects individuals who are 40 years of age or older from employment discrimination based on age. The ADEA's protections apply to both employees and job applicants. Under the ADEA, it is unlawful to discriminate against a person because of his/her age with respect to any term, condition, or privilege of employment—including, but not limited to, hiring, firing, promotion, layoff, compensation, benefits, job assignments, and training.

It is also unlawful to retaliate against an individual for opposing employment practices that discriminate based on age or for filing an age discrimination charge, testifying, or participating in any way in an investigation, proceeding, or litigation under the ADEA.

The ADEA applies to employers with 20 or more employees, including state and local governments. It also applies to employment agencies and to labor organizations, as well as to the federal government.

APPRENTICESHIP PROGRAMS
It is generally unlawful for apprenticeship programs, including joint labor-management apprenticeship programs, to discriminate on the basis of an individual's age. Age limitations in apprenticeship programs are valid only if they fall within certain specific exceptions under the ADEA or if the EEOC grants a specific exemption.

JOB NOTICES
AND ADVERTISEMENTS
The ADEA makes it unlawful to include age preferences, limitations, or specifications in job notices or advertisements. As a narrow exception to that general rule, a job notice or advertisement may specify an age limit in the rare circumstances where age is shown to be a "bona fide occupational qualification" (BFOQ) reasonably necessary to the essence of the business.

PRE-EMPLOYMENT INQUIRIES
The ADEA does not specifically prohibit an employer from asking an applicant's age or date of birth. However, because such inquiries may deter older workers from applying for employment or may otherwise indicate possible intent to discriminate based on age, requests for age information will be closely scrutinized to make sure that the inquiry was made for a lawful purpose, rather than for a purpose prohibited by the ADEA.

BENEFITS
The Older Workers Benefit Protection Act of 1990 (OWBPA) amended the ADEA to specifically prohibit employers from denying benefits to older employees. An employer may reduce benefits based on age only if the cost of providing the reduced benefits to older workers is the same as the cost of providing benefits to younger workers.

(continues)

DIRECTOR'S RESOURCE 10-3
(continued)

WAIVERS OF ADEA RIGHTS

At an employer's request, an individual may agree to waive his/her rights or claims under the ADEA. However, the ADEA, as amended by OWBPA, sets out specific minimum standards that must be met in order for a waiver to be considered knowing and voluntary and, therefore, valid. Among other requirements, a valid ADEA waiver: (1) must be in writing and be understandable; (2) must specifically refer to ADEA rights or claims; (3) may not waive rights or claims that may arise in the future; (4) must be in exchange for valuable consideration; (5) must advise the individual in writing to consult an attorney before signing the waiver; and (6) must provide the individual at least 21 days to consider the agreement and at least 7 days to revoke the agreement after signing it. In addition, if an employer requests an ADEA waiver in connection with an exit incentive program or other employment termination program, the minimum requirements for a valid waiver are more extensive.

Facts About National Origin Discrimination

Title VII of the Civil Rights Act of 1964 protects individuals against employment discrimination on the basis of national origin as well as race, color, religion, and sex.

It is unlawful to discriminate against any employee or applicant because of the individual's national origin. No one can be denied equal employment opportunity because of birthplace, ancestry, culture, or linguistic characteristics common to a specific ethnic group. Equal employment opportunity cannot be denied because of marriage or association with persons of a national origin group; membership or association with specific ethnic promotion groups; attendance or participation in schools, churches, temples or mosques generally associated with a national origin group; or a surname associated with a national origin group.

SPEAK-ENGLISH-ONLY RULE

A rule requiring employees to speak only English at all times on the job may violate Title VII, unless an employer shows it is necessary for conducting business. If an employer believes the English-only rule is critical for business purposes, employees have to be told when they must speak English and the consequences for violating the rule. Any negative employment decision based on breaking the English-only rule will be considered evidence of discrimination if the employer did not tell employees of the rule.

ACCENT

An employer must show a legitimate nondiscriminatory reason for the denial of employment opportunity because of an individual's accent or manner of speaking. Investigations will focus on the qualifications of the person and whether his or her accent or manner of speaking had a detrimental effect on job performance. Requiring employees or applicants to be fluent in English may violate Title VII if the rule is adopted to exclude individuals of a particular national origin and is not related to job performance.

HARASSMENT

Harassment on the basis of national origin is a violation of Title VII. An ethnic slur or other verbal or physical conduct because of an individual's nationality constitutes harassment if it creates an intimidating, hostile or offensive working environment, unreasonably interferes with work performance or negatively affects an individual's employment opportunities.

(continues)

DIRECTOR'S RESOURCE 10-3
(continued)

Employers have a responsibility to maintain a workplace free of national origin harassment. Employers may be responsible for any on-the-job harassment by their agents and supervisory employees, regardless of whether the acts were authorized or specifically forbidden by the employer. Under certain circumstances, an employer may be responsible for the acts of non-employees who harass their employees at work.

IMMIGRATION-RELATED PRACTICES WHICH MAY BE DISCRIMINATORY

The Immigration Reform and Control Act of 1986 (IRCA) requires employers to prove all employees hired after November 6, 1986, are legally authorized to work in the United States. IRCA also prohibits discrimination based on national origin or citizenship. An employer who singles out individuals of a particular national origin or individuals who appear to be foreign to provide employment verification may have violated both IRCA and Title VII. Employers who impose citizenship requirements or give preference to U.S. citizens in hiring or employment opportunities may have violated IRCA, unless these are legal or contractual requirements for particular jobs. Employers also may have violated Title VII if a requirement or preference has the purpose or effect of discriminating against individuals of a particular national origin.

Facts About Pregnancy Discrimination

The Pregnancy Discrimination Act is an amendment to *Title VII of the Civil Rights Act of 1964.* Discrimination on the basis of pregnancy, childbirth or related medical conditions constitutes unlawful sex discrimination under Title VII. Women affected by pregnancy or related conditions must be treated in the same manner as other applicants or employees with similar abilities or limitations.

HIRING

An employer cannot refuse to hire a woman because of her pregnancy related condition as long as she is able to perform the major functions of her job. An employer cannot refuse to hire her because of its prejudices against pregnant workers or the prejudices of co-workers, clients or customers.

PREGNANCY AND MATERNITY LEAVE

An employer may not single out pregnancy related conditions for special procedures to determine an employee's ability to work. However, an employer may use any procedure used to screen other employees' ability to work. For example, if an employer requires its employees to submit a doctor's statement concerning their inability to work before granting leave or paying sick benefits, the employer may require employees affected by pregnancy related conditions to submit such statements.

If an employee is temporarily unable to perform her job due to pregnancy, the employer must treat her the same as any other temporarily disabled employee; for example, by providing modified tasks, alternative assignments, disability leave or leave without pay.

Pregnant employees must be permitted to work as long as they are able to perform their jobs. If an employee has been absent from work as a result of a pregnancy related condition and recovers, her employer may not require her to remain on leave until the baby's birth. An employer may not have a rule which prohibits an employee from returning to work for a predetermined length of time after childbirth.

Employers must hold open a job for a pregnancy related absence the same length of time jobs are held open for employees on sick or disability leave.

(continues)

DIRECTOR'S RESOURCE 10-3
(continued)

HEALTH INSURANCE

Any health insurance provided by an employer must cover expenses for pregnancy related conditions on the same basis as costs for other medical conditions. Health insurance for expenses arising from abortion is not required, except where the life of the mother is endangered.

Pregnancy related expenses should be reimbursed exactly as those incurred for other medical conditions, whether payment is on a fixed basis or a percentage of reasonable and customary charge basis.

The amounts payable by the insurance provider can be limited only to the same extent as costs for other conditions. No additional, increased or larger deductible can be imposed.

If a health insurance plan excludes benefit payments for pre-existing conditions when the insured's coverage becomes effective, benefits can be denied for medical costs arising from an existing pregnancy.

Employers must provide the same level of health benefits for spouses of male employees as they do for spouses of female employees.

FRINGE BENEFITS

Pregnancy related benefits cannot be limited to married employees. In an all-female workforce or job classification, benefits must be provided for pregnancy related conditions if benefits are provided for other medical conditions.

If an employer provides any benefits to workers on leave, the employer must provide the same benefits for those on leave for pregnancy related conditions.

Employees with pregnancy related disabilities must be treated the same as other temporarily disabled employees for accrual and crediting of seniority, vacation calculation, pay increases and temporary disability benefits.

Facts About Religious Discrimination

Title VII of the Civil Rights Act of 1964 prohibits employers from discriminating against individuals because of their religion in hiring, firing, and other terms and conditions of employment. The Act also requires employers to reasonably accommodate the religious practices of an employee or prospective employee, unless to do so would create an undue hardship upon the employer (see also 29 CFR 1605). Flexible scheduling, voluntary substitutions or swaps, job reassignments and lateral transfers are examples of accommodating an employee's religious beliefs.

Employers cannot schedule examinations or other selection activities in conflict with a current or prospective employee's religious needs, inquire about an applicant's future availability at certain times, maintain a restrictive dress code, or refuse to allow observance of a Sabbath or religious holiday, unless the employer can prove that not doing so would cause an undue hardship.

An employer can claim undue hardship when accommodating an employee's religious practices if allowing such practices requires more than ordinary administrative costs. Undue hardship also may be shown if changing a bona fide seniority system to accommodate one employee's religious practices denies another employee the job or shift preference guaranteed by the seniority system.

An employee whose religious practices prohibit payment of union dues to a labor organization cannot be required to pay the dues, but may pay an equal sum to a charitable organization.

Mandatory "new age" training programs, designed to improve employee motivation, cooperation or productivity through meditation, yoga, biofeedback or other practices, may conflict with the nondiscriminatory provisions of Title VII. Employers must accommodate any employee who gives notice that these programs are inconsistent with the employee's religious beliefs, whether or not the employer believes there is a religious basis for the employee's objection.

DIRECTOR'S RESOURCE 10-4

INTERVIEW QUESTIONS

(In the interest of time and to ensure fairness, consider choosing four or five questions that are particularly applicable to your program to ask of all candidates. Ask additional questions as time allows.)

Degreed Candidate

1. Tell us about your past experiences in this field—both your previous work experience and/or your practicum placements.

2. Of all the theories and ideas you studied in school, what had the greatest impact on you with regards to discipline in the classroom?

3. How do you think children learn? Give an example of how you would set up an experience for learning about a simple machine like an inclined plane or a pulley.

4. What would you do when an irate parent approaches you about an incident (such as biting in the classroom)? How would you handle that?

5. How would you handle problem solving in the classroom? For example, if two children are arguing over a basket of Lego® blocks, each saying she had it first, what would you do?

6. Choose an area of the curriculum (e.g., science, math, music, etc.). Tell us how you would set it up.

7. How do you view your role as a preschool teacher?

8. What would you strive for in a parent/caregiver relationship?

9. What do you see as strong points in our program? Weak points?

10. How do you feel about themes when planning a curriculum?

11. How do you feel separation issues should be handled? For example, a child comes in with a special toy from home, and he is very reluctant to have Mom leave him. How might you handle that situation?

12. What are your long-term professional goals?

13. Since consistency is important in every program, how do you feel about committing to one year here?

Nondegreed Candidate

1. Tell us about your experience in the field of early childhood education, as well as any other work experience you have had.

2. What do you see as your particular strengths that would apply to a position like this?

(continues)

DIRECTOR'S RESOURCE 10-4
(continued)

3. What are your professional goals? Would you be willing to attend some training sessions in the fall?

4. How would you handle an irate parent who approaches you at the end of the day when the teacher has gone?

5. If two children are arguing over Legos, each saying she had them first, what would you do?

6. What do you see as your role in the classroom?

7. What do you think the purpose of child care should be?

8. How would you handle a situation where a child has just knocked down another child's block building?

9. How do you think discipline is different from punishment?

10. What did you see during your tour of our center that you particularly liked? What were some of your questions as you toured the classroom?

11. What special skills and abilities do you feel you can bring to our program?

*Adapted and used with permission from CELC-Cincinnati, OH.

Second Interview

Select three or four questions that seem appropriate for the candidate being interviewed.

1. What was the parenting style of the person who cared for you (mother, father, other)?

2. Do you think babies can be spoiled? How?

3. How can you help a child (baby, toddler, preschooler) who cries when his parent leaves in the morning?

4. How would you handle a situation when two children (toddlers, preschoolers) are holding the same toy and both are shouting, "mine?"

5. What is your favorite book to read to children?

6. What was the last book you read for your own information or pleasure?

7. What did you like best (least) about the last job you had?

8. What are some things you might talk about when a parent comes to pick up a child at the end of the day and asks, "How was my child's day?"

DIRECTOR'S RESOURCE 10-5

SAMPLE STAFFING PLAN–INFANT PROGRAM

The sample staffing schedule offered here can be used to staff a small program or an individual class in a larger program. Guidelines for its use in programs with varying numbers of children follow. This schedule assumes a 1:3 adult-child ratio, for twelve infants.

Schedule for One Classroom of 12 Infants

B = paid rest break of 15 minutes　　　　　　　　　　**Lunch = unpaid lunch break of 30 minutes**
　= 15-minute intervals (i.e., 8:15, 8:30, 8:45)

	7:30	8	9	10	11	12	1	2	3	4	5	6
Assistant A (6 hrs; 7:30–2)				B		Lunch						
Assistant B (6 hrs; 7:30–2)				B			Lunch					
Assistant C (8 hrs; 8:30–5)					B			Lunch		B		
Teacher* (8 hrs; 9–5:30)					B			Lunch		B		
Assistant D (6 hrs; 11:30–6)								Lunch		B		
Assistant E (4 hrs; 2–6)										B		

*These 8 teacher hours may be covered by more than one qualified teacher.
Note: This schedule shows child care staff only. Hours for administration and housekeeper or other maintenance personnel are not included.

From "Staffing Schedules," by L. Gordon, 1996. In Setting Up for Infant Care: Guidelines for Centers and Family Child Care Homes, *(p. 50), A. Godwin and L. Schrag, (Eds.), Washington, DC: NAEYC. Reprinted with permission from NAEYC.*

DIRECTOR'S RESOURCE 10-6

SAMPLE STAFFING PLAN–MULTIPLE PROGRAM B

Staff Plan by Staff Member

Title	How Many	Schedule	Recommended Salary	Total Yearly
Director/Administrator	1	MWF 7:30am–TTH 12:00pm	$11.00/hr $22,880/yr	$22,880
Head Teachers	5	7:30–3:00pm 30-min break between 12:00–1:30pm	$8.50/hr $17,680/yr	$88,400
Teachers	5	11:00–7:00pm 30-min. break between 1:00–2:30pm	$7.00/hr $14,560/yr	$72,800
Morning Assistants	5	7:30–12:30pm 15-min. break between 11:00–12:00pm	$5.00/hr $6,500/yr	$32,500
Afternoon Assistants	5	12:30–7:00pm 15-min. break between 2:30–3:00pm	$5.00/hr $8,450/yr	$42,250
Secretary/Bookkeeper	1	9:00–5:30 1-hr. lunch	$6.00/hr $10,400/yr	$12,480
Custodian	1	5:00–10:00pm Mon.–Thur. 5 hrs. on Sat. 15-min. break	$5.00/hr $6,500/yr	$6,500
Cook	1	7:30–3:00pm 30-min. lunch	$5.00/hr $10,400/yr	$10,400
Total Yearly Salaries:				$288,210

(continues)

DIRECTOR'S RESOURCE 10-6
(continued)

STAFF PLAN BY CLASSROOM

Classroom	No. of Children	Staff/Child Ratio
Infants Rm: 101	8	required: 5:1 maximum: 8:3 minimum: 8:2
Toddlers Rm: 201	11	required: 7:1 maximum: 11:3 minimum: 11:2
3-Year-olds Rm: 202	17	required: 12:1 maximum: 17:3 minimum: 17:2
3- and 4-Year-olds Rm: 203	17	required: 12:1 maximum: 17:3 minimum: 17:2
4-Year-olds Rm: 204	17	required: 14:1 maximum: 14:3 minimum: 14:2

Each classroom will be staffed as follows:

1 Head Teacher	7:30–3:00pm
1 Teacher	11:00–7:00pm
1 Assistant	7:30–12:30pm
1 Assistant	12:30–7:00pm

This flexible schedule allows ample time for classroom planning in the morning and evening when the ratios will be low because most children arrive at the center between 8:00–9:00 am and leave between 5:00–6:00 pm. Nap time is when team planning and communication takes place.

(continues)

DIRECTOR'S RESOURCE 10-6
(continued)

ADDITIONAL COMMENTS ABOUT STAFFING

- Breaks must maintain staff-to-child ratio at all times.
- Flexibility in scheduling breaks is necessary to meet the immediate needs of the classrooms.
- Short restroom breaks or emergency phone calls could be arranged as needed, as long as ratio is maintained.
- Staff schedules are designed for enhancing staff communications and for meeting the needs of the children.
- Swing scheduling for directors is designed to encourage and maintain communication with all staff members, family members, board, and community contacts.
- It is the teacher's responsibility to take care of housekeeping emergencies during the day.
- The cook is solely responsible for cleaning the kitchen, other than the cleanup after the afternoon snack, which is the teacher's responsibility.
- One morning snack, one afternoon snack, and one full meal will be provided each day.
- Encourage male applicants for all positions to balance male–female models.
- Parent(s)/surrogate(s) provide transportation.
- Tuition is $95/week for infants and $85/week for all others.
- Eighty percent of tuition income goes for salaries.

DIRECTOR'S RESOURCE 10-7

JOB DESCRIPTION—PRESCHOOL TEACHER

Description:

The Teacher is a member of the teaching team who shares responsibility with the Lead Teacher for the care and education of an assigned group of children. The Teacher is responsible for implementing curriculum, supervising children, communicating with parents, and providing a healthy and safe environment for children.

Accountability: The Teacher reports to the Education Coordinator.

Minimum Qualifications:

Successful completion of 30 semester hours of college coursework, including or supplemented by 12 semester hours of credit in child development or early childhood education or the completion of a training program to acquire the CDA or CCP credential.

Responsibilities:

To establish and maintain a safe and healthy learning environment

1. Designs appropriate room arrangement to support the goals of the classroom
2. Plans and implements a nutritious snack program
3. Promotes healthy eating practices
4. Maintains a safe environment
5. Posts necessary information to ensure the safety and well-being of the children
6. Maintains an orderly learning environment

To advance physical and intellectual competence

1. Provides a balance between child-initiated and teacher-initiated activities
2. Provides a balance between quiet and active learning activities
3. Uses equipment and materials for indoor and outdoor play that promote children's physical development
4. Involves children in planning and implementing learning activities
5. Provides an integrated curriculum that meets the needs of individual children
6. Plans and implements experiences that promote language and literacy development
7. Plans and implements activities that promote the acquisition of number concepts

To support social and emotional development and provide positive guidance

1. Plans and implements hands-on activities that develop positive self-esteem
2. Plans and implements hands-on activities that develop social skills
3. Plans and implements culturally diverse experiences
4. Uses and promotes positive guidance techniques
5. Provides a wide variety of creative and expressive activities
6. Establishes routines with smooth transition periods
7. Communicates with children at their developmental level
8. Encourages children to be independent

(continues)

DIRECTOR'S RESOURCE 10-7
(continued)

To establish positive and productive relationships with families

1. Relates assessment information to parents and offers support for dealing with children at different developmental stages
2. Plans and conducts home visits
3. Promotes communication with parents through weekly progress notes, a monthly newsletter, and semi-annual parent conferences
4. Provides a variety of ways that families can participate in the program
5. Encourages parents to participate in the program

To ensure a well-run, purposeful program responsive to participant needs

1. Assesses program supplies and materials needed prior to implementing activities
2. Coordinates and helps supervise aides and volunteers working in the classroom
3. Maintains written plans on a weekly basis
4. Assesses children's needs and developmental progress on an ongoing basis
5. Uses the results of assessment to plan activities

To maintain a commitment to professionalism

1. Promotes the center's philosophy and educational objectives
2. Supports the center's code of ethical conduct
3. Engages in ongoing staff development to improve personal and professional skills
4. Supports the professional growth and development of colleagues by sharing materials and information and providing helpful feedback and encouragement
5. Attends staff meetings, workshops, and in-service training provided by the center

Personal Qualities:

Must be physically able to perform the job of a preschool teacher. Must have a warm, supportive attitude toward children. Must be reliable. Must be flexible in receiving assignments or adapting to changes in the program. Must be willing to accept supervision in order to improve work performance. Must be willing to perform other duties as required.

From Blueprint for Action: Achieving Center-Based Change through Staff Development (Rev. Ed.), *by P. J. Bloom, M. Sheerer and J. Britz, 2005. Lake Forest, IL. New Horizons. Reprinted with permission.*

DIRECTOR'S RESOURCE 10-8

ANNUAL PERFORMANCE EVALUATION
JOB-SPECIFIC STANDARDS EVALUATION
(60% OF TOTAL RATING)
(Required for all non-management employees)

Employee Name: _____ Position: _____ **Lead Teacher** _____

Performance Standard	4	3	2	1	0
1. Has a high level of knowledge of early childhood and maintains up-to-date professional knowledge through attendance at continuing education activities, including state-required courses.					
2. Maintains confidentiality with parents, children, and staff members and treats them with respect.					
3. Serves as an ethical and professional model; follows and promotes OAEYC Code of Ethics and Children's for Children's philosophies.					
4. Provides constructive feedback to classroom teachers; provides feedback to master teacher for immediate co-workers' evaluations.					
5. Maintains knowledge of and compliance with accreditation standards and city and state licensing.					
6. Prepares meaningful daily reports/journals and reviews those of classroom teachers; is responsible for the preparation of insightful progress reports and solicits input from classroom teachers; submits all progress reports to master teacher for review; conducts parent conferences twice a year; prepares monthly classroom newsletter.					
7. Understands and articulates childhood developmental stages and the concept of learning in children's play.					
8. Plans developmentally appropriate (individual and group) activities that are success-oriented and open-ended in relevant curriculum areas (art, dramatic play, music, blocks, sensory, science, manipulatives, language, math, and gross/fine motor); encourages classroom teachers to plan as well; submits lesson plans to master teacher for review.					
9. Integrates family traditions and cultural practices in the classroom; promotes diversity in the classroom; respects parents' requests and individual children's rhythms and tempos.					
10. Uses developmentally appropriate techniques for guiding children's behavior, such as redirection, verbalizing feelings, and encouraging problem solving; sets consistent limits to help children develop inner control.					
11. Respects and accepts all children, including those with special needs; seeks resources in the community and gathers written information on individual children's special needs; communicates with parents and staff in a nonjudgmental, sensitive, and confidential manner in regards to the special need.					

(continues)

DIRECTOR'S RESOURCE 10-8
(continued)

Performance Standard	4	3	2	1	0
12. Addresses children by name, speaks to them at their eye level, and walks over to the child to speak; uses appropriate voice and body language.					
13. Plans smooth transitions for children's moves to new classrooms and transitions throughout the day.					
14. Facilitates the orientation of new families and children. Prepares updated Welcome Packet, orients child and family to classroom and seeks family history and child-specific information.					
15. Initiates meetings with master teacher and communicates effectively with master teacher; approaches constructive criticism and feedback with a positive attitude and as a learning opportunity.					
16. Is viewed as approachable by parents and staff and assumes responsibility for positive problem solving with parents, staff, and supervisors.					
17. Communicates in a constructive way (verbal or written); avoids gossip.					
18. Conducts regular meetings with classroom staff that create systems for reflection and peer collaboration.					
19. Guides, mentors, and welcomes Teacher I's, Teacher II's, and student teachers; helps foster an understanding of developmentally appropriate practice; conducts classroom orientation with new staff.					
20. Demonstrates and models flexibility in meeting program needs (i.e. changes schedule to orient new staff, works in other classrooms when requested, accommodates parents' schedules); seeks approval from supervisor for overtime.					
21. Is willing to take initiatives and risks and to make mistakes in order to learn; continually evaluates new initiatives.					
22. Maintains communication with Business Director regarding classroom budgets; contributes suggestions for replacement and enhancement materials for budget preparation; oversees petty cash and minor equipment expenditures.					
Totals					

(continues)

DIRECTOR'S RESOURCE 10-8
(continued)

POSITION DESCRIPTION

POSITION TITLE: Lead Teacher

DEPARTMENT: Child Care (Children's For Children)

ORGANIZATIONAL RELATIONSHIPS: Procter & Gamble

SUPERVISOR'S TITLE: Manager or Master Teacher

COLLABORATIVE RELATIONSHIPS: Kindergarten Teacher, Kindergarten Assistant, Director, Cook, Service Coordinator II, Site Manager, Clerk, Business Manager

TITLES SUPERVISED: Teacher I and Teacher II (indirect)

TOTAL NUMBER OF FTE's DIRECTLY OR INDIRECTLY SUPERVISED: 6 (indirect)

PURPOSE OF POSITION: To plan and implement age-appropriate programming for a Child Care Center dedicated to the care of infants and children and to mentor colleagues.

MAJOR DUTIES AND RESPONSIBILITIES:

1. Maintain positive relationship with parents and co-workers.
2. Provide supervision and coaching to Teacher I and Teacher II and volunteers. Review and provide feedback to Teacher I and Teacher II on all written communications and prepared materials, checking for accuracy and content. Contribute to probationary and annual reviews.
3. Assume immediate responsibility for children in assigned group; maintain hygiene and safety of assigned children.
4. Plan and implement age-appropriate programs which address individual, small and large group needs. Provide related activities and growth opportunities in language, art, music, science, math and gross and fine motor movement. Assure activities are safe and success-oriented.
5. Create appropriate learning environment. Create teacher-made materials.
6. Follow oral and/or written instructions of parents and center administrators.
7. Prepare daily reports for parents regarding child. Design meaningful report format.
8. Assess each child's development; plan individual activities based on assessments.
9. Post written lesson plans for parental review. Design format which incorporates art, music, literature, dramatic play, math, science. Submit plan to supervisor.
10. Attend scheduled in-service training and maintain updated knowledge of current issues and studies related to early childhood education. Develop training as requested.
11. Conduct parent-teacher conferences a minimum of 2 times annually.
12. Report problems and concerns to Manager and/or Master Teacher.
13. Maintain orderliness of classroom area(s) and shared areas.
14. Serve as educational resource to parents, coworkers and the larger community.
15. Contribute to Child Care department newsletter.
16. Prepare classroom orientation packets prior to a family's first day. Orient families to classroom procedures.
17. Provide leadership to center sponsored events, projects and committees.

(continues)

DIRECTOR'S RESOURCE 10-8
(continued)

18. Conduct total staff meetings twice a year. Attend staff meetings.

19. Lead tours on request.

20. Contribute to equipment budget requests, select equipment for purchase, maintain petty cash allocation.

21. Respect patient rights for informed consent and the handling of confidential information as defined by CHMC's mission and applicable laws and regulations. Review timeliness, accuracy, availability and security of information.

22. Provide services in a manner to be regularly and conveniently available to meet the needs of user, families as determined by department management and CHMC's governing body.

23. Develop knowledge and professional skills through cross-training, literature and attendance at department meetings. Attend center required training.

24. Participate in improving organizational performance through recommending areas or approaches for improvement activities, performing new procedures, collecting data and providing input to department discussions.

25. Ensure that work areas are organized and present a safe, accessible, effective and efficient environment for employees, patients and families. Comply with Infection Control policies and procedures.

26. Participate in establishing job requirements and goals; perform duties at the desired level of competency.

27. Maintain knowledge of and compliance with code of ethics established by Ohio Association for the Education of Young Children. Maintain knowledge of and compliance with city and state regulations governing Child Care Programs.

28. Perform other duties as assigned.

REQUIRED SKILLS: Excellent verbal, written and interpersonal communication skills. Capable of relating to diverse age and demographic backgrounds. Physical ability sufficient to frequently bend, stoop and lift up to 50 pounds. Possess sound knowledge of the procedures and regulations specific to the care and education of infants and children. Possess a willingness to learn necessary skills and knowledge and to strive for continuous improvement. Demonstrate diplomacy, tact and professional demeanor.

EDUCATION/WORK EXPERIENCE: Associate's Degree in Early Childhood Education or equivalent and current certification in first aid, recognizing child abuse and recognition of common childhood diseases required; Bachelor's Degree preferred. Minimum 2 years experience as a teacher. Professional level knowledge of educational theory, child development and teaching skills.

_____	_____
DATE	DIRECTOR/MANAGER
_____	_____
DATE	HUMAN RESOURCES

Reprinted with permission from Children's for Children *at Cincinnati Children's Hospital.*

DIRECTOR'S RESOURCE 10-9

U.S. Department of Justice
Immigration and Naturalization Service

OMB No. 1115-0136

Employment Eligibility Verification

Please read instructions carefully before completing this form. The instructions must be available during completion of this form. **ANTI-DISCRIMINATION NOTICE:** It is illegal to discriminate against work eligible individuals. Employers CANNOT specify which document(s) they will accept from an employee. The refusal to hire an individual because of a future expiration date may also constitute illegal discrimination.

Section 1. Employee Information and Verification. To be completed and signed by employee at the time employment begins.

Print Name: Last	First	Middle Initial	Maiden Name

Address (Street Name and Number)	Apt. #	Date of Birth (month/day/year)

City	State	Zip Code	Social Security #

I am aware that federal law provides for imprisonment and/or fines for false statements or use of false documents in connection with the completion of this form.

I attest, under penalty of perjury, that I am (check one of the following):
☐ A citizen or national of the United States
☐ A Lawful Permanent Resident (Alien # A
☐ An alien authorized to work until ___/___/___
(Alien # or Admission #)

Employee's Signature	Date (month/day/year)

Preparer and/or Translator Certification.   *(To be completed and signed if Section 1 is prepared by a person other than the employee.) I attest, under penalty of perjury, that I have assisted in the completion of this form and that to the best of my knowledge the information is true and correct.*

Preparer's/Translator's Signature	Print Name

Address (Street Name and Number, City, State, Zip Code)	Date (month/day/year)

Section 2. Employer Review and Verification. To be completed and signed by employer. Examine one document from List A OR examine one document from List B and one from List C, as listed on the reverse of this form, and record the title, number and expiration date, if any, of the document(s)

	List A	OR	List B	AND	List C
Document title:	_____		_____		_____
Issuing authority:	_____		_____		_____
Document #:	_____		_____		_____
Expiration Date (if any):	___/___/___		___/___/___		___/___/___
Document #:	_____				
Expiration Date (if any):	___/___/___				

CERTIFICATION - I attest, under penalty of perjury, that I have examined the document(s) presented by the above-named employee, that the above-listed document(s) appear to be genuine and to relate to the employee named, that the employee began employment on *(month/day/year)* ___/___/___ **and that to the best of my knowledge the employee is eligible to work in the United States. (State employment agencies may omit the date the employee began employment.)**

Signature of Employer or Authorized Representative	Print Name	Title

Business or Organization Name	Address (Street Name and Number, City, State, Zip Code)	Date (month/day/year)

Section 3. Updating and Reverification. To be completed and signed by employer.

A. New Name (if applicable)	B. Date of rehire (month/day/year) (if applicable)

C. If employee's previous grant of work authorization has expired, provide the information below for the document that establishes current employment eligibility.

Document Title:_____   Document #: _____   Expiration Date (if any): ___/___/___

I attest, under penalty of perjury, that to the best of my knowledge, this employee is eligible to work in the United States, and if the employee presented document(s), the document(s) I have examined appear to be genuine and to relate to the individual.

Signature of Employer or Authorized Representative	Date (month/day/year)

Form I-9 (Rev. 11-21-91)N Page 2

(continues)

DIRECTOR'S RESOURCE 10-9
(continued)

LISTS OF ACCEPTABLE DOCUMENTS

LIST A		LIST B		LIST C
Documents that Establish Both Identity and Employment Eligibility	**OR**	**Documents that Establish Identity**	**AND**	**Documents that Establish Employment Eligibility**

LIST A — Documents that Establish Both Identity and Employment Eligibility

1. U.S. Passport (unexpired or expired)

2. Certificate of U.S. Citizenship *(INS Form N-560 or N-561)*

3. Certificate of Naturalization *(INS Form N-550 or N-570)*

4. Unexpired foreign passport, with *I-551 stamp or* attached INS Form I-94 indicating unexpired employment authorization

5. Permanent Resident Card or Alien Registration Receipt Card with photograph *(INS Form I-151 or I-551)*

6. Unexpired Temporary Resident Card *(INS Form I-688)*

7. Unexpired Employment Authorization Card *(INS Form I-688A)*

8. Unexpired Reentry Permit *(INS Form I-327)*

9. Unexpired Refugee Travel Document *(INS Form I-571)*

10. Unexpired Employment Authorization Document issued by the INS which contains a photograph *(INS Form I-688B)*

LIST B — Documents that Establish Identity

1. Driver's license or ID card issued by a state or outlying possession of the United States provided it contains a photograph or information such as name, date of birth, gender, height, eye color and address

2. ID card issued by federal, state or local government agencies or entities, provided it contains a photograph or information such as name, date of birth, gender, height, eye color and address

3. School ID card with a photograph

4. Voter's registration card

5. U.S. Military card or draft record

6. Military dependent's ID card

7. U.S. Coast Guard Merchant Mariner Card

8. Native American tribal document

9. Driver's license issued by a Canadian government authority

For persons under age 18 who are unable to present a document listed above:

10. School record or report card

11. Clinic, doctor or hospital record

12. Day-care or nursery school record

LIST C — Documents that Establish Employment Eligibility

1. U.S. social security card issued by the Social Security Administration *(other than a card stating it is not valid for employment)*

2. Certification of Birth Abroad issued by the Department of State *(Form FS-545 or Form DS-1350)*

3. Original or certified copy of a birth certificate issued by a state, county, municipal authority or outlying possession of the United States bearing an official seal

4. Native American tribal document

5. U.S. Citizen ID Card *(INS Form I-197)*

6. ID Card for use of Resident Citizen in the United States *(INS Form I-179)*

7. Unexpired employment authorization document issued by the INS *(other than those listed under List A)*

Illustrations of many of these documents appear in Part 8 of the Handbook for Employers (M-274)

Form I-9 (Rev. 10/4/00)Y Page 3

REFERENCES

The Americans with Disabilities Act: Questions and answers. (1991, July). U.S. Equal Opportunity Commission, Washington, DC.

Bloom, P. J., Sheerer, M., & Britz, J. (2005). *Blueprint for action: Achieving center-based change through staff development.* Lake Forest, IL: New Horizon.

Carter, M. (1998). Principles and strategies for coaching and mentoring. In R. Neugebauer and B. Neugebauer (Eds.), *The art of leadership: Managing early childhood organizations.* Redmond, WA: CCIE.

Cohen, A. J. (1998). Bettering your odds of not getting sued. In R. Neugebauer & B. Neugebauer (Eds.), *The art of leadership: Managing early childhood organizations.* Redmond, WA: CCIE.

Greenberg, P. (1991). *Character development: Encouraging self-esteem and self-discipline in infants,* toddlers and two-year olds. Washington, DC: NAEYC.

Hamrick, J. (2000). Reduce staff turnover through effective interviewing. *Child Care Information Exchange, 134,* 26–28.

Sciarra, D. J., & Dorsey, A. G. (2002). *Leaders and supervisors in child care programs.* Clifton Park, NY: Thomson Delmar Learning.

Surr, J. (1992). *Early childhood programs and the American with disabilities act (ADA).* Young Children, Vol. 47, No. 5, p. 18.

Whitebrook, M., & Bellm, D. (1999). *Taking on turnover: An action plan for child care teachers and directors.* Washington, DC: Center for Child Care Workforce.

Additional resources for this chapter can be found on the Online Companion™ at http://www.earlychilded.delmar.com. This supplemental material includes relevant Web links, Web activities, and case studies that apply the concepts presented in this chapter. In addition, the Working Papers and Director's Resources are available for download, allowing you to complete Class Exercises and Class Assignments electronically.

CHAPTER 11

Marketing the Program and Selecting the Children

Some centers adopt a symbol to use on all brochures, ads, stationery, and newsletters.

OBJECTIVES

After reading this chapter, you should be able to:

- List items typically included in a brochure.
- Identify the types of places and materials used to market a program.
- Understand the implications of the laws pertaining to serving children with disabilities in a child care setting.

An important part of the director's job, in both new and ongoing programs, is marketing and publicizing the center. Decisions about the total population of children to be served by the center will determine the nature of the focus for marketing and the publicity that is written as well as the audience to whom it is addressed. Marketing is related to recruitment and selection of children, staff recruitment, and the center's public relations program. When your center has a good reputation, families want to be there and staff want to work there.

MARKETING

Marketing a program and publicizing a center can be done through newspaper, magazine, or journal advertising; a Web site; a listing in the Yellow Pages®; radio or television advertising; fliers or posters; and neighborhood papers or church bulletins. The director's first task is to decide where to direct the major thrust of the marketing and how the materials will look.

Where and How to Market the Program

The direction that marketing takes is based on competition in the area as well as consideration of families that need to be reached in order to recruit children and promote the program. Obviously, young families are the first to come to mind since most programs are set up to serve children from infancy to five years of age or primary school-aged children in before- and after-school programs. However, there are other considerations. If program survival depends on tuition, the target population is clearly limited to those who can afford to pay for the service. On the other hand, if outside funding sources exist, it will be necessary to increase the scope of the publicity effort so that a greater portion of the potential clientele can be reached. Whether or not the program will serve families within walking distance of the center or will draw from a broader geographical area by transporting children from rural areas, surrounding suburbs, or nearby businesses will affect the publicity effort. Likewise, the program sponsorship and program location will exert an influence in this regard. For example, sometimes program sponsors limit the population to be served to university families, poverty-level families, children of hospital personnel, children of families who are employed in a particular factory or office complex, children of club or church members, and so forth.

There will be minimal gains from marketing in an area where competing programs are limited to specific populations such as those just mentioned. Similarly, marketing will have a limited effect on families who choose a preschool program offered by an exclusive private school because that guarantees the child access to this private school's elementary school. Such a choice presents a dilemma for a center that may have provided care for these children since they were infants. Here the marketing efforts must be focused on the quality of the preschool program offered at the early childhood education center and the benefits of continuity of care. In addition, if the preschooler has younger siblings, the center can stress the advantage of having the preschooler in the same center as her siblings.

The increase in public school preschools as well as other publicly funded programs affects enrollment in early childhood education centers. Some of these publicly funded programs serve only preschool-aged children, which means some families are eligible for and choose these preschools. Because the publicly funded programs are free, even though children have been in a center since infancy, families are likely to make the choice to leave the center-based program for economic reasons, and marketing efforts directed to these families are unlikely to succeed.

All these factors and others that you may have thought about will enter into the decision about where and how to promote the program. Newspaper ads and radio announcements reach a wide audience, while a more limited population is reached through direct mailing of brochures or circulars; display of window placards; door-to-door solicitation; and advertisements in local papers, church bulletins, and military newsletters. Be sure to consider the ethnic and cultural makeup of your audience, as well as reading level and language skills, as you write and design promotional materials.

As a director, it behooves you to take advantage of opportunities to invite reporters to the center so that they can do newspaper or television pieces on your center. If you are affiliated with a large business or hospital, their public relations staff may help you. Television and newspaper reporters are interested in what is new at your center. If there is a new infant room opening or you have a new custom-designed playground, reporters and cameramen will come to you. Other newsworthy items might be a new teacher who signs for deaf children, installation of a ramp to accommodate children and adults with disabilities, or the use of senior citizen volunteers in the preschool classrooms.

Taking your message to the local lodge or church gathering, PTA groups, or community meetings where it will reach parents whose busy lives may limit the time spent reading publications or listening to radio or television is still another way to publicize the program. Taking slides, videotapes, DVDs, or a PowerPoint presentation to these meetings to show what children and teachers do in child care centers will enrich your promotional materials. Always have an ample supply of business cards to distribute to your audience.

At community events that draw parents of young children, it is often useful to arrange to have a booth where a display of photos taken at the center and promotional materials will attract families who are interested in child care. Arrange for the director or a competent staff member who can answer questions and distribute admission applications to be available at these events. This is an excellent way to reach out to the community and capitalize on an opportunity to establish a personal contact with potential clients.

It is important to get your message out to companies in the community, as well as to individuals and community groups. The first wave of companies interested in addressing the child care needs of their employees typically were attracted to setting up on-site child care centers. However, some companies are more inclined to look to existing community child care centers where they can purchase slots, buy priority status, or negotiate for corporate group rates for their employees. Developing a professional presentation that is designed for use with corporate clients and timely follow-up with appropriate contacts within the corporation will enhance your chances of attracting corporate clients (Duncan & Thornton, 1993).

It is important to consider various ways to market your program, but do not underestimate the value of "word of mouth" from parents who are enthusiastic about the quality of your program. Nothing sells better than offering a high-quality program worthy of accreditation and led by well-trained, qualified early childhood teachers.

Marketing Materials

The choice of words and the photographs used in the printed materials distributed by the center should reflect a subtle message of concern, respect, and appreciation for children and should express the philosophy behind the center's program. These materials project the image of the center and should exemplify your professionalism (Tiger, 1995).

Develop marketing materials that send a distinctive and powerful message. They must define your specialties and exactly what you offer that sets you apart from your competitors. The fundamentals of "quality care," "developmentally appropriate practice (DAP)," and "trained caring staff" are descriptive but not distinctive. Brainstorm with staff, parents, board members, and consultants about how you are different, and put down some sample statements that will tell that story in the printed materials that you develop. Examples follow:

- soft, cozy spaces in a homelike environment (use pictures if possible)
- innovative, cutting-edge social/emotional focus
- family-centered practice where we think of family/child/teacher as a unit

Find unique ways to identify your program with a logo that appears on all business cards, stationery, telephone book or newspaper ads, and so on. Use of a particular "tagline" with the logo can become your mark of distinction. In marketing circles, this is called "branding." It is something potential clients recognize and remember. Taglines give a quick and easily remembered clip of what a program is about. Examples follow:

- "Where Every Child Is Special"
- "We Strengthen Children Emotionally and Academically"
- "Child Care That Nurtures Our Future"

Keep in mind that you are endeavoring to attract the attention of the current generation of young parents, most of whom can be identified as Generation Xers. Select techniques and content for the marketing materials that appeal and entice this target generational group. For eye appeal and influence, consider:

- using color and emotion in taglines and photos
- mixing pictures and graphics (a photo of a teacher and child, a parent event, your accreditation credential)
- bulleting the benefits so there is a quick and easy way to sum up *what they will get from you*—a bit different from what you have to offer
- quoting testimonials from the current parent population

Using the talents of staff and parents to do creative marketing will help you build your enrollment.

DIRECTOR'S CORNER

"The thing we had the most success with when we opened our second center was the newspaper piece about using the 'pod' concept for our infant program. It not only helped our infant enrollment, but it helped fill all the groups in that center. That notion about the 'pod' bringing together the richness of group care and the individualized nurturance of home was very appealing—it seemed to give parents a solid idea to hold onto. It was the best public relations piece we ever had."

—Director, independent not-for-profit center

Brochures and Promotional Materials

The content and appearance of brochures or fliers make a statement to parents. The words should be informative and spell out the philosophy of the center's program; the photographs or some creative, clever artwork should convey, in less obvious ways, the fact that the staff of the center is professional and creative. It is the creative design of these materials that will attract attention, and attention is the first step to generating interest. The message for parents should be clear: any child who is sent to this center will share in the professionalism and creativity of the staff. When unsolicited letters from parents are available, using statements from those letters in brochures or publicity releases is an excellent way to get your message across. Every detail of any mailing piece to be used for initial advertising or in response to inquiries about the program should be carefully scrutinized.

The director is responsible for the preparation and the mailing of brochures, but other staff members as well as parents can contribute to the effort by providing artistic talents, access to a printer they know about, or some other expertise. When a brochure is prepared, two major considerations are cost and content.

Costs vary depending on number, length, quality of paper, use of color, and use of photographs. Therefore, it is wise to discuss ideas for the brochure with a printer as soon as possible. Costs increase when the professionally done brochure includes photos or a logo that requires artwork, but it is these unique features that may be precisely what attracts the attention of prospective clients. The distinctive logo and tagline on every promotional piece becomes a familiar identifying symbol to potential customers. Money spent on an attractive brochure may be a good investment. Using a single color on heavyweight, standard-size paper will give a look of high quality yet keep the costs down.

If the brochure is to be used over a long period of time, it is wise to avoid using items that are subject to change such as the school calendar or the fee schedule. These variable items can be detailed in a short insert. The brochure itself should contain information that remains constant from year to year. The following list includes some of the more stable items typically included in a brochure:

1. name, address, and telephone number of the center
2. a map showing location of the program
3. description of the program
4. sponsorship of the program
5. enrollment procedures and children served (ages, inclusive program, diversity, and so forth)
6. licensing and/or accreditation status of the center

It is important to include the hours, days, and months for the program. The stability of the operational schedule will determine whether such information should go into the brochure itself or be part of the insert.

Centers sell services to families who seek solutions to concerns and questions about quality child care. It is helpful to them when promotional materials cover all the services available at the center. Prospective customers, especially those with more than one child, will want to have information about availability of services such as before- and after-school care, summer programs for school-age children, care for the mildly ill child, and backup care for older children on school holidays or for the baby cared for at home when the regular caregiver is ill.

Other selling points to cover in promotional materials might be:

- accreditation by NAEYC
- parenting workshops
- the ability to borrow books from the center's lending library
- a baby-sitting referral service
- the center's Web site address to help keep potential clients up to date on all center activities
- an e-mail address to keep in touch with administrators

Keep in mind that promotional materials are designed to tell prospective families that the center offers solutions for them and is there to help and support them and their children.

Public Relations

The center's image is an important consideration in all aspects of the public information and public relations efforts. The appearance of the physical setting and the behavior of personnel in that setting are fundamental factors in creating good public relations and sound relationships with the children and with their parents. These factors are what convey professionalism and concern about children and families. The director serves as a model and encourages the staff to be mindful of their role as community advocates for children. Parents entering the building should see an interior prepared for use by children. Furthermore, parents should be greeted by a warm, caring person who expresses interest in them and in their children. A "Director's Coffee" once a month is a way to encourage parents to take a few minutes to chat before rushing off to work. When parents or others telephone the center, the person who answers must be pleasant, tactful, and knowledgeable.

An open house for parents who have made inquiries or have responded to your marketing efforts is a good way to expand the public relations program for the center. Remember to invite current parents, current staff members, and board members to these social events. An open house affords an opportunity for the staff to have an informal meeting with others who are interested in the center's activities. In the case of a new program, publicizing the open house can be part of the initial efforts at promotion. In the case of ongoing programs, staff and board members also will reap benefits from this kind of gathering, since it provides a time for interaction and communication among adults who have common concerns and share an interest in the children attending the program.

When the center is opened to visitors, the environment should be prepared just as it would be for the children. In this way, you can demonstrate how a well-planned environment should look and also provide an opportunity for parents to participate and use available materials. What better way to give parents a feeling for what happens each day than to have them use the materials in the classrooms! In addition, slides, a scrapbook of photos, or a videotape or PowerPoint presentation of children actively participating in the classroom can give parents further insights into what a quality program can offer their children.

Planning for the open house is done by people who understand the lifestyles and expectations of the clients who are likely to show interest in the event. Careful and sensitive planning regarding the time of the event and the level of informality communicates to members of the community that the people at the center understand and care about them and their children.

REFLECTION

Think about a center you have been in on a regular basis. You are sitting outside in the parking lot as parents arrive. Is the building inviting? Does it really welcome children and families? Now imagine yourself inside, observing the way children are greeted. Do adults stoop down and extend a friendly welcome to the children? Are parents recognized and called by name? As you walk farther into the building, how does it look? What sounds do you hear? How does it smell? The impressions you are reliving are the same parents and children experience each day that they enter the center.

SELECTING THE CHILDREN

Ultimately, the director is responsible for the decisions about which children will be admitted to the program. The teachers often are called on to assist in this decision, and sometimes a standing committee authorized by the board is asked to make policy or give advice. An Admissions and Recruitment Committee might be charged with policy-making decisions about the population to be served. There also are decisions about the admission of children with disabilities or who are atypical, and about the grouping of children.

Other factors such as readiness of the child, needs of the child and family, and age of the child may enter into the final selection. Of course, there are pressures to admit all applicants when enrollment is not full. However, it always is important for the director to exercise good professional judgment about which children to admit, basing admission decisions on what is in the best interests of the child. The number of children to be served by the program will be determined by the size of the space and the number of adults available for the children's programs. In many areas, criteria set by licensing regulations must be satisfied (see Chapter 4).

Readiness of Children and Families

The director or a member of the professional staff must assess the child's readiness to enter the program. It is essential that this assessment be made with the participation of the family. In some situations, the age of the child is the only consideration, but that is clearly a tenuous criterion if it is the only one used in deciding whether or not a child can manage a group experience in a particular center. Indeed, it is analogous to the idea of judging a book by its cover. Chronological age is only one factor among many that will determine whether a child will be able to move into a program and profit from the experience. Other determinants are the emotional, social, and intellectual development of the child and, of course, the child's health.

This is not to suggest that a child who does not meet some arbitrary standard or norm should be rejected on that basis alone, unless licensing regulations prohibit admission of children before a certain age. What it does mean is that the professionals at the center must decide if the available staff and the particular program offerings at the center can be adapted to provide the most enriching experience for a particular child. In other words, can *this* program provide what *this* child needs to develop to her fullest potential? If there is any doubt in the minds of either the members of the family or the director, careful consideration should be given to a number of questions. Can the program be adjusted to accommodate this child? Is there another program with a different focus that would provide a better match for this child and the lifestyle of this family? Is it better for the child and the family to consider waiting a while longer before placing the child in the center so that all will be more prepared for an initial separation, even though the family is seeking placement for the child so the parents can work? What other arrangements can be made for the care of the child?

What about the child who must be placed in full-day care to meet a family need that is both urgent and imminent? Perhaps there is some financial crisis or some tragedy or illness that makes it impossible to keep the child at home. That need must be heard. However, an experienced person with a strong sense of professional integrity certainly would avoid admitting a child to a program if the program, as it is currently set up, could be potentially damaging to the child. In special cases, a child could be accepted on a trial basis. Alternatives such as a family child care home, coming for half days for a short period of time, or finding a qualified baby-sitter might be recommended for the child. In any case, as a director you must remember that your decisions are affecting the lives of children and families who are looking to you for help in the decision-making process. Your task is to provide help that is educationally and professionally sound.

There also is another side to the issue. Not only must the child be ready for the separation and the

group environment, but the family and, most important, the primary caregiver must be ready to leave the child. Members of the professional staff at the center may have excellent skills when it comes to adapting the learning environment to each child, regardless of the child's age or level of readiness. However, coping with the reluctant parent is another problem that may be much more difficult to manage. For this very reason, the assessment of readiness and the final decision on admission must be a cooperative effort between a member of the professional staff and the family. Interviews, visits to the home and to the center, and careful observation of the child in the context of the family are all helpful in making a final admission decision.

Admission of Children with Disabilities

The general question of readiness applies to all children and families seeking admission, whether the children are atypical or developmentally typical. The critical questions in each case are the same.

Will the child's needs be met?

Will the family's needs be met?

Will the program meet the needs of both the child and the family while also serving the needs of all other children and families involved in the program?

In 1986, Congress enacted Public Law 99–457, amending the Education of Handicapped Act (EHA, PL 94–142). The reauthorization of both PL 94–142

Directors attend to the importance of inclusion.

and PL 99–457 came in 1990 with the passage of PL 101–476, Individuals with Disabilities Education Act, known by the acronym IDEA. It was further amended in 1997 as PL 105–17. The law requires that states provide a free, *appropriate* public education to everyone with disabilities, age 3 to 21. (See the following section for a discussion of *discretionary legislation* for exceptions.) States that fail to comply will no longer receive certain public funding for preschoolers. Knowledge of the ADA, enacted in 1990, is also important as directors review requests for admission of children with disabilities. Centers are prohibited from denying admission to a child simply because of a disability *unless* such admission would fundamentally "alter the nature of the program" or would be an "undue burden" on the program (*Child Care Information Exchange*, 1995, p. 81). In the 21st century, directors in early childhood education programs must be prepared to address the challenge of providing quality inclusion environments for increasing numbers of preschool children with disabilities.

Directors are obligated to understand that a child may not be excluded simply because he has a disability. It is important for them to know how the law applies to infants, toddlers, and preschoolers and to understand how preschools and child care centers are likely to fit into the scheme of services for atypical children. They also should know what role they and their staff can play as part of the interdisciplinary, interagency team effort to give these children the benefit of quality early childhood education experiences. The well-being of the child is best served when families are a part of the team.

Provisions of IDEA

IDEA, as amended by PL 105–17, the Individuals with Disabilities Act Amendments of 1997, extends all rights and due process protection to children with disabilities ages three to five. Therefore, preschool children with exceptionalities are ensured free public education in a least restrictive environment based on an individualized education plan (IEP) developed by a team that includes the child's parents. The programs are to be administered through state or local education agencies (LEA), which may contract with other service providers to offer a range of service models. The designated state agency ultimately is responsible for monitoring overall services and use of the federal funds. Other sources of funding such as Medicaid or Maternal and Child Health also must be utilized when the children are eligible, and the new funds are to supplement, not supplant, these existing sources. Therefore, the new funds may be used *in addition to* but not *instead of* existing sources of

funding. Some states do not require the reporting of children by disability category, thereby eliminating the necessity to categorically label these children because of data collection requirements. IDEA also establishes a state grant program to provide financial assistance to states to maintain and implement a comprehensive, multidisciplinary system of services for infants and toddlers with disabilities. Part C of IDEA, known as *discretionary legislation*, says that states may serve this age group but are not required to do so. The exception is for those states that serve nondisabled infants and toddlers; they must serve those children who are disabled in that age group. The governor of each state designates a lead agency in the state to administer the program. That agency develops eligibility criteria, and the law allows but does not require extension of services to those babies viewed as "at risk" for developmental delay based on medical or environmental factors, in addition to identified infants with disabilities. A case manager, sometimes called a service coordinator, must be designated for each child. That person, who is the liaison between agencies and services needed, also is responsible for the development of the individualized family service plan (IFSP), which must have evidence of multidisciplinary input and include information about the child's level of development, the family's strengths and needs as these relate to the child, the specific intervention services planned, and the projected outcomes for the child and the family. Therefore, the IFSP is somewhat comparable to the IEP required for the age three-to-five population and brings the focus to the importance of the family in each young child's life. (Most of the information in this section is from Allen & Cowdery, 2005.)

Role of Child Care Centers

The law allows for variation in length of day, as well as range and variety of programs, which means part-time or full-time home-based or center-based services can be utilized. This is likely to lead to more inclusion models as state and local agencies contract with half-day and full-day child care programs to expand the continuum of services to include more center-based care in integrated settings. Now that the values of early childhood education programs are sufficiently high and demand public notice, state education agencies that have almost unlimited discretion to choose program models see that these programs offer viable alternatives to the current typical public school categorical model. In many public school models, children with disabilities may be in the same wing of the regular school building. The only time they share space with "normal children" is on the

 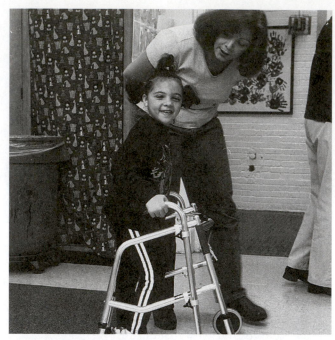

The needs of applicants with disabilities must be carefully assessed to ensure that this is the best possible program for them.

playground or at lunch. A major exception to this principle is when Head Start is housed in public schools. Ten percent of Head Start's classroom slots must be reserved for children with disabilities.

The vast majority of unserved atypical children who come into programs under the new law are mildly disabled. Most severely disabled children already receive services and may or may not be included in preschools or child care centers depending on how well their needs would be met in an inclusion environment. However, based on ADA, you must consider each applicant on a case-by-case basis and may not exclude a child merely because of a severe disabling condition. If your program could include the child by making reasonable accommodations in the environment, you are expected to do that. You need not make changes that put an undue burden on the resources readily available at your center (*Child Care Information Exchange,* 1995).

The law requires that these children identified with special needs be in a "least restrictive environment" (LRE). Legally, this means that every effort must be made to maintain developmentally disabled children with their peers in a regular educational setting. When placements are made away from normal peers, the state bears the burden of proof to demonstrate that the integrated setting is not appropriate (Smith & Strain, 1988). In practice, the least restrictive environment is one that facilitates opportunities to function and grow optimally in all areas of development. Directors of centers with inclusion models

are responsible for providing such an environment for children with disabilities who are admitted and funded under the law. Children must share the pedagogical and social environment, and teachers are expected to be specifically trained to facilitate interaction among and between typically developing children and those who have special needs.

Although there is evidence that significant benefits accrue to children with special needs who participate in groups with normal peers, these benefits are not the result of merely being in the same classroom. The factors that determine how well children with special needs do in an inclusion environment depends on the quality of the program and the presence of a teacher who has developed specific intervention plans to support interaction between and among the atypical and their normal peers (Allen & Cowdery, 2005).

When available staff do not have sufficient time or background to provide the special support for children with special needs in the classroom, it may be possible to reach out into the community for additional help. Volunteers from parent groups, senior citizens, service organizations, or students from early childhood or special education programs can help in the classroom. Special training for the volunteers and the staff can be arranged through special educators at the local school or university, or from other community agencies (Appendix B and Allen & Cowdery, 2005, pp. 425–427).

Including children who have been identified with special needs is a challenge for both the teaching staff and the director. However, because so many resources are available to them and their families, it can work out to benefit everyone involved. The more vexing challenges are those faced when a new child enters the program and, soon after admission, begins to manifest social and/or emotional problems through disruptive emotional outbursts in the classroom. In these cases, neither the director nor the teaching staff has had a chance to prepare themselves or the children for this new student. It becomes stressful and time consuming to work with this new family and to provide the necessary support for the troubled child and the classroom teacher. In these situations, directors are pulled in many directions, sometimes struggling with a screaming, angry child; sometimes talking with hostile, defensive, or bewildered parents; sometimes taking time after hours to give support to an exhausted teacher. These are the times when directors must call on all their professional skills to help the child, the family, and the teacher cope and eventually move forward toward resolution.

DIRECTOR'S CORNER

"When I put a child with special needs in a classroom, I always talk at length with the teacher, telling her how I feel she can make it work—how I understand that it's important for all of us and for this child to really find ways to integrate this child into this group. It's very important for a staff member to tell me when she thinks it isn't working. I have to be able to confirm that it's not working both for the group and for the child, but I must also be able to tell her that there are ways to make it work if that, indeed, is the case, and help her find those ways."

—Director, for-profit corporate center

ROLE OF THE DIRECTOR IN AN INTERDISCIPLINARY/ INTERAGENCY EFFORT

"Cooperation among education agencies, social service agencies, Head Start, and private providers will be crucial, especially if much greater numbers of children are to be served in the least restrictive environment" (Barrett, 1988, p. 22). Directors conversant in the law and its implications for child care programs

will be able to respond more knowledgeably to professionals from related agencies who make inquiries about placements for children with special needs. These directors may be called on to make decisions about whether or not their programs can meet the needs of the selected special needs children; to serve on interdisciplinary teams where IEPs are developed and referral decisions are made; and to support their teachers who will be working with special educators, therapists, and the children's families. If the children are to benefit from what early childhood educators have to offer, turf guarding must be set aside; yet they must assertively advocate developmentally appropriate practice, which is the area of expertise they bring to the interdisciplinary and interagency team.

To facilitate communication between and among members of interdisciplinary teams and to support their work, directors must understand how and why inclusion works and what makes it work or prevents it from working. That often means directors must learn more about children with special needs through additional training and reading in order to prepare themselves for coaching classroom staff and for working with an interdisciplinary team. When members of the interdisciplinary team view each other as colleagues, all of whom bring special skills and training to the situation, and when they keep in mind that their common goal is to provide the best environment for the children and their families, they can work together to that end.

SUMMARY

Marketing materials for the center must be drafted and directed to the population that the program is designed to serve. Successful recruitment of children and families will depend on the content and dissemination of the promotional materials about the program, as well as on the total public relations effort. The written materials advertising the center must be planned carefully to attract the families to be served. Any other efforts or activities to market the center deserve considerable thought and attention as well. After the families have indicated their interest, it is the responsibility of the professional staff to select children for the program, taking into account the readiness of the children and the capacity of the program to serve their needs and those of their families. The mandate to provide services for three- to five-year-old children with disabilities continues to have far-reaching implications for early childhood programs in the 21st century. It will influence the selection of children to be enrolled and affect the dynamics within classrooms. For inclusion programs to be successful, early childhood teachers and special educators must forge new relationships.

CLASS ASSIGNMENTS

1. Interview the director of a full-day or half-day program. Ask the questions listed on Working Paper 11–1.

2. Analyze the brochures, newsletters, or any advertisements you have seen on the program you inquired about in Class Assignment 1. Using Working Paper 11–2, evaluate the printed material as it relates to the information from your interview with the director of the program.

CLASS EXERCISES

1. Working in small groups (three to five students), discuss the questions and issues pertaining to inclusion of special needs children in early childhood education programs. Record the ideas of the group on Working Paper 11–3.

2. Using the information from the small group discussions and other ideas generated from class discussion, summarize what your class views as the most critical issues and concerns facing early childhood educators during the next decade of IDEA.

WORKING PAPER 11-1

(for use with Class Assignment 1)

INTERVIEW QUESTIONS

Following are interview questions for a director of an early childhood education program:

Are you the director of a full-day program? _____

Are you the director of a half-day program? _____

Who is enrolled in the program?

1. Tell me about your program.

   ■ How many children are enrolled? _____

   ■ What is the age range of the children? _____

   ■ How many groups of infants? _____

   Toddlers? _____

   Prekindergartners?_____

2. Tell me about availability of service.

   ■ What are your hours? _____

   ■ What days do children come? _____

   ■ What holidays do you observe? _____

3. Can you give me an idea about the population you serve?

   ■ Are most of your parents working? _____

   ■ What is the racial and ethnic mix of your population? _____

   ■ How would you describe the socioeconomic status of the families (upper class, middle class, impoverished)? _____

4. Could you give me an idea about the center's philosophy and the program goals?

5. May I have copies of your brochures or any newsletters you distribute in the community or to your prospective clients?

WORKING PAPER 11-2

(for use with Class Assignment 2)

EVALUATION FORM

Using the printed materials you collected from the director you interviewed (Class Assignment 1), describe and discuss how well these materials reflect what the director said about the program in each of the following areas:

1. Ages served and groupings of children

2. Availability of service in terms of hours, days of the week, time of the year, and so forth

3. Suitability of writing level, layout, and photographs for the target population

4. Power of logo/tagline/content

5. Clarify what the program is about as to the philosophy and goals mentioned in the printed material and how these match what you were told.

WORKING PAPER 11-3

(for use with Class Exercise 1)

GROUP IDEAS

Discuss and record the responses of the group to the following issues related to PL 99–457.

1. How will an early childhood director determine if a program is the least restrictive environment for a specific developmentally disabled child?

   ■ What factors must be considered in the determination?

   ■ Where can the director go for help?

2. What are some of the strategies early childhood education professionals can use to communicate to other professionals (special educators, physicians, psychologists, social workers, and the like) about "developmentally appropriate practice" and its importance for all children?

3. What are the major things early childhood educators need to learn from special educators?

4. What are some of the specific classroom strategies a director can share with the teaching staff that will facilitate interaction between and among atypical children and their typically developing peers?

REFERENCES

Allen, K. E., & Cowdery, G. E. (2005). *The exceptional child: Inclusion in early childhood education* (5th ed.). Clifton Park, NY: Thomson Delmar Learning.

Barrett, W. S. (1988). The economies of preschool education under Public Law 99–457. *Topics in Early Childhood Special Education, 8*(1).

Child Care Information Exchange. (1995). Redmond, WA: CCIE, *106,* 81–84.

Duncan, S., & Thornton, D. (1993, January). Marketing your center's services to employers. *Child Care Information Exchange.* pp. 53–56.

Smith, B. J., & Strain, P. S. (1988). Early childhood special education in the next decade: Implementing and expanding PL 99–457. *Topics in Early Childhood Special Education, 8*(1), 37–47.

Tiger, F. (1995). The art of brochure. *Child Care Information Exchange, 107,* March/April 1995, p. 24.

Additional resources for this chapter can be found on the Online Companion™ at http://www.earlychilded.delmar.com. This supplemental material includes relevant Web links, Web activities, and case studies that apply the concepts presented in this chapter. In addition, the Working Papers and Director's Resources are available for download, allowing you to complete Class Exercises and Class Assignments electronically.

CHAPTER 12

Grouping and Enrolling the Children

Grouping patterns should be determined before the enrollment process begins.

Group 1		Group 2	
Andrew R.	Alex A.	Sarita W.	Karen V.
Allison N.	Joey B.	Peter N.	Marcy S.
Ned R.	Nadine C.	Sammy B.	Kenny L.
Dion J.	Sally Z.	Brad A.	Tommy P.

OBJECTIVES

After reading this chapter, you should be able to:

- Make informed decisions about grouping children in centers.
- List steps in the intake process.
- Understand the rationale for different types of grouping.

Decisions about grouping the children must be reached before making the group assignments and pursuing all the subsequent steps in the enrollment procedure. Decisions about group size, ages of children, and composition of the groups should be made before the children are assigned. Once assignments have been made, teachers can contact families and initiate the enrollment process. Although the degree of flexibility around grouping in ongoing early childhood education programs is sometimes more limited than in half-day programs, even there the cyclical nature of demand usually follows the public school year, thereby giving rise to numerous grouping decisions for newcomers in the fall.

GROUPING THE CHILDREN

A number of factors are considered in dealing with the complex question of how children should be grouped appropriately. The size of groups is determined by a variety of factors, including the physical space available, the licensing requirements, the number of staff members, and the program philosophy. Appropriate group size has a positive influence on both children and teachers (Decker & Decker, 2005). Other factors that relate to grouping of children are the needs and skills of the staff, the needs of the children, the question of chronological age grouping versus vertical (sometimes called family) multi-age grouping, the number of children with special needs to be enrolled, and the nature of their disabilities.

Total Number of Children

To a large extent, the number of children available and the size of the physical space determine the total number of children in a center. If it is a new program, once the needs assessment in the community has been completed (Chapter 3) and the facility has been selected (Chapter 8), the final decision about the total number of children in the center must be made. Often, this decision is simply to take all children available. However, when the requests for service are overwhelming or when the available space can accommodate large numbers of children, the director and/or the board may want to limit the enrollment. Accreditation standards and many state licensing regulations limit total group size as well as adult-to-child ratios, both of which affect program quality. (See Chapter 4 for further details.)

Centers for young children must radiate a feeling of intimacy and warmth. Little children often feel frightened and uncomfortable about entering a large, forbidding building. The noise, the inevitable confusion, and the motion created by many people concentrated in one area can provoke anxiety in young children. It is difficult to maintain an inviting, comfortable atmosphere for small children when buildings are very large and when children are moved through crowded play yards, hallways, or receiving areas before they reach *their* room and *their* teacher.

Because the atmosphere in large public school buildings can be overwhelming for very young children, it is important for early childhood professionals and public school educators to give special attention to the selection of the classroom and play yard space for the preschool children. Partnerships between early childhood educators and public school personnel can result in site selection for public-school-sponsored programs that may be in a separate wing of the building or in a facility completely separate from the school building. Greater stability and insulation from political attack and protection from sudden economic shifts may be some of the advantages of funneling preschool and full-day child care services into public school sponsorship. However, early childhood educators must guard the safety and well-being of the children when site selection for these programs is under discussion.

Space and Group Size

Group size varies according to the licensing regulations and how the available space is organized. Licensing regulations often limit the number of children in a room and usually dictate the adult-to-child ratio for children of different ages. Since space requirements and adult-to-child ratio standards in the licensing regulations are not always based on the knowledge of experienced professionals, it is wise to follow a standard of small groups with low teacher-to-child ratios (NAEYC, 1998).

DIRECTOR'S CORNER

"I had to go down the hall and upstairs when I wanted to take the children to the gym for large-muscle activities. I always tried to avoid having them in the halls of the school building when the older children were moving in and out of the auditorium or the lunchroom. It was very confusing for the preschoolers to be taken through the long lines of older children—especially if remarks were made like, 'make room for the baby group' by the children or the elementary teachers."

—Director, Head Start program in a public school building

The organization or plan of the available space affects the size of the groups that can be accommodated. When bathrooms are two floors down or outside areas are not directly adjacent to the classroom, groups must be smaller to be manageable during the transition periods when children move from one place to another. If fenced-in play areas outside can be reached directly from the classroom, the total space can be supervised more easily and a larger group could be assigned to the space.

REFLECTION

REFLECTION

Can you recall how you felt as a first-year high school student when you initially entered your big high school building? Were you afraid and anxious? How did it feel to be the youngest or the smallest in the whole school? Did you feel that you might not be able to find your room or your locker? Did you ever have nightmares about forgetting your schedule or losing your most important notebook? If you can recall any of those feelings, perhaps you can begin to relate to the young child who leaves a familiar home environment and enters a large, strange, crowded place called a child care center or school.

When space is adequate to accommodate large numbers of young children, some directors and teachers find creative ways to use dividers, draperies, or movable partitions to break the space into smaller units. Even where available space would accommodate larger groups, smaller groups are viewed as optimal (NAEYC, 1998).

Skills of Staff and Group Size

In deciding on the size of groups, the director considers the skill level of the staff and factors that into the decision about how many children should be assigned to each classroom. The staff for each group must be available to provide frequent personal contact; promote age-appropriate, meaningful learning experiences; create a nurturing environment using effective classroom management strategies; and respond immediately to all emergencies.

Needs of Children and Group Size

It is beyond the scope of this book to discuss the policy of making group size or placement decisions on the basis of differing individual family and child needs or ages of children, even though every director must consider such needs carefully. However, some basic considerations apply to all children, whether infant, toddler, preschool, or school age.

The needs of children will vary depending on their experiences, their level of development in all areas, and their ages. However, it is generally agreed that very young children in their first group experience find it most satisfying to relate to a constant

Very young children in their first group experience find it most satisfying to relate to a constant adult.

adult. After the initial shift in attachment from the primary caregiver (usually the mother) to a constant adult at the center, the child begins to branch out and relate to other adults and other children in the group. This developmental progression suggests that the child's first experience should be in a small, intimate group with a constant adult. The children in this group may be the same chronological age, or they may range over a year or two in age. Volunteers, student teachers, or parent helpers may rotate through the classroom, but the one, primary constant caregiver becomes the trusted adult figure to whom children can turn when they need caring and attention. Consistency of care is especially important for infants and toddlers, who should have an assigned primary caregiver that works closely with the parents.

For young children spending the full day in a center, it is wise to consider small, intimate grouping patterns. Since children in full-day programs spend practically all of their waking hours in the center, it becomes a surrogate home for them. Young children who are dealing with all the stimulation and interpersonal relationships of a large group for an extended period of time may be exhausted by the end of their long day. Small groups in a carefully planned space provide both time and space for the child to be alone, to establish close relationships with just one or two children, or to spend time alone with just one adult. Quiet and intimacy in a comfortable setting with a few people more closely resembles the home environment and can soften the institutional atmosphere that prevails in many large centers.

REFLECTION

Think about your first practicum experience in a classroom. Think about how many children you were able to manage at one time. Could you comfortably work with 5 children? If you were asked to work with 10 children without a second person to help, did you still feel that you could practice effective management skills? What adult-to-child ratio and total group size is most comfortable for you, keeping in mind your philosophy of early childhood education?

Chronological versus Vertical Age Grouping

There is no consensus on the best grouping practice. Although there has been some movement toward greater homogeneity in classrooms for young children, which usually results from chronological age grouping, there is a resurgence of interest in multi-age or vertical grouping (Decker & Decker, 2005). Program philosophy may dictate the preferred approach to grouping the children. However, unless licensing regulates how children should be grouped, the way classrooms are organized within the program is left to the discretion of the director and the professional staff.

Directors are faced with the challenge of maintaining full enrollment while keeping groups balanced and exercising caution when decisions are made about moving children among established center groupings. When infant-toddler groups are at capacity but there are openings in the preschool, it is tempting to move some of the older toddlers to the preschool to make space for families on the waiting list. It is important to balance the need for full enrollment to

meet budget requirements against the social-emotional readiness of these very young children and their ability to manage a more complex environment with older children and new adults.

Too often, children are moved based solely on their chronological age or in response to pressure to make room for new children, rather than on a careful analysis of the readiness of the children involved in the move. The first step is to give careful consideration to a child's readiness to thrive and grow with the older children. Then take note of the challenges to the family and teachers involved in supporting the child through this critical adjustment to many unknowns, such as different spaces with new adults and few familiar faces. The transition process for any child to a new group in the center can be eased by setting up a transition plan that parallels the phasing-in process described in the Intake Procedures section of this chapter (page 346). The family and the teachers from both rooms will be involved in the transition process, just as a parent and the teacher are involved when a new child enters the program.

Parents may need a special conference with the director to clarify the importance of the parent role in the transition process, not only when the child enters the program but also for all subsequent transitions from one group to another and the final one when the child leaves the center. Meeting with the child's parents as these transition times approach offers the director the opportunity to help them understand how their presence in the new room can help reduce stress for their child as both are adjusting to the families and staff. It is helpful to parents if they understand that taking time there for their child during potentially stressful changes will contribute to the emotional well-being of their child.

Chronological Grouping

Grouping by age traditionally has been a more popular practice in early childhood programs than vertical grouping. It involves grouping based solely on the basis of age: three- and four-years-olds are in different groups, and toddlers are separated from infants. When children are grouped chronologically, there is little discussion about which group a given child will join. The director's task is simplified because in accepting the center program, parents understand that their three-year-old will be in Group 1 and their four-year-old will be in Group 2. Of course, there will be ranges of ability and behavior within an age group due to individual differences, but the child's exposure to differences is inevitably lessened when chronological grouping is used. Therefore, the child's opportunity to develop a broad appreciation for diversity is diminished. On the other hand, there are advantages to age grouping such as simplifying the planning of the learning environment and making classroom management less troublesome. The less experienced teacher may find this type of grouping more comfortable.

Chronological age grouping is based on the assumption that children of the same age are within the same range in ability and level of development. Because children of the same age are not homogeneous, many programs go to multi-age grouping where children advance at their own rate through individualized programming. Multi-age grouping allows for children's uneven development and provides an environment in which younger children engage in more interactive and complex types of play with older children who are easily accessible (Katz, Evangelou, & Hartman, 1990).

REFLECTION

Think about the progression of your feelings when you have spent an entire day in large, crowded classrooms; a busy, noisy cafeteria; community bathrooms; and noisy student centers. Consider those long days when you have found no privacy, no place to be alone and talk to a friend about a problem, or listen to music either by yourself or with a special person. Your day on campus may be like this. If you can think through how you feel when following such a pattern, you will develop greater insight into how a child feels when placed in a large group for a full-day program. The lack of intimacy and warmth in an institutional setting creates both anxiety and fatigue.

Vertical Grouping

Vertical grouping, or family grouping as it is sometimes called, involves placing children of different ages in the same group; the children in any one group may range in age as much as two to three years. This multi-age grouping more closely resembles one that would occur in a family, hence the label *family grouping*. Depending on licensing requirements, infants and sometimes even toddlers must be kept in separate groups. When vertical grouping is the pattern,

decisions about the size and the composition of each group, as well as the number of adults needed for each one, become more complex. The broad age range also complicates managing the children and planning their learning environment.

Sometimes, parents object to having their two-year-old with older children who may be viewed by the toddler's parents as being loud and rough. These parents often are concerned about the safety of their toddler and sometimes fear that their young child will be unable to cope in a group covering a wide age range. However, many of these parents can be helped to see that a young child in a multi-age group has more opportunity to learn from older children in the group and that every child has a chance to teach the other group members. Peer teaching and learning has intrinsic value because it not only enhances a child's sense of mastery and worth but also facilitates cooperation and appreciation of others. For example, two-year-olds may not be as efficient as five-year-olds about putting equipment back on the shelf, but the total concentration they give to an activity like water play and the curiosity they show in exploring this material may help their more controlled three- or five-year-old counterparts to try splashing in the water.

The director must cope with the dubious parents and with the teachers who are reaching out for support as they work with a broad age range. However, sometimes the advantages of multi-age grouping such as peer modeling and peer tutoring are outweighed by the challenges of planning for the age span and equipping and managing the classroom. Directors become coaches and sources of support for staff as they try to meet these challenges. Teachers who are able to individualize planning for a multi-age group also will be better qualified to create culturally consistent and inclusive programs for children with special needs. These teachers develop a keen awareness of the fact that "one size does not fit all."

Inclusion of Children with Exceptionalities

When children with exceptionalities are included in the group, the size and composition of the group must be adjusted accordingly to ensure that enough adults will be available to respond to their needs. Consider which group can offer something to the child with a disability, as well as how that child can offer something to the group. Unless the child is truly integrated into the group, each offering something to the other, there is a risk that the child with the disability will be ignored and become an isolate, thereby *not* in the *least restrictive* environment. The least restrictive ruling is not necessarily a mandate to enroll all children with a disability into regular programs; however, the advantages of inclusion for both nondisabled children and children with developmental disabilities are numerous and well documented (Allen & Cowdery, 2005). Social competence and the ability to maintain higher levels of play is enhanced for children with exceptionalities who have the opportunity to interact with normally developing peers in inclusive classrooms. At the same time, their language and cognitive gains are comparable to their peers in self-contained special education classrooms. On the other hand, children without disabilities in inclusive classrooms become more accepting of others who are different and become more comfortable with those differences.

There is no ideal exceptional-to-normal ratio, and recommendations range from at least two or more to an even balance (50–50), to more disabled than nondisabled, sometimes called "reverse mainstreaming" where nondisabled make up one-quarter to one-third of the enrollment (Allen & Cowdery, 2005, p. 3). The best ratio of special needs to nonspecial needs children is the one with which teachers, administrators, and parents are most comfortable. Variables that must be considered include the following:

- the severity of the disabling conditions of the children with special needs in the group
- the characteristics of the nondisabled children
- how to explain and understand the disabilities of peers
- the expertise of the available adults who are to work with the inclusive group (Taylor, 2002)

Multi-age groups are advantageous for children with special needs because they provide peer models with a broad range of skills and abilities. The atypical child is exposed to the peer model who has higher level skills or abilities and also will have a chance to develop friendships with younger children who may be more compatible developmentally.

Decisions about group size or group patterns will affect program planning, child and teacher behaviors, group atmosphere, and ultimately the experiences of both teacher and child in the learning environment. An inclusive program must consider the uniqueness of every child and family in the classroom and how each child's strengths and needs will be addressed (Allen & Cowdery, 2005). Therefore, grouping the children is a complex issue that has far-reaching results.

ENROLLING THE CHILDREN

Filling out forms, interviewing parents, and visiting back and forth between home and school are the major components of the enrollment procedure. The director is responsible for developing forms that will provide the center staff members with the information they need about the families and the children. The director also manages the planning and timing of this procedure; however, these plans must be discussed with staff members and parents who will be required to carry them out.

Information on Families and Children

The director first determines what information is needed from each family, then develops a plan for obtaining it. Forms and interviews can both be used for this purpose. It is up to the director to design the forms and to develop the plan for interviews or conferences. The ultimate goal is to assemble the necessary information for each child and family and to make it available to selected adults at the center who will be responsible for the child and the family.

The following list includes the type of preenrollment information that is typically obtained from the family. Note that all the information is important to efficient business operation of the center, to the health and safety of the children, or to the better understanding of the child and the family.

1. name of the child (including nickname)
2. names of family members and ages of siblings
3. names of other members of the household and their relationship to the child
4. home address and phone number
5. name, address, telephone number (home, work, cell), and e-mail addresses of employer(s) of parent(s)
6. arrangement for payment of fees
7. transportation plans for the child (including how the child will be transported and by whom)
8. medical history and record of a recent physical examination of the child by a physician
9. social-emotional history of the child
10. name, address, and telephone number of the child's physician or clinic
11. emergency medical treatment authorization
12. name, address, and telephone number of a person (outside the family) to contact in an

emergency if a member of the family cannot be reached

13. Permission to participate in the total school program (field trips, photos, videotaping, research, and so on)

To ensure that you have all the information and signed releases required to satisfy licensing and to cover liability questions, contact your local licensing agent and consult an attorney.

Forms

A number of sample forms included in the Director's Resources at the back of this chapter demonstrate various ways in which the information listed above can be recorded. These are only sample forms and cannot be used in the exact format presented, but they can provide a basis for developing appropriate forms to meet the specific needs of each center. For example, the director of a small cooperative preschool does not need all the data on family income that is required by Head Start or public-funded programs but needs details on family schedules to plan for parent participation.

Public-school-sponsored programs may or may not require family income information but will require a Medicaid number for those children entitled to the benefits of that program and also may need a birth certificate to validate the age of the child.

Because there is so much variation among programs about information required on children and families, directors must develop forms that meet the specific needs of the program.

In the case of early childhood education centers and preschools, applications for admission are mailed to interested families in response to their initial inquiry about the center. In fact, sometimes the application is enclosed in a brochure or is actually part of it. On receipt of the applications, the director can begin to arrange the groups, based on whatever guidelines have been adopted for grouping the children, or in ongoing child care programs, select an appropriate group placement for the new child. If selection and grouping of the children require more subjective data than can be gleaned from the application form or any other written information that has been collected prior to admission, the director can arrange to talk with the parent(s).

After most of the children have been admitted and assigned to groups, those who have not yet been placed are held for deferred enrollment, or in the case of ongoing programs, put on a waiting list. If a child is rejected for reasons other than full enrollment,

the reasons should be discussed with the family to avoid any misunderstandings that quickly could undermine the public relations efforts of the center staff and impair communication between the staff and potential clients from the community.

Confidentiality

Information on families and children that is recorded on forms or obtained by staff members during interviews or home visits is confidential and *must not be released* to unauthorized persons without parental consent. Furthermore, a federal law provides that any public or private educational institution that is the recipient of federal funds made available under any federal program administered by the U.S. Department of Education must give parents access to their children's educational records. Since all information in the files must remain available to parents, it is important that staff members use discretion when recording information to be placed in a child's permanent record. Parents should be informed of what information will be kept confidential and what will be available to teaching staff, office staff, and other support staff. Parents decide how much detail they are willing to release. They realize that emergency telephone numbers and authorized persons to pick up the child will be needed by all teaching and office staff. However, they may choose to have medical histories and income information available only to the director and the lead teacher (Taylor, 2002).

Records and other confidential information should not be disclosed to anyone other than center personnel without written consent of the parent or guardian, unless its disclosure is necessary to protect the health or safety of the child. Written parental consent is required in order to pass information on to the public school by any preschool or Head Start program. As a general rule, parental consent should be obtained except in emergency cases or where it appears that the parent is a threat to the child (Family Educational Rights and Privacy Act, 1974). Centers that receive funds from government sources should be familiar with any regulations or guidelines on confidentiality and privacy that are tied to the funding source.

Center directors in collaboration with staff, parents, and board members can develop written policies for the protection of confidentiality and the disclosure of children's records. These policies should be made available to all program personnel and families (Feeney & Freeman, n.d.). The trust that develops between staff and families will be damaged if there is a breach of confidentiality. Setting aside one staff meeting each year to review the confidentiality policies is one way to encourage the staff to reaffirm their pledge to maintain confidentiality.

Intake Procedures

The director decides which staff members will be involved in each step of the intake procedure, but it is imperative that the child's teacher actively be involved throughout. The adult who will work directly with the child must interact with the child and family to begin to establish feelings of mutual trust among the child, the family, and the teacher.

Parents often feel guilty and apprehensive about placing children in an early childhood program. A carefully planned intake process that provides frequent opportunities to talk with the teacher, the director, and the social services staff (if available) can help parents cope with their feelings. At the same time, young children are upset when they first are separated from their parents and family. Children worry about who will take care of them or how they will get home. Some children display regressive behaviors. Both teachers and parents need help to understand that children are uneasy about this new experience and must have special attention and care during this initial transition. Because children feel frightened and lonely, their transition to a new physical and social environment is done gradually and must be accompanied by continuous support from family members. For the mental health of both the parents and children, the sequences followed in the intake process should be arranged so that everyone involved will be able to cope successfully with the separation experience. Four steps are commonly employed in introducing the family and the child to the center program and to the teacher. They are discussed here because it is the director's responsibility to ensure that this careful intake procedure is implemented.

Initial Interview with Parents

The purpose of an initial interview is to get acquainted with the parent(s), answer their questions about the center program, communicate what will be expected of them, take them on a tour of the center, and familiarize them with the forms that must be filled out before their child can be admitted. It may be useful to go over the family information, the child's social history, the medical history, the emergency information record, and the various release and permission forms during the interview to answer questions about any confusing items. The sample forms in the Director's Resources give some idea of the way these forms may look. The informality and friendliness of this first personal contact will set the tone for all future contacts. Since this is precisely the time to establish the foundation for mutual trust among director, teacher, parent, and child, it is important that these interviews be conducted in a nonthreatening manner.

Scheduling the interview usually is done at the convenience of the family. Even though the teacher or the office staff may do the interview scheduling, it is essential that the director monitor it to ensure that families are not unduly inconvenienced. Careful consideration of family needs indicates that the center staff is sensitive to individual lifestyles and family preferences. When parents work, evenings or weekends may be best for interviews. Center staff members also must consider the transportation problems for some families, the availability of babysitters, and the schedules of other children in the family.

Home Visit with the Family

A home visit may be the next step in the intake procedure. The director first describes the purpose of home visits to the staff and goes over a home visit report with them before family appointments are made (see Working Paper 12–2). The purpose is not to evaluate the home, but rather to gather information that will enable the staff to have a better understanding of the child. Trust between the parent(s) and the staff will be destroyed and communication impaired if the family interprets the purpose of these home visits as evaluative. Observing a family at home will help the teacher understand the family lifestyle and the family attitudes toward the child.

DIRECTOR'S CORNER

"We make it clear at the outset and are fairly firm with parents about spending some time here with their child because we know, from experience, that even a child who comes in with apparent ease may have a problem two months hence, which harks back to skipping the gradual transition into the group. Even if a parent can spend only 15 minutes in the morning with a child for a week or two, we accept that and make it clear we expect it. My staff is sold on the importance of gradual separation and will even come in 15 or 30 minutes early—before we open—to give a new child time in the classroom with both the parent and the teacher present."

—Director, corporate-sponsored center

The child's first visit to the classroom is made with a parent or some trusted caregiver who stays with the child throughout the visit and gives the child time to feel comfortable with the teacher.

Initial Visit to the Center

The scheduling of the initial visits to the center is arranged by the director and the staff before home visits begin so that information about visiting the center can be given to parents during the home visit.

This initial visit to the classroom is planned to help the child make that first big step from home and the trusted caregiver to the center and a new caring adult. For preschool children, the visit can last from 30 to 45 minutes and should terminate before the child is tired or bored. This entire orientation process is longer and more complex for infants and toddlers. Although the teacher is clearly responsible for working with the child and the accompanying adult during preliminary visits, it is important for the director to be available to greet the newcomers and answer any questions that might arise. It provides a perfect opportunity for the director and the parent(s) to get to know each other better and is a good time to give them a copy of the parent handbook (see Chapter 16 for further discussion of and a sample of a Handbook).

Phasing In the Children

The first three intake steps for preschool children described here can be implemented in all types of center-based programs. The scheduling of each step should be adjusted to individual family needs and obviously is much more difficult for working parents. In fact, the scheduling of these steps may seem to be somewhat unrealistic for full-day child care programs but can be done through very creative planning. Implementing the intake procedures for all ages of children in child care programs could involve evenings, early mornings, or weekends. The director, therefore, must work out the scheduling with the staff and may give comp time to professional staff or overtime for hourly employees.

The phasing in or staggered entrance, which is the fourth and last step in the intake procedure, will, of necessity, be very different in ongoing child care programs than in programs that are just starting, or in those based on the typical school calendar. (For a detailed discussion of staggered entrance, see Read, Gardner, & Mahler, 1993.)

Arranging for the staggered entrance of a group of 12 to 15 preschool children at the beginning of the year poses a complex scheduling problem, but it is an essential step in the orientation process. Since scheduling is very involved, it is important for the director and staff to consult with parents about convenient times for them to come and stay with their child. Successful implementation of the plan depends on staff and family commitment to it. Extended intake procedures for younger children can require special planning.

In public-school-sponsored programs where there is usually no precedent for gradual intake of new children, early childhood staff will have to meet with administrators and building principals to explain the importance of this procedure for the well-being of children and families. Because some early childhood programs in public schools are considered part of the elementary school and are accredited with the elementary school in the local school district, they usually are expected to provide a given number of instructional days to maximize the amount of state funds they receive. Developmentally appropriate practices like phasing in children often is one of the first issues that creates conflict between developmental early childhood educators and the academic-school readiness elementary educators.

In full-day child care programs, the major problem is to find a trusted adult to stay with the child until all persons involved feel comfortable about the child being at the center every day for the full day. When a family needs full-day care for a child, both parents usually are working, or the child may be a member of a one-parent family or in foster care. In these special cases, a grandparent or other member of the extended family may be the best person to provide the emotional support that is necessary for the child during the phasing-in period.

If there is any question among staff members about the importance of the gradual orientation program for the child, the family, and the success of the total program, it is up to the director to help everyone understand that this process represents the next logical step in developing mutual trust within the teacher-child-family unit. Orienting children is usually exciting and productive for the teacher, but it is also time consuming and energy draining. The process can be successful only if the entire staff understands its relevance to the total program and recognizes it as being consistent with developmentally appropriate practice.

SUMMARY

Most of the decisions about grouping children appropriately are made by the director, who must consider the unique needs of the children, space available, and licensing regulations about ratios and group size. Policy decisions about chronological or multi-age grouping must be made before children are assigned to groups. Skills and experience of staff, ages of children, and the numbers and types of children with special needs selected for admission are all factors that will affect where children will be assigned.

Enrolling children involves filling out forms, interviewing parents, making home visits, and gradually phasing in the children. Although the staggered-enrollment procedure is complex and time consuming, it is a critical step in the process of building trust among the school, the child, and the family.

CLASS ASSIGNMENTS

1. Using Working Paper 12–1, work out a staggered enrollment schedule for 12 children.

2. Talk with at least two directors of child care programs in your community. Find out how children are grouped (chronologically or vertically) and how grouping decisions are made. Write a one-page paper, comparing and contrasting the grouping practices in each program and the rationale for each.

CLASS EXERCISES

1. Working with another student, role-play an initial interview with a young mother who is sending an only child who is three years old to your program. The Sample Personal History (Director's Resource 12–5) and the Permission Form (Director's Resources 12–8) are to be explained during this interview. At the close of the interview, discuss reactions to this role-play with the entire group.

2. In groups of four, role-play a home visit with a mother, father, and their three-year-old daughter. When you arrive, you see no evidence of toys in the home, and you find the child dressed and sitting in a chair with her hands folded, apparently having been told to "be good and sit quietly while we talk to your teacher." The purpose of the visit is to explain the initial visit to the center and the staggered enrollment plan for the child.

After the role-play, stay in groups of four and evaluate your reaction to the child and to the family. Evaluate your reactions as you played teacher, mother, father, or child. Consider how successful the teacher was at developing a relationship with the child. Fill in the Home Visit Report (Working Paper 12–2) in sufficient detail so the director will have a clear picture of what transpired during the visit.

WORKING PAPER 12-1

(for use with Class Assignment 1)

DEVELOP A STAGGERED ENROLLMENT PLAN

■ Enroll 12 children over a period of eight days.

■ The plan is for a half-day preschool that meets from 9:00 a.m. to 11:30 a.m. daily.

■ Remember to have children come for shorter hours, in small groups, and gradually move toward having all children together for the full 2 1/2 hours on the ninth day of school.

■ Fill in the time slots with the child's number—1, 2, 3, . . . 12.

■ Time slots can be adjusted to suit your plan.

Week 1	Monday—1	Tuesday—2	Wednesday—3	Thursday—4	Friday—5
9:00					
9:30					
10:00					
10:30					
11:00					
11:30					
Week 2	Monday—6	Tuesday—7	Wednesday—8	Thursday—9	Friday
9:00				Children 1–12	Children 1–12
9:30					
10:00					
10:30					
11:00					
11:30				↓	↓

WORKING PAPER 12-2

(for use with Class Exercise 2)

SAMPLE HOME VISIT/PARENT CONTACT REPORT

Center _____

Type of Program _____

1. Name of interviewer _____ Title _____

2. Child's name _____

3. Parent or guardian _____

4. Address _____

5. Date and time of visit or meeting _____

6. Purpose of visit or meeting _____

_____

_____

7. Specific action taken as result of visit or meeting _____

_____

_____

_____

_____

_____

_____

8. Observations and comments _____

_____

_____

_____

_____

_____

_____

_____

_____

DIRECTOR'S RESOURCE 12-1

SAMPLE CHILD CARE APPLICATION (requesting income information)

<u>For office use only</u>
District Status: _____
Income Status: _____
Priority Status: _____
Date Application Received: _____
Date Eligible for Entrance: _____
Enrollment Age: _____

Child's Name: _____ Date of Birth: _____ Sex: _____
Race, Nationality, or Ethnic Group: _____
Address: _____ Phone: _____

Mother's Name: _____ Date of Birth: _____ SS # _____
Father's Name: _____ Date of Birth: _____ SS # _____
Child lives with _____

Children attend the center-based program four (4) half days per week; they eat lunch and snack at the center. Transportation is provided for handicapped or special needs children.

Do you wish to apply for center-based program? Yes _____ No _____
    Session preferred A.M. _____ 8:45 – 11:45
                      P.M. _____ 12:45 – 3:45

Children and families in the home-based program are visited once per week in the home and are transported to the center on Friday for a group experience. The home-based teacher will assist parents in creating a home environment to promote children's growth and development. This program is in the morning only.

Do you wish to apply for home-based program? Yes _____ No _____

* *

Family Size:

Family Income:
    $ _____ per week $ _____ per month $ _____ per year

Source of Reimbursement or Services (Circle "Yes" or "No" for each source)
    YES   NO   EPSDT/Medicaid (Latest certification #): _____
    YES   NO   Federal, State or Local Agency: _____
    YES   NO   In-kind Provider: _____
    YES   NO   Insurance: _____
                 I.D. #: _____
    YES   NO   WIC
    YES   NO   Food Stamps

Does this child or any of your family members have a disability or special need? Describe: _____
_____

How well does your child speak and understand English? _____
_____

How did you obtain information about this program? _____
_____

DIRECTOR'S RESOURCE 12-2

SAMPLE APPLICATION (no income information requested)

Walnut Corner Children's Center Preregistration Form

CHILD'S FAMILY INFORMATION

Child's Name _____   Name Used _____

Date of Birth, or Expected Date of Birth _____

Child's Address _____

Father/Guardian Name _____   Mother/Guardian Name _____

Home Address _____   Home Address _____

_____   _____

Employer _____   Employer _____

Address _____   Address _____

_____   _____

Business Phone _____   Business Phone _____

REQUESTED DAYS OF ATTENDANCE

Days: M   T   W   TH   F   Hours: _____ AM _____ PM

Requested Start Date: _____

HOW DID YOU LEARN ABOUT WALNUT CORNER CHILDREN'S CENTER?

Personal Referral/If so, who? _____

Newspaper _____   Radio _____   Web site _____   Other _____

Thank you for this information

PLEASE INCLUDE THE NONREFUNDABLE $25 REGISTRATION FEE WITH THIS FORM.

THIS FEE WILL SECURE YOUR CHILD'S NAME ON OUR WAITING LIST.

DIRECTOR'S RESOURCE 12-3

SAMPLE STUDENT ENROLLMENT FORM

(Public School-Sponsored Program)

STUDENT ENROLLMENT FORM

(MUST BE RETAINED IN STUDENT'S CUMULATIVE RECORD)

DO NOT WRITE IN THIS BOX

Assigned to:	Gr_____ Hr_____
SDF sent to Census	_____
Type a new CR	_____
CR in office file	_____
CR requested	_____
Health Record	Yes _____ No _____
Rec'd. 4-part SDF	_____

Name of school student is entering _____   Grade Entering* _____   Special Ed _____

Name _____

Student's Legal Name (as listed on birth certificate)

Circle   Sex: Male   Female   Circle   Race: Black   White   Other

Address_____   Apt. No._____   Zip Code _____   Phone No. _____

Place of birth _____   Date of birth _____

City   State   County   Mo.   Day   Yr.

Check one of the birth verifications listed below:

❏ Birth Certificate No. _____   ❏ Baptismal Certificate _____   ❏ Physician's Record   ❏ Passport

	DPT	Polio	Measles	Rubella	Mumps
IMMUNIZATION DATA					

Name		Place of birth		Deceased (Date)
		State	County	
Father:				
Mother:				
Step-Parent:				
Guardian:				

SOCIAL RECORD

	Occupation	Place of Employment	Business Phone No.
Father's occupation			
Mother's occupation			

If family is supported by another source indicate: _____

Name of Brothers and Sisters— School of Attendance	Still in School:	
	Preschool	

Family Status: of Parents:

Circle one: Married   Single   Divorced   Separated   Remarried

Student is living with _____   Relationship _____

LANGUAGE OTHER THAN ENGLISH SPOKEN IN HOME: _____

Did student attend this school last year?

❏ Yes

❏ No   Name of school _____   Address _____

❏ Yes – Privacy Requested: If this box is checked, no information pertaining to this student will be released to any person or institution (including colleges or universities) without your written approval.

❏ No – Privacy is not requested

Parent/Guardian's Signature _____   Date: _____

In case of emergency, call _____

Name   Relationship   Phone No.

NAME   Last   First   Middle

STUDENT NUMBER

SOCIAL SECURITY NO.

DIRECTOR'S RESOURCE 12-4

SAMPLE DEVELOPMENTAL HISTORY

Arlitt Child Development Center
Developmental History

Child's Name _____

How do you want your child's name written in the classroom? _____

Address _____ Zip Code _____ Phone _____

Birth Date _____ Race _____ Sex _____

I. Child's Family

Parents or Guardians

A. Name _____ Birth Date _____

Education (include highest grade completed or degrees) _____

Occupation _____ Usual working hours _____ Work phone _____

B. Name _____ Birth Date _____

Education (include highest grade completed or degrees) _____

Occupation _____ Usual working hours _____ Work phone _____

Status of Parents (check one): Living Together _____ Living Apart _____

Child lives with _____

If parents work or are students, who keeps the child in their absence? (check all appropriate)

Grandparent _____ Other relative _____ Friend _____ Paid sitter _____ Other _____

Other children in the family: (list in order of birth)

Name	Sex	Birth Date	What grade if in school

Sisters or brothers who attend Arlitt _____

Has your child ever been separated from his parents for long periods of time, and if so why?

_____

(continues)

DIRECTOR'S RESOURCE 12-4
(continued)

Have you moved frequently? _____

What language is spoken at home? _____

If more than one, what other language(s) are spoken? _____

II. Development in Early Childhood

Comment on the health of the mother during pregnancy _____

Comment on the health of your child during delivery and pregnancy _____

When did your child walk? _____ When did your child talk? _____

Is your child adopted? _____ Does he/she know it? _____

Does your child have bladder control? _____ Child's terminology _____

Does your child have bowel control? _____ Child's terminology _____

Does your child need reminding about going to the bathroom? _____

Does your child usually take a nap? _____ At what time? _____

Describe any special needs, handicaps, or health problems _____

_____

Does your child have any difficulty saying what he/she wants or do you have any trouble
understanding his/her speech? _____

III. Health Record

List all allergies and any special precautions and treatment indicated for these allergies:

_____

_____

List any medications (food supplements, modified diets or fluoride supplements currently being
administered to the child): _____

_____

List any chronic physical problems and any history of hospitalization: _____

_____

List any diseases, serious illnesses, operations or accidents the child has had: _____

_____

Has your child ever had a hearing examination or treatment? _____ When? _____

By Whom? _____ Results: _____

Has your child ever had a vision examination or treatment? _____ When? _____

By Whom? _____ Results: _____

(continues)

DIRECTOR'S RESOURCE 12-4
(continued)

IV. Eating Habits

1. What foods does your child especially like or dislike? _____
_____

2. List any food your child should net eat for medical, religious, or personal reasons? (this also requires a separate form) _____

3. Does your child take a bottle? _____

4. Does your child eat or chew things that aren't food? _____

5. Does your child have trouble chewing or swallowing? _____

6. How often does your child have diarrhea? _____ Constipation _____

7. Do you have any concerns about what your child eats? _____

V. Play and Social Experiences

1. Has your child participated in any group experiences?_____
   Where? _____

2. Did your child enjoy it?_____

3. Do other playmates visit the child? _____

4. Does your child visit other playmates in their homes? _____

5. What are your child's favorite toys and/or activities? _____
_____

6. How long does your child watch TV each day?_____

7. What is your child's favorite TV program?_____

8. What are your child's favorite books? _____

9. How many times a week is your child read to? _____

10. Is there anything else about your child's play or playmates which the school should know? _____
_____
_____

VI. Discipline

In most circumstances, do you consider your child easily managed, fairly easy to manage, or difficult to manage?_____

What concerns do you presently have about your child? _____
_____

How are these concerns dealt with? _____
_____

(continues)

DIRECTOR'S RESOURCE 12-4
(continued)

VII. *Parents' Impressions and Attitudes*

From your point of view, what were the events which seemed to have had the greatest impact on your child (moving, births, deaths, severe illness of family members, divorce)? _____

_____

_____

In what ways would you like to see your child develop during the school year? _____

_____

_____

VIII. *Additional Information*

_____

_____

_____

_____

School Year   **Date**   **Signature**

_____   _____   _____

_____   _____   _____

_____   _____   _____

Reprinted with permission from Arlitt Child & Family Research and Education Center, University of Cincinnati.

DIRECTOR'S RESOURCE 12-5

(for use with Class Exercise 1)

SAMPLE PERSONAL HISTORY—YOUR CHILD'S DEVELOPMENT

Date _____

Child's Name _____ Nickname _____

Address _____ Zip _____ Phone _____

Date of Birth _____ Place of birth _____ Race _____

I. The Child's Family   Sex _____

   Parents or Guardians

   A. Name _____ Birthdate _____

      Education (include highest grade completed or degrees)_____

      _____

      Occupation _____ Usual working hours _____

                                                  Work phone _____

   B. Name _____ Birthdate _____

      Education (include highest grade completed or degrees)_____

      _____

      Occupation _____ Usual working hours _____

                                                  Work phone _____

Status of Parents (Check)   Living together _____   Living apart_____

Child lives with _____

If parents work or are students, who keeps the child in their absence?

Circle one   Grandparent   Other Relative   Friend   Paid Sitter   Other

Other children in the family (list in order of birth)

Name	Sex	Birthdate	What grade if in school

Additional members of household (give number)

Friends _____   Others_____

Boarders _____   Relatives_____

                                                                 (Indicate relationships)

(continues)

DIRECTOR'S RESOURCE 12-5
(continued)

(for use with Class Exercise 1)

What part do these other persons have in the care of your child? _____
_____

Has your child been separated from his parents for long periods of time, and if so, why?
_____

Have you moved frequently? _____

What language is usually spoken at home?_____

(If more than one, what other language(s) are spoken?) _____

C. Income _____ (per month) _____(per year) _____

D. Medical card number _____ (parent)

     Child's number _____

II. Development in Early Childhood

Comment on the health of the mother during pregnancy _____

Comment on the health of your child during delivery and infancy _____
_____

When did you child walk? _____ When did your child talk? _____

Is your child adopted? _____ Does he/she know it? _____

Does your child have bladder control? _____ Child's terminology _____

Does your child have bowel control? _____ Child's terminology _____

Does your child need help when going to the bathroom? _____

Does your child need reminding about going to the bathroom?_____

Does your child usually take a nap? _____ At what time? _____

Describe any special needs, handicaps, or health problems. _____
_____

Does your child have any difficulty saying what he/she wants or do you have any trouble understanding his/her speech? _____

III. Eating Habits

What is your child's general attitude toward eating? _____

What foods does your child especially like? _____

For which meal is your child most hungry? _____

Does the child feed himself/herself entirely? _____

Does your child dislike any food in particular? _____

Is your child on a special diet? _____

Does your child take a bottle? _____

(continues)

DIRECTOR'S RESOURCE 12-5
(continued)

(for use with Class Exercise 1)

Does your child eat or chew things that are not food? Explain. _____

Do you have any concerns about your child's eating habits? Explain. _____

_____

Is there any food your child should not eat for medical, religious, or personal reasons? _____

_____

IV. Play and Social Experiences

Has your child participated in any group experiences?_____

Where? _____

Did your child enjoy it? _____

Do other playmates visit the child? _____

Does your child visit other playmates in their homes? _____

How does your child relate to other children?_____

Does your child prefer to play alone? _____ With other children?_____

Does your child worry a lot or is he/she very afraid of anything?_____

What causes worry or fear?_____

Does your child have any imaginary playmates? _____ Explain _____

_____

Does your child have any pets? _____

What are your child's favorite toys and/or activities?_____

_____

What is your child's favorite TV program? _____

How long does your child watch TV each day?_____

What are your child's favorite books? _____

How many times a week is your child read to?_____

Is there anything else about your child's play or playmates which the school should know? _____

_____

_____

V. Discipline

In most circumstances, do you consider your child easily managed, fairly easy to manage, or difficult
to manage? _____

What concerns do you presently have about your child? _____

_____

How are these concerns dealt with? _____

_____

(continues)

DIRECTOR'S RESOURCE 12-5
(continued)

(for use with Class Exercise 1)

VI. Parent's Impression and Attitudes

From your point of view, what were the events which seemed to have had the greatest impact on your child (moving, births, deaths, severe illness of family members, divorce)? _____

_____

_____

How would you describe your child at the present time? What changes have you seen in your child during the past year? _____

_____

Does your child have any behavior characteristics which you hope will change? Please describe.

_____

In what ways would you like to see your child develop during the school year?

_____

_____

_____

_____

_____

_____

_____
Signature(s) of person(s) filling out this questionnaire

DIRECTOR'S RESOURCE 12-6

SAMPLE CHILD'S MEDICAL STATEMENT

Enrollment Date _____

Day Care Center/Preschool Certificate of Medical Examination
To be Completed by Family Physician or Clinic

This is to certify that _____   _____
                                                Child's Name   Birth Date

Child of _____   _____   _____
                              Mother   Address   Phone

_____   _____   _____
                      Father   Address   Phone

was examined by me on _____, and based on his/her medical history
                                                Date of Examination

and physical condition at the time of this examination, is free from apparent communicable disease, and
is in suitable condition for enrollment in a child day care facility; and has had the immunizations required
by Section 3313.671 of the Revised Code for admission to school, or has had the immunizations required
by the State Department of Health for infants and toddlers, or is to be exempted from these requirements
for medical reasons.

Tuberculin Test
(within last year
for new enrollee)   Date _____   Type of test _____   Results_____

DPT Series and
booster dates   1st _____   2nd _____   3rd _____   4th _____   5th* _____

Oral Polio
Series dates   1st _____   2nd _____   3rd _____   4th* _____

                        *The 5th DPT and 4th polio are normally administered just prior to kindergarten.

Measles (Rubella,
10-day)   Date _____
Rubella (3-day)   Date _____
Mumps   Date _____
Haemophilus b
Polysaccharide (HIB)   Date _____   (HIB vaccine is required for children ages
                                                        2 years through 4 years)

Is able to participate in all regular activities except _____
_____

Remarks _____
Physician's Signature _____   Date _____
Clinic Name _____   Phone _____
Office Location_____
City, State, Zip _____

Parent should retain this sheet when child withdraws from center

DIRECTOR'S RESOURCE 12-7

SAMPLE EMERGENCY INFORMATION RECORD

Child's Name _____

Home Address _____

Father's name/Husband (or guardian)	Place of Employment	Bus. Phone

Mother's name/Wife (or guardian)	Place of Employment	Bus. Phone

Please fill in information below so that the school may act more effectively in event of illness or injury to the child.

EMERGENCY: Person to be called if parent (husband or wife) cannot be reached

Name	Address	Phone

Date	Parent's Signature (or guardian)

DIRECTOR'S RESOURCE 12-8

(for use with Class Exercise 1)

SAMPLE PERMISSION FORM

While your child is enrolled in this program, he/she will be involved in a number of special activities for which we need your permission. Please read the following information carefully. You are encouraged to ask questions about anything that is unclear to you. You, of course, have the option of withdrawing permission at any time.

_____

(Child's Name)

(Please circle your choice)

A. I DO DO NOT give my permission for my child to go on walks with the classroom teacher and class in the nearby neighborhood.

B. I DO DO NOT give my permission for my child to be screened for speech and language.

C. I DO DO NOT give my permission for my child to be screened for hearing.

D. I DO DO NOT give my permission for my child to be screened for specific educational needs.

E. From time to time photographs of our preschool program will be made for educational and publicity purposes. These pictures will be representative of the enriching experiences offered your child during the year.

I DO DO NOT give my permission for my child to be photographed for use in educational, nonprofit publications/presentations intended to further the cause of public education. This permission is applicable for current as well as future project use.

As part of this program, your child's records may be included in research that evaluates the value of the program. In all cases, the confidentiality of individual children's records is maintained.

_____

Parent's Signature

_____

Date

DIRECTOR'S RESOURCE 12-9

SAMPLE TRANSPORTATION AND ATTENDANCE RELEASE FORM

Escort Form
Transportation of Children to & from School*

1. Child's Name: _____ Teacher: _____

   Parent Signature: _____ Date: _____

2. I authorize these people to assume responsibility for my child to and from school:

   _____

   _____

   _____

   _____

   _____

   _____

   If someone other than myself or these people are going to bring or pick up my child I will send a note or phone the school office 556-3802.

3. My child carpools with these children on these days:

Child's Name	Days
_____	_____
_____	_____
_____	_____
_____	_____
_____	
_____	

*It is our policy not to send a child home with anyone other than the parent without written permission.

Reprinted by permission of Cincinnati Youth Collaborative.

REFERENCES

Allen, K. E., & Cowdery, G. E. (2005). *The exceptional child: Inclusion in early childhood education* (5th ed.). Clifton Park, NY: Thomson Delmar Learning.

Decker, C. A., & Decker, J. R. (2005). *Planning and administering early childhood programs* (8th ed.). Upper Saddle River, NJ: Prentice Hall.

The Family Educational Rights and Privacy Act (Buckley Amendment). (1974). The 1974 Education Amendments, Sec. 513,88, Stat. 571.20, U.S.C.A., Sec 1232g. (Supp. 1875).

Feeney, S., & Freeman, N. (n.d.). *Ethics and the early childhood educator.* Using the NAEYC Code of Ethics, Section ll. Washington, DC: NAEYC.

Katz, L. G., Evangelou, D., & Hartman, J. A. (1990). *The case for mixed-age grouping in early childhood education.* Washington, DC: NAEYC.

NAEYC. (1998). *Accreditation criteria and procedures of the National Academy of Early Childhood Programs.* Washington, DC: Author.

Read, K., Gardner, P., & Mahler, B. (1993). *Early childhood programs: Early childhood relationships and learning* (9th ed.). Orlando, FL: Harcourt.

Taylor, B. (2002). *Early childhood program management: People and procedures.* Columbus OH: Merrill.

Additional resources for this chapter can be found on the Online Companion™ at http://www.earlychilded.delmar.com. This supplemental material includes relevant Web links, Web activities, and case studies that apply the concepts presented in this chapter. In addition, the Working Papers and Director's Resources are available for download, allowing you to complete Class Exercises and Class Assignments electronically.

CHAPTER 13

Managing the Food and the Health and Safety Programs

Health and safety information should be posted where both parents and teachers can see it.

OBJECTIVES

After reading this chapter, you should be able to:

- Understand the need for staff training and reporting in the area of abuse.
- List components for providing a complete food service program.
- Describe the process for monitoring procedures for caring for injured or sick children.
- Formulate plans for various emergencies, including natural or national disasters.

The director ultimately is responsible for the center's food service and health and safety programs, despite the fact that the components of these programs may be the immediate responsibility of assigned staff members. In large programs, a nutritionist and/or food service coordinator and a cook may have full responsibility for the center's food service, but the director should be knowledgeable about the program and is accountable to the board, the funding agencies, and the center's families. Similarly, a social service or health coordinator may plan and implement the health and safety program, but again, the accountability for the program is with the director. Directors of small programs often have full responsibility for both planning and implementing the food service and health and safety programs. Since you, as a director, will be expected to supervise and monitor these programs, or in small centers to fully implement them, you must be informed about the elements of the food service and the health and safety programs and about the importance of these programs to the children and families in your center.

FOOD SERVICE PROGRAMS

The total food service program, whether it is limited to midmorning snack, or consists of a two- or even a three-meal-a-day program, is important, not only because nutrition affects the mental functioning and the physical well-being of the child, but also because nutritional habits and attitudes toward eating are established during the early years. Providing variety in food choices, the style of serving the food, and establishing an appropriate emotional atmosphere for mealtime are foremost considerations, whether the children's meals and snacks are catered, served from frozen prepackaged microwave dinners, come from public school or company cafeterias, or are prepared completely from start to finish in the center's kitchen. In some programs, children bring "brown bag" lunches, a practice that can be a boon to your budget and provide an opportunity to help parents learn more about good nutrition. All brown bag lunches must be dated and properly labeled. They must be refrigerated and all leftover foods discarded and not sent home in the child's lunch box. It is also important to make certain that children do not trade food with their friends. Nutritious foods should be offered daily, using variations in serving styles such as self-help and group snacks, family-style and cafeteria-style meals, picnics, bag lunches, and more casual food service for special occasions.

It should be understood that the adults in the classroom sit down with the children when food is served, that the adults eat the same food that is served to the children, and that the adults take charge of creating pleasant conversation among the entire group during snack time or mealtime. Conversation can focus on food, on what children have been doing or expect to do later in the day, or on any topic that is of interest to most children. An accepting adult who avoids having children wait to be served, who encourages but doesn't demand tasting new foods, who uses utensils appropriately and suggests that children try to manipulate their own small forks or spoons, and who avoids associating unpleasantness or punishment with food is demonstrating healthy habits and attitudes toward eating.

For the young infant, a caring familiar adult who is unrushed is important during feeding time. Infants should be held while taking a bottle but encouraged to begin to hold it for self-feeding as voluntary control progresses. Staff must be reminded *not* to prop bottles for infants because of dangers of choking, and falling asleep with milk or juice in the mouth, which is detrimental to healthy gums and teeth and could lead to a possible increase in ear infections. In addition, for their emotional and social well-being, it is critical that babies be held and cuddled while being fed.

Older infants benefit from sitting in adapted chairs near the table with older toddlers and preschoolers, whenever that is possible. They often can enjoy finger foods with the toddlers and participate in the pleasant atmosphere of eating time. Since choking may be a problem for babies who are beginning to feed themselves, a caregiver must be close by at all times. Foods should be cut in bite-size pieces, be of proper consistency, and at the very beginning, be offered one piece at a time. Make sure the cook and the caregivers in the program know that there are high-risk foods that are likely to cause choking in young children. Ninety percent of all fatal chokings occur in children under age four.

Foods that may cause choking include the following (American Academy of Pediatrics, 2002):

- frankfurters
- raw carrots
- marshmallows
- peanut butter(spoonfuls) pretzels
- whole grapes
- raw celery
- large pieces of fruit
- nuts and seeds
- chunks of meat
- chips
- hard candy
- cherries with pits
- popcorn
- raisins

Some of these food can be offered if served in a different form.

- frankfurters cut in strips
- carrots or celery cooked until slightly soft (cut in sticks)
- grapes or cherries cut in small pieces (U.S. Department of Agriculture [USDA], 1999)

It also is essential for children to sit down while eating or drinking to further avoid the dangers of choking.

Since directors are responsible for all aspects of the food service program, they must monitor and supervise the atmosphere, health, and safety features of mealtimes. They also must oversee the planning, buying, and preparation of food and provide opportunities for in-service training to the food service staff members and other adults who work with the children during snack and mealtime.

MyPyramid: Steps to a Healthier you (*Courtesy of the U.S. Department of Agriculture*)

Menu Planning

The proportion of the total daily food requirement provided by the center depends on the total number of hours the child spends in the center. Licensing regulations vary, but general guidelines state

- children in care eight hours or less shall be offered at least one meal and two snacks, or two meals and one snack.

- children in care for nine hours or more shall be offered at least two meals and two snacks, or one meal and three snacks.

- a nutritious snack shall be offered to all children in midmorning and in midafternoon.

- children shall be offered food at intervals of not less than two hours and not more than three hours apart unless the child is asleep. (American Academy of Pediatrics, 2002)

Of course, infants in group care have very different needs and require individualized eating schedules with carefully prepared formulas and special diets.

The 2005 version of the Food Guide Pyramid includes the food groups listed on the "MyPyramid Steps to a Healthier You."

The USDA Food Pyramid plus the portion sizes and food selections for young children are available from the Center for Nutrition Policy and Promotion, an agency of USDA (see Appendix B for contact information).

At the time this book went to press, the new and revised "My Food Pyramid" had been published, but the agency was still working out the details of the new food pyramid for school-age children as well as the one for preschoolers, infants, and toddlers.

Nutritious meals and snacks can be selected from among the following food groups:

- bread, rice, cereal, and pasta group
- vegetable group
- fruit group
- milk, yogurt, and cheese group
- meat, poultry, fish, dry beans, eggs, and nuts group
- fats, oils, and sweets group

Careful planning involves including ample choices of fruits and vegetables along with dairy products; some meat, fish, and poultry; and some selected items from the bread and pasta group. It is important to check local licensing standards for additional details on nutrition requirements. For centers involved in the USDA Child and Adult Care Food Program (CACFP), nutritional standards for meal and snack serving sizes for children birth through age 12 can be found in the USDA/CACFP materials.

Every precaution must be taken to ensure that children with food allergies or other conditions requiring a special diet are served only those foods on their prescribed diet. Both the cook and all classroom staff must be alerted to these special dietary requirements, and both the director and the staff must know the emergency procedures to follow in the event a particular child has an allergic reaction. With the increasing incidences of peanut allergies among young children, some programs choose to eliminate all peanut products, including peanut butter, from their menus. For some special diet cases, parents may choose to send food for the child. It is important that these packed lunches be properly refrigerated until served and *not* be shared with other children. Any food from home must be labeled, showing the child's name and date.

Nutritional considerations in meal planning for young children are necessary but not sufficient to guarantee that children will be adequately nourished. Children's appetites and food preferences also must be taken into consideration when meals are planned. Three- and four-year-old children tend to have small, unpredictable appetites, and they are prone to food sprees. Their foods must be neither too hot nor too cold, not too spicy or gluey, and it is best if they are cut into bite-size and manageable portions. Variation in texture, color, and flavor also are important considerations in planning children's meals. Every effort should be made to limit use of salt and sugar as well as foods high in fat. Serving certain ethnic foods will provide wider variation for all the children and make available familiar foods to the children from specific ethnic groups represented in the classroom. It is always a good idea to introduce a new food along with old familiar favorites.

Further considerations that affect menu planning are the availability of equipment and utensils and the preparation time for each menu item when all foods are prepared in the center kitchen. It is virtually impossible to prepare hot breads, an oven-cooked main dish, and a baked dessert for one meal if only one oven is available. Also, the number and sizes of pots and pans must be checked when menus are planned to ensure that there is an adequate supply of equipment of an appropriate size to prepare the foods for a particular meal. Preparation time is another factor that influences meal planning. Meals that require too much last-minute preparation create problems for the cook, which, in turn, could delay the serving time. Hungry children who are forced to wait for their food become impatient and restless, and teachers then must find ways to help them cope with these unnecessary delays.

Meal and menu planning can be systematized and simplified by using meal planning guides, standardized recipes, and sample menus. A number of government booklets and other menu planning guides are useful in planning four to six weeks of basic menus. Menu changes based on the availability of seasonal or plentiful foods can be made on a weekly basis. But beyond those minor changes, basic menu patterns can be repeated every four to six weeks.

Teachers and parents often have helpful suggestions about changes in the basic menu patterns. Some lunches include too many items that are difficult for children to manage or too time consuming to serve. For example, soup, banana sections that have to be peeled, and packaged crackers that have to be opened is a menu both difficult to serve and a problem for children to manage. If the cook has a way to get input from the teachers, menu adjustments can be made easily.

Inviting the cook to lunch with the children and having a "cook's mailbox" provide an opportunity for her to hear comments from the children about the food and to observe how well they manage the foods served. A "cook's mailbox" not only invites children to write requests for favorite foods and send thank-you notes to the cook but serves as an excellent meaningful literacy experience as well. The mailbox and the lunch with the children also give the cook a chance to feel more a part of the total center program, rather than one who spends all day in the kitchen and away from the children.

Since parents often are interested in what children have been served for snacks and/or for breakfast and lunch, it is helpful to post weekly menus or publish them regularly in the parent newsletter. Posting menus not only helps the parents plan for a child's meals at home but also serves as a model for parents who may be inexperienced with planning balanced family meals.

An interesting feature to add to the menu posting area is a pictorial menu for the children. The cook, another staff member, or an interested parent may be willing to collect food pictures and post each day's snack and/or lunch on an eye-level bulletin board for children to "read." It creates interest among the children who can look forward to a dish they especially enjoy, and it becomes part of the center's nutrition program.

Food Buying

Careful menu planning reduces cost and waste and provides a clear-cut basis for setting up shopping lists for daily, weekly, and monthly food buying. Whether meals are catered, partially prepared from prepackaged meals especially designed for children, or fully prepared in the center kitchen, the food budget will affect both meal planning and food purchasing. Quantity buying and cooperative buying arrangements among a group of centers sometimes results in lower prices, but also might limit choices, increase the pressure to purchase foods of lesser quality, and create storage problems when quantity purchases exceed the available storage space. Therefore, although price is an important consideration, quality, available storage space, and, of course, food preferences of the children must be taken into consideration when food purchasing decisions are made.

Catered meal services require practically no shopping time, no storage space, and very little time selecting foods and developing the shopping lists. They also eliminate the need for a complete meal preparation space and a full-time cook, but the services may be more expensive than meals that are prepared at the

center. However, the food could turn out to be less satisfying to the children and the choices likely to give the director less control over the entire food service entity.

The prepackaged frozen meals that are prepared in convection or microwave ovens are a very expensive convenience. This type of food service requires large freezers and special ovens yet requires neither a full-time cook nor complete meal preparation space. The director must select carefully so the choices are appropriate for young children and there is variety in the menu. Fresh foods and beverages must be bought daily or weekly as needed to supplement prepackaged meals.

Using company or public school cafeterias requires planning with the cafeteria manager and staff. Foods brought from cafeterias serving adults or older children are sometimes served in containers or in portions difficult for young children to manage. A whole hamburger, a large strip of dill pickle, catsup in a sealed foil container, and milk in a sealed carton are all difficult for young children to handle. But since that is standard public school cafeteria fare, you may find no other choices for your children. Also, cafeteria service customarily means self-help and carrying trays. That is out of the question for young children. It is important to develop clear-cut guidelines for portion sizes, family-style service, and alternative menus so you can work with the cafeteria food service staff to find ways to make appropriate adjustments for young children.

DIRECTOR'S CORNER

"One of the things I learned quickly when I started to work with this program in the public school was to become friendly with the cafeteria manager. Now she cuts the hamburgers in quarters, sends pickle slices instead of those huge strips of dill pickles, and includes a sharp knife for my use when there are apples to be cored and sliced or oranges to be quartered."

—Director, public school Head Start program

Meals prepared at the center mean that the center must have a complete meal preparation space that meets all licensing requirements and must employ a full-time cook if it is a full-day child care program. Preferably, the cook will have planning and buying skills. If not, a staff person (sometimes the director) plans and purchases the foods in consultation with the cook. Planning purchases, doing the shopping, and checking deliveries are all time consuming; however, total meal preparation at the center allows for greater variation in foods served and more involvement of the children in shopping, preparation, and serving. It also guarantees that items on the menu will be prepared and served with young children in mind.

USDA Child and Adult Care Food Program

Some centers serve children who are eligible for free or reduced-price meals from the USDA Child and Adult Care Food Program (CACFP). Based on income eligibility of families enrolled, child care centers (not-for-profit or for-profit), home-based programs, and after-school care programs are eligible to participate in the CACFP. The Child Nutrition and WIC Reauthorization Act of 2004 permits for-profit centers to participate when 25 percent of the center's enrollment or licensed capacity receives either Title XX assistance or is eligible for free or reduced meals. For those providers who may not qualify under the Title XX criteria, they may meet other qualification expectations. The National Child Care Association (NCCA) is a helpful resource for the for-profit programs. Although some programs may have a designated staff person or the cook do some of the paperwork in order to receive the USDA reimbursement, in most cases the director does the necessary paperwork or at least is responsible for making sure it is done correctly.

Eligibility of children for free or reduced-price meals is based on family income. Income levels for family eligibility and reimbursement rates for providers are adjusted annually effective July 1 of each year. Therefore, to determine which families in your center are eligible and what the reimbursement rate will be for those meals, contact the USDA Communication and Government Affairs office (see Appendix B for contact information). Other helpful sources of information include the National Food Service Management Institute (see Appendix B), your state licensing agent (see Chapter 4), or your state agency that administers the Child Nutrition Program (http://www. fns.usda.gov).

An Income Eligibility Application (Figure 13–1) must be on file for every child who receives meals under the USDA Child Care Food Program. These forms must be kept on file for at least three years to ensure that they will be available at the time your agency undergoes a Verification Review. It is essential that the information on the forms be complete and accurate to avoid the possibility of penalties if errors are discovered at the time of the review. USDA forms vary from state to state, so samples shown may not match those required by your state. Also, new forms are issued yearly with updated income guidelines.

To get forms from your state, contact your state agency that administers the Child Nutrition Program. The list of these state agencies can be found at the USDA Web site (http://www.fns.usda.gov). The state agency will provide not only updated application forms but also worksheets that can be used to determine eligibility of your clients and worksheets for record keeping and for applying for reimbursement. Most states require centers to submit the final information and request for reimbursement on-line.

Providers who fit into one of the following categories may receive USDA reimbursement for eligible children enrolled:

- nonresidential public or private not-for-profit child care and ADC centers (some forms or documents replace ADC with Temporary Assistance for Needy Families [TANF])
- profit-making child care centers that receive Title XX compensation for at least 25 percent of the children attending
- Head Start programs
- settlement houses and recreation programs
- family child care homes (only if they participate in the CACFP under a sponsoring organization that has tax-exempt status)

All participating agencies must serve meals that meet the standards for the Special Food Service Program for Infants, Preschool Age and School Age Children. Following USDA guidelines ensures well-balanced meals; however, some recommended serving sizes may be overwhelming for young children if put on the plate all at one time.

The USDA Child and Adult Care Food Program meal patterns requires extensive paperwork that must be done accurately and on a regular basis. A Claim for Reimbursement form and a Monthly Financial Report must be filed monthly with the State Division of School Food Service, and report data on

- attendance.
- number of meals served.
- cost of food, which is calculated on the basis of information obtained from a monthly food inventory.
- labor and purchased service costs.
- income from reduced-lunch fees and other sources.

To complete these claim forms, you must have accurate attendance records, invoices or cash tapes and receipts for all food, and some nonfood purchases, canceled checks and financial records on all cash received from those families who pay full or

CHILD AND ADULT CARE FOOD PROGRAM: <u>CHILD CARE COMPONENT</u>
INCOME ELIGIBILITY APPLICATION FOR FREE AND REDUCED PRICE MEALS

INSTRUCTIONS: To apply for free and reduced price meals, read the Household Letter/instructions on backside. Complete application and return to the center. In Accordance with the NSLA, information on this application may be disclosed to other Child Nutrition Programs or applicable enforcement agencies. Parents/guardians are not required to consent to this disclosure. *Part 1* is to be completed by all households. *Part 2* is to be used only for a child living in a household receiving Food Stamps or Ohio Works First (OWF) benefits. *Part 3* is only for children NOT receiving Food Stamp or OWF benefits. *Part 4* is to be completed for foster children.
*Asterisk items must be filled in for each part you complete. Form must be updated annually and is valid for only 12 months including the month signed.

PART 1 – PRINT INFORMATION FOR ALL CHILDREN ENROLLED AT CENTER			PART 2 – LIST EACH CHILD'S FOOD STAMP OR OWF CASE NUMBER, IF ANY, A VALID CASE NUMBER CONTAINS 10 TO 12 DIGITS.
*CHILD (REN) NAME	AGE	BIRTH DATE	*FOOD STAMP OR OWF CASE NUMBER
1.			
2.			
3.			
4.			

PART 3 – HOUSEHOLD SIZE AND HOUSEHOLD INCOME: If Part 2 completed skip to Part 5.

Monthly Income Conversion: Weekly × 4.33, Every 2 weeks × 2.15, Twice a Month × 2

*LIST NAMES OF ALL HOUSEHOLD MEMBERS INCLUDING CHILDREN LISTED ABOVE IN PART 1	*Gross MONTHLY Earnings (before deductibles)		*MONTHLY Welfare Payments, Child Support, Alimony	*MONTHLY Pensions, Retirement, Social Security	*ANY OTHER MONTHLY income
	Job 1	Job 2			
1.	$	$	$	$	$
2.	$	$	$	$	$
3.	$	$	$	$	$
4.	$	$	$	$	$
5.	$	$	$	$	$
6.	$	$	$	$	$
7.	$	$	$	$	$

PART 4 – FOSTER CHILD: [] (check) List foster child's monthly personal use income. Enter "0" if one. $

PART 5 – SIGNATURE AND SOCIAL SECURITY NUMBER: I certify that the above information is true and correct and that all income is reported. I understand that this information is being given for receipt of federal funds; that program officials may verify the information on the application; and that deliberate misrepresentation of the information may subject me to prosecution under applicable state and federal criminal statutes.

X_____ X_____ X_____
*SIGNATURE OF ADULT HOUSEHOLD MEMBER   **DATE**   **SOCIAL SECURITY NUMBER (SSN) Required only for Part 3) Write "None" if adult signer doesn't have a SSN.**

Print Name:	Daytime Phone Number:	Work Phone Number:
Street/Apt:	City/State/Zip:	County:

PART 6 – RACIAL/ETHNIC IDENTITY: Optional Question: Please check appropriate box to identify the race or ethnicity of your child (ren).

American Indian or Alaska Native	Black or African American	Native Hawaiian or Other Pacific Islander
Asian	Hispanic or Latino	White

Privacy Act Statement: Section 9 of the National School Lunch Act (NSLA) requires that, unless your child's food stamp or OWF case number is provided, you must include the social security number of the adult household member signing the application or indicate that the household member does not have a social security number. Provision of a social security number is not mandatory, but if a social security number is not given or an indication is not made that the signer does not have such a number, the application cannot be approved. This notice must be brought to the attention of the household member whose social security number is disclosed. The social security number may be used to identify the household member in carrying out efforts to verify the correctness of information stated on the application or shared with other persons directly connected with the administration or enforcement of the program under the NSLA or Child Nutrition Act of 1966 to determine program eligibility. These verification efforts may be carried out through program reviews, audits, and investigations and may include contacting employers to determine income, contacting a food stamp or welfare office to determine current certification for receipt of food stamps or OWF benefits, contacting the state employment security office to determine the amount of benefits received and checking the documentation produced by household members to prove the amount of income received. These efforts may result in a loss of reduction of benefits, administrative claims or legal action if incorrect information is reported.   State Distribution: Week of 6/21/04

SPONSOR USE ONLY: COMPLETE THESE TWO SECTIONS TO CATEGORIZE FORM	CHECK ONE:
A VALID FOOD STAMP OR OWF CASE NUMBER HAS BEEN PROVIDED: (circle one) YES NO IF YES AND FORM IS COMPLETE, CHILD MAY BE CLAIMED AS FREE. IF NO, MUST CATEGORIZE BY INCOME.	APPROVED FREE []
	APPROVED REDUCED []
TOTAL HOUSEHOLD SIZE:_____ TOTAL MONTHLY INCOME, ALL SOURCES: $_____	
SIGNATURE OF STAFF CATEGORIZING FORM:_____ DATE CATEGORIZED:	NOT ELIGIBLE (PAID) []

Revised 6/04

Figure 13–1

Sample application for free and reduced price meals.

HOUSEHOLD LETTER

Dear Parent or Guardian:

Our child care center must provide a copy of this letter with the Application for Free and Reduced Price Meals. It explains how your family can apply for free or reduced price meals and learn more about receiving free medical benefits. To apply for free and reduced price meals, complete the application on the reverse side using the instructions for your type of household. An application must contain complete information to be considered for free or reduced price meals. Once completed, you must report to your child's center any changes in your income of $50 per month or $600 per year, any change in your household size and any termination of your child's certification to receive food stamps or OWF benefit. During periods of unemployment, your child(ren) is eligible for meal reimbursement provided the loss of income during this time causes the family to be within eligibility standards for meals.

PART 1 – CHILD INFORMATION: ALL HOUSEHOLDS COMPLETE THIS PART.
- (a) Print the name of the child(ren) enrolled at the child care center. Children from the same household (except foster children) may be listed on the same application.
- (b) List their age and birthday.

PART 2 – HOUSEHOLDS GETTING FOOD STAMPS OR OWF: COMPLETE THIS PART AND PART 5. – If a child is a member of a food stamp or OWF household, the child is automatically eligible to receive free CACFP benefits subject to application completion.
- (a) List a current food stamp or OWF case number for each child. This will be a 10 or 12-digit number.
- (b) Sign the application in PART 5. An adult household member must sign.

SKIP PART 3 – Do not list names of household members or income if you list a food stamp or OWF case number for each child.

PART 3 – ALL OTHER HOUSEHOLDS: COMPLETE THIS PART AND PART 5
- (a) Write the names of all household members including yourself and the child(ren) that attends the child care center, whether they receive income or not. A household is defined as a group of related or unrelated individuals who are living as one economic unit that share housing and/or significant income and expenses of its members. Attach another piece of paper if you need more space to list all household members.
- (b) Income is any money received on a recurring basis, including gross earned income. Write the amount of income each household member received the previous month, before taxes or anything else is taken out, in the appropriate column. If any amount during the previous month was more or less than usual, write that person's usual monthly income. To figure monthly income: weekly income × 4.33, income paid every 2 weeks × 2.15, income paid twice a month × 2. Examples of household sources of income may include: Earnings from work such as wages, salaries, tips, strike benefits, unemployment compensation, worker's compensation, net income from self-owned business or farm; welfare, public assistance, child support payments, and alimony; pensions, retirement income, social security, veteran's payments, or supplemental security income; other income such as disability benefits, cash withdrawn from savings, interest/dividends, income from estates/trusts/investments, regular contributions from persons not living in the household, net royalties/annuities, net rental income, or other income.
- (c) An adult household member must sign the application and give his/her social security number (SS#) or indicate that they do not have a SS# in PART 5.

PART 4 – HOUSEHOLDS WITH A FOSTER CHILD: COMPLETE THIS PART AND PART 5. – In certain cases, foster children are eligible for free or reduced price meals regardless of the income of such household with whom they reside. If you wish to apply for such benefits for a foster child living with you, complete the application as if for a family of one since a foster child is the legal responsibility of a welfare agency or court. Complete a separate application for each foster child.
- (a) List the foster child's monthly "personal use" income. Write "0" if the foster child does not receive "personal use" income.
- (b) An adult member of the foster home must sign the application in PART 5.
- (c) A social security number is not needed for the foster child's application.
"Personal use" income is: (1) money given by the welfare office identified by category for the child's personal use, such as for clothing, school fees, and allowances; and (2) all other money the child receives, such as money from his/her family and money from the child's full-time or regular part-time jobs.

PART 5 – SIGNATURE AND SOCIAL SECURITY NUMBER: ALL HOUSEHOLDS COMPLETE THIS PART.
- (1) All applications must have the signature of an adult household member.
- (2) An application that lists monthly income must have the social security number of the adult who signs. If the adult does not have a social security number, write "none" or something else to show that the adult does not have a social security number. If you listed a food stamp or OWF number for each child or if you are applying for a foster child, a social security number is not needed.

PART 6 – RACIAL/ETHNIC IDENTITY

Complete the racial/ethnic identity question if you wish. You are not required to answer this question to be eligible to get free or reduced price meals. This information is collected to make sure that everyone is treated fairly and will be kept confidential. No child will be discriminated against because of race, color, national origin, gender, age or disability.

HEALTHY START & HEALTHY FAMILIES

Families with children eligible for free or reduced price meals may be eligible for FREE health care coverage through Ohio's Healthy Start & Healthy Families programs. These programs include coverage for doctor visits, immunizations, physicals, prescriptions, dental, vision, mental health, substance abuse and more. Please call 1-800-324-8680 for more information or to request an application. Information can also be found on the web at www.state.oh.us/odifs/ohp/bcps/hshf/index.stm. *Note: If you already have an Ohio Medicaid Care, you are already getting these services.

NON-DISCRIMINATION STATEMENT: "In accordance with Federal law and U.S. Department of Agriculture policy, this institution is prohibited from discriminating on the basis of race, color, national origin, gender, age or disability. To file a complaint of discrimination, write USDA, Director, Office of Civil Rights. Room 326-W, Whitten Building, 1400 Independence Avenue, SW, Washington, D.C. 20250-9410 or call (202)5964 (voice and TDD). USDA is an equal opportunity provider and employer."

REDUCED INCOME ELIGIBILITY GUIDELINES

Guidelines to be effective from July 1, 2004 through June 30, 2005

Households with incomes less than or equal to the reduced price values below are eligible for free meal benefits.

HOUSEHOLD SIZE	YEAR	MONTH	WEEK
1	17,224	1,436	332
2	23,107	1,926	445
3	28,990	2,416	558
4	34,873	2,907	671
5	40,756	3,397	784
6	46,639	3,887	897
7	52,522	4,377	1,011
8	58,405	4,868	1,124
For each additional household member add:	5,883	491	114

Revised 6/04

Figure 13–1

(continued)

reduced-lunch costs. The reimbursement form helps with record keeping. Some states provide worksheets to assist with record keeping. Directors may also develop their own worksheets.

Even when there is an extra person on staff to do the USDA paperwork, data collection for the reports and preparation for the Verification Review involve the director, the cook, and the teaching staff. Some states require regular training for all staff involved in the food program. Items such as point-of-service meal counts, safe and sanitary food handling, and size of servings are appropriate topics for these mandatory staff training sessions. Although the sessions are time consuming and costly, it is important that all staff understand details of the requirements to qualify for reimbursement from the CACFP because it is the center's primary source of revenue to finance the food program for eligible families.

Each program is subject to a Verification Review by the state agency every three years. The purpose of the review is to determine that all the income eligibility forms since the last review have been filled out correctly; that each family is properly classified as free, reduced, or paid; and that the figures reported to the state on the monthly claim forms are accurate. When the CACFP consultant comes to the center to do the Verification Review, you must provide the following:

- all income eligibility forms
- attendance records
- enrollment forms (to confirm that children listed as eligible for reimbursement are enrolled)

In addition to reviewing records on children, the consultant also will review administrative records. For that review, you must provide the following:

- record of meal counts
- menus
- monthly food inventories
- documentation of food and supply costs
- documentation of labor costs
- documentation of Title XX enrollments if it is a proprietary center

Auditors who do the Verification Review send information prior to their visit giving instructions about what they expect to review and what documentation must be prepared and available to them.

As a director, it is essential that you understand the USDA program so you can do the paperwork if it is part of your job description, or delegate the responsibility and then coach those who are doing the detailed record keeping and reporting.

Food Storage

Storing food requires careful planning so that sufficient quantities of food items are conveniently accessible to the preparation area and storage areas and containers are sanitary and chilled. The available shelf space and containers must be appropriate to accommodate the packaged size of the food items as they are delivered from the supplier. All food items should be stored separately from nonfood items, and food storage rooms should be dry, relatively cool (60°F to 70°F), and free from insect or rodent infestation. Commodities should be stored in tightly covered, labeled metal or heavy plastic containers that are at least six inches above the floor level to permit air circulation and to protect them from dirt. Dating containers ensures food supplies will be used in the order received.

Perishable foods must be stored at temperatures that prevent spoilage. Refrigerator temperature must be 40°F or lower; freezer temperature should be at 0°F or lower. Shelf space must allow for air circulation around the refrigerated foods, and thermometers in the warmest sections of refrigerators and freezers should be checked daily.

Food Preparation

Cooks must be instructed to follow recipes in meal preparation, and are expected to adhere to directions about cooking times and temperatures, proper techniques, temperatures for holding prepared foods, and proper methods for storing and using leftovers. Sanitation in the food preparation area is of utmost importance. The food service staff must follow sanitary food-handling practices and maintain good personal hygiene while handling foods and cleaning food preparation equipment and utensils. Even though there may be a nutritionist or other staff member responsible for the total food service program in the center, it is advisable for you, as director, to make periodic checks on the food preparation techniques and the sanitation practices of the cook as food is prepared and served to the children. It often becomes the director's responsibility to coach the cook when correct preparation procedures are not being followed.

Sanitation guidelines are available from your local health department or your state or local licensing agent. The licensing regulations at all levels include clearly stated sanitation requirements related to food preparation in child care centers. A local health department staff member or your center licensing agent are

It is advisable for you, as the director, to make periodic checks on food preparation and service.

excellent resources for helping interpret and implement the sanitation regulations applicable in your area.

Resources

Every state has a child nutrition agency (http://www.fns.usda.gov). These agencies can supply copies of laws, regulations, and guidelines in response to questions about nutrition and health. The following list includes additional places to go for printed material and for consultation on the center's nutrition component:

- public health nutritionists in state or local health department, or the county extension agency
- nutritionists in local dairy councils or comprehensive health centers
- USDA extension home economists
- dietitians in nearby high schools or universities
- dietitians in local hospitals

HEALTH AND SAFETY PROGRAM

The center staff members are responsible for the health and safety of the children while they are at the center; therefore, directors must be knowledgeable about health and safety regulations as stipulated in the licensing regulations, staff liability in cases of accidents at school, and procedures for protection from and reporting of communicable disease and child abuse. Although some large centers may have a health consultant on staff, in most places, the director is the designated individual responsible for the health program.

The health services provided through the child care center may range from no service at all to comprehensive service, including regular physicals, dental checkups and treatment, vision screening, hearing screening, and mental health services. The scope of the health services program depends on the program health policies set by the funding agent, the socioeconomic status of the families, the family expectations, and the licensing regulations. All centers should maintain up-to-date health and immunization records on the children, whether or not direct health services are provided.

Health Records for Children and Staff

Children's health records cover information up to the time of registration and any new health or medical information received while the child is in the program. Formats for these records vary and may be set by local health departments. The information provided (in addition to the basic demographics such as name, birth date, parent's names, and the like) should include medical and developmental information and must be completed and signed by the child's health care provider. The medical report on the child should include the following:

- records of the child's immunizations
- description of any disability, sensory impairment, developmental variation, seizure disorder, and emotional or behavioral disturbance that may affect adaptation to child care
- assessment of the child's growth based on height, weight, and head circumference (percentile for these if the child is younger than 24 months)
- results of screenings for vision, hearing, dental, nutrition, developmental, tuberculosis, hemoglobin, urine, lead, and so forth
- dates of significant communicable diseases (for example, chicken pox)

- prescribed medications, including information on recognizing and reporting potential side effects
- description of current acute or chronic health problems under or needing treatment
- description of serious injuries sustained by the child in the past
- special instructions for the caregiver
- Medical Treatment Authorization Form (American Academy of Pediatrics, 2002)

It is preferable to have the child's medical report on file prior to or on admission but imperative that it be completed within six weeks after admission or as required by licensing laws. These records should be updated every six months for children under two years and every year for children age two to six.

The preceding list indicates a dental screening should be included in the medical report. An authorized health care provider often does the dental screening on children under age three, at which time the child should visit a dentist. If the earlier dental screenings reveal special oral/dental problems, the child should see a dentist immediately.

Staff medical records that follow the licensing requirements must be on file at the center. Even when not required by licensing, there should be a medical record on every adult who has regular contact with the children, including substitutes, volunteers, practicum students, cooks, and van drivers. The staff records should include not only a physical assessment but also an evaluation of the emotional fitness of those who are to care for the children. The staff health appraisal should include the following:

- health history
- physical exam
- vision and hearing screening
- tuberculosis (TB) screening by the Mantoux method
- a review of immunizations (measles, mumps, rubella, diphtheria, tetanus, polio)
- a review of occupational health concerns
- assessment of need for immunizations against influenza, pneumococcus, and hepatitis B
- assessment of orthopedic, psychological, neurological, or sensory limitations and communicable diseases that may impair a staff member's ability to perform the job (American Academy of Pediatrics, 2002)

Unless licensing regulations require more frequent updating of staff health records, it is recommended this be done every two years. After many years of decreasing numbers of cases, tuberculosis seems to be on the rise again, so it is wise to consult your local health authorities to determine the frequency of repeat TB testing.

Currently, there are no screening or self-appraisal tools to identify specific health conditions that may seriously impair a caregiver's ability to provide safe and healthy experiences for children. However, there are some obvious things that a director can assess. These include the ability or willingness to

- move quickly to supervise and assist the children.
- lift children, equipment, and supplies.
- sit on the floor and on child-size chairs.
- practice frequent hand washing.
- eat the same food served to the children.
- hear and see at a distance for playground supervision. (American Academy of Pediatrics, 2002)

Communicable Disease

Cases of communicable diseases at the child care center must be reported to all center families and to the local health authorities. The usual children's diseases, as well as cases of meningitis, scarlet fever, infectious hepatitis, and head lice, must be reported so that necessary precautions can be taken immediately. It is important that pregnant staff members consult their physician about precautions related to exposure to communicable diseases at the workplace.

Directors and some of the teaching staff should have training in communicable diseases to enable them to recognize symptoms and make decisions about exclusion of children from the group. Communicable disease training is available in most communities through the Red Cross or the local health department. Licensing usually requires updated communicable disease training for classroom staff. Every center should provide easy access to a communicable disease chart (Director's Resource 13–1) to help staff recognize symptoms and make exclusion decisions. The most important measure in preventing spread of disease in child care centers is hand washing, not only after toileting or diapering but also after nose blowing or helping a child with a runny nose or cough, and before handling dishes or serving food (for details on proper hand-washing procedures, see Decker & Decker, 2005, p. 292). Sanitizing surfaces after diapering or on tables before using for eating also will help cut down on the spread of disease. Cleanliness is the major contributing factor to effective disease control in child care environments.

Staff members responsible for giving first aid to children and those likely to come in contact with blood or body fluids should have special training in dealing with blood-borne pathogens such as HIV or hepatitis B. Child care programs are required to offer free hepatitis B immunizations to employees when hired, or within 24 hours following exposure to blood or body fluids containing blood (Marotz, Cross, & Rush, 2005).

The spread of disease also is minimized through precautionary measures for handling situations where children become ill during the day and when children are ill on arrival. A written policy regarding management of sick children must be conveyed to parents when children are enrolled. Since very few centers have facilities to care for a sick child who must be separated from the other children, the usual practice is to call the parent or a designated adult to come for the child. In the meantime, the child usually is removed from the classroom and rests or plays quietly under adult supervision. Often, the director is the only staff person who has a schedule flexible enough to allow for time to stay with the sick child. An extra cot and a few toys for use while children are waiting to be picked up by a parent is standard equipment in many directors' offices.

Exclusion Policy

Exclusion policies must be made clear to parents and to the child care staff. If the purpose of excluding an ill child is to prevent the spread of infection to others in the group, it is important to specify which types of illnesses require exclusion. This list should include infectious diarrhea and vomiting, untreated conjunctivitis, impetigo, ringworm, head lice, and scabies (Aronson, 1986). Most centers develop special policies and procedures for excluding ill children so that all staff members and parents are aware of the specific criteria for exclusion. A rise in body temperature is common in young children and may or may not be a symptom of a contagious or serious illness. Nonetheless, most centers have strict policies about exclusion of children with a fever. Following are guidelines for when a child should be kept home or will be sent home:

- a fever over 100°F (37.8°C) orally or 99°F (37.2°C) axillary (under the arm)
- signs of newly developing cold or uncontrollable coughing
- diarrhea, vomiting, or an upset stomach
- unusual or unexplained loss of appetite, fatigue, irritability, or headache
- any discharge or drainage from eyes, nose, or ears, or open sores (Marotz, Cross, & Rush, 2005)

When the policy is clear, it helps both parents and staff make decisions about when to exclude children from the group. Programs that have staffed facilities to care for mildly ill children can have more liberal exclusion policies than those with no staff or space for these children to receive the extra rest and supervision they require. For working parents, finding alternative care arrangements for sick children is often a real problem. If parents don't have family leave time to use, it is helpful to provide resources for finding alternate care for an ill or recuperating child. Referring them to community agencies such as a "sitters on call" or a nanny service may be an answer for some families. If you locate alternative services in your community, they could be posted on the center Web site or published in a newsletter as a way of letting parents know that you will try to help as much as possible when their sick child is temporarily excluded from the classroom (Stephens, 2003).

Although there is an ever-increasing amount of information on the risks posed by children infected with HIV (a viral infection that can lead to AIDS) attending child care programs, evidence is inconclusive at this time. Since new information about HIV and AIDS is being generated constantly, stay in touch with local health authorities or the Centers for Disease Control (CDC) for updated information and guidance. If a child infected with HIV applies for admission, the public health department and the child's physician can help determine if it is safe for the child to be in a group situation. They also will provide help in determining whether the presence of this child exposes other children and adults to undue risk.

The number of children in group care infected with HIV may increase because newer medications and treatments are making it possible for infected children to live longer (Marotz, Cross, & Rush, 2005). These HIV-positive children are protected under the Americans with Disabilities Act and, therefore, cannot be denied access to educational programs. The overwhelming majority of children in this country who are infected acquired the HIV virus from their mother during pregnancy and delivery (Kendrick, Kaufman, & Messenger, 1995). The primary risk of admitting children with AIDS is that these children run a greater risk of contracting illnesses and infections from the other children because their immune systems are not functioning properly. These infections pose a serious threat to the child's life (Marotz, Cross, & Rush, 2005). The current information regarding HIV and the hepatitis B virus (similar to HIV but more infectious) is that neither is easily transmitted in school or child care environments, nor through casual contact such as touching, hugging, eating together, or sharing bathrooms. However, many centers are choosing to have a written policy on HIV and hepatitis B to protect the rights of an infected child and the other children in the center.

The CDC is recommending that children with HIV be excluded from the group *only* if they have open sores or bleeding that would put other children at risk from exposure to the infected child's body fluids (Marotz, Cross, & Rush, 2005). Whether or not there are known cases of HIV/AIDS among enrolled children, it is essential that staff follow universal precautions to prevent transmission of blood-borne pathogens. In addition to wearing latex gloves when serving food, changing diapers, or handling a bleeding wound, special care must be taken in dealing with blood-soiled areas and clothing or bedding (Decker & Decker, 2005, p. 292). To obtain updated information on this question or others involving infectious diseases, contact the CDC (see Appendix B for information).

Sick Child Care

As more children under five require some type of care outside the home, there is the consequent increase in the need for sick child care. The first alternative is to have the child at home with a caring parent whose employer allows time off for that purpose. Being at home may be the best alternative, but it is not always the most realistic. That means child care professionals, with the help of health professionals, are beginning to develop alternative sick child care models. For example, sick children might be accommodated in

- a sick bay at the center (a "Get Well" room).
- a center in a separate building that might be the cooperative venture of several child care programs.
- a center in a wing of a hospital or on hospital grounds that is available to the general public.
- a "satellite" system of family child care homes linked to a child care center.
- the child's own home under the supervision of a trained person sent from the center or local health agency.

"Deciding how to meet sick children's needs and parents' needs for child care is often difficult. Isolation and exclusion is not necessary for many illnesses. A balance must be struck between the needs of the child, the other children in the group, and an arrangement made that does not strain the staffing resources of the day care program" (Deitch, 1987, p. 16). Since children with AIDS are extremely vulnerable to infection from other children, it probably is unwise to have them in a sick child care facility where they would be exposed to other sick children.

Disaster Plan

Although licensing regulations do not always require disaster plans, it is important to plan for building evacuation in the event of fire and to detail additional measures to be taken during tornadoes, earthquakes, smog alerts, floods, sudden loss of heat or air conditioning, or any other major emergency or national disaster. The director must instruct all staff members on the best ways to evacuate the premises and the safe places to shelter children in weather or other emergencies. It is important to practice all emergency procedures with staff so they are conditioned to respond and less likely to panic. An evacuation plan should be posted in every classroom (Figure 13–2). Fire emergency plans show alternative exit routes, and evacuation drills should be held regularly so children become familiar with this routine. Parents must be informed in advance about alternative shelters so they know the whereabouts of their children during emergencies.

DIRECTOR'S CORNER

"I'm very interested in sick child care because of my background in nursing, and I know how much kids need Mom or Dad when they are sick! I also know there is a critical need for sick child care for those cases where job pressures force parents to get to work, even when their baby is sick. My dream is to develop a satellite family child care home system that will use our center as a base."

—Director, proprietary for-profit center

Daily attendance records and information needed to reach parents must be maintained in a convenient location and removed from the building by the designated adults as part of the evacuation procedure. The "chain of command" regarding who will call for emergency fire or police help, who will secure the building and make a final check that everyone is out, how the building will be secured, and who will contact the parents all must be arranged in advance and communicated to staff by the director. Fire alarms, fire extinguishers, and emergency exit lights should be checked regularly to ensure they are in working order.

Supplies stored in emergency evacuation areas and to be taken to the alternative shelter include the following:

- first aid kit
- blankets
- food and water

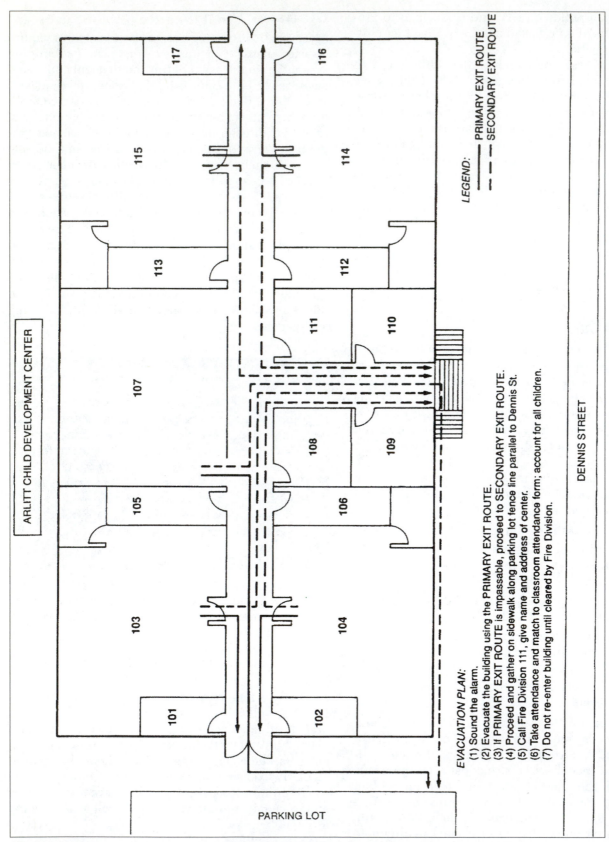

Figure 13–2

Sample evacuation plan.

- battery-operated radio
- flashlight
- children's books, crayons, paper, and the like

Fire, earthquake, tornado, and national emergency plans and drills are important, but keep in mind that there are many other disasters that can impact the child care center in addition to those that require building evacuation. Rehearsals for building evacuation are a necessity, but how will the staff respond when a sleeping child stops breathing, when an angry noncustodial parent appears with a gun, or an inebriated person harasses departing parents and children? How will the staff deal with a warning of a terrorist threat? There are resources in most communities to call on for help as you develop emergency plans for a vast array of possible emergencies and as you train the staff to deal with unexpected events. Invite local law enforcement personnel, health professionals, Red Cross, legal aid, and social service people to assist you with developing procedures and doing staff training. General steps and procedures to keep in mind when you write emergency plans are

included in "Suggestions for Code Blue Design" (Figure 13–3) and the sample national preparedness plan (Figure 13–5).

Directors' responsibilities do not end with plan development, training and rehearsing staff on procedures, and carrying out the plan when a real disaster strikes. They also must deal with the follow-up for parents and children and deal with the press. After a crisis such as a fire, a shooting, the death of a child at the center, of an allegation of child abuse, or a national disaster, it is critical that accurate information be presented to families and to the public through the press. Although this responsibility usually falls to the director, it is wise to consider who else might serve as a spokesperson. A carefully selected, knowledgeable spokesperson who is savvy about handling the press can help protect the center and its families when serious emergencies or damaging allegations arise. Choices for spokesperson may be

- the center's lawyer.
- the director of public relations or human resources if it is an employer-sponsored center.

Suggestions for Code Blue Design

Review the organization chart and the chain of command. Each time the director leaves the building, it should be clear who is in charge.

Make it a priority that no adult is left alone in the building. In cases where this is necessary, program a phone and teach one of the older children to use it to call for help if something happens to the caregiver.

Assume the program loses power—how will communication be maintained? Is there a back-up lighting system? A cellular phone? A laptop computer?

Get to know the press in the area over positive issues first! Invite them to the center, refer positive information to them on a regular basis, put announcements in their calendars, etc. so that their first encounter with the center is not over an emergency.

Train the receptionist or designate someone to answer the phone who is unflappable and will deliver a succinct message to all callers.

Make it clear that all staff will stay at the center until the Code Blue is over. Ask other staff to come in to help.

Update Code Blue materials every September when new information peaks.

Reassure staff and board that this planning is preventative—it will probably not be needed, but if it is, every attempt has been made to minimize the damage.

Figure 13–3

Suggestions for Code Blue Design (from "Code Blue! Establishing a Child Care Emergency Plan," by M. Copeland, 1996, *Child Care Information Exchange, 107*, p. 18. http://www.ChildCareExchange.com).

Procedures for Medical Emergencies

1. Each classroom teacher shall assume responsibility for care in any emergency that occurs on school property.
2. Assistant teachers or volunteers should contact the classroom teacher in case of emergency. If the teacher is not available, contact should be made with another classroom teacher in the building or the director.
3. If, in the judgment of the teacher, the injury needs medical attention, the director will call the parent of the child. If the parent cannot be reached, the director will call the emergency number on the Emergency Information Record.
4. If the injury requires immediate emergency treatment, call for medical assistance and transportation to the Emergency Room of the hospital authorized by the parent. Ambulance number is _____. The classroom teacher will accompany the child to the hospital and the director will call the parent.

Staff Instructions for Ill Children

1. If a child should become ill after arrival at school, contact the parent to come and take the child home. If parents cannot be reached, the director will call the emergency number on the Emergency Information Record.
2. If no transportation is available, provisions will be made for the child to remain at school until the regular departure time. The child will be removed from the classroom and will be cared for in the director's office.

Additional Instructions for Staff

1. An accident report must be filled out for any injury requiring medical attention. The report is to be filled out by the teacher and given to the director to be placed in the office health file with a copy in the child's file.
2. Any incident or injury occurring at school that appears to be upsetting or traumatic to the child shall be related to the parent by the teacher.
3. The center maintains a $25 deductible insurance policy on each child. If injuries sustained by a child incur costs above this amount, the parent should be told to contact the director for appropriate insurance forms for coverage.

Figure 13–4

Sample emergency medical plan.

- the priest, rabbi, or minister if a center has a religious affiliation.
- a board member or other volunteer who has a vested interest in the center, is respected in the community, and is trained in public relations. (Copeland, 1996)

All staff must be trained to deflect media questions to the spokesperson or director and to answer informal questions from parents and others by quoting center written policy or by referring these inquiries to the director.

To obtain more information on the best methods to provide protection in particular areas, directors can contact local health and fire department and national security officials, building inspectors, the Environmental Protection Agency (EPA), or the Occupational Safety and Health Administration (OSHA). Also, make sure *all foreseeable issues* are covered by various insurance policies.

Emergency Safety, Health, and Accident Planning

The 21st century presents those who care for children with new challenges relative to planning not only for children's health, injury and accidents, and natural disasters but also for the possibility of terrorist attacks. All of these plans are usually developed by the director with input from parents, staff, the board, and community groups responsible for homeland security.

Some centers may have disaster plans that are in place in case of hurricanes or other weather-related events. In some cases, they will suffice for possible national security alerts as well. However, these plans need to be reviewed to make sure they are broad enough to cover bomb threats, exposure to hazardous material, and various potentially violent situations (Figure 13–5).

An emergency health plan is also developed by the director. It includes the step-by-step procedures to be followed when a child is injured at the center. The purpose of this plan is to provide the center staff with a detailed set of instructions to follow when giving an injured or sick child the best and quickest treatment, notifying the family, and filling out the necessary papers for maximum liability and insurance protection for both staff and family (Figure 13–4).

Some states require that centers have a Medical Treatment Authorization Form on file for every child in the program. This form, when properly completed, will give the center the authority to obtain medical treatment in an emergency situation. These forms usually contain specific information related to the child such as the child's name, date of birth, address, known allergies, the child's physician, and medical insurance information. Often, there is a requirement to have this form notarized. A good resource for information on what is required for this form is the Paramedic or Emergency Department at a local hospital.

If the child must be taken away from the center for emergency care, the caregiver must stay with that child until the parent arrives or accompanies the child to the hospital. A signed consent form from parents that gives detailed information on where the child should be taken for emergency treatment and permission to transport the child for emergency treatment, should be in each child's folder (Figure 13–6). Since the parent cannot give informed consent in advance for emergency treatment because the nature of the injury is not known, it is essential that parents understand that the center must know their whereabouts or that of another responsible adult at all times. It is suggested that the telephone numbers on the child's emergency record, including those for the child's usual source of health care, be updated several times a year.

The director, as well as some members of the teaching staff, must have first aid training including cardiopulmonary resuscitation (CPR) so that preliminary emergency treatment can begin before professional help arrives and minor injuries will be handled correctly. An injury report must be filled out any time a child is hurt, and it should be filed in a central location with a copy in the child's file (Figure 13–7). It is essential to follow the accident plans, have staff properly trained to deal with injuries, and fill out injury reports, both for the safety and well-being of children and the protection of staff. Directors and board members must understand that taking all these precautions may not protect the staff from liability completely. Therefore, the center should carry accident insurance on the children and have liability coverage for the staff as additional precautionary measures. It is wise to consult an attorney and an insurance agent about what constitutes adequate coverage.

Child Abuse

Directors must be vigilant and take steps to prevent the possibility of abuse on the premises, recognize signs of abuse on children who come to the program, and make certain suspected cases of abuse are properly reported.

Prevention on the Premises

Precautions must be taken to prevent both physical and sexual abuse on the premises. Physical abuse occurs most often when adults are stressed; further, the abusive act is unplanned and explosive and usually occurs when other adults are not around. Sexual abuse, on the other hand, although it also occurs when other adults are not around, is frequently planned ahead, and pedophiles may seek employment in child care centers to gain access to children. In the latter case, careful preemployment screening and use of criminal record checks and fingerprinting may provide helpful information, but how effective these expensive measures really are is still unknown (American Academy of Pediatrics, 1996).

Since abuse of all types usually occurs when other adults are not around, the preventive measures mentioned in connection with staffing patterns (Chapter 10) and developing the facility (Chapter 8) and making it clear to everyone that parents may visit at any time should help eliminate the possibility of abuse occurring in your center.

Recognizing and Reporting Abuse

All directors and members of the teaching staff in child care programs should have some training in recognizing the physical and behavioral signs of

SAMPLE NATIONAL PREPAREDNESS PLAN

CHILDREN'S FOR CHILDREN—CCHMC and P&G
EMERGENCY PREPAREDNESS PLAN DURING NATIONAL EMERGENCIES

Supplies to purchase for each center:

- flashlight and batteries for each classroom, office, kitchen
- portable radio and batteries for each "wing" or partner room
- drinking water
- modified first aid kits for each classroom, office, and kitchen

In all situations, staff remain calm and under emotional control.

Staff must remain focused on their responsibilities and reassure the children.

While we cannot force parents to remain at the center during an emergency, we can certainly strongly encourage them to remain at the center for their family's safety. A lockdown is not permitted at CCHMC.

If there is a warning (conditions seem real):

- follow procedures for tornado emergency
- remain on first floor of building
- take books, simple toys, portable radios, first aid supplies, flashlights and attendance chart
- quickly note the names of every child and adult in your room or area
- take parent roster if readily available
- if parents or staff relatives/friends arrive, encourage them to remain at the center

If there is an explosion:

- do not retrieve personal items
- do not stop to use the phone
- go to the first floor, away from windows or potential projectile objects
- if debris is falling, protect children and move under tables, desks or sturdy furnishings
- stay low to floor, below smoke level
- cover your mouth and nose with cloth, preferably dampened, then cover mouths and noses of children

If you are trapped in an area:

- do not move, to avoid stirring up dust
- cover your mouth and nose with cloth and then the children's (use damp washcloth or surgical mask if possible)
- tap on wall or pipe to alert rescuers
- avoid shouting unless you are fairly confident that a rescuer is nearby

Figure 13–5

Sample national preparedness plan. (Reprinted with permission from Children's for Children at Cincinnati Children's Hospital.)

Emergency Contact Information

Child's Name _____ Date of Birth _____

Address _____ Home Phone _____

Mother's Name _____ Business Phone _____

Father's Name _____ Business Phone _____

Name of other person to be contacted in case of an emergency:

1. _____ Address _____

Relationship (sitter, relative, friend, etc.) _____ Phone _____

2. _____ Address _____

Relationship (sitter, relative, friend, etc.) _____ Phone _____

Authorization is hereby given for the Child Development Center Staff to release the above named child to the following persons, provided proper identification is first established (list all names of authorized persons, including immediate family):

1. _____ Relation: _____

2. _____ Relation: _____

3. _____ Relation: _____

Physician to be called in an emergency:

1. _____ Phone _____ or _____

2. _____ Phone _____ or _____

I, the undersigned, authorize the staff of the Child Development Center to take what emergency medical measures are deemed necessary for the care and protection of my child enrolled in the Child Development Center program.

_____

(Signature of Parent or Guardian/date)

Signature witnessed by:
(Notary)

_____

(Signature of Parent or Guardian/date)

The above statement sworn
before me on:

_____

_____

Figure 13–6

Sample emergency contact information (from *Health, Safety, and Nutrition for the Young Child*, by L. R. Marotz, M. Z. Cross, and J. M. Rush, 2005. (Reprinted with permission from Delmar Learning, a division of Thomson Learning, http://www.thomsonrights.com.)

abuse, whether or not licensing requires it. In most states, professionals involved with children are required to report suspected cases of abuse. When mandated to report suspicion of abuse, those reporting are not required to prove their allegations. Nonetheless, reports should be made carefully because much harm can come to children and families when the accusations are unfounded. The director should be notified of all suspected cases of abuse and review the case with the staff member who has

Injury Report Form

Name of Child _____ Birth Date _____

Parent Name _____

Address _____ Phone Number _____

Usual Source of Health Care_____

Date of Injury _____ Time _____ Age _____ Sex _____

Type of Injury (circle)   Bite   Broken Bone   Bruise   Burn   Choking   Cut   Eye Injury   Foreign
Body   Head Injury   Poisoning   Scrape   Sliver   Sprain   Sting
Other _____

Location Where Injury Occurred _____
e.g., child care room, bathroom, hall, playground, large-muscle
room, bus, car, walk

Type of Equipment Involved _____

How Injury Happened (details of who, what, when, how): _____

_____

_____

_____

_____

Type of Treatment Required _____
e.g, first aid only in day care, visit to doctor's office or clinic, emergency room, hospitalized, sutures, cast, bandage, medication given

Signature of Person Filling Out the Report _____

Signatures of Witnesses _____

Name of Medical Professional Consulted _____

Date _____Time _____ Advice_____

Figure 13–7

Sample injury report form.

found evidence of abuse before the case is reported to the authorities. In most states, information is given to law enforcement agencies or child protective agencies. Familiarity with state laws and local rules for reporting is essential for all child care directors.

Legal Issues: Health and Safety

Lawsuits by parents resulting from injury to a child in playground accidents, exposure to serious illnesses such as HIV or AIDS, injuries inflicted by other children, or alleged child abuse are a major concern of almost all center staff, administrators, and board members. Lawsuits are to be avoided, not only for reasons of wanting children in our care to be kept safe and healthy but also because the suits can be won by plaintiffs even when the center staff is right. These unfortunate results can occur as a consequence of the sympathies engendered in the courts and in the press. Centers risk losing insurance coverage and suffer irreparable damage to their reputations. A chart showing self-defense strategies is presented in Figure 13–8.

The possibility of being sued for any reason, whether for an accident, a suspicion of child abuse, or alleged wrongful exclusion of a child, can be minimized by building preventive steps into your day-to-day practices.

1. Promote open, trusting communication with parents from the time they walk in the door. When parents trust center staff, they are less

Self–Defense Strategies

Plaintiff's attorney might . . .	Child care provider should . . .
Claim that staff member was a "dangerous instrumentality."	Warn staff that their actions (or inactions) could result in their being termed a dangerous instrumentality. Document unsafe, imprudent actions (inactions) of staff and take necessary personnel actions.
Join forces with the District Attorney's investigation.	Warn staff in advance that in the beginning it might look like everyone is against them. Develop a plan on what support accused staff members may expect from the center.
Agree that the acts were unintentional.	Be aware that a plaintiff's attorney is not necessarily doing you or your staff a favor—intentional acts are usually not insured, so chances of a large settlement are decreased if the acts are intentional.
Threaten to sue everybody even remotely related to the case, then try to drive a wedge between defendants.	Within limits bounded by truth and ethical behavior, ask your affected staff to cooperate with your defense attorney. The investigation you conduct into the incident with or on behalf of your defense attorney should not be hampered by lack of cooperation from staff.
Expect institutional defendants, including churches, youth organizations, and related groups, to underrate their culpability—to not fathom how they could have any liability.	Work with boards of directors and policy groups to stay on target in reviewing and making policy—neither delegating everything to the director or trying to fund all administrative functions.
Subpoena agendas, minutes of board of directors meetings, staff meetings, training sessions, memos, phone logs, appointment books, and other files and records.	Keep good records. Check with your attorney about the kind of gratuitous and careless misinformation that should not be recorded. Information regarding fundraising should be limited to resolutions so that your meeting history doesn't unfairly condemn you as an organization beset with, and overwhelmed by, funding problems to the exclusion of safety concerns.
Spend a great deal of time reviewing management decisions looking for patterns which would prove negligence.	At least annually, take time to review your own management decisions. Ask all staff, board members, parents, and others involved to help look for things that you had not noticed or which might be misinterpreted.
Interview past employees and call them as witnesses.	When possible, try to part as friends with all staff. Establish formal exiting procedures for staff, asking that they share with you any concerns they have about the way children are treated and asking if there were any instances they can remember (but have not previously reported) where a child may have been injured, abused, molested, neglected, or endangered. Where possible, obtain such concerns in writing.
Attempt to prove that you participated in deceptive practices by promising safety or security for children and then not exercising due diligence in that safety or security.	Have your attorney review all advertising or promotional trade materials. Establish an active parent involvement risk management program, and keep parents well informed of providing problems.

Figure 13–8

Self-defense strategies. Republished with permission from CCIE (Neugebauer) from CCIE exchange; permission conveyed through Copyright Clearance Center, Inc.

likely to sue when things go wrong. The positive regard they hold for the staff encourages them to talk it through and make more rational decisions before calling in their lawyers.

2. Maintain a well-trained staff in adequate numbers to ensure proper supervision, and appropriate health and safety procedures throughout each day. Train staff to inspect all toys and equipment for safety hazards, report all problems in writing, and carefully fill out detailed accident reports.

3. Purchase adequate liability insurance and accident insurance on all the children, even when parents have health insurance. It promotes good will and means some parents will not have to cover a deductible or co-pay requirement.

4. Check all applicants' references carefully and question any gaps in their employment history. Document that references have been checked under the applicant's current name as well as all previous names.

5. Keep records of all board meetings, staff meetings, licensing monitoring reports, and staff training sessions. A plaintiff's attorney can subpoena copies of any or all of these documents, in addition to other related materials such as personnel files, memos, and appointment books.

6. Have your lawyer review all promotional and marketing materials for information that might be viewed as "deceptive" under your state's consumer protection legislation.

7. Choose an attorney who is very familiar with both liability and child care laws in your state, and periodically check with your legal advisers.

Keep in mind that individual staff are rarely held personally responsible for claims against the center. It is the employer who is held responsible, provided the act in question occurred within the scope of employment. Staff members may be held individually responsible only when they cause harm outside their legitimate scope of authority.

Centers are especially vulnerable to legal actions over issues of playground equipment safety and playground supervision and performance of specialized health procedures to children with special needs. Recently, centers have become vulnerable over transportation issues based on changes by the National Highway Traffic Safety Administration regulating bus and van safety, as well as other changes in state regulations. (Material in this section is taken from Cohen, 1998, and Strickland & Lenbarg, 1998.)

SUMMARY

Directors are responsible for overseeing the food service and the health and safety programs in the child care center. Although a designated staff person and the center cook may plan menus, order food, and prepare meals, the director is accountable to both the center families and the sponsoring or funding agency for the quality of the food service program.

Monitoring the health program and implementing plans to care for children in the event of a national or natural disaster or those who are injured or sick also is part of the director's responsibility. It is important to have written policies and reporting procedures for all emergencies and rehearsal for various emergency procedures. Plans for caring for sick children with specific exclusion guidelines are helpful. It also is important to take preventive precautions regarding child abuse in the center and to make certain that suspected cases of abuse are detected and reported. Consult with your attorney on a regular basis and take the necessary precautions to avoid legal action against your agency.

CLASS ASSIGNMENTS

1. Contact your regional USDA office, local child care center, or a Head Start program to obtain the current reimbursement rates for both free and reduced rate meals for eligible children.

   a. Using Working Paper 13–1, record reimbursement allowances in the spaces provided.

   b. Using information from Working Paper 13–1 (Assignment 1–a) and the information given in the chart "Number of Meals Served" (Working Paper 13–2), complete Working Paper 13–2 by calculating the amount to be reimbursed for meals served during the month.

2. Using Working Paper 13–3, fill in the emergency numbers for the services listed. Include the name of the agency and a contact person, where indicated.

CLASS EXERCISES

1. Work with another student and role-play a conference between a director and a cook, assuming the two roles as follows:

Director: As a director, you are responsible for monitoring food preparation and serving methods. You have checked carefully with the home economist at the local utilities company and you have read numerous government publications on the best way to prepare vegetables to retain nutrients. You know that cooking time should be short, that the amount of water used should be small, and that the vegetables should be prepared only minutes before eating. Furthermore, you know that children's foods should be cut in bite-size portions; that is, stew meat in half-inch cubes, bread slices in quarters, fish sticks halved, and so forth. Your cook prepares all vegetables early in the day and keeps them over low heat until serving time. Even though the recipes indicate that meat should be served in bite-size pieces and portions should be small, the meat comes from the kitchen in the same sizes in which it was delivered from the meat market.

Cook: You were hired for this job in the child care center after being an assistant cook in a restaurant for five years. You have looked forward to having your own kitchen, and you are proud of your previous experience and what you know about preparation of food in quantity.

As director, you must call the conference and deal with the problem. Keep in mind that you are committed to maintaining open communication and to promoting the personal and professional growth of your staff.

2. As a group, discuss the evacuation plan for the room in which you are now having class. Do you see exit signs or evacuation directions in this room or in the adjacent hallways?

   a. If you were responsible for this building, what steps would you take to develop a building evacuation plan and inform the staff about it?

   b. If you had to use this room for a children's classroom, how would you evacuate the children and how would you prepare the children for an emergency evacuation procedure without creating anxiety and fear?

WORKING PAPER 13-1

(for use with Class Assignment 1a)

FOOD REIMBURSEMENT ALLOWANCES

	Free	*Reduced*
Breakfast	_____ per child	_____ per child
Lunch/dinner	_____ per child	_____ per child
Snack (supplements)	_____ per child	_____ per child

Fill in the above chart with information from your regional USDA office, a local child care center, or a Head Start program. Use this information to complete the assignment on Working Paper 13–2.

WORKING PAPER 13-2

(for use with Class Assignment 1b)

NUMBER OF MEALS SERVED

Date	Breakfast		Lunch/Dinner		Snack	
	Free	Reduced	Free	Reduced	Free	Reduce
3	12	2	21	3	21	3
4	13	2	20	3	20	3
5	11	1	18	2	19	2
6	15	1	18	2	19	2
7	15	2	18	1	18	1
10	12	1	17	1	18	1
11	14	2	21	1	20	1
12	15	1	20	2	20	2
13	15	2	18	3	18	3
14	13	2	18	3	18	3
17	12	2	19	2	19	2
18	11	2	19	1	19	2
19	13	1	18	3	19	3
20	13	1	17	3	19	3
21	14	2	19	3	18	3
24	13	2	19	2	19	2
25	14	1	18	3	18	3
26	15	1	18	2	18	2
27	16	0	19	3	19	3
28	14	2	18	3	18	3
31	14	2	20	3	20	2
TOTAL						

Using the information from Working Paper 13–1 on reimbursement amounts for free and reduced meals and the information from the chart "Number of Meals Served," fill in the following table:

Breakfast	number of free meals × rate =	_____
	number of reduced meals × reduced rate =	_____
Lunch/dinner	number of free meals × free rate =	_____
	number of reduced meals × reduced rate =	_____
Snack	number of free meals × free rate =	_____
(supplement)	number of reduced meals × reduced rate =	_____
	Total claim for reimbursement	_____

WORKING PAPER 13-3

(for use with Class Assignment 2)

EMERGENCY TELEPHONE NUMBERS

Record the following emergency telephone numbers and contact person, where that information is requested:

- General emergency number (for example, 911)   _____
- Police   _____
- Fire   _____
- Ambulance   _____
- Poison Control Center   _____
- Health Department   _____

                                            Contact Person

- Report child abuse   _____

                                            _____
                                            Agency

                                            _____
                                            Contact Person

DIRECTOR'S RESOURCE 13-1

COMMON COMMUNICABLE DISEASES

AIRBORNE TRANSMITTED ILLNESS

Communicable Illness	Signs and Symptoms	Infectious Agent	Methods of Transmission	Incubation Period	Length of Communicability	Control Measures
Chicken pox	Slight fever, irritability, cold-like symptoms. Red rash that develops blister-like head, scabs later. Most abundant on covered parts of body, e.g., chest, back, neck, forearm.	Virus	Airborne through contact with secretions from the respiratory tract. Transmission from contact with blisters less common.	2–3 weeks after exposure	2–3 days prior to the onset of symptoms until 5–6 days after first eruptions. Scabs are not contagious.	Specific control measures: (1) exclusion of sick children and (2) practice of good personal hygiene, especially careful handwashing. Children can return to group care when all blisters have formed a dry scab (approximately 1 week). Immunization is now available.
Common Cold	Highly contagious infection of the upper respiratory tract accompanied by slight fever, chills, runny nose, fatigue, muscle aches, and headaches. Onset may be sudden.	Virus	Airborne through contact with secretions from the respiratory tract, e.g., coughs, sneezes, eating utensils, etc.	12–72 hours	About 1 day before onset of symptoms to 2–3 days after acute illness.	Prevention through education and good personal hygiene. Avoid exposure. Exclude first day or two. Antibiotics not effective against viruses. Avoid aspirin products (possible link to Reye's syndrome). Watch for complications, e.g., earaches, bronchitis, croup, pneumonia.
Fifth's disease	Appearance of bright red rash on face, especially cheeks.	Virus	Airborne contact with secretions from the nose/mouth of infected person.	4–14 days	Prior to appearance of rash; probably not after rash develops.	Don't need to exclude children once rash appears. Frequent handwashing; frequent washing/disinfecting of toys/surfaces. Use care when handling tissues/nasal secretions.

(continues)

© 2007 by Thomson Delmar Learning

DIRECTOR'S RESOURCE 13-1
(continued)

Communicable Illness	Signs and Symptoms	Infectious Agent	Methods of Transmission	Incubation Period	Length of Communicability	Control Measures
Heamophilus influenza Type b	An acute respiratory infection; frequently causes meningitis. Other complications include pneumonia, epiglottitis, arthritis, infections of the bloodstream and conjunctivitis	Bacteria	Airborne via secretions of the respiratory tract (nose, throat). Persons can also be carriers with or without symptoms.	2–4 days	Throughout acute phase; as long as organism is present. Noncommunicable 36–48 hours after treatment with antibiotics.	Identify and exclude sick children. Treatment with antibiotics 3–4 days before returning to group care. Notify parents of exposed children to contact their physician. Immunize children. Practice good handwashing techniques; sanitize contaminated objects.
Measles (Rubeola)	Fever, cough, runny nose, eyes sensitive to light. Dark red blotchy rash that often begins on the face and neck, then spreads over the entire body. Highly communicable.	Virus	Airborne through coughs, sneezes and contact with contaminated articles.	8–13 days; rash develops approximately 14 days after exposure	From beginning of symptoms until 4 days after rash appears.	Most effective control method is immunization. Good personal hygiene, especially handwashing and covering coughs. Exclude child for at least 4 days after rash appears.
Meningitis	Sudden onset of fever, stiff neck, headache, irritability, and vomiting; gradual loss of consciousness, seizures, and death.	Bacteria	Airborne through coughs, nasal secretions; direct contact with saliva/nasal discharges.	Varies with the infecting organism; 2–4 days average	Throughout acute phase; noncommunicable after antibiotic treatment.	Encourage immunization. Exclude child from care until medical treatment is completed. Use Universal Precautions when handling saliva/nasal secretions, frequent handwashing, and disinfecting of toys/surfaces.
Mononucleosis	Characteristic symptoms include sore throat, intermittent fever, fatigue, and enlarged lymph glands in the neck. May also be accompanied by headache and enlarged liver or spleen.	Virus	Airborne; also direct contact with saliva of an infected person.	2–4 weeks for children; 4–6 weeks for adults	Unknown. Organisms may be present in oral secretions for as long as one year following illness.	None known. Child should be kept home until over the acute phase (6–10 days). Use frequent handwashing and careful disposal of tissues after coughing or blowing nose.

(continues)

DIRECTOR'S RESOURCE 13-1
(continued)

Communicable Illness	Signs and Symptoms	Infectious Agent	Methods of Transmission	Incubation Period	Length of Communicability	Control Measures
Mumps	Sudden onset of fever with swelling of the salivary glands.	Virus	Airborne through coughs and sneezes; direct contact with oral secretions of infected persons.	12–26 days	6–7 days prior to the onset of symptoms until swelling in the salivary glands is gone (7–9 days).	Immunization provides permanent protection. Peak incidence is in winter and spring. Exclude children from school or group settings until all symptoms have disappeared.
Roseola Infantum (6–24 mo.)	Most common in the spring and fall. Fever rises abruptly (102°–105°F) and lasts 3–4 days; loss of appetite, listlessness, runny nose, rash on trunk, arms, and neck lasting 1–2 days.	Virus	Person to person; method unknown.	10–15 days	1–2 days before onset to several days following fading of the rash.	Exclude from school or group care until rash and fever are gone.
Rubella (German Measles)	Mild fever; rash begins on face and neck and rarely lasts more than 3 days. May have arthritis-like discomfort and swelling in joints.	Virus	Airborne through contact with respiratory secretions, e.g., coughs, sneezes.	4–21 days	From one week prior to 5 days following onset of the rash.	Immunization offers permanent protection. Children must be excluded from school for at least 7 days after appearance of rash.
Streptococcal Infections (strep throat, scarlatina, rheumatic fever)	Sudden, onset. High fever accompanied by sore, red throat; may also have nausea, vomiting, headache, white patches on tonsils, and enlarged glands. Development of a rash depends on the infectious organism.	Bacteria	Airborne via droplets from coughs or sneezes. May also be transmitted by food and raw milk.	1–4 days	Throughout the illness and for approximately 10 days afterward, unless treated with antibiotics. Medical treatment eliminates communicability within 36 hours. Can develop rheumatic fever or become a carrier if not treated.	Exclude child with symptoms. Antibiotic treatment is essential. Avoid crowding in classrooms. Practice frequent handwashing, educating children, and careful supervision of food handlers.

(continues)

DIRECTOR'S RESOURCE 13-1
(continued)

Communicable Illness	Signs and Symptoms	Infectious Agent	Methods of Transmission	Incubation Period	Length of Communicability	Control Measures
Tuberculosis	Many people have no symptoms. Active disease causes productive cough, weight loss, fatigue, loss of appetite, chills, night sweats.	Bacteria	Airborne via coughs or sneezes.	2–3 months	As long as disease is untreated; usually noncontagious after 2–3 weeks on medication.	TB skin testing, especially babies and young children, if there has been contact with an infected person. Seek prompt diagnosis and treatment if experiencing symptoms; complete drug therapy. Cover coughs/sneezes. Practice good handwashing.
BLOOD-BORNE TRANSMITTED ILLNESSES						
Acquired immunodeficiency Syndrome (AIDS)	Flu-like symptoms, including fatigue, weight loss, enlarged lymph glands, persistent cough, fever, and diarrhea.	Virus	Children acquire virus when born to infected mothers from contaminated blood transfusions and possibly from breast milk of infected mothers. Adults acquire the virus via sexual transmission, contaminated drug needles, and blood transfusions.	6 weeks to 8 years	Lifetime	Exclude children 0–5 yrs if they have open lesions, uncontrollable nosebleeds, bloody diarrhea, or are at high risk for exposing others to blood-contaminated body fluids. Use Universal Precautions when handling body fluids, including good handwashing techniques. Seal contaminated items, e.g., diapers, paper towels in plastic bags. Disinfect surfaces with bleach/water solution (1:10) or other disinfectant.
Hepatitis B	Slow onset; loss of appetite, nausea, vomiting, abdominal pain, and jaundice. May also be asymptomatic.	Virus	Through contact with blood/body fluids containing blood.	45–180 days; average 60–80 days	Varies; some persons are lifetime carriers.	Immunization is preferable. Use Universal Precautions when handling any blood/body fluids; use frequent handwashing.

(continues)

asymptomatic—*having no symptoms.*

DIRECTOR'S RESOURCE 13-1
(continued)

(continues)

CONTACT (direct and indirect) TRANSMITTED ILLNESSES

Communicable Illness	Signs and Symptoms	Infectious Agent	Methods of Transmission	Incubation Period	Length of Communicability	Control Measures
Conjunctivitis (Pinkeye)	Redness of the white portion (conjunctiva) of the eye and inner eyelid, swelling of the lids, yellow discharge from eyes and itching.	Bacteria or virus	Direct contact with discharge from eyes or upper respiratory tract of an infected person; through contaminated fingers and objects, e.g., tissues, washcloths, towels.	1–3 days	Throughout active infection; several days up to 2–3 weeks.	Antibiotic treatment. Exclude child for 24 hours after medication is started. Frequent handwashing and disinfection of toys/surfaces is necessary.
Cytomegalo-virus (CMV)	Often no symptoms in children under 2 yrs.; sore throat, fever, fatigue in older children. High risk of fetal damage if mother is infected during pregnancy.	Virus	Person to person contact with body fluids, e.g., saliva, blood, urine, breast milk, in utero.	Unknown; may be 4–8 weeks	Virus present (in saliva, urine) for months following infection.	No need to exclude children. Always wash hands after changing diapers or contact with saliva. Avoid kissing children's mouths or sharing eating utensils. Practice careful handwashing with children; wash/disinfect toys and surfaces frequently.
Hand, Foot, and Mouth Disease	Affects children under 10 yrs. Onset of fever, followed by blistered sores in the mouth/cheeks; 1–2 days later raised rash appears on palms of hands and soles of feet.	Virus	Person to person through direct contact with saliva, nasal discharge, or feces.	3–6 days	7–10 days	Exclude sick children for several days. Practice frequent handwashing, especially after changing diapers. Clean/disinfect surfaces.
Herpes simplex (Cold sores)	Clear blisters develop on face, lips, and other body parts that crust and heal within a few days	Virus	Direct contact with saliva, on hands, or sexual contact.	Up to 2 weeks	Virus remains in saliva for as long as 7 weeks following recovery.	No specific control. Frequent handwashing. Child does not have to be excluded from school.

DIRECTOR'S RESOURCE 13-1
(continued)

Communicable Illness	Signs and Symptoms	Infectious Agent	Methods of Transmission	Incubation Period	Length of Communicability	Control Measures
Impetigo	Infection of the skin forming crusty, moist lesions usually on the face, ears, and around the nose. Highly contagious. Common among children.	Bacteria	Direct contact with discharge from sores; indirect contact with contaminated articles of clothing, tissues, etc.	2–5 days; may be as long as 10 days.	Until lesions are healed.	Exclude from group settings until lesions have been treated with antibiotics for 24–48 hours. Cover areas with bandage until treated.
Lice (head)	Lice are seldom visible to the naked eye. White nits (eggs) are visible on hair shafts. The most obvious symptom is itching of the scalp, especially behind the ears and at the base of the neck.	Head louse	Direct contact with infected persons or with their personal articles, e.g., hats, hair brushes, combs, or clothing. Lice can survive for 2–3 weeks on bedding, carpet, furniture, car seats, clothing, etc.	Nits hatch in 1 week and reach maturity within 8–10 days.	While lice remain alive on infested persons or clothing; until nits have been destroyed.	Infested children should be excluded from group settings until treated. Hair should be washed with a special medicated shampoo and rinsed with a vinegar/water solution (any concentration will work) to ease removal of all nits (using a fine-toothed comb). Heat from a hair dryer also helps destroy eggs. All friends and family should be carefully checked. Thoroughly clean child's environment; vacuum carpets/upholstery, wash/dry or dry clean bedding, clothing, hair-brushes. Seal nonwashable items in plastic bag for 2 weeks.

(continues)

DIRECTOR'S RESOURCE 13-1
(continued)

Communicable Illness	Signs and Symptoms	Infectious Agent	Methods of Transmission	Incubation Period	Length of Communicability	Control Measures
Ringworm	An infection of the scalp, skin, or nails. Causes flat, spreading, oval-shaped lesions that may become dry and scaly or moist and crusted. When it is present on the feet it is commonly called athlete's foot. Infected nails may become discolored, brittle, or chalky or they may disintegrate.	Fungus	Direct or indirect contact with infected persons, their personal items, showers, swimming pools, theater seats, etc. Dogs and cats may also be infected and transmit it to children or adults.	4–10 days, (unknown for athlete's foot)	As long as lesions are present.	Exclude children from gyms, pools, or activities where they are likely to expose others. May return to group care following medical treatment with a fungicidal ointment. All shared areas, such as pools and showers should be thoroughly cleansed with a fungicide.
Rocky Mountain Spotted Fever	Onset usually abrupt; fever (101°–104°F); joint and muscle pain, severe nausea and vomiting, and white coating on tongue. Rash appears on 2nd to 5th day over forehead, wrist, and ankles; later covers entire body. Can be fatal if untreated.	Bacteria	Indirect transmission; tick bite.	2–14 days; average 7 days	Not contagious from person to person.	Prompt removal of ticks; not all ticks cause illness. Administration of antibiotics. Use insect repellent on clothes when outdoors.
Scabies	Characteristic burrows or linear tunnels under the skin, especially between the fingers and around the wrists, elbows, waist, things, and buttocks. Causes intense itching.	Parasite	Direct contact with an infected person.	Several days to 2–4 weeks	Until all mites and eggs are destroyed.	Children should be excluded from school or group care until treated. Affected persons should bathe with prescribed soap and carefully launder all bedding and clothing. All contacts of the infected person should be notified.

(continues)

DIRECTOR'S RESOURCE 13-1
(continued)

Communicable Illness	Infectious Agent	Signs and Symptoms	Methods of Transmission	Incubation Period	Length of Communicability	Control Measures
Tetanus	Bacteria	Muscular spasms and stiffness, especially in the muscles around the neck and mouth. Can lead to convulsions, inability to breathe, and death.	Indirect: organisms live in soil and dust; enter body through wounds, especially puncture-type injuries, burns and unnoticed cuts.	4 days to 2 weeks	Not contagious.	Immunization every 8–10 years affords complete protection.
FECAL/ORAL TRANSMITTED ILLNESSES						
Dysentery (Shigellosis)	Bacteria	Sudden onset of vomiting; diarrhea, may be accompanied by high fever, headache, abdominal pain. Stools may contain blood, pus or mucus. Can be fatal in young children.	Fecal-oral transmission via contaminated objects or indirectly through ingestion of contaminated food or water and via flies.	1–7 days	Variable; may last up to 4 weeks or longer in the carrier state.	Exclude child during acute illness. Careful handwashing after bowel movements. Proper disposal of human feces; control on flies. Strict adherence to sanitary procedures for food preparation
E. coli	Bacteria	Diarrhea, often bloody	Spread through contaminated food, dirty hands.	3–4 days; can be as long as 10 days	For duration of diarrhea; usually several days.	Exclude infected children until no diarrhea; practice frequent handwashing, especially after toileting and before preparing food.

(continues)

DIRECTOR'S RESOURCE 13-1
(continued)

Communicable Illness	Signs and Symptoms	Infectious Agent	Methods of Transmission	Incubation Period	Length of Communicability	Control Measures
Encephalitis	Sudden onset of headache, high fever, convulsions, vomiting, confusion, neck and back stiffness, tremors, and coma.	Virus	Indirect spread by bites from disease-carrying mosquitoes; in some areas transmitted by tick bites.	5–15 days	Man is not contagious.	Spraying of mosquito breeding areas and use of insect repellents; public education.
Giardiasis	Many persons are asymptomatic. Typical symptoms include chronic diarrhea, abdominal cramping, bloating, pale and foul-smelling stools, weight loss, and fatigue.	Parasite (protozoa)	Fecal-oral transmission; through contact with infected stool (e.g., diaper changes, helping child with soiled underwear), poor handwashing, passed from hands to mouth (toys, food). Also transmitted through contaminated water sources.	7–10 days average; can be as long as 5–25 days	As long as parasite is present in the stool.	Exclude children until diarrhea ends. Scrupulous hand-washing before eating, preparing food, and after using the bathroom. Maintain sanitary conditions in bathroom areas.
Hepatitis (Infectious; Type A)	Fever, fatigue, loss of appetite, nausea abdominal pain (in region of liver). Illness may be accompanied by yellowing of the skin and eyeballs (jaundice) in adults, but not always in children. Acute onset.	Virus	Fecal-oral route. Also spread via contaminated food, water, milk, and objects.	10–50 days (average range 25–30 days)	7–10 days prior to onset of symptoms to not more than 7 days after onset of jaundice.	Exclude from group settings a minimum of 1 week following onset. Special attention to careful hand-washing after going to the bathroom and before eating is critical following an outbreak. Report disease incidents to public health authorities. Immunoglobulin (IG) recommended for protection of close contacts.

(continues)

DIRECTOR'S RESOURCE 13-1

(continued)

Communicable Illness	Signs and Symptoms	Infectious Agent	Methods of Transmission	Incubation Period	Length of Communicability	Control Measures
Pinworms	Irritability, and itching of the rectal area. Common among young children. Some children have no symptoms.	Parasite; not contagious from animals.	Infectious eggs are transferred from person to person by contaminated hands (oral-fecal route). Indirectly spread by contaminated bedding, food, clothing, swimming pool.	Life cycle of the worm is 3–6 weeks; persons can also reinfect themselves.	2–8 weeks or as long as a source of infection remains present.	Infected children must be excluded from school until treated with medication; may return after initial dose. All infected and noninfected family members must be treated at one time. Frequent handwashing is essential; discourage nail biting or sucking of fingers. Daily baths and change of linen are necessary. Disinfect school toilet seats and sink handles at least once a day. Vacuum carpeted areas daily. Eggs are also destroyed when exposed to temperatures over 132°F. Education and good personal hygiene are vital to control.
Salmonellosis	Abdominal pain and cramping, sudden fever, severe diarrhea (may contain blood), nausea and vomiting lasts 5–7 days.	Bacteria	Fecal-oral transmission: via dirty hands. Also contaminated food (especially improperly cooked poultry, milk, eggs) water supplies, and infected animals.	12–36 hours	Throughout acute illness; may remain a carrier for months.	Attempt to identify source. Exclude children/adults with diarrhea; may return when symptoms end. Carriers should not handle or prepare food until stool cultures are negative. Practice good handwashing and sanitizing procedures.

From Health, Safety, and Nutrition for the Young Child, (6th ed.), by L. R. Marotz, M. Z. Cross, and J. M. Rush, © 2005. Reprinted with permission from Delmar Learning, a division of Thomson Learning, http://www.thomsonrights.com.

REFERENCES

American Academy of Pediatrics, American Public Health Association, & Maternal and Child Health Bureau. (2002). *Caring for our children: National health and safety performance standards: Guidelines for out-of-home child care programs.* Denver, CO: National Resource Center for Health and Safety in Child Care.

Aronson, S. S. (1986, May). Exclusion criteria for ill children in child care. *Child Care Information Exchange, 14.*

Cohen, A. J. (1998). Bettering the odds of not getting sued. In R. Neugebauer and B. Neugebauer (Eds.). *The art of leadership: Managing early childhood organizations.* Redmond, WA: CCIE.

Copeland, M. L. (1996). Code blue! Establishing a child care emergency plan. *Child Care Information Exchange, 107,* 17–21.

Decker, C. A., & Decker J. R. (2005). *Planning and administering early-childhood programs* (9th ed.). Upper Saddle River, NJ: Pearson, Merrill, Prentice Hall.

Deitch, S. R. (Ed.). (1987). *Health in daycare: A manual for professionals.* Elk Grove, IL: American Academy of Pediatrics.

Kendrick, A. S., Kaufman, R., & Messenger, K. P. (Eds.). (1995). *Healthy young children: A manual for programs.* Washington, DC: NAEYC.

Marotz, L. R., Cross, M. Z., & Rush, J. M. (2005). *Health, safety, and nutrition for the young child* (6th ed.). Clifton Park, NY: Thomson Delmar Learning.

Stephens, K. (2003, Winter). Parent partnerships: What programs can do to make them happen. *The Director's Link.*

Strickland, J., & Lenbarg, M. (1998). Teachers aides and other dangerous instruments: Lessons in self-defense. In R. Neugebauer & B. Neugebauer (Eds.). *The art of leadership: Managing early childhood organizations.* Redmond, WA: CCIE.

U.S. Department of Agriculture. (1999). *Tips for using the Food Guide Pyramid for young children 2 to 6 years old.* (Program Aid 1647). Washington, DC: USDA's Center for Nutrition Policy and Promotion.

Additional resources for this chapter can be found on the Online Companion™ at http://www.earlychilded.delmar.com. This supplemental material includes relevant Web links, Web activities, and case studies that apply the concepts presented in this chapter. In addition, the Working Papers and Director's Resources are available for download, allowing you to complete Class Exercises and Class Assignments electronically.

CHAPTER 14

Evaluating Center Components

Staff members participate in NAEYC accreditation self-study by becoming familiar with accreditation materials and by discussing their program.

OBJECTIVES

After reading this chapter, you should be able to:
- Describe the director's role in evaluation.
- List criteria for selecting an assessment tool.
- List several methods of assessing children's progress.

Evaluation is an ongoing process. An evaluation can take the form of an analysis of a person's behavior, of an administrative procedure, or of some other component of an early childhood education program in terms of its usefulness or worth. Once an early childhood education program has been planned, the evaluation of that program should be designed immediately because continuation of an ineffective aspect of the program is fruitless and frequently expensive. Inappropriate staff behavior may be detrimental to children's development or to staff relations. Desirable behavior, on the other hand, should be recognized and encouraged as a result of the evaluation process.

Evaluation that is planned during the early stages of program development facilitates the process and notifies everyone from the start how the evaluation process will be conducted. The evaluator uses the goals or mission statement that was prepared prior to the opening of the center as the basis for making judgments about what is valuable in the program. The goals and objectives that grow from the mission statement provide guidelines for assessing the center's program and the performance of individuals affiliated with that program.

Assuming that the director has worked to create a "we" feeling described in Chapter 2, evaluation also will take on a collaborative tone. Rather than being threatening or punitive, evaluation will be a way to note and celebrate progress. Whether the evaluation being addressed is focused on the center, the staff, or the children, participants can work together to assess current conditions and to decide on future goals. Then they can support one another in reaching those goals.

EVALUATION PLAN

The director usually conducts staff evaluations, although a committee of the center's board also may be involved. In some centers, staff members evaluate other employees whom they supervise (for instance, teachers evaluate their aides) or employees evaluate all fellow employees whose jobs are related. Therefore, teachers may evaluate each other, aides and teachers may evaluate each other, and everyone working under the director may evaluate and be evaluated by him. It is unlikely, however, to find auxiliary staff evaluating teaching staff because the decision about who does the evaluating is based on how the assigned jobs relate to one another. In other words, the maintenance staff and the nurse would not evaluate the teaching staff, even though teachers might be asked to evaluate the janitor's or nurse's work in relation to their role.

Often, parents are asked to give their opinions about the center, its personnel, and its operation to enable the center staff to understand how people directly affected by the program feel about it. In corporate systems, a national or regional staff member may plan and conduct some or all of the evaluation. When funds are received from a governmental or private agency, an employee of that agency may be assigned to perform an evaluation. When public schools operate preschool or child care programs, the principal usually is responsible for evaluating the staff.

Purpose of Evaluation

Since the major purpose of evaluation is to determine whether the center's goals are being met, the evaluators need to know what these goals are before gathering data. In effect, the evaluators must know who the clients are, what their needs are, and which of these needs the center is attempting to meet. In a community where the local high school is expressing concern about the high number of dropouts due to pregnancy, a center director may decide to work with the school system to assess how many students could return to school if care were provided for their infants and toddlers. Together, the center and the school may be able to obtain funding to provide this service. In such a situation, particularly if tax dollars are to be used, community education would be important since many taxpayers may believe that the program would cause teen pregnancy rather than prevent school dropouts.

A further purpose of evaluation is to determine how effective the program is in meeting the needs of clients and how efficient it is in terms of cost, time, and energy. Are needs met to the satisfaction of the center and the clients? Are they partially met or not met at all? More important, are significantly more teen parents returning to and staying in school when their babies receive child care? Even if needs are met, could the same job have been done for less money or by using less time or energy? Funding agencies, board members, and clients expect documentation that the center is doing what it has agreed to do. An evaluation provides the data for such documentation and possibly the basis for further funding.

A final reason for evaluation is the need to have a solid basis for future planning. The director uses the data from the current evaluation to determine the strengths and weaknesses of the program and to adapt the plan for the following year appropriately to correct any deficiencies or to respond to newly perceived needs. For example, if one of the goals of the center is to provide a parent education program for all parents and the data show that only 10 percent of the parents participated, then the director needs to determine whether the goal is inappropriate or whether the method of achieving it is not meeting the needs of the clients. If a thorough evaluation has been done, the director will have information from parents regarding how they felt about the parent program and why they did or did not attend. The information then can be used to plan changes in next year's program or to ascertain that this community does not need parent education from this particular center.

It would be easy to arrive at the conclusion that parents in the preceding example do not want or need parent education. But the director has to consider other factors and perhaps ask himself the following questions:

- Have parents been involved in the planning so that they feel as though they are part of the program?

- Is there another parent education program already established in the community that is meeting these parents' needs?

- Is the timing, format, or content inappropriate for these parents?

- Has there been a breakdown in communication so that parents do not feel welcome or comfortable about coming?

- Are there other, more pressing matters, confronting the parents?

- Are there ancillary problems such as baby-sitting or transportation?

Since one or more of these factors may have had a major effect on parent participation, the director should address them to make sure that the evaluation is accurate.

Evaluation Principles

Evaluation plans should be based on certain principles that reduce anxiety and increase cooperation among the individuals being evaluated.

1. The evaluation process is open, that is, the people or groups being evaluated know about the evaluation process in advance and have access to their own evaluation data. Furthermore, the people being evaluated have an opportunity to give input into their own evaluation.

2. Evaluation relates directly to program goals and objectives.

3. Each person being evaluated knows why, when, where, how, and by whom the evaluation is to be done.

4. Evaluation is conducted on an individual basis. However, for reporting purposes, the results are compiled and group data rather than individual data are presented.

5. The individual's evaluation is a confidential matter and is accessible only to those who need to know such as an employee's supervisor or a child's teacher.

6. Evaluation is built into the program so that it occurs on a regular basis.

An early childhood education evaluation plan involves three components: staff, children, and total program evaluation. A plan for each of these components includes delineating who will evaluate what, how, and when the evaluation will be conducted, and for what purposes a particular evaluation is being done.

STAFF EVALUATION

Staff evaluation is a natural outgrowth of supervision, one of the basic duties of the director. Every staff member should be evaluated on a regular basis according to the procedure included in the policies and procedures manual.

REFLECTION

We have discussed the purpose of conducting an evaluation in early childhood centers and the people who conduct these investigations. Now think about the people who evaluate you. Who are they? Why do they evaluate you? Some of you may think of relatives or friends who evaluate your behavior on an ongoing basis. Others may immediately associate evaluation with teachers and employers. Do all these people see you in the same way? If not, why do some of them evaluate you in different ways? What is the purpose of their evaluation?

DIRECTOR'S CORNER

"The steering committee conducts an annual parent survey. One parent gathers all the information and then gives each classroom a printout of what the parents in their room specifically said. The parents' names aren't included though. Parents seem willing to write things that they might not take time to say in person, and it's been real helpful to the staff to get this kind of feedback."

—Director, agency-sponsored child care center

Staff evaluation is conducted to enable the director and the staff member to analyze what the staff member is doing well and in what areas growth and change are desirable or required. This type of evaluation provides information to the funding agency and the board about how employees spend their time; it also validates the work of the employees.

The first form of evaluation is *employee selection*. In assessing an applicant's ability to work well with other employees, the director must be cautious, avoiding the selection of only those people who fit a mold. A successful choice is based on a careful evaluation of credentials and behavior, rather than on an overgeneralization of positive or negative traits. For example, the candidate who answers an early question to the interviewer's liking then may be regarded as being highly qualified, although he actually may be poorly skilled in working with young children. On the other hand, the candidate with an unusual style of clothing may be considered initially as incompetent when, in reality, that person might work quite well with young children. The director should avoid hiring only those applicants who are very similar to current employees but still must consider whether or not the qualifications of a particular candidate will combine well with those of current employees to provide the total staff strength that is needed to meet center goals. In any case, the most important criterion is: "Is this the best person available to do the job?"

Process and Procedures

Ongoing evaluation of staff members begins when they accept a position. At this time, the director and the new staff member go over the job description together carefully and make adjustments as needed to fit the circumstances, writing these changes (if any) into the job description. A comprehensive evaluation is based on this job description. The director makes it clear to employees from the beginning that they will be evaluated. However, another important component to be discussed with the employee is the support that will be provided to assist new staff members as they become acclimated to a new role. This support is particularly helpful for first-year teachers.

The director informs each employee why, when, where, and by whom the evaluation will be done; outlines the basis for the evaluation; and describes the method to be used. Sometimes, a new employee is evaluated after a two- or three-month probationary period. If the employee's work is found to be satisfactory at this time, the employee and director then plan together for further growth by writing out what the employee expects to accomplish prior to the next evaluation. In this initial step in the evaluation cycle, the employee writes out goals and brings them to a meeting with the director, at which time both must agree on their importance and reasonableness. The goals must relate to the job description, and the subsequent evaluation is based on the mutually agreed-upon objectives.

For example, if one of the teacher's goals is to maintain a more orderly classroom, that teacher's procedural plan may include teaching the children to return things to the proper shelf, rearranging the classroom, or working with the classroom aide to develop a mutually agreeable plan for keeping materials in order. Sometimes, the director gives help at

Teachers are aware that observation by the director is a regular part of the evaluation process.

this stage, either by assisting the employee in finding ways of meeting an objective or by designating areas in which specific objectives should be defined. The primary goal at this step is to draw up a workable plan that the staff member can follow and that will enhance the overall program.

Next, the director and employee decide how data will be gathered. Will the director observe? Will parents be asked for their opinions? Will the teacher be asked to engage in a self-evaluation process? Will the teachers observe each other? Will children's behavior be used as a criterion? Again, both director and staff member reach agreement on what is the best plan to use. Some centers use checklists or rating scales. These tools are most useful in large centers in which a number of staff are working on comparable skills such as fostering a relaxed classroom atmosphere or preparing appropriate classroom materials.

The objectives and evaluation format are called a *work plan*, which is the formative component of staff evaluation. Once the plan has been written, the director and the staff member each receive a copy for reference as they work to achieve the objectives and to evaluate the progress that is made. They plan a specific time period for the next meeting: in one month, at the end of the semester, or whatever length of time fits their needs.

The Director's Role

The director's role in staff evaluation is to observe and analyze the work of a staff person, encourage the development of that person's strengths, and look for ways to promote growth in weaker areas. If the weak areas considerably outweigh the strong, then the director must terminate the employment of that individual because the director's role (except in special cases) is to promote growth rather than to provide total on-the-job training. The staff member's role is to work out the details of meeting the agreed-upon goals and to implement these plans.

In some centers, a standard form is used to evaluate each teacher. Although this may be seen as more equitable, it sets the same expectations for beginners as for experienced teachers. An alternative method is to evaluate all teachers with a standard form that addresses basic requirements. In addition, provide individualized planning and evaluation for each teacher.

Some directors observe each teacher weekly, biweekly, or monthly and have a conference informally after making the observation. The director may take notes during the observation or write notes afterward, but any notes should be shared with the teacher because they are useful in helping to fulfill the specific objectives that have been set. It sometimes is easy to pick out and focus on the weak spots in a teacher's style, which leaves the teacher feeling incompetent. Other directors concentrate only on the positive aspects and are unable to address problem areas. The teacher who is aware of a problem knows that the director is not providing appropriate guidance; the teacher who is unaware of a problem receives unofficial sanction of the behavior when the director ignores it. In either case, some of the center's objectives are not met, and the observation and informal conference times are nonproductive.

Some directors make videotapes, DVDs, or audio tapes of teachers and review them with that teacher afterward. The advantage is that both are viewing the same situation during the conference. The disadvantage is that taping is intimidating to some staff. Of course, the tapes are confidential information and the subject's permission must be obtained if they are to be shown to others.

When the agreed-upon observations have been completed and other assessments have been made, the director meets with the staff member for a comprehensive evaluation of the work that is based on the work plan set up earlier. The staff member may bring a self-evaluation in a form preselected by the director to be completed by the employee, in a narrative form that is written by the employee, or in an unwritten form that the employee has planned to discuss with the director. During the conference, a work plan, including the objectives and an evaluation format, is drawn up again for the next evaluation cycle, and the director summarizes the staff person's evaluation for the previous cycle in a written form that is dated. The staff member may add written comments if desired, then both the staff member and the director sign the evaluation form and the new work plan. Although this process is somewhat formal, the director's evaluation role becomes businesslike, as well as personal, if it is followed.

Professional Approach

In all staff evaluation situations, a professional approach must be taken. Such an approach conveys to each staff member the importance of the role and of the staff member's performance. Because this may seem difficult in the rather informal child care setting, the director may want to discuss with the staff what an important professional responsibility evaluation and planning should be.

Arranging unhurried, uninterrupted time and space for evaluation sessions is essential. Such procedures may seem superfluous in the majority of situations. However, establishing the pattern sets the stage for the occasional very difficult evaluation conference

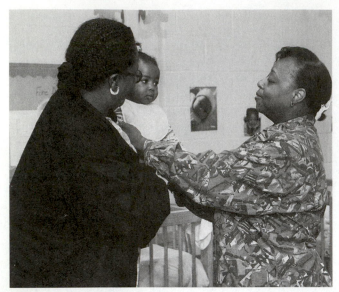 

When teachers interact with individual children, their observations are important sources of data about the child's development.

and should make it easier to proceed in a professional manner in those instances. Careful and thoughtful evaluation also sends a message to all staff that their work is indeed serious and can leave them feeling quite positive about what they have accomplished and ready to work toward continued development.

A similar evaluation process is followed for the director, and the board is usually responsible for its implementation. In a multisite corporate system, a regional representative may conduct the director's evaluation. Since the staff members in a well-run center may feel very close to one another and may consider the director a personal friend, it is wise to maintain structure in the evaluation process to allow everyone to be as objective as possible. Parents' perspectives on the director's performance are significant and may be gathered by means of a survey.

Since the director is responsible for the overall quality of the center, logically, evaluation focuses on reaching quality indicators. These include low staff turnover, low rate of staff absenteeism, high occupancy rates by clients, and sufficient resources in terms of teacher salaries, along with classroom equipment and supplies (Neugebauer, 1998).

Beyond that, however, managing the ever-changing needs of children, families, and staff requires tremendous organizational ability on the part of the director. Programs for children are complex, as evidenced by the fact that the director's day may involve developing new enrollment policies, assisting a struggling teacher in the classroom, and meeting with funders from a national organization. The complexity of the director's role reflects the unpredictable, interconnectedness described by complexity theory. According to this theory, "the world is spontaneous, alive and disorderly—in other words, complex. This results in organizations where there are no simple answers and where people and program continually interact with a constantly changing environment" (VanderVen, 2000). In evaluating directors, the complex nature of their role must be taken into account. Refer to Director's Resource 14–1.

As director credentialing becomes more available, the board may want to require obtaining the credential as part of the evaluation. Currently, the credential is gaining in popularity as a way to improve center quality and to market the center to families.

CHILD ASSESSMENT

Although the terms *assessment* and *evaluation* are often used as synonyms, Gullo (2005) offers the following definitions:

> *Assessment*: the process of gathering information about children in order to make educational decisions
>
> *Evaluation*: the process of making judgments about the merits, value, or worth of educational programs, projects, materials, or techniques (Gullo, 2005, pp. 159–160)

As was mentioned in Chapter 1, the curriculum plan is determined by the director in consultation with the teaching staff. The assessment plan is also the ultimate responsibility of the director. This plan should

Directors help teachers recognize the importance of understanding each child's own strengths and needs.

be designed to relate to the curriculum. Because the major goals of an early childhood education center revolve around expectations about the development of children, the evaluation most commonly thought of to demonstrate the program's efficacy is child outcomes. Note that assessing young children's development has always been part of the responsibility of early childhood programs. Those assessments have focused on all aspects of development. In some cases, child assessment has been haphazard or overlooked. When directors do not take responsibility for ensuring that assessment is a regular part of the program, it may not occur, or inappropriate assessment may be done.

Because every state has created academic standards for K–12 programs, and because most states have also created academic standards for prekindergarten, assessment related to those standards has assumed a prominent position in decision making by funders, families, the media, and even by early childhood educators.

Since young children develop rapidly, it is important that the progress they make in their normal development is not attributed solely to the center's program. Many other conditions affect the child's development, including parental behavior, cultural background, nutrition, and general health. Any one of these variables or combinations of them can affect the child's development positively or negatively, just as the center's program may have a positive or negative influence. The child's total development is a result

of the interaction of many factors, which makes it almost impossible to evaluate the influence of one variable such as a specific child care or preschool experience.

Professional Recommendations

NAEYC and the National Association of Early Childhood Specialists in State Departments of Education (NAECS/SDE) issued an important and informative joint statement in 2003 titled *Early Childhood Curriculum, Assessment, and Program Evaluation: Building an Effective Accountable System in Programs for Children Birth through Age 8.* The statement can be found on the NAEYC Web site. An earlier joint position statement, *Early Learning Standards: Creating the Conditions for Success* (2002), reiterates the long-held belief that early childhood must provide appropriate opportunities for *all* children to develop in all areas. The document encourages professionals to assume responsibility for recognizing the benefits and risks of the expanded standards movement and for ensuring that essential features of effective and appropriate standards be understood and delivered.

The *Early Childhood Curriculum* joint statement reminds us to "Make ethical, appropriate, valid, and reliable assessment a central part of all early childhood programs. To assess young children's strengths, progress, and needs, use assessment methods that are developmentally appropriate, culturally and linguistically responsive, tied to children's daily activities, supported by professional development, inclusive of families, and connected to specific, beneficial purposes (2003)." This strong, well-researched recommendation makes it clear that assessment is a significant responsibility. The director's role is to ensure that the responsibility is met.

Methods for Assessing Child Progress

This segment examines the recommendation in terms of the director's responsibility. The recommendation delineates *criteria* for assessment. It must be ethical, valid, and reliable. The recommendation calls for *appropriate methods* of assessing children. Therefore, directors must ensure that only appropriate methods are employed. They must evaluate the methods based on the following criteria:

1. *Developmental appropriateness of the methods.* Does the teacher use appropriate questions to help understand the child's thinking? Is the teacher aware of emerging knowledge and skills being exhibited by each child? Have a wide variety of related opportunities been provided to support children's interests? Is the level of materials appropriate so that every child's need can be met?

2. *Cultural and linguistic responsiveness of the methods.* Is there evidence that the teachers are familiar with each child's culture and are using it as they plan curriculum? Is there at least one adult available who speaks the child's home language? If that is not possible, are teachers finding ways to communicate with each child?

3. *Connection of the methods to children's daily activities.* Do teachers plan and implement daily activities in ways that allow them to assess what children are learning? Do they use that information to plan additional or modified daily activities?

4. *Support of the methods by professional development.* Has the director provided opportunities for teachers to learn about the expected standards? Has professional development been provided to help teachers plan ways to help children meet the standards in meaningful ways?

5. *Inclusion of families.* Has the director provided opportunities for families to become acquainted with program goals? Have they had opportunities to observe in the classroom and to receive information about how the program is designed to meet goals?

6. *Connection of the methods to specific, beneficial purposes.* Are methods of assessment designed to provide information that supports teachers as they modify curriculum for each child and for the group? Will the information obtained be helpful to families? Will the information demonstrate to funders the significance of the program?

Tools for Assessing Child Progress

The director, in consultation with the teaching staff, decides on the tools to be used to document each child's progress. They discuss goals, time lines, and process. The assessment should also lead to planning to meet each child's needs. In cases involving researchers or funders needing to collect data, the director should consider whether this data collection presents an ethical dilemma. If so, the director must determine what course of action to take.

The first question to ask regarding any child assessment tool is, "Is it ethical to use this procedure?" Early childhood educators must be aware of and follow the Code of Ethical Conduct. (The Code can be found in Director's Resource 15–2, is on the NAEYC Web site, and can be purchased inexpensively from NAEYC in brochure form. Providing a copy for each staff member and family helps everyone understand what is expected. The Code of Ethical Conduct addresses a breadth of principles related to early care and education and makes an excellent starting point for staff discussions of appropriate assessment.) The principle, *We shall do no harm to children,* supersedes all other principles in the code and can be used as a first consideration.

Important issues include the following:

- Will children be put in a stressful situation?
- Will individual children be evaluated unfairly because the test was normed on a specific population?
- Will children have had the opportunity to learn the material being assessed?
- Will the results of the assessment help the child by enabling families, teachers, and other professionals to plan for the child's continued progress?
- Will the use of the testing program or other assessment detract from other important opportunities for the children (such as physical activity, arts, and opportunity to explore a wide range of materials)?

Among the tools to be considered are teacher observations, checklists, rating scales, portfolios, reports from other professionals, and standardized tests. The next section consists of a brief look at each of these tools. Keep in mind the relationship between appropriate curriculum and appropriate assessment, but remember that assessment should not drive curriculum.

REFLECTION

Think about your own feelings about being evaluated. Are your feelings positive? Negative? Mixed? How does the evaluator influence these feelings? What is the behavior of an evaluator who helps you feel positive? Can you recall the behavior of an evaluator who left you feeling incompetent?

Teacher Observations

Throughout the year, the teacher may keep anecdotal and running records on each child. These notes, recorded on file cards or in a logbook, are summarized by the teacher at the end of the year. Boehm and Weinberg (1997), Genishi (1992), and Nicolson and Shipstead (1998) are among the authors who describe general guidelines for observing children. The teacher notes the changes in developmental level and the specific objectives that the child has met. Using this method, the teacher is able to make statements about each child individually, placing emphasis on what the child's needs were based on initial observations, and how the needs were met. This method uses subjective data provided by the teacher and is valuable only if the teacher is a skilled observer and collects data regularly. In a center that is minimally staffed, use of this method may be difficult. However, NAEYC, in a brochure on testing of young children, states, "The systematic observations of trained teachers and other professionals, in conjunction with information obtained from parents and other family members, are the best sources of information" (NAEYC, 1988).

Checklists

The director may find or create a checklist that names the behaviors toward which the center's objectives are aimed. Then the teacher merely checks whether or not the child exhibits the listed behavior. A question arises when the child sometimes does the task and sometimes does not, either because the task is just being learned, because the child chooses not to do it, or because no opportunity is made available. For example, an item might be "Buttons own coat." The child who does this occasionally may be in the process of learning and may not be ready to struggle with buttons on some days, or the child may be asking the teacher for help because he needs attention rather than help.

Rating Scales

The director may create or locate a rating scale that lists the behaviors aimed at in the center's objectives. The rating scale alleviates the problem created by a checklist by providing a way for teachers to qualify their answers. The teacher rates each child at least at the beginning and the end of the school year and perhaps more frequently.

The rating may be based on numbers; for example:

Speaks clearly enough for a stranger to understand.

1 2 3 4 5

with an explanation of whether 1 or 5 is high.

The rating may involve descriptive words such as:

Participates in group activities:
never
seldom
occasionally
usually
always

The problems with rating scales are that each teacher may interpret the categories differently, and most teachers are reluctant to use the two ends of the scale (1 and 5, or never and always). Such scales, however, can be useful in pointing out general strengths and weaknesses in any child's development and in the functioning of the group. Rating scales are relatively quick to complete, and the teacher can do them when the children are not present.

Both checklists and rating scales are suitable for use if they are viewed as a particular teacher's assessment of an individual child instead of as a comparison of one child or class with another. In reporting data from checklists and rating scales, the director may comment on how many children recognize their name in print or play cooperatively in a group of two or more children. But this information must be placed in proper context by pointing out the children's ages and other factors that may influence the data. In any case, group data of this sort should be deemphasized. Refer to Director's Resource 14–2 for a sample.

Portfolios

One type of record keeping that can provide valuable information about each child is the portfolio. Some teachers use a two-part system with one folder in a locked cabinet and a second folder in the classroom readily accessible to the child. Folder one contains forms and information from families; the teacher's written observations such as anecdotal records; notes on plans for that child; progress reports; medical reports; and reports from previous teachers, agencies, or consultants who have worked with the child. This information is confidential and should be available only to those who have a legitimate right to it. The second folder provides the child with an opportunity to save products that he has created. The teacher may add photos, videos, and audio tapes although the availability of these records depends on the center's budget and the time available to teachers to prepare these records. Periodically, the records must be sorted and decisions made about what is to be retained, since the record is intended to follow the child throughout school years. The child should participate in deciding what is to be retained, and the family, too, may want to be involved. Some records, however, must be retained by school policy or by law. (See Nilsen, 1997 for other ideas about portfolios.)

Other Observers

The director may observe a particular child when a teacher has concerns about that child. Sometimes, an outside observer such as the director or a consultant brings a more objective analysis or may see factors in the environment or even in the teacher's behavior that appear to be influencing the child's behavior. After collecting data, the observer confers with the teacher, and together they design a plan for working with the child. When an individual child is being evaluated to an extent that is beyond the center's regularly scheduled observation plan, parental permission must be obtained, and parental participation in planning is preferable and sometimes required by law.

When a child with identified special needs is enrolled, the director, with written parental permission, contacts agencies familiar with the child to obtain previous evaluations. The director and representatives of other agencies also may meet to share information that would be useful in working with the child and family.

Reporting a child's behavior to parents usually is handled in a conference (Chapter 16). Written information may be provided, but the use of checklists and rating scales for this purpose often is misleading. Parents may misunderstand the significance of this type of written report and categorize their child as a success or a failure. A more appropriate written evaluation for parents is a narrative report that describes the child's strengths and progress at school and discusses areas in which the child has difficulty (Horm-Wingard, 1992). The teacher also may confer with parents about ways to help the child continue progressing toward future educational goals.

Parents have the right to review information from their child's folder at any time. In some cases, they feel that it is damaging to the child to have certain information passed along to the next teacher. In other cases, they are eager for the new teacher to understand as much as possible about their child immediately so that the child does not have to endure a time period in which the teacher is discovering a hearing loss or some other condition for which an instructional plan should be designed. In any case, the teacher and parent discuss available information about the child, and together determine which data should be sent forward to the next teacher. When a child has an individual family services plan (IFSP) or an individual education plan (IEP), the new teacher should have access to that plan and participate with the IEP team in updating the plan on a regular basis. Keep in mind that the family is part of the team.

Standardized Tests

Until recently, limited attention was paid to using standardized tests with young children. Several reasons are apparent. First, young children can't be tested in a group because they can write only in a limited way, if at all. In a group situation, they have trouble attending to the type of test form typically used in such standardized tests. Even if their task is to draw a circle around one of three pictures for each question, they may be focused on an aspect of the question or of the pictures that is not related to the presumed correct answer.

For example, one kindergartner was asked to circle the picture of two characters from a story. The three choices were a picture of Jack and Jill falling down the hill, a picture of the three bears, and a picture of Little Red Riding Hood. After the test, the teacher talked with a child who she was certain had well-developed concepts of twoness and threeness. She asked why he had circled the three bears. He replied, "Well, you see, there's two bears and one left over." She asked what he thought about circling Jack and Jill, and he quickly responded, "Jack and Jill is not a story; it's a poem." While that thinking may not be typical, we have no way of knowing why young children respond the way they do in a standardized testing situation. For this reason, standardized tests, if used at all with young children, must be carefully reviewed.

Even when tests are administered to young children individually, results are often spurious. The answer a young child gives today may differ from the answer he provides a few days later. Children do not learn in small isolated bits. As they examine their world, they form relationships with what they already know. Those relationships initially are not always accurate from an adult perspective but are meaningful to the child. As the child encounters additional situations, he creates new relationships, which may or may not be more realistic from an adult perspective. The information that a child learns by rote may be lost relatively quickly if it is meaningless to the child. It is this kind of information that is often assessed on standardized tests.

In a critique of the Head Start National Reporting System (NRS) introduced recently, Meisels and Atkins-Burnett (2004) describe this high-stakes achievement test for four- and five-year-olds as containing "items that are rife with class prejudice and are developmentally inappropriate." The authors present a number of examples of NRS test items, explaining, in each case, the inadequacies of each. The authors conclude that "(t)his test is not good early education practice. It is not good psychometric practice. It is not good public policy. And it is certainly not good for young children." Yet when the pretest and posttest results reach Congress, funding may be affected. An even worse case would be that more than half a million children will be subjected to a curriculum that teaches to this test and that may allow little or no time for the real learning that four- and five-year-olds should be doing. Raver and Zigler (2004) argue that "the application of a strictly cognitive focus to assessments of school readiness runs counter to what the best developmental research tells us and what past policy experience has shown."

REFLECTION

REFLECTION

Find out what has happened to the National Reporting System since the Meisels and Atkins-Burnett and Raver and Zigler articles were written. Reflect on what you would have done if you had been a Head Start director when this testing system was inaugurated.

The director's role is to understand and use an appropriate assessment program and to work to modify or eliminate high-stakes testing. In some cases, the director's ethical decision may be to refuse to allow such testing in his center. Such a decision may involve issues such as cessation of funding based on the refusal, thus impacting many children, families, and staff. A concerted effort over time, however, with supportive position statements by professional organizations and reasoned discussions with legislators, educators, funders, and other interested parties may prove more beneficial to children in the long run.

If tests are to be administered, the director is professionally responsible for determining whether the test in question is appropriate for the children to be assessed. The director should understand what the test measures, how it is to be administered, by whom, and for what purpose. What effect will it have on the curriculum and, more important, on the children? What provisions will be made for assessing children for whom the test is culturally inappropriate based on language, other aspects of culture, or special needs? The director is expected to know or learn about terms related to testing, such as what the scores mean, what different types of tests are designed to measure, what the results mean, and how they will be used. The director is also responsible for ensuring that staff members understand these topics. A clear description appears in Gullo's (2005) book on assessment and evaluation.

If we find that a particular test meets the criteria described earlier in this section, the next questions include the reliability and validity of the test.

- Would the results obtained by a particular data collector be similar enough to those of another trained data collector?
- If teachers are expected to test their own classes, what preparation will they receive? Who will teach the class while the teacher tests one child at a time?
- Does the test measure what it purports to measure?
- How will the results be reported?
- What do the results mean to teachers? To families?
- Will the persons who receive the results know how to interpret them?
- What will be done with the results? Will they be used for the purpose for which the test was designed? Are the results beneficial to the children? If not, will the benefits to someone else outweigh the impact on the children and prorgam?

Some misuses of standardized tests of young children include the following:

1. keeping a child from entering kindergarten when he is chronologically eligible
2. rating a program
3. evaluating teachers
4. making curricular decisions based on specific test content

Part of the director's role is to ensure that, if standardized tests are administered, the results are not misused.

REFLECTION

Think about report card day when you were in elementary school. Can you recall any of your feelings about receiving a report card? If the experience was not always a good one for you, who could have changed? You? The teacher? Your parents? Other children?

When you consider what you will include in a child's folder, try to remember your own grade school days. Think about the effects that the inclusion of data about your behavior may have had on your relationships with teachers and your parents.

TOTAL PROGRAM EVALUATION

The program goals of the center, and the program itself, are designed to fulfill the particular needs that the center was established to meet. Consequently, at evaluation time, the needs, the goals, and the program are evaluated.

At regular intervals, the community's needs must be assessed so that the center can plan for current and future populations. (The methodology for conducting a community needs assessment is discussed in Chapter 3.) Since goals are closely tied to the philosophy of the center program, they change slowly. Nonetheless, they should be examined periodically, perhaps every few years, to determine whether they still are applicable. Because the objectives are more directly related to the individuals served at a given time, they may change more rapidly than the goals; therefore, the objectives should

be examined annually prior to the start of a new school year.

In addition, the director or the board may prepare checklists or rating scales for the evaluation of the program that can be distributed to staff members, parents, and community representatives; or these people may be asked to provide their evaluations in written or oral forms. Board members and funding agency representatives may contribute to the evaluation by reviewing aspects of the overall program such as the physical environment, curriculum, parent program, ancillary services, and board operations. They also may evaluate the staff performance in general, rather than individual, terms. Periodically, perhaps every few years, the policies and procedures manual, the job descriptions, and the board bylaws are reviewed. Even the evaluation plans and procedures are evaluated!

A widely used center-evaluation tool is the *Early Childhood Environment Rating Scale* (Harms, Clifford, & Cryer, 2005). Seven areas are covered in separate subscales. These are personal care routines, furnishings and display for children, language-reasoning experiences, fine and gross motor activities, creative activities, social development, and adult needs. After observing, the rater circles the appropriate category from 1 (inadequate) to 7 (excellent). Each subscale total rating is plotted on a profile sheet. Center staff then can decide in which areas they wish to make improvements. Profiles produced at different points in time can be used to determine changes in the center's program during that time period. Similar scales have been produced for rating infant-toddler programs and family child care. Instructional guides for observers are available in print and on videocassette.

Perhaps the most important evaluation a director can conduct is to look at quality of work life. Jorde-Bloom points out that high staff turnover rate, stress, and burnout soon affect commitment to the profession. When staff experience these tensions, it becomes impossible for directors to maintain high-quality programs.

Jorde-Bloom (1988) recommends, therefore, that the director examine 10 dimensions necessary to create a professional climate. Among these are supervisor support, opportunities for professional growth, and amount of staff autonomy in decision making. She further recommends surveying the staff, then using the resulting data to plan changes.

Talan and Bloom (2005) have created a publication that provides guidance related to all aspects of early childhood program assessment, focusing on the leadership and management practices of center-based early childhood organizations. The format is

10 categories of items, including center operations, fiscal management, program planning and evaluation, technology, and marketing and public relations. Each category is addressed on a wide two-page spread. A list of what to look for, such as needed documents, and questions to ask appear on the left. The evaluator takes notes based on review of components of the category during the data-gathering phase. For example, when completing the section titled Assessment in Support of Learning, evaluators would probably ask the director how curriculum is planned. They would also determine whether reliable and valid assessments are being used. Next the evaluator completes the rating scale. This scale appears on the facing page, allowing the rater to refer back to notes made during the data-gathering phase. Using a seven-point scale for each item assessed, the evaluator can create a profile depicting the center's leadership and management strengths and areas in which improvement can be considered. When completed, these documents provide valuable planning tools for directors.

Another form of staff survey is included in the NAEYC center accreditation package. Werner (1996) suggests a climate survey of from 30 to 80 items. Using a scale of 1 to 5 such as "poor" to "outstanding" or "strongly disagree" to "strongly agree," the survey might consist of a series of positive statements that relate to job satisfaction.

Staff surveys usually are anonymous, although in large centers, individuals may be asked to indicate age, job type, level of education completed, or any other category that will provide productive information. The purpose is to use the data for revising administrative practice and planning realistic changes in the center. Items that are obviously unattainable should, of course, not be included. For instance, one would not list "The center shall allow monthly unpaid mental health days" if such a policy would not be workable.

Many center directors and staff members are aware that they need to check the quality of their relations with parents, children, and staff members from a variety of cultures. Although it was not designed specifically for child care centers, the *Cultural Competence Agency Self-Assessment Instrument* (Child Welfare League of America, 2002) may help directors provide leadership in analyzing areas of strength and areas where improvement is needed. This publication includes sections titled Valuing Diversity, Documents Checklist, Governance, Administration, Program and Policy Development, Service Delivery, Clients, and Interpreting Your Results. Refer to Director's Resources 14–3, 14–4, 14–5, and 14–6.

DIRECTOR'S CORNER

"We decided as a staff to do more fun things together. This past year hasn't been much fun because everybody has been putting in overtime since we had two teachers on maternity leave. The steering committee gave us some money from a fund-raiser, and we're meeting next week to decide how to have fun together with it. It's a real morale booster."

—Director, agency-sponsored child care center

Accreditation

One type of center evaluation, accreditation, is conducted by an outside agency, usually a professional organization. Several groups currently offer some type of early childhood education accreditation. These include NAEYC, the National Association of Child Care Professionals (NACCP), and the National Child Care Association (NCCA). The NAEYC plan is the most widely used (Surr, 2004). Since its inception in 1985, that accreditation system has awarded accreditation to well over 10,000 centers and has many more than that involved at some stage of the process.

In 1999, "to increase the reliability and accountability of NAEYC accreditation," the organization began its Project to Reinvent NAEYC Accreditation. Employing its usual process of study, data and response gathering, and decision making, the accreditation reinvention commission reviewed 3,000 responses to current standards and draft proposals. The next step involved the American Institutes for Research (AIR) and the Center for Improving Child Care Quality at the University of California in Los Angeles to advise staff on the development of accreditation assessment instruments.

In developing the new system, NAEYC prepared lists of the values and of evidence-based criteria to be used in decision making. In the new system, early childhood programs are required to be in substantial compliance with the 10 standards, thus providing a more reliable indicator of high quality than the earlier system. Under the new plan, the public and staff of accredited centers will know that the centers are providing the quality that leads to positive outcomes for children.

The process, scheduled to be fully operational in 2006, includes, three steps:

1. self-study
2. self-assessment
3. external review process (Goffin, 2004a, 2004b, 2004c).

However, NAEYC views the self-study as an important way to begin program improvement whether or not the center decides to continue with the accreditation process.

Some directors may decide not to get involved because their centers are not perfect or because the process seems too complicated. In many communities, directors' support groups are springing up to encourage directors, answer their questions, and dispel myths. In some cases, these groups have obtained funding from community agencies or from business groups to provide technical assistance to centers that recognize the need to improve their programs.

Materials for the accreditation process may be obtained from NAEYC. Most directors find that when they take the time to read through the documents, the steps they need to take are all laid out for them and the procedures no longer seem intimidating. The director's role then is to obtain the support of the board and of the staff by letting them know what is expected, and that they will be engaging in a worthwhile team effort. Sharing the accreditation materials with confidence and being open to addressing staff members' questions and concerns will help everyone get started willingly.

Some changes may be needed. Everyone involved may feel stressed as change is discussed. Here again, the disrector must listen to concerns and help the group decide how to address them. Making changes is less stressful when the group feels ownership. Some changes may be out of the question, often because of the finances involved. This does not necessarily mean that the center cannot become accredited, but the program report will have to describe how the staff has designed an appropriate alternate approach. In many cases, the staff will have to set priorities and create a schedule for working on various components within a certain time frame. Trying to tackle everything at once can be overwhelming and counterproductive.

Completing the accreditation self-study and the related paperwork takes time. Often, successful directors find that the support of the board, parents, and colleagues makes a major difference. Preparing a time line and sticking to it also is helpful. One way to get staff involved is to begin with a discussion of the program's strengths. Encouraged by that discussion, your team will be ready to address areas that need to be improved and ways to accomplish that improvement (Eisenberg, 2000).

The board and the director must consider the cost of accreditation and the value to the children, families, and staff. In addition, the center may profit financially by being accredited as the community begins to recognize that the new process involves demonstration of quality in all aspects of the center's operation. If the decision is to move forward, the director submits the required documentation to the NAEYC Academy. The Academy will then review the documents and decide whether the program is ready for review.

Once assured that the center is ready for a visit, assessors will be sent to the site. They will use a tool to enable them to assess whether criteria demonstrate substantial compliance with each standard. Although it is not necessary that each criteria be met, each of the standards must be met in order to be accredited. The assessors will recommend the accreditation decision to the NAEYC Academy (Goffin, 2004c).

Accreditation from NAEYC will be valid for five years. The director will submit regular reports to maintain accreditation. In addition, assessors will make unannounced visits to randomly selected sites. This practice provides further assurance to all concerned that the accreditation process is reliable.

Current information about the NAEYC accreditation process and procedures is available on the NAEYC Web site.

Some directors may feel that they do not need to bother with accreditation because they have a long waiting list and their programs seem to be doing well. However, directors who take a professional approach will lead their staff in a self-study periodically, whether or not they choose to participate in a particular form of accreditation (Talley, 1997). Many center directors are finding that a number of states are encouraging early childhood programs to seek accreditation. Some are indicating that programs seeking funding must be accredited. Some states provide differentiated pay rates for subsidies for programs that are accredited. They also may provide training and technical assistance related to the accreditation process and even may offer funding for fees and for some needed improvements (Warman, 1998).

SUMMARIZING DATA

The director is responsible for summarizing the data that is collected from all aspects of the evaluation process, showing the progress or regression since the last evaluation rather than focusing solely on the current performance level. The summary should provide a clear data picture for the reader and should reflect accurately the facts, ideas, and opinions provided by those who participated. A comment that occurs frequently should receive more weight in the summary than an item that seldom appears in the data, no matter how striking or impressive that item appears. Furthermore, no new information should appear in the summary.

The summary is written, dated, and signed by the summarizer and should include a listing of sources used in its compilation. Some data may appear in graph or chart form, particularly if this format makes it easier to understand or more likely to be read. Appropriate computer software makes this task much easier.

Analyzing and Using the Data

The director or a designated committee uses the summary to cull out information. For example, in analyzing enrollment records, the dropout rate of children whose transportation is provided by the school may be compared to the dropout rate of those children who get to school by some other means.

In examining this information, it is necessary to keep other factors constant. For example, if all the children receiving transportation are from low-income families, and if some or all of the other children are from middle-income families, the dropout rate might be more closely related to income level than to mode of transportation. To clarify the situation, additional data would be needed.

Once the data have been analyzed, the director prepares a report for the funding agency, the board, and the other people or groups to whom the center is responsible. This type of report usually is prepared annually, although interim reports may be compiled. The report should be expressed clearly, easily comprehensible, and professional in appearance. Current software simplifies this task and enhances the results.

Each board member receives a copy of the report, one or more copies are submitted to each funding agency that is involved, and one or more copies are filed at the center. The narrative may be enhanced and clarified by the addition of appropriate graphs, charts, or tables. A pie chart showing the use of the director's time, for example, can be more effective than a lengthy narrative that contains the same information. Graphs and charts can be computer generated and add an extra professional touch to a report. The fact that the report is read by people from a variety of backgrounds should be considered.

Usually, by the time the report for a given year is complete and is in the hands of board members, the planning process for the new year has been completed and put into operation. The report then is used primarily for future planning. The board looks at the report, which includes the director's recommendations, to determine the areas that need modification. For example, if there is a high rate of turnover among the teaching staff, the board looks further to see if the cause can be determined from the evaluation data. Perhaps the salaries at this center are much lower than those of other centers in the community, or perhaps the physical environment is poor. Decisions for change are based on available evidence that grows out of the total evaluation process.

SUMMARY

From the center's inception, an evaluation plan is an essential component of the total program. The purpose of the plan is to determine the value of the center's operation; to evaluate the individuals within it through an analysis of the progress and functioning of the staff, the children, and the overall program; and to provide a basis for future planning. The evaluation process is open and ongoing and relates to the goals and objectives of the center. The process includes collecting, summarizing, analyzing, and using data according to a prespecified plan that lets everyone involved know by whom, how, when, where, and why evaluation is being done.

CLASS ASSIGNMENTS

1. Ask the director of an early childhood center about the evaluation plan used in that center. Find out who conducts evaluations and why, when, where, and how they are conducted. Perhaps the director will share with you copies of the forms that are used. Be sure to ask about all three components of the plan (staff, children, and general program). Write your responses on Working Paper 14–1.

2. Create a rating scale by which the director of a center could be evaluated. You may want to prepare a sample director's job description. Write your responses on Working Paper 14–2.

3. Using Working Paper 14–3, assess two preschool children you know. This procedure should be carried out by recalling what the children have done and by observing them in the classroom or home. It should not be conducted as a test situation for the children. (Note that Working Paper 14–3 represents a small portion of a child assessment tool. This brief form is used to allow the student to complete the assignment within a reasonable amount of time.)

CLASS EXERCISES

1. Work with a partner and role-play a conference in which a teacher and a director set up a work plan for the next six months. If you are assuming the role of teacher, try to use your own current classroom skills and areas in which you need improvement as a basis for the objectives in your work plan. If you are playing the director, use your communication skills to find out what help this teacher seems to need and where his strengths lie. After the role-play, ask your classmates for a brief evaluation of the conference. Then have two other students repeat the role-play. Is the second work plan different from the one formulated in the first role-play?

2. You are a teacher responsible for evaluating your aide. The aide lives in the inner-city community in which the center is located and seems to be highly skilled at interacting with the children and at guiding them. The aide wants them to succeed in kindergarten, and as a consequence, frequently insists that they practice writing the alphabet and doing addition and subtraction problems. Role-play with a classmate a midyear evaluation conference you might have with this aide.

WORKING PAPER 14-1

(for use with Class Assignment 1)

EVALUATION RESPONSE FORM

Name of center _____

1. Who conducts evaluations?

2. When is the evaluation done?

3. Where does the evaluation occur? (classrooms, director's office, parents' homes)

4. Describe the evaluation procedures for each of the components of the plan:

   ■ Staff

   ■ Children

   ■ General program

WORKING PAPER 14-2

(for use with Class Assignment 2)

RATING SCALE FOR EVALUATING DIRECTOR FORM

List at least five items on which a director could be evaluated. Include the format you would use to indicate the level of performance.

WORKING PAPER 14-3

(for use with Class Assignment 3)

PRESCHOOL CHILD ASSESSMENT FORM

CHILD ASSESSMENT (1st child)

Child's name _____ Birth date _____

School _____ Teacher _____

Form completed by _____ Date _____

Note: These items are listed to give a sense of long-range goals. Preschool children are not expected to accomplish all of them.

	Consistent	Frequent	Beginning	Not yet
1. Comments on number and numerical relationships	_____	_____	_____	_____
2. Rote counts to _____	_____	_____	_____	_____
3. Counts sometimes using double counting or skipping items	_____	_____	_____	_____
4. Counts in one-to-one correspondence	_____	_____	_____	_____
5. Recognizes last number counted as total quantity	_____	_____	_____	_____
6. Compares quantities globally (more)	_____	_____	_____	_____
7. Compares quantities globally (less)	_____	_____	_____	_____

(continues)

WORKING PAPER 14-3
(continued)

(for use with Class Assignment 3)

CHILD ASSESSMENT (2nd child)

Child's name _____ Birth date _____

School _____ Teacher _____

Form completed by _____ Date _____

Note: These items are listed to give a sense of long-range goals. Preschool children are not expected to accomplish all of them.

	Consistent	Frequent	Beginning	Not yet
1. Comments on number and numerical relationships	_____	_____	_____	_____
2. Rote counts to _____	_____	_____	_____	_____
3. Counts sometimes using double counting or skipping items	_____	_____	_____	_____
4. Counts in one-to-one correspondence	_____	_____	_____	_____
5. Recognizes last number counted as total quantity	_____	_____	_____	_____
6. Compares quantities globally (more)	_____	_____	_____	_____
7. Compares quantities globally (less)	_____	_____	_____	_____

DIRECTOR'S RESOURCE 14-1

DIRECTOR SELF-EVALUATION

This assessment process is to help you be a successful program director. It separates the *management* and *leadership* responsibilities of directing an early childhood program. In each section, you will identify your strengths and weaknesses and consider how you will use these insights about your skills and competencies to improve your personal performance, invest your energies, and assure the effectiveness and success of your center's program.

Program Management

Read the following statements that describe a director's *management* responsibilities. Identify your strengths (s) and weaknesses (w).

I implement effective orientation for new staff to help them learn the program's
___1. goals and philosophy
___2. emergency procedures
___3. special needs of children, including allergies, dietary restrictions, illnesses or medical conditions
___4. written policies and procedures including hours, holidays, guidelines for handling illness
___5. written personnel policies including job descriptions, salary scale, resignation/termination procedures, benefits, grievance procedures, and nondiscriminatory hiring procedures

I implement effective communication strategies for informing parents about the program's
___6. goals and philosophy
___7. emergency procedures
___8. written policies and procedures including tuition rates and policies, hours, holidays, guidelines for handling illness
___9. specific classroom assignments

I have effective strategies in place to
___10. maintain a fair and open waiting list
___11. help families when their child first enrolls in the center
___12. ease children's and family's transitions from one classroom to the next

I keep accurate records of
___13. staff qualifications and inservice training
___14. food services and nutritional plans
___15. administrative activities
___16. annual program assessment
___17. staff and student attendance
___18. fee payments
___19. Long- and short-term budgets

In *each section*, check √ the *two* items you think are your greatest strengths; mark with an X the *two* items you want to work on that are relative weaknesses.

(continues)

DIRECTOR'S RESOURCE 14-1
(continued)

Program Leadership

Read the following statements that describe a director's *leadership* responsibilities. Identify your **strengths (s)** and **weaknesses (w).**

I am an ethical leader when

___1. I model reflective practice that demonstrates an understanding of my personal learning and teaching style.

___2. I am knowledgeable about and strive to model established standards of best practice within the profession.

___3. I translate my knowledge of child development into effective programming for young children.

___4. I translate my knowledge of appropriate curriculum into effective programming for young children.

___5. I convey my knowledge of child development and curriculum effectively to teachers and parents.

___6. I model respect for individual differences and value cultural and ethnic diversity.

___7. My interactions with children, parents, and employees reflect my respect of each individual's dignity, worth, and uniqueness.

___8. I involve parents as partners in their children's care and education.

___9. I contribute to the creation of a positive climate at the center and encourage collaboration and cooperation.

___10. I plan and regularly provide effective inservice opportunities for staff development.

___11. I am a resource for parents and effectively share my professional knowledge.

___12. I am a resource for instructional staff and effectively share my professional knowledge.

___13. I conduct regular staff meetings that are well planned and make good use of our time together.

___14. I plan and implement effective staff evaluation procedures that are carried out in a spirit of professionalism and collegiality.

___15. I support the development of a community that nurtures employees, families, and children.

___16. I make appropriate use of community resources, including social services, and educational programs such as museums, libraries, and community centers.

I consistently work to improve my practice:

___17. I keep abreast of current developments in child development and appropriate curriculum design.

___18. I assume appropriate advocacy responsibilities.

___19. I assume leadership roles in professional organizations, including presenting at conferences and taking an active role in professional organizations' work.

After you have identified *strengths,* you might choose to

capitalize on your aptitude and ability and increase the emphasis on this dimension of program management or program leadership

OR

maintain your current expertise and emphasis, investing your efforts to develop yourself and the center elsewhere.

(continues)

DIRECTOR'S RESOURCE 14-1
(continued)

I have these specific plans to use my identified *management strengths:*

- ▪
- ▪

I have these specific plans to use my identified *leadership strengths:*

- ▪
- ▪

I am making a *deliberate effort* to establish and clarify my long-term personal career goals and set realistic objectives. I am currently

__collecting and studying information pertaining to professional development activities.

__seeking assistance in the development of professional development plan. _____
   is helping me.

__actively progressing through a planned continuing education program.

❏ CDA	❏ A.A.	❏ Ph.D.
❏ B.A.	❏ M.Ed.	❏ Other _____

I am actively involved in professional organization(s) concerned with children:

❏ ACEI	❏ SECA	❏ CEC
❏ NAEYC	❏ NBCDI	❏ Other _____

After you have identified *weaknesses,* you might choose to

delegate these responsibilities, recognizing that they are not, and may well never be, skills you will elect to develop

OR

develop these abilities by pursuing additional training and education.

I have these specific plans to address my identified *management weaknesses:*

- ▪
- ▪

I have these specific plans to address my identified *leadership weaknesses:*

- ▪
- ▪

Other comments

Program year _____

Name _____

Title _____

Date _____

Date of last evaluation _____

From *"Evaluating the Child Care Director: The Collaborative Assessment Process,"* by N. K. Freeman and M. H. Brown, 2000, Young Children, 55*(5), pp. 20–28. Reprinted with permission from NAEYC.*

DIRECTOR'S RESOURCE 14-2

CHILD EVALUATION FORM

Use different color for each assessment. Record date in that color.

Child's name: _____ Birth date: _____

School: _____ Teacher: _____

Form completed by: _____

Date: _____   Date: _____   Date: _____

General Autonomy

	Consistent	Frequent	Beginning	Not yet	Comments
A. Initiative					
1. Develops and pursues own ideas in activities	_____	_____	_____	_____	_____
2. Expands ideas of others	_____	_____	_____	_____	_____
B. Self-confidence					
1. Assured in expressing ideas and convictions	_____	_____	_____	_____	_____
2. Copes well with new experiences	_____	_____	_____	_____	_____
3. Manifests general feeling of self-satisfaction	_____	_____	_____	_____	_____
4. Verbalizes feelings	_____	_____	_____	_____	_____
C. Independence					
1. Cares for self (bathroom, dressing)	_____	_____	_____	_____	_____
2. Chooses activities	_____	_____	_____	_____	_____
3. Separates comfortably from parent	_____	_____	_____	_____	_____
4. Seeks attention, help, and recognition when appropriate	_____	_____	_____	_____	_____
D. Responsibility					
1. Cares for materials	_____	_____	_____	_____	_____
2. Cleans up (with minimal prompting)	_____	_____	_____	_____	_____
3. Keeps up with own belongings	_____	_____	_____	_____	_____
E. Appears psychologically engaged in child-selected activity	_____	_____	_____	_____	_____

Sociomoral Development

	Consistent	Frequent	Beginning	Not yet	Comments
A. Responsibility					
1. Can verbalize classroom guidelines	_____	_____	_____	_____	_____
2. Adheres to classroom guidelines	_____	_____	_____	_____	_____
*3. Participates in setting classroom guidelines	_____	_____	_____	_____	_____
*4. Participates in enforcing classroom guidelines	_____	_____	_____	_____	_____
*5. Initiates or participates in a discussion of classroom problems	_____	_____	_____	_____	_____

(continues)

DIRECTOR'S RESOURCE 14-2
(continued)

	Consistent	Frequent	Beginning	Not yet	Comments
6. Facilitates and participates in classroom routine (by anticipating transitions, etc.)	_____	_____	_____	_____	_____

B. Cooperation

	Consistent	Frequent	Beginning	Not yet	Comments
*1. Uses appropriate assertive behavior and language to resolve conflicts	_____	_____	_____	_____	_____
*2. Takes up for others' rights and attempts to help others in conflict situations	_____	_____	_____	_____	_____
3. Channels feelings of anger, frustration, etc. in appropriate ways	_____	_____	_____	_____	_____
4. Generates game rules	_____	_____	_____	_____	_____
*5. Follows game rules agreed upon by players	_____	_____	_____	_____	_____
*6. Considers others' point of view	_____	_____	_____	_____	_____
*7. Discusses moral dilemmas (extra guests, enough cookies for class)	_____	_____	_____	_____	_____
*8. Takes turns	_____	_____	_____	_____	_____
9. Invites others to participate in activities	_____	_____	_____	_____	_____
10. Responds to invitations to participate in activities	_____	_____	_____	_____	_____
*11. Recognizes rights of others (may not act on)	_____	_____	_____	_____	_____
*12. Channels competitive impulses in cooperative direction (enjoys the process and accepts the outcome)	_____	_____	_____	_____	_____

C. Relating to Group

	Consistent	Frequent	Beginning	Not yet	Comments
1. Calls children and adults by name	_____	_____	_____	_____	_____
2. Identifies which children are absent	_____	_____	_____	_____	_____
3. Notices others' needs (such as getting tissue for another)	_____	_____	_____	_____	_____
4. Interested in doing things for group (such as preparing snack)	_____	_____	_____	_____	_____
5. Spontaneously expresses caring for others (solutions when another is hurt)	_____	_____	_____	_____	_____
6. Shows interest in what others at grouptime say	_____	_____	_____	_____	_____
7. Participates in voting process	_____	_____	_____	_____	_____

Cognitive Development

A. Writing

	Consistent	Frequent	Beginning	Not yet	Comments
1. Writes using personal cursive	_____	_____	_____	_____	_____
2. Writes pseudoletters	_____	_____	_____	_____	_____
*3. Copies letter and numbers	_____	_____	_____	_____	_____
*4. Writes own name	_____	_____	_____	_____	_____
*5. Writes other words	_____	_____	_____	_____	_____
*6. Writes from left to right	_____	_____	_____	_____	_____
*7. Experiments with conventions of writing (such as writing from right to left)	_____	_____	_____	_____	_____

(continues)

DIRECTOR'S RESOURCE 14-2
(continued)

	Consistent	Frequent	Beginning	Not yet	Comments
*8. Asks for models (how to write a letter or word or how to spell a word)	_____	_____	_____	_____	_____
9. Uses writing with intention of communicating	_____	_____	_____	_____	_____
10. Asks to dictate messages	_____	_____	_____	_____	_____

B. Reading

	Consistent	Frequent	Beginning	Not yet	Comments
1. Enjoys stories	_____	_____	_____	_____	_____
2. Requests stories	_____	_____	_____	_____	_____
3. Holds book properly and turns pages	_____	_____	_____	_____	_____
4. Pretends to read	_____	_____	_____	_____	_____
5. Distinguishes between print and picture	_____	_____	_____	_____	_____
6. Recognizes first letter of own name	_____	_____	_____	_____	_____
7. Recognizes own name in print	_____	_____	_____	_____	_____
8. Recognizes printed names of other children	_____	_____	_____	_____	_____
9. Recognizes meanings of signs	_____	_____	_____	_____	_____
10. Matches words in print	_____	_____	_____	_____	_____
*11. Knows what a word is	_____	_____	_____	_____	_____
12. Recognizes letters	_____	_____	_____	_____	_____
13. Reads own writing	_____	_____	_____	_____	_____
14. Attempts voice print pairing	_____	_____	_____	_____	_____
*15. Generates rhyming words	_____	_____	_____	_____	_____
*16. Generates words that begin alike	_____	_____	_____	_____	_____
17. Knows one reads from left to right, front to back, and top to bottom	_____	_____	_____	_____	_____
*18. Reads predictable books	_____	_____	_____	_____	_____

C. Language

1. Spoken

	Consistent	Frequent	Beginning	Not yet	Comments
a. Speaks clearly enough for a stranger to understand	_____	_____	_____	_____	_____
b. Modulates tone of voice based on situation	_____	_____	_____	_____	_____

2. Understood Language

	Consistent	Frequent	Beginning	Not yet	Comments
a. Responds appropriately to questions including who, what, when, and how	_____	_____	_____	_____	_____
b. Responds appropriately to why questions	_____	_____	_____	_____	_____
c. Carries on meaningful conversations	_____	_____	_____	_____	_____
d. Stays on topic in group discussion	_____	_____	_____	_____	_____

Cognitive Dispositions

A. Autonomy

	Consistent	Frequent	Beginning	Not yet	Comments
1. Generates several alternatives in play situations	_____	_____	_____	_____	_____
2. Has "wonderful ideas" (thinks of new ideas in relation to objects and activities)	_____	_____	_____	_____	_____

(continues)

DIRECTOR'S RESOURCE 14-2
(continued)

	Consistent	Frequent	Beginning	Not yet	Comments
B. Physical Knowledge					
1. Experiments with objects (water, sand, art media, pendulum, and other mechanical apparatus)	_____	_____	_____	_____	_____
2. Makes and verifies predictions (such as water will come out hole in side of container)	_____	_____	_____	_____	_____
3. Notices effects of actions on objects	_____	_____	_____	_____	_____
4. Notices changes in objects	_____	_____	_____	_____	_____
C. Logico-Mathematical Knowledge					
1. Comments on number and numerical relationships	_____	_____	_____	_____	_____
2. Rote counts to ___	_____	_____	_____	_____	_____
3. Counts sometimes using double counting or skipping items	_____	_____	_____	_____	_____
4. Counts in 1 to 1 correspondence	_____	_____	_____	_____	_____
5. Recognizes last number counted as total quantity	_____	_____	_____	_____	_____
6. Compares quantities globally (more)	_____	_____	_____	_____	_____
7. Compares quantities globally (less)	_____	_____	_____	_____	_____
8. Compares quantities globally (as much as, etc.)	_____	_____	_____	_____	_____
9. Reasons about addition and subtraction in classroom situations	_____	_____	_____	_____	_____
10. Compares quantities numerically (5 is more than 3)	_____	_____	_____	_____	_____
*11. Identifies numerals	_____	_____	_____	_____	_____
12. Thinks about spatial relationships	_____	_____	_____	_____	_____
a. Follows path on game board	_____	_____	_____	_____	_____
1. Own path	_____	_____	_____	_____	_____
2. Common path (straight)	_____	_____	_____	_____	_____
3. Curved path	_____	_____	_____	_____	_____
b. Reasons about spatial problems '(as in aiming at target)	_____	_____	_____	_____	_____
c. Reasons about body fitting in space	_____	_____	_____	_____	_____
d. Uses prepositions such as in, on, over, etc. appropriately	_____	_____	_____	_____	_____
*e. Uses "first" appropriately	_____	_____	_____	_____	_____
*f. Uses "last" appropriately	_____	_____	_____	_____	_____
*g. Uses "middle" appropriately	_____	_____	_____	_____	_____
*h. Uses "second" appropriately	_____	_____	_____	_____	_____
*i. Uses "in between" appropriately	_____	_____	_____	_____	_____

(continues)

DIRECTOR'S RESOURCE 14-2

(continued)

	Consistent	Frequent	Beginning	Not yet	Comments
13. Reasons about classes and relations	___	___	___	___	___
a. Groups objects according to similarities and differences in games and other classroom situations	___	___	___	___	___
*b. Conceptualizes part/whole relations in sets of objects (as in card games with suits)	___	___	___	___	___
14. Temporal reasoning					
a. Knows order of classroom routine	___	___	___	___	___
b. Refers to clock to monitor routines	___	___	___	___	___
*c. Understands "today"	___	___	___	___	___
*d. Understands "tomorrow"	___	___	___	___	___
*e. Understands "yesterday"	___	___	___	___	___
*f. Global understanding of past and future ("a long time ago," "a long time from now," etc.)	___	___	___	___	___
g. Knows order of events in familiar stories	___	___	___	___	___
15. Patterns					
a. Recognizes patterns	___	___	___	___	___
b. Matches patterns	___	___	___	___	___
c. Creates patterns	___	___	___	___	___
d. Extends patterns	___	___	___	___	___
16. Constructs matching sets					
a. 1–3	___	___	___	___	___
b. 4–6	___	___	___	___	___
*c. 7–12	___	___	___	___	___
17. Makes count-cardinal transitions	___	___	___	___	___

*Asterisk indicates that it would not be expected until at least four years of age.
(This form was drawn from previous work of Rheta deVries and Brenda Hieronymus and Sally Moomaw.)

DIRECTOR'S RESOURCE 14-3

PROGRAM EVALUATION

Parents and teachers have valuable information about the quality of our child care program. We hope you will answer these questions carefully and thoughtfully. We appreciate your involvement and cooperation as we work to provide our children the best possible environment for living and learning.

Please check the box that most closely reflects your view. If you have no information or opinion about an item, please circle its number.

I am a   ❏ **parent**   ❏ **staff member**   ❏ **other** _____

Program year _____	Needs immediate attention	Less than ideal	Satisfactory	Above average	Exemplary: Other programs should visit us
1. The program has a clearly stated philosophy and goals.					
2. The curriculum, environment, and activities reflect the stated philosophy and goals.					
3. Indoor and outdoor areas are clean, safe, and attractive.					
4. There is an adequate supply of age-appropriate equipment and materials. Materials are durable, in good repair, and are readily accessible to children.					
5. Appropriate play activities to develop children's small and large muscles are planned and encouraged both indoors and outdoors.					
6. The program's activities reflect an appreciation and respect for cultural diversity.					
7. Orientation practices and routines help welcome new families and smooth children's transitions from one class to another.					
8. Staff/parent communications give adults opportunities to share information about childrearing practices.					
9. Parents are welcome to visit and encouraged to become involved in center activities.					

(continues)

DIRECTOR'S RESOURCE 14-3
(continued)

Program year _____	Needs immediate attention	Less than ideal	Satisfactory	Above average	Exemplary: Other programs should visit us
10. There are effective routines for oral and/or written day-to-day parent/teacher communications.					
11. Conferences about children's progress and accomplishments are scheduled when parents or teachers feel they are needed, and are conducted at least once a year.					
12. There are safe arrival and departure routines that allow for appropriate staff-parent interactions.					
13. Routines are in place to protect children's and teachers' health and well-being. Surfaces and toys are cleaned appropriately. There are provisions for sanitary disposal of diapers as well as bloody waste. Gloves and other protective equipment are available for teachers to use when changing diapers and treating ill or injured children. There are adequate facilities for children and staff to toilet and wash their hands.					
14. Meals and snacks are nutritious and appealing. Parents receive the menu information they need.					
15. We can be proud of how our program . . .					
16. The first improvement we should make is . . .					

Other comments

From "Evaluating the Child Care Director: The Collaborative Assessment Process," by N. K. Freeman and M. H. Brown, 2000, Young Children, 55(5), pp. 20–28. Reprinted with permission from NAEYC.

DIRECTOR'S RESOURCE 14-4

QUESTIONS TO ASK IN EVALUATING A PROGRAM'S ASSESSMENT PROCEDURES

1. Is the assessment procedure based on the goals and objectives of the specific curriculum used in the program?

2. Are the results of the assessment used to benefit children, i.e., to plan for individual children, improve instruction, identify children's interests and needs, and individualize instruction, rather than label, track, or fail children?

3. Does the assessment procedure address all domains of learning and development—social, emotional, physical, and cognitive—as well as children's feelings and dispositions toward learning?

4. Does assessment provide useful information to teachers to help them do a better job?

5. Does the assessment procedure rely on teachers' regular and periodic observations and record keeping of children's everyday activities and performance so that results reflect children's behavior over time?

6. Does the assessment procedure occur as part of the ongoing life of the classroom rather than in an artificial, contrived context?

7. Is the assessment procedure performance-based, rather than only testing skills in isolation?

8. Does the assessment rely on multiple sources of information about children, such as collections of their work, results of teacher interviews and dialogues, as well as observations?

9. Does the assessment procedure reflect individual, cultural, and linguistic diversity? Is it free of cultural, language, and gender biases?

10. Do children appear comfortable and relaxed during assessment rather than tense or anxious?

11. Does the assessment procedure support parents' confidence in their children and their ability as parents rather than threaten or undermine parents' confidence?

12. Does the assessment examine children's strengths and capabilities rather than just their weaknesses or what they do not know?

13. Is the teacher the primary assessor, and are teachers adequately trained for this role?

14. Does the assessment procedure involve collaboration among teachers, children, administrators, and parents? Is information from parents used in planning instruction and evaluating children's learning? Are parents informed about assessment information?

15. Do children have an opportunity to reflect on and evaluate their own learning?

16. Are children assessed in supportive contexts to determine what they are capable of doing with assistance as well as what they can do independently?

17. Is there a systematic procedure for collecting assessment data that facilitates its use in planning instruction and communicating with parents?

18. Is there a regular procedure for communicating the results of assessment to parents in meaningful language, rather than letter or number grades, that reports children's individual progress?

From "Assessment in Context: Teachers and Children at Work," by T. W. Hills, 1993, *Young Children, 48(5)*, pp. 20–28. Reprinted with permission from NAEYC.

DIRECTOR'S RESOURCE 14-5

CHILD ASSESSMENT

Assessment in Support of Learning

Notes	Questions
Documents needed: child assessment form, developmental checklist, written record of use of aggregated assessment data for evaluation and/or planning, and an example of a child's portfolio.	How do teaching staff assess children's learning and development?
	■ Do teaching staff conduct formal observations of children?
* Reliable and valid assessments include research-based checklists (e.g., High/Scope COR, Work Sampling System, Creative Curriculum).	■ Do teaching staff use assessment tools with established reliability and validity?
	■ Do teaching staff maintain a portfolio of individual children's work?
** Standards refer to published professional standards (e.g., NAEYC, NSACCA, Head Start Outcomes Framework) or individual state learning standards.	How is the curriculum planned at the center?
	■ Is the curriculum based on professional standards?
	■ Are children's individual outcomes considered?
	■ Are data regarding children's assessments aggregated and used for curriculum planning?

(continues)

DIRECTOR'S RESOURCE 14-5
(continued)

Assessment in Support of Learning

1	2	3	4	5	6	7
Inadequate		**Minimal**		**Good**		**Excellent**
1.1 No formal assessment system is in place for observing children and assessing their learning and development.		3.1 D Assessment system includes teaching staff making judgments using assessment checklists (may be teacher-made).		5.1 D Assessment system includes teaching staff making judgments using assessment checklists that are reliable and valid.*		7.1 D Assessment system includes teaching staff making judgments using reliable and valid checklists as well as other measures (e.g., portfolios of children's work, teacher's observational notes).*
1.2 Standards are not considered in curriculum planning.**		3.2 Standards are considered in curriculum planning.**		5.2 Individual assessment results regarding child outcomes are utilized in curriculum planning.		7.2 D Aggregated assessment results regarding child outcomes are utilized in long-range curriculum planning and/or in program evaluation.

Circle the final score based on the scoring rules on page 9

1	2	3	4	5	6	7

Assessment in Support of Learning

Comments:

From Program Administration Scale: Measuring Early Childhood Leadership and Management, by A. Talan and J. Bloom, 2005. Reprinted with permission from Teachers College Press.

DIRECTOR'S RESOURCE 14-6

FISCAL MANAGEMENT

Accounting Practices

Notes

Documents needed: quarterly financial statements, most recent audit, policy regarding separation of financial duties, and examples of cancelled checks with multiple signatures.

* The elements of a system of checks and balances might include: two or more signatures required on checks, restricted funds (grants) and major capital funds are separate from general operating funds, and the separation of duties (e.g., the same person does not receive cash and authorize cash disbursements).

** Independent review means that the reviewer is not an employee of the organization. A board member or parent can conduct an independent review.

Questions

How often are income and expense statements prepared?

Does the on-site Administrator have access to income and expense statements?

■ Provide an example of how this information is used to make program decisions.

Does the center have a system of checks-and-balances?

■ Describe the elements of this system.

Is there an independent review of accounting records?

■ By whom?

■ How often?

(continues)

DIRECTOR'S RESOURCE 14-6

(continued)

Accounting Practices

Inadequate		Minimal		Good		Excellent	
1	2	3	4	5	6	7	

1.1 A system does not exist to generate quarterly income and expense statements.

3.1 A system exists to generate quarterly income and expense statements.

5.1 D The on-site Administrator has access to or generates quarterly income and expense statements.

7.1 D The on-site Administrator uses quarterly income and expense statements to monitor the center's fiscal status and make programmatic decisions.

1.2 There is no accounting system of checks and balances.*

3.2 D There is one element of a checks-and-balances system.*

5.2 D There are two elements of a checks-and-balances system.*

7.2 D There are three elements of a checks-and-balances system.*

1.3 There is no independent review of the accounting records (reconciliation of the bank statements to the general ledger).**

3.3 There is an independent review of the accounting records (reconciliation of bank statements to the general ledger).**

5.3 There is a quarterly review of the accounting records by an independent third party who has accounting or bookkeeping expertise.**

7.3 D An outside audit is conducted annually by a certified public accountant.

Comments:

Circle the final score based on the scoring rules on page 9

| 1 | 2 | 3 | 4 | 5 | 6 | 7 |

Accounting Practices

From Program Administration Scale: Measuring Early Childhood Leadership and Management, by A. Talon and J. Bloom, 2005. Reprinted with permission from Teachers College Press.

REFERENCES

Boehm, A. E., & Weinberg, R. A. (1997). *The classroom observer: Developing observational skills in early childhood settings* (3rd ed.). New York: Teachers College Press.

Child Welfare League of America. (2002). *Cultural competence agency self-assessment instrument* (revised). Washington, DC: Author.

Eisenberg, E. (2000). Accreditation, strategies, benefits and practical tips. *Child Care Information Exchange, 131*, 70–73.

Genishi, C. (Ed.). (1992). *Ways of assessing children and curriculum: Stories of early childhood practice.* New York: Teachers College Press.

Goffin, S. (2004a, May). Moving into the next phase: Developing new accreditation assessment tools and addressing questions. *Young Children, 59*(3), 70–72.

Goffin, S. (2004b, September). Update on key differences in reinvented and current systems. *Young Children, 59*(5), 89–90.

Goffin, S. (2004c, November). New policies, procedures, and fees for the NAEYC accreditation system. *Young Children, 59*(6), 62–63.

Gullo, D. F. (2005). *Understanding assessment and evaluation in early childhood education* (2nd ed.). New York: Teachers College Press.

Harms, T., Clifford, R., & Cryer, D. (2005). *Early Childhood Environment Rating Scale* (Rev. ed.). New York: Teachers College Press. (Also available in Spanish)

Horm-Wingard, D. (1992). Reporting children's development: The narrative report. *Dimensions of Early Childhood, 21*(1).

Jorde-Bloom, P. (1988). *A great place to work: Improving conditions for staff in young children's programs.* Washington, DC: National Association for the Education of Young Children.

Meisels, S., & Atkins-Burnett, S. (2004). The Head Start National Reporting System: A critique. *Young Children, 59*(1) 64–66.

National Association for the Education of Young Children. (1988). *Testing of young children: Concerns and cautions.* Washington, DC: Author.

Neugebauer, R. (1998). *Out of the box ideas for evaluation.* In R. Neugebauer, & B. Neugebauer (Eds.), *The art of leadership: Managing early childhood organizations,* Vol. 2 (pp. 291–294). Redmond, WA: Child Care Information Exchange.

Nicolson, S., & Shipstead, S. G. (1998). *Through the looking glass: Observations in the early childhood classroom* (2nd ed.). Upper Saddle River, NJ: Merrill/Prentice Hall.

Nilsen, B. A. (1997). *Week by week: Plans for observing and recording young children.* Clifton Park, NY: Thomson Delmar Learning.

Raver, C., & Zigler, E. (2004). Another step back? Assessing readiness in Head Start. *Young Children, 59*(1), 58–63.

Surr, J. (2004, March). Who's accredited? What and how the states are doing on best practices in child care. *Child Care Information Exchange, 156*, 14–19.

Talan, T., & Bloom, P. (2005). *Program administrators' scale measuring early childhood leadership and management.* New York: Teacher College Press.

Talley, K. (1997). National accreditation: Why do some programs stall in self-study? *Young Children, 52*(3), 31–37.

VanderVen, K. (2000). Capturing the breadth and depth of the job: The administrator as influential leader in a complex world. In M. Culkin (Ed.), *Managing quality in young children's programs: The leaders role* (pp. 112–128). New York: Teachers College Press.

Warman, B. (1998). Trends in state accreditation policies. *Young Children, 53*(5), 52–55.

Werner, S. (1996). Need a barometer for assessing the climate of your center? *Child Care Information Exchange, 109*, 29–31.

For additional references on assessment, see the January 2004 issue of *Young Children* published by NAEYC.

Additional resources for this chapter can be found on the Online Companion™ at http://www.earlychilded.delmar.com. This supplemental material includes relevant Web links, Web activities, and case studies that apply the concepts presented in this chapter. In addition, the Working Papers and Director's Resources are available for download, allowing you to complete Class Exercises and Class Assignments electronically.

CHAPTER 15

Providing for Personal and Professional Staff Development

The staff meeting agenda includes the time as well as the name of the person responsible for each agenda item.

Agenda
Staff Meeting

12:30 Convene and present agenda
12:40 Present plan for self-study
for NAEYC accreditation - Joan
1:15 Discuss use of manipulative/
art storage room - Yvette
1:30 Plan a winter parent meeting - Sue
date? program? staff responsibilities
1:45 Report on meeting with carpenter
on new outdoor sandbox - Joan
2:00 Adjourn

OBJECTIVES

After reading this chapter, you should be able to:

- Identify the career levels of teachers to plan professional development strategies.
- Describe the process of scheduling and planning for staff meetings and in-service training.
- List the four principles of supervision.

The center director is responsible for the personal and professional development of the staff. In very large centers or in corporate systems, the business and fiscal maintenance functions may be separated from the educational program maintenance, in which case the education director is accountable for the educational program and the accompanying staff development programs. However, in most centers, one person is responsible for both the business and educational program components.

A basic assumption underlying staff development programs is that learning is a lifelong process, and adults have the capacity to change and grow. This capacity is, in a sense, similar to that manifested by children in their growth processes. Likewise, the director's responsibility as it relates to the center staff parallels that of the classroom teacher: to create a favorable environment for optimum growth and development of all the people in the environment. Having the director serve as a model of professionalism in handling staff meetings, staff training programs, staff supervision, and assessing staff problems facilitates and enhances the personal and professional development of the center staff. The specific content or the specific strategy employed in any aspect of the staff development program depends on group composition. In the same way that classroom teachers assess the needs of children in planning appropriate learning environments, directors evaluate staff needs and plan staff development programs accordingly. In addition, just like teaching young children, where the responsible adult offers many opportunities to make decisions but there are times when children are expected to follow certain rules and expectations, so the director establishes expectations for teachers that represent the bottom line and are expected to be followed (Jones, 1993).

STAFF MEETINGS

The director is responsible for planning and conducting staff meetings. Bloom states that meetings are very important. In fact, she says meetings are ". . . the glue that holds the organization together" (Bloom, 2002, p. 1). Although conducting a staff meeting may seem to be a routine and relatively easy task, holding meetings that are satisfying and worthwhile for both the director and the staff requires careful planning and preparation. Effective implementation of the planned agenda is dependent, largely, on the director's ability to maintain open communication among those attending the meeting.

Purpose of Staff Meetings

Communication is the main purpose of staff meetings. Although much can be communicated through memorandums and newsletters, posting bulletin board notices, using e-mail, and exchanging information on a casual one-to-one basis, many issues and problems are resolved most effectively in a meeting.

Two-way communication in a meeting permits an interchange of ideas and feelings and provides a forum for thoughtful discussion and clarification of problems and issues. The final outcome for each individual should be a better understanding of problems and issues and of self and others. When staff members are involved in discussing program issues

The director, with input from staff, is responsible for preparing the agenda for staff meetings.

or problems, when their opinions have been heard, and when they have had some voice in decision making, they feel a greater sense of self-worth and consider themselves to be a more integral part of the total center community. To be comfortable for everyone, staff meetings must provide a safe environment where staff members can ask questions, challenge others by presenting alternative ideas, and share feelings with the group.

To prevent the meeting from deteriorating into a "gripe session," the director can take an active role in channeling the complaints and concerns toward improvement strategies. Open communication during staff meetings is one way to develop cooperation and harmony and to encourage the "we" feeling among staff members. This is further advanced when staff members are encouraged to suggest staff meeting agenda items. As mentioned in Chapter 2, the sense of community is fundamental for the creation of a favorable environment for the personal growth of staff members, children, and families who participate in the center program.

When the director becomes aware that there is an undercurrent of discontent among the staff, a staff meeting discussion focused on concerns and issues may be useful, but only after talking informally with several staff to see if the problem can be remedied, thereby leaving staff meeting time for other agenda items. If, however, staff unrest persists, it may be necessary to assess staff morale through the use of a *climate survey*. A well-designed survey tool that includes items related to motivation, commitment, satisfaction-dissatisfaction, and other concerns can yield useful information that directors then can use to provide a framework for a staff meeting discussion. The climate survey becomes a means to an end because it helps staff focus on their most urgent issues, and it helps the director bring the staff meeting discussion toward problem resolution. Bloom (2005) suggests that climate of the organization is akin to the personality of the center. Although both director and staff can have input into the design of the survey tool, calling in an expert to help design the questions is often the best way to proceed (Werner, 1996).

Staff meeting discussions may involve specific questions such as which piece of outdoor equipment to buy, or whether to buy tricycles or books with the equipment money available at the end of the year. Sometimes, discussions focus on the use of available building or outdoor space, or on the appropriateness of timing the meal service or the monthly fire drill. The director may decide to use staff meeting time to discuss more general philosophical or educational program issues such as, "What changes should we

consider in our program planning in order to focus more attention on emerging literacy?" A question that logically follows is, "How do we, as a staff, learn more about the application of a whole language approach in the classroom?" Discussions about both educational program and general program philosophy often lead to group decisions about the focus and content of future in-service training sessions. If the group makes decisions about the training needs of the teaching staff, there undoubtedly will be a greater commitment to the training program than if the director makes those decisions without group input.

Directors and teachers sometimes decide to use part of each staff meeting to discuss individual children and their needs. This is a place where teachers not only set the agenda but may lead the discussion. These discussions, which are confidential among those involved, are particularly productive for the total staff when the center program is open and free flowing, and the children regularly interact with different staff members. Although it may seem less productive to involve the total staff in a discussion of one child when that child is in a self-contained classroom, if others feel free to contribute, they often can lend a degree of objectivity to the discussion.

Nonetheless, when staff meeting discussions are not of particular relevance to those in attendance, boredom and restlessness become apparent, and members feel that the time is wasted. To maintain interest and open communication, try to select agenda items that are of concern to most of the staff members who are expected to attend the regular staff meetings. Remember to use icebreakers and various problem-solving strategies that will help maintain interest and keep staff focused. Make certain that the purpose of the meeting, whatever it may be, is clearly stated and understood by everyone at the meeting (Bloom, 2002). The agenda items that pertain only to the work of a few can be reserved for special meetings or assigned to small committees for discussion and subsequent decision making.

DIRECTOR'S CORNER

"Our staff scheduling problems are so complex, there is no way I can plan a staff meeting during the day. We have evening meetings and everyone is expected to attend. Each new employee is advised of that expectation and assured that she will receive overtime pay or hours for work will be adjusted."

—*Director, employer-sponsored child care center in hospital setting*

Timing of Staff Meetings

The frequency and timing of staff meetings vary, depending on the amount of business typically transacted and the amount of time devoted to each meeting. Weekly or biweekly meetings that are well planned and brief may be more productive than long sessions that are held less frequently. Although staff members usually prefer daytime meetings because they need evenings and weekends to rest and take care of personal matters, evenings may be the only time everyone can meet together.

In half-day programs, staff meetings can be scheduled after the children leave at noon, or in centers with double sessions, either early in the morning or late in the afternoon. However, full-day programs present special problems because the centers are open from early morning until very late afternoon, and the center staff usually works a staggered schedule. Nap time is often the time set aside for meetings because most staff members are present in the middle of the day; however, sleeping children must be supervised. Use of volunteers or parents for nap time supervision is an alternative but one that licensing disallows in some places. In smaller centers, hiring substitutes to cover nap rooms may be a better solution.

The center staff and the director decide which staff members, in addition to classroom staff, should be encouraged to attend staff meetings. It may be beneficial to have the bus driver, the cook, or the receptionist at staff meetings because the kind of contact these staff members have with the children and families enables them to make a unique contribution to staff meeting discussions. Directors also may find it useful to ask the consulting psychologist, the special education resource teacher, or other professionals who are involved in the program to attend staff meetings. Anyone who can profit from, or contribute to, the discussions should be encouraged to come to the meetings.

DIRECTOR'S CORNER

"I reserve one-half hour at the end of each monthly staff meeting and have one staff member take over the meeting. Last month a teacher talked about a workshop she had attended on dealing with stress. It was great! We all participated in some of the stress-relieving exercises she had learned."

–Director, church-sponsored early education program

Preparation for Staff Meetings

Both the director and the staff members must prepare for a staff meeting so that the meeting will be productive for everyone. The director is responsible for obtaining staff input on agenda items, preparing and posting the agenda, and distributing any material that should be read by the staff before the meeting. Even though the director holds final responsibility for planning the agenda, all staff members should be invited to suggest agenda items either before or after it is posted. The posted agenda usually includes a brief description of each item and the action to be taken. For example, if the agenda item about the use of outdoor space is to cover the timing for its use, the responsibility for setting up and cleaning up, and the equipment needs, then all these subjects for discussion would be listed. The agenda also should state clearly which items are open for discussion *and* group decision, and which items are open only for discussion. In the latter case, the director hears the discussion, considers the ideas and feelings of the staff, and subsequently makes the decision. In the case of the outdoor space questions, the classroom staff probably should decide about the timing for the use of outdoor space; the total staff, including the janitor or housekeeper, should be involved in the discussion and decision about setting up and cleaning up the space; the final decision about equipment purchase is made by the director after hearing the preferences of the entire staff. When all these expectations are spelled out clearly on the posted agenda, there is little room for confusion or misunderstanding about what will occur during the meeting.

Each item on the posted agenda includes the name of the person responsible for presenting the item and leading the discussion and a rough time estimate for adequate coverage of the item. This procedure notifies staff members about their responsibility during the meeting and ensures coverage of the entire agenda within a specified meeting time. Giving staff members responsibility for selected agenda items is an excellent way to encourage interest in center operations. Reserving part of each meeting to have a staff member present on a topic of interest also contributes to the feeling of collegiality.

The director should distribute copies of readings, minutes from previous staff or board meetings, and any other information that will provide a common basis for discussion to enhance the quality of the dialogue during the meeting. For example, if there is to be a discussion about curriculum planning as it relates to emerging literacy, research studies and program ideas on this topic could be duplicated and given to staff members several days before the meeting. Individual staff members also can be encouraged to search out additional information on the topic so the time spent during the meeting is productive and informative for everyone. Occasionally, a specialist from the community can be invited to a staff meeting to contribute to a discussion that requires particular expertise, such as services provided by the local children's protective agency or new information on infectious diseases in child care centers. When the director prepares the agenda carefully, and both the director and the staff members come well informed, the outcome is more likely to be satisfying for everyone.

Staff Meeting Procedure

The director usually serves as the convener and assumes the responsibility for moving the group through the agenda by facilitating but not dominating the discussion and helping the group maintain a balance between dealing with tasks and dealing with interpersonal processes.

At the outset, it is important that the meeting begin at the stated time and end on schedule. When the convener does not call the meeting to order on time and moves immediately to the first agenda item, group members are inclined to come late because they assume the meeting will not start on time. When the discussion of an agenda item extends beyond the time assigned, the convener should call attention to that fact and have the group decide whether more time should be spent on that item.

Perhaps all this emphasis on time seems unimportant, but time management is important. Time is finite, and you and your staff must develop good time management skills to accomplish as much as you can within a specified time frame. The staff meeting is an excellent place for you, as a director, to demonstrate good time management.

Clearly, conducting an effective staff meeting takes careful planning and requires special skills on the part of the director. However, when meetings are satisfying and productive for the staff, they serve as a vehicle for communication and promote cooperation and good feeling among staff. Furthermore, staff meetings give the director a chance to model interpersonal communication skills that serve as the basis for all interactions with children, parents, and other staff members.

STAFF TRAINING/ PROFESSIONAL DEVELOPMENT

The staff training and professional development program begins with the orientation of new staff members and includes all aspects of in-service training. Planning the total staff training program depends on the composition of the center staff. Just as the classroom teacher individualizes approaches to children, so the director recognizes the developmental level of each teacher and plans training accordingly. The training must be adjusted to the experience level and career stage, as well as to the specific concerns, capabilities, and perspectives of each person and should focus on long-term growth and change in individuals' thinking skills (Bloom, 2005).

Fully trained and qualified classroom teaching staff members should have basic child development information and should be able to plan curriculum and classroom management strategies with minimum additional training. However, they may be ready for some help on working with the special education resource teacher who comes to consult with them about the children with disabilities in the center. Because special classroom strategies must be employed in order to truly include children with disabilities into a noncategorical classroom, training in techniques and strategies to accomplish that integration also will be helpful to the experienced teacher. The interdisciplinary classroom team of early childhood and special educators must work together to provide quality programming for all children in an inclusive environment. An interdisciplinary team building and staff development approach for both the special educators and the early childhood staff is to provide mutual training so these professionals together develop their own professional skills, as well as come to appreciate more fully the knowledge and skills of other members of the team. As team members come to accept and extend the skills and knowledge of fellow professionals, mutual respect and camaraderie are reinforced. Further, with more preschools in public schools where program expectations and philosophies are often incongruent with early childhood principles, team building and staff development programs for both preschool and public school personnel in these settings is clearly indicated.

On the other hand, paraprofessional classroom staff may need training in preparing classroom materials, in understanding growth and development, or in developing basic management skills. Custodians, food service staff, or clerical staff will need different levels and types of assistance. When planning a staff training program, the director will have to assess the training needs of everyone, then make decisions about time, content, and training methods for the sessions. An experienced director can assess training needs by observing staff as they carry out their job responsibilities and by having conferences with them to discover more about their own analysis of training needs and their interest in professional advancement. Assessment of training needs is an ongoing process, and, as personal and professional development proceeds, the director's task is to present more challenging training opportunities.

Time and Place for Training

Finding a suitable time for training meetings is even more difficult than finding a suitable time for staff meetings. In the case of regularly scheduled staff meetings, the staff can plan ahead for the full year and schedule their other duties and commitments around the meeting times. However, training sessions that usually occur with less regularity often require a larger block of time than a staff meeting and have to be planned to coincide with the schedules of consultants or outside experts whose services are needed. If the director and center staff members are the only people involved in the training, scheduling difficulties are alleviated somewhat. Nonetheless, the problems of late afternoon or evening fatigue, and the inability of the staff to leave the classroom during the day, create special problems for the training of child care staff, unless the training can be planned for nap time or incorporated into the staff meetings. Since most training requires larger time blocks, it may be

necessary to discuss the possibility of a Saturday meeting or a weekend retreat. Half-day preschool programs that usually meet during the public school academic year often have training meetings in the early autumn before school begins or in the spring after school closes. In any case, if in-service training attendance is mandatory, this point must be included in the employee's job description and spelled out during orientation of new employees.

Whether attendance at training sessions should be mandatory or optional is a question that must be decided by the director or by the group. In some places where licensing requires a given number of clock hours of training each year, the planned training could be mandatory for some staff and not for others. If attendance is mandatory, the feelings of resentment may negate the possible benefits. On the other hand, if attendance is not mandatory, those who attend may feel resentment toward those who have decided not to attend. As a director, you will have to work closely with your staff to get a feel for their commitment to the training program and their possible reactions to mandatory or voluntary attendance.

REFLECTION

REFLECTION

Think about your personal feelings when you were told that you had to attend some function such as a meeting, a party, or a class, as opposed to the times when you were given a choice. When it was a matter of choice, what were the factors that motivated you to attend? Was it curiosity about who would be there or what would take place? Was it interest in what you expected would take place? Was it to please the person who requested you attend or who told you about the event? Can you analyze your feelings and reactions when you went someplace to please someone else as opposed to the times when you went because you were intrinsically motivated?

When there is a comfortable lounge or conference room at the center, the staff may prefer to stay in the building for the training sessions. The comfort and familiarity of the center will help create a feeling of openness, which could be very important if the success of the training is dependent on dialogue and exchanging ideas among staff members. If the training is a cooperative effort and several centers are

On-site workshops are useful mechanisms for encouraging direct involvement of the staff in a special content area.

involved, a space in a centrally located community building may be more convenient for the trainees. Sometimes, it is helpful to get away from the center.

Training Methods and Resources

The methods or strategies employed in the in-service training program will depend on the amount of time and the resources available and the nature of the content selected. For example, if one hour of a staff meeting is set aside for a refresher course in first aid, the best way to present that information may be in a lecture given by a representative from the health department or with a film presentation. If, on the other hand, there is more time to spend on the topic of first aid, it may be desirable to plan a full-day session with a Red Cross specialist. Enrolling some staff members who do not have first aid certificates in a Red Cross course that extends over several weeks and is available evenings or on Saturday is yet another alternative. First aid training can be expanded to include health, nutrition, and safety. The expansion of the program creates new training strategy possibilities. Group discussions led by the director would be an appropriate method to use in making the staff more aware of safety issues in the center. The program could include discussions about safety when using outdoor equipment, when planning cooking experiences, or when organizing field trips. The health or nutrition questions might be handled best by a nurse, physician, or a dietitian who would come for a seminar. A special educator might come to discuss

health and safety issues as these relate to special-needs children. When outside consultants are brought in, the director's role is to sit in on the training in order to be able to do follow-up with the staff, thereby extending the new information to specific situations each teacher encounters in the classroom. There are any number of possible methods from which to choose, each one requiring different amounts of time and different resources and all individualized to meet the needs of the trainee. A list of training resources in the community as well as national opportunities should be available in the director's library at the center.

On-site workshops are useful mechanisms for encouraging direct involvement of the staff in a special content area. Implicit in the workshop concept is the idea that those who attend participate actively in the program. Frequently, workshops are planned for a staff that expresses a need to know more about curriculum areas such as developing writing centers, math or science experiences for young children, or music in the classroom. Other areas, such as building skills for more effective conferences with parents or for ways to interact with volunteers, also can be handled in a workshop format that involves participants in a series of role-plays or simulation games. Workshops require active involvement from the participants and are more suitable for some training needs than are lectures, films, or seminars.

There should be planned follow-up for all types of training. Behavior change is not likely to follow a one-shot session or even a series of meetings unless there is follow-up by the director or supervisor at the center. Teachers need feedback and support to integrate new information into their day-to-day practice.

Visits to other centers are encouraged by some directors and can be a very helpful piece of the total staff training program. Watching other teachers and children is refreshing and interesting for some staff members. After such visits, they bring back program ideas, new and different ways to set up the physical environment, and sometimes a renewed interest in developing classroom materials such as math games or interactive charts. Some teachers who are able to move beyond the more obvious things like equipment or curriculum ideas may begin to compare and contrast classroom environments and teaching strategies, relating these differences to the differences in the stated philosophies of the programs. Follow-up group discussions will help teachers refine their understanding of how theory relates to practice. Why are the children in one program encouraged to negotiate with one another about dividing up the play dough, while the teacher controls amounts for each child in another center? The two strategies clearly reflect different program goals. Group discussions also may encourage teachers to reexamine the theoretical basis for the center program in which they work and reevaluate the curriculum to ascertain how closely it reflects the stated philosophy of the center, as well as their own philosophy of early childhood education.

DIRECTOR'S CORNER

"One of the most helpful things we did in my administration class at college was role-playing. I especially remember role-playing a parent conference. Now I use that technique all the time with my staff. In staff training sessions, when we are discussing an issue like dealing with a difficult parent, I ask for a specific example and immediately turn it into a role-play. 'OK—now I'm the parent and here is my concern—you are the teacher,' and we play it out. Then we often reverse roles so I take the role of the teacher. It works very well for me as a director."

–Director, YMCA-sponsored center

Professional conferences and workshops provide excellent training opportunities for staff. Directors who commit to a personal program of professional development by attending professional meetings set a standard of excellence for their teachers to emulate. It is important to encourage staff to take advantage of these opportunities and to facilitate their attending conferences by allowing time off from work and subsidizing their travel and registration expenses if at all possible. Some child care programs not only subsidize conference attendance but also pay for teachers' memberships in professional organizations such as NAEYC, which includes membership in local affiliates, the Council for Exceptional Children (CEC), the Association for Childhood Education International (ACEI) or the National Association of Child Care Professionals (NACCP).

Staff members who express an interest in professional advancement are to be commended for their ambitious goals and encouraged to take courses toward a college degree in child development or early childhood education, or the Child Development Associate (CDA) certificate in communities where these types of training programs are available. The availability of on-line courses offers easy access to educational opportunities for many. Some centers will help pay tuition for relevant courses as well as adjust work schedules to allow staff to attend daytime classes. Directors can lend further support to these part-time students by showing interest in what they are learning and guiding them to helpful resources available at the center.

To provide on-site materials to support and enhance all aspects of the staff training program, it is the job of the director to establish a professional library and a teachers' resource center. The library books should cover information on child development, curriculum, classroom management, special-needs children, diversity, and working with other professionals and with families. Books on specific curriculum areas such as literacy, math, science, cooking, or music will help the staff plan for the children. Recent copies of professional journals and newsletters should be available in the teachers' library, along with a collection of audiovisual materials, including tapes, slides, videotapes, DVDs, and computers to provide a rich source of information on curriculum development and classroom management.

The teachers' resource center should be a space where teachers can make math games, charts, big books, and other teacher-made classroom materials. Supplies like paper, tagboard, paper cutter, scissors, glue, tape, plain die, marking pens, and so forth must be available in addition to a large working surface. It is a luxury to have things like a laminating machine or an Elison machine for stamping out letters and shapes for charts. When teachers have materials and space to work, they are more likely to develop individualized teacher-made classroom materials that will enrich the program for the children.

Training Content

A number of ideas for the staff training program already have been mentioned in the previous discussions on methods of training. Training needs will vary according to the previous training and experience of the center staff. Many teachers constantly are seeking new curriculum ideas and resource materials for the classroom; consequently, training in curriculum areas is usually welcomed. There is always interest in strategies for dealing with the difficult, challenging, disruptive child or the withdrawn child. Furthermore, most teachers are interested in learning more about community resources where they can get advice about how to handle children with special needs, or about where to refer children and families for additional help. Although staff will rarely request it, directors are obligated to hold at least one staff meeting per year or set aside a time at a regularly scheduled staff retreat to review the NAEYC Code of Ethical Conduct and Statement of Commitment (see Director's Resource 15–2). Although the orientation of new employees includes mention of the NAEYC Code of Ethics, yearly review of this important document will renew staff members' awareness of their professional commitment to ethical practice.

The director should determine if staff members need special coaching in conducting a home visit or a parent conference. These duties are taxing, produce anxiety, and require very special culturally sensitive communication skills that are suitable for the particular parent population being served. It is important to know that some families may be slow to accept a stranger and will draw back from a person whom they perceive as too intrusive. Attitudes about accepting newcomers, about education, and about child rearing vary among cultural, ethnic, and socioeconomic groups, and it is essential for staff to know what those differences are when they work with children and families. Staff members also find it helpful to have special guidance from the director in effective interpersonal communications.

There is a pressing need to assist staff with dealing with diversity in the classroom. Including children with disabilities and children from diverse cultural and ethnic groups into early childhood education programs means there must be training programs that focus on providing information about ways to meet the individual needs of children and families from these groups. Teachers may also need help handling issues regarding children of divorce, single-parent families, hospitalization of a parent or sibling, children who have been abused, and so forth.

When the staff is experienced and fully capable of coping with the day-to-day, here-and-now events in the classroom, training can move on to the questions that challenge us in the 21st century. What do children need to know to survive in the 21st century? How will life change in the next 50 years, and what personality characteristics and thinking dispositions will be essential to function competently during those 50 years? The job of staff training is never complete because there are always new challenges.

DIRECTOR'S CORNER

"When the central office in Dallas called to offer me the director's position at our center in Topeka, I accepted. I knew I was a good teacher—that is one of the things that qualified me for the promotion. But I was not prepared for the challenge of supervising the adults at the center. Without a doubt, supervising the staff was the hardest thing for me to handle when I stepped into the director's position."

–Director–large corporate for-profit center

STAFF SUPERVISION AND COACHING

The director, or the educational director in the case of large centers or some corporate chains, is responsible for supervision of classroom staff. (The director will be referred to as supervisor for the purposes of this discussion.) By observing, doing one-to-one coaching, and working in the classroom with the children and the staff, the supervisor gives support and guidance to each staff member and establishes a trusting relationship with each one. As a coach, the director's job is to ". . . encourage and provide opportunities for problem definition and problem-solving, for self-reflection and collaboration. It is important that you (the director) model the kind of behavior you want staff to use with children—providing for self-initiated learning, risk taking and exploration" (Carter & Curtis, 1998, p. 119). The trust and mutual respect that develop between coach and teacher provide the basis for building a teaching-learning relationship that parallels the relationship between adult and child. Then the supervisor is able to create a favorable environment in which each staff member can gain new understandings of children, of self, and of the supervisor's expectations.

An experienced supervisor knows that sometimes growth and change take place slowly. Working together, talking together, and planning together will promote personal and professional competence on the part of classroom staff members, provided the supervisor is supportive and encouraging and is not perceived as being critical or threatening.

Principles of Supervision

A number of basic principles or assumptions should be kept in mind as you think about the director as staff supervisor. The same principles apply to the supervisory role, whether you are working with a new, inexperienced staff member or a mature, qualified, experienced teacher or are a new director moving into a fully staffed center.

- Supervision is a dynamic, evolutionary process that is based on trust.
- Supervision is individualized and adapted to the personality and teaching style of each staff member.
- Supervision provides a support system for each staff member.
- Supervision provides a framework within which the supervisor demonstrates professional skills for the entire staff.

However, an individualized model of staff development means you must use a developmental approach to supervision, and teachers who are at different stages in their careers will require qualitatively different supervisory strategies.

Supervisory Process

As classroom staff members grow and change, the thrust and focus of the supervisory process shifts accordingly. The process begins by providing support and guidance for a new staff member, who is integrating past learning experiences into a personal teaching style that is compatible with the center philosophy. The process changes as the staff member adjusts and develops into an accomplished teacher, who will, in turn, supervise assistants, aides, student teachers, or be paired with a new teacher and become a mentor. If you think of this supervisory process on a continuum, it moves from a very directive approach for new teachers where the control is in the hands of the supervisor, to a collaborative model where an accomplished teacher and the supervisor share control of the process.

One-to-one coaching is the essential ingredient of the supervisory process, whether working with the beginning teacher or the accomplished professional who, in turn, will coach others in the center. Coaching includes encouraging, modeling, observing, and the giving of specific feedback. A coach is a cheerleader who watches and listens and shares skills, resources, and experience. Communicating with staff after an observation usually is handled in a conference, but, when time is short, a brief note with some specific feedback may have to suffice.

The director must ensure that staff engage in high-quality practices at all times. When there are questions and concerns about teacher performance, it always is a challenge to communicate those concerns in a way that addresses the issues but maintains program quality and does not compromise staff morale. Depending on the level of training and experience of the staff, you, as the director, will find that you will have to deal with questions and concerns about classroom practices on a regular basis. There may be issues about curriculum, classroom management, staff relationships, or interactions with parents. On any given day, you will see and hear things that must be addressed. Following are some examples:

- How should I approach Estella, who continues to call across the room to set limits for children who are not doing what she thinks they should be doing?
- I must talk with Consuelo about using positive redirection instead of the constant, "Stop running in the room" or "Don't spill your milk."
- Colin's group times are not rich or challenging these days. I must call him in and talk about that.
- What is the best way to tell Betsy that she and her assistant should be sitting with the children at lunch and eating what children eat? I also will have to tell them that they must wait until they are on break to have coffee or a Coke.

Dealing with questionable practices is especially distasteful for directors who prefer to avoid conflict and confrontations, but it is an important part of the supervisory process and goes to the core of what it takes to maintain the integrity of the program.

REFLECTION

REFLECTION

Think about some of the staffing issues you, as a director, may have to handle. When you are short-staffed and the late afternoon toddler teacher calls at noon to say she is sick today, you must deal with that immediately. Would you cover the toddler room from 4:00 p.m. to 6:00 p.m.? Would you ask the teacher who has been working in there since 8:00 a.m. to stay for an extra two hours? Would you try to call someone on your list of substitutes? How would you find individuals who would be willing to be on your substitute list? Can you think of other alternative solutions?

The method and intensity of supervision varies from actually teaching in the classroom with the classroom teacher in order to coach and model exemplary practice, to frequently scheduled classroom observations and conferences, or occasional observations and conferences. In addition to this ongoing supervisory process, there also must be a regularly scheduled, more formal review of all teaching staff. After the notes or checklists from supervisory classroom observations are shared with the staff member, they become part of that teacher's file and are subsequently utilized as a basis for the regularly scheduled teacher evaluation and review process. (See Chapter 10, Director's Resource 10–8 for a sample teacher performance evaluation; Director's Resource 15–1 at the end of this chapter for a sample checklist for supervisory classroom observations; and Chapter 14 for additional discussion of teacher evaluation.) When staff have been effectively supervised and coached through ongoing observations and conferences, they usually know what to expect when it is time for their formal evaluation review. (See Sciarra & Dorsey, 2002, for a detailed discussion of the supervisory process.)

Supervising New Teachers

New teachers need daily or even hourly support; therefore, the supervisor must plan to spend some time each day observing and teaching with the new teacher. If a new teacher is recently trained, that teacher will be developing a personal teaching style and will profit from the example that is set by an experienced supervisor. It is very important for a supervisor to work beside a new teacher with the children in the classroom. This supervisory procedure creates a rich learning environment for the new teacher and often provides a more favorable transition for the children and families who know the supervisor but are not yet well acquainted with the new teacher. As a supervisor, you must make sure to remove yourself gradually so that the new teacher can build a relationship with the children and families and begin to manage the classroom without your constant support. What you are doing, in effect, is providing hourly or daily support during the initial trust-building period but stepping back when the new teacher is able to function independently. However,

stay nearby because your ongoing support is still important when things do not go well.

CORNER

"Since I am new here I haven't developed a schedule for regular observations as yet, but I make the rounds at least twice a day, if only to let my teachers know I am available. Of course, I have a chance to catch things going on in each room—maybe a new chart or a teacher reading a book to a sleepy child. I make sure I leave a short note in each teacher's box, mentioning some little thing I noticed when I came by. If I see an activity or a procedure that concerns me, I mention it. 'I noticed you had the toddlers finger painting with chocolate pudding today. Drop by when you have a chance—I have some ideas about that that I would like to share with you.' It seems to work well for me."

—Director, community-agency-sponsored center

Supervising Experienced Teachers

As teachers develop their skills and become more competent, they continue to profit from the supervisor's support. Positive reinforcement and constructive criticism from supervisors are excellent motivating factors. But experienced teachers also are ready for expansion and growth in new directions. They still are integrating and reorganizing what they have learned in the past, but they are now able to reach out for new learning opportunities. These teachers now are comfortable with their teaching style and can direct more attention to curriculum development. They are ready for the intellectual stimulation they can draw from taking course work, reading new publications, and attending professional meetings. Therefore, although the supervisor continues to observe these teachers and have conferences with them on a regular basis, emphasis now is placed on the supervisor as a resource person. The supervisor can supply new program ideas, new theoretical information, articles from professional journals and Web sites, research materials, and as many opportunities as possible for teachers to participate actively in professional organizations and conferences.

While experienced teachers are perfecting their teaching skills under the guidance of the supervisor, they also should be developing self-evaluation skills. With encouragement and help from a supervisor, experienced teachers feel secure enough to step back

By observing and holding conferences with individual teachers, the director gives support and guidance to each staff member.

and evaluate their teaching. They can begin to ask themselves some of the questions a supervisor has been asking them and engage in some self-searching about their methodology. For example, one teacher might make the inquiry, "How could I have better handled the situation between those two children who had a conflict over the sand bucket? What I did was really not productive. I must find alternative ways of handling those two children." Another teacher might ask, "How can I adjust my questioning techniques for all the children in order to help them become better problem solvers? I heard you mention Rheta deVries. Maybe you could give me something she has written on that topic that will help me."

Supervising the Accomplished Teacher

The accomplished, long-term teacher still is perfecting teaching and self-evaluation skills and revising curriculum. However, having reached a new level of mastery, this teacher is ready to develop supervisory skills. While working with the teachers, the supervisor has not only exemplified teaching and self-evaluation skills but also supervisory skills. In working with accomplished teachers, the supervisor now turns to coaching them in supervisory skills. This teacher is preparing to assume responsibility for the supervision of assistants, aides, and, in some situations, student teachers. To serve in this capacity, the teacher will need instruction and support to develop the necessary skills for fulfilling supervisory responsibilities. The supervisor still is observing and having conferences

on a regular basis, giving attention to teaching strategies and self-evaluation. However, the new thrust is directed to this teacher's interaction with, and supervision of, other adults in the classroom.

Involving accomplished teachers with novice teachers in a mentoring program is an ideal way to offer the benefit of job enrichment for both. The director's role becomes one of modeling for the mentor by engaging in reflective practice and helping this teacher, who is very skilled at working with young children, learn more about the characteristics of the adult learner. The director models ways to use many of the same skills that teachers use when caring for young children, and now explores ways to "care for a fellow caregiver." Pairing mentors with novices is a challenge for the director who must observe, reflect, and confer with staff in order to ensure a "good fit" in each pairing. A successful peer mentoring program contributes to the well-being of staff and children alike. It is connected to both staff development and supervision, but at the same time, separate. It provides unique opportunities for both mentors and novices to learn from each other and grow professionally.

Supervision is one of the most difficult and anxiety-producing aspects of the director's job. It draws on every bit of professional skill the director has because it demands expertise in interpersonal communication, children's programming, teaching strategies, and self-evaluation. It also helps the director focus on the importance of being a model for the staff by making positive suggestions to coach and motivate and by using supportive, caring gestures and voice tone. This sets the tone for staff who, in turn, are more likely to follow a similar pattern in their interactions with children and families.

REFLECTION
REFLECTION

Think about the cooperating teacher who supervised your practicum. Did you receive support and constructive criticism? Did that person serve as a model of good supervisory skills for you? Think about how your cooperating teacher might have been more helpful. What do you feel you need before you can become a supervisor of a center classroom staff?

ASSESSING STAFF PROBLEMS

Assessing what the staff members view as work-related problems provides the basis for designing the staff development program and focusing individualized supervision activities. Once you have identified what teachers feel to be their major problems, you can take the first steps toward helping them solve those problems (Bloom, 2005). The expressed needs of staff can be addressed directly. If a teacher has problems handling the aggressive behaviors of a child, the director can respond in various direct ways, including offering relevant readings, observing or participating in the classroom, discussing various management strategies, calling in a consultant to observe and conference with the classroom staff, or discussing the general problem of dealing with aggression in a staff meeting. This direct response to an expressed need may motivate the staff member to become involved in a training plan offered by the director. On the other hand, when the selection of staff development activities is based on those issues the director views as problems, motivating staff interest will be more difficult. For example, if a new director finds the long-term staff using punitive and age-inappropriate techniques in response to unacceptable classroom behaviors, but the teachers are comfortable with their management methods, those teachers will resist making a commitment to any training designed to encourage them to use more positive management strategies. The new director will have to spend time establishing a trusting working relationship with the professional staff before training related to the classroom management question

will be accepted. Since the use of punitive management techniques can be hard on children, the new director may choose to bring in a consultant to work with individual staff members or may even consider making staff changes. A new director is well advised to design the initial staff development activities in response to the teachers' expressed needs.

Expressed Teacher Concerns

Expressed teacher concerns cluster around a number of problem areas (Bloom, 2005). The director's task is to identify and then respond to these concerns. The areas of greatest concern include those points discussed in the following paragraphs.

Dealing with Assisting Staff

Teachers have a problem getting their assistants to follow through on assigned responsibilities and to work as a member of a cooperative team. In response to this problem, effective directing, evaluating, and giving feedback to subordinate staff would be appropriate areas to address in the staff training program for the teachers. The best way for the director to help teachers with this problem is to model exemplary supervisory skills.

Managing the Classroom

Teachers report problems with managing children's challenging behaviors. Included in their list are things like aggression and violence, not picking up, not sharing, and not cooperating. In addressing the problem of working with these children, the director first might focus on developmental expectations for the specific age group in question, followed by ways to encourage prosocial behaviors. This is a sensitive problem area because the perceived problem sometimes results from teachers' unrealistic expectations. Directors must model developmentally appropriate responses to children's behaviors whenever they have encounters with children in the center. Managing children who present extremely oppositional or violent behaviors often requires the help of a mental health specialist.

Helping Children with Special Needs and Their Families

Teachers report that they do not know enough about how to deal appropriately with children with special needs. This becomes a serious problem when children with previously unidentified social-emotional problems join the group. Teachers suddenly realize that this child is, indeed, disturbed and in need of special help, but they are not prepared for the disruption and management challenges this new child presents. They want help on how to provide rich environments for these children as well as ways to work effectively with the family. Providing reading materials and planning special meetings on this topic will be helpful to teachers who are searching for better ways to help these special children. Directors also must watch for upcoming conferences and meetings on the topic and encourage staff to attend. Because teachers and directors are seeing an increase in the number of children who exhibit challenging behaviors, some center directors are seeking funding for more mental health services or for a mental health specialist on the staff.

Relating to Supervisors

Directors often face the reality that they can be perceived as a major problem by staff members. Teachers complain about not being treated fairly and not being respected as professionals. The response to this problem is clearly in the director's hands. Directors must work on their own professional development to enable them to become better staff managers.

Maintaining Parent Cooperation

Teachers have problems with parents who send a sick child to school, who are not prompt about picking their child up after school, and those who do not cooperate with the teachers' efforts with things like encouraging use of messy materials. Here, the director can reinforce center policies by reviewing the parent handbook material with the parent, as well as participating in parent conferences when necessary, to mediate and to give support to both the teacher and the parent. In-service training focused on working with parents and becoming sensitive to their needs may help teachers feel more secure about handling difficult situations with parents.

Managing Time

Time to deal with nonteaching tasks like cleaning, planning, making materials, or doing other paperwork is a problem for teachers. Since time management is also a major problem for directors, it is something they have in common. Time management seminars under the guidance of an experienced trainer can be part of the staff development program. It is especially important for the director to be a part of this training and to model good time management.

Although staff concerns always are situation specific, there is a common core of recurring problems that fall into the categories just listed. It can be reassuring to you, as a director, to know that your teachers' expressed needs are much like those of most teaching staffs.

SUMMARY

The staff development program contributes to both the personal and professional growth of the center staff. Through the planning and implementation of effective staff meetings, staff training programs, and staff supervision, the director creates an enriched learning environment for the staff. Given the benefits of an enriched environment and a director who demonstrates good interpersonal and professional skills, the staff members have the opportunity to enjoy the inevitable personal satisfaction and excitement that result from positive, individualized professional growth experiences.

CLASS ASSIGNMENTS

1. Contact a director in the community and request permission to attend a staff meeting. Answer the questions on Working Paper 15–1 after attending the meeting. (Do not take notes during the meeting!)

2. Use the list of expressed teacher problems on Working Paper 15–2, and complete a. and b. below.

   a. Based on your experience with children, rank order the list of teacher problems from most difficult (1) to least difficult (10).

   b. Select one from the first three in your ranking. Complete a staff training plan for that particular teacher concern by responding to the items listed on Working Paper 15–2.

CLASS EXERCISES

1. Role-play a child care center staff meeting and discuss one agenda item, "Timing for weekly staff meetings." It has been decided by the director that the entire staff (including the cook, the janitor, and the secretary) must meet every week. The question open for discussion is the day of the week on which the staff should meet, and when and how long the

meetings should be. Assign the following roles to class members:

a.   Director: works Monday through Friday 9:00 a.m. to 5:00 p.m.

b.   Teacher A: works Monday through Friday 9:00 a.m. to 5:00 p.m.

c.   Teacher B: works Monday through Friday 6:00 a.m. to 2:00 p.m.

d.   Assistant teacher C: works Monday through Friday 10:00 a.m. to 6:00 p.m.

e.   Assistant teacher D: works Monday through Friday 6:00 a.m. to 2:00 p.m.

f.   Part-time teacher E: works Monday through Friday 10:00 a.m. to 2:00 p.m.

g.   Cook: works Monday through Friday 9:00 a.m. to 3:00 p.m.

h.   Janitor: works Monday through Friday 3:00 p.m. to 8:00 p.m.

There are 35 children in the program who arrive on a staggered schedule between 6:15 a.m. and 9:30 a.m. and leave between 2:30 p.m. and 5:30 p.m. The children occupy two classrooms and two sleeping rooms. Sleeping rooms are adjacent to one another and to the outdoor area.

The staff meeting discussion is to be led by the director, and the group is to come to some decision about when the regular staff meeting will be held. Use the blackboard or newsprint for note taking, if you need it. Practice good listening skills; make sure that everyone participates.

2. Role-play a special staff meeting that has been called by the director to discuss and reach a decision about allocation of classroom space at the child care center. There will be one additional classroom available beginning in September, and a new teacher, Mark, will be employed. The new classroom is larger than the others and opens directly to the playground.

Sandra currently has the best classroom, which has its own bathroom. The other four rooms share a bathroom down the hall. Jean will be working with a new pilot program and will have many parents participating in her classroom. She was responsible for getting the pilot program funded, and it is a real asset for the center. Bob's classroom is far from the outside play area and from the storage room. Bob feels that this location is inconvenient. Sheila would like to keep her current classroom because she recently made curtains and painted the walls. Barbara feels that her 10 years of teaching qualify her for the new classroom.

Name	Years at Center	Degree	Current Classroom
Sandra	6	M.S.	Excellent
Barbara	10	B.S.	Very good
Sheila	4	B.S.	Very good
Bob	6	A.S.	Good
Jean	1	A.S.	Poor
Mark	0	B.S.	

The staff has allocated 30 minutes for making this decision. After the group has arrived at a decision, individually rate your level of satisfaction with the decision from 1 (low) to 5 (high). Also, rate your level of participation from 1 to 5. Tally the results on the chalkboard. As a group, discuss the factors that contributed to the level of satisfaction or dissatisfaction. Was the level of participation a factor?

WORKING PAPER 15-1

(for use with Class Assignment 1)

STAFF MEETING QUESTIONS

Based on your experience at the staff meeting you attended, answer the following questions.

1. Did the director fulfill the role of keeping the group focused on the agenda items? How?

2. Was there any attempt to follow a time line? If not, what effect do you suspect that had on the feelings of the staff?

3. Were there any notable incidents where staff members seemed not to be heard? Describe them, and indicate the behaviors that you observed in those staff members after the incidents.

WORKING PAPER 15-2

(for use with Class Assignment 2)

EXPRESSED TEACHER PROBLEMS

1. Based on your experience up to this point in your professional career, rank order the expressed teacher problems listed below from most difficult (1) to least difficult (10).

   _____ Finding time to play and do paperwork

   _____ Getting the supervisor to respect my opinion

   _____ Knowing how to handle aggressive or violent children

   _____ Handling a child with a physically disabling condition

   _____ Handling a child who requires constant attention without neglecting the other children

   _____ Handling a parent who is very punitive with her child when she picks him up

   _____ Getting the other adults in the room to do their share of cleanup and "dirty" work

   _____ Keeping children's attention during group time

   _____ Motivating myself to be involved with professional organizations

   _____ Dealing with criticism from my supervisor

2. Select problem 1, 2, or 3 from your rankings from the above list and complete a staff-training plan that addresses that problem. Then address the following:

   What relevant material would you provide in the staff resource room for the staff to read or check?

   ■ Books

   ■ Journals (give name of articles and authors)

   ■ Audiovisuals

   ■ Web sites

Develop an agenda for a staff meeting addressing the problem. Include:

   ■ Format (panel, speaker, role-playing, and the like)

   ■ Outline of content

   ■ Discussion of the direct steps you would take, as a director, to support the staff as they deal with this problem on a day-to-day basis

DIRECTOR'S RESOURCE 15-1

SAMPLE CHECKLIST FOR SUPERVISORY CLASSROOM OBSERVATIONS

Ratings:

5	Consistently exceeds performance standard
4	Consistently meets and often exceeds performance standard
3	Consistently meets performance standard
2	Usually meets performance standard
1	Seldom meets performance standard
0	Does not meet performance standard
N/O	Not Observed
N/A	Not Applicable

(Note: Supervisor may choose to evaluate section V on professionalism semiannually or prior to regular teacher evaluation conferences.)

Performance Standard	Date			
The staff person:				
I. PROVIDES A PROGRAM TO MEET THE DEVELOPMENTAL NEEDS OF THE CHILDREN IN A SAFE, HEALTHY AND EDUCATIONALLY CHALLENGING ENVIRONMENT.				
■ shows awareness of the importance of safety in the environment.				
■ adjusts the space to ensure safety of children.				
■ positions self in the environment to optimize and maintain total group awareness.				
■ arranges space with clear pathways so children can move about without disturbing others.				
■ provides open space for crawling infants.				
■ provides protected play space for infants.				
■ washes hands carefully before handling food and/or after toileting or changing a child.				
■ washes tables and toys regularly with sanitizing solution.				
■ is alert to sharp edges or splinters on toys and equipment.				
■ provides only objects that could not be swallowed by infants or toddlers.				
■ provides toddlers and/or preschoolers spaces for a variety of individual and small group activities including block building, dramatic play, art, music, science, math, quiet book reading, and writing.				
■ provides water and other sensory activities both indoors and outside on a regular basis.				
■ provides private areas where a child can play alone or with a friend.				
■ provides soft, cozy places where children can relax on rugs, cushions, in a rocking chair with an adult, etc.				

(continues)

DIRECTOR'S RESOURCE 15-1
(continued)

Performance Standard	Date			
The staff person:				
■ keeps floor spaces relatively free of clutter to maintain safety for all children.				
■ makes certain that children are *never* left alone—school age may be out of sight, but adult knows where they are and checks on them.				
■ takes cues from other adults in the room and moves to those areas where needed.				
II. **PLANS ACTIVITIES THAT WILL PROVIDE OPPORTUNITIES FOR CHILDREN TO CREATE, EXPLORE THE ENVIRONMENT, SOLVE PROBLEMS AND HAVE HANDS-ON EXPERIENCES WITH AGE-APPROPRIATE MATERIALS. (For assistants, evaluate in terms of how well s/he works with the teacher to carry out the program plans.)**				
■ plans experiences that reflect awareness of developmental skills of the age group.				
■ plans experiences that reflect awareness of previous experiences in the same area.				
■ plans experiences relevant to the children's life experiences.				
■ plans experiences that have children focus on experimentation and exploration.				
■ plans experiences that focus on process as opposed to product (as in art activities).				
■ carefully sets up the spaces for each planned experience, making all supplies and materials accessible to children and staff.				
■ plans for backup materials for activities in order to be able to increase complexity of tasks as needed.				
■ utilizes multiracial, nonsexist, nonstereotyping pictures, dolls, books and materials in the room.				
■ provides developmentally appropriate materials for: infants: rattles, squeak toys, music, cuddly toys, teething toys, mobiles, mirrors, books, sturdy places to pull up self, objects for reaching and grasping. toddlers: push and pull toys, stacking toys, large wooden beads/spools/cubes, picture books, music, pounding bench, telephones, dolls, pretend props, large paper and crayons or markers, sand and water toys, sturdy furniture to hold onto while walking, active play equipment for climbing.				

(continues)

DIRECTOR'S RESOURCE 15-1
(continued)

Performance Standard	Date			
The staff person:				
preschool: active play equipment for climbing and balancing; unit blocks and accessories; puzzles and manipulatives; books; records; musical instruments; art materials such as paint, glue, scissors, tape, staplers, paper, etc.; dramatic play materials including dolls, dress-ups, props, child-size furniture, etc.; water and sensory materials such as homemade play dough, clay, silly putty, etc.; materials for writing.				
school-age: active play equipment such as balls and bats, basketballs, construction materials such as blocks, woodworking, materials for hobbies such as art, science or sewing projects, materials for creative drama and cooking, books, records, musical instruments, board and card games.				
III. PROVIDES PLAY OPPORTUNITIES FOR CHILDREN TO INITIATE THE SELECTION AND EXPLORATION OF MATERIALS IN ORDER TO PROMOTE INDEPENDENCE, AUTONOMY, SELF-ESTEEM, AND A SENSE OF MASTERY.				
■ provides choices for the child for most of the day and carries through on the choices the child makes.				
■ uses questioning and encouragement to guide children toward successful experiences.				
■ encourages self-help by having children set tables, clean up place at table, dress or undress, etc. (depending on age of child).				
■ respects the rights of a child *not* to participate in some activities.				
■ has school-age children help prepare, plan, and choose their own activities most of the time.				
■ prepares space so children can independently wash hands, put on smocks for painting, hang paintings to dry, hang up clothes, etc.				
■ tells children about transitions that are about to occur.				
■ does not require that children always move as a group from one place to another (inside to outside, large motor room, room to bathroom).				
■ prepares the new activity or the space (room, outside, large motor room) *before* the transition from the previous space takes place.				
■ allows school-age children to help plan and prepare for transitions.				
■ allows school-age children a block of time to adjust to the transition from school to the center.				

(continues)

DIRECTOR'S RESOURCE 15-1
(continued)

Performance Standard	Date			
The staff person:				
■ uses age-appropriate transition strategies (songs, chants, poems) and/or quiet, individual directions to the children who are to be involved in the transition.				
IV. **SERVES AS A POSITIVE ROLE MODEL AND PROVIDES CARE THAT IS SUPPORTIVE, NURTURING, WARM, AND RESPONSIVE TO INDIVIDUAL CHILDREN'S AND PARENT'S NEEDS.**				
■ uses correct grammar when speaking to the children and parents.				
■ uses a soft, effective teaching voice.				
■ when talking to a child, stoops down, gets eye contact, and speaks clearly and quietly to the child.				
■ uses appropriate manuscript printing for all labels, charts, and messages in the classroom.				
■ checks spelling on all written materials used in the classroom to ensure that all writing samples are spelled correctly.				
■ talks with children of all ages and encourages them to talk.				
■ listens carefully to what children of all ages say (repeats sounds that infants make).				
■ communicates acceptance of children of all ages nonverbally by smiling, touching, holding.				
■ quickly comforts distressed children of all ages by reassuring, comforting, listening to concerns, and reflecting feelings the child seems to have (sad, lonely, angry, fearful).				
■ uses positive methods for controlling and redirecting unacceptable behavior.				
■ individualizes responses to unacceptable behavior based on the context of the situation and the particular child involved.				
■ plans ahead to avoid problems.				
■ encourages prosocial behavior by modeling turn taking, cooperation, etc.				
■ helps children negotiate with each other in conflict situations, rather than using adult power to solve the situation for them.				
■ uses feeding time and changing times with infants for affectionate chatting, singing, peek-a-boo games, etc.				
■ sits with children at snack and meals and converses with them to model vocabulary, conversational turn taking, good grammar, etc.				

(continues)

DIRECTOR'S RESOURCE 15-1
(continued)

Performance Standard	Date			
The staff person:				
■ builds trust with children and with parents by being friendly, sincere, respectful of individual interests and needs and by being a good listener.				
V. SHOWS PROFESSIONALISM				
■ understands the importance of confidentiality regarding *all* events, conversations, and interactions that take place at the work site.				
■ focuses on the classroom and does not allow personal problems to affect the work with children and parents.				
■ shows a willingness to go beyond the minimum requirements set out in the job description.				
■ is interested and enthusiastic about learning new things in the field of early childhood education.				
■ understands the importance of being a good role model for children and parents (in social interactions at the center, correct grammar and spelling, use of correct printing, interest in learning and attitudes toward schooling, etc.).				
■ comes to work dressed appropriately for full classroom and indoor/outdoor participation in the planned program.				
■ is rarely absent or tardy and always notifies director when absence or tardiness is unavoidable.				
■ completes all written tasks (lesson plans, child evaluations, notes on parent conferences, etc.) in a neat and timely fashion.				
■ is able to self-evaluate realistically in order to plan for future goals as a growing professional.				
■ shows self-control in the educational environment.				
■ takes the initiative to develop materials for the classroom.				
■ establishes positive working relationships with other staff members but avoids becoming a part of cliques or groups within the group, which could lead to divisiveness among staff or to undermining the position of the administrator or others responsible for the total operation.				

COMMENTS:

DIRECTOR'S RESOURCE 15-2

CODE OF ETHICAL CONDUCT

Preamble

NAEYC recognizes that many daily decisions required of those who work with young children are of a moral and ethical nature. The NAEYC Code of Ethical Conduct offers guidelines for responsible behavior and sets forth a common basis for resolving the principal ethical dilemmas encountered in early childhood care and education. The primary focus is on daily practice with children and their families in programs for children from birth through 8 years of age, such as infant/toddler programs, preschools, child care centers, family child care homes, kindergartens, and primary classrooms. Many of the provisions also apply to specialists who do not work directly with children, including program administrators, parent and vocational educators, college professors, and child care licensing specialists.

Core values

Standards of ethical behavior in early childhood care and education are based on commitment to core values that are deeply rooted in the history of our field. We have committed ourselves to

- Appreciating childhood as a unique and valuable stage of the human life cycle.
- Basing our work with children on knowledge of child development.
- Appreciating and supporting the close ties between the child and family.
- Recognizing that children are best understood and supported in the context of family, culture, community, and society.
- Respecting the dignity, worth, and uniqueness of each individual (child, family member, and colleague).
- Helping children and adults achieve their full potential in the context of relationships that are based on trust, respect, and positive regard.

Conceptual framework

The code sets forth a conception of our professional responsibilities in four sections, each addressing an arena of professional relationships: (1) children, (2) families, (3) colleagues, and (4) community and society. Each section includes an introduction to the primary responsibilities of the early childhood practitioner in that arena, a set of ideals pointing in the direction of exemplary professional practice, and a set of principles defining practices that are required, prohibited, and permitted.

The ideals reflect the aspirations of practitioners. **The principles** are intended to guide conduct and assist practitioners in resolving ethical dilemmas encountered in the field. There is not necessarily a corresponding principle for each ideal. Both ideals and principles are intended to direct practitioners to those questions which, when responsibly answered, will provide the basis for conscientious decision-making. While the Code provides specific direction and suggestions for addressing some ethical dilemmas, many others will require the practitioner to combine the guidance of the Code with sound professional judgment.

The ideals and principles in this Code present a shared conception of professional responsibility that affirms our commitment to the core values of our field. The Code publicly acknowledges the responsibilities that we in the field have assumed and in so doing supports ethical behavior in our work. Practitioners who face ethical dilemmas are urged to seek guidance in the applicable parts of this Code and in the spirit that informs the whole.

(continues)

DIRECTOR'S RESOURCE 15-2

(continued)

Ethical dilemmas always exist

Often, "the right answer"—the best ethical course of action to take—is not obvious. There may be no readily apparent, positive way to handle a situation. One important value may contradict another. When we are caught "on the horns of a dilemma," it is our professional responsibility to consult with all relevant parties in seeking the most ethical course of action to take.

Section I:
Ethical responsibilities to children

Childhood is a unique and valuable stage in the life cycle. Our paramount responsibility is to provide safe, healthy, nurturing, and responsive settings for children. We are committed to supporting children's development, respecting individual differences, helping children learn to live and work cooperatively, and promoting health, self-awareness, competence, self-worth, and resiliency.

Ideals

I-1.1—To be familiar with the knowledge base of early childhood care and education and to keep current through continuing education and in-service training.

I-1.2—To base program practices upon current knowledge in the field of child development and related disciplines and upon particular knowledge of each child.

I-1.3—To recognize and respect the uniqueness and the potential of each child.

I-1.4—To appreciate the special vulnerability of children.

I-1.5—To create and maintain safe and healthy settings that foster children's social, emotional, intellectual, and physical development and that respect their dignity and their contributions.

I-1.6—To support the right of each child to play and learn in inclusive early childhood programs to the fullest extent consistent with the best interests of all involved. As with adults who are disabled in the larger community, children with disabilities are ideally served in the same settings in which they would participate if they did not have a disability.

I-1.7—To ensure that children with disabilities have access to appropriate and convenient support services and to advocate for the resources necessary to provide the most appropriate settings for all children.

Principles:

P-1.1—**Above all, we shall not harm children. We shall not participate in practices that are disrespectful, degrading, dangerous, exploitative, intimidating, emotionally damaging, or physically harmful to children.** *This principle has precedence over all others in this Code.*

P-1.2—We shall not participate in practices that discriminate against children by denying benefits, giving special advantages, or excluding them from programs or activities on the basis of their race, ethnicity, religion, sex, national origin, language, ability, or the status, behavior, or beliefs of their parents. (This principles does not apply to programs that have a lawful mandate to provide services to a particular population of children.)

P-1.3—We shall involve all of those with relevant knowledge (including staff and parents) in decisions concerning a child.

(continues)

DIRECTOR'S RESOURCE 15-2
(continued)

P-1.4—For every child's we shall implement adaptations in teaching strategies, learning environment, and curricula, consult with the family, and seek recommendations from appropriate specialists to maximize the potential of the child to benefit from the program. If, after these efforts have been made to work with a child and family, the child does not appear to be benefiting from a program, or the child is seriously jeopardizing the ability of other children to benefit from the program, we shall communicate with the family and appropriate specialists to determine the child's current needs, identify the setting and services most suited to meeting these needs, and assist the family in placing the child in an appropriate setting.

P-1.5—We shall be familiar with the symptoms of child abuse, including physical, sexual, verbal, and emotional abuse, and neglect. We shall know and follow state laws and community procedures that protect children against abuse and neglect.

P-1.6—When we have reasonable cause a suspect child abuse or neglect, we shall report it to the appropriate community agency and follow up to ensure that appropriate action has been taken. When appropriate, parents or guardians will be informed that the referral has been made.

P-1.7—When another person tells us of a suspicion that a child is being abused or neglected, we shall assist that person in taking appropriate action to protect the child.

P-1.8—When a child protective agency fails to provide adequate protection for abused or neglected children, we acknowledge a collective ethical responsibility to work toward improvement of these services.

P-1.9—When we become aware of a practice or situation that endangers the health or safety of children, but has not been previously known to do so, we have an ethical responsibility to inform those who can remedy the situation and who can protect children from similar danger.

Section II:
Ethical responsibilities to families

Families are of primary importance in children's development. (The term *family* may include others, besides parents, who are responsibly involved with the child.) Because the family and the early childhood practitioner have a common interest in the child's welfare, we acknowledge a primary responsibility to bring about collaboration between the home and school in ways that enhance the child's development.

Ideals:

I-2.1—To develop relationships of mutual trust with families we serve.

I-2.2—To acknowledge and build upon strengths and competencies as we support families in their task of nurturing children.

I-2.3—To respect the dignity of each family and its culture, language, customs, and beliefs.

I-2.4—To respect families' childrearing values and their right to make decisions for their children.

I-2.5—To interpret each child's progress to parents within the framework of a developmental perspective and to help families understand and appreciate the value of developmentally appropriate early childhood practices.

I-2.6—To help family members improve their understanding of their children and to enhance their skills as parents.

I-2.7—To participate in building support networks for families by providing them with opportunities to interact with program staff, other families, community resources, and professional services.

(continues)

DIRECTOR'S RESOURCE 15-2
(continued)

Principles:

P-2.1—We shall not deny family members access to their child's classroom or program setting.

P-2.2—We shall inform families of program philosophy, policies, and personnel qualifications, and explain why we teach as we do—which should be in accordance with our ethical responsibilities to children (see Section I).

P-2.3—We shall inform families of and, when appropriate, involve them in policy decisions.

P-2.4—We shall involve families in significant decisions affecting their child.

P-2.5—We shall inform the family of accidents involving their child, of risks such as exposures to contagious disease that may result in infection, and of occurrences that might result in emotional stress.

P-2.6—To improve the quality of early childhood care and education, we shall cooperate with qualified child development researchers. Families shall be fully informed of any proposed research projects involving their children and shall have the opportunity to give or withhold consent without penalty. We shall not permit or participate in research that could in any way hinder the education, development, or well-being of children.

P-2.7—We shall not engage in or support exploitation of families. We shall not use our relationship with a family for private advantage or personal gain, or enter into relationships with family members that might impair our effectiveness in working with children.

P-2.8—We shall develop written policies for the protection of confidentiality and the disclosure of children's records. These policy documents shall be made available to all program personnel and families. Disclosure of children's records beyond family members, program personnel, and consultants having an obligation of confidentiality shall require familial consent (except in cases of abuse or neglect).

P-2.9—We shall maintain confidentiality and shall respect the family's right to privacy, refraining from disclosure of confidential information and intrusion into family life. However, when we have reason to believe that a child's welfare is at risk, it is permissible to share confidential information with agencies and individuals who may be able to intervene in the child's interest.

P-2.10—In cases where family members are in conflict, we shall work openly, sharing our observations of the child, to help all parties involved make informed decisions. We shall refrain from becoming an advocate for one party.

P-2.11—We shall be familiar with and appropriately use community resources and professional services that support families. After a referral has been made, we shall follow up to ensure that services have been appropriately provided.

Section III:
Ethical responsibilities to colleagues

In a caring, cooperative workplace, human dignity is respected, professional satisfaction is promoted, and positive relationships are modeled. Based upon our core values, our primary responsibility in this arena is to establish and maintain settings and relationships that support productive work and meet professional needs. The same ideals that apply to children are inherent in our responsibilities to adults.

A—Responsibilities to co-workers

Ideals:

I-3A.1—To establish and maintain relationships of respect, trust, and cooperation with co-workers.

I-3A.2—To share resources and information with co-workers.

I-3A.3—To support co-workers in meeting their professional needs and in their professional development.

I-3A.4—To accord co-workers due recognition of professional achievement.

(continues)

DIRECTOR'S RESOURCE 15-2
(continued)

Principles:

P-3A.1—When we have a concern about the professional behavior of a co-worker, we shall first let that person know of our concern, in a way that shows respect for personal dignity and for the diversity to be found among staff members, and then attempt to resolve the matter collegially.

P-3A.2—We shall exercise care in expressing views regarding the personal attributes or professional conduct of co-workers. Statements should be based on firsthand knowledge and relevant to the interests of children and programs.

B—Responsibilities to employers

Ideals:

I-3B.1—To assist the program in providing the highest quality of service.

I-3B.2—To do nothing that diminishes the reputation of the program in which we work unless it is violating laws and regulations designed to protect children or the provisions of this Code.

Principles:

P-3B.1—When we do not agree with program policies, we shall first attempt to effect change through constructive action within the organization.

P-3B.2—We shall speak or act on behalf of an organization only when authorized. We shall take care to acknowledge when we are speaking for the organization and when we are expressing a personal judgment.

P-3B.3—We shall not violate laws or regulations designed to protect children and shall take appropriate action consistent with this Code when aware of such violations.

C—Responsibilities to employees

Ideals:

I-3C.1—To promote policies and working conditions that foster mutual respect, competence, well-being, and positive self-esteem in staff members.

I-3C.2—To create a climate of trust and candor that will enable staff to speak and act in the best interests of children, families, and the field of early childhood care and education.

I-3C.3—To strive to secure equitable compensation (salary and benefits) for those who work with or on behalf of young children.

Principles:

P-3C.1—In decisions concerning children and programs, we shall appropriately utilize the education, training, experience, and expertise of staff members.

P-3C.2—We shall provide staff members with safe and supportive working conditions that permit them to carry out their responsibilities, timely and nonthreatening evaluation procedures, written grievance procedures, constructive feedback, and opportunities for continuing professional development and advancement.

P-3C.3—We shall develop and maintain comprehensive written personnel policies that define program standards and, when applicable, that specify the extent to which employees are accountable for their conduct outside the workplace. These policies shall be given to new staff members and shall be available for review by all staff members.

(continues)

DIRECTOR'S RESOURCE 15-2
(continued)

P-3C.4—Employees who do not meet program standards shall be informed of areas of concern and, when possible, assisted in improving their performance.

P-3C.5—Employees who are dismissed shall be informed of the reasons for their termination. When a dismissal is for cause, justification must be based on evidence of inadequate or inappropriate behavior that is accurately documented, current, and available for the employee to review.

P-3C.6—In making evaluations and recommendations, judgments shall be based on fact and relevant to the interests of children and programs.

P-3C.7—Hiring and promotion shall be based solely on a person's record of accomplishment and ability to carry out the responsibilities of the position.

P-3C.8—In hiring, promotion, and provision of training, we shall not participate in any form of discrimination based on race, ethnicity, religion, gender, national origin, culture, disability, age, or sexual preference. We shall be familiar with and observe laws and regulations that pertain to employment discrimination.

Section IV:
Ethical responsibilities to community and society

Early childhood programs operate within a context of an immediate community made up of families and other institutions concerned with children's welfare. Our responsibilities to the community are to provide programs that meet its needs, to cooperate with agencies and professions that share responsibility for children, and to develop needed programs that are not currently available. Because the larger society has a measure of responsibility for the welfare and protection of children, and because of our specialized expertise in child development, we acknowledge an obligation to serve as a voice for children everywhere.

Ideals:

I-4.1—To provide the community with high-quality (age and individually appropriate, and culturally and socially sensitive) education/care programs and services.

I-4.2—To promote cooperation among agencies and interdisciplinary collaboration among professions concerned with the welfare of young children, their families, and their teachers.

I-4.3—To work, through education, research, and advocacy, toward an environmentally safe world in which all children receive adequate health care, food, and shelter, are nurtured, and live free from violence.

I-4.4—To work, through education, research, and advocacy, toward a society in which all young children have access to high-quality education/care programs.

I-4.5—To promote knowledge and understanding of young children and their needs. To work toward greater social acknowledgment of children's rights and greater social acceptance of responsibility for their well-being.

I-4.6—To support policies and laws that promote the well-being of children and families, and to oppose those that impair their well-being. To participate in developing policies and laws that are needed, and to cooperate with other individuals and groups in these efforts.

I-4.7—To further the professional development of the field of early childhood care and education and to strengthen its commitment to realizing its core values as reflected in this Code.

Principles:

P-4.1—We shall communicate openly and truthfully about the nature and extent of services that we provide.

P-4.2—We shall not accept or continue to work in positions for which we are personally unsuited or professionally unqualified. We shall not offer services that we do not have the competence, qualifications, or resources to provide.

(continues)

DIRECTOR'S RESOURCE 15-2
(continued)

P-4.3—We shall be objective and accurate in reporting the knowledge upon which we base our program practices.

P-4.4—We shall cooperate with other professionals who work with children and their families.

P-4.5—We shall not hire or recommend for employment any person whose competence, qualifications, or character makes him or her unsuited for the position.

P-4.6—We shall report the unethical or incompetent behavior of a colleague to a supervisor when informal resolution is not effective.

P-4.7—We shall be familiar with laws and regulations that serve to protect the children in our programs.

P-4.8—We shall not participate in practices which are in violation of laws and regulations that protect the children in our programs.

P-4.9—When we have evidence that an early childhood program is violating laws or regulations protecting children, we shall report it to persons responsible for the program. If compliance is not accomplished within a reasonable time, we will report the violation to appropriate authorities who can be expected to remedy the situation.

P-4.10—When we have evidence that an agency or a professional charged with providing services to children, families, or teachers is failing to meet its obligations, we acknowledge a collective ethical responsibility to report the problem to appropriate authorities or to the public.

P-4.11—When a program violates or requires its employees to violate this Code, it is permissible, after fair assessment of the evidence, to disclose the identity of that program.

STATEMENT OF COMMITMENT

As an individual who works with young children, I commit myself to furthering the values of early childhood education as they are reflected in the NAEYC Code of Ethical Conduct.

To the best of my ability I will

- Ensure that programs for young children are based on current knowledge of child development and early childhood education.

- Respect and support families in their task of nurturing children.

- Respect colleagues in early childhood education and support them in maintaining the NAEYC Code of Ethical Conduct.

- Serve as an advocate for children, their families, and their teachers in community and society.

- Maintain high standards of professional conduct.

- Recognize how personal values, opinions, and biases can affect professional judgment.

- Be open to new ideas and be willing to learn from the suggestions of others.

- Continue to learn, grow, and contribute as a professional.

- Honor the ideals and principles of the NAEYC Code of Ethical Conduct.

The statement of commitment expresses those basic personal commitments that individuals must make in order to align themselves with the profession's responsibilities as set forth in the NAEYC Code of Ethical Conduct.

Reprinted with permission of the National Association for the Education of Young Children.

REFERENCES

Bloom, P. J. (2002). *Making the most of meetings: A practical guide.* Lake Forest, IL: New Horizons.

Bloom, P. J. (2005). *Blueprint for action.* Lake Forest, IL: New Horizons.

Carter, M., & Curtis, D. (1998). *The visionary director: A handbook for dreaming, organizing and improving.* St. Paul, MN: Redleaf Press.

Jones, E. (Ed). (1993). *Growing teachers: Partnerships in staff development.* Washington, DC: NAEYC.

Sciarra, D. J., & Dorsey, A. G. (2002). *Leaders and supervisors in child care programs.* Clifton Park, NY: Thomson Delmar Learning.

Werner, S. (1996, May/June). Need a barometer for assessing the climate of your center? *Child Care Information Exchange, 109,* 29.

Additional resources for this chapter can be found on the Online Companion™ at http://www.earlychilded.delmar.com. This supplemental material includes relevant Web links, Web activities, and case studies that apply the concepts presented in this chapter. In addition, the Working Papers and Director's Resources are available for download, allowing you to complete Class Exercises and Class Assignments electronically.

CHAPTER 16

Working with Families, Volunteers, and the Community

The community volunteer who comes to the center to discuss fire prevention and safety must be prepared for children's questions and their desire to handle and touch the equipment.

OBJECTIVES

After reading this chapter, you should be able to:

- Identify components of a parent program.
- List items to be included in a parent handbook.
- Understand the process of recruiting and adding volunteers and becoming active in the community where services are provided.

According to Ellen Galinsky, "The job of the child care center director is one that calls for enormous skill, particularly in working with parents. It is being a professional who simultaneously creates a friendly atmosphere yet retains an appropriate distance; an expert who builds competence in others, who is understanding, empathetic, yet at times firm. Most important is the role of the model—whose words or way of handling a sad, tired or exuberant child are inspiring to parents" (Galinsky, 1984, p. 4). Developing a first-class program for children is the primary goal of the child care center administrator. But many centers have a secondary focus on special programming for parents that requires the director to assume an additional major role as leader of the parent program or as supervisor of the staff members who are responsible for the parent program. Work with volunteers and community organizations or agencies also is an integral part of the total center program that falls within the director's purview in some centers. Creating a positive climate based on good communication is essential for the success of this part of the program (see Chapter 2 section titled Creating a Positive Climate.)

PARENT PROGRAM

Although center directors are not always responsible for the total planning and implementation of all aspects of the parent program, they are held accountable for the program. Classroom staff members or someone designated as a parent coordinator may assume some responsibility for parts of the program, but directors monitor the work, train those who are working with the parents, supervise the program, and serve as a resource for both the staff and the parents.

A positive attitude toward families and what they can contribute to the center program must be demonstrated by the director. With the significant alterations in the American family, the changing complexion of center families requires a multicultural mind-set that values diversity (Gordon & Browne, 2004). There are a number of reasons why parents may be hesitant about coming to the child care center or preschool program over and above language and cultural differences. They may feel threatened by the idea that the teacher is very knowledgeable about children and fearful that their child-rearing practices will be criticized. Some parents, particularly from impoverished backgrounds, may feel inhibited around the school environment because of their limited or unsuccessful school experiences (Decker & Decker, 2005). It also is difficult for parents who have other special problems such as having a child with a disability, being a potential abuser, a single parent, or one who is unable to read or write. Staff behavior and the atmosphere at the center must communicate to parents that each is valued as an individual, that each is highly regarded as the child's first teacher and as someone who knows a great deal about the child. All parents should be aware that they are welcome to come as frequently (or as infrequently) as they wish.

Any number of things can communicate this feeling of acceptance and trust to parents, although some are more tangible than others. A parent-receiving area is the place where parents establish their first impressions of the center. Take time to look at this transition space from the perspective of a rushed parent who is late for work or a tired grandmother or uncle who enters the building to drop off or pick up a child. Is it welcoming and aesthetically pleasing, softly lit, freshly painted, carpeted, and clean? It can be made to feel "homey" and more pleasant if there is a comfy adult seating area and maybe even the smell of freshly brewed coffee. Parent information folders in this space sometimes contain information about the center, highlight interesting articles, and display a calendar of coming events. Pamphlets and journals on child rearing, toy selection, nutrition, and how to make play dough or finger paint can be made available in the parent-receiving area. A parent and child book lending library or toy lending library might be located nearby. Sometimes, interested parents are asked to manage the entire lending program.

Some centers choose to offer families a few ancillary services, including take-out meals or dry cleaning pickup. When James Hymes originally presented this idea, he was responding to a need during World War II when mothers worked seven days a week, and many did not drive or had a limited gasoline supply if they did drive. Although few present-day parents work day or night shifts seven days a week, many find themselves using time-saving, affordable measures that help them meet their family's needs. These "family friendly" offerings can help ease some of the nagging stresses on young parents. If you choose to offer these "extras" to your families, you must consider the space and staffing requirements, as well as costs to you and your staff in time and energy. All related expenses then should be factored into your cost per child.

The less tangible things that make parents feel welcome include the manner in which their calls are handled by the staff member who answers the telephone or the greeting they receive from the van driver who picks up their child each day. Parents' feelings about the center program and staff also are substantially influenced by their first contacts with their child's teacher or the center director. Since it is very difficult to perceive what is having the most significant impact on the parents' reactions to a center program, directors have to be alert to any number of subtle factors that may be influencing parental attitudes and feelings.

The success of the entire parent program depends on the feelings of trust that are established among the center staff, the children, and the families who use the center. Such trust begins to develop at the first contact and will continue to grow as it is nurtured by center staff.

The parent program can be divided into three major categories.

1. parent contacts
2. parent education
3. parent involvement

Clearly, these three aspects of the parent program overlap; however, they are separated here for the purpose of discussion.

Parent Contacts

Parent contacts range from the most informal arrival or departure greetings to formal interviews, regularly scheduled conferences, and special conferences when problems are encountered. Whatever the occasion, contacts with parents can be useful channels for communication. It is through these contacts that the center staff members communicate to parents that they have important information to share with one another and that they have a very special mutual concern for a child whom they both value. Viewing parents as partners rather than as "we" versus "they" enhances the family/center staff relationship. Details of initial interviews and intake procedures were discussed in Chapter 12. When staff members are not fully prepared to handle initial contacts with parents, inservice training time should be devoted to discussion or role-play of parent interviews and intake procedures. (See Chapter 15 for the discussion of inservice training.)

It is important to plan regularly scheduled parent conferences where parents and teachers meet at a mutually agreed-upon time and place to discuss the child. It may take several scheduled conferences and unscheduled calls or casual contacts before a teacher can be successful in creating a totally relaxed environment in which both parent and teacher can discuss the child comfortably. When a good relationship exists, the scheduled conference is a time when parents and teachers can discuss the child's progress, present their concerns and their satisfaction about the child's progress, and develop a plan to follow both at home and at school that will help the child grow to full potential. In the interval between scheduled conferences, casual telephone calls and informal contacts at the center are both excellent ways to converse about how the plan for the child is working.

Preconference planning sheets can be a useful tool in planning some parent conferences. Depending on the parent population being served, you, as a director, may have both the parents and the teachers complete a preconference planning sheet (Figure 16–1). Those parents who may have limited writing or reading skills may feel uncomfortable filling out a form with open-ended questions like those in the sample. In cases like this, teachers can call or chat with parents when children are brought to the classroom. When dates and times are set in these casual conversations, it probably is wise for the teacher to remind families when their scheduled conference time draws near. Experienced teachers can plan the conference based on information from their notes and observations of the child, the information supplied by the parent, and their knowledge of the characteristics of an effective parent conference. The director can model and provide some coaching for inexperienced staff before they conference with parents. Role-playing works well when coaching teachers.

After the preconference planning sheet has been developed, it can be used as a basis for outlining the conference itself. Items on the conference outline might include the following:

- greeting and stating the plan for this conference
- sharing a positive experience the child had within the past couple of days
- asking parents how things are at home and actively listening to their responses
- showing work samples from the child's portfolio and discussing developmental expectations in various areas represented in the samples (for example, art, writing, and the like)
- sharing anecdotes that will focus discussion on the child's strengths as well as on those areas

Child's Name: _____

Parent(s) Name: _____

Date and Time of Conference: _____

Above is the date and time of your parent/teacher conference. Please call the office and reschedule if the assigned time is not convenient.

    I look forward to talking with you about your child. Some of the things I have planned to share with you are:

    I am specifically interested in finding out about the areas of interest or concern that you would like to discuss with me. Please use the space below to tell me what those things are.

Please return this to my box in the office at least a week before the scheduled conference.

Thank you very much.

Figure 16–1

Sample preconference planning sheet.

for potential growth (for example, math concepts, social interactions, self-help and independence, self-control, and so forth)

- asking the parents to share what they would like to see happening for their child in the classroom during the ensuing months
- developing a plan that will facilitate the child's progress toward the agreed-upon goals and expectations discussed during this conference
- closing with consensus on when the next conference should be held, while making sure the door is left open for ongoing dialogue

It is important that parent conferences start and end on a positive note and that incidents or samples of work be used to make specific points about the child's progress. Parents must be given time to express concerns while teachers practice their best listening skills. Just as early childhood professionals build trust with children by listening to concerns and reflecting those feelings, so they build trust with parents by practicing those same listening skills. Putting parents at ease and avoiding arousing anxiety enhances the quality of the relationship during the conference and carries over to the daily interactions with parents as well.

Special conferences sometimes are necessary when either parents or teachers have a need to discuss particular concerns about a child or the center program. The special conferences are likely to produce anxiety for everyone because they are called most often when a problem arises. Sometimes, the director is asked to sit in on a special conference to give support to both teacher and parent and to help clarify what is being said and heard. The teacher may have a conference with the director prior to a particularly difficult parent conference so that they both have a clear understanding of the problem to be discussed. The teacher also may ask the director to recommend the best way to present a problem and to offer some suggestions on how to handle the parents' questions and reactions during the conference. Sometimes, these special conferences include other specialists or consultants from referral agencies, such as a mental health clinic or a speech and hearing center. Both the teacher and the director should be well prepared for special conferences because they will be expected to make a knowledgeable contribution to the discussion about the child. In some cases, they will have to provide support for the parent who may feel tense and threatened.

Uninterrupted time and a comfortable space are essential for successful parent conferences. Timing is important; the time of day or evening that is chosen must suit both the staff members and the parents so that no one feels pressured or rushed. The time allotted must be long enough to discuss matters thoroughly, but not so long that the discussion becomes tedious. Consider allowing at least 30 minutes of uninterrupted conversation time for a conference. Both parents should be encouraged to attend conferences, and, in cases of divorce or separation, teachers may be expected to arrange a conference with each parent. Both teacher and parents leave a successful conference feeling that they have accomplished their goals. In addition, parents should go away with an awareness that their child is valued and appreciated. Finally, it is *critical* that parents have complete confidence that confidentiality will be maintained. The parent-teacher trust relationship will be seriously damaged if a parent should learn from some outside source that shared information about the family or the child was not kept confidential.

A postconference review will help teachers evaluate the quality of their participation. The following checklist will help them focus on their responses during the conference. Directors may want to review the following questions with their teachers after their encounters with parents (adapted from Hewes & Hartman, 1988).

- Did you give the parents plenty of time to talk about their concerns?
- Did you remain an accepting listener?
- Were you able to restrain yourself from giving advice? Did you ask rather than tell?
- Did you remember that suggestions usually are nothing more than advice under a different guise?
- Did the parents do most of the talking?
- Were you able to restate to the parent the feelings just expressed, always using your best active listening skills?
- Are you comfortable that the parent left feeling that you really cared?

Parent Feedback

Parents' viewpoints and suggestions can be solicited by using a parent rating scale with items addressing center ambience, childrens' program, and the center communication network. Many questions can be addressed during a parent-teacher conference where parents can respond to family-specific inquiries like, "Are your needs for information on your child's daily activity being met?" or "What are the best times for me to call you when I have questions about how Betsy is handling the arrival of the new baby?" But written evaluations or rating scales with items that may draw parents' attention to features of your high-quality service give parents an opportunity to ponder and reflect on their reactions to the center. Find ways to let parents know that you are interested in hearing from them and that you are eager to partner with them to provide the richest possible experiences for their child.

DIRECTOR'S CORNER

"I realize now that I really have to keep in touch with what parents are thinking about our program and how they see us. Last year we had two or three families leave our program, and I wasn't really sure why they were making a move. When I contacted several of them, I realized that they were feeling the quality of our program was not what they had come to expect from us. Of course, I acted on that immediately, but I also developed a rating scale for parents to complete so they could let us know how we're doing."

—*Director, suburban for-profit center*

Parent Education

Typically, the parent education program is designed to improve parenting skills or to interpret the center program to the parent group. In some centers, there are more ambitious goals for the parent education program, including education on consumerism, nutrition, stress management, or time management. A popular program in some communities is English as a Second Language (ESL). Some centers provide vocational education programs or special remedial classes to help parents complete high school or take the General Education Development test (GED). (A successful score on the GED leads to a high school equivalency certificate.)

Planning parent education programs is the responsibility of the director, but the planning group should include parent and staff representatives. Format and content must reflect the needs and interests of the parents and be adjusted to the level of education and previous training of the parent population. Centers that serve families from diverse educational, cultural, and socio-economic backgrounds should present a wide variety of choices from which the parents can select the programs that are best suited to their needs.

Activities in the parent education program may be as informal as casual classroom observations followed by one-to-one or small-group discussions with a staff member or as formal as a planned lecture, workshop, panel discussion, or seminar. The planned activities should meet the parents' needs in terms of timing, content, and presentation strategy. Casual classroom observations are particularly helpful to parents who are curious about how their child's behavior compares with that of peers. For example, a mother who feels great concern about the explosive yelling and unacceptable language of her preschool son may feel reassured when she observes other four-year-olds who also are noisy and explosive. It also is helpful for that mother to discuss these erratic outbursts with a staff member who can interpret the behavior in terms of expected behaviors at this developmental stage. Group discussions, lectures, films, videotapes, DVDs, or workshops that are offered by center staff members or by outside consultants are all useful tools for providing parents with information on child rearing, child development, or topics related to parental problems and concerns. Including a social time along with information sharing creates a nonthreatening, relaxed learning atmosphere.

Topics of interest and concern to parents range from specific questions like, "What do I do about my child who awakens at 4:30 A.M. every day and wants to get up?" to broader issues facing employed parents who struggle with the stresses of job, home, and family. Programs should focus on building parents' sense of expertise. In planning parent education programs, consider emphasis on empowering parents to explore ways to cope with their concerns and issues around parenting.

Directors are responsible for ensuring that parent education programs and parent meetings are both timely and responsive to the parents' interests and concerns. A designated parent educator may select some of the topics for parent meetings, but when parents are involved in planning parent meetings, the topics are more likely to be relevant to parents' interests (Hildebrand & Hearron, 2002).

Parent meetings usually are considered part of the total parent education program. The frequency of scheduled parent meetings varies widely from program to program. Some programs offer monthly meetings, while others have as few as one, or two meetings a year. The first meeting of the year for a preschool on the typical public school calendar often is devoted to introducing the staff and taking parents through a typical day at school by using slides, videos, DVDs, or classroom visitation. The format for all parent meetings should include time for questions and for informal socialization. Regular parent meetings are a good way to create a parent support group that can be mobilized to act as a strong political force when threats to child care programs arise in your community.

Low parent turnout is a chronic issue and often very discouraging for center directors and staff who plan for parent visits to the classroom, prepare refreshments, and look forward to meeting and sharing with parents. It requires creative planning, taking time to find out the best timing for meetings, and exploring what might interest this particular population of parents. Maybe they want to learn about using the Internet or have a tasting party of Thai foods. Shifting from an exclusive focus on parenting sometimes can encourage more families to attend center functions. As center gatherings become popular, parents may begin to ask for more meetings that focus on parenting issues or child development.

Parent Involvement

Parent conferences and parent education are, indeed, parent involvement, but the parent involvement concept implies a more extensive parental commitment than participation in parent conferences or in selected parts of the parent education program. Although parents should be encouraged to become involved, they also should have the option to remain uninvolved. It is an imposition on the parents' right to choose if they are made to feel that they must become involved in the center program. Of course, if the program is a co-op, then by definition it requires full parent participation.

The purpose of a parent involvement program is to get them active in planning, implementing, and evaluating the total program. In some comprehensive child care programs such as Head Start, parents may serve on advisory and policy boards, participate in all aspects of program planning and classroom activity, take part in the evaluation of staff and program, participate in budget and personnel decisions, and come to understand their role as advocates for their children.

Parents sometimes enjoy working regularly in the classroom or helping with children's parties or field trips, and some center programs depend on the help that parents can provide. Before parents participate in any aspect of the children's program, they should know something about classroom ground rules, routines, and what to expect of the children. The mother

Planning parent education programs is the responsibility of the director, but the planning group should include parent representatives.

who comes to read to the children may need some help on how to include children other than her own in a small, informal, shared reading experience. The father who takes a morning off to come and read to the children may be disappointed when only three or four children are interested enough to stay for more than one book. He must be helped to understand that children have choices and that they are free to choose not to participate. It also is helpful if he knows the ground rules about deciding who chooses books to be read and techniques for helping children wait to have their choice read. Parents who work in the classroom on a regular basis should be expected to participate in a more extensive orientation program before being assigned specific tasks when they come to the center. Both parents and volunteers can attend the same orientation sessions.

There are innumerable ways for parents to be involved in the center program other than direct classroom participation. They can do clerical work, repair or make equipment, take responsibility for the lending library, baby-sit during conference periods or committee meetings, drive carpools, and participate in advocacy endeavors with help from staff. If they have special talents or interests in fund-raising, they can serve as a resource for the center board or the director. If they have special language skills, they can provide priceless service in bilingual programs. There also are many opportunities for parents to serve in a variety of ways on the board, on advisory committees, or on any number of standing or ad hoc committees. (See Chapter 5 for the discussion of the composition of the center board and of the committee structure.)

Clearly, when the director is committed to a parent involvement program and that attitude prevails throughout the center, it is possible to find a special place for every parent to participate, provided the parent has the time and interest to become involved. However, it is important for the director to be sensitive to individual family situations. Employed parents who are unable to be involved with center activities must be reassured that they are free to choose not to participate. A successful parent involvement program does require some management; therefore, the center staff must make a commitment to the program to give it the time and attention it requires.

Working with Demanding Parents

The best centers work to empower parents. Administrators and teachers develop partnerships over time with parents who gradually come to feel they are a valued participant in their child's care at the center. There always will be angry parents and some "high maintenance" parents who will challenge the staff. Staff members will have to remember and practice their best communication and problem-solving skills when faced with these parents.

There are situations where staff feelings and perceptions work against forming partnerships with parents. Parents can become "they" when these staff

A parent who enjoys reading to the children will need some guidelines on how to include children other than her own in a small, informal group.

members get together for staff meetings. "They don't tell us what is happening at home." "They don't follow through at home." "They don't set any limits at home." Or "They are too restrictive at home." Staff might comment, "they don't care" when referring to a parent who seems to have no interest in discussing child-related issues. On the other side of that coin, a staff member may comment, "She will not leave me alone—she questions me about everything he did or said while he was here at school and wants to know exactly what I did in response to his actions." Helping staff value diversity in family lifestyles and attitudes, as well as how various parents choose to communicate or not communicate with staff about their concerns, is something directors can plan to discuss at staff meetings and staff retreats and can model in their interactions with families (adapted from Greenman, 1998). It is helpful if staff can manage to view parents as partners and find ways to see situations from the parents' point of view.

Every program, sooner or later, will have to deal with angry and/or "high maintenance," demanding parents. Directors can encourage all staff to make encounters and exchanges with these, as well as all parents, as customer friendly as possible. Child care staff may not view families and children as customers, but a review of what customers are may clarify for all that the center clients are its customers. Customers are

■ people who buy products or services from you.
■ not dependent on you; you are dependent on them.

■ not interruptions to your work; they are the purpose of your work.
■ not persons you argue with; they are persons you value and serve (adapted from Phipps, 1998).

Directors and all center staff are obliged to work on building positive relationships with children and center families (customers). When confronted with the angry parent's tirade or the needy "high maintenance" parent's demands on their time, it is an opportunity for center staff to make effective conflict-resolution strategies part of their customer service plan.

PREPARING A PARENT HANDBOOK

A handbook for parents is a convenient way to communicate basic program information and should be distributed to all families at some point in the enrollment procedure. Since the contents may change from year to year and vary from program to program, directors will have to use some general guidelines for developing a handbook, then adapt those to their specific program. Some items, like program philosophy or grouping children, may or may not be part of the marketing brochure but could be repeated in the handbook. As a director, you will have to decide what information parents need to know and the best way to convey it to them. If a handbook seems too overwhelming for the particular parent population in your program, consider putting an item or two on colorful single sheets to be handed out over a period of several weeks after admission to the program.

The suggested list of items that follows is not exhaustive but provides broad guidelines for developing a parent handbook (see sample parent handbook in Director's Resource 16–1). Directors often choose to avoid including items likely to change, such as names of staff and fees.

- Brief statement of the program philosophy.
- Outline of the daily program and an explanation of how it fits the program philosophy.
- Fees and arrangements for payment, including details about reimbursement possibilities and credit for absences.
- Car-pool and/or transportation arrangements. If transportation is not provided, indicate that fact and state what information you need to have about the family's transportation arrangements for the child.
- Expected arrival and pickup times and procedures.
- Center policy on health and safety precautions to be taken by the family and the center staff, to ensure the health and safety of children. State your policy about bringing medication to the center and children coming to the center when symptoms of illness are apparent, and cover the procedures used by the center staff when a child becomes ill at school and so on.
- Explanation of liability and medical insurance carried by and/or available through the center.
- Sample menus for snacks and/or meals and any expectations the staff may have about eating.
- Services the center staff will offer to children and families, such as opportunities for having conferences, special medical or psychological services or referrals, discussion groups, group meetings, and so on.
- Center discipline policy.
- Requests for help from parents such as for time spent in the classroom, help on field trips, clerical help, making materials for the classroom, and so on.
- Summary of scheduled events at the center and what families may do at the center to celebrate holidays and birthdays. Make the policies in this regard reflect the program philosophy by including what to send, what to expect the child to bring home, which holidays will be celebrated, and so on.
- Expectations about the child's use of transition objects while getting adjusted to the center and

policies about bringing other items or food from home, making clear how these policies are developed to meet the needs of children and to reflect the program philosophy.
- Description of the legal obligations of center staff to report any evidence of child abuse.

This list provides guidelines for developing a handbook that ultimately must be fashioned to fit your program and your parent population. In writing material for a handbook, it is important to consider content, format, length, and, most important, style of writing. Should the style be scholarly or chatty, formal or informal, general or detailed? Answers to these questions can be found by giving careful consideration to the families being served by the program.

The parent handbook is a useful tool to acquaint parents with the center program initially and to help them understand what to expect. However, it must be supplemented with other written and verbal communications to keep them abreast of center events and the progress of their children. Other details concerning your program can be listed on your Web site. In some communities it will be necessary to publish not only the handbook but all written materials in another language in addition to English.

Some directors send parents a chatty newsletter describing special events that are being planned for children or families. It is important for parents to know that one family brought their new baby to visit the classroom or that a musician from a symphony orchestra came to show the children a slide trombone. Such information will help parents understand a child's questions and any ideas that are expressed at home. Newsletters can keep parents informed about the center's progress, program philosophy, special programs, and future plans. It can include a monthly calendar, information about fund-raisers, updates of staff changes, and activities. Including a profile of a staff person, another parent, or a center volunteer is a sure way to generate readership and enthusiasm about your newsletter. News items from each classroom are always welcome, especially if children's names are mentioned. Parents will search the pages to find a mention of their child or their child's teacher. Best of all, parents are eager to read the "Director's Message," which is a must for each issue. Remember, the director sets the "feeling tone" for the center, and the tone of a "Director's Message" communicates that to parents (Jones, 1996).

Other ways to communicate with parents include meetings, regularly scheduled parent conferences, use of e-mail, a center Web site, and telephone calls to tell parents about happy experiences that their children had at school. Center staff must take advantage of every opportunity to communicate with the family, to share ideas about the child, and to strengthen the basic trust in the relationship.

VOLUNTEER PROGRAM

Volunteers are welcomed in most early childhood education centers, and the volunteer program usually is managed by the center director. Occasionally, a member of the center staff other than the director or a volunteer who is willing to undertake the coordinating responsibilities manages the volunteer activities. The coordinating function includes recruiting, orienting, and scheduling the volunteers. Other aspects of the volunteer program, such as planning activities for the volunteers and handling the supervision and record-keeping responsibilities connected with a volunteer program, either must be delegated or performed by the director. Volunteers are often interested in ways to advocate for children.

Volunteer Recruitment

Recruiting volunteers is time consuming and often frustrating, but there are individuals in every community who are potential volunteers. Finding those people who have both the time and the interest in serving a child care center may present a problem at the outset; however, a program that provides both challenge and appropriate incentives soon will build up a roster of available volunteers who come regularly.

Available sources for recruiting volunteers will vary, depending on the size of the community and the demands of other agencies in the community. Larger cities have organized volunteer bureaus, Junior Leagues, universities with student volunteer programs, child advocacy groups, and any number of philanthropic groups that can supply volunteers. Church groups, high schools, senior citizen groups, and business groups are other sources that can be found and approached in both large urban communities or small rural areas. The volunteers must feel that they are welcome and needed; in addition, they must feel a sense of personal regard for their efforts.

Volunteer Orientation

Participation in the volunteer orientation program should be a requirement for every person who chooses to give time to the center program. Although it may seem presumptuous to insist that volunteers participate in an orientation, it is essential that they become completely familiar with the operation of the center and that they have a clear understanding of how their services fit into the total service offered by the center program. Furthermore, the volunteers usually recognize that a center staff that will take the time to plan and carry through a meaningful and helpful orientation program for them also will value their involvement in the center program.

Orientation meetings should provide volunteers with a staff directory and introduction to as many staff members as possible. The director should talk about the organizational structure of the agency, the goals and objectives of the center program, and the importance of volunteer help in meeting those goals and objectives. Further, licensing standards and health requirements for volunteers must be explained. That will clarify what is expected of them regarding immunizations, health examination, and classroom health and safety procedures and help them understand the rationale for restrictions on their participation. For example, in most places, a volunteer may not be alone at any time with a group of children because of licensing and insurance requirements. When the rationale for that ruling is understood, volunteers are less likely to be offended when told they may not take the children on a walk or drive them the few blocks to the park.

Confidentiality is an issue for everyone at the center, including the volunteers. It is wonderful to have volunteers who become ambassadors for the program in the community, but it is essential that they adhere to a strict policy of absolute confidentiality. Volunteers who share their general enthusiasm about working with the children or doing other work for the center can be a great asset, but talking about specific children, families, or teachers can be very damaging to your program.

Other details that should be covered at the orientation meeting include sign-in and sign-out procedures for volunteers, and where they should call if they expect to be absent. Record keeping is necessary because many publicly funded centers must report volunteer hours, and some private agencies often choose to keep records and reward volunteers based on their hours of service. Evidence of a strong commitment to a program by volunteers is useful when applying for grant money.

Volunteer Activities

Volunteers can do most things that parents do in a center program, and they often have more free time than working parents or parents with young families. Volunteers, like parents, must be made to feel welcome; and like parents they must leave with a sense of satisfaction and a feeling that their services are needed and appreciated. Since they do not have the reward of seeing the joy their own children experience by having them participate in the program, it is

Volunteers are sometimes asked to participate in setting up classroom activities.

doubly important for the center staff to make them feel welcome, to define their task for them, and to let them know how highly their service is regarded. Volunteers will continue to serve only in situations where they feel needed.

REFLECTION

Think about your own volunteer activities. Perhaps you tutor younger students or work in a program for children with disabilities. What motivates you to be there at the scheduled time? Do you look for excuses not to go? If not, why not? How do you feel about yourself after you spend time volunteering? What rewards do you receive?

ORGANIZATIONS AND AGENCIES

In addition to working with parents and volunteers, the director is responsible for involvement with professional organizations, referral agencies, and the community in which the center is located. In each case, the amount of time and degree of involvement varies according to the type of center and the director's individual style.

Professional Organizations

Directors frequently join one or more local, regional, and national professional organizations. Sometimes, the board encourages and assists them by paying their dues (a list of professional organizations is presented in Appendix B). Through these memberships, directors can accomplish several goals.

First, directors can obtain information and make contacts that may be personally and professionally helpful. Therefore, they may select organizations that focus on development of administrative skills, presentation of research data, and provision of information about legislation and funding. Through contacts at group meetings, the director may meet potential staff members, although "pirating" staff from other centers certainly should be avoided. Directors also may see professional organizations as providing a forum for their ideas, a place where they can speak before a group and discuss their concerns with other professionals. They may volunteer to hold meetings at their centers, thereby providing opportunities for others in the field to see different early childhood education facilities.

When directors join a professional organization, the organization is enhanced since the directors have had a number of years of education and experience and carry some influence in the community. As a result of their having belonged to these organizations or similar groups for a number of years, they have expertise that can help move the group forward, and they can give guidance to newer, less experienced members.

Directors may join professional organizations to become part of a group that effects change. The professional groups offer many advocacy opportunities. Legislators who will not listen to an individual's recommendations on teacher-to-child ratios or low wage issues may be persuaded by an organization's stand, and directors can have input through their membership in the organization.

In some communities, directors form support groups because they need a forum to discuss problems unique to their particular position. They can share information and ideas and work out cooperative plans for staff training. With the increased, widespread focus on child care, national support groups are forming to provide hot lines, Web sites, consultation services, and management retreats.

When they join organizations, directors serve as models for staff members. In some cases, the staff profits more directly from the organization than the director, but staff members put off joining or may even be hesitant about attending meetings if they do not know other members. Directors can provide an incentive by offering to accompany teachers to the first meeting and by notifying staff members of upcoming meetings. Directors may work out a plan for released time from center duties that staff members can use to participate in the work of professional organizations. They also may provide staff meeting time for members who have attended sessions to share their information.

For similar reasons, directors should attend (and facilitate staff members' attending) lectures, courses, and conferences that are related to early childhood education. Directors also have the responsibility for reading current books, periodicals, and resources on the Internet and passing relevant materials on to staff members (a list of periodicals appears in Appendix C). Most staff members will respond positively to an article from the director that is marked to indicate a personal application such as, "This article addresses an interest of yours, new ways of teaching math concepts." Or, "Have you seen the reviews of these new multiethnic books? Which ones should we order?" This personal touch encourages the staff member to read the article and perhaps discuss it further with the director. When the director has provided a model of this behavior, staff members may begin to circulate articles or books that they have found to be worthwhile.

Referral Agencies

Directors contact referral agencies and advise staff members to use special services when that is appropriate. Directors also help staff members delineate the boundaries of their own professional expertise and recognize those circumstances under which an opinion obtained from another type of professional could be useful.

The job of relating to referral agencies begins with the collection of a list of services that are available in the surrounding community. In some areas, a booklet is published that contains the names of all the social service agencies, their addresses, telephone numbers, fax numbers, Web sites, hours, charges, what services are provided and to whom, and whether a referral from a physician or caseworker is required. Some communities add other kinds of information such as lists of recreation centers, churches, schools, and government agencies and officials. If this type of directory is not available, a center director can develop a referral list. Writing the data on file cards provides a convenient reference that can be updated easily.

After determining which agencies provide services related to the clients' needs, directors should attempt to make personal contact with as many of these agencies as possible. This contact can be accomplished by visiting the agency, attending programs sponsored by the agency, and meeting its staff members at professional meetings. Later, when the need for services from such an organization arises, it will be easier for the director to make contacts with the people whom he already knows. The director also is in a good position to explain the nature of the services provided by these agencies to the center staff and to parents when that is necessary.

DIRECTOR'S CORNER

"When I first became a director, one of the things I had trouble finding out about was the whole referral network, and I realize that takes time and comes with experience. You have to know the agencies, how they work, and the particular people to contact before you can help your teachers or your families with referrals. I always feel better when I can call a specific person whom I have already met."

—Director, YMCA-sponsored center

In addition to working with the staff in referring children and families for care and treatment, directors make use of agencies in other ways. For example, agencies usually have personnel and material resources available for in-service training or parent meetings. Some agencies in the community such as Community Coordinated Child Care (4Cs) or resource and referral agencies provide consultation and technical assistance. A range of services may be available from other types of agencies such as the public library, which usually offers storytellers, films, and teachers' collections of books.

If the center's program includes the provision of medical, dental, and mental health services to children, the director may be able to provide these services at low cost and with convenience in scheduling through agency contacts. For example, arrangements can be made for a physician to come to the center to do routine physical checkups so that children do not have to endure long trips, boring waiting rooms, and frightening strange buildings. The director, who is well acquainted with physicians, psychologists, speech therapists, and social workers, is able to depend on their services but is sensitive to the needs and limitations under which they operate. It is important that directors establish reciprocal relationships with these professionals by being open to accepting children referred to the center by them and their agencies.

WORK WITH THE COMMUNITY

The director explains the center to the community and, in turn, explains the community to the staff. This function requires familiarity with the community in which the center is located. If some or all of the children who attend the center live in other communities, the director should become informed about those areas as well.

In marketing and publicizing the center to the community, the director uses public relations and communications techniques that were covered in Chapter 11. These include news releases, open houses, and tours of the center. The effective use of the interpersonal skills that were discussed in Chapter 2 is particularly appropriate when working with the community. The appearance and maintenance of the center's building and grounds also can have an influence on the relationship with the community.

Sometimes, individual members of the community become interested in the center and its work through the director's efforts. For example, the owner of a lumberyard may agree to provide scrap lumber for the children's woodworking projects, or a printer will offer to save all the paper ends from print jobs for the children's use. If the director and staff have met the local grocer and other shopkeepers, these businesspeople may be far more responsive to the children when they visit on field trips or when they walk by as they explore the area with classmates. A university in the area may be interested in sending architecture or product design students or may come to do research. In addition, there are child advocacy groups in the community that will offer information and support to center staff and families.

Directors help their staff members understand the community by encouraging involvement in community activity and by providing information about life in the community. Having knowledge of the historical background of the area and the cultural or ethnic groups that live there will increase staff awareness of the needs of families who come to the center. The director is responsible for making center staff members sensitive to the customs, language, and values of the people they serve. Frequently, staff members live in other communities and represent different cultural or ethnic groups. It is impossible for staff members to work effectively with children and parents from a culture about which they have no knowledge.

When the director has done a good job of understanding the community, and when all the pertinent information is conveyed to the staff, everyone at the center gains a greater appreciation of the community, and a strong working relationship can emerge. The center's team of staff, parents, and children working together can be expanded to incorporate community members as well.

SUMMARY

The director works with or is accountable for the parent program. A major aspect of this role is helping staff members establish effective parent relationships. The parent program includes parent contacts, parent education, and parent involvement and places emphasis on the participation of the individual parent to the degree that is appropriate and comfortable for her. Directors also are involved in recruiting and orienting volunteers and in providing recognition for their services. In addition, they work closely with professional organizations, referral agencies, and members of the community. Part of their role involves setting an example for staff members of an appropriate amount of professional involvement, and training them in the techniques of working with a variety of resources. Directors also provide information to staff members and give them opportunities to make use of the services that professional organizations, referral agencies, and the community at large have to offer.

CLASS ASSIGNMENTS

1. Using Working Paper 16–1, develop a list of specific tasks a volunteer could do in the specified classroom areas.

2. Find out if you have a directory of social and health service agencies in your community. Use your directory to locate five agencies that an early childhood education director might use for referrals. If you do not have a directory, compile a list of five agencies that an early childhood center director might use for referrals. Include each agency's name, address, telephone number, type of services provided, and charges.

CLASS EXERCISE

1. Divide into groups of three for the purpose of role-playing a parent conference. The situation is one in which a young mother has requested a conference about her three-year-old son who spends a great deal of time in the housekeeping area in the classroom. He also plays with dolls, washes dishes, and dresses up in a skirt and high heels at home. The father is very upset and annoyed by this behavior and has pressured the mother into calling for a conference. The father is unable to attend the conference. The roles are as follows:

■ male teacher
■ mother
■ female director

Using the checklist in Working paper 16–2, discuss each item listed. If you were director or mother in the role-play, give your perception of how well the teacher handled the questions asked.

WORKING PAPER 16-1

(for use with Class Assignment 1)

VOLUNTEER TASKS FORM

List specific tasks a volunteer could be assigned to do in each of the classroom areas or activities listed below. Think beyond supervising children. Consider care and development of materials, enriching the area, or making it more aesthetically pleasing.

Dramatic play (expand beyond house-type play)

Carpentry

Literature/library area

Writing center

Lunchtime

Nap time

WORKING PAPER 16-2

(for use with Class Exercise 1)

ROLE-PLAY CHECKLIST

After the role-play in Class Exercise 1 is completed, discuss the items in this checklist. If your role was that of director or parent, respond to the questions in terms of your perception of how well the teacher handled the conference. You are expected to give more than yes or no answers. Document your answers with examples from the conference.

Did you give the parent time to talk about her concerns?

Were you a receptive listener?

When you made comments, did you talk in terms of the parent's feelings?

Were you able to restrain yourself from giving advice?

Did the parent do most of the talking?

What was accomplished during the conference?

DIRECTOR'S RESOURCE 16-1

HANDBOOK

for Families, Visitors, Volunteers
& Other Friends of Young Children

Children's for Children
The employer-sponsored child care and
education centers managed by Cincinnati
Children's Hospital Medical Center

3333 Burnet Avenue
Cincinnati, Ohio 45229
(513)636-4999

520 Linton Street
Cincinnati, Ohio 45219
(513)636-2640

(continues)

DIRECTOR'S RESOURCE 16-1
(continued)

Children's for Children

The employer-sponsored child care and education centers managed by Cincinnati Children's Hospital Medical Center

3333 Burnet Avenue
Cincinnati, Ohio 45229
(513)636-4999

520 Linton Street
Cincinnati, Ohio 45219
(513)636-2640

~~~~~~~~~~~~~~~~~~~~

Ron McKinley
Vice President
Human Resources
513-636-4417

Chris Burroughs
Director
Child Care
513-636-4055

Yvonne Olsen
Business Director
Child Care
513-636-2645

Mary Alice Callahan
Manager
CFC-CCHMC
513-636-4056

Kathy Haders
Manager
CFC-P&G
513-636-0429

1

(continues)

DIRECTOR'S RESOURCE 16-1
(continued)

Table of Contents

2

(continues)

Our Mission

The Child Care Division of Cincinnati Children's Hospital Medical Center, Children's for Children, provides unparalleled services in early child care and education. We are the preferred source for care and developmental information to the families of our corporate sponsors. We are an active resource to the larger community.

3

(continues)

DIRECTOR'S RESOURCE 16-1
(continued)

Hello!

We bring you a warm welcome to Children's for Children, the child development centers of Cincinnati Children's Hospital Medical Center. Founded in 1987, the child care division offers two of Cincinnati's largest, loveliest, and liveliest child care facilities. We like to think of Children's for Children as a place that children and adults consider their second home...a place where they are accepted and loved...a place where laughter and play are cherished...a place where children's rhythms are caught and given warm response.

We hold special pride in the center's professional staff. Selected for their knowledge of child development as well as their strong interpersonal skills, they are the strength of our program. When visiting Children's for Children, please take time to listen, to watch, and to learn from this unique group. You will be enriched.

It is the role of all staff members to not only facilitate the learning of children, parents, and one another, but also to work as enablers to the important work of the parents at our outstanding hospital medical center and second sponsor, Procter & Gamble. We are pleased to embrace these roles.

Sincerely

Chris Burroughs
Director

Mary Alice Callahan
Manager
CFC-CCHMC

Kathy Haders
Manager
CFC-P&G

4

(continues)

DIRECTOR'S RESOURCE 16-1
(continued)

Philosophically Speaking

Childhood is a time like no other. It's a time for exploring... for creating... for discovering about oneself... for meeting the world... for learning how to learn... for being accepted "just the way I am". It's a time for blossoming and being cherished... a time for being allowed the time to be a child.

Our child care center administrators and caregivers are committed to the belief that children have achieved... that is, they CAN DO a lot. It is the role of the caregivers to build upon those things that children are able to do. We believe that most of life's learning –

5

(continues)

DIRECTOR'S RESOURCE 16-1
(continued)

including how to learn – occurs in the first five years of life. Since each child learns at her own pace, our staff will look to her to determine the next stage of development. This "can do" approach is the basis of our philosophy. This "can do" viewpoint allows the children we serve to become confident and to enjoy successes in an atmosphere of respect, warmth, and love.

Time and again, research shows us that <u>THE</u> main component of sound, quality child care is the trained, sensitive adult who is the caregiver. We carefully select staff trained in early childhood development who value, respect, and sensitively respond to the unique needs of children. We feel that children learn best with highly trained staff. The time that they are away from Mommy and Daddy must be a blossoming time. We respect parents as the most significant providers of care and nurturing. We are pleased to serve as extended family members. As such, we encourage parents and children to use our first names.

6

(continues)

DIRECTOR'S RESOURCE 16-1
(continued)

Some Background

Child care centers are special places. And centers become even more special when created to serve a unique population. So it is at Cincinnati Children's Hospital Medical Center (CCHMC). Our child care centers, Children's for Children, provide services primarily to the children of Cincinnati Children's Hospital and Procter & Gamble personnel in convenient settings. The hours vary at each site to meet the needs of our families. We offer full weekday service for children from 12 weeks old to kindergarten age. The hospital site does includes a kindergarten program.

CFC-CCHMC   CFC-P&G
6:00am – 6:30pm   7:00am – 6:30pm

Our centers are accredited by the National Academy of Early Childhood Programs (NAEYC). We have also been successfully evaluated by Comprehensive Community Child Care on several occasions. CFC-CCHMC was selected in 1998 as one of eight exemplary centers, identified nationally by NAEYC and the High/Scope Research Foundation.

Our services stretch beyond child care to support the whole family. Families using the center receive daily written communications on their child's day, prompt attention to any concerns, and parent-teacher

7

(continues)

DIRECTOR'S RESOURCE 16-1
(continued)

conferences twice a year. Families gather during the year for social events. Child Care Center Support Teams include parents and are an important resource to the centers. Each site manager prepares a newsletter monthly, providing an overview of center activities and policy changes. Many classrooms have newsletters specific to the activities of their rooms.

A Brown Bag series is offered throughout the year to any employee of CCHMC or P&G, held at their respective sites. Topics focus on issues facing today's families.

The center does not discriminate in the enrollment of children or selection of staff or volunteers upon the basis of race, color, creed, age, religion, sex, national origin, varying ability or status as a veteran.

Persons desiring to be employees, to register their children, or to apply for tuition assistance must follow the established procedures. No child may be in the program until the parent has submitted a completed registration packet, including health forms. Upon enrollment, parents must arrange an orientation with the site manager. Families are encouraged to visit the center frequently before the day of admission as the center staff and families begin building a collaborative relationship early.

8

(continues)

DIRECTOR'S RESOURCE 16-1
(continued)

It is to the benefit of our children, families, and staff to collaborate with an extensive network of agencies and individuals.

Resources held by affiliated institutions, such as the Cincinnati Center for Developmental Disorders, of Cincinnati Children's are used by the professional staff of the centers. All these groups focus on the healthy development of children, providing the family ultimate support and advocating for safe environments for young ones. In addition, we may use consultants from the Children's Home or Childreach.

The center is licensed to operate by both the Ohio Department of Job and Family Services (ODJFS) and by the City of Cincinnati. Licenses are posted in the lobbies. We are also licensed for food service operation, with documentation displayed in each kitchen. Our compliance with all licensing requirements is monitored regularly. Licenses are renewed in a timely manner. To receive a copy of current state day care laws and rules, contact ODJFS office, 1-866-635-3748, option 2, extension 2 . Our compliance reports, as well as evaluations from the health, building, and fire departments are also available from ODJFS. Recent licensing compliance reports are also posted in our lobbies. To report any suspected violation of the state law, please contact the local Department of Job and Family Services' office, (513) 852-3296. City regulations and compliance reports are

9

(continues)

DIRECTOR'S RESOURCE 16-1
(continued)

available from the Cincinnati Department of
Health, (513) 357-7460. All state rules are also
available at each center or from
www.state.oh.us/odjfs/cdc. City rules are located
in each manager's office.

Employees of Children's for Children have advocated
and testified on numerous occasions to strengthen the
city and state laws governing child care settings to
their current level. We are pleased to cooperate in the
important role of protecting children.

We participate in the professional development
program of Comprehensive Community Child Care (4C).
Individual staff members belong to various professional
groups, such as the National Association for the
Education of Young Children (NAEYC). We uphold the
Ohio AEYC Code of Ethics.

Students from community colleges and universities may
be assigned to the centers to complete their teaching
internships. In addition, student nurses and medical
residents/fellows may come to observe healthy
children at play.

Doctoral, corporate, or other research is conducted at
the center with parental permission only. On occasion,
we have the opportunity to participate in consumer
research (toy design firms, etc.). Sometimes we have

10

(continues)

DIRECTOR'S RESOURCE 16-1
(continued)

assisted with research projects of CCHMC. No research is completed without the approval of the Center's Support Teams. Parental permission is secured.

Our staff also joins hands with hospital, community, and parent volunteers. All volunteers are carefully screened and trained for their "jobs" by center administrators and lead teachers. We require medical statements to be on file for volunteers who interact with our children. Classroom or field trip volunteers are to support the staff but are never left in charge of the children. (Children are supervised at all times by center staff members.)

11

(continues)

DIRECTOR'S RESOURCE 16-1
(continued)

Our Facilities

Both child care centers have been designed and occasionally renovated with the needs of children topmost on our minds. Cincinnati Children's Protective Services personnel monitor the safety of our children, families and staff members. Each center has a security camera system and there are visits by Protective Services officers. Telephones are located for emergency contacts in areas in which children play and adults work. Both centers are cleaned by Marriott housekeeping during the evening hours.

Children's for Children – CCHMC became an official part of the medical center "family" in 1989. The building, just a few years old then, was renovated to better meet the needs of the children and staff members. The large outdoor play spaces include a separate area for infants and toddlers. Preschool and kindergarten children enjoy contemporary play equipment and also have opportunities for traditional bike riding on their trail or gardening in the warmer months. Indoors, there are eight classrooms, roomy lobbies, a muscle room, full-service kitchen, laundry area and several offices. Recent renovations made a staff planning and relaxation space available. All center spaces, including the playgrounds, are equipped with security cameras and limited access to non-

12

(continues)

DIRECTOR'S RESOURCE 16-1
(continued)

program persons. CFC-CCHMC is licensed to care for
128 children at a time.

Children's for Children – P&G is specially designed to
provide safe, stimulating and inviting play spaces. Some of
the special areas are the fine arts room, airy indoor
muscle room and garden plots. Two outdoor playgrounds
provide sand, water, climbing and tricycling experiences.
The 14 classrooms are spacious, have observation windows,
and natural light. The colorful artwork in the hallways
helps celebrate diversity as well as the playfulness of
children. CCHMC security personnel visit frequently and
monitor 5 security cameras. Entrance is by controlled key
card only. Parking is conveniently located at the front of
the building. The full-service kitchen, resource room and
offices complete this center. CFC-P&G is licensed to care
for 190 children at a time.

13

(continues)

DIRECTOR'S RESOURCE 16-1
(continued)

Our Disciplinary Approach

Children at our center will not receive physical punishment. Children who have conflicts or problems with others while at our center will be encouraged to verbalize their feelings and concerns. Even infants without verbal skills will hear their caregivers describing problems, solutions and logical consequences. The role of the adult at school is to be a helper to positive problem solving. Our staff members view discipline as guidance, not punishment.

We want children to value cooperation and teamwork. We help them to learn peaceful approaches as ways to get along.

Our spaces are set up with preventative measures in mind. Multiples of toys are provided. Verbalizing feelings, redirection and explaining to children what they <u>may</u> do are some of the techniques we use.

Children whose behavior endangers others will be supervised away from other children. The child will then process the problem with a staff member and any other concerned parties. Staff rarely use "time out" unless a child is emotionally out of control and needs private time to regain composure. Verbal processing is our preferred approach.

14

(continues)

DIRECTOR'S RESOURCE 16-1
(continued)

Discipline, i.e., guidance, will always be positive, productive and immediate when behavior is inappropriate. Many of the staff members have had extensive course work in Dr. Thomas Gordon's Teacher Effectiveness Training (TET) and utilize TET techniques in assisting children with problems.

No child will be humiliated, shamed, frightened, or subjected to verbal or physical abuse by an employee or by parents or any other person on the premises or during field trips.

Every employee of Children's for Children understands and follows our disciplinary approach as well as the standards on guidance and management in state licensing rule 5101:2:12.22.

15

(continues)

DIRECTOR'S RESOURCE 16-1
(continued)

Our Staff

We employ people who are mature, warm and nurturing, who understand child development, who can apply their knowledge in the classroom, and who respect each child as an individual. We seek employees who value working as a team with parents, colleagues, and volunteers.

We select our staff carefully in order to provide the best possible care and education for the children. The director and managers have degrees or advanced coursework in early childhood education and experience as center administrators. Master teachers are selected for their levels of expertise with children and adults. They supervise the teaching staff, and are available to parents by appointment. Lead teachers have degrees in early childhood education and experience as teachers of young children. Teachers I and II have special training as well as demonstrated competence with young children. They must have a high school diploma and most have graduated from vocational school programs or universities with degrees in early childhood. Our business director oversees the finances of both sites. Our staff includes two services coordinators who have billing and scheduling responsibilities. Our cooks prepare all food on site. CFC-P&G also has a clerk to support the staff.

16

(continues)

DIRECTOR'S RESOURCE 16-1
(continued)

Each staff person has on file three written references as well as a police record check, proof of a physical examination, and drug screening.

Continuing education is an important part of working at Children's for Children. Each staff person attends training in first aid, recognizing communicable diseases, recognizing and preventing child abuse, child development, and teaching methods. A required number of staff also have CPR training. We offer tuition reimbursement for those desiring to take college classes.

No medical personnel are directly on staff. However, physicians and nurses at Cincinnati Children's Hospital Medical Center are available as consultants.

17

(continues)

DIRECTOR'S RESOURCE 16-1
(continued)

Parent Involvement

We welcome parents to share their interests, talents and occupations with the classes. Our registration packet includes a "time and talents" survey for parents to complete. Parents may see their child's teacher to explore these opportunities.

Teachers meet with individual parents to review each child's progress throughout the year. Conferences may be scheduled at any time. Parents of our children receive daily written information regarding their child.

Parents may serve on the Center's Support Teams to help guarantee a setting designed to reflect the needs of today's families. Each team has smaller working groups focused on environmental rounds, staff appreciation and adult programs.

Rosters of names and telephone numbers of parents, custodians, or guardians of children attending the center are available. The rosters will not include the name and telephone numbers of any parent, custodian, or guardian who requests not to be included.

Social and educational events are held throughout the year to encourage interactions between staff and families.

18

(continues)

DIRECTOR'S RESOURCE 16-1

(continued)

If parents have concerns or need assistance with problems related to the child development center, they may discuss the issue, if applicable, with the staff involved. If they are not satisfied, they may discuss their concerns with the master teacher or site manager.

Parent surveys are completed regularly in order to measure satisfaction and to gain ideas for improvements.

Employees with concerns would follow the same procedure but also have available the Human Resources personnel.

19

(continues)

DIRECTOR'S RESOURCE 16-1
(continued)

Center Ratios and Group Sizes

We ask that parents with fluctuating schedules inform us in a timely manner. Schedules are due the Monday prior to the week of service. In order to operate smoothly, we appreciate cooperation in this regard. Our staff schedules will "go with the flow."

We are authorized to serve a licensed capacity of:

	CCHMC	P&G
Infants (3 months – 17 months)	26	48
Toddlers (18 months – 36 months)	32	65
Preschoolers (36 months & up)	53	75
School-age (must be 5 years old by start of the school year)	17	2

We maintain these child/adult ratios and class sizes:

Infants	4:1 licensed for groups no larger than 14
Toddlers	5:1 licensed for groups no larger than 15
Preschoolers	10:1 licensed for groups no larger than 15
School-agers	15:1 licensed for groups no larger than 20

20

(continues)

DIRECTOR'S RESOURCE 16-1
(continued)

Typical Daytime Schedule

Parents must always deliver the child directly to the teacher and sign in. At departure, the parent must inform staff that the child is leaving for the day and sign out.

Although each classroom's daily schedule varies, activities alternate between quiet and active, free play, and total group experiences. Daily lesson plans are posted in classrooms of the oldest groups of children. Infant schedules are at the baby's preference. An example of a daily schedule for older groups is:

Opening – 8:00	Arrival, warm greeting, play with parents and staff, free play
8:00 – 8:30	Wash hands, breakfast
8:30 – 8:45	Wash table space, brush teeth, transition to outdoors
8:45 – 9:30	Outdoor play*
9:30 – 9:50	Language or music activities in whole group
9:50 – 10:00	Transition to free play
10:00 – 11:15	Self-selection in all learning areas
11:15 – 11:30	Preparation for lunch, wash hands
11:30 – 12:15	Lunch in small groups
12:15 – 12:30	Wash hands, brush teeth, toileting
12:30 – 2:30	Soft music, back rubs, naptime

21

(continues)

DIRECTOR'S RESOURCE 16-1
(continued)

2:30 – 3:00	Toileting, wash hands, snack, some departures
3:00 – 3:45	Self-selected activities
3:45 – 4:15	Outdoor play*
4:15 – 4:45	Grouptime (songs, stories)
4:45 – 6:30	Free choice of activities or muscle room; transition to parent

Note: Attendance sheets are kept with the children throughout the day to assure that all children are accounted for.

*Outdoor Play

The center provides outdoor play each day in suitable weather for all children in attendance for four or more consecutive daylight hours.

22

(continues)

DIRECTOR'S RESOURCE 16-1
(continued)

What to Bring from Home

(Please check with classroom staff as well.) All items brought from home must be permanently labeled. Food and formula must be labeled <u>and</u> dated.

Infants:

- baby food
- prepared formula
- pacifiers
- favorite soft crib toy or crib mobile, if desired
- disposable diapers or cloth diapers with pail
- sweater or jacket
- blankets
- 1 or 2 changes of clothes
- security items
- photo of family
- a smile

Toddlers:

- pacifiers
- naptime toy
- blanket and pillow
- pillowcase
- disposable diapers or cloth diapers with pail
- 1 or 2 changes of clothes
- sweater or jacket
- security items
- toothbrush

23

(continues)

DIRECTOR'S RESOURCE 16-1
(continued)

	toothpaste
	comb or pick
	photo of family
	bike helmet
	a smile
Preschoolers and Kindergartners:	naptime toy
	blanket and pillow
	pillowcase
	1 change of clothes
	jacket or sweater
	toothbrush
	toothpaste
	comb or pick
	security items
	photo of family
	bike helmet
	a smile

Note: Some classrooms require a blank video, one-time use camera or a roll of film to document your child's growth. Please ask the classroom staff for their preference.

24

(continues)

DIRECTOR'S RESOURCE 16-1
(continued)

What Not to Bring from Home
(please check with classroom staff as well)

Toys of violence
Candy
Chewing gum
"jellies", sandals
Crib bumper pads
Anything unlabeled
A frown

CFC-P&G is a "nut-free" environment. Please, no foods
with nuts or nut by-products at CFC-P&G.

25

(continues)

DIRECTOR'S RESOURCE 16-1
(continued)

The Infant Program

Our program for infants sets its pace around the needs and unique differences of each child. Our infants have a "primary" caregiver who centers her day around the schedules of those for whom she cares. This care, while meeting basic needs for food, diapering and adequate rest, goes beyond that. This keen observer plans and enhances the interactions and activities the infant's behavior is identifying.

Routines are the curriculum for an infant's day. Every moment of a young child's day offers opportunities for learning. The skilled educator catches these moments and helps each baby establish trust, discover and feel good about herself, tackle a motor task, realize the power of language, and begin to understand this strange new world from many angles. This is accomplished as each teacher keys into the verbal and non-verbal messages the child is sending.

An infant teacher, with the education and understanding of early childhood development, knows that rich verbal interactions with children help them to understand that language is a tool for identifying and expressing their needs, ideas, and feelings in later life. Each of our caregivers accepts that infants, developmentally, need to explore the world through mouthing and touching and allows for this, viewing it as

26

(continues)

DIRECTOR'S RESOURCE 16-1
(continued)

a valuable learning experience. This teacher is alert to the need for proper sanitation measures and follows them consistently and conscientiously. As the trained adult looks at the environment, she views it from the child's eye and creates a cozy, inviting, and stimulating place for children. She understands that what is made available for children to use depends on who the children are and what their developmental needs. This might necessitate frequent rotation of toys to "keep up" with a growing child, or prompt a teacher to make a toy that focuses on the child's interest or need.

Infants should view the world from many angles and are allowed that experience. This includes crawling, being carried, stroller rides, outdoor play, climbing, and rocking so that various perspectives are gained. Diaper changing, feeding, and other routines are viewed as vital times for communication, self discovery, and socializing. They are encouraged to master feeding themselves despite the messiness that accompanies this activity. While being supportive of infants in their quest for competence, our teachers look to the parents as the best resource in working with their children. Early childhood educators view themselves as professionals with children and with parents.

Special health and cleaning practices are used in our infant rooms. All toys are removed from the play space

27

(continues)

DIRECTOR'S RESOURCE 16-1
(continued)

once mouthed, then sterilized. All shelves and climbing equipment are cleaned with a bleach solution daily. Staff wash their hands before and upon entering the room and during any diapering, nose-wiping or food service. Infant formula and partially eaten baby food (jars) must be removed each day by the parent. Any adult or child visiting an infant room should use shoe covers to limit any "street dirt" to the playspace.

The Toddler Program

In providing a program for toddlers, our teachers understand that these children learn with their whole bodies. They learn more by doing than by being told. Toddlers discover their world on a physical level, so it is expected that they will prefer walking, climbing, carrying objects, dumping, or dropping objects over sitting, picking up toys, or playing only in a designated space. These large muscle activities are the legitimate activity of toddlerhood.

In planning for toddlers, our educators are prepared to be flexible and spontaneous. Because they are active explorers, toddlers are eager to try new things and use materials in different ways. Our understanding teachers will go with the cues of the child and view that as learning-extending it even if it isn't

28

(continues)

DIRECTOR'S RESOURCE 16-1
(continued)

part of the day's planned curriculum. Toddlers are working on becoming autonomous. The educated teacher respects this and allows opportunities for the child to be responsible and to make choices. This teacher also understands why certain behaviors must be limited, and sets limits that are fair and consistent. Expectations for behaviors are developmentally appropriate and allow the child to be challenged yet to feel support from the teacher. Consequently, frustration is kept to a minimum and the child's dignity and self-concept remain intact.

Our teachers, with patience, warmth and respect, redirect toddlers to help guide them toward controlling their impulses and behaviors. The teacher draws more attention to a child's appropriate behavior than to the inappropriate because she understands that toddlers will act in the way that draws the most attention. Constant testing and expressions of opposition are viewed as the child's development of a healthy sense of self. The teacher accepts this and offers positively worded directions to avoid getting into power struggles. The teacher views herself as a model for how she wants the children to develop. She does this in her verbal interactions because she understands that

29

(continues)

DIRECTOR'S RESOURCE 16-1
(continued)

toddlers lack the skills to cope with frustrating situations and might act out in a physical way without her guidance.

The teacher recognizes that routine times are important moments to help children learn about themselves and others. An early childhood educator views play as valuable and facilitates this so that children stay interested and move from simple to more complex aspects of their play. The classroom includes materials for children to engage in imaginative play, appropriate art experiences for creative exploration, various manipulatives to develop cognitive and physical skills, as well as building blocks, music, and books. The environment allows for the children to choose activities. The teacher respects the child's need for ample time to use and reuse activities because repeated experiences foster competence. The setting is stimulating and inviting. It offers comfortable spaces for privacy and for interacting in small groups. Children's art is displayed proudly and respected for what it is. The little ones are encouraged by a knowing adult to care for the belongings and the environment in ways they can handle. The teacher creates and adapts the environment and activities to meet the children's changing needs from day to day.

30

(continues)

DIRECTOR'S RESOURCE 16-1
(continued)

The Preschool Program

Preschoolers are usually most responsive to activities in which they are involved in a "hands-on" manner. Our teachers accept that and design their classroom spaces with "learning centers" at which children can freely choose whether to participate or not and for how long. Our quality staff rotate and add materials frequently to maintain and extend the child's interest. Often our teachers create their own games and materials if commercial ones do not offer the challenge needed or do not reflect the interests of the children. Young children seem to learn best when trained teachers build on the interests and abilities of the children. This reflects the currently recognized theory that endorses non-pressured, child-centered activities guided by an adult with a solid child development base and strong problem-solving skills. Open-ended questioning and activities are offered so that children develop creative thinking skills. In such a program, parents can truly become partners with the professional staff. Information or discoveries about the child's development are mutually shared, resulting in a program tailored to the individual child.

31

(continues)

DIRECTOR'S RESOURCE 16-1
(continued)

The preschool curriculum includes activities centering on communication, science, math, social studies, music, art, large and small motor development. An enrichment program, which includes field trips and visitors, is offered. Dramatic play opportunities reinforce learning of practical life experiences.

LANGUAGE/COMMUNICATION – The whole language approach is our model. This is one in which children are exposed to print and language that is integrated into each activity center. Each classroom offers many opportunities for literacy awareness. Books are readily available for children's use. Thomas Gordon's communication system is used by staff to facilitate problem-solving and language building.

SCIENCE – Hands-on activities include using simple machines, sensory table play, plant and animal life. Nutrition awareness and weekly cooking activities are offered. Open-ended questions by the trained teacher help the children learn how to question… how to be thinkers.

MATH – Activities include concepts of introductory geometry, seriation, classification, sets, number, quantity, length, weight, use of simple graphs, simple addition/subtraction (more/less), and money.

32

(continues)

DIRECTOR'S RESOURCE 16-1
(continued)

SOCIAL STUDIES – Learning about the "world around us" is the focus of this curriculum area. Field trips and studies of occupations are included. Discovering new customs, traditions, music and foods from many cultures heightens the children's appreciation of others.

MUSIC – Exposure to and involvement with simple rhythm instruments is part of our music program. Rhythms are also "practiced" by the learning of songs and finger plays. Guest musicians visit the children to give exposure to a variety of sounds and diverse musical styles. Tone, volume, and pitch awareness is part of the music curriculum.

ART – Exploratory, sensory art activities help the child experience a variety of media. Collages and creating mobiles are offered. Paints, chalk, pencils, paper, markers, glue, paste, and play dough are all available in a "free choice" activity center for the children to use as they wish.

LARGE MOTOR – Movement activities including free dance, parachute handling, climbing, crawling, running and balancing are just a small part of the large motor program.

33

(continues)

DIRECTOR'S RESOURCE 16-1
(continued)

SMALL MOTOR – From the handling of simple tools to completing pegboards, children are continually offered opportunities to develop their smaller muscles, an important prerequisite for writing.

FIELD TRIPS – Trips are taken approximately three times a year to nearby places such as the Art Museum, the Zoo and the Museum of Natural History. Field trip fees may be requested. Parents may ask the manager about field trip fee assistance. Our desire is to have all children participate in trips. Periodic walks to Levine Park, adjacent to the Medical College, are taken by the children at CFC-CCHMC. Occasional walks to the Civic Garden Center, at Reading and Oak, are taken by the CFC-P&G preschoolers.

VISITORS – Classroom visitors might describe a career or hobby. They could include SPCA and zoo representatives with animals. Visiting parents describe hobbies, occupations or cultural practices.

DRAMATIC PLAY – From "playing house" to being a cashier in a pretend grocery store to repairing cardboard automobiles in a child-sized garage, the children are able to practice roles that productive adults hold.

34

(continues)

DIRECTOR'S RESOURCE 16-1
(continued)

Kindergarten Program at CFC-CCHMC

The kindergartners are actively learning about our world and community. Our teachers place strong emphasis on cooperation, problem-solving and the joy of literature. The children are participants in the learning process as they are encouraged to work collaboratively to explore areas of interest. The teachers create a supportive, accepting climate and value both effort and achievement. The small group size allows for much hands-on exploration and discovery and individual teaching and learning.

Our kindergarten room looks similar to a preschool space, but the schedule is a bit more structured. Children work frequently in small groups and focus on individual tasks. Many of the materials are open-ended, allowing brain-storming and creativity to happen. Children practice turn-taking, following directions and respecting the rights and thoughts of others.

The kindergarten program is literature based, with many opportunities for children to see, hear, and eventually read, quality children's literature. Creativity is shown through writing experiences and exploration of rich art materials. Math and science are learned

35

(continues)

DIRECTOR'S RESOURCE 16-1
(continued)

through a variety of activities including experimentation, cooking, graphing and patterning. Field trips are taken regularly and include the library and the Children's Theatre. There is a $10 monthly fee to cover the cost of these activities.

The kindergarten teacher and assistant are certified by the State of Ohio.

Transitions

Transitions to a new group can be very exciting and sometimes a little scary. We strive to make every move into a new classroom a pleasant, "seamless" experience for all. We always allow for a transitional period so that the child and parents gain gradual exposure to the room and its practices. This also allows the "new" teachers to learn about the child, family and their customs. Usually a transitional period lasts two weeks. Each day the child's visits become a bit longer, gradually working up to a full day. A written transition plan is provided prior to the visits.

36

(continues)

DIRECTOR'S RESOURCE 16-1
(continued)

Field Trips and Walks

Preschool and kindergarten children are well prepared for trips through relevant classroom activities and conversations. Parents must sign a permission slip for each trip. This form includes the child's name, date and destination of trip, as well as parent signature and date signed. The ratios maintained on trips vary according to the means of travel, destination and the "personality" of the class. For example, a ratio of 6:1 may be determined for a trip to the firehouse, but 1:1 may be more appropriate for the heliport. Parents are always informed of ratios on the permission form.

A lack of adequate staff and chaperones to meet the stated ratio will cause a trip to be postponed.

Ratios for walking trips also differ from those within the building. Infants and young toddlers at CFC-CCHMC limit their walks to the hospital grounds, avoiding the Erkenbrecher/Burnet corner. The older toddlers, preschoolers and kindergartners at CFC-CCHMC traverse the CCHMC grounds and, on occasion, walk to Levine Park. Our preschoolers at CFC-P&G occasionally walk to the Civic Garden Center at Reading Road and Oak. Kindergartners and preschoolers who take such walks meet the ratio of 6:1. At CFC-P&G, stroller rides occur only on the sidewalks around the parking lot.

37

(continues)

DIRECTOR'S RESOURCE 16-1
(continued)

The ratios for infant/toddler outings are:

Infants in strollers: 3:1
Infants on foot: 2:1
Toddlers in strollers: 4:1
Toddlers on foot: 3:1

A minimum of two staff members are part of each field trip or walk.

Transportation for most trips is provided by public transit or yellow bus. A staff person trained in first aid goes on all trips, taking a complete first aid kit and emergency permission forms for each child. Children wear tags that include the center's name, address, and phone number. Attendance sheets accompany each outing, including brief stroller rides or trips to the playgrounds.

No trips to waterparks or pools are taken.

38

(continues)

DIRECTOR'S RESOURCE 16-1
(continued)

Health

Our center operates for well children and staff only. Children who are mildly ill (e.g. minor cold symptoms) may remain at the center only with the manager's approval. Children should be fully able to participate in all activities, including outdoor play. Parents should provide appropriate changes of clothing so children do not become either chilled or overheated. Snow pants and boots are needed for snowy days. Swimsuits are needed for toasty days. Light sweaters or jackets should be made available, as well. "Jellies", "flip-flops", and sandals are not appropriate for wear at school. Sun screens or diaper lotions may be applied by staff with the written permission of the parent on a center-supplied form.

Children with symptoms of communicable disease remain with a staff member until the parent or designated family representative arrives for the child. We take temperatures two times to assure accuracy. We make every effort, including cell phones and e-mail, to reach the parents when a child is ill, but after 30 minutes, we will attempt to reach the emergency contacts indicated by the parents.

We will not serve children with:

- vomiting two or more times within a 24-hour period
- vomiting one time with another symptom

39

(continues)

DIRECTOR'S RESOURCE 16-1
(continued)

a fever between 100°F - 100.9°F, axillary, if combined with another symptom

- a fever of 101°F or higher, axillary
- unusual spots, skin rashes or untreated, infected skin patches
- diarrhea two or more times in a day
- evidence of head lice, scabies or other parasites
- severe coughing causing red or blue coloration on face
- severe coughing that causes a "whooping" sound
- rapid or difficult breathing
- yellowish skin or eyes
- redness of eye with obvious discharge, matted eyelashes, burning or itching of the eye
- unusually dark urine and/or gray or white stool
- sore throat or difficulty swallowing
- stiff neck with elevated temperature
- excessive fatigue
- an infant or toddler may not remain with an open sore in or around the mouth

Children who show these signs are separated from other children, supervised, provided a cot and made comfortable until their parent or family representative arrives to take them home.

40

(continues)

DIRECTOR'S RESOURCE 16-1
(continued)

Children may be readmitted:

- with a physician's statement that the child is free from communicable disease and that returning poses no risk to the child or others.

  OR

- if visibly free from communicable disease, fever-free without benefit of fever reducing medications for 24 hours, and free of vomiting/diarrhea for 24 hours while on a normal diet.

The center retains the right to continue to exclude a child despite a physician's statement if that statement contradicts the center's policies or does not seem to be in the child's best interest. When any youngster in a child's class has a communicable disease, parents are informed in writing within 24 hours.

It is our policy that staff with symptoms of illness remain away from the center.

Our staff members have special training in recognizing communicable diseases. The staff rely on their training, as well as the disease chart posted in the first floor lobby (CFC-CCHMC) and in the resource room (CFC-P&G), to determine indicated diseases. We follow strict handwashing and disinfection procedures. The disinfection policy is posted in each classroom and reviewed with any adult working in that space.

41

(continues)

DIRECTOR'S RESOURCE 16-1
(continued)

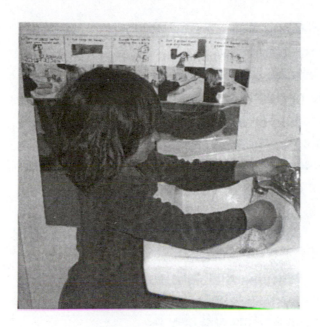

Medication is given only if parents sign a center-supplied permission form. Prescription medication must have a prescription label with the child's name and date on it. Medical samples and over-the-counter oral medicines MUST have a written note from the doctor as well as a parent-signed form. Permission forms must be renewed every six months. We may only administer oral, non-prescription medication for three consecutive days. Topical, non-prescription products may only be used for fourteen consecutive days for treatment (not preventative) purposes. Medication is administered by the lead teacher or her designee. Such administering is documented. Lip balm, sun screen and diaper rash

42

(continues)

medications do not require a physician's signature, but do need a parent's written instruction and permission. Such items must be labeled, given to a teacher, and taken home once the period of use has ended. Medications are kept in locked cabinets or the room's refrigerator. No medications are to be stored in cubbies or backpacks. No child will "help" to administer medication, inhalers or epi-pens to himself or others.

If a child's diet must be modified for health reasons, a physician's written explanation is required. If a child's diet is modified for cultural or religious reasons, the parent is asked to put the request in writing and may be asked to provide supplemental foods.

Children of all ages go outdoors for fresh air daily unless the temperature (or temperature combined with wind chill) is 20 degrees or below. We do not take the children outdoors when the temperature exceeds 90 degrees. Children must be prepared to be dressed for outdoor experiences. On days of weather extremes, all children have opportunities to use the large muscle room.

In warm weather, sprinklers and wading pools are used. Pools are emptied immediately after use and sanitized before the next use. A staff member remains at the side of pools. Parents of infants and toddlers must sign a permission form for their child to use a wading pool.

43

(continues)

DIRECTOR'S RESOURCE 16-1
(continued)

Nutrition

We provide nutritionally balanced snacks, meals (breakfast and lunch), and cooking activities. Menus are posted in each classroom and copies are made available to parents on Friday afternoons for the coming week. We encourage the children to have a "hello" bite, that is – to try a taste of everything. We limit sugars and prefer birthday celebrations sent by parents to be fruits, yogurt-sicles or juice-sicles, or other nutritious alternatives to cake and ice cream. CFC-P&G is a "nut free" environment and never serves nuts or their by-products.

The center supplies whole milk for children 24 months and younger. Children 25 months of age and older are served 2% milk. Parents may provide breast milk or formula. CFC-CCHMC families are offered formula as part of the USDA program for non-profit centers.

We provide approximately two-thirds of the child's daily nutritional needs. Seconds are offered to the children. Adults eat seated with the children, except the infant staff. Meal times are relaxed times, rich with conversation and fellowship. Parents may join us for lunch if the kitchen is aware by 9:30 am. Cost of lunch is $3 per adult except staff, for whom meals are provided.

Parents are sometimes asked to donate snack items.

44

(continues)

Safety

We ask that parents closely supervise their children in parking lots and garages, lobbies and elsewhere on the premises. It is recommended that as children exit from cars, they be offered a hand to hold. Sticking together seems to be a reasonable safety request. When going to the classroom, the family is asked to stay together. Sending the child on the elevator while the adult uses the stairs (or vice versa) is a safety concern. Likewise, older children should accompany parents to infant rooms and not be left in a lobby. So much could happen in a moment or two, and we request your cooperation.

Children must be signed in and out each day in the front lobby. This is extremely important since this list is used to check attendance during emergency drills or events. Children are released only to persons for whom the staff has written permission from the parents. Parents should provide us with the birth date or special identifying word of any person designated to pick up a child. We ask to see photo identification, which also indicates date of birth. We may release children to either parent unless there is a restraining order or custody arrangement of which we have a copy.

No child is ever left alone or unsupervised. At arrival, parents are expected to help the child settle into play, which may require ten minutes or so per child. Parents

45

(continues)

DIRECTOR'S RESOURCE 16-1
(continued)

complete a portion of the daily report form before departing for work or training. Parents are permitted access to all parts of the center at all times, including nap times and pre-admission tours or observations. Parents may request controlled key cards for building entry from the services coordinator.

Incident or injury reports are completed whenever first aid is given, there is a blow to the head, whenever 911 or CCHMC's internal code alert (emergency medical services) is contacted or any unexpected event has occurred which jeopardizes the safety of others.

Admittance to the building is by a buzzer/doorbell or key card. All doors are locked at all times for security. Doors are easily opened from the inside in case of emergency. Parents have keys (access cards) for immediate entry through the front door or, at CCHMC, via Building E or the South Garage. P&G access cards operate the front door. Parents and staff members are to be aware of others at the door who may "slip in" behind them. Parents and employees are asked to never admit an unfamiliar person.

There is always immediate access to a phone at the centers. Telephones are located in the entries, all offices, and in most classrooms.

46

(continues)

DIRECTOR'S RESOURCE 16-1

(continued)

Aerosol sprays are not used when children are present. Smoking is not permitted in the building or on the playgrounds.

Housekeeping is provided by the Marriott's Environmental Services department. Most cleaning is done after 6 p.m.

CCHMC plant engineers assume responsibility for maintaining the equipment and facility when feasible. Otherwise, specialists are called in for certain repairs.

The center is monitored indoors and outdoors by camera surveillance.

All center employees are required under Section 2151.421 of the Ohio Revised Code to report any suspicion of child abuse or child neglect. All teaching staff have training to recognize signs of neglect and abuse. We will report any suspected child abuse or neglect to the appropriate authorities. Policies are in place to suspend for investigation a staff member suspected of abuse, in the unlikely event that it occurs.

47

(continues)

DIRECTOR'S RESOURCE 16-1
(continued)

Emergencies

Monthly emergency drills are held at varying times and are documented by the Protective Services Department. In addition, documentation is posted in lobbies. The following procedures are rehearsed:

FIRE: Staff members remain calm and reassure the children. The person noting the fire sounds the alarm and calls the fire department, 6-8877. Staff members escort second floor children to the nearest safe exit and congregate at their assigned locations. First floor children walk to their assigned area. The infants are placed in a single crib and wheeled outdoors with the other first floor children. The staff members take attendance forms which are compared to the daily sign-in sheets. The manager and/or services coordinator checks classrooms, bathrooms, kitchen, playground, and all other areas. Plans for evacuation are posted in each classroom. Elevators are not used for evacuation.

WEATHER ALERT: CCHMC's Protective Services Department alerts us to dangerous weather concerns. In addition, each center owns a weather monitor. In the case of a weather emergency (eg, a tornado warning), the staff members remain calm and reassure children. Children are escorted to the inner hallways of the first floor, as far as possible from potential flying window glass. Staff may bring books or

48

(continues)

DIRECTOR'S RESOURCE 16-1
(continued)

manipulative games for the children. Parents who arrive to take their children are strongly encouraged to remain at the center until the weather alert has been lifted. Elevators are not used during weather alerts.

ACCIDENT: The first aid boxes are kept in the offices of both services coordinators as well as in the preschool wing. Emergency numbers for children are filed in the first floor file cabinets; for staff and volunteers in the first floor business office. All staff have first aid training and many have CPR training. In a serious emergency, the life squad, CCHMC code alert team and/or hospital Protective Services personnel are notified, as well as the relevant parents and center administrator. When going for treatment, the child's complete file and injury report form (if applicable) is taken. This contains a summary of the child's medical history as well as medical emergency permission forms. Children not requiring treatment or observation remain supervised and reassured that their friend is being well cared for. Any incident or accident, that occurs on the center premises, including the emergency transportation of a child, will be reported to the parent in written form. A copy of the form is forwarded to ODJFS.

Emergency closings occur when weather is so severe that the Mayor issues a travel ban, if there are problems with our physical plant, or if the Board of Health orders closure for disease control or other reasons. Each of these instances is highly unlikely. CFC-CCHMC

49

(continues)

DIRECTOR'S RESOURCE 16-1
(continued)

staff members are considered "essential" to the work of the medical center and are to report to work even in inclement weather. Closures at CFC-P&G are placed on the center's phone line (513) 636-2640; at CFC-CCHMC, call (513) 635-4999. The center has policies for managing emergency preparedness due to national disasters, acts of terrorism, explosion or entrapment in areas of the facilities. These are available on request.

Emergency Transportation

Each center obtains written emergency transportation authorization from each parent or guardian before the child begins attending the program. We will not accept any children whose parents or guardians refuse to grant permission for emergency transportation.

If a child is seriously injured and needs treatment immediately, the center will call the life squad or CCHMC code alert team, and/or hospital Protective Services personnel for assistance transporting the child. A staff member will go the hospital with the child and will take the child's records. The parents will be called to meet the child and staff person at the hospital. The staff person remains at the hospital until the parent arrives or longer if possible.

50

(continues)

"Occasional" Child Care

The center will offer "occasional" services to children 18 months up to kindergarten age, whose regular care arrangements have fallen through. Examples might be a child care facility having plumbing concerns, or a home care provider being ill. Parents choosing to participate must complete all the required forms, including a medical form, prior to using the service. Parents must confirm availability with the center before bringing their child. Parents of currently enrolled children will be expected to either arrive at the center by 9:30 am or contact the center by that time for a planned later arrival. If they do not, their child's space may be made available to a child for occasional service. No refunds are provided to the current family for non-attendance, whether the center is informed or not. A full daily rate is assessed for occasional service regardless of the number of hours utilized. Fees for occasional care are due on the day of service, payable directly to the center. This service has an annual non-refundable fee at CFC-P&G. This service has a one-time non-refundable registration fee at CFC-CCHMC. The intent of this policy is to allow the center, when openings permit, to also provide support to other corporate families in emergency situations. Complete policies are available upon request.

51

(continues)

DIRECTOR'S RESOURCE 16-1
(continued)

Financial Information

Fees are determined by a group of childcare representatives. The rates are based on those charged by programs of similar quality and do not meet the actual cost of care that we provide. Our corporate sponsors generously subsidize our programs.

We offer full-day service for children from 12 weeks of age through preschool age with kindergarten age at the CCHMC center. Tuition fees are collected by automatic payroll deduction. Fees vary according to the ratio of the group the child enjoys.

Part-time care (Tuesday, Wednesday and Thursday) is available for toddlers and preschoolers at the P&G location only. A non-refundable fee is due at the time of registration, and annually thereafter, for all "occasional" services and for all families at the P&G site.

No sick or vacation allowances are made. No reimbursements are given for unforeseen center closings or for center holidays.

There are miscellaneous fees for field trips, speech screening, insufficient funds, additional meals, late tuition and late pick-up. The Kindergarten program also has a shirt fee.

52

(continues)

DIRECTOR'S RESOURCE 16-1
(continued)

Parents receive complete financial policies prior to enrollment. The Business Director and Services Coordinator II are available to clarify policies of a financial nature.

Children who have not departed the building by 6:30pm are considered "late pick-ups". After closing hours, if a child has not been picked up, staff members make all possible efforts to reach the parents and secondary contacts. Families pay $2.00 per minute; $1 per minute paid directly to each inconvenienced staff member. Payment is due the night of late pick-up or the next business day.

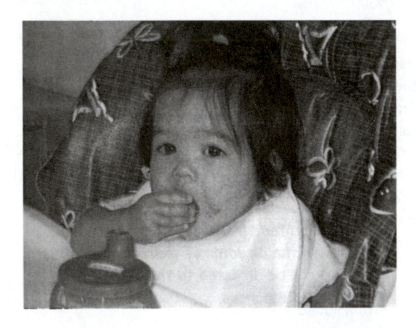

53

(continues)

DIRECTOR'S RESOURCE 16-1
(continued)

Termination of Services

If a family is enrolled and then leaves the employment of either CCHMC or P&G, ninety days of child care service may be used after the date of termination. Assistance in locating new child care may be obtained by calling 4C, (513) 221-0033.

A parent's right to withdraw a child from Children's for Children is respected. Each center has specific advance written notice requirements. Information regarding termination is included as part of each center's financial policy.

There may be situations in which termination of service to an individual child or family is initiated by center management. Although each circumstance is unique, efforts will be made by the parties concerned to improve the situation prior to a termination decision. Should termination become necessary, a two-week written notice is generally provided. Parents disagreeing with the decision can address their concerns with the center's manager. If not satisfied, they may meet with the director of child care services. Further concerns can be directed to the CCHMC Vice President of Human Resources.

54

(continues)

DIRECTOR'S RESOURCE 16-1
(continued)

Closing Statement

We hope that visitors and participants will sense that we have created a home away from home for our children. We appreciate feedback from any visitor or family member. We are pleased to elaborate on any facets of our program. Tours are available by prior arrangement to small groups of persons wishing to see quality programming for children.

Thank you for your continuing interest in quality child care in our community.

Important Phone Numbers, area code 513:

	CFC-CCHMC	CFC-P&G
Main Number	636-4999	636-2640
Manager	636-4056	636-0429
Director	636-4055	636-4055
Business Director	636-2645	636-2645
Scheduling Office	636-4065	636-2641
Business Office	636-1854	636-2642

55

Reprinted with permission from Children's for Children, Cincinnati, OH.

REFERENCES

Decker, C. A., & Decker, J. R. (2005). *Planning and administering early childhood programs* (8th ed.). Upper Saddle River, NJ: Prentice Hall.

Galinsky, E. (1984, July). How to work with working parents. *Child Care Information Exchange.*

Gordon, A. M., & Browne, K. W. (2004). *Beginnings and beyond: Foundations in early education* (6th ed.). Clifton Park, NY: Thomson Delmar Learning.

Greenman, J. (1998). Plans for childhood includes parents too. In R. Neugebauer & B. Neugebauer (Eds.), *The art of leadership: Managing early childhood organizations.* Redmond, WA: Child Care Information Exchange.

Hewes, D., & Hartman, B. (1988). *Early childhood education: A workbook for administrators.* San Francisco: R&E Research Associates.

Hildebrand, V., & Hearron, P. F. (2002). *Management of child development centers* (4th ed.). Colmbus, OH: Merrill.

Jones, R. (1996). Producing a school newsletter parents will read. *Child Care Information Exchange: The Director's Magazine*, pp. 91–93.

Phipps, P. A. (1998). Working with angry parents: Taking the customer service approach. In R. Neugebauer & B. Neugebauer (Eds.), *The art of leadership: Managing early childhood organizations.* Redmond, WA: Child Care Information Exchange.

Additional resources for this chapter can be found on the Online Companion™ at http://www.earlychilded.delmar.com. This supplemental material includes relevant Web links, Web activities, and case studies that apply the concepts presented in this chapter. In addition, the Working Papers and Director's Resources are available for download, allowing you to complete Class Exercises and Class Assignments electronically.

APPENDIX A

ABC School Supply
2920 Old Tree Drive
Lancaster, PA 17603
(800) 669-4222
http://www.abcschoolsupply.com

African American Images
1909 West 95th Street
Chicago, IL 60643-1105
(773) 445-0322

The Angeles Group
9 Capper Drive
Daily Industrial Park
Pacific, MO 63069
(800) 346-6313
http://www.angeles-group.com

Atari, Inc.
417 Fifth Avenue
New York, NY 10016
(212) 726-6500
http://www.atari.com/atarikids

Becker's School Supplies
12300 McNulty Road
Philadelphia, PA 19154
(800) 523-1490
http://www.shopbecker.com

Broderbund Software, Inc.
Riverdeep, Inc.
100 Pine Street, Suite 1900
San Francisco, CA 94111
http://www.broderbund.com

Busy Kids, LLC
937 139th Avenue NW
Andover, MN 55304-4124
(800) 344-7155

Childcraft Education Corp.
P.O. Box 3239
Lancaster, PA 17603
(800) 631-5652

Childforms
110 Charleston Drive, Suite 106
Mooresville, NC 28117
(800) 447-3349
http://www.childforms.com

Child Life Play Specialties, Inc.
55 Whitney Street
Holliston, MA 01746
(800) 467-9464

Child Plus Software
1117 Perimeter Center West
Suite W 300
Atlanta, GA 30338
(404) 252-6674
http://www.childplus.com

Children's Press
Grolier Publishing Co.
Sherman Turnpike, P.O. Box 1796
Danbury, CT 06816
(800) 621-1115
http://www.scholasticlibrary.com

Clarion Books
Division of Houghton-Mifflin
222 Berkeley Street
Boston, MA 02116
(617) 351-5000

Community Playthings
359 Gibson Hill Road
Chester, NY 10918
(800) 777-4244
http://www.communityplaythings.com

Creative Educational Materials
2600 Frenbrook Lane, Suite 100
Plymouth, MN 55447
(800) 328-3360
http://www.triarcoarts.com

Custom Recreation Products
1821 Garden Road
Pearland, TX 77581
(800) 597-4896
http://www.customplayground.com

Developmental Learning Materials (DLM)
P.O. Box 4000
One DLM Park
Allen, TX 75002
(800) 537-5030

Dick Blick Art Materials
P.O. Box 1267
Galesburg, IL 61402-1267
(800) 723-2787
http://www.dickblick.com

Didax Educational Resources, Inc.
395 Main Street
Rowley, MA 01969
(800) 458-0024
http://www.didaxinc.com

The Discovery Channel
P.O. Box 788
Florence, KY 41022-0788
(800) 627-9399
http://www.discovery.com

Don Johnston Inc.
26799 West Commerce Drive
Volo, IL 60073
(800) 999-4660
http://www.donjohnston.com

Edmark Corp.
Riverdeep, Inc.
100 Pine Street, Suite 1900
San Francisco, CA 94111
(800) 542-4222

Environments, Inc.
P.O. Box 1348
Beaufort, SC 29901
(800) 342-4453
http://www.eichild.com

Flagship Carpets
1546 Progress Road
P.O. Box 507
Ellijay, GA 30540
(800) 848-4055
http://www.flagshipcarpets.com

John R. Green
411 West 6th Street
Covington, KY 41011
(800) 354-9737
http://www.johnrgreenco.com

GroundScape Technologies
4595 Van Epps Road
Brooklyn Heights, OH 44131
(877) 922-7529
http://www.groundscapekids.com

Growing Tree Toys
202 South Allen Street
State College, PA 16801
(800) 993-8697
http://www.growingtreetoys.com

Gryphon House, Inc.
P.O. Box 207
10726 Tucker Street
Beltsville, MD 20705-0207
(800) 638-0928
http://www.gryphonhouse.com

Harcourt School Publishers
6277 Sea Harbor Drive
Orlando, FL 32887
(800) 225-5425
http://www.harcourt.com

Harper Collins Children's Books
10 East 53rd Street
New York, NY 10022-5299
(212) 207-7000
http://www.harpercollins.com

Holcomb's Educational Materials
P.O. Box 94636
Cleveland, OH 44101
216-341-3000 Ohio
(800) 362-9907
(800) 321-2543
http://www.holcombs.com

Houghton-Mifflin Publishers
222 Berkeley Street
Boston, MA 02116
(617) 351-5000
http://www.hmco.com

Insect Lore
Box 1535
Shafter, CA 93263
(800) 548-3284
http://www.insectlore.com

International Playthings Inc.
75D Lackawanna Avenue
Parsippany, NJ 07054
(800) 445-8347
http://www.intplay.com

Johnson & Johnson Consumer Products, Inc.
Johnson & Johnson Place
New Brunswick, NJ 08933
(800) 526-3967
http://www.jnj.com

Jonti-Craft, Inc.
P.O. Box 30
171 Highway 68
Wabasso, MN 56293
(800) 543-4149
http://www.jonti-craft.com

Kaplan School Supply Corp.
P.O. Box 609
Lewisville, NC 27023
(800) 334-2014
http://www.kaplanco.com

Lakeshore Learning Materials
2695 East Dominguez Street
P.O. Box 6261
Carson, CA 90810
(800) 421-5354
http://www.lakeshorelearning.com

Landscape Structures Inc.
601 7th Street South
P.O. Box 198
Delano, MN 55328-0198
http://www.playlsi.com

Learning Resources, Inc.
380 North Fairway Drive
Vernon Hills, Illinois 60061
(800) 333-8281
http://www.learningresources.com

Lego Education
P.O. Box 1707
Pittsburg, KS 66762-1707
(800) 362-4308
http://www.legoeducation.com

Little, Brown & Company
Time and Life Building
1271 Avenue of the Americas
New York, NY 10020
(800) 343-9204
http://www.thebookmark.com

The Little Tikes Co.
2180 Barlow Road
Hudson, OH 44236-9984
(800) 321-0183
http://www.littletikes.com

Micro Revisions, Inc.
5301 Hollister, Suite 170
Houston, TX 77040
(713) 690-6676

Mindscape (UK) Limited
Gainsborough House
28-32 High Street
Crawley
RH10 1BW
http://www.mindscape.com

Mulberry Hill Press, Inc.
2710 South Washington Street
Englewood, CO 80110
(303) 781-8974
(800) 294-4714
http://www.mulberryhillpress.com

Music For Little People
P.O. Box 1460
Redway, CA 95560-1460
(800) 346-4445
http://www.mflp.com

Music Together LLC
66 Witherspoon Street
Princeton, NJ 05842
(800) 728-2692
http://www.musictogether.com

New Horizons
P.O. Box 863
Lake Forest, IL 60045
info@newhorizons.org
http://www.newhorizons.org

Penguin USA (Lodester Books)
375 Hudson Street
New York, NY 10014-3657
(212) 366-2000
http://www.penguingroup.com

Picture Book Studio/Simon & Schuster
12310 Avenue of the Americas
New York, NY 10020
http://www.simonsays.com

Playtime Equipment and School Supply, Inc.
5310 North 99th Street, Suite 2
Omaha, NE 68134
(800) 28–TEACH

Private Advantage Center
Management Software for Macintosh Computer
Mt. Taylor Programs
716 College Avenue, Suite B
Santa Rosa, CA 95404
(800) 238-7015
http://www.privateadv.com

PRO-ED, Inc.
8700 Shoal Creek Boulevard
Austin, TX 78757
(800) 897-3202
http://www.proedinc.com

Redleaf Press
10 Yorkton CR. Court
St. Paul, MN 55117
(800) 423-8309
http://www.redleafpress.org

Rhythm Band Instruments, Inc.
P.O. Box 126
Fort Worth, TX 76101
(800) 424-4724
http://www.rhythmband.com

SofterWare, Inc.
540 Pennsylvania Avenue, Suite 200
Fort Washington, PA 19034
(215) 628-0400
(800) 220-4111
http://www.softerware.com

Sunburst Technology
1550 Executive Drive
Elgin, IL 60123-9979
(800) 321-7511
http://www.sunburst.com

Teachers College Press
P.O. Box 20
Williston, VT 05495
(800) 575-6566
http://www.teacherscollegepress.com

Terrapin Software
955 Massachusetts Avenue
Cambridge, MA 02139-3233
(800) 774-LOGO
http://www.terrapinlogo.com

Things From Bell, Inc.
S+S Worldwide
P.O. Box 513
Colchester, CT 06415
(800) 543-1458
http://www.ssww.com

Thomson Delmar Learning
Executive Woods
5 Maxwell Drive
Clifton Park, NY 12065
(518) 348-2300
http://www.delmarlearning.com

Tom Snyder Productions
80 Coolidge Hill Road
Watertown MA 02472-5003
(800) 342-0236
http://www.tomsnyder.com

Toys to Grow On/Lakeshore
  Learning Materials
2695 East Dominguez Street
P.O. Box 17
Long Beach, CA 90801
(800) 542-8338
http://www.tgo.com

Tree Blocks
1187 Coast Village Road, #112
Santa Barbara, CA 93108
(800) 873-4960
http://www.treeblocks.com

U.S. Toy Company
Constructive Playthings
13201 Arrington Road
Grandview, MO 64030-1117
(800) 841-6478
http://www.ustoy.com

Willow Tree Press
P.O. Box 428
Naperville, IL 60540-9725
(800) 453-7148
http://www.willowtreepress.com

APPENDIX B

Administration for Children and Families
370 L'Enfant Promenade, SW
Washington, DC 20201
(202) 670-6782
http://www.acf.hhs.gov

Administration for Children, Youth and
  Families (ACYF)
Head Start Division
330 C Street, SW
Washington, DC 20447
(202) 205-8572
http://www.acf.dhhs.gov

American Academy of Pediatrics
141 Northwest Point Boulevard
Elk Grove Village, IL 60007-0927
(800) 433-9016
(847) 228-5005
http://www.aap.org

American Association for Gifted Children—
  Duke University
Box 90270
Durham, NC 27708-0270
(919) 783-6152
http://www.aagc.org

American Association of Families
  and Consumer Sciences
400 North Columbus Street, Suite 202
Alexandria, VA 22314
(703) 706-4600
(800) 424-8080
http://www.aafcs.org

American Association of School Administrators
1801 North Quincey Street, Suite 700
Arlington, VA 22203
(703) 528-0700
http://www.aasa.org

American Council on Education (ACE)
1 Dupont Circle, NW, Suite 800
Washington, DC 20036
(202) 939-9300
http://www.acenet.edu

American Educational Research Association (AERA)
1230 17th Street, NW
Washington, DC 20036-3078
(202) 223-9485
http://www.aera.net

American Federation of Teachers (AFT)
555 New Jersey Avenue, NW
Washington, DC 20001
(202) 879-4400
http://www.aft.org

American Medical Association
515 North State Street
Chicago, IL 60610
(800) 621-8335
http://www.ama-assn.org

American Montessori Society (AMS)
281 Park Avenue South, 6th Floor
New York, NY 11237
(212) 358-1250
http://www.amshof.org

American Speech, Language and Hearing Association
10801 Rockville Pike
Rockville, MD 20852
(800) 638-8255
http://www.asha.org

The Annie Casey Foundation
701 Saint Paul Street
Baltimore, MD 21202
(410) 547-6600
http://www.aecf.org

Appalachian Regional Commission
1666 Connecticut Avenue, NW, Suite 700
Washington, DC 20009-1068
(202) 884-7799
http://www.arc.gov

Association for Childhood Education
    International (ACEI)
1790 Georgia Avenue, Suite 215
Olney, MD 20832
(800) 423-3563
http://www.acei.org

Association for Library Service to Children
American Library Association
50 East Huron
Chicago, IL 60611
(800) 545-2433
http://www.ala.org

Association Montessori Internationale, USA
410 Alexander Street
Rochester, NY 14607
(800) 872-2643
http://www.montessori-ami.org

Association for Supervision and Curriculum
    Development (ASCD)
1703 North Beauregard Street
Alexandria, VA 22311
(800) 933-2723
http://www.ascd.org

California Child Care Resource and Referral Agency
111 New Montgomery, 7th Floor
San Francisco, CA 94105
(415) 882-0234
http://www.rrnetwork.org

Center for Career Development in Early Care
    and Education
Center for Parenting Studies
Wheelock College
200 The Riverway
Boston, MA 02215-4176
(617) 879-2000
http://www.wheelock.edu/ccd/ccdearlychildhood.htm

Center for Child Care Workforce
555 New Jersey Avenue, NW
Washington, DC 20001
(202) 662-8005
http://www.ccw.org

Center for Policy Alternatives
1875 Connecticut Avenue, NW, Suite 710
Washington, DC 20009
(202) 387–6030
http://www.cfpa.org

Centers for Disease Control & Prevention
1600 Clifton Road N.E.
Atlanta, GA 30333
(404) 639-3311 or (800) 311-3435
http://www.cdc.gov

Center for Early Childhood Leadership
National-Louis University
6310 Capitol Drive
Wheeling, IL 60090-7201
(800) 443-5522
http://www.cecl.nl.edu/

Center for Nutrition Policy and Promotion
3101 Park Center Drive
Alexandria, VA 23202-1594
(703) 305-7600
http://www.cnpp.usda.gov

Child Care Action Campaign
330 7th Avenue, 14th Floor
New York, NY 10001
http://www.wecaretoo.com

Child Care in Health Care (formerly National Association
    of Hospital Affiliated Child Care Programs)
1100 South 105 Street
Edwardsville, KS 66111
(913) 441-4065 (CCHC)
http://www.childcareinhealth.org

Child Care Information Exchange
P.O. Box 2890
Redmond, WA 98073-2890
(800) 221-2864
http://www.ccie.com

Child Care Law Center
221 Pine Street, 3rd Floor
San Francisco, CA 94104
(415) 395-7144
http://www.childcarelaw.org

Child Care Services Association
1829 East Franklin Street, Building 1000
P.O. Box 901
Chapel Hill, NC 27514
(919) 967-3272
http://www.childcareservices.org/

Child Welfare League of America (CWLA)
440 1st Street, NW, 3rd Floor
Washington, DC 20001-2085
(202) 638-2952
http://www.cwla.org

The Children's Book Council, Inc.
12 West 37th Street
New York, NY 10018
(212) 966-1990
http://www.cbcbooks.org

Children's Defense Fund
25 E Street, NW
Washington, DC 20001
(202) 628-8787
http://www.childrensdefense.org

Children's Foundation
725 15th Street, NW, Suite 505
Washington, DC 20005
(202) 347-3300
http://www.childrensfoundation.net

Community Development Institute Head Start
CDI Head Start
9745 East Hampden Avenue, Suite 310
Denver, CO 80231
(877) 789-4900
http://www.cdiheadstart.org

Council of Chief State School Officers
One Massachusetts Avenue, NW, Suite 700
Washington, DC 20001-1431
(202) 336-7000
http://www.ccsso.org/

Council for Early Childhood Professional
    Recognition (CDA)
2640 16th Street, NW
Washington, DC 20009-3573
(800) 424-4310
(202) 265-9090
http://www.cdacouncil.org

Council for Exceptional Children (CEC)
1110 North Glebe Road, Suite 300
Arlington, VA 22201-5704
(888) CEC-SPED
http://www.cec.sped.org

Council for Indian Education
1240 Burlington Avenue
Billings, MT 59102
(406) 248-3465
http://www.cie-mt.org

Division for Early Childhood
634 Eddy Avenue
Missoula, MT 59812
(406) 243-5898
http://www.dec-sped.org/

Early Childhood Directors Association
450 North Syndicate, Suite 80
Saint Paul, MN 55104
(763) 603-5853

Education Development Center (EDC)
55 Chapel Street
Newton, MA 02458

Education Funding Research Council
4301 North Fairfax, Suite 875
Arlington, VA 22203
(703) 528-1000

Eric Project
c/o Computer Science Corp.
4483-A Forbes Boulevard
Lanham, MD 20706
(800) LET-ERIC
http://www.eric.ed.gov

Families and Work Institute
267 Fifth Avenue, 2nd Floor
New York, NY 10006
(212) 465-2044
http://www.familiesandwork.org

The Feminist Press
    at the Graduate Center, CUNY
365 Fifth Avenue, Suite 5406
New York, NY 10016
(212) 817-7920
http://www.feministpress.org

Forum for Early Childhood Organization
    and Leadership Development
Midwest Center for Nonprofit Leadership
University of Missouri—Kansas City
Bloch School, Room 310
5100 Rockhill Road
Kansas City, MO 64110-2499
http://www.bloch.umkc.edu/mwcnl

The Foundation Center
79 Fifth Avenue/16th Street
New York, NY 10003-3076
(212) 620-4230
http://www.fdncenter.org

Foundation for Child Development
145 East 32nd Street, 14th Floor
New York, NY 10016-6055
(212) 213-8337
http://www.fcd-us.org

Handicapped Children's Early Education
    Program (HCEEP)
Office of Special Education and Rehabilitation Services
U.S. Department of Education
400 Maryland Avenue, SW
Washington, DC 20202-7600
(202) 245-7531

Head Start Bureau
Department of Health and Human Services
330 C Street, SW, Room 2018
Washington, DC 20201
(202) 205-8575
http://www.acf.hhs.gov/programs/hsb

Head Start—Johnson and Johnson Management
    Fellows Program
University of California, Los Angeles/The Anderson
    School of UCLA
110 Westwood Plaza
Box 951481
Los Angeles, CA 90095
(301) 825-6306
http://www.anderson.ucla.edu/

Head Start State Collaborative Project
Center for Schools and Communities
275 Grandview Avenue, Suite 200
Camp Hill, PA 17011
(717) 763-1661
http://www.center-school.org

High/Scope Educational Research Foundation
600 North River Street
Ypsilanti, MI 48198-2898
(734) 485-2000
(800) 407-7377
http://www.highscope.org

International Child Resource Institute
1581 Leroy Avenue
Berkeley, CA 94708
(510) 644-1000
http://www.icrichild.org

International Reading Association
800 Barksdale Road
P.O. Box 8139
Newark, DE 19714-8139
(302) 731-1600
http://www.ira.org

Kids and the Power of Work
1501 Broadway
New York, NY 10036
(212) 840-1801
http://www.kapow.org

Leadership Development Program
Bank Street College of Education
610 West 112th Street
New York, NY 10025
(212) 875-4400
http://www.bnkst.edu

National Academy of Early Childhood
    Programs NAEYC
1509 16th Street, NW
Washington, DC 20036
(800) 424-2460
http://www.naeyc.org

National After School Association
1137 Washington Street
Dorchester, MA 02124
(617) 298-5012
(800) 617-8242
http://www.naaweb.org

National Association for Bilingual Education
1030 15th Street, NW
Suite 470
Washington, DC 20005
(202) 898-1829
http://www.nabe.org

National Association of Child Care Professionals (NACCP)
7610 Highway 71 West, Suite E
Austin, TX 78735
(800) 537-1118
http://www.naccp.org

National Association of Child Care Resource
    and Referral Agencies
1319 F Street, NW, Suite 500
Washington, DC 20004
(202) 393-5501
http://www.naccrra.org

National Association for the Education
    of Young Children (NAEYC)
1509 16th Street, NW
Washington, DC 20036
(202) 232-8777
(800) 424-2460
http://www.naeyc.org

National Association of Elementary School Principals
1615 Duke Street
Alexandria, VA 22314-3483
(703) 684-3345
(800) 386-2371
http://www.naesp.org

National Association for Family Child Care
5202 Pinemont Drive
Salt Lake City, UT 84123
(801) 269-9338
http://www.nafcc.org

National Association for Gifted Children
1707 L Street, NW, Suite 550
Washington, DC 20036
(202) 785-4268
http://www.nagc.org

National Association for Sick Child Daycare
1716 5th Avenue North
Birmingham, AL 35203
(205) 324-8447
http://www.nascd.com

National Association of State Boards of Education
277 South Washington Street, Suite 100
Alexandria, VA 22314
(703) 684-4000
http://www.nasbe.org

National Association of State Directors of Special
   Education (NASDSE)
1800 Diagonal Road
Suite 320
Alexandria, VA 22314
(703) 519-3800
http://www.nasdse.org

National Black Child Development
   Institute (NBCDI)
1101 15th Street, NW, Suite 900
Washington, DC 20005
(202) 833-2220
http://www.nbcdi.org

National Center for Children in Poverty
215 West 125th Street, 3rd Floor
New York, NY 10027
(646) 284-9600
http://www.nccp.org

National Center for Education in Maternal
   and Child Health
2000 15th Street, North, Suite 701
Arlington, VA 22201-2617
(888) 434-4624
http://www.ncemch.org

National Child Care Association (NCCA)
1016 Rosser Street
Conyers, GA 30012
(800) 543-7161
http://www.nccanet.org

National Coalition for Campus
   Children's Centers
119 Shindler Education Court
University of Iowa
Cedarfalls, IA 50614
(800) 813-8207
http://www.campuschildren.org

National Community Capital Association
Public Ledger Building
620 Chestnut Street, Suite 572
Philadelphia, PA 19106
(215) 923-4754
http://www.communitycapital.org

National Council of Jewish Women (NCJW)
Center for the Child
53 West 23rd Street, 6th Floor
New York, NY 10010
(800) 829-6259
http://www.ncjw.org

National Education Association (NEA)
1201 16th Street, NW
Washington, DC 20036
(202) 833-4000
http://www.nea.org

National Food Service Management
   Institute (NFSMI)
The University of Mississippi
6 Jeanette Phillips Drive
P.O. Drawer 188
University, MS 38677-0188
(800) 943-5463 (helpdesk)

National Head Start Association
1651 Prince Street
Alexandria, VA 22314
(703) 739-0875
http://www.nhsa.org

National Institute of Child Health and Human
   Development
NIH Building 31, Room 2A32, MSC 2425
31 Center Drive
Bethesda, MD 20892
(301) 496-5133
http://www.nichd.nih.gov

National Institute on Out-of-School Time
Wellesley College
Center for Research on Women
106 Central Street
Wellesley, MA 02481
(781) 283-2547
http://www.niost.org

National League of Cities
1301 Pennsylvania Avenue, NW
Suite 550
Washington, DC 20004
(202) 626-3000
(202) 626-3043
http://www.nlc.org

National PTA
330 North Wabash Avenue
Suite 2100
Chicago, IL 60611
(312) 670-6782
http://www.pta.org

National Resource Center for Health and Safety
    in Child Care
UCHSC at Fitzsimons
Campus Mail Stop F541, P.O. Box 6508
Aurora, CO 80045-0508
(800) 598-KIDS (5437)
http://www.nrc.uchsc.edu

National Women's Law Center
11 Dupont Circle, NW, Suite 800
Washington, DC 20036
(202) 588-5180
http://www.nwlc.org

North American Montessori Teachers
    Association (NAMTA)
13693 Butternut Road
Burton, OH 44021
(404) 834-4011
http://www.montessori-namta.org

Office of Child Development
U.S. Department of Health and Human Services
200 Independence Avenue, SW
Washington, DC 20201
(877) 696-6775

Parent Cooperative Preschools International,
    U.S. Office
National Business Center
1401 New York Avenue, NW, Suite 1100
Washington, DC 20005
(800) 636-6222
http://www.preschools.coop/

Puerto Rican Association for Community Affairs
853 Broadway, 5th Floor
New York, NY 10003
(212) 673-7320

Save the Children Federation
54 Wilton Road
Westport, CT 06880
(800) 728-3843
http://www.savethechildren.org

Society for Research in Child Development (SRCD)
University of Michigan
3131 South State Street, Suite 302
Ann Arbor, MI 48108
(734) 998-6578
http://www.sred.org

Southern Early Childhood Association (SECA)
P.O. Box 55930
Little Rock, AR 72215-5930
(800) 305-7322
http://www.southernearlychildhood.org

Southern Institute of Children and Families
500 Taylor Street, Suite 202
Columbia, SC 29201
(803) 779-2607
http://www.kidsouth.org

Superintendent of Documents
Government Printing Office
732 North Capital Street, NW
Washington, DC 20401
(202) 512-1800
http://www.gpoaccess.gov

The Trust for Early Education
1250 H Street, NW, Suite 700
Washington, DC 20005
(202) 293-1245
http://www.trustforearly.org

United Way of America
701 North Fairfax Street
Alexandria, VA 22314
(703) 836-7112
http://www.unitedway.org

USA Child Care
(703) 875-8100
http://www.usachildcare.org

U.S. Consumer Product Safety Commission
Washington, DC 20207
301-505-0580
(800) 638-CPSC
http://www.cpsc.gov

USDA Communication and Governmental Affairs Office
3101 Park Center Drive
Alexandria, VA 22302
(703) 305-2276
http://www.usda.gov

U.S. Department of Agriculture
14th & Independence Avenue, SW
Washington, DC 20250
(202) 720-2791
http://www.usda.gov

U.S. Department of Education
400 Maryland Avenue, SW
Washington, DC 20202
(800) USA–LEARN
http://www.ed.gov

U.S. National Committee of OMEP
World Organization for Early Childhood Education
1314 G Street, NW
Washington, DC 20005-3105
(800) 424-4310
http://www.omep-usnc.org

The White House
Head Start Policy Book
1600 Pennsylvania Avenue, NW
Washington, DC 20500
(202) 456-1111
http://www.whitehouse.gov/infocus/earlychildhood,
   hspolicybook/03.html

Work/Family Directions, Inc.
200 Talcott Avenue West
Watertown, MA 02472
(800) 447-0543
http://www.wfd.com

Work and Family Life Studies/Research Division
Bank Street College
610 West 112th Street
New York, NY 10025
(212) 875-4400
http://www.bankst.edu

Zero to Three—National Center for Infants,
   Toddlers and Families
2000 M Street, NW, Suite 200
Washington, DC 20036
(202) 638-1144
http://www.zerotothree.org

APPENDIX C
Partial List: Early Childhood Periodicals and Media

Periodicals

Access Child Care: News and Information on the Americans With Disabilities Act
Disability Resource Group, Inc.
8 East Long Street
Columbus, OH 43215-2914

Beginnings
Exchange Press, Inc.
P.O. Box 3249
Redmond, WA 98073-2890
(800) 221-2864
http://www.childcareexchange.com

The Black Child Advocate
National Black Child Development Institute
1101 15th Street, NW, Suite 900
Washington, DC 20005
(202) 833-2220
http://www.nbcdi.org

Byte
BYTE Publications, Inc.
70 Main Street
Peterborough, NH 03458
(603) 924-9281

CCI&R Issues (Child Care Information and Referral)
Child Care Resources and Referral Network
126 Woodlake Drive SE
Rochester, MN 55904
http://www.c2r2.org

CDF Reports and Child Watch Updates
Children's Defense Fund
25 E Street, NW
Washington, DC 20001
(202) 628-8787
http://www.childrensdefense.org

Campus Child Care News
National Coalition for Campus Children's Center
119 Shindler Education Center
University of Northern Iowa
Cedar Falls, IA 50614
(800) 813-8207
http://www.campuschildren.org

Center for Parent Education Newsletter
81 Wyman Street, No. 6
Waban, MA 02168-1519
(617) 964-2442

Child Care Information Exchange
P.O. Box 3249
Redmond, WA 98073-2890
(800) 221-2864
http://www.ccie.com

Child Care Quarterly
Day Care And Early Education
Human Sciences Press
233 Spring Street
New York, NY 10013
(212) 620-8000
(800) 221-9369
http://www.childcarequarterly.com

Child Development
Society for Research in Child Development
University of Michigan
3131 South State Street, Suite 302
Anne Arbor, MI 48104
(734) 998-6578

Child Development Media, Inc.
5632 Van Nuys Blvd., Suite 286
Van Nuys, CA 91401
(800) 405-8942
http://www.childdevmedia.com

Child Health Alert
P.O. Box 610228
Newton Highlands, MA 02161
(781) 239-1762
http://www.childhealthalert.com

Child Health Talk
National Black Child Development Institute, Inc.
1101 15th Street, NW, Suite 600
Washington, DC 20005
(202) 833-2220

Childhood Education
Association for Childhood Education International
17904 Georgia Avenue, Suite 215
Olney, MD 20832
(800) 423-3563
http://www.udel.edu

Children and Families
National Head Start Association
1651 Prince Street
Alexandria, VA 22314
(703) 793-0875
http://www.nhsa.org

Children Now
1212 Broadway, 5th Floor
Oakland, CA 94612
(510) 763-2444
http://www.childrennow.org

Children Today
Office of Human Development Services
P.O. Box 371954
Pittsburgh, PA 15250-7954
(202) 783-3238

Children's Voice
Child Welfare League of America
440 First Street, NW, Suite 310
Washington, DC 20001-2085
(202) 638-2952
http://www.cwla.org

Competence: News for CDA Community
Council for Early Childhood Professional
    Recognition
2640 16th Street, NW
Washington, DC 20009-3573
(800) 424-4310

Council News and Views
Council for Early Childhood Professional
    Recognition
2640 16th Street, NW
Washington, DC 20009-3573
(800) 424-4310

Day Care and Early Education
Human Sciences Press, Inc.
233 Spring Street
New York, NY 10013-1587
(212) 620-8000

Dimensions
SECA
P.O. Box 55930
Little Rock, AR 72215-5930
(501) 663-0353
(800) 305-7322
http://www.southernearlychildhood.org

Early Childhood Research Quarterly
Ablex Publishing Corporation
355 Chestnut Street
Norwood, NJ 07648-2090
(201) 767-8450 or 8455

Education Week
4301 Connecticut Avenue, NW, Suite 432
Washington, DC 20077-6796
(202) 364-4114

Eric Project
c/o Computer Science Corporation
4483-A Forbes Boulevard
Lanham, MD 20706
(800) LET–ERIC
http://www.eric.ed.gov

Exceptional Children
Council for Exceptional Children
1110 North Glebe Road, Suite 300
Arlington, VA 22201-5704
(888) 232-7733
http://www.cec.sped.org

Food and Nutrition
Superintendent of Documents
732 North Capital Street, NW
U.S. Government Printing Office
Washington, DC 20401
(202) 512-0000
http://www.gpo.gov

Growing Child
22 North Second Street
P.O. Box 620
Lafayette, IN 47902-0620
(317) 423-2624
(800) 927-7289
http://www.growingchild.com

Growing Child Research Review
22 N. Second Street, P.O. Box 620
Lafayette, IN 47902-1100
(317) 423-2624

InfoWorld
InfoWorld
155 Bovet Road, Suite 800
San Mateo, CA 94402
(415) 572-7341

Journal of Child Care Administration
Prakken Publications
3970 Varsity Drive
Ann Arbor, MI 48108
(800) 530-9673

MacWorld
501 2nd Street, 5th Floor
San Francisco, CA 94107
(415) 243-0505

PC Magazine
Ziff-Davis Media, Inc.
28 East 28th Street
New York, NY 10016
(212) 503-3500
http://www.ziffdavis.com

PC World
PCW Communications, Inc.
501 2nd Street, Suite 600
San Francisco, CA 94107
(415) 243-0500

Reading Today and *Reading Teacher*
International Reading Association, Inc.
800 Barksdale Road, Box 8139
Newark, DE 19714
(302) 731-1600
http://www.ira.org

Report on Preschool Programs
8737 Colesville Road, Suite 1100
Silver Springs, MD 20910-3928
301-587-6300
(800) 274-6737

Resource
High-Scope Educational Research Foundation
600 North River Street
Ypsilanti, MI 48198-2898
734-485-2000
(800) 407-7377
http://www.highscope.org

School Age Notes
P.O. Box 40205
Nashville, TN 37204
(615) 242-8464

Software Digest Ratings Report
625 Ridge Pike, Building D
Conshohochen, PA 19426
(610) 941-9600
(800) 220-NSTL

Teaching Pre K–8: The Professional Magazine for Teachers
Early Years, Inc.
325 Post Road W.
Westport, CT 06880
(800) 999-0384

The Well-Centered Child
P.O. Box 428
Naperville, IL 60566-9725
(800) 453-7148

Young Children
National Association for the Education of Young Children
1509 16th Street, NW
Washington, DC 20036
(800) 424-2460
http://www.naeyc.org

Zero to Three
Zero to Three—National Center for Infants,
　Toddlers and Families
2000 M Street, NW
Washington, DC 20036
(202) 638-1144
(800) 899-4301 (publications only)

Media

C&J Videos
3127 Davenport Avenue
Saginaw, MI 48609
(517) 790-5911
Videocassettes:
What Does It Look Like? Developmentally Appropriate
　Learner-Centered Classrooms in Public Schools—1994
The Challenge: Quality Public School Programs for Four
　Year Olds—1996

CRM/McGraw-Hill Films
P.O. Box 641
DelMar, CA 92014
(619) 453-5000
Videocassettes:
Communicating Non-Defensively: Don't Take It Personally
Communications: The Nonverbal Agenda
Decisions
A New Look at Motivation
Performance Appraisal: The Human Dynamics
Verbal Communication
Power of Listening

Davidson Films, Inc.
735 Tank Farm Road, Suite 210
San Luis, Obisbo, CA 93401
(888) 437-4200
http://www.davidsonfilms.com
Davidson Films supplies videos and DVDs featuring many
of the most well-known thinkers who have influenced
early childhood education. Its "Acclaimed Giants" series
includes Piaget, Elkind, Montessori, Ainsworth, and
Bandura.

National Association for the Education of Young Children
1509 16th Street, NW
Washington, DC 20036-1426
(800) 424-2460
Videocassettes:
Cultivating Roots—Home/School Partnerships—1996
Seeds of Change—Leadership and Staff Development—1996
Celebrating Early Childhood Teachers—1986
Partnerships with Parents—1989
Quality Family Child Care—1993
*The Early Childhood Program: A Place to Learn and
    Grow: (7 program series)*—1996
Places to Grow—The Learning Environment—1996
*Safe Active Play: A Guide to Avoiding Play Area
    Hazards Caring for Our Children*—1997

National Institute of Child Care Management
The Mount Community Center
751 South 8th Street
Atchison, KS 66002
(913) 367-2936
Audiocassettes:
Creating Harmony in Your Center—1994
*Interviewing Strategies: Moving from Survival to
    Success*—1995
Supervising Your Child Care Staff Effectively—1994
Success as an Effective Director—1994

Teachers College Press
Teachers College—Columbia University
1234 Amsterdam Avenue
New York, NY 10027
(800) 575-6566
Videocassettes:
*Video Observations for the Early Childhood Ratings
    Scale (ECERS)*—1992

APPENDIX D

CHILD DEVELOPMENT

Charlesworth, R. (2004). *Understanding child development* (6th ed.). **Clifton Park, NY: Thomson Delmar Learning.**

This sixth edition introduces the reader to the unique qualities of the young child as distinguished from older children and demonstrates how to work with young children in ways that match their developmental level. The author also includes critical social and emotional factors that relate to and have an effect on development.

Puckett, M. B. & Black, J. K. (2001). *The young child: Development from prebirth through age eight* (3rd ed.). **Upper Saddle River, NJ: Pearson/Prentice Hall.**

A comprehensive coverage of child development written at a level appropriate for CDA programs and beyond.

CHILDREN WITH SPECIAL NEEDS

Allen, K. E. & Cowdery, G. E. (2005). *The exceptional child: Inclusion in early childhood education.* **Clifton Park, NY: Thomson Delmar Learning.**

Although this edition focuses on inclusion of children with special needs, Allen and Cowdery again place emphasis on the fact that teachers of children with special needs must have a thorough knowledge of normal growth and development. When the teachers see developmental deviations, they are able to judge where and how to work with each child and identify when there is a need for clinical evaluations and referrals. This book offers a comprehensive and inclusive overview of early intervention and public policy and discusses types and causes of developmental disabilities, working with parents, and day-to-day "how to" strategies for classroom teachers.

Benner, S. M. (2003). *Assessment of young children with special needs: A context-based approach.* **Clifton Park, NY: Thomson Delmar Learning.**

This book is an excellent tool for directors to evaluate the skills of the children with special needs that they have enrolled at their centers. It focuses on infant, toddler, and preschool children with developmental delays and those considered at risk to experience developmental difficulties. There is discussion of the importance of considering the environment when thinking about assessment of children with special needs.

Child Care Law Center. (1993). *Caring for children with special needs: The Americans with Disabilities Act and child care.* **ADA Series.**

A well-written booklet that discusses admitting and accommodating children with special needs and includes a discussion of liability and record-keeping issues when children with disabilities are enrolled. The booklet contains an extensive list of resources for center directors.

Child Care Law Center. *Caring for children with special needs: The Americans with Disabilities Act.*

This 44-page booklet covers questions and issues about admitting children with disabilities, what are viewed as "reasonable accommodations" for these children, and who will cover the extra costs of inclusion.

Deiner, P. L. (2005). *Resources for educating children with diverse abilities: Birth through eight* (4th ed.). **Clifton Park, NY: Thomson Delmar Learning.**

This book is a very comprehensive, detailed resource for information relating to working with children with diverse abilities. The first section of the book, Educating Children with Diverse Abilities, covers legal issues, inclusion questions, assessment and entitlement decisions, and focusing on families. The second section, Resources and Activities for Children with Diverse Abilities, deals with a span of practical guides to classroom application, including curriculum ideas and pedagogical strategies for classroom teachers.

Guralnick, M. J. (2001). *Early childhood inclusions: Focus on change.* **Baltimore: Paul H. Brookes Publishing.**

The focus of this book is on early childhood inclusion, and it is about change, or the hope for change. Guralnick notes that, on the surface, the press for inclusion of children with disabilities is, what he calls, "benign." On closer inspection, it is clear that successful inclusion requires considerable change in how the society thinks, feels, and acts in order to achieve the expected and needed profound changes in the lives of many children and families.

COMPUTER INFORMATION

ERIC/EECE Publications. (1997). *A to Z: The early childhood educator's guide to the Internet.*

This guide is a basic primer and tool for finding and using resources on the Internet that are of interest to early childhood educators. The guide cites resources accessible by various Internet tools (Telnet, Gopher, World Wide Web browsers, newsgroups, electronic discussion lists) produced by various organizations and institutions in the field of education.

It is arranged by broad subject areas and has subject, organizational, geographic, and personnel indexes.

DIVERSITY/ANTI-BIASED CURRICULUM

Copple, E. (Ed.). (2003). *A world of difference.* **Washington, DC: NAEYC.**

This collection of readings provides a knowledge base and a thought-provoking discussion of issues relative to culture, language, religion, inclusion, and socioeconomic status. Emphasis is on building mutual respect and understanding between and among child care staff, children, and families.

Derman-Sparks, L. & the A.B.C. Task Force. (1989). *Anti-bias curriculum: Tools for empowering young children.* **Washington, DC: NAEYC.**

Teachers can use principles and methodology from this book to create an anti-bias curriculum in relation to the specific groups of children and families in their settings.

Gonzalez-Mena, J. (1993). *Multicultural issues in child care.* **Mountain View, CA: Mayfield Publishing.**

This booklet is a companion to Louise Derman-Sparks's *Anti-Bias Curriculum*. This author takes off from where Derman-Sparks stopped. Derman-Sparks's focus is on an anti-bias approach to preschool curriculum; the focus here is on an anti-bias approach to cultural information, adult relations, and conflicts in goals, values, expectations, and child-rearing practices.

Kendall, F. E. (1996). *Diversity in the classroom: New approaches to the education of young children.* **New York: Teachers College Press.**

This new edition builds on the theory presented in the earlier edition and also incorporates the perspectives of Michael Cole, Howard Gardner, and Lev Vygotsky. The author addresses many aspects of anti-bias education, focusing particularly on the teacher's role as a change agent.

Parlakian, R. (2004). *How culture shapes social-emotional development: Implications for practice in infant-family programs.* **Washington, DC: Zero to Three Press.**

This is for leaders and practitioners, and it examines how culture shapes children's fundamental learning about themselves and their world. It provides a framework for resolving cultural dilemmas.

EVALUATION

Bredekamp, S. & Rosegrant, T. (Eds.). (1992). *Reaching potentials: Appropriate curriculum and assessment for young children,* **Vol. 1. Washington, DC: NAEYC.**

This book presents guidelines for curriculum and assessment practices that will make it more likely for both teachers and children to reach their potential.

Harms, T., Cryer, D., & Clifford, R. *Early Childhood Environment Rating Scale.* **New York: Teachers College Press.**

There are four Harms, Cryer, and Clifford Rating Scales. They are:

Infant/Toddler Environment Rating Scale (ITERS)
Early Childhood Environment Rating Scale (ECERS)
School-Age Care Environment Rating Scale (SACERS)
Family Daycare Rating Scale (FDCRS)

These easy-to-use evaluation instruments answer many questions about the adequacy of early childhood settings. The ratings cover issues such as space, care routines, language, reasoning skills, social development, and adult needs.

Jorde-Bloom, P. (1986). *Improving the quality of work life: A guide for enhancing organizational climate in the early childhood setting.* **Evanston, IL: Early Childhood Professional**

Development Project, National College of Education.

After an overview of the concept of organizational climate as it relates to the quality of work life in the early childhood setting, an assessment tool for measuring organizational climate is provided. Helpful suggestions for how a center director can improve the overall quality of work life are also included.

FINANCIAL MANAGEMENT FUND-RAISING AND MARKETING

American Appraisal Associates, Inc. (1986). *Appraisal of an operating day-care center: Real estate valuation guide.* Milwaukee, WI.

This booklet is designed to facilitate the appraisal of the real estate, equipment, and the operation itself of a child care center. There is discussion of three valuation approaches—the cost approach, the income approach, and the market data approach.

Children's Defense Fund. (1990). *An advocate's guide to fund-raising.* Washington, DC: Children's Defense Fund Publications.

This booklet covers the basics of how to raise money from foundations, corporations, and individuals.

Finn, M. (1982). *Fund-raising for early childhood programs: Getting started and getting results.* Washington, DC: NAEYC.

This booklet describes techniques used by nonprofit institutions to raise money by contacting sources of support, including individual donors, corporations, foundations, and government. It also includes a section on proposal writing and an updated bibliography.

Gross, M. & Warshauer, W. (1995). *Financial and accounting guide for nonprofit organizations.* New York: John Wiley and Sons.

Comprehensive, well-written resource. Detailed advice on cash, accrual, and fund accounting; financial statements; budgeting; internal control; tax requirements; and bookkeeping.

Morgan, G. (1992). *Managing the day care dollars: A financial handbook* (Rev. ed.). Cambridge, MA: Steam Press.

A practical guide to financial management in the child care setting. Addresses budgeting, accounting, financial statements, and meeting insurance needs.

National Governors' Association. *Taking care: State developments in child care.* Washington, DC: Center for Policy Research.

This report summarizes state funding resources for child care services as states begin to implement the federally mandated Family Support Act. Citing evidence from a recent survey, the report suggests that states will continue to expand their role as regulators, system builders, and employers in support of child care assistance for families.

On-target marketing: Promotion strategies for child care centers. (1996). Redmond, WA: Child Care Information Exchange.

A compilation of articles that first appeared in *Child Care Information Exchange: The Director's Magazine.* Very helpful articles on courting the press, advertising your center, and handling parents' visits to your center.

Young, J. (1981). *Fund-raising for nonprofit groups.* Seattle, WA: Self-Counsel Press.

A practical fund-raising guide with ideas on developing strategies; approaching corporations, foundations, and government agencies; direct mail solicitation; and fund-raising in small communities.

FUNDING

Bowker, R. R. (Ed.). (1997). *Annual register of grant support.*

A comprehensive guide to various types of grant support, both governmental and private.

Getting a grant: How to write successful proposals. (1990).

A general guide to writing proposals for funding.

National databook, 7th ed., 2 vols. (1983).

A listing of grant-making foundations in the United States. Chiefly of use in seeking grants for groups or projects.

The foundation directory. (1993).

Nonprofit, nongovernmental organizations with resources of $1 million or more, or those making grants of $500,000 or more per year. Covers both grants to individual grant seekers and grants to organizations. Excellent index by subject field.

HEALTH, SAFETY, AND SICK CHILD CARE

American Academy of Pediatrics, American Public Health Association, & Maternal and Child Health Bureau. (2004). *Caring for our children: National health and safety performance standards: Guidelines for out-of-home child care programs* (2nd ed.). Denver, CO: National Resource for Health and Safety in Child Care.

This new edition is the one manual of health and safety guidelines that offers nine comprehensive chapters of the latest information and program activities for child care providers, licensors, and policy makers in the early child care field. It covers healthy development, safe play facilities, supplies and equipment, infectious diseases, principles for including and caring for children with special needs, and much more.

Aronson, S. & Shope, T. (2004). *Managing infectious diseases in child care and schools: A quick reference guide.* Grove Village, IL: American Academy of Pediatrics.

This is a convenient, easy-to-reference guide specifically designed for use by child care teachers. It offers a quick resource to industry standards and proven policies for protecting the children in your care, the center staff, and the organization's liability.

Marotz, L. R., Cross, M. Z., & Rush, J. M. (2005). *Health, safety and nutrition for the young child.* (5th ed.). Clifton Park, NY: Thomson Delmar Learning.

This up-to-date, comprehensive text covers the essential aspects of health, safety, and nutrition for young children. It includes material on infant nutrition, AIDS, and sanitary procedures in group care facilities.

Work/Family Directions. (1986). *A little bit under the weather: A look at care for mildly ill children.*

A comprehensive coverage of the need for sick child care and how it is viewed by child care professionals, families, employers, medical professionals, and the child.

INFANT/TODDLER CARE

Gonzalez-Mena, J. & Widmeyer Eyer, D. (2001). *Infants, toddlers, and caregivers.* Mountain View, CA: Mayfield Publishing.

This book offers excellent coverage of infant/toddler development. It serves as a complete resource on attachment as well as infant and toddler care in group settings.

Greenman, J. & Stonehouse, A. (1996). *Prime times: A handbook for excellence in infant and toddler programs.* St. Paul, MN: Redleaf Press.

Greenman and Stonehouse explore the topic of what makes for quality in infant and toddler programs, emphasizing the need for primary caregivers, small groups, responsive interactions, and environments that are safe, secure, and "filled with learning." This is a "hands on" guide for practitioners.

Hast, F. & Hollyfield, A. (1999). *Infant and toddler experiences.* St. Paul, MN: Redleaf Press.

These authors differentiate between an activity and an experience. They describe experiences in detail, including materials needed and procedures to keep in mind that help caregivers promote healthy development for infants and toddlers.

Honig, A. (2001). *Secure relationships: Nurturing infant/toddler attachment in early care settings.* Washington, DC: NAEYC.

Based on knowledge of research and theory, Honig describes how loving, responsive, and consistent care from primary caregivers is the foundation for how children learn to form relationships.

Parlakian, R. (2001). *The Power of questions: Building quality relationships with infants and families.* Washington, DC: Zero to Three Press.

This book focuses on direct work with parents of very young children. It is a resource that explores reflective approaches and practices that staff can use to establish relationships with families. Strategies that define boundary setting and managing one's reactions to families address the complex interpersonal situations that staff face every day when working in infant/toddler settings.

LEADERSHIP

Bloom, P. J. (2002). *Making the most of meetings: A practical guide.* Lake Forest, IL: New Horizons.

A rich resource for guiding the planning and preparation of meetings, with helpful strategies for carrying out a successful meeting plus ways one can enhance effectiveness of meetings. This book will help directors preside over stimulating and inspiring staff and parent meetings.

Bloom, P. J. (2003). *Leadership in action: How effective directors get things done.* Lake Forest, IL: New Horizons.

This book includes discussion of many facets of leadership, including leadership roles, leadership as a way of thinking, knowing thyself, and becoming a facilitative leader. Bloom discusses the essential functions of a leader in early childhood education—to inspire, to inform, to motivate, and to serve as a symbol for the collective identity of the group.

Culkin, M. L. (Ed.). (2000). *Managing quality in young children's programs: The leader's role.* New York: Teachers College Press.

This book, which focuses on and acknowledges the importance of effective leadership in early childhood programs, is one of the first of its kind. The articles, written by respected early childhood scholars and practitioners, cover the development of center directors and the director's credential. With growing interest in a credential for directors, this is a timely and much needed source of information.

Gordon, T. (1984). *Leadership effectiveness training (LET)*. E. Rutherford, NJ: The Penguin Group.

The basic skills for effective interpersonal communication including active listening, "I" messages, and no-lose problem solving are covered. These skills are analogues to those covered in Gordon's *Teacher Effectiveness Training* and *Parent Effectiveness Training*.

Neugebauer, B. & Neugebauer, R. (Eds.). (1998). *The art of leadership: Managing early childhood organizations*. Redmond, WA: Child Care Information Exchange.

The Neugebauers have carefully selected articles covering a wide range of topics of interest to directors. This is a collection of more than 80 articles written by respected specialists and covering leadership, organizational management, financial management, personnel management, program development, and community relations. Those directors who find *Child Care Information Exchange: A Magazine for Directors* helpful will find this compilation of informative articles assembled by the Neugebauers an excellent resource.

Sciarra, D. J. & Dorsey, A. G. (2002). *Leaders and supervisors in child care programs*. Clifton Park, NY: Thomson Delmar Learning.

The book is about leadership and supervision in the field of early child care and education. It is divided into three sections. Section I, Describing the Leader, draws on principles from business that leaders in early childhood can apply to the business of child care. Section II, Supervision 101, offers an in-depth discussion of supervision that will guide directors through the specific steps of an effective supervisory program. Section III considers other aspects of the leader's role. It addresses the issues faced by leaders as change agents and the leader's role as a professional in the field. This textbook has features similar to Sciarra and Dorsey's *Developing and Administering a Child Care Center* that makes it a suitable companion for use in a college-level course as well as for working directors.

PLANNING SPACES

Curtis, D. & Carter, M. (2002). *Designs for living and learning: Transforming early childhood environments*. St. Paul, MN: Redleaf Press.

This book will inspire directors and teachers to create wonderful environments that are comfortable and inviting for children, families, and staff.

Greenman, J. (1988). *Caring spaces, learning places: Children's environments that work*. Redmond, WA: Exchange Press.

This is a helpful guide to planning spaces for young children. It is full of ideas and observations, as well as problems and solutions for those responsible for planning spaces for child care.

PROGRAM DEVELOPMENT, CURRICULUM, AND GUIDANCE

Albrecht, K. & Miller, L. G. (2000). *The Comprehensive infant curriculum: A complete interactive curriculum for infants from birth to 18 months*. Beltsville, MD: Gryphon House.

Albrecht, K. & Miller, L. G. (2000). *The Comprehensive toddler curriculum: A complete interactive curriculum for toddlers from 18 months to 36 months*. Beltsville, MD: Gryphon House.

Albrecht, K. & Miller, L. G. (2004). *The Comprehensive preschool curriculum*. Beltsville, MD: Gryphon House.

These three volumes by Albrecht and Miller offer a complete review of child development for each age group followed by sections on interactions, relationships, communicating, making friends, and age-appropriate activities. It is very comprehensive series that presents a convincing position that curriculum is much more than well-arranged rooms and interesting activities.

Branscombe, N. A., Castle, K., Dorsey, A. G., Surbeck, E., & Taylor, J. B. (2003). *Early childhood curriculum: A constructivist perspective*. Boston and New York: Houghton Mifflin.

This comprehensive book explores the ways teachers can integrate constructivist principles in all areas of the curriculum, linking learning and development to the needs of children. It also invites the reader to become actively engaged in the construction of knowledge as it is presented in this book.

Bredekamp, S. & Coppel, C. (Eds). (1997). *Developmentally appropriate practice in early childhood programs*. Washington, DC: NAEYC.

This book is intended to explain the position of NAEYC on what is developmentally appropriate practice birth through age eight. It will help teachers, directors, parents, and board members better understand sound practice that should reverse the current trend toward a narrow focus on academics for young children.

Colker, L., Heroman, C., & Trister-Dodge, D. (2004). *The creative curriculum for preschool*. Washington, DC: Teaching Strategies.

This edition, like previous editions of this book, maintains the environmentally based approach but also clearly defines the teacher's role in connecting content, teaching, and learning. It applies recent research to the practice and strategies that help meet the needs of all children, including those with special needs as well as those who are second language learners.

Crowther, I. (2003). *Creating effective learning environments.* **Scarborough, Ontario: Thomson Nelson.**

This author expresses the strong conviction that the fundamental truth about curriculum is that it must be based on the strengths and needs of children. She believes that the cornerstones of curriculum development are careful observation and documentation followed by planning and implementation. There are chapters covering areas of play, including sand and water play, block play, and dramatic play. Other specific learning environments addressed are creative arts, math/science, and manipulative experiences.

Gartrell, D. J. (2004). *The power of guidance: Teaching social-emotional skills in early childhood classrooms.* **Clifton Park, NY: Thomson Delmar Learning.**

This book is well titled because it is, indeed, a powerful book as it explores age-appropriate and developmentally appropriate ways to teach social-emotional skills in the classroom through the use of thoughtful guidance practices. Gartrell has an informal, friendly writing style and he uses many anecdotes to help the reader reflect on and apply his suggested approaches that promote the emotional well-being of young children.

Gordon, A. M. & Williams Browne, K. (2004). *Beginnings and beyond* **(6th ed.). Clifton Park, NY: Thomson Delmar Learning.**

A comprehensive text covering many of the traditional questions that are of interest to early childhood educators including What Is The Field of Early Childhood? Who Is the Young Child? Who Are the Teachers of the Young Child? What Is the Setting? What Is Being Taught? and How Do We Teach for Tomorrow?

Jackman, H. (2005). *Early education curriculum: A child's connection to the world.* **Clifton Park, NY: Thomson Delmar Learning.**

This third edition is designed for teachers who are looking for current early childhood education philosophies, fresh ideas, and new insight into curriculum planning. Interconnecting philosophies are underscored here, focusing not only on child-initiated curriculum but also on cultural context, learning by doing, physical activity and play, plus helpful discussions of interpersonal relationships as well.

Miller, D. F. (2000). *Positive child guidance* **(3rd ed.). Clifton Park, NY: Thomson Delmar Learning.**

Child guidance is a challenging process of finding ways to help children become responsible, cooperative members of their group. This book is for caregivers who spend a great deal of time helping children become self-disciplined members of society. It is intended as a road map to guide adults as they work to meet the individual needs of children from infancy through early childhood.

Moomaw, S. (1997). *More than singing.* **St. Paul, MN: Redleaf Press.**

This book, which includes a cassette recording, offers a wealth of wonderful musical experiences that teachers can plan, even though they may not be trained musicians. Teachers will learn to make resonant, inexpensive instruments as well as gain knowledge about how to select songs and rhythm activities and coordinate these with their whole language curriculum.

Moomaw, S. & Hieronymous, B. (1995). *More than counting: Whole math activities for preschool and kindergarten.* **St. Paul, MN: Redleaf Press.**

An excellent resource for use with teachers and parents as they come to understand the "whole math" curriculum based on the constructivist model of cognitive development. The math games and materials described here in detail are not just additions to enrich the curriculum, they are the math curriculum for preschool and kindergarten.

Moomaw, S. & Hieronymous, B. (1997). *More than magnets.* **St. Paul, MN: Redleaf Press.**

The science curriculum in early childhood classrooms has typically consisted of a classroom "display," usually with a plant/animal focus, or teacher-directed experiments. This book offers a comprehensive, developmentally appropriate approach to science education with young children, with special attention to physics and math. It has more than 100 activities that engage children in interactive science explorations in many areas of the classroom.

Moomaw, S. & Hieronymous, B. (2001). *More than letters: Literacy activities for preschool, kindergarten and first grade.* **St. Paul, MN: Redleaf Press.**

This excellent book is an extensive compilation of emergent-literacy materials and activities that translate theory and research into a dynamic, effective literacy program for young children. The curriculum evolved following the emergence of the whole language movement and took shape as the authors explored their interest in how children construct literacy concepts.

Read, K., Gardner, P., & Mahler, B. (1993). *Early childhood programs: Human relations and learning* **(9th ed.). San Diego, CA: Harcourt, Brace, Jovanovich.**

No director's library should be without this time-tested book, now in its ninth edition. Play is emphasized as the most important mode of learning for young children, and there is a major focus on understanding and guiding children's personality development. The authors point out the importance of a trusting, close relationship between the child and the teacher.

PROGRAM MANAGEMENT

Child Welfare League of America. (rev.) (1991). *Guide for establishing and operating day care centers for young children.*

This booklet provides a brief and concise overview of essential information in the areas of licensing, budgeting, housing and equipping, staffing, and dealing with health and safety issues for those who are responsible for operating a child care center.

RESEARCH

Eager to learn: Educating our preschoolers. (2000). National Research Council.

This booklet is about the education of children ages two to five. It focuses on programs outside the home such as preschool, Head Start, and child care centers. It covers the major trends that will influence our thinking about the education of young children during the early part of the 21st century.

Gopnik, A., Meltzoff, A., & Kuhl, P. (1999). *The Scientist in the crib: Minds, brains, and how children learn.* New York: William Morrow & Company.

This book tells the story of the new science of children's minds. These authors have united cognitive science with psychology, philosophy, linguistics, computer science, and neuroscience. Their research demonstrates that babies and young children know and learn more about the world than we ever imagined. It shows that very young children think, draw conclusions, and make predictions. This book lays out the science of babies' minds.

Shore, R. (1997). *Rethinking the brain: New insights into early development.* Families and Work Institute.

This book presents an overview of neuroscientists' recent findings about the brain and suggests how these insights can guide and support our efforts to promote healthy development and learning of young children.

WORKING WITH STAFF, BOARD, COMMUNITY, AND PARENTS

Bloom P. J. (2005). *Blueprint for action: Achieving center-based change through staff development.* Lake Forest, IL: New Horizons.

This book is based on two basic assumptions, namely, that high-quality programs are distinguished by their

willingness to deal with their imperfections and that organizational change can come about only through change in individuals. The blueprint Bloom presents in this excellent book serves as a guide for enhancing the professional development of all who work together to achieve changes that will move them toward their shared vision of excellence.

Carter, M. & Curtis, D. (1998). *The visionary director: A handbook for dreaming, organizing and improvising in your center.* St. Paul, MN: Redleaf Press.

The major thrust of this handbook is to help directors and managers claim their potential as leaders. These authors help directors move beyond their "to do" lists and become visionaries who shape their organizational culture and create learning communities. The leader is the one who guides a program with a vision while building and supporting the learning community. Each principle presented in this book is followed by practical strategies that serve as guides for the professional development of the leader who, in turn, creates a thriving community for staff, families, and children.

Caruso, J. J. & Faucett, M. T. (1999). *Supervision in early childhood education: A developmental perspective.* New York: Teachers College Press.

This book addresses supervisory issues pertinent to personnel in both public and private settings. The focus of this book is staff development, and it is both descriptive and practical.

Diffily, D. & Morrison, K. (Eds.). (1996). *Family-friendly communication for early childhood programs.* Washington, DC: NAEYC.

This practical resource for directors includes samples of messages to include in newsletters for parents. Each item is designed so it can be photocopied and included in your correspondence to parents. No permission is required to use the material. The messages, written for laypersons, address the many facets of developmentally appropriate practice.

Greenman, J. T. & Fuqua, R. W. (Eds.). (1986). *Making day care better: Training, evaluation and the process of change.* New York: Teachers College Press.

Descriptions of the current status of the child care field and recommendations on how to promote positive changes. Issues dealt with include environments, caregivers, marketing, evaluation, regulation, training, consultation, and information and referral.

Jones, E. (Ed.). (1993). *Growing teachers: Partnerships in staff development.* Washington, DC: NAEYC.

This book applies a constructivist model for staff development. It describes activities that are open in design, where philosophy and process are defined, but not outcomes. Using these approaches, teachers are expected to participate actively in the construction of knowledge about their work and about how they can grow professionally.

Jorde-Bloom, P. (2000). *Circle of influence: Implementing shared decision making and participative management.* **Lake Forest, IL: New Horizons.**

In this book, you learn that participative management is both a philosophy and a set of behaviors that define your interactions with people. You will explore techniques for managing the daily business of your center. If you implement these strategies and expand your staff's circle of influence over decision making, you will have true collaboration and commitment to shared goals.

Stonehouse, A. (1995). *How does it feel?* **Redmond, WA: Child Care Information Exchange.**

This book aims to help child care staff get a clearer idea of how child care feels to a parent. Because it is so important for all staff to understand the importance of seeing the child in the context of the family, this booklet is one a director must share with the teaching staff.

INDEX

Page numbers followed by italic *f* indicate figures.